Political Psychology

*Contemporary Problems
and Issues*

Margaret G. Hermann

General Editor

Political
Psychology

Jossey-Bass Publishers
San Francisco • London • 1986

POLITICAL PSYCHOLOGY
CONTEMPORARY PROBLEMS AND ISSUES
Margaret G. Hermann, *General Editor*

Library of Congress Cataloging-in-Publication Data

Main entry under title:

Political psychology.

  (The Jossey-Bass social and behavioral science series)
  Includes bibliographies and indexes.
  1. Political psychology.   I. Hermann, Margaret G.
II. Series.
JA74.5.P633   1986   320'.01'9   85-45905
ISBN 0-87589-682-0

Manufactured in the United States of America

The paper in this book meets the guidelines for
permanence and durability of the Committee on
Production Guidelines for Book Longevity of the
Council on Library Resources.

JACKET DESIGN BY WILLI BAUM

FIRST EDITION

Code 8613

The Jossey-Bass
Social and Behavioral Science Series

Preface

Since the 1973 publication of the *Handbook of Political Psychology*, edited by Jeanne Knutson, the field of political psychology has attracted both attention and people. An international network of scholars and practitioners has begun to coalesce around the many issues and topics described in the *Handbook* as interest has grown in understanding how psychological and political phenomena interrelate. Information has accumulated rapidly. To help those just becoming acquainted with political psychology gain some perspective on what is currently occurring in the field, to consolidate the knowledge of those already working on a particular topic, and to suggest to all how the field has expanded, there has been a recurring call for an update to the *Handbook*. This volume represents that update indicating the growth in our knowledge and the present shape of the field. It brings together in one place discussions of the topics that are the focus of most theory and research in political psychology at this point in time. And it explores the problems that confront political psychologists as they work to expand their understanding of the psychological roots and effects of political behavior.

This book is premised on a bidirectional approach to political psychology. Thus, chapters examine how psychological factors affect political behavior as well as how political factors affect psychological functioning and performance. Part One of the book, "Humans as Political Animals," examines the first half of this equation, suggesting how an individual's biological makeup, needs, values, beliefs, life experiences, and psychodynamics help shape his political views of the world and his political activity. Part Three, "The Political Environment," explores the reverse question, namely the effects of the political environment on what people believe and value and how they act. This section considers what is involved in political socialization; what the effects of cultural beliefs and values are; and what constraints in the political environment lead people to form and join protest movements and to engage in terrorism. Part Two, "Political Decision Making," focuses on the interaction between individuals' characteristics and the political environment with respect to specific types of political activity—voting, political leadership, foreign policy making, and conflict resolution.

The authors of the individual chapters were selected because of their expertise on a particular topic and their interest in synthesizing a body of knowledge.

Contributors were asked to review the literature in their areas of expertise and to propose a fresh way of organizing the information that would advance our understanding of each topic. More specifically, each author was asked to indicate the underlying themes and concepts that guide theory and research in his or her area, what some of the puzzles are that people face who are interested in learning more about the topic, and where the gaps in our knowledge are. The contributors to the volume represent several disciplines—psychology, political science, history, and sociology—and thus bring different points of view to the topics under discussion. An effort was made to seek chapter authors who are actively interested in learning how those in other disciplines perceive and deal with their topics.

To ensure that the volume captures the international flavor of political psychology, the last section of the book, Part Four, is devoted to exploring the state of the field worldwide. The chapters in this section suggest the exciting work in political psychology that is going on in Latin America, Western Europe, and Asia. The authors of these chapters provide insights into such questions as how different cultural contexts have shaped what are considered relevant topics to study in political psychology, the kinds of theories that are needed to explain political behavior cross-culturally, and the extent to which generalization is possible across cultural contexts.

Enclosing the individual chapters are a prologue and an epilogue. The purpose of the prologue is to set the stage for what follows by suggesting some of the assumptions that undergird work in political psychology and some of the issues that arouse continuing debate and dialogue among political psychologists. The chapters fall within the basic tenets that are outlined in the prologue but they present different ways of dealing with the issues. The epilogue explores four themes that recur across the chapters and indicates how the chapters have begun to elaborate and shape the themes. These cross-cutting themes provide a basis by which individuals working on the different topics that comprise political psychology can communicate and build on each other's work. They suggest several paradigms of importance to political psychologists.

Monies to support the editorial tasks required in putting this volume together were generously provided by the Mershon Center of Ohio State University and are gratefully acknowledged. Vigorous debates with members of the International Society of Political Psychology on what constitutes political psychology played an important role in the development of the material in the prologue and epilogue. Too numerous to mention by name, their help is greatly appreciated.

A debt of thanks is also owed Jeanne Knutson, to whom the contributors would like to dedicate this book. Jeanne Knutson served as a catalyst for the field of political psychology. With the publication of the *Handbook* and the founding of the International Society of Political Psychology, she helped give legitimacy to political psychology as a field of inquiry. She was a mentor, patron, colleague, salesman, and friend to political psychologists worldwide as she worked to forge an international community—inside and outside academia—interested in how psychological and political phenomena interrelate. Before her untimely death in December 1981, Jeanne had begun plans for this update to the *Handbook*. The contributors hope that this book will follow in the footsteps of its predecessor and lay the groundwork for the continued growth and development in our knowledge about human nature in politics that Jeanne worked so hard to foster.

Columbus, Ohio Margaret G. Hermann
February 1986

Contents

Contributors

Tom Bryder is a professor of social science at the University of Lulea, Sweden, and is affiliated with the Academy of Abo, Finland, as an honorary research associate in political science. He is presently directing a comparative political psychology project on adolescence, unemployment, and political involvement in Denmark, Finland, Norway, and Sweden. A regular contributor to the *Swedish Political Science Review*, he is the author of several studies on content analysis, political leadership, and the history of social science.

Geoffrey Cocks is an assistant professor of history at Albion College. He received his Ph.D degree from the University of California at Los Angeles, specializing in modern Germany and psychohistory. Among his publications are psychohistorical essays on A. A. Milne, Thomas Pynchon's *Gravity's Rainbow*, and Adolf Hitler. He is also the author of *Psychotherapy in the Third Reich: The Göring Institute* (1985).

Martha Crenshaw is an associate professor of government at Wesleyan University. She received her Ph.D. degree in government and foreign affairs from the University of Virginia. Her major research interest is the politics of terrorism. She is the author of *Revolutionary Terrorism: The FLN in Algeria, 1954–1962* (1978) and the editor of *Terrorism, Legitimacy, and Power: The Consequences of Political Violence* (1982, with Y. Dror and C. O'Brien). Her research has been facilitated by fellowships from the National Endowment for the Humanities and the Russell Sage Foundation.

James Chowning Davies is a professor emeritus of political science at the University of Oregon. He received his Ph.D degree in political science from the University of California at Berkeley and has held fellowships from the Social Science Research Council, the Carnegie Corporation, and the Rockefeller Foundation. He is the author of *Human Nature in Politics* (1963), the editor of *When Men Revolt and Why* (1971), and has published numerous articles on political socialization, revolution, leadership, political biology, and political fiction. He has served on the Council of the American Political Science Association, as president of the Western Political Science Association, and as councillor of the International Society of Political Psychology.

Morton Deutsch is Edward Lee Thorndike Professor of Psychology and Education at Teachers College, Columbia University. He received his Ph.D. degree from the Massachusetts Institute of Technology and has taught at New York University and directed research on interpersonal processes at Bell Telephone Laboratories in Murray Hill, New Jersey. He is the author of *The Resolution of Conflict: Constructive and Destructive Processes* (1973), *Applying Social Psychology* (1975), and *Distributive Justice: A Social Psychological Perspective* (1985). Among his many honors are the Kurt Lewin Memorial Award (1968), the Gordon Allport Prize (1973), and the Nevitt Sanford Award (1984). He has served as president of the Society for the Psychological Study of Social Issues, the Eastern Psychological Association, the Division of Personality and Social Psychology of the American Psychological Association, and the International Society of Political Psychology.

Susan T. Fiske is an associate professor of social psychology in the Department of Psychology and Social Sciences at Carnegie-Mellon University. She received her Ph.D. degree from the Department of Psychology and Social Relations at Harvard University. Her published articles include work on political cognition (particularly images of candidates and political events) and on social cognition (particularly social categorization, stereotyping, and interpersonal affect). She is the author of *Social Cognition* (1984, with S. E. Taylor), editor of *Affect and Cognition: The 17th Annual Carnegie Symposium on Cognition* (1982, with M. S. Clark), and editor of the *Journal of Social Issues* special issue on images of nuclear war (1983, with B. Fischhoff and M. Milburn).

Margaret G. Hermann is a senior research associate at the Mershon Center, Ohio State University. She received her Ph.D. degree in psychology from Northwestern University and held a National Institute of Mental Health (NIMH) postdoctoral fellowship at the Educational Testing Service. Her major research interests include political leadership, the role of personality in politics, and psychological factors in foreign policymaking. She is the editor and a contributor to *A Psychological Examination of Political Leaders* (1977) and *Describing Foreign Policy Behavior* (1982, with P. Callahan and L. Brady). She has served as a vice-president of the International Studies Association and the International Society of Political Psychology and as editor of the journal *Political Psychology*.

Donald R. Kinder is an associate professor of political science and psychology and an associate research scientist at the Center of Political Studies, University of Michigan. He received his Ph.D. degree in psychology from the University of California at Los Angeles. Before moving to Michigan, he headed the Yale program in political psychology. He has written widely on matters of voting and public opinion and is at present completing a book (with S. Iyengar) on television news.

Gerda Lederer has been associated with the Institute for Conflict Research in Vienna and the recipient of research grants from the Konrad-Adenauer-Stiftung, the Deutsche Forschungsgemeinschaft, and the Fritz-Thyssen-Stiftung. She received her Ph.D. degree in sociology from Columbia University. Her research has focused on authoritarianism and dogmatism and on political protest in the Federal Republic of Germany. She has lectured widely in Europe and the United States and has written numerous articles. Her cross-cultural study on trends in authoritarianism earned her the International Society of Political Psychology's Erik Erikson Award in 1981. Her book, *Jugend und Autoritaet*, was published in West Germany in 1983.

Robert Mandel is an associate professor of international affairs at Lewis and Clark College. His major research interests include psychological, economic, and environmental approaches to international relations, with a primary focus on conflict. He is the author of *Perception, Decision Making, and Conflict* (1978) and numerous book chapters and articles. He is currently working on studies of shows-of-force and irrationality in world politics.

Richard M. Merelman is a professor of political science at the University of Wisconsin at Madison. He received his Ph.D. degree in political science from Yale University and has taught at Wesleyan University, the University of California at Los Angeles, and the University of Essex (England). He has written extensively in the areas of political psychology and sociology and on political socialization. His book *Making Something of Ourselves: On Culture and Politics in the United States* was published in 1984.

Lester W. Milbrath is director of the Environmental Studies Center and professor of political science at the State University of New York at Buffalo. He has taught at Northwestern University, Duke University, and the University of Tennessee, and has twice been a Fulbright scholar to Norway as well as a visiting professor at the University of Aarhus in Denmark and a visiting scholar in the Center for Resource and Environmental Studies at the Australian National University, Canberra. He has built on his past research on political beliefs, political participation, and lobbying in studying environmental questions. His current research focuses on environmental beliefs and values, on public participation in environmental policy decisions, on assessing environmental quality and quality of life, and on forecasting and planning for environmental futures. He is the author of *The Washington Lobbyists* (1963), *Political Participation* (1977), *The Politics of Environmental Policy* (1975), and *Environmentalists: Vanguard for a New Society* (1984).

Maritza Montero is an associate professor of social psychology at the Universidad Central de Venezuela in Caracas. She received her magister degree in psychology from the Universidad Simón Bolívar and her Ph.D. degree in sociology from Paris University (École des Hautes Études en Sciences Sociales). Her major research interest is in the psychology of dependency. She is the author of *Ideologia, Alienacion y Identidad Nacional* (1984), which she worked on while a senior fellow at Saint Antony's College, Oxford University.

Steven A. Peterson is a professor of political science at Alfred University. He received his Ph.D. degree from the State University of New York at Buffalo. His major research interests include biopolitics, political behavior, and judicial processes. His articles have appeared in such journals as the *Journal of Politics, Western Political Quarterly, Political Psychology,* and *Micropolitics.*

Lucian W. Pye is Ford Professor of Political Science at the Massachusetts Institute of Technology. As a specialist in comparative politics, his research has concentrated on the psychological bases of the political cultures of Asian societies. As chairman of the Committee on Comparative Politics of the Social Science Research Council (1967–1972), he contributed to the growth of the field of political development and modernization. His books on Asian political psychology include *Politics, Personality, and Nation Building* (1962), *Mao Tse-Tung: The Man in the Leader* (1976), and *The Dynamics of Chinese Politics* (1981).

Ofira Seliktar is a fellow in residence in the Middle East Research Institute at the University of Pennsylvania. She received her Ph.D. degree from Strathclyde University, where she was a British council fellow and was formerly on the political science faculty of the University of Haifa, Israel. Her major research interests include comparative political psychology, conflict behavior, and the psychology of military intelligence. She is the author of numerous articles and of the forthcoming book, *New Zionism and Israel's Foreign Policy System.*

Shula Shichman is an assistant vice-president of Citibank, where she works as an organizational development consultant on strategic issues. She received her Ph.D. degree in social and organizational psychology from Columbia University. She also holds a graduate degree in clinical psychology from Tel-Aviv University and was a practicing clinician in Israel. Her areas of interest and research include managing conflict, organizational culture, organizational assessment, and managing change. She has published articles on psychopathology, managerial competencies, the development of organizational culture, and conflict resolution.

Paul M. Sniderman is a professor of political science at Stanford University. He received his Ph.D. degree from the University of California at Berkeley. His major research interests include public opinion and ideology, political alienation and allegiance, and the idea of race in American politics. He is the author of *Personality and Democratic Politics* (1975) and *A Question of Loyalty* (1981). He has been both a Guggenheim fellow and fellow at the Center for Advanced Study in the Behavioral Sciences.

Albert Somit is a professor of political science and president of Southern Illinois University. Previous faculty appointments were at New York University, the State University of New York at Buffalo, and visiting professor at the Naval War College. He has been chair of the International Political Science Association's Committee on Biology and Politics since 1970 and was a founding member of the Association for Politics and the Life Sciences. He is author of *Biology and Politics* (1976) and the near annual "The Literature of Biopolitics" (with S. A. Peterson).

Philip E. Tetlock is an associate professor of psychology at the University of California at Berkeley and is affiliated with the Survey Research Center at the same institution. He received his Ph.D. degree from Yale University. His areas of major research interest include social cognition and decision making, impression management and other forms of strategic behavior, and psychological processes that shape political attitudes and opinions. He is the author of numerous articles, including "Psychological Research on Foreign Policy" in *Review of Personality and Social Psychology* (1983) and "Policymakers' Images of International Conflict" in the *Journal of Social Issues* (1983).

Political Psychology

*Contemporary Problems
and Issues*

PROLOGUE

‽‽‽‽‽‽‽‽‽‽‽‽‽‽‽‽‽‽‽‽‽‽‽‽

What Is
Political Psychology?

Margaret G. Hermann

Political psychology is coming of age. In 1973, in the preface to the *Handbook of Political Psychology,* Jeanne Knutson urged that the collaborative efforts evidenced in that book be but a beginning to further theoretical and empirical study of the interaction of psychological and political phenomena. During the ensuing years, the International Society of Political Psychology has been established; the journal *Political Psychology* has been started; and those interested in political psychology have become more identifiable to one another. Some basic tenets of the field have also become more obvious during this period, as have certain issues that continue to arouse debate and discussion. Since both the tenets and the issues help to define the field of political psychology as it has evolved to date, a discussion of them sets the stage for the chapters that follow.

Five Apparent Tenets of Political Psychology

1. *Focus Is on the Interaction of Political and Psychological Phenomena.* There is a growing consensus that the focus of political psychology is on what happens when political and psychological phenomena interact (see, for example, Forum sections of *Political Psychology,* 1979–1985; "Political Dimensions of Psychology," 1983; Merelman, 1979; Schaffner and Alker, 1981–82). How do psycho-

Note: I wish to acknowledge the help of Charles Snare in the preparation of this prologue. His curiosity about just what political psychology is sparked many lively discussions. The remarks made by Morton Deutsch, Hilde Himmelweit, Robert Lane, and Helmut Moser during a roundtable entitled "What Is Political Psychology" at the International Society of Political Psychology meeting at Oxford University in 1983 and the animated audience debate that followed have also contributed to shaping the contents of this prologue.

logical factors help to determine political behavior, and how do political actions affect psychological factors? This interaction is viewed as bidirectional (see Deutsch, 1983). That is, the perceptions, beliefs, motives, opinions, values, interests, styles, defenses, and experiences of individuals—be they citizens, leaders, group members, bureaucrats, terrorists, or revolutionaries—are seen as influencing what they do politically; and, in turn, the political culture, political system, mechanisms of political socialization, political movements and parties, and the international system are perceived as having an impact on what people are like.

As a result of this focus, political psychology engages persons from multiple disciplines. Psychologists become involved because they are interested in explaining personal and group behavior in a political context. Political scientists see that individuals have an effect in the political arena and wonder why. They also are intrigued by the effects that variations in the political context can have on individuals. Sociologists are interested in exploring why individuals become part of political groups and organizations. Historians examine the place of the individual in forming and being formed by political events at certain points in time. Psychiatrists seek to understand how intrapsychic phenomena and life experiences affect people's political behavior. Anthropologists want to know how the political aspects of culture influence members of that culture, and vice versa. Members of these various disciplines bring a different perspective to examining how psychological and political phenomena interact; they ask different questions and begin to fill in different pieces of the puzzle.

2. *Research Is Responsive and Relevant to Societal Problems.* Many persons studying and interested in political psychology have been drawn to the field in response to what they perceive to be societal problems that have become politicized: environmental issues, fear of nuclear war, the crisis in public leadership, the growing discrepancy between "the haves and the have-nots," increasing dissatisfaction with government, terrorism, increased dominance of the mass media, growing interdependence among all sectors of society, prolonged ethnic conflicts, and discrimination. Knutson (1973, p. vii) has observed that problems like these "crucially affect the quality and the quantity of human life today," and their solutions demand the combination of insights about people and politics.

But, as both Mack (1983) and Moser (1983) have remarked, there is a sense of urgency about these problems. And for many of those in political psychology, there is a tension between wanting to make a difference and maintaining an analytical perspective. Some have reacted to this tension by trying out possible solutions and learning from what happens (Burton, 1969, 1979; Doob, 1970, 1974; Doob and Foltz, 1973; Kelman, 1979b; Kelman and Cohen, 1979); others have become participant observers (Dukakis, 1980; Lockard, 1959; Nixon, 1982; Stewart, 1985a, 1985b). Still others have tried to educate policy makers and the general public to understand why certain things are happening and what some possible alternatives are for dealing with the problem (Bennis and Nanus, 1985; Fisher and Ury, 1981; Harvard Nuclear Study Group, 1983; Maccoby 1976; Ury, 1985). Most, though, have simply attempted to make their research more relevant and more directly focused on a specific problem.

3. *Context Can Make a Difference.* Lane (1983) has observed that political psychology is the study of the person in a particular time and situation. One could add to this as well "in a particular political system and culture." How a researcher defines time, situation, political system, and culture has implications for both

what he perceives is an important societal problem and how psychological and political phenomena are viewed as interacting. There is growing recognition that such contextual factors help not only to shape what an individual is like but also to limit what an individual can do politically. Thus individuals appear to be shaped and constrained differently in turbulent times than in stable times, in autocratic regimes than in democratic regimes, in the Japanese culture than in the American culture.

Within political psychology there is a healthy dialogue and debate between those who search for the more general aspects of time, situation, culture, and political system that play critical roles in bounding how psychological and political phenomena interact and those who work within a specific context (with a particular problem located at a given point in time, in a specific culture and political system). Each contributes to the mosaic that is political psychology—the latter group working on a particular picture or square of the mosaic, the former group identifying the colors, texture, dimensions that will characterize the entire mosaic.

Greenstein (1973), Merelman (1979), and Moser (1979) note that political psychology weaves together the results from studies done by researchers (usually political scientists, historians, or anthropologists) that focus on context-specific material with the results from studies done by researchers (usually psychologists, sociologists, or psychiatrists) that examine cross-context material. According to Knutson (personal communication, April 8, 1980), one of her main purposes for establishing the International Society of Political Psychology (ISPP) was to foster interaction among those examining the effects of the context in these various ways—enabling each to appreciate the perspective and vista of the other.

4. *Emphasis Is on Process as Well as Outcome.* Those engaged in political psychology are as interested in how a particular political behavior came about (process) as in the behavior itself (outcome) (see Deutsch, 1983). How do voters decide? How can political conflicts be resolved? How do policy makers process information? How do leaders mobilize followers? How do young people become politically socialized? Psychological and political phenomena often seem to have their most direct impact on one another in determining political processes as opposed to political outcomes. Once delineated in one political setting, descriptions of processes offer the possibility of generalization to other political contexts with somewhat similar characteristics. By ascertaining what some of these cross-cutting processes are, political psychologists can begin to build more general explanations and theories.

5. *There Is a Tolerance of Multiple Methods for Gathering Data.* Political psychology appears not to be wedded to one type of methodology. Its practitioners employ a variety of methods: scientifically oriented research, case studies, historical narratives, "intensive" or more qualitative research. Instead of pressure to adopt and use one approach, there is encouragement of the multiple approaches because of the variety of information that is thus gained about a topic. Much as the clinician or physician does in arriving at a diagnosis, the political psychologist appears interested in examining systematic quantitative and qualitative data as well as subjective reactions and the historical record in considering what is happening in the political arena.

This tolerance for various methods has grown out of the multidisciplinary nature of political psychology. In order to encourage a sharing of perspectives among people from the various disciplines who are engaged in studying how psychological and political phenomena interact, there has been a need to accept and understand the variety of techniques used by the disciplines. Arguments are less likely over what methods are appropriate as over criteria for assessing how well the information gleaned from the various techniques matches or overlaps.

Issues in Political Psychology

In addition to the basic assumptions just discussed—assumptions about which there is growing agreement among those in the field—there are also, as is inevitable in a relatively young field, certain assumptions that continue to arouse much debate and discussion. The following are five issues over which opinion is divided.

1. *Should We Be Searching for a Single, Unifying Paradigm or Reinforcing the Pluralism That Presently Exists?* In the concluding chapter to the *Handbook of Political Psychology*, Greenstein (1973, p. 469) suggests that it is important to "let many flowers bloom" in the study of political psychology and to encourage the pluralism he sees as existing in the field. Merelman (1979, p. 106), on the other hand, comparing political psychology to Humpty-Dumpty, worries that in its fragmented condition it may never get back together again. Currently, those involved in political psychology tend to focus on particular problems (or topics)—terrorism, leadership, conflict resolution, ideology, socialization—or on areas of the world—the Middle East, East-West relations—with little communication among persons working in these various arenas. Interdisciplinary networks are emerging around these topics and areas, but there is little cross-fertilization among the networks. Within each problem or area focus, there is a growing attempt to develop theories or models that explain the particular phenomenon. The theories often take into account the multiple perspectives of the disciplines represented in the networks. In general, however, little effort has been made to find cross-cutting themes or processes that link these topics or areas together. That is, there are few proposals to suggest how ways of explaining phenomena in one of these arenas may be similar to ways of explaining phenomena in another arena.

Smith's (1968, 1973) functional map of the relationship between personality and politics has been offered as one way of organizing the field of political psychology (see, for example, Deutsch, 1983; Schaffner and Alker, 1981–82). This map, shown in Figure 1, suggests what kinds of phenomena are likely to influence what other phenomena and the kinds of factors that need to be taken into account in understanding political behavior. Individual studies in political psychology emphasize one of the factors indicated in the map or focus on one of the sets of relationships stipulated in the map. Were we to juxtapose these studies, could we begin to fill in the map and develop propositions linking the various factors? The astute reader may be puzzled at this point, observing that the map focuses on the individual. How can such a map help us account for group, organizational, national, cultural, or intergroup political behavior? Can we simply change the labels—substituting, for example, "group" for "self," "person," or "personality"; or must additional factors be considered or the factors on the map rearranged?

At issue is whether political psychologists are ready to develop a map of the terrain or are still deciding what features should be highlighted on such a map and even whether a single map is possible or relevant.

Figure 1. A Functional Map: Political Attitudes in Their Personal and Social Context.

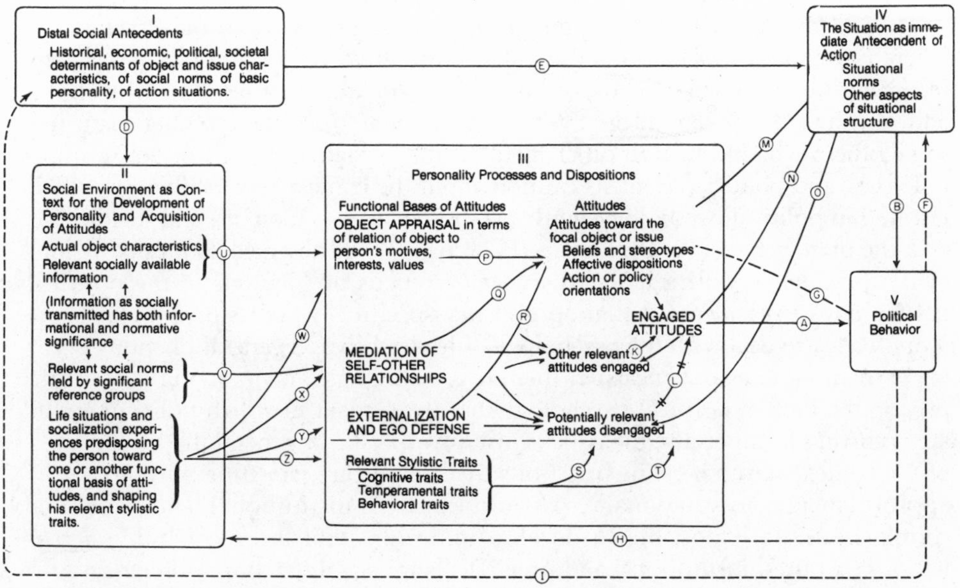

Source: Adapted from Smith, 1968.

2. *What Is the Appropriate Unit of Analysis for Political Psychology?* Knutson (1973, p. ix) has noted that the integrating focus of political psychology "remains a concern with individual-level determinants of political behavior." Yet an overview of the International Society of Political Psychology's programs and of the journal *Political Psychology* shows as much emphasis on group, organizational, and governmental dynamics as on individuals. As Eulau (1968, p. 209) has observed, political psychologists face a dilemma: "Although concrete political action is invariably the behavior of individual human actors, the politically significant units of action are groups, associations, organizations, communities, states, and other collectivities. . . . The problem involves constructing, not only theoretically but also empirically, the chain of interactions and transactions that links the individual actor to the collectivities of which he is a part."

This dilemma presents a challenge to those in political psychology. It suggests that no single level of analysis can dominate research; that the emphasis, indeed, needs to be on developing the rules for moving from one level of analysis to another—from the individual to the collectivity, from the collectivity to the individual. There are many pitfalls strewn in the path of such cross-level analysis. How do we go about aggregating individual data; are there characteristics of collectivities that are independent of the aggregated characteristics of individual members? Can we extrapolate or treat as analogous explanations of political behavior at the individual level and those made at the level of a collectivity? Under what conditions is it appropriate to generalize from observations of a sample of individuals in a collectivity to the nature of the collectivity as a whole? Those in political psychology are just beginning to wrestle with such questions. The initial tendency is to treat these issues from a disciplinary perspective—we as psychologists do this, as political scientists we do this, while as historians we do something else. This reaction has led to debate and the growing recognition that political psychologists as a group may need to consider these issues anew, given the importance of the interrelationship between individuals and collectivities in this field.

3. *How Important Is a Comparative Approach to Political Psychology?* There is a natural tension among the disciplines involved in political psychology regarding the uniqueness of any situation, individual, or group. The Kluckhohn and Murray (1948, p. 35) adage "We are at the same time like no other man, like some other men, and like all other men" is appropriate here. Historians, anthropologists, and political scientists caution about the context-specific nature of their research in political psychology, while psychologists, psychiatrists, and sociologists seek the more general. As Greenstein (1973, p. 457) has observed about discussions of the presidency, political scientists tend to focus on "aspects of the political psychology of presidents that are presidency-specific," whereas psychologists are more likely "to deal with the psychology of leadership as a general phenomenon."

Although, as noted earlier, there is growing agreement among those comprising the field of political psychology that the context in which political events are occurring is important, the issue is just how specific or general the specification of the context has to be. The questions that people are wrestling with are: How appropriate are cross-national, cross-cultural, cross-institutional, and cross-time comparisons? Is it possible to develop indicators that are comparable across nations, cultures, institutions, and time? Do language differences, different norms and values, and different historical experiences distort such comparisons? Is there a set of factors that, if identified, could establish comparability between what appear on the surface to be similar contexts? The multidisciplinary nature of political psychology heightens this debate; and the debate at times overshadows the substantive questions that the various disciplinary representatives are asking. It is often easier to indicate how context factors have dictated another's findings than to deal with the substantive findings and conclusions themselves. In some areas of political psychology, however, interaction among psychologists, sociologists, historians, and political scientists has led to the initial formulation of rules for determining what contexts are comparable and what types of comparisons are more and less appropriate (for example, see Himmelweit's 1983 discussion of political socialization). Increased interdisciplinary action is likely to have a similar effect on other areas of political psychology as disciplinary representatives begin to understand and share each other's views on context effects.

4. *What Are the Boundaries Between Research and Action?* Given the problem focus of much of the research undertaken in political psychology and the focus on problems that have often become politicized, there is a growing debate among those working in the field on the nature of their ethical imperatives and social responsibilities. Some of the questions being raised include: How do we learn to recognize the extent to which our own cultural and political biases color the policies we propose and the research we conduct? How do we avoid confusing an individual's "political correctness with the validity or scientific worth of whatever it is that he or she is producing" (Kaplan, 1979, p. 99)? How do we avoid the problem in more action-oriented research of "creating the phenomena that we are observing" (Kelman, 1979a, p. 101)? How does the level of analysis that we choose to focus on in our research—individual, group, organization, or nation—influence the assumptions we make about where the problem lies and possible solutions for dealing with it? "If we define the problem as the psychological problem of a certain group of people, then we're more likely to develop policies that involve

changing these people, rather than policies that involve changing the social structures that help sustain their powerlessness" (Kelman, 1979a, p. 102). What is the appropriate knowledge base on which to rest policy proposals and action? Which types of action are most appropriate (for example, facilitating exchange between researchers and policy makers, or social intervention, or developing propaganda materials)?

These issues are not peculiar to political psychology or to this point in time. The problem focus of political psychology, however, gives these debates more urgency, since many become engaged in the field because they want to translate knowledge into action, to work toward solutions to problems. Political psychologists need to be encouraged to develop the possible responses to these issues in more detail than has been done to date. (For guides that might facilitate more systematic consideration of the questions we have raised, see Kelman, 1968; Lindblom and Cohen, 1979; McHale, Hughes, and Grundy, 1980; Organization for Economic Cooperation and Development, 1977; Rappaport, 1977; Rein, 1980; Segall, 1977; Snyder, Hermann, and Lasswell, 1976; Weiss, 1977.)

5. *What Kind of Training Does a Political Psychologist Need?* Since political psychology includes among its ranks people with a variety of disciplinary backgrounds and with a variety of research and problem concerns, the question of what should be involved in training in political psychology becomes nontrivial. Merelman (1979) has observed that at present training in political psychology is "haphazard." Most people receive degrees in one of the disciplines—anthropology, history, political science, psychiatry, psychology, sociology—involved in the study of political psychology. With luck they take several courses within their disciplinary focus that examine political behavior or one of the topics in political psychology, or they are permitted to take several courses in one of the other disciplines that compose political psychology. The student, however, is responsible for integrating the materials across disciplinary and topical boundaries. Academic and research positions also are generally available along disciplinary lines. As a result of these factors, individuals interested in political psychology usually design their own courses of training and, often, receive what training they do get after they are on the job and can afford time to look at topics of interest to them outside of purely disciplinary professional demands. Thus, what training there is tends to be topic and discipline specific and does not cut across the set of topics or disciplines included under political psychology.

Were the circumstances different and were we asked to design a course of study in political psychology, what would it entail? Schaffner (1981-82) and Schaffner and Alker (1981-1982, in reviewing five texts in political psychology (Elms, 1976; Freedman and Freedman, 1975; Manheim, 1982; Segall, 1977; Stone, 1974), found that there is no consensus on the topics, theories, and methods that should be emphasized. The pluralism we noted earlier that pervades political psychology is evident in the texts. The five texts "share a core conception of the importance of psychological processes in political events, but they differ profoundly in their topical interests and their theoretical perspectives insofar as they are made available" (Schaffner and Alker, 1981-82, p. 219). In effect, students will get a different picture of political psychology from each of the five texts. These reviewers suggest that political psychology, as represented by these texts, is experiencing some of the "identity confusion" found in relatively new fields as those working in the area seek to construct a professional identity.

In addition to questions of curriculum, there are queries about whether students of political psychology need to be trained in more than one discipline and, if so, which ones. Is political psychology training more appropriate at the postdoctoral than the predoctoral level? Can political psychology be learned only by having an interdisciplinary team of teachers who present different perspectives on a topic or by joining an interdisciplinary team of researchers or network of individuals involved in examining a particular topic? As political psychology becomes a more established, legitimate field of inquiry, questions such as these are arousing more attention and discussion.

Chapters in This Book

The chapters in this book exhibit the apparent tenets of political psychology outlined earlier in this prologue. They examine how political and psychological phenomena interact; they reflect a responsiveness to and interest in societal problems; they suggest how contextual factors can make a difference; they emphasize political processes as well as political outcomes; and they report research based on a variety of techniques and methods. The chapters also wrestle with the issues that political psychologists are currently discussing and debating. Each contributor believes that his or her topic is at the heart of what political psychology is; each would argue that the topic should be a part of any curriculum in political psychology. Yet there is very little overlap among the theories that are espoused or the literature that is reviewed. The unit of analysis in the chapters that follow is not always the individual; and, indeed, several of the chapters make suggestions about how to move from the individual as the unit of analysis to the collectivity while still examining problems of importance to political psychologists. The chapters differ in the degree to which they are context specific and the degree to which the authors are willing to generalize the frameworks that they propose to other settings and times. Moreover, there is consideration of the boundaries between research and action. In the epilogue, we will return to these issues and explore the alternative ways the chapters have responded to these dilemmas. Readers should keep these issues in mind as they examine the chapters and consider the effects on what is presented of choosing one route in dealing with these dilemmas over another.

References

Bennis, W., and Nanus, B. *Leaders: The Strategies for Taking Charge.* New York: Harper & Row, 1985.

Burton, J. *Controlled Communication: The Use of Controlled Communication in International Relations.* London: Macmillan, 1969.

Burton, J. *Deviance, Terrorism, and War: The Process of Solving Unsolved Social and Political Problems.* New York: St. Martin's Press, 1979.

Deutsch, M. "What Is Political Psychology?" *International Social Science Journal,* 1983, *35,* 221–236.

Doob, L. W. *Resolving Conflict in Africa: The Fermeda Workshop.* New Haven, Conn.: Yale University Press, 1970.

Doob, L. W. "A Cyprus Workshop." *Journal of Social Psychology,* 1974, *94,* 161–178.

Doob, L. W., and Foltz, W. J. "The Belfast Workshop." *Journal of Conflict Resolution,* 1973, *17,* 489–512.

Dukakis, M. "The Psychology of Victory and the Psychology of Defeat: The Governorship of Massachusetts." Paper presented at meeting of the International Society of Political Psychology, Boston, June 4–7, 1980.

Elms, A. *Personality in Politics.* San Diego: Harcourt Brace Jovanovich, 1976.

Eulau, H. "Political Behavior." In D. L. Sills (ed.), *International Encyclopedia of the Social Sciences.* Vol. 12. New York: Macmillan, 1968.

Fisher, R., and Ury, W. L. *Getting to Yes: Negotiating Agreement Without Giving In.* Boston: Houghton Mifflin, 1981.

Freedman, A. E., and Freedman, P. E. *The Psychology of Political Control.* New York: St. Martin's Press, 1975.

Greenstein, F. I. "Political Psychology: A Pluralistic Universe." In J. N. Knutson (ed.), *Handbook of Political Psychology.* San Francisco: Jossey-Bass, 1973.

Harvard Nuclear Study Group (Carnesale, A., Doty, P., Hoffmann, S., Huntington, S. P., Nye, J. S., Jr., and Sagan, S. D.). *Living with Nuclear Weapons.* New York: Bantam Books, 1983.

Himmelweit, H. T. "Political Socialization." *International Social Science Journal,* 1983, *35,* 237–356.

Kaplan, A. "Ethical Imperatives and Social Responsibility in the Practice of Political Psychology." *Political Psychology,* 1979, *1,* 99–100.

Kelman, H. C. *A Time to Speak: On Human Values and Social Research.* San Francisco: Jossey-Bass, 1968.

Kelman, H. C. "Ethical Imperatives and Social Responsibility in the Practice of Political Psychology." *Political Psychology,* 1979a, *1,* 100–102.

Kelman, H. C. "An Interactional Approach to Conflict Resolution and Its Application to Israeli-Palestinian Relations." *International Interactions,* 1979b, *6,* 99–122.

Kelman, H. C., and Cohen, S. P. "Reduction of International Conflict: An Interactional Approach." In W. G. Austin and J. Worchel (eds.), *The Social Psychology of Intergroup Relations.* Monterey, Calif.: Brooks/Cole, 1979.

Kluckhohn, C., and Murray, H. A. "Personality Development: The Determinants." In C. Kluckhohn and H. A. Murray (eds.), *Personality in Nature, Society and Culture.* New York: Knopf, 1948.

Knutson, J. N. "Preface." In J. N. Knutson (ed.), *Handbook of Political Psychology.* San Francisco: Jossey-Bass, 1973.

Lane, R. E. "What Is Political Psychology?" Remarks made during a roundtable at meeting of the International Society of Political Psychology, St. Catherine's College, Oxford University, July 19–22, 1983.

Lindblom, C. A., and Cohen, D. K. *Usable Knowledge: Social Science and Social Problem Solving.* New Haven, Conn.: Yale University Press, 1979.

Lockard, D. "The Tribulations of a State Senator." In J. C. Wahlke and H. Eulau (eds.), *Legislative Behavior: A Reader in Theory and Research.* New York: Free Press, 1959.

Maccoby, M. *The Gamesman.* New York: Simon & Schuster, 1976.

McHale, V. E., Hughes, B. B., and Grundy, K. W. *Evaluating Transnational Programs in Government and Business.* Elmsford, N.Y.: Pergamon Press, 1980.

Mack, J. "What Is Political Psychology?" Remarks made during a roundtable at meeting of the International Society of Political Psychology, St. Catherine's College, Oxford University, July 19-22, 1983.

Manheim, J. B. *The Politics Within: A Primer in Political Attitudes and Behavior.* (2nd. ed.) New York: Longman, 1982.

Merelman, R. M. "On the Asking of Relevant Questions: Discussion Notes Towards Understanding the Training of Political Psychologists." *Political Psychology*, 1979, *1*, 104-109.

Moser, H. "Ansätze und inhaltliche Struktur einer politischen Psychologie" [Definitions and issues in political psychology]. In H. Moser (ed.), *Politische Psychologie* [Political psychology]. Weinheim, West Germany: Beltz, 1979.

Moser, H. "What Is Political Psychology?" Remarks made during a roundtable at meeting of the International Society of Political Psychology, St. Catherine's College, Oxford University, July 19-22, 1983.

Nixon, R. M. *Leaders.* New York: Warner Books, 1982.

Organization for Economic Cooperation and Development. *The Utilization of the Social Sciences in Policy Making.* Paris: Organization for Economic Cooperation and Development, 1977.

"Political Dimensions of Psychology." *International Social Science Journal*, 1983, *35* (2), 221-351.

Rappaport, J. *Community Psychology: Values, Research, and Action.* New York: Holt, Rinehart & Winston, 1977.

Rein, M. "Methodology for the Study of the Interplay Between Social Science and Social Policy." *International Social Science Journal*, 1980, *32*, 361-368.

Schaffner, P. E. "Texts in Political Psychology: II." *Political Psychology*, 1981-82, *3* (3/4), 189-195.

Schaffner, P. E., and Alker, H. "Toward Disciplinary Identity: Texts in Political Psychology." *Political Psychology*, 1981-82, *3* (1/2), 184-225.

Segall, M. H. *Human Behavior and Public Policy: A Political Psychology.* Elmsford, N.Y.: Pergamon Press, 1977.

Smith, M. B. "A Map for the Analysis of Personality and Politics." *Journal of Social Issues*, 1968, *24*, 15-28.

Smith, M. B. "Political Attitudes." In J. N. Knutson (ed.), *Handbook of Political Psychology.* San Francisco: Jossey-Bass, 1973.

Snyder, R. C., Hermann, C. F., and Lasswell, H. D. "A Global Monitoring System: Appraising the Effects of Government on Human Dignity." *International Studies Quarterly*, 1976, *20*, 221-260.

Stewart, P. D. "Informal Diplomacy: The Dartmouth Conference Experience." In D. D. Newsom (ed.), *Private Diplomacy with the Soviet Union.* Washington, D.C.: Institute for Study of Diplomacy, School of Foreign Service, Georgetown University, 1985a.

Stewart, P. D. "Private Citizens and the Process of International Communication: A Study of 20 Years of the Dartmouth Conference." In A. Vanderven (ed.), *Citizens and the Political Process: The Kettering Experience.* Dayton, Ohio: Kettering Foundation, 1985b.

Stone, W. F. *The Psychology of Politics.* New York: Free Press, 1974.

Ury, W. L. *Beyond the Hotline.* Boston: Houghton Mifflin, 1985.

Weiss, C. H. (ed.). *Using Social Research in Public Policy.* Lexington, Mass.: Lexington Books, 1977.

ONE

❧❧❧❧❧❧❧❧❧❧❧❧❧❧❧❧❧❧❧❧

Biological Correlates
of Political Behavior

Albert Somit
Steven A. Peterson

Any discussion of recent attempts to apply biological concepts and techniques to political behavior should begin with two reminders: first, that there is a long tradition of using biological metaphors and ideas in political philosophy; second, that barely a century ago there was a remarkably unsuccessful attempt to build a social science on what was mistakenly thought to be scientifically sound biological theory.

Biology in Classical Political Thought

As even a casual survey of the literature testifies, political theorists have traditionally based their ideas on assumptions about the biological basis of human nature. Plato insisted, in his *Republic,* that there are essentially three different types of human nature; and he justified the structure of his ultimate "utopia" on the different political aptitudes that he associated with each. His distinguished critic and rival Aristotle rested much of the argument in his *Politics* on the proposition that "man is by nature a political animal." Subsequently, Aristotle introduced two other biological premises: (1) that those who are slaves are in that servile role by virtue of their biological nature; and, perhaps currently more controversial, (2) that women are intellectually inferior to men because of their different biological makeup.

Roman Stoic thought, with Cicero an excellent case in point, took for granted the essential biological and intellectual equality of mankind. Centuries later John of Salisbury utilized an extended biological metaphor to describe the state—depicting, for instance, the king as the "head," and the church as the "heart" or "soul." Machiavelli's *Prince* testifies to the Florentine's explicit and unflattering conception of "innate" human nature. And, it need hardly be said, both Thomas Hobbes and John Locke based their divergent theories of the origin of the state on diametrically opposed conceptions of human nature.

The regularity with which political and social philosophers have turned to biology requires little explanation, since the pivotal question underlying all political speculation is that of the "nature of human nature" (see Somit, 1981). The major differences among philosophers, and between philosophical schools, in large part turn on this issue. Is man a political animal by nature, as Aristotle insisted, or is he made into a social being by society, as Plato would have it? Are humans inherently unselfish and good, as Locke claimed, or are they fundamentally self-seeking, as Hobbes maintained? What is the nature of political man—good, bad, or neutral? Is human nature relatively fixed, a view that tends to prevail among conservative philosophers, or is it reasonably plastic, as liberals and most utopian theorists believe? Are there differences in moral and legal "rights" between one person and another, which can be justified, as Aristotle argued, on the basis of their different biological makeup?

From these basic questions follow issues of major import: To what extent are present political institutions well or ill adapted to "human nature"? What political goals are "realistic," given what we understand (or believe) to be the malleability, or lack thereof, of human nature? These and similar questions make it abundantly clear why the nature of human nature remains a central issue in political philosophy. They also explain why political philosophers have so often turned to biology in their search for answers.

Social Darwinism and Its Aftermath

The attempt to use biology, in one form or another, was not limited simply to political philosophy. In the late nineteenth century, there occurred a concerted, if misguided, effort to build a social science on the basis of what was then understood to be the Darwinian theory of evolution. Arguing from alleged biological principles, Herbert Spencer and William Graham Sumner drew one set of conclusions, Lester Frank Ward and Peter Kropotkin quite different ones; and, in the most notorious version of Social Darwinism, Joseph de Gobineau, Alfred Rosenberg, and their fellow racists also claimed a "scientific" basis for their doctrines.

There were two major defects in these various attempts to move from biology to social science: They entailed grave misreadings and misinterpretations of Darwinian thought; furthermore, Darwinian biology itself left too many questions unanswered. The net effect of Social Darwinism was to discredit for almost a half century (from approximately 1900 to the mid-1950s) the notion that human social and political behavior is in any way influenced by biological makeup. American social scientists essentially rejected the possibility that genetic factors in any significant way influenced the phenomena with which they were concerned.

Mid-Twentieth-Century Resurgence of Interest in Biology

During the first half of the twentieth century, then, the prevailing "paradigm" in American social science was based on the assumption that human behavior is primarily the product of learning and social conditioning. By mid-century, though, there was increasing evidence of a renewed interest among social scientists in possible biological influences. Several factors contributed to this shift in outlook.

Freudian Psychology. Among the more important of these influences was a growing receptivity to Freudian thought, either in its original form or as modified by Freud's disciples. Freudian doctrine holds, fundamentally, that human behavior is the product of nonrational innate tendencies and that these drives are an intrinsic aspect of man's biological makeup. While Freud conceded the importance, for the individual psyche, of events that occur during infancy and youth, he nonetheless claimed that human nature is essentially universal—that is, largely independent of cultural influences—and that this universality stems ultimately from our common genetic legacy (for example, see Davies, 1963).

The Psychopharmacological Revolution. About the same time, there occurred a profound transformation in the treatment of mental disorders. Prior to mid-century, there were basically two modes of treatment for psychoses and neuroses. For the fairly mild ailments, there was the familiar therapeutic session. When the illness was more severe, the individual was removed from society and placed in some type of "mental hospital." Whether public or private, these were basically designed as custodial institutions and primarily concerned with keeping the patients from injuring themselves or others; real therapy was limited or nonexistent.

These practices began to change in the 1950s as researchers discovered a variety of drugs capable of achieving striking behavioral modifications. Some drugs quieted manic and disordered patients to the point where they could be reasonably self-sustaining. Other drugs were employed to energize depressed and melancholic patients, thereby enabling them to resume a more normal existence. This approach had the further advantage of "opening" the patient, once calm, to nonpharmacological therapeutic procedures.

The "psychopharmacological revolution" had two major consequences. It greatly altered much of existing psychiatric treatment and brought about sweeping reductions in the number of persons held in mental institutions. Second, and from the standpoint of this discussion more germane, it demonstrated a clear-cut linkage between the physiological functioning of the body and the functioning of the mind. Subsequent developments in psychopharmacology and brain science have further reaffirmed that link.

Brainwashing. During the 1950s the close relationship between the body and the mind had already been grasped by students of the phenomenon popularly termed "brainwashing." As the Soviets and, subsequently, the Chinese demonstrated, brainwashing (or coercive indoctrination) could radically alter an individual's value systems and beliefs. That is, brainwashing could bring an individual to give up one set of beliefs and accept diametrically opposed values.

Central to the brainwashing technique, in both the Soviet and Chinese versions, was a determined and calculated assault on the body, as well as the mind. Once the body was weakened by a sharply reduced diet, physical abuse, unremitting stress, and drastic interference with sleeping patterns, the desired psychological and ideological changes could be achieved with relative ease. Even more clearly than the use of psychopharmaceuticals, brainwashing demonstratd the close interplay between "body" and "mind."

The Rise of Ethology. By 1950 the "neo-Darwinian synthesis" made it possible for biologists to describe, in reasonably satisfactory fashion, the basic processes operative in evolution. Neo-Darwinism, consequently, is a far more powerful explanatory tool than its nineteenth-century precursor. Ordinarily, such a development would have been of primary interest only to biologists, but one branch of the new biology had a much wider impact. We refer, of course, to the amazing popularity of the ethological writings of Lorenz (1952, 1966), Ardrey (1961, 1966, 1970), and Morris (1967, 1969), who attracted a vast readership by their explanations of why animals behave as they do and by their unabashed readiness to apply their explanatory concepts to human social and political behavior. These ethological best-sellers did much to win acceptance, among the public at large and among many social scientists, for the idea that biological and genetic makeup play a significant role in shaping social behavior.

Sociobiology. Closely related to, and coming almost immediately on the heels of, ethology was the attention attracted by what is now called sociobiology—the study of the evolutionary bases of social behavior. Sociobiology proposes a solution to a problem that has long puzzled ethologists—altruistic behavior. If altruism is the willingness to sacrifice oneself for the benefit of others, how is such a trait successfully transmitted to succeeding generations? The solution advanced by the sociobiologists shifts emphasis from "reproductive fitness" to "inclusive fitness." They explain altruistic behavior by looking not only at the individual's reproductive potential but also at that of those who are closely related, in genetic terms, to that individual. Inclusive fitness is defined as "the sum of an individual's fitness as measured by personal reproductive success and that of relatives, with relatives devalued in proportion to their genetic distance; that is, as they share fewer genes" (Barash, 1977, p. 329). A mother, for example, shares half her genes with each of her children. If, by some self-sacrificing altruistic act, a mother ensures the survival of three of her children, she achieves a 50 percent gain in inclusive fitness. For, even though that act causes her own death, there remain alive three offspring, each carrying 50 percent of the mother's genes and each potentially capable of transmitting those genes to succeeding generations. As another illustration we note that cousins carry one eighth of an individual's genes; thus, in order to justify an altruistic act, one would have to save at least nine cousins before perishing.

The logic of sociobiology has aroused some disagreement when applied to nonhuman species. However, when applied to humans, sociobiology has generated heated debate. The final chapter of Wilson's (1975) classic *Sociobiology,* with its attempt to apply to *Homo sapiens* an explanatory theory based on the study of animal and insect species, stirred up a violent and continuing controversy. In the process, it also undoubtedly contributed to the growing plausibility of the idea that human behavior can at least partially be explained in biological and genetic terms.

Public Policy Issues. The last contributing factor that requires mention here is the emergence, in the 1950s and 1960s, of a number of urgent public policy issues with "biological" components. Among these issues were population pressures, the danger of nuclear war, environmental pollution (including the use of pesticides and herbicides), genetic engineering, aging, and a variety of prickly medical questions ranging from abortion to euthanasia. A growing public concern with these topics led more and more political scientists in particular to study the substantive, as well as the philosophical and political, aspects of these problems (Somit and others, 1980, pp. 11–12, 69–74).

Biopolitics

"Biopolitics" is the shorthand, if not entirely felicitous, term used to describe the attempt by social scientists, in particular political scientists, to employ biological concepts and techniques for the better understanding of political phenomena. Although biopoliticians share the belief that biological techniques and concepts can be useful in examining political behavior, their research moves in three quite different directions: (1) applying ethological and sociobiological perspectives to political behavior; (2) studying physiological influences on political behavior; and (3) utilizing research techniques borrowed from the biological sciences. This tripartite classification, we should add, does not include two additional categories—namely, a literature arguing the pros and cons of applying biology to political phenomena and items focusing primarily on public policy issues. For reasons of space, these two will not be covered in this chapter.

Table 1 depicts the relative popularity of each of the three areas of research in biopolitics that we will examine. The ethological/sociobiological/evolutionary approach has consistently comprised about 50 percent of the literature. The corpus of work on physiological aspects has varied somewhat but has tended to stay at around 30 percent. The research techniques studies are the least abundant. Overall, we can discern no compelling shifts among these three areas of research over the past decade.

Table 1. Trends in Biopolitical Research, by Subarea.

Subarea	1963–1969	1970–1974	1975–1979	1980–1982	Total
Ethological/ Evolutionary/ Sociobiological	7 (47%)	35 (51%)	66 (48%)	80 (52%)	188 (50%)
Physiological	6 (40%)	22 (32%)	36 (26%)	47 (31%)	111 (30%)
Research Techniques	2 (13%)	11 (16%)	35 (26%)	26 (17%)	74 (20%)
Total	15	68	137	153	373

Source: Data for the first three time periods are taken from Somit and others, 1980; numbers for the final period, from Peterson and others, 1982, 1983.

In the following sections, we will describe the central features of each of the areas mentioned, briefly summarize recent trends, and discuss the literature.

Ethological/Sociobiological/Evolutionary Approach

The concepts used in ethology and sociobiology to explain and describe animal behavior are almost guaranteed to elicit the interest of those studying political behavior. Among these are dominance and subordination, aggression and altruism, territoriality, and imprinting, all of which seem to have human analogues. Works in this subarea tend to deal with the "big" issues, such as the nature of human nature, war, aggression and political conflict, and the origins of political hierarchy.

The basic assumption on which ethology proceeds is that evolution (operating primarily via natural selection) fashions characteristic behavioral patterns for each species. These patterns, developed over millions of years (for a different time scale, see Eldredge, 1971; Eldredge and Gould, 1972), shape the manner in which a species conducts functions essential to its survival: nesting, hunting, defense, courtship, mating, care of the young, and relations with fellow speciates. To be sure, these genetically transmitted "instructions" vary from species to species in the degree to which they influence behavior. They are most controlling and inflexible among the lower forms of life but allow increasing variety of response to changing environmental conditions and learning as one moves up the "Great Ladder of Being." From worm to primate, however, they play an important part in the behavior of all organisms.

Does this also hold true for mankind? Practically all ethologists answer in the affirmative. *Homo sapiens*, they maintain, is the product of the same selective, evolutionary process that has molded all other species; humans are subject to the same biological laws as other forms of life. Needless to say, this viewpoint is not universally held by nonethologists; there is also considerable disagreement among ethologists about the *degree* to which human behavior is influenced by our genetic legacy. As might be expected, the lavish claims of some sociobiologists on this matter have generated a voluminous literature (for example, see Caplan, 1978).

There are trends apparent in this branch of biopolitics. First, attempts have been made to apply sociobiology to politics. Wilson's (1975) *Sociobiology* sparked considerable interest, and a 1977 meeting at Temple University featured a discussion involving a leading sociobiologist, political scientists, and other social and biological scientists on the relevance of sociobiology for the study of political behavior. (White's 1981b volume on *Sociobiology and Human Politics* presents, in part, the results of this meeting.) In fact, about half of the literature produced in this subarea since 1975 reflects a sociobiological perspective.

A second trend has been a more "sophisticated" use of ethology, sociobiology, and evolutionary theory. In the late 1960s and early 1970s, there was an innocent enthusiasm about the work of Ardrey and Lorenz (for example, Adrian, 1969; Masters, 1975; Pranger, 1967; Willhoite, 1971). Since then there has been manifest a wider array of theoretical approaches and a greater awareness of the difficulties associated with these various perspectives (for perceptive criticisms of sociobiology, for example, see G. Schubert, 1981b, 1982b).

In the following pages, we summarize the literature that adopts an ethological, sociobiological, or evolutionary framework to explain political phenomena. For the most part, the studies are grouped according to the "ethological" or "sociobiological" concepts around which literature has developed. Where the item does not fit conveniently into this format, we let the subject matter suggest the appropriate label.

Inclusive Fitness. Here is the central defining concept of mainstream sociobiology. As noted earlier, inclusive fitness implies that individuals should behave in such a way as to maximize the number of their genes that appear in the next generation. Since relatives have many genes in common, individuals should behave so as to increase their relatives' reproductive success as well.

One subject studied from this viewpoint is altruism and cooperation. For the sociobiologist altruism is self-sacrifice that benefits another. Kort (1977) contends that support for civil liberties in the United States may be, in part, an expression of the genetics of altruism. He argues that allowing others to exercise freedom may conflict with one's own desires. Thus, permitting blacks to vote (a civil liberty) may appear to a segregationist to undermine his power and position in society. To allow a black to vote under such circumstances is a form of altruism. Willhoite (1981) claims that the "norm of reciprocity" found in many human societies also is perfectly consistent with the inclusive fitness ideas from sociobiological theory (see also Beam, 1981; Masters, 1978). Using the familiar Prisoner's Dilemma game to examine the evolution of cooperative behavior, Axelrod and Hamilton (1981) conclude that cooperation based on reciprocity is a likely outcome and an evolutionarily stable strategy (ESS). (For an exploration of some problems with this approach, see Losco, 1981.)

A number of biopoliticians have discussed the emergence of bureaucracy as an example of genetically based altruistic or cooperative tendencies. Adrian (1970, p. 7), who does not adopt a sociobiological perspective, suggests that a need for cooperation partially explains the origins of bureaucracy: "Participation in organizational activities and goals . . . can be viewed as innately satisfying to the individual as part of his preprogrammed commitment to group preservation." Gulick (1977) also claims that bureaucracy helps fulfill a biologically based concern for one's fellow humans. On the other hand, Caldwell (1980, p. 2) argues that sociobiology confronts bureaucracy with a real challenge, for it calls into question assumptions long accepted in public law and policy: "An apparent human tendency to develop large, impersonal, centralized bureaucracies to cope with social needs could be a monumental error compounded by man's misunderstanding of his innate needs and limitations." Since *Homo sapiens* evolved in small, face-to-face groups, he may not be "programmed" to function well in impersonal bureaucratic structures; therefore, large-scale bureaucratic society may be doomed to fail (see also Masters, 1981c).

Finally, some have adopted a sociobiological orientation to explore cost-benefit thinking in humans. Margolis (1981) posits a model of human rationality based on a cost-benefit calculus that takes account of both individual and group interests. He argues that following one's own self-interest springs from inclusive fitness principles; behaving in terms of group interests comes from group selection. Both processes are operative in decision making. He concludes that the purely egoistical underpinning of classical economics ignores group interest as a motivation and, consequently, provides too limited a picture. Peterson and Somit (1981) hypothesize an evolutionary root for the human propensity to think—and often to behave—in cost-benefit terms. They note a similar tendency among male chimpanzees, which is reflected in their coalition behavior. Both chimpanzee and human decision making in small groups is characterized by shifts in alliances among group members to advance individuals' interests. Peterson and Somit speculate that there may be a common evolutionary pattern.

Aggression, Violence, and Defense. Aggressive behavior among animals has long fascinated ethologists, and those interested in biopolitics quickly attempted biological explanations of its human manifestations (for a more detailed summary, see Peterson and Somit, 1983). Corning (1971, 1973; Corning and Corning, 1972) presents a detailed evolutionary analysis of aggression but does not deal with its political aspects. Weiner (1974), concerned with the control of political violence, assumes that humans are innately aggressive and argues that this reality must be accepted in any solution to the problem. Among Weiner's proposals for minimizing outbreaks of violence is the creation of small political units. Strate (1981, p. 2), adopting a sociobiological framework, contends: "The single function of political systems is defense of their members from the attacks of hostile political systems." According to Strate, human intergroup conflict is the basic force producing social behavior (see also Schonscheck and Boyd, 1982; Ross, 1981).

One factor that some ethologists believe may affect aggressive behavior is excessive crowding, and those working in biopolitics have attempted to apply this idea to *Homo sapiens*. Singer and his colleagues (Bremer, Singer, and Luterbacher,

1973) used aggregate data to test the relationship between crowding (population density) and combat (battle-connected deaths) in Europe from 1815 to 1965. The outcome is inconclusive. Welch and Booth (1974), examining the association between crowding (for instance, household density) and mass violence in sixty-five nations, used a similar research strategy. Their results indicate that certain types of crowding have a modest relationship with violence. (See Welch, 1976, for a study of crowding effects at the individual level.)

Parent-Offspring Relations. Studies of primate behavior demonstrate that a male's status is often a function of his mother's standing in the group. Willhoite (1975) observes that, for humans, there is a tendency for the young to end up in the same social class as their parents. He believes that this cross-species similarity is evidence of evolutionary continuity and deduces that high-status human parents will pass on their own advantages to their offspring. In the process, equality of opportunity suffers, since some begin with a substantial head start in the "race of life." White (1981a, 1981b, 1981c) argues that Trivers's (1974) work on the sociobiology of parent-offspring conflict provides a theoretical basis with which to explain the generational conflict frequently observed in politics.

Dominance and Leadership Behavior. Many primate species have a clear-cut hierarchical social structure, and several students of biopolitics have sought to relate this structure to human politics. Willhoite (1976) suggests that stratification of political power and authority may be inherent in human social existence and that it will tend toward a mild leadership type, such as that evidenced in James Madison's "pluralism" (see also Kort, 1983).

Ethologist M. R. A. Chance has developed an "attention structure" theory, which views dominance as largely the result of an individual's ability to attract the attention of other group members. Two types of interaction—agonic (threat or force) and hedonic (facilitation, reassurance, reward)—are related to gaining attention and, hence, dominance. Several persons have sought to apply Chance's ideas to politics. (For a cogent critique of attention structure theory, see G. Schubert, 1982a, 1983b.) Barner-Barry (1977, 1978, 1979, 1981b, 1982a, 1982b) discusses the formation and maintenance of leadership among children. She observes that hedonic factors are more important in establishing leadership than agonic behavior. Masters (1976, 1981a, 1981b, 1982b) examined photographs of presidential candidates to determine the presence of nonverbal cues and their possible effects on mass support. He concludes that hedonic nonverbal cues (such as Nixon's reassuring facial expressions in the 1972 election) have an impact on electoral success (see also Beck, 1976).

Increased stress seems to produce more rigid dominance orders in many animal species. Madsen (1976) surveyed the literature on human political development, human political-social evolution, and primate behavior with respect to the impact of resource scarcity (a form of stress) on centralization of authority structures. His results were inconclusive. In an experimental study, however, Madsen (1982) found a relationship between stress and an increase in the influence of human small-group leaders.

Hummel (1970) has developed a biosocial model of "crisis charisma"; that is, the emergence of a strong, charismatic leader under conditions of social stress. In Hummel's view, stresses that threaten social stability produce, as one outcome, the prerequisites for charismatic leadership. He notes that the existence of crisis charisma has survival value for *Homo sapiens* and is, therefore, a predictable evolution-derived response.

Xenophobia. Many animal species live in groups; many of these, in turn, manifest hostility toward other groups of conspecifics. Willhoite (1977) hypothesizes that collective human intolerance (that is, hostility toward some out-group) may have a genetic basis. Observing that xenophobia seems present in many primate species, he advances the possibility of a common evolutionary cause. Ronen (1980) asserts that the quest for national self-determination has possible biological roots. One contemporary outcome is ethnic nationalism.

Evolution of the State. How did the state originate? This is one of the oldest questions in political philosophy. Over the last decade or so, several researchers interested in biopolitics have explored this issue. Claude Phillips first posited the relevance of evolutionary models for political development in 1971; he further elaborated the argument in 1973, noting that cultural evolution is the selective retention of cultural variation as culture adapts to environmental change. Phillips claims that the political component of a culture has the critical role of selecting choices from among existing variations; that is, the political sector decides which available options to take. These two essays provide the background for Phillips's (1981, p. 16) statement: "The evolutionary approach . . . views the origin of the state as a cultural adaptation to the environmental changes associated with the Agricultural Revolution. . . . The societies which responded to these changes by inventing states were the best adapted. . . . Those which did not invent states were generally absorbed by states, pushed into marginal areas, or isolated from contact with states."

Corning has also formulated an evolutionary theory of the state and politics (see, for example, Corning, 1974, 1981, 1982a, 1982b, 1983). He conceptualizes political society as a cybernetic system: " 'Positive' synergistic (combinatorial) effects of various kinds have been the underlying cause of 'progressive' sociocultural and political evolution" (1982b, p. 1). He emphasizes the functional, teleonomic (goal-oriented) nature of general evolutionary processes (whether sociocultural, political, or biological). This interactive (synergistic) feature of evolution, he holds, has led to increasingly complex, hierarchically organized political systems. As society has become larger and increasingly interdependent, hierarchy has become more pronounced. (Among others who have also investigated this issue are Geiger, 1982; Hines, 1981; MacKenzie, 1978; Masters, 1982a; Thorson, 1970.)

Physiological Influences on Behavior

In this subfield, the primary concern is the manner in which the physiological state of the human organism may modify social and political behavior. We have already noted that brainwashing, with its combined assault on mind and body, can be used to alter political beliefs. To date, more than a dozen physiological variables have been seen as affecting political attitudes and behavior. (Kort, 1983, has argued that it is arbitrary to separate physiological from evolutionary approaches in explaining political behavior. We draw this distinction because the two literatures have moved in rather diverse directions.)

A couple of trends are evident. First, there appears to be a decrease in the number of quantitative, empirical studies. From the origins of the contemporary biopolitics movement until 1975, roughly seventeen such projects were initiated (although the results may have been made public later); from 1976 through 1982, about eight. Only in the areas of stress, nutrition, and political cognition have there been any significant new efforts. A second, and perhaps related, trend is a move toward speculation about the neurophysiological bases of political thinking and behavior. Between 1980 and 1982, eighteen of the thirty-nine works in the "physiological aspects" subfield reflect this thrust. Prior to 1980 a much smaller proportion of the literature could be so labeled.

In the following sections, we summarize studies that have explored the physiology-politics linkage.

Health Status and Physical Fitness. It seems reasonable to hypothesize that health influences political behavior. Someone who is chronically ill, for example, is ordinarily less able to engage in such activity. Schwartz (1976a, 1976b, 1978; Schwartz and others, 1975) has conducted several studies of the relationship between health and political activity, using as his subjects a national adult sample, high school students in New Jersey, adults in the urban Northeast, members of Congress, top-level administrators in Washington, D.C., and federal appeals court judges. He found that poorer health was associated with depressed levels of participation, more negative views toward the political world, and more passive views toward politics. Peterson (1974) employed a much less precise self-report measure and discovered that health status bore little relationship to students' involvement in either protest activity or more traditional participation. Booth and Welch (1976) relied on fairly complete health data (derived from a medical examination) for a Toronto sample and detected a modest relationship with political activity—but in a direction contrary to Schwartz's findings. McBride (1980) replicated Schwartz's studies on a sample of Southern Illinois University students but was unable to confirm Schwartz's results.

Closely allied to health status is physical fitness. One investigator (Peterson, 1974) found that greater fitness was associated with higher levels of student political protest. Wiegele and colleagues (1975) utilized the treadmill test as a measure of fitness and report little relationship between college students' fitness and such attitudes as powerlessness, anxiety, world-mindedness, and isolationism. The only statistically significant correlation suggests that greater fitness is linked with lower levels of anomie. Booth and Welch (1976) used chest expansion, a general indicator of physical condition, as a possible predictor. They found it unrelated to three different dimensions of political behavior (working with others to try to influence community decision making, campaign efforts, and protest activity).

Energy Level. Some persons feel more energetic than others and often behave more energetically. Conceivably, energy level might affect political attitudes and behavior. Two studies look at this possible relationship, both using self-reports of energy level. Schwartz (1970), sampling University of Pennsylvania students and faculty, found that (controlling for political alienation) higher energy levels were correlated with less conformity and greater support for reformism. Peterson and Somit (1978b) used Schwartz's measure on a State University of New York at Buffalo student sample. Here energy level associated reasonably well with student protest activities, although not with standard dimensions of political participation. The relationship was considerably stronger for female respondents than for males.

Body Image. Psychological research suggests that people with more positive perceptions about their bodies tend to have greater self-esteem and self-acceptance than those with poorer body images (Fisher and Cleveland, 1968). In a pioneer study of body image as a predictor of political attitudes and behavior, Schwartz and colleagues (1975) found that body image is an intervening variable between health status and political participation and that it predicts participation fairly well. Shubs (1973) discovered that individuals perceive and evaluate politics on the same dimensions as they perceive and evaluate their own bodies (for example, well versus ill, strong versus weak). According to Peterson (1973, 1974, 1978, 1983a), body image has little effect on student protest behavior, but female respondents with positive body images are much more likely to engage in different dimensions of conventional participatory behavior than those with negative images. Finally, McBride (1980) reports that as body image becomes more positive, political participation decreases.

Height and Weight. Peterson (1974) found that height and weight were unrelated to student protest; however, with campaign activity and campus political behavior as dependent variables, increased female weight was associated with decreased activity. Booth and Welch (1976) discerned a small influence of height and weight on political activity; that is, both height and weight were inversely correlated with campaign activity. Waist size also was inversely linked with community-oriented political behavior. (No study has been conducted thus far on the impact of foot size.)

Stress. Preliminary efforts have been made to establish a link between stress and political behavior. Wiegele, relying on anecdotal evidence, asserts that the stress associated with foreign policy decision making affects adversely the quality of elites' decisions (see Wiegele, 1973, 1976; Wiegele and Plowman, 1974). Booth and Welch employed physiological indicators of stress to determine whether these indicators have any relationship with political attitudes or behavior. They report that "people who are politically involved in communal and protest activities show more signs of short-term stress than individuals not so involved. The signs of stress were most pronounced among actives with a low sense of political efficacy" (1976, p. 14). Overall, though, they found no clear connection between stress and political behavior.

Lehnen and Silberberg (1977) reversed the causal sequence to see whether stressful events in the larger political system (for instance, George Wallace's near assassination) may be related to an individual's sense of well-being. Their results are inconclusive, and the study can most profitably be deemed "heuristic," given the admittedly crude measures employed. Schulman (1975) also reversed the causal direction. He examined the impact of Richard Nixon's "Saturday Night Massacre" by comparing responses on a health and stress questionnaire before the massacre with those received afterward. Schulman concludes that such political events may have some effect on how persons feel about themselves.

Geigle (1977) relied on self-reports of life-change stress (the Social Readjustment Rating Questionnaire) to predict variances in political conservatism and cynicism. He found that "increasing amount of life experience successfully managed is positively associated with decreasing conservatism and increasing trust" (p. 30). Rosenberg and Lupfer (1981) used a variation of the same questionnaire to explore the relationship between (1) life stress and (2) political attitudes and behavior for a sample of Memphis adults. They discovered no clearly defined pattern of significant correlations.

Sex. The thesis that biological differences between males and females are related to differences in political behavior has been repeatedly advanced (see, for example, Baer, 1980; Baer and Bositis, 1983; Cook, 1983; Tiger, 1969; Watts, 1982). At a theoretical level, G. Schubert (1981a, 1981c) hypothesizes that there may be differences in political thinking between men and women because the female brain is less lateralized than the male brain; that is, females may be more "holistic" than males in making political decisions and, hence, capable of making "better" decisions than males—an issue to which we return later.

Several researchers have examined sex differences in behavior via survey research techniques. Dearden (1974) used Almond and Verba's (1963) five-nation study, plus a student sample, as data bases to explore sex differences in political behavior. He found a greater level of male political activity, consistent with predictions based on Tiger's (1969) work. However, there is no way of assuring that the observed differences are, in fact, physiologically based, since no biological variables were included in the data bases. (On general problems with this literature, see Baer and Bositis, 1982.) Both Andersen (1975) and Welch (1977) reanalyzed Survey Research Center data to investigate the relationship between sex and behavior. They discovered that sex differences in socioeconomic status, employment status, and educational attainment seem to explain many of the observed disparities in behavior; and they suggest that differences in political behavior by gender will diminish as more women complete their education and become part of the work force (compare with McDonagh, 1982).

Two investigators have tried to tie physiological factors to female political attitudes and behavior. Jaros (1976) looked at effects of the menstrual cycle: Female students indicated at which point in their cycle they were when they filled out a questionnaire on political attitudes (information on whether or not the respondent was using birth control pills was gathered as a control). Jaros discerned no strong relationships between the cycle and political attitudes. Peterson (1978) used a "menstrual distress" measure on a questionnaire administered to college students and discovered that degree of distress during the several phases of the menstrual cycle was unrelated to political behavior or attitudes.

Age at Puberty. Psychologists have observed that late-maturing males are more likely to have negative self-conceptions and feelings of inadequacy. Could age at puberty influence political attitudes and behavior? Ferguson, Ferguson, and Bouterline-Young (1970) tested this hypothesis on males from Palermo, Italy— many of whom had subsequently moved either to Rome (Italy) or Boston—and discovered that, in all three cities, age of puberty was linked with political attitudes. Late maturers manifested less political interest, less political information gathering, and lower levels of political efficacy. Peterson (1973, 1974) employed pubertal age as an independent variable and noted that, although it had no significant statistical relationship with student protest behavior, the direction of the correlation was different for males than for females. On the other hand, there was no correlation between onset of puberty and conventional forms of participation.

Intelligence. According to several investigators (Easton and Dennis, 1967; Hess and Torney, 1967; White, 1968), IQ scores of elementary school children are directly associated with sense of political efficacy. Harvey and Harvey (1970) administered a political questionnaire to high school students, using scores on a standardized aptitude test (the Differential Aptitude Test) as a measure of intelligence. Even when the authors controlled for standard predictors (such as socioeconomic status of parents), intelligence continued to bear a statistically significant relationship to both political knowledge and sense of civic duty. In most cases the Harveys found that intelligence was a better predictor of these dependent variables than socioeconomic status, parents' education, family wealth, or media exposure. Path analysis suggests that intelligence is an intervening variable between socioeconomic status and political attitudes and behavior. Rogers's (1972) data indicate that college student activists (whether on the right, left, or middle part of the ideological spectrum) have higher intelligence scores than the nonactivist student population.

Psychophysiological Arousal. Arousal is defined as an individual's general psychophysiological excitation. (For a very different view, however, see McGuinness and Pribram, 1980; Vanderwolf and Robinson, 1981.) Schwartz and Zill (1971, p. 2) hypothesize that *"ceteris paribus,* individuals characterized by a high level of overall arousal are more likely to be participants in a wide variety of interpersonal, social, and political contexts than are individuals with lower generalized arousal levels." They measured general arousal via posture and nonspeech verbal patterns, such as hesitations between words. Their results testify to a strong association of arousal with predisposition to participate in politics and reported level of actual political participation. Peterson's (1974, 1981b) data indicate that arousal, as measured by Thayer's adjective checklist, has only a modest relationship with student protest at the zero-order level. However, when standard socioeconomic variables were controlled for, the correlation increased dramatically, suggesting a "suppressor" or "threshold" effect. Peterson also detected a smaller degree of influence of arousal on more conventional participatory behavior.

Brain Structure. Several scholars have speculated about the manner in which the structure of the human brain might influence political thinking and behavior (for a lucid introduction, see Manheim, 1982, chap. 9). G. Schubert (1981a, 1981c) maintains that the brain's structure militates against the likelihood of "rational" decisions, because the human brain is "programmed" to perceive the environment selectively, depending on the subjective relevance of stimuli for the individual. The upshot is that decisions are likely to be skewed, given the flawed information base. Peterson (1982) also questions the rationality of human political behavior. Drawing heavily on Paul MacLean's concept of the triune brain, recent information on the brain's chemistry, and cognitive psychology, Peterson (1981c, 1983b) asserts that the brain's triune structure leads to the human propensity to "hypostatize"—that is, to attribute reality to human-created abstractions, to accept these abstractions as givens, and even blindly to adhere to them (see also Pettman, 1981).

Davies (1970, 1980) is perhaps the first political scientist to explore the physiological roots of aggression, calling attention to brain structure and endocrine factors. He has also provided a speculative framework—a neurophysiological prototheory—for explaining outbreaks of mass violence, such as revolution (Davies, 1976). Stegenga (1978) and Corning and Corning (1972) have summarized literature that focuses on the brain-aggression linkage.

Somewhat more cheerful implications have been drawn, as well, from the brain sciences. Davies (1971) contends that the brain provides the substrates for the drive toward Maslowian "self-actualization." White (1981a, 1981b) holds that human neurobiology supports the view that individuals are more "the captains of their fate" than traditional treatments of political socialization concede. That is, the young do not merely accept the political views transmitted by parents, schools, and other media of socialization but, rather, are active agents in their own socialization. Furthermore, both White (1982) and Losco (1982a, 1982b)—basing their conclusions on neurophysiological research—argue that adults are conscious agents directing their own behavior and cannot be viewed simply as responding either to genetic determinants or to environmental stimuli.

A related issue is the impact of cognitive development on political learning. There is some evidence of a neurophysiological base for cognitive development (see Peterson, 1981a). Connell (1971) reports changes in Australian children's political orientations consistent with expectations derived from Piagetian theory (see also Bailey and Gravning, 1979a, 1979b). Similarly, Peterson and Somit (1982) argue that cognitive development theory casts doubts on the validity of the primacy principle (the assumption that what is learned earliest significantly shapes later political learning). As children proceed through various stages of cognitive development, and as cognitive structures change through accommodation to new information, their views of the "political" are transformed.

Finally, some of those interested in biopolitics have considered the implications of the brain's hemispheric specialization for political behavior. Although considerable disagreement still exists (compare Sperry, 1964; Levy, 1980; McGlone, 1980; Bradshaw and Nettleton, 1981), neurophysiologists generally believe that in most people the left hemisphere specializes in analytical, "logical" processes and the right brain is more disposed toward holistic, "intuitive" thought. G. Schubert (1981a, 1981c) holds that males generally—and male political elites specifically—tend to be left lateralized. Thus, male elites tend to think in "analytical" as opposed to "holistic" terms. However, as noted above, Schubert believes that humans perceive their environment selectively and use information for decision making on the basis of subjective (rather than objective) relevance. As a result, male leaders may think "logically" or "analytically"—but the information on which their decisions are based is often biased. In the end, Schubert says, it is hardly surprising that political leaders frequently make bad decisions. (On lateralization and politics, see also Hines, 1982; Kitchin, 1982a, 1982b; Laponce, 1976, 1981.)

Drugs. Given the known effects of many psychotropic drugs, one could anticipate that drugs might be used to manipulate political behavior (see Somit, 1968; Stauffer, 1970). Jaros (1972, p. 1) studied the influence of a mild depressant (pentobarbital) on political attitudes and behavior, in order to test the propositions that "(1) depressant drugs modify substantive political choices; (2) depressants increase the quantity of political responses which individuals manifest; (3) drugs induce dependency, which results in increased probability of manipulation of political acts; . . ." The data yielded little support for any of these propositions, although there was a tendency for experimental subjects to have diminished ability to discriminate among political stimuli.

Biological Rhythm. What is the influence of cyclical patterns on human political behavior? Bailey (1978b), exploring the possible role of "biorhythm" in politics, claims that several of President Nixon's emotional outbursts coincided with some critical or near-critical points in his alleged cycles (see also Bailey, 1978a). Elsewhere, Peterson and Somit (1978b) investigated the effects of being a "morning person" or "night person" on political activity for a college student sample. Those who reported being more active in the morning or early afternoon tended to participate more in student protest activity. This variable, though, seems unrelated to conventional political participation.

Nutrition. Some investigators speculate that a diminished nutritional level may influence political attitudes and behavior through physiologically induced irritability and lowered cognitive capability (see Davies, 1963; Stauffer, 1969; Wiegele, 1979a; G. Schubert, 1981a). Others reason that diminished levels of nutrition may, depending on the situation, produce a sense of frustration, which, in turn, increases the probability of aggression or violence. As Davies (1963, p. 15) notes: "A momentary worsening of the food supply may produce local food riots, which may broaden and deepen into revolution. But extreme hunger, as starvation approaches, produces apathy and manipulability." J. Schubert (1981), using aggregate data, has analyzed the relationship between malnutrition and political violence in less developed countries. In societies that are relatively nonrepressive, severe malnutrition is associated with lowered levels of political violence; in moderately repressive societies, the greater the malnutrition, the greater the political violence. The former pattern conforms to the physiological hypothesis, the latter to the frustration-aggression hypothesis. (For a more elaborate theoretical argument, see J. Schubert, 1982b.) Schubert's conclusions are only suggestive, but they testify to the desirability of follow-up studies at the individual level. (For one idiosyncratic quantitative test at the individual level, see Bhaskaran, 1982.)

Biologically Derived Research Techniques

For those working in this subfield, the primary influence has been technical and technological rather than conceptual or substantive. Over the long run, perhaps the most important borrowing will be from the ethologists, whose striking advances can be attributed largely to their painstaking and systematic study of actual animal behavior, observed in natural surroundings whenever possible. What happens? How does the organism behave under what circumstances and in response to what environmental stresses and stimuli? The plea of Wahlke (1979) and others that those interested in political behavior turn away from attitude surveys and look, instead, at actual behavior stems mainly from this source. (It is, we should add, a plea that can be traced in American political science as far back as Woodrow Wilson.)

In this general category, there has been slow and uneven development in both the variety and the sophistication of research technology drawing on the life sciences. One encouraging development has been the move to increased use of observational methods. Within the past six years, several scholars have begun to report findings based on this mode of study.

Observation. Barner-Barry (1981a, 1981b) has applied nonparticipant observation methods to the formation and maintenance of authority structures among children. Drawing on her previous work (Barner-Barry, 1977, 1978, 1979, 1982b) and a careful reading of the ethological literature on observational methodology, she has produced a research guidebook (Barner-Barry, 1982a), in which she discusses such subjects as sampling (for instance, length of each observational episode and subject versus behavior sampling) and recording of data (for example, pencil-and-paper behavioral checklists, event recorders, videotapes, and tape recorders). (On problems with observational methodology, see Barner-Barry, 1981a; Peterson and Somit, 1978a.)

J. Schubert (1982a) is applying observational techniques to small political groups—specifically, city councils (for a similar early effort, see Barber, 1966). He has developed a list of behaviors that can be easily measured—for instance, how long are the various speakers' comments, who pays attention to whom, and how supportive or nonsupportive are individuals toward one another? Preliminary results demonstrate the viability of Schubert's framework and its potential value for understanding the dynamics of the decision-making process.

Nonverbal Communication. Nonverbal communication is the most important mode of information transmission for nonhuman species; it was doubtless the primary mode of communication for our prehominid and early hominid ancestors;

there is reason to believe that body posture, facial expression, and so on, still play a far more important role in human communication than we have realized (for example, see Masters, 1976).

Schwartz and Zill (1971) utilized measures of postural and vocal arousal (for instance, total number of hesitations in responses divided by total number of words), unobtrusively recorded during a standard preelection interview. These variables were correlated with political attitudes and participation (as noted in the section on "Psychophysiological Arousal"). Frank (1977) used videotapes of a 1972 presidential primary debate between Hubert Humphrey and George McGovern to analyze eye-blink rates and other nonverbal and paralinguistic measures of stress (such as head nods, gross bodily movements, and speech disturbances).

Masters (1981a, 1981b, 1982b) has coded presidential candidates' photographs in selected print media in 1960 and 1972 to identify the nonverbal cues associated with winners and losers. His ultimate goal is to determine the impact of such nonverbal communication on election outcomes, although how this is to be accomplished remains unclear. (On the use of photographs, see also Bernstein and Schwartz, 1973.) G. Schubert (1982a, 1982b) observed Swiss judges during public court sessions. After analyzing the statements exchanged by judges (categorized as assertive, reactive, or emotive) and judges' level of arousal (defined in terms of facial expression and degree of movement during interaction), he concludes that nonverbal and paralinguistic communication played an important role in their deliberations and ultimate decisions.

Physiological Measurement. Several political scientists have adapted psychophysiological research techniques to the study of political behavior. The Stony Brook researchers (that is, Milton Lodge, Joseph Tanenhaus, Bernard Tursky, and their colleagues), for example, have developed cross-modal analyses whereby psychophysiological data are gathered from experimental subjects in conjunction with the subjects' responses to attitudinal survey questions. Whereas the "normal" survey approach calls only for verbal responses to questionnaire items, the cross-modal approach derives attitude scores from *both* verbal responses *and* physiological and psychophysiological measures, such as heartbeat rate, galvanic skin response, and blood pressure (Lodge and Tursky, 1981; Tursky and others, 1976; Watts, 1981).

The cross-modal technique is particularly useful for assessing the intensity of the attitudes under study in a manner apparently superior to traditional category scaling (Wahlke and Lodge, 1976; Lodge, 1981). Of particular interest is the discovery that psychophysiological responses do not always correspond with standard Likert-scaled categories. For instance, on a Likert scale the respondents reported a minimal level of dislike for black leaders; the psychophysiological measures suggested much greater intensity (Wahlke and Lodge, 1976). The Stony Brook team members have also developed a pencil-and-paper technique for assessing intensity of reaction. Researchers ask respondents to a survey question to draw lines representing, by their length, the intensity of their feelings. Line length appears to be preferable to the traditional category scaling of political opinions (see Andrus, 1982; Finkel and Norpoth, 1982; Lodge and Tursky, 1979; Norpoth and Lodge, 1983).

A related project has been the development of self-report attitude scales validated by psychophysiological measures. Watts and Sumi (1979), for instance, have developed a violence acceptance scale along these lines, and the Stony Brook researchers have designed a political support scale (Lodge, Cross, and Tursky, 1975; Lodge and Tursky, 1981).

Still another approach is the study of vocal patterns, pioneered by Wiegele (for a summary of the method and its applications, see Wiegele, 1978, 1980a; Hirsch and Wiegele, 1981). To investigate the effect of stress on elite international decision-making behavior, Wiegele employs the Psychological Stress Evaluator (PSE), an instrument that transforms vocal utterances into electronic signals and permits the identification of even subtle speech differences by the same individual, thus pinpointing those sections of speeches apparently most stressful or arousing for the speaker. Wiegele has examined several crisis speeches—among them, Lyndon Johnson's Gulf of Tonkin speech in 1964, his 1968 Pueblo speech, and John Kennedy's 1962 "Cuban missile crisis" speech (see Wiegele, 1978, 1979b, 1980b, 1981). Policy-oriented applications of this technique, once perfected, require little comment.

A related effort to examine speech patterns has a different goal—to identify neurophysiological processes within individuals. Kitchin (1982b, p. 2) assumes that "the holistic, integrative style of the right hemisphere yields three cognitive systems—visual, auditory, and kinesthetic. The digital, logical style of the left hemisphere reveals itself in a logical, a temporal, and/or a detachment system." Key words related to the three right hemisphere cognitive systems indicate activity/dominance of that hemisphere: visual (colors or spatial arrangements, such as "broad" or "wide"), auditory (for example, "hear" or "tell"), and kinesthetic (for instance, "feel" or "pain"). For evidence of left hemisphere activity, the following are indicators: logical ("therefore," "because"), temporal ("when," "until"), and detachment ("I think," "I believe"). Kitchin has used a computerized text search program to examine press conferences of presidents Ford, Carter, and Reagan, seeking to ascertain the cognitive styles characteristic of each (based on underlying neurophysiological processes). Although there is some question about Kitchin's basic assumption that word usage reflects hemispheric involvement, his approach deserves careful attention. If it proves valid, we will be able to assess—or at least infer—the internal cognitive processes of political actors.

Booth and Welch (1976) have used fairly direct measures of physiological functioning as biological independent variables. They have taken chest expansion as a metric of physical fitness and diastolic blood pressure and uric acid level as measures of stress. These variables are then correlated with standard survey indicators of political participation. (The biomedical data themselves were collected from a probability sample of Toronto residents by trained medical personnel.) Their results are inconclusive, but the study clearly demonstrates that gathering direct, "hard" measures of biological variables is feasible. In biosociology Mazur and Lamb (1980) also have used direct measures, such as testosterone levels.

Tanenhaus (1977) was the first person, we believe, to suggest the relevance of reaction time (RT) methodology (an important tool in cognitive psychology) for the study of politics. Essentially, RT involves presentation of a stimulus or problem to a respondent—usually on a computer terminal or projected on a screen. The person then presses a key to respond. The interval between stimulus presentation and key pressing is the reaction time. Lodge and Wahlke (1982) have found that politically oriented subjects react more rapidly to political stimuli than apolitical subjects do. Tanenhaus and Foley (1982) discovered that respondents differ in the speed with which they associate such items as the president, the Supreme Court, the Postal Service, and the electoral college with "government in Washington," depending on the specificity with which the "government in Washington" is defined.

Problems and Prospects

We turn now to some of the problems that may hinder substantive biopolitical contributions to our understanding of political behavior. We will attempt to suggest what advances, in light of these problems, can reasonably be expected over the next half decade or so.

Ethological/Sociobiological/Evolutionary Approach. This subfield explores the ways in which political behavior might be shaped by our genetic legacy. For a number of reasons, it seems unrealistic to expect any significant "breakthroughs" in the immediate future. As mentioned earlier, there is considerable disagreement among biologists themselves over the validity of many aspects of contemporary ethological/sociobiological/evolutionary theory. This means, at a minimum, that those interested in biopolitics will have to move cautiously in applying these concepts to political behavior.

A further major limitation of this approach is essentially methodological and has two major aspects. First, almost all of the ethological/sociobiological/ evolutionary research has been conducted on species other than our own. As a result, much of the thinking in human ethology entails comparing nonhuman animal behavior with human behavior and then deducing common biological roots when there is an apparent similarity—a very hazardous process (see, for example, Peterson, 1977; compare with G. Schubert, 1983a). Second, no research design has yet enabled us reliably to distinguish between, let alone separate, the learned and the genetic components of behavior. This problem is extremely difficult to resolve when one is dealing with lower forms of life; it is even more so when one is dealing with mammals; so far, it has been insoluble with respect to *Homo sapiens*. These methodological constraints may be overcome, but it would be unrealistic to expect solutions in the immediate future.

Physiological Influences on Behavior. In this area, the major problems are methodological rather than conceptual. Whether one is investigating chemical, biological, or environmental factors, the development of research designs that control for the effects of possible intervening variables poses serious difficulties. There are also complex measurement problems when the impact of, say, brain structure, malnutrition, disease, drug ingestion, or overcrowding is assessed. Laboratory experimentation, quite correctly, is also severely limited by ethical and legal constraints; in any event, laboratory experimentation, without the counterweight of field studies, is unlikely to be very convincing.

Despite these formidable obstacles, it is not unreasonable to think that our understanding of the manner in which physiological factors affect political behavior will be substantially enlarged in the next few years. Studies of the relationship between health, perception of health, and body image, on the one hand, and political participation, on the other, have already provided suggestive results; the attempt to relate findings from brain science to political behavior holds great promise; and, finally, preliminary analyses of the nutrition and politics nexus seem encouraging.

Biologically Derived Research Techniques. Here the basic objective is to apply research methods derived from various fields—that is, from ethology, semiotics, experimental biology, psychology, kinesics, and related specializations—to political behavior. The problems are more technical than conceptual and, therefore, more likely to be solved in a relatively short span of time. Consequently, the use of biologically derived research techniques promises to provide the most immediate and applicable—though in the long run not necessarily the most important—results of the three subfields. Among the more promising methods are direct observation, voice analysis, and studies of nonverbal communication.

General Prospects. Biopolitics has been an active area of research for some fifteen years now. During this time it has attracted many new practitioners and generated a sizable body of literature. This work reflects, we are happy to say, a steadily increasing familiarity with, and sophisticated grasp of, biological theory and findings, even in some highly technical areas. In this context we think that the debate under way in evolutionary circles over the punctuated equilibria model of evolution (see Eldredge, 1971; Eldredge and Gould, 1972; Gould, 1982) may have a significant impact on future biopolitical writing. Punctuationalists accept two major interlinked postulates: (1) rapid rather than gradual evolutionary change; (2) natural selection operating at various levels (that is, individual, group, species)—not just at the individual level. As a corollary, punctuationalists suggest that traits (including behavior) of species are not necessarily adaptive.

There appear to be two obvious implications for the study of politics if the punctuational perspective is valid. First, much of the work in biopolitics explicitly or tacitly assumes that political institutions and even political behavior are necessarily adaptive (for example, Corning's essays on the evolution of political society accept the creativity of natural selection with the accompanying assumption that existing institutions are de facto adaptive). According to the punctuationalists, however, much behavior is nonadaptive, and we cannot conclude that a behavior or institution has survival value simply because it exists. A second implication relates to the nature of sociopolitical change. Classical conservatives, Spencerian liberals, evolutionary socialists, and functionalists accept the notion that social and political change is slow and adaptive. The analogy is with the "natural" evolutionary process. Models of change based on punctuational theory, though, would stress the nonadaptive nature of existing institutions and behavior and the possible benefits of rapid—that is, revolutionary—change.

We would expect other, less obvious, implications to be explored in the very near future. This brief discussion—based on one model of evolutionary change—illustrates how new views in biology may help to alter our understanding of politics. Given the many advances now occurring in the life sciences, we would expect even greater cross-fertilization between biology and politics in the future.

References

Adrian, C. "Implications for Political Science and Public Policy of Recent Ethological Research." Paper presented at Sinological Conference, Taipei, Taiwan, 1969.

Adrian, C. "Ethology and Bureaucracy." Paper presented at meeting of the International Political Science Association, Munich, 1970.

Almond, G. A., and Verba, S. *The Civic Culture.* Princeton, N.J.: Princeton University Press, 1963.

Andersen, K. "Working Women and Political Participation, 1952-1972." *American Journal of Political Science,* 1975, *19,* 439-454.

Andrus, D. C. "Policy Evaluations, Policy Preferences, and the Magnitude Measurement of Ideological Consistency." Paper presented at meeting of the American Political Science Association, Denver, 1982.

Ardrey, R. *African Genesis.* New York: Atheneum, 1961.

Ardrey, R. *The Territorial Imperative.* New York: Atheneum, 1966.

Ardrey, R. *Social Contract.* New York: Atheneum, 1970.

Axelrod, R., and Hamilton, W. D. "The Evolution of Cooperation." *Science,* 1981, *211,* 1390–1396.

Baer, D. "Disentangling Gender Differences: An Inquiry into the Biological and Learning Based Explanations." Paper presented at meeting of the Midwest Political Science Association, Chicago, 1980.

Baer, D., and Bositis, D. A. "Biology, Gender, and Politics: An Assessment and Critique." Paper presented at meeting of the Midwest Political Science Association, Milwaukee, 1982.

Baer, D., and Bositis, D. A. "The Political Socialization of Gender." *Politics and the Life Sciences,* 1983, *1,* 125–134.

Bailey, K. D. "Biological Time and Cops and Robbers." Paper presented at meeting of the American Society of Criminology, Dallas, 1978a.

Bailey, K. D. "Biological Time and Political Behavior." Paper presented at meeting of the American Political Science Association, New York, 1978b.

Bailey, K. D., and Gravning, P. S. "Genetic Maturity, IQ, and Political Learning in Children." Paper presented at meeting of the Southern Political Science Association, Gatlinburg, Tenn., 1979a.

Bailey, K. D., and Gravning, P. S. "Physiological Growth, IQ, and the Development of Political Awareness in Pre-Adolescence." Paper presented at meeting of the Southwestern Political Science Association, Fort Worth, Texas, 1979b.

Barash, D. P. *Sociobiology and Behavior.* New York: Elsevier Science, 1977.

Barber, J. D. *Power in Committees.* Skokie, Ill.: Rand McNally, 1966.

Barner-Barry, C. "An Observational Study of Authority in a Preschool Peer Group." *Political Methodology,* 1977, *4,* 415–449.

Barner-Barry, C. "The Structure of Young Children's Authority Relationships." In D. R. Omark and others (eds.), *Power Relationships.* New York: Garland, 1978.

Barner-Barry, C. "The Utility of Attention Structure and the Problem of Human Diversity." Paper presented at meeting of the International Political Science Association, Moscow, 1979.

Barner-Barry, C. "An Introduction to Nonparticipant Observational Research Techniques." Paper presented at meeting of the American Political Science Association, New York, 1981a.

Barner-Barry, C. "Longitudinal Observational Research and the Study of Basic Forms of Political Socialization." In M. W. Watts (ed.), *Biopolitics: Ethological and Physiological Approaches.* New Directions for Methodology of Social and Behavioral Science, no. 7. San Francisco: Jossey-Bass, 1981b.

Barner-Barry, C. "Ethological Methods in the Study of Political Behavior." Paper presented at meeting of the American Association for the Advancement of Science, Washington, D.C., 1982a.

Barner-Barry, C. "An Ethological Study of a Leadership Succession." *Ethology and Sociobiology,* 1982b, *3,* 199–207.

Beam, D. R. "Altruism vs. Egoism in Public Affairs: Hobbes, Darwin, and Humankind." Paper presented at meeting of the American Political Science Association, New York, 1981.

Beck, H. "Attentional Struggles and Silencing Strategies in a Human Political Conflict." In M. R. A. Chance and R. D. Larson (eds.), *The Social Structure of Attention.* New York: Wiley, 1976.

Bernstein, P., and Schwartz, D. C. "A Note on the Impact of Health on Presidential Decision Making." Paper presented at meeting of the International Political Science Association, Montreal, 1973.

Bhaskaran, S. "Linkage Between Malnutrition and Political Apathy." Paper presented at meeting of the International Political Science Association, Rio de Janeiro, 1982.

Booth, A., and Welch, S. "Stress, Health, and Political Participation." Paper presented at meeting of the International Political Science Association, Edinburgh, 1976.

Bradshaw, J. L., and Nettleton, N. C. "The Nature of Hemispheric Specialization in Man." *Behavioral and Brain Sciences*, 1981, *4*, 51-92.

Bremer, S. J., Singer, J. D., and Luterbacher, U. "The Population Density and War Proneness of European Nations, 1816-1965." *Comparative Political Studies*, 1973, *6*, 329-348.

Caldwell, L. "Biology and Bureaucracy: The Coming Confrontation." *Public Administration Review*, 1980, *40*, 1-12.

Caplan, A. L. (ed.). *The Sociobiology Debate*. New York: Harper & Row, 1978.

Connell, R. W. *The Child's Construction of Politics*. Victoria: Melbourne University Press, 1971.

Cook, T. E. " 'Misbegotten Males?' Innate Differences and Stratified Choice in the Subjection of Women." *Western Political Quarterly*, 1983, *36*, 194-220.

Corning, P. A. "The Biological Bases of Behavior and Some Implications for Political Science." *World Politics*, 1971, *23*, 312-370.

Corning, P. A. "Human Violence: Some Causes and Implications." In C. Beitz and T. Herman (eds.), *Peace and War*. New York: W. H. Freeman, 1973.

Corning, P. A. "Politics and the Evolutionary Process." *Evolutionary Biology*, 1974, *7*, 253-293.

Corning, P. A. "A Synopsis of a General Theory of Politics." Paper presented at meeting of the American Political Science Association, New York, 1981.

Corning, P. A. "Empirical Evidence for a Cybernetic Theory of Politics." Paper presented at meeting of the American Political Science Association, Denver, 1982a.

Corning, P. A. "Political Development Versus Political Evolution." Paper presented at meeting of the Northeastern Political Science Association, New Haven, Conn., 1982b.

Corning, P. A. *The Synergism Hypothesis*. New York: McGraw-Hill, 1983.

Corning, P. A., and Corning, C. H. "Toward a General Theory of Violent Aggression." *Social Science Information*, 1972, *11*, 7-35.

Davies, J. C. *Human Nature in Politics*. New York: Wiley, 1963.

Davies, J. C. "Violence and Aggression: Innate or Not?" *Western Political Quarterly*, 1970, *23*, 611-623.

Davies, J. C. "Biology, Darwinism, and Political Science." Paper presented at meeting of the American Political Science Association, Chicago, 1971.

Davies, J. C. "Ions of Emotion and Political Behavior: A Prototheory." In A. Somit (ed.), *Biology and Politics*. The Hague: Mouton, 1976.

Davies, J. C. "Biological Perspectives on Human Conflict." In T. R. Gurr (ed.), *Handbook of Political Conflict*. New York: Free Press, 1980.

Dearden, J. "Sex-Linked Differences in Political Behavior: An Investigation of Their Possibly Innate Origins." *Social Science Information*, 1974, *13*, 19-45.

Easton, D., and Dennis, J. "The Child's Acquisition of Regime Norms: Political Efficacy." *American Political Science Review*, 1967, *66*, 25-38..

Eldredge, N. "The Allopatric Model and Phylogeny in Paleozoic Vertebrates." *Evolution*, 1971, *25*, 156-167.

Eldredge, N., and Gould, S. J. "Punctuated Equilibria: Alternative to Phyletic Gradualism." In T. J. M. Schopf (ed.), *Models in Paleobiology*. San Francisco: Freeman, Cooper, 1972.

Ferguson, L., Ferguson, L., and Bouterline-Young, J. "An Attempt to Correlate Rate of Physical Maturation with Attitudes Toward Politics." Paper presented at meeting of the International Political Science Association, Munich, 1970.

Finkel, S., and Norpoth, H. "Ideological Recognition of Issues and Candidates in the 1980 Election." Paper presented at meeting of the Midwest Political Science Association, Chicago, 1982.

Fisher, S., and Cleveland, S. E. *Body Image and Personality*. (2nd ed.) Mineola, N.Y.: Dover, 1968.

Frank, R. S. "Nonverbal and Paralinguistic Analysis of Political Behavior." In M. Hermann (ed.), *A Psychological Examination of Political Leaders*. New York: Free Press, 1977.

Geiger, G. "Primordial State Formation as an Evolutionary Process." Paper presented at meeting of the International Political Science Association, Rio de Janeiro, 1982.

Geigle, R. A. "Psychobiological Adaptation and the Political Response Predisposition." Paper presented at meeting of the American Political Science Association, Washington, D.C., 1977.

Gould, S. J. "Darwinism and the Expansion of Evolutionary Theory." *Science*, 1982, *216*, 380–387.

Gulick, L. "Democracy and Administration Face the Future." *Public Administration Review*, 1977, *37*, 706–711.

Harvey, S. K., and Harvey, T. G. "Adolescent Political Outlooks: The Effects of Intelligence as an Independent Variable." *Midwest Journal of Political Science*, 1970, *14*, 565–595.

Hess, R., and Torney, J. V. *The Development of Political Attitudes in Children*. Hawthorne, N.Y.: Aldine, 1967.

Hines, S. M., Jr. "Recent Empirical Evidence on the Origins of the State." Paper presented at meeting of the American Political Science Association, New York, 1981.

Hines, S. M., Jr. "Ordering Political Space." Paper presented at meeting of the Western Political Science Association, San Diego, 1982.

Hirsch, L., and Wiegele, T. C. "Methodological Aspects of Voice Stress Analysis." In M. W. Watts (ed.), *Biopolitics: Ethological and Physiological Approaches*. New Directions for Methodology of Social and Behavioral Science, no. 7. San Francisco: Jossey-Bass, 1981.

Hummel, R. "A Case for a Bio-Social Model of Charisma." Paper presented at meeting of the International Political Science Association, Munich, 1970.

Jaros, D. "Biochemical Desocialization." *Midwest Journal of Political Science*, 1972, *16*, 1–28.

Jaros, D. "Sex, Psychophysiology, and Political Behavior." Paper presented at meeting of the Midwest Political Science Association, Chicago, 1976.

Kitchin, W. "Hemispheric Lateralization and Political Communication." Paper presented at meeting of the American Political Science Association, Denver, 1982a.

Kitchin, W. "The Split Brain and Political Behavior: A Preliminary Analysis of the Cognitive Systems of Ronald Reagan." Paper presented at meeting of the Northeastern Political Science Association, New Haven, Conn., 1982b.

Kort, F. "A Biological Base of Civil Rights and Liberties." Paper presented at meeting of the Midwest Political Science Association, Chicago, 1977.

Kort, F. "An Evolutionary-Neurobiological Explanation of Political Behaviour and the Lumsden-Wilson 'Thousand Year Rule.' " *Journal of Social and Biological Structures,* 1983, *6,* 219-230.

Laponce, J. "The Left-Hander and Politics." In A. Somit (ed.), *Biology and Politics.* The Hague: Mouton, 1976.

Laponce, J. *Left and Right: The Topography of Political Perceptions.* Toronto: University of Toronto Press, 1981.

Lehnen, R., and Silberberg, Y. "Some Social and Health-Related Consequences of Threatening Political Events for the Life Style of a Metropolitan Area." Paper presented at the William Munro Seminar, Stanford, Calif., 1977.

Levy, J. "Cerebral Symmetry and the Psychology of Man." In M. C. Wittrock (ed.), *The Brain and Psychology.* Orlando, Fla.: Academic Press, 1980.

Lodge, M. *Magnitude Scaling.* Beverly Hills, Calif.: Sage, 1981.

Lodge, M., and Tursky, B. "Comparisons Between Category and Magnitude Scaling of Political Opinions." *American Political Science Review,* 1979, *73,* 50-66.

Lodge, M., and Tursky, B. "On the Magnitude Scaling of Political Opinion in Survey Research." *American Journal of Political Science,* 1981, *25,* 376-419.

Lodge, M., and Wahlke, J. "Politicos, Apoliticals, and the Processing of Political Information." *International Political Science Review,* 1982, *3,* 131-150.

Lodge, M., Cross, D., and Tursky, B. "The Psychophysical Scaling and Validation of a Political Support Scale." *American Journal of Political Science,* 1975, *19,* 611-649.

Lorenz, K. Z. *King Solomon's Ring.* New York: Crowell, 1952.

Lorenz, K. Z. *On Aggression.* San Diego: Harcourt Brace Jovanovich, 1966.

Losco, J. "Understanding Altruism: An Exploration of Various Contemporary Approaches." Paper presented at meeting of the American Political Science Association, New York, 1981.

Losco, J. "Evolution, Consciousness, and Political Thought." Paper presented at meeting of the American Political Science Association, Denver, 1982a.

Losco, J. "Teleonomic Selection, Rational Preselection, and Politics." Paper presented at meeting of the Northeastern Political Science Association, New Haven, Conn., 1982b.

McBride, A. "Health and Body Image." Paper presented at meeting of the Midwest Political Science Association, Chicago, 1980.

McDonagh, E. L. "To Work or Not to Work: The Differential Impact of Achieved and Derived Status upon the Political Participation of Women, 1956-1976." *American Journal of Political Science,* 1982, *26,* 280-297.

McGlone, J. "Sex Differences in Human Brain Asymmetry: A Critical Survey." *Behavioral and Brain Sciences,* 1980, *4,* 51-92 (with accompanying commentaries).

McGuinness, D., and Pribram, K. "The Neuropsychology of Attention: Emotional and Motivational Controls." In M. C. Wittrock (ed.), *The Brain and Psychology.* Orlando, Fla.: Academic Press, 1980.

MacKenzie, W. J. M. *Biological Ideas in Politics.* New York: Viking Penguin, 1978.

Madsen, D. "Synecology and Social Structure: A Comparative Review." Paper presented at meeting of the International Political Science Association, Edinburgh, 1976.

Madsen, D. "The Effect of Psychological Stress on Influence Distributions." *International Political Science Review,* 1982, *3,* 91-106.

Manheim, J. B. *The Politics Within.* (2nd ed.) New York: Longman, 1982.

Margolis, H. "A New Model of Rational Choice." *Ethics*, 1981, *91*, 265-279.

Masters, R. D. "Politics as a Biological Phenomenon." *Social Science Information*, 1975, *14*, 7-63.

Masters, R. D. "The Impact of Ethology on Political Science." In A. Somit (ed.), *Biology and Politics*. The Hague: Mouton, 1976.

Masters, R. D. "Of Marmots and Men." In L. Wispe (ed.), *Altruism, Sympathy, Helping*. Orlando, Fla.: Academic Press, 1978.

Masters, R. D. "Empirical Analysis of Photographs in Presidential Elections." Paper presented at meeting of the American Political Science Association, New York, 1981a.

Masters, R. D. "Linking Ethology and Political Science: Photographs, Political Attention, and Presidential Elections." In M. W. Watts (ed.), *Biopolitics: Ethological and Physiological Approaches*. New Directions for Methodology of Social and Behavioral Science, no. 7. San Francisco: Jossey-Bass, 1981b.

Masters, R. D. "Social Biology and the Welfare State." Paper presented at meeting of the American Political Science Association, New York, 1981c.

Masters, R. D. "Evolutionary Biology, Political Theory, and the State." *Journal of Social and Biological Structures*, 1982a, *5*, 439-450.

Masters, R. D. "Nice Guys Don't Finish Last: Aggressive and Appeasement Gestures in Media Images of Politicians." Paper presented at meeting of the American Association for the Advancement of Science, Washington, D.C., 1982b.

Mazur, A., and Lamb, T. A. "Testosterone, Status, and Mood in Human Males." *Hormones and Behavior*, 1980, *14*, 236-246.

Morris, D. *The Naked Ape*. New York: McGraw-Hill, 1967.

Morris, D. *The Human Zoo*. New York: McGraw-Hill, 1969.

Norpoth, H., and Lodge, M. "Partisanship, Ideological Self-Image, and Policy Preferences." Paper presented at meeting of the Midwest Political Science Association, Chicago, 1983.

Peterson, S. A. "The Effects of Physiological Variables upon Student Protest Behavior." Paper presented at meeting of the International Political Science Association, Montreal, 1973.

Peterson, S. A. "The Biological Bases of Student Protest." Unpublished doctoral dissertation, Department of Political Science, State University of New York at Buffalo, 1974.

Peterson, S. A. "On the Hazards of Cross-Species Comparison." Paper presented at meeting of the International Political Science Association, Bellagio, Italy, 1977.

Peterson, S. A. "The Menstrual Cycle and Politics." *Social Science Information*, 1978, *17*, 993-1001.

Peterson, S. A. "Cognitive Development, Biology, and Political Socialization." Paper presented at meeting of the International Society of Political Psychology, Mannheim, Federal Republic of Germany, 1981a.

Peterson, S. A. "Psychophysiological Arousal as a Predictor of Student Protest." *Journal of Political Science*, 1981b, *8*, 108-113.

Peterson, S. A. "Sociobiology and Ideas-Become-Real." *Journal of Social and Biological Structures*, 1981c, *4*, 125-143.

Peterson, S. A. "Neurophysiology and Rationality in Political Thinking." Paper presented at meeting of the American Political Science Association, Denver, 1982.

Peterson, S. A. "The Body and Politics." *Southeastern Political Review*, 1983a, *11*, 147-156.

Peterson, S. A. "The Psychobiology of Hypostatizing." *Micropolitics*, 1983b, *2*, 423-451.

Peterson, S. A., and Somit, A. "Methodological Problems Associated with a More Biologically Oriented Social Science." *Journal of Social and Biological Structures*, 1978a, *1*, 11-25.

Peterson, S. A., and Somit, A. "Student Protest: A Biomedical Perspective." *Journal of Higher Education*, 1978b, *3*, 233-244.

Peterson, S. A., and Somit, A. "Primates, Coalitions, and Small Group Politics." Paper presented at meeting of the International Studies Association, Philadelphia, 1981.

Peterson, S. A., and Somit, A. "Cognitive Development and Childhood Political Socialization."*American Behavioral Scientist*, 1982, *25*, 313-334.

Peterson, S. A., and Somit, A. "Biology and Political Violence: An Assessment." Paper presented at meeting of the International Society of Political Psychology, Oxford, England, 1983.

Peterson, S. A., and others. "Biopolitics: 1980-1981 Update." *Politics and the Life Sciences*, 1982, *1*, 52-57.

Peterson, S. A., and others. "Biopolitics in 1982." *Politics and the Life Sciences*, 1983, *2*, 76-80.

Pettman, R. *Biopolitics and International Values.* Elmsford, N.Y.: Pergamon Press, 1981.

Phillips, C. S. "The Revival of Cultural Evolution in Social Science Theory." *Journal of Developing Areas*, 1971, *5*, 337-370.

Phillips, C. S. "Biology, Cultural Evolution, and the Political Process." Paper presented at meeting of the International Political Science Association, Montreal, 1973.

Phillips, C. S. "The Origin of the State: Fortuitous or Evolutionary?" Paper presented at meeting of the American Political Science Association, New York, 1981.

Pranger, R. "Ethology and Politics: The Work of Konrad Lorenz." Paper presented at meeting of the Southern Political Science Association, New Orleans, 1967.

Rogers, E. D. "Intelligence and Student Activism." *Social Science Quarterly*, 1972, *53*, 557-562.

Ronen, D. "Ethnic Nationalism and the Energy Crisis: Their Origins in 'Human Nature.' " Paper presented at meeting of the International Society of Political Psychology, Boston, 1980.

Rosenberg, J. P., and Lupfer, M. "Is One What One Experiences? The Effect of Milestone Events on the Political Attitudes of Memphis Adults." Paper presented at meeting of the Midwest Political Science Association, Cincinnati, 1981.

Ross, M. H. "When Does Ethnic Antagonism Displace Class Conflict? A Sociobiological Hypothesis in Urban Africa." *Comparative Urban Research*, 1981, *8*, 5-28.

Schonscheck, J., and Boyd, J. B. "Natural Selection and Nation-States." Paper presented at meeting of the International Studies Association, Cincinnati, 1982.

Schubert, G. "Brain Science and Political Thinking." Paper presented at meeting of the International Society of Political Psychology, Mannheim, Federal Republic of Germany, 1981a.

Schubert, G. "The Sociobiology of Political Behavior." In E. White (ed.), *Sociobiology and Human Politics.* Lexington, Mass.: Heath, 1981b.

Schubert, G. "Some Implications of Brain Science for Political Science." Paper presented at meeting of the Western Political Science Association, Denver, 1981c.

Schubert, G. "Ethological Politics." Paper presented at meeting of the American Association for the Advancement of Science, Washington, D.C., 1982a.

Schubert, G. "Infanticide by Usurper Hanuman Langur Males: A Sociobiological Myth." *Social Science Information,* 1982b, *20,* 199–244.

Schubert, G. "Nonverbal Communication as Political Behavior." In M. Key (ed.), *Nonverbal Communication Today.* The Hague: Mouton, 1982c.

Schubert, G. "Evolutionary Politics." *Western Political Quarterly,* 1983a, *36,* 175–193.

Schubert, G. "The Structure of Attention: A Critical Review." *Journal of Social and Biological Structures,* 1983b, *6,* 65–80.

Schubert, J. N. "Malnutrition and Political Violence." Paper presented at meeting of the Western Political Science Association, Denver, 1981.

Schubert, J. N. "An Ethological Approach to Analyzing the Interaction Process in Small Group Legislative Decision-Making." Paper presented at meeting of the American Political Science Association, Denver, 1982a.

Schubert, J. N. "Toward a Psychobiological Model of Malnutrition and Political Violence." Paper presented at meeting of the International Political Science Association, Rio de Janeiro, 1982b.

Schulman, M. "The Saturday Night Massacre: A Quasi-Experimental Study of Psychophysiology and Politics; Or, Is Politics Harmful to Your Health?" Paper presented at meeting of the Southern Political Science Association, Nashville, 1975.

Schwartz, D. C. "Perceptions of Personal Energy and the Adoption of Basic Behavioral Orientations to Politics." Paper presented at meeting of the International Political Science Association, Munich, 1970.

Schwartz, D. C. "The Influence of Health Status on Basic Attitudes in an American Political Elite." Paper presented at meeting of the International Political Science Association, Edinburgh, 1976a.

Schwartz, D. C. "Somatic States and Political Behavior: An Interpretation and Empirical Extension of Biopolitics." In A. Somit (ed.), *Biology and Politics.* The Hague: Mouton, 1976b.

Schwartz, D. C. "Health Status, Self-Image, and Political Behavior in America's Governmental Elite." Paper presented at meeting of the Western Political Science Association, Los Angeles, 1978.

Schwartz, D. C., and Zill, N. "Psychophysiological Arousal as a Predictor of Political Participation." Paper presented at meeting of the American Political Science Association, Chicago, 1971.

Schwartz, D. C., and others. "Health, Body Images, and Political Participation." In D. C. Schwartz and S. K. Schwartz (eds.), *New Directions in Political Socialization.* New York: Free Press, 1975.

Shubs, P. "Self Body-Image Correlates of Political Attitudes and Behavior." Paper presented at meeting of the International Political Science Association, Montreal, 1973.

Somit, A. "Toward a More Biologically Oriented Political Science." *Midwest Journal of Political Science,* 1968, *12,* 550–567.

Somit, A. "Human Nature as the Central Issue in Political Philosophy." In E. White (ed.), *Sociobiology and Human Politics.* Lexington, Mass.: Heath, 1981.

Somit, A., and others. *The Literature of Biopolitics.* (2nd ed.) DeKalb, Ill.: Center for Biopolitical Research, 1980.

Sperry, R. "The Great Cerebral Commissure." *Scientific American,* 1964, *210,* 42–54.

Stauffer, R. "The Biopolitics of Underdevelopment." *Comparative Political Studies,* 1969, *2,* 361–387.

Stauffer, R. "The Role of Drugs in Political Change." Paper presented at meeting of the International Political Science Association, Munich, 1970.

Stegenga, J. A. "The Physiology of Aggression (and Warfare?)." *International Journal of Group Tensions,* 1978, *8,* 51-67.

Strate, J. M. "The Sovereign as Protector: The Functional Priority of Defense." Paper presented at meeting of the American Political Science Association, New York, 1981.

Tanenhaus, J. "Psychophysiology, Psychophysics, and Reaction Time Methodology in Political Science." Paper presented at meeting of the International Political Science Association, Bellagio, Italy, 1977.

Tanenhaus, J., and Foley, M. A. "'The Words of Things Entangle and Confuse': The Ambiguous Political Concept." *International Political Science Review,* 1982, *3,* 107-129.

Thorson, T. L. *Biopolitics.* New York: Holt, Rinehart & Winston, 1970.

Tiger, L. *Men in Groups.* New York: Random House, 1969.

Trivers, R. "Parent-Offspring Conflict." *American Zoologist,* 1974, *14,* 249-264.

Tursky, B., and others. "A Bio-Behavioral Framework for the Analysis of Political Behavior." In A. Somit (ed.), *Biology and Politics.* The Hague: Mouton, 1976.

Vanderwolf, C. H., and Robinson, T. E. "Reticulo-Cortical Activity and Behavior: A Critique of the Arousal Theory and a New Synthesis." *Behavioral and Brain Sciences,* 1981, *4,* 459-515 (with accompanying commentaries).

Wahlke, J. C. "Pre-Behavioralism in Political Science." *American Political Science Review,* 1979, *73,* 9-32.

Wahlke, J. C., and Lodge, M. "Psychophysiological Measures of Political Attitudes and Behavior." *Midwest Journal of Political Science,* 1976, *16,* 505-537.

Watts, M. W. "Individual Differences in Skin Conductance Response to Vicariously Modeled Violence and Pathos." In M. W. Watts (ed.), *Biopolitics: Ethological and Physiological Approaches.* New Directions for Methodology of Social and Behavioral Science, no. 7. San Francisco: Jossey-Bass, 1981.

Watts, M. W. "Biopolitics and Sex Differences." Paper presented at meeting of the Western Political Science Association, San Diego, 1982.

Watts, M. W., and Sumi, D. "Studies of the Physiological Component of Aggression-Related Social Attitudes." *American Journal of Political Science,* 1979, *23,* 538-558.

Weiner, S. B. "Toward the City-State: An Ethological Approach in the Problem of Political Violence." Unpublished doctoral dissertation, Department of Political Science, University of Maryland, 1974.

Welch, S. "Crowding and Political Activity." *Polity,* 1976, *9,* 40-62.

Welch, S. "Women as Political Animals?" *American Journal of Political Science,* 1977, *21,* 711-730.

Welch, S., and Booth, A. "Crowding as a Factor in Political Aggression." *Social Science Information,* 1974, *13,* 151-162.

White, E. "Intelligence and Sense of Political Efficacy." *Journal of Politics,* 1968, *30,* 710-731.

White, E. "The Neurobiological Basis of Human Action." Paper presented at meeting of the Western Political Science Association, Denver, 1981a.

White, E. "Political Socialization from the Perspective of Generational and Evolutionary Change." In E. White (ed.), *Sociobiology and Human Politics.* Lexington, Mass.: Heath, 1981b.

White, E. "Sociobiology, Neurobiology, and Political Socialization." *Micropolitics,* 1981c, *1,* 113-144.

White, E. "Self-Direction and Political Action." Paper presented at meeting of the Northeastern Political Science Association, New Haven, Conn., 1982.

Wiegele, T. C. "Decision-Making in an International Crisis: Some Biological Factors." *International Studies Quarterly*, 1973, *17*, 295–335.

Wiegele, T. C. "Health and Stress During International Crisis: Neglected Input Variables in the Foreign Policy Decision-Making Process." *Journal of Political Science*, 1976, *3*, 139–144.

Wiegele, T. C. "The Psychophysiology of Elite Stress in Five International Crises." *International Studies Quarterly*, 1978, *22*, 467–511.

Wiegele, T. C. *Biopolitics: Search for a More Human Political Science*. Boulder, Colo.: Westview Press, 1979a.

Wiegele, T. C. "Physiological Traces During the 1961 Berlin Crisis." Paper presented at meeting of the International Political Science Association, Moscow, 1979b.

Wiegele, T. C. *Psycholinguistic Analyses of Physiological Stress During International Crises*. DeKalb, Ill.: Center for Biopolitical Research, 1980a.

Wiegele, T. C. "Voice Stress and the International Crisis: A Psychophysiological Analysis of Richard Nixon During the Cambodian Invasion." Paper presented at meeting of the International Studies Association, Los Angeles, 1980b.

Wiegele, T. C. "A Comparative Psycholinguistic Analysis of International Crises." Paper presented at meeting of the International Studies Association, Philadelphia, 1981.

Wiegele, T. C., and Plowman, S. "Stress Tolerance and International Crisis: The Significance of Biologically-Oriented Experimental Research to the Behavior of Political Decision-Makers." *Experimental Study of Politics*, 1974, *3*, 63–92.

Wiegele, T. C., and others. "Cardiorespiratory Health and Dimensions of Subject Attitudes Toward International Affairs: A Pilot Study." *Experimental Study of Politics*, 1975, *5*, 36–54.

Willhoite, F., Jr. "Ethology and the Tradition of Political Thought." *Journal of Politics*, 1971, *33*, 615–641.

Willhoite, F., Jr. "Equal Opportunity and Primate Particularism." *Journal of Politics*, 1975, *37*, 270–276.

Willhoite, F., Jr. "Primates and Political Authority: A Biobehavioral Perspective." *American Political Science Review*, 1976, *70*, 1110–1126.

Willhoite, F., Jr. "Evolution and Collective Intolerance." *Journal of Politics*, 1977, *39*, 667–684.

Willhoite, F., Jr. "Rank and Reciprocity: Speculations on Human Emotions and Political Life." In E. White (ed.), *Sociobiology and Human Politics*. Lexington, Mass.: Heath, 1981.

Wilson, E. O. *Sociobiology: The New Synthesis*. Cambridge, Mass.: Harvard University Press, 1975.

TWO

Roots of Political Behavior

James Chowning Davies

In the 1980s the state of political psychology specifically, and the social sciences generally, may be characterized as in transition. At best the transition promises new, deeper understanding of why people behave politically as they do. This understanding calls for pursuit of basic causes of political behavior, not just in stable circumstances in developed nations, where people behave rather predictably within the effective framework of constitutional democracies, but also in unstable circumstances in both developed and developing nations, where behavior is unpredictable and established institutions are being violently disestablished. At worst the transition can give rise to a malaise, a lack of interest in distinguishing what is important to investigate from what is repetitive trivialization—in short, a fragmentation of research into bits that are too small to serve as building stones for some really new social science.

There is a dearth of new theory and a superabundance of research. The very term "new," in both theory and research, fails to distinguish fundamental contributions from trendy confirmations and disconfirmations. It sometimes seems that all living social theories are like trees to which vines cling and grow. These vines threaten theorizing with extinction, in a suffocating embrace of research that unquestioningly accepts theory as fixed. Extant social theory, like Euclid's in geometry or Darwin's in evolution, is to be merely cited, or at most the extant is merely to be confirmed or disconfirmed. New theory is not to be generated. References to established social theory in research writings tend to be like recitations of ritual, invoking Freud or Marx or Lasswell—or even Plato—in a manner that fails to integrate the basic contributions of these pioneers with what the researcher is saying.

To say that the most fundamental contribution to political psychology was made by Freud is not to invoke an icon. Among his contributions to psychology generally, it is said that the most fundamental is his theory of the unconscious (Jones, 1953, p. 397); that is, his assertion that the deepest determinants of our behavior are buried in the unconscious. Consciously or unconsciously, both Freud and his protagonists and antagonists sometimes suffocated this theory in arguments over his separate assertion that all (well, nearly all; see Jones, 1953, p. 254; 1955, pp. 293–284) neuroses and perhaps all behavior are ultimately embedded in the sex drive.

To say that the most fundamental contribution to the analysis of social systems and institutions was made by Marx is also not invoking an icon. One of Marx's major contributions is the argument that social, economic, and political institutions develop through orderly, successive stages. Tribalism is followed by feudalism, out of which emerges private capitalism and the factory system. Then comes socialism and finally communism, in which the means of production are owned and operated by "the masses." Among Marx's protagonists and antagonists, this theory of institutional development has sometimes been suffocated by the dispute over the merits of his radical condemnation of the capitalistic mode of industrial organization and production.

I am not attempting the impossible: an integration of orthodox or heterodox Freudianism with orthodox or heterodox Marxism. Rather, I am attempting to show how (usually unconscious) forces in individuals interact with (usually ignored) systemic, institutional forces that help to determine the limits within which individuals behave. Freud and Marx are only the most distinguished of many students of people and society whose relevant work is used here. In this chapter I will attempt to indicate briefly the prior theory and research that seem to me to be most fundamental to understanding political behavior, in both stable and unstable circumstances. Then I will outline at somewhat greater length a theory that can help improve our understanding of the roots of political behavior in varying circumstances.

Specifically, I am venturing to present a new theory that reciprocally relates two fundamental processes: the successive stages of development of individuals from infancy to maturity and the successive stages of development of political institutions. In my view, these political stages start with the primitive anarchy that appears in tribal and feudal societies (even in the twentieth-century latifundia of developing nations in Southeast Asia, Latin America, and perhaps southern Africa) and progress to the civilized anarchy that can emerge only out of the highly integrated industrial societies that have helped to produce democracy. The process is likely to take hundreds of years.

Like all theories—whether those who generate or employ them are conscious of it or not—this theory includes basic ideas whose incorporation has a few implications. One is that the theory provides a basis for evaluating our political past, present, and future. Another is that human nature, being determined by the genes, is a long-range constant, alterable only by genetic mutation or by what Darwin called natural selection. Another is that overt human behavior, including political behavior, is a product of the interaction of genes with pre- and postnatal environments. As such a product, human behavior can be changed only if the environment is changed so that it is more nurturant and can facilitate the full realization of the genetic potential—of human nature.

Prior Theory and Research

In one sense, my theory of political development is merely an explication of Freud's gigantic contribution to understanding human behavior: his discovery of the unconscious. Most of the forces that determine human behavior have always been unknown to human beings, and even when known have been taken for granted. Until recently, for example, few people have considered physical health as related to the ability to write or read, perhaps because people who write and read are healthy and assume that everyone else is. But could I write this and could you read it if I or you were voraciously hungry or grievously ill?

Freud's assertion that unconscious forces operate, often with overriding power, is a statement of well-nigh universal applicability and validity and represents an intellectual act of enormous courage. His assertion that sexual desire is the ultimate cause, the ultimate moving force, of all action is similarly gigantic; as an explanation for all kinds of human interaction, however, it does not appear to be as universally applicable and valid. As someone has said, it is impossible to overestimate the role of sex in human activity, but Freud achieved the impossible.

Beyond his emphasis on the unconscious, Freud's real and present contribution to the following theory is in a sense latter-day Freud. While categorically refusing to deny the ultimate role of sex, he eventually expanded the term "Eros" to make it include not only the sex but also the tenderness and altruism connotations of the German word "Liebe" and the English word "love" (Freud, 1922, pp. 37–40). In the following theory, I argue that love in all its connotations is a very fundamental drive but that it is overridden by the drive (or the need) to survive. In the middle-class milieu and among his middle-class patients in Vienna before World War I, Freud never really had the opportunity to see the circumstances in which love—the desire to get together, be together, and stay together, and not just the desire for sex—could be quite destroyed by the stronger desire to survive.

World War I began when Freud was fifty-eight years old, long after he had established his basic theses about the unconscious and sex. When he did see the ferocity of survival behavior in wartime, it profoundly influenced his fundamental outlook and perhaps had much to do with his introduction of the death instinct as a force that countervails Eros. The savage 1914–1918 war was a profound trauma to Freud. It may have unconsciously contributed to his assertion, in the exchange with Einstein (Einstein and Freud, 1932), that aggression is an instinctive drive rather than a phenomenon that accompanies profound changes within individuals and social systems.

Other psychologists, starting with James ([1890] 1950, vol. 2, chap. 24) and continuing with McDougall (1908) and Murray (1938), asserted that there are many other innate drives in addition to sex and to survival. And so did two great sociologists, Thomas (1923) and Sorokin (1925, p. 33). But as I see it, the greatest advance in motivation theory was made by Maslow (1943), who said not only that there are many basic, innate drives but also that they are arranged in a rank order, priority, or hierarchy. Without such a concept of priority, it is impossible to explain why all human beings whose circumstances allow them to enjoy their lives freely most of the time (because they need not worry about subsistence most of the time) nevertheless eat when they are hungry and sleep when they are tired. If intellectuals and other members of that heterogeneous body called the elite did not genetically share with all other human beings the physical, bodily needs for food and rest, then they would be able to do their highly mental work without pausing for restoration. And so would those who benefit or suffer from the work of elites. Maslow was aware of priority in the pursuit of what he called "instinctoid" needs;

and, as I shall attempt to show in presenting my theory below, his theory is a most helpful, even I think an essential, element in understanding both individual development and political development.

Psychological research has been as valuable as psychological theory in developing a theory of political development. Among the investigators whose work has been most critical to me are Spitz (1949, 1965) and Bowlby (1969, 1973) in their studies of the disintegrating consequences of depriving very young children of normal maternal care. Harlow, in his decades-long study of primates (summarized in Harlow and Mears, 1979), has shown the disintegrating consequences of depriving infant monkeys of normal maternal care. Such deprivation of love, as we shall see, is quite separate from food deprivation; and it, too, sheds light on a theory of the priority of innate needs.

Additionally, psychological research shows the close relationship between physical deprivation and family and community life. Aronoff (1967), for example, applied the theoretical framework of the need hierarchy in his study of a community of cane cutters and a community of fishermen on a Caribbean island. He found that malnutrition among the cane cutters made relationships between husband and wife and between parents and children enormously difficult. In contrast, when good nutrition prevailed, as in the fishing village, more stable marital and parent-child relationships and more integrated communities began to emerge. While Aronoff's study may seem a redundant confirmation of Marx and Engels, its theoretical base is in individual psychology and not in social institutions, and it marks an empirical and direct validation of the need hierarchy.

Probably most sociologists in the 1980s no longer accept the premise that society, as the central object of their attention, is the sole determinant of human behavior. Logically, they should therefore consider the forces that generate within human beings—the set of directed energies, drives, and motivations that are innate in origin. But, perhaps on grounds that groups and not individuals are the units of their analysis, sociologists have tended to overlook the human brain as a source of determinants that have much to do with human behavior in society.

Some sociologists, however, have considered basic drives. I have already mentioned that Thomas and Sorokin briefly discussed them. So, initially and sketchily, did Marx and Engels. In one of their earliest works, *The German Ideology* (written in 1845-46 but not published until 1932; see Tucker, 1972, p. 110), Marx and Engels said, in talking about fundamental causes, "the root is man." But they evidently abandoned their concern for looking at the root and turned their attention to the sequence in which social systems and institutions develop, fixing their anger on the greedy but emotionless way in which industry, as it developed under private capitalism, heartlessly ground down and voraciously ground up human beings. Marx's theory of institutional development is a major but often ignored starting point in analysis of the evolution of all social systems, not just the economic and political ones. But Marx allows genetically established basic motivations to enter only implicitly into his angry analysis.

Émile Durkheim, like Marx, was a social determinist. But some of his thinking was influenced by Jean Jacques Rousseau, who was not a social determinist (see Rousseau's discourse on education, *Émile*, 1762; for Rousseau's influence on Durkheim, see Durkheim, [1893] 1933, pp. 201, 399; [1902] 1961, pp. 168-169). Durkheim argued that moral systems are an outgrowth of human interaction within developing social systems. In his study of suicide, Durkheim ([1897]

1951) found that he did have to consider individual human beings as well as groups. But he insistently viewed them not as actors endowed with innate drives but only as *reactors* to social change. He categorically asserted that the social solidarity and cooperation that develop in industrial societies are primarily the consequence of the division of labor in societies undergoing industrialization.

For Durkheim the formation of moral society is a product of interaction, but interaction between people rather than interaction between human nature and the environment. He avoided the question of whether interaction itself is something that people *innately* want and asserted that interaction occurs only because people cannot do alone most of the things they do: have families and jobs as well as live decent or even good lives. Durkheim's ([1893] 1933) intense and meticulous analysis of human behavior in the transition from a rural to an urban society, from agrarian to industrial life, represented a major breaking of intellectual ground; but, like Marx and Engels, he ignored the developing human organism as a determining force. And his reasoning, like that of Marx and Engels, makes social, economic, and political development a self-contained, self-initiating, and self-perpetuating process that ignores genetic forces.

Marx and Engels used the word "alienation" (*Entfremdung* in German) to describe the consequence of separating people from their ties to land and family. Durkheim used the term "anomy" (*anomie* in French) to describe the product of this severing of ties. The deep understanding that Marx, Engels, and Durkheim had of the transition from rural to urban life is altogether essential to understanding stages of political development. But, to reiterate, there is no systematic psychological consideration of the interaction between the human psyche and the social system in Marx, Engels, or Durkheim. The psyche is a passive product of social relations.

These are some of the major roots of the theory of political development presented here. The strength of psychological contributions, starting but not ending with Freud, has been an awareness of dynamic forces within the human organism. Their weakness has been an unawareness of the long history of the development of social institutions. The strength of sociological contributions, starting but not ending with Marx, has been their awareness of these institutional forces in the environment. Their weakness has been an unawareness of intrahuman forces. Other theoretical and research materials pertaining to the theory that follows are mentioned where specifically relevant to the presentation of the theory.

A New Theory of Political Development

In a century of profound change and worldwide political turmoil, theory has been lacking that can explain why that change is so deep and why that turmoil is so universal. There are theories to justify democracy or to explain why it must fail. There are theories to justify dictatorship or to explain why it must fail. But there is no dynamic theory to explain fundamentally when and why irresponsible tyranny and responsible democracy emerge or to say whether either of these is the ultimate political institution. In short, we have very little basis for understanding the circumstances that lead to tyranny and democracy and, therefore, no solid basis for predicting when and whether government of the people, by the people, and for the people will emerge, endure, perish from the earth, or be replaced by a higher form of government.

I will argue that both the demand for fundamental change and the sequence in which political institutions emerge are initially and ultimately a product of human nature. Furthermore, there is an orderly sequence in the emergence of political institutions, and neither tyranny nor democracy is the final political form. Anarchy is both the earliest and the ultimate society-wide institution, but anarchy of two very different kinds: primitive and civilized.

The two most turbulent, anarchic centuries out of the last five have been the sixteenth and the twentieth. In the sixteenth century, the first major efforts were undertaken in Europe to establish nation-states with governments that in a small but portentous degree were responsible to their citizens. In the twentieth century, these major efforts have become worldwide. In these centuries and between them, anarchy, tyranny, and democracy have succeeded each other in seemingly random order. This apparent disorder is, however, much less significant than meets the eye, and the underlying sequence in which these political forms emerge is much more orderly than meets the eye.

I have defined human nature biologically, as the genetic components of all human behavior. It can also be defined psychologically, as the innate ingredients of overt behavior. Some of these innate ingredients remain inactive when individuals grow in less than optimal circumstances. Individuals behave differently and more complexly as they move from infancy to childhood, adolescence, adulthood, and old age. This change in behavior is the result of the interaction of the slowly maturing human organism with its environment.

If the environment provides at least the opportunity to stay alive and well and to gain social integration with at least the family, the chances are good that the organism will survive. When the environment provides no more, human beings share with lower animals a nearly exclusive concern with self-survival and species survival, and their particularly human potential for growth is stunted. This kind of environment prevails for most people in the world. But when the environment is optimally nurturant, the chances are good that the individual will blossom, realizing rather fully his or her unique potential. The *realized* potential is the product of innate, genetic potential and an environment that is complex and challenging enough to elicit the innate capabilities of the human organism with its enormously and discriminatingly absorbent and creative brain.

Over tens of thousands of years, the environment has changed, so that in the most advanced cultures some people have the opportunity to choose from a vast and growing array of things to do. The process has involved a change from the primitive political anarchy of hunting and gathering societies and of feudal agrarian society all the way to the point where people are groping for institutional changes that can take us beyond the urban industrial society and beyond democracy. Thus is the genetic potential being realized and thus is human nature emerging.

My thesis is that emergent human nature leads to political development and, reciprocally, that political development makes possible the further emergence of human nature. The sequence is nonrandom because political development is related to the nonrandom sequence in which human beings move from infancy to childhood, adolescence, and maturity. Just as there is a trend in human beings to move from an infantile nature to a fully realized human nature, so also there is a comparable political trend. There is a continuous interaction between the processes in which individual human potential is gradually realized and political institutions gradually evolve.

Theorists and Their Environment

It has been hard for political theorists to see an orderly, nonrandom relationship because they themselves are located in a specific epoch in a particular part of the very slowly civilizing world. Before the portentous theorizing by Marx a century ago, about sequence in the emergence of social institutions, it was difficult for people to see any orderly succession. Before the likewise portentous work of Mannheim ([1929] 1954) in showing the subjective relationship between observer and observed social phenomena, it was difficult to see the dynamic relationship between human beings as *both* causes and consequences of social, including political, events. The German physicist Werner Heisenberg, in showing that the observation of natural phenomena interacts with the phenomena themselves, further broke down the notion of pure objectivity. Marx, Mannheim, and Heisenberg made possible two major steps in progress toward basic theorizing: an understanding of sequence and an understanding of matrix. By matrix I mean here the accumulation of culture, including political culture, over many centuries, as this culture, like a developing language, is internalized and becomes part of each human being in his or her environment.

Only in our time, then, has it become possible for us—as individuals who themselves are involved in the developing process—to see the dynamic interaction between emergent individuals and emergent political institutions. We need no longer base our analyses of instability, anarchy, and order on theory that is unaware of where human beings have come from, where we are in particular cultures, and where we are going.

Hobbes in the Seventeenth-Century Jungle. The first modern political theory (after Machiavelli) was generated by Hobbes ([1651] 1962). Both sequence and historical matrix were quite lacking in Hobbes's analysis. Thanks to Marx and Mannheim, we can now see both sequence and matrix in the epoch when Hobbes generated his theory. A complex, integrated society was starting to emerge out of the subsistence economy and decentralized society that is called feudalism. Hobbes was writing in the midst of the most turbulent, violent part of this great era. Long-established institutional loyalties had been profoundly disestablished. A century before Hobbes and the Puritan Revolution, Henry VIII and England had fractured the pervasive political power of the Roman church.

But these were only the recent events. Changes in economic institutions, at a seemingly glacial rate, had already been profoundly altering English society. Several hundred years before Hobbes observed and wrote, the exchange of goods and services for money had slowly begun to erode a subsistence, barter economy. Starting in the twelfth century, English landlords undertook the enclosure of common lands, in order to increase the production of grain and sheep for the national and even international market. This action led to the dire impoverishment of peasants, whose existence already was almost exclusively a matter of staying alive and well. Enclosures pushed them off the land and into cities, where they worked for wages. The great plague of 1348–49 was a major catalyst of these social and economic changes, because the plague so reduced the population—somewhere between a fourth and a third—that labor became scarce and wages rose.

These epochal events in England, possibly the earliest nation to begin to abandon feudalism and venture into the modern world, were generated and sustained over five centuries before the Reformation and the Puritan Revolution.

Familial, economic, social, religious, and political institutions were slowly but radically re-forming. Hobbes was reacting to the crisis in political institutions at the heart of the Puritan Revolution. In turn, that revolution was an epiphenomenon of long-developing change in most, if not all, social structures.

The changes were accompanied by violence that reached a peak at the very time that Hobbes came to his conclusion that it is man's nature to search perpetually for power and that individual power must be surrendered to government if the suicidal war of individual against individual is to be avoided. Hobbes could observe this savage conflict on the London docks, where poor people fought each other for jobs that would let them stay alive. Himself briefly exiled to France, he could sense in his bones the savage conflict between factions among the elite for control of the state. In Hobbes's ([1651] 1962, p. 64) view, rich and poor alike fought so savagely because of "a general inclination of all mankind, a perpetual and restless desire of power after power." It was hard for Hobbes to search for the fundamental causes of civil strife when he was in the very midst of the centuries-long and violent process of modernization.

Marx, Engels, and Freud and Their Historical Times. In the nineteenth century, following early reflections on the enormous human cost of establishing an exchange economy and finally of industrialization, Engels ([1850] 1967) wrote a brief history of the socioeconomic roots of the German Protestant Reformation. Seventeen years later, Marx ([1867] 1967) came out with the first major theory of the growth and change of social institutions. In his view, conflict in economic institutions was the result of the movement from a feudal, agrarian barter economy to a capitalist, urban market economy. Marx replaced the largely static theorizing of earlier writers with a statement of dynamic institutional sequence. The exploitation of "the masses," he concluded, leads to class conflict when the exploited become conscious of their exploitation. Violence, he thundered, stems from the immiseration of the poor by the rich who seize political power; it does not come from human nature.

In *The German Ideology*, Marx and Engels ([1932] 1976) briefly mentioned human needs, but they came to believe that human nature is altogether the product of the ensemble of social and particularly of class relations. To my knowledge, Marx never systematically looked at a radical implication of his class-conflict theory: If people are altogether the *product* of their social circumstances, where does the resistance to miserable, stunting circumstances come from? If becoming conscious of misery is enough, why not tolerate misery as readily as well-being? Within the human organism and brain, he saw no organizing, developing, directing forces that relate to the sequential emergence of social institutions.

It took Freud and many motivational psychologists who came after him to begin to generate a theory of individual human development. But Freud and those who came after him developed their views of basic human needs by observing the middle-class patients who had progressed far beyond mere concern with staying alive and healthy. They did not really know what poverty—and impoverishment—does to human beings. Marx was intensely conscious of the modern society and economy and unaware of himself. Freud was intensely aware of himself and had little consciousness of his own socioeconomic matrix.

Contrasts Between and Within Centuries and Countries. Marx established the profound import of context, both temporal and spatial, and of sequence in socioeconomic institutional development. And Mannheim and Heisenberg broke down the false notion that there is a clear-cut subjective-objective dichotomy. Nevertheless, people still find it difficult to see themselves in their own times and in their cultural context. Perhaps in most societies that have moved beyond survival, those who have so moved find it hard to imagine another and less comfortable world. They find it hard to see that some other people in their own society are still mainly preoccupied with staying alive, healthy, and out of jail—and that virtually all people in developing societies may be similarly preoccupied. A middle-class American or Western European who is concerned with payments on his new car or boat may be effectively unaware of the survival preoccupations of migrant workers in the fields of vast and efficient mechanized farms. Virtually all Americans may be effectively unaware that in most of the world migrant farm workers in America would be seen as well off. The large flow of Central Americans into the United States in the 1970s and 1980s is one indicator of relativity in well-being.

In consequence, there is a reluctance to establish the quantitative appraisal necessary to say that in advanced industrialized societies the struggle to survive has been replaced with other concerns in the minds of most people—at the very same time on the very same planet when survival is the preoccupation of most people in unadvanced, still slowly industrializing societies. In *The Revolt of the Masses,* Ortega y Gasset ([1930] 1957) observed a scene in Spain much like what Hobbes saw three centuries earlier in England. But in addition to observing the growing turbulence in Spain as it slowly moved toward popularly responsible government, Ortega y Gasset saw with some disdain the resistance to civilization, to enculturation, among "the masses." He could not see that poor people then, as now, in Spain and everywhere, found it difficult to share his exquisite refinement and his detached, civilized values, which were appropriate to his needs but not to theirs. Poor people lived and live in a different world from Ortega y Gasset's.

In sum, it is necessary to recognize the range—the standard deviation—of development within particular nations and also the mean. Only thus can one avoid saying that the circumstances and the *predominant, active* needs of all people in all societies, everywhere and in all times, are the same. To reiterate, *genetically* the basic drives of every member of our society may be taken to be the same. *Environmentally* the basic drives, which are not dormant but active, vary enormously with circumstances. And in consequence so do the familial, socioeconomic, and political institutions change as their older forms become dysfunctional to newly emerging needs. People who respond to the struggle of each against all by accepting, as Hobbes said they should, totalitarian government are genetically the same as people who respond to totalitarian government by seeking its overthrow, once the struggle to survive has diminished throughout a society.

Underlying a theory of human and political development is the interaction between the organism and the environment. This interaction commences before birth, as is most readily apparent in birth defects caused by excessive or deficient prenatal intake of hormones and nutrients. The interaction continues after birth, most notably for our purposes as the newborn child begins to establish bonds to parents and to learn language and (somewhat later) patterns of belief and modes of social interaction. The developing human organism *selectively* assimilates environmental influences—familial, social, economic, and political loyalties, habits, customs, and institutions.

Developing customs and institutions interact with human beings as they develop, as new needs emerge, and as people individually and collectively establish new loyalties and make new demands on established customs and institutions. The human organism is both an encultured and an enculturating force and, thus, causes customs and institutions to emerge and grow in ways that help fulfill human nature.

This theory is presented as a statement of the orderly way in which human wants emerge in sequence, as people move from their preoccupation with survival, starting at birth, to their mature preoccupation with fulfilling their unique, individual potential, a process that starts no later than adolescence and continues throughout life. Human beings share some basic needs with all other life forms—notably, self-preservation and species preservation—and some with at least all vertebrates, from snakes on up—notably, the social needs. Social needs, which are very highly developed in *Homo sapiens,* have particular significance in the emergence of political institutions that respond to needs beyond survival and aggregation.

Human nature has already been defined both biologically and psychologically. Now, within the psychological field, it needs to be defined motivationally: as the total set of innate, genetically established needs that form the goal-oriented ingredients of overt human action, including political behavior. Human nature, so conceived, is constant and unchangeable; human needs do not change short of genetic mutation. However, they do not all emerge at the time of conception and require time and favorable conditions to become manifest. Their emergence in more or less regular order may be so impeded by the environment (including institutions) that, for most individuals in most societies on earth, not much more than mere survival and procreation is possible. And so *most* governments in the twentieth century—as Hobbes in the seventeenth century too readily concluded for *all* governments in *all* times—deal with the problems of policing the struggle to survive and helping to allocate the goods and services that people need to survive. And the innate human potential remains dormant for most of the human race.

Basic Human Needs

Homo sapiens shares some innate drives with *all* other species, some with *some* other species, and some with *no other* species. The differences in these drives appear to be related principally to brain development. Even one-celled life forms, lacking a distinct nervous system, "want" to survive, and human beings share this drive with them. Even lizards, which are among the lowest vertebrates but have a central nervous system and a rudimentary cortex in their brains, engage in courtship and mating behavior, select and protect home sites and foraging areas, form groups, and establish societies with a rudimentary hierarchy (MacLean, 1975).

Mammalian species that are easily observable by humans—for instance, domestic cats, dogs, and horses—do all the things that one-celled animals and reptiles do, and they even exhibit behavior that human beings unfamiliar with these mammals may suppose to be characteristic only of primates. Cats, dogs, and horses desire affection and therefore get lonesome when deprived of companionship (whether human or conspecific). To their human owners at least, they appear to desire minimal recognition and praise and therefore occasionally get bad-tempered if they are ignored or treated with contempt. Moreover, they have some rudimentary desires to do their particular feline, canine, and equine things—cats to play with balls of yarn and, even when they are well fed, to catch birds; dogs to chase cats and hunt a variety of animals; and horses to run.

Humans, who do all these things that life forms from one-celled animals to primates do, also engage in complex information-gathering and decision-making activity. People usually engage in this activity in the process of fulfilling needs that range from survival itself to satisfying the love drive and gaining recognition. When the environment is supportive, people also do things that fulfill their unique, individual, idiosyncratic pattern of genetic endowment.

The basic needs, which are genetic to every human being, include (1) substantive needs and (2) instrumental needs.

Substantive Needs. Substantive needs, in a sequence modified from Abraham Maslow's pioneering 1943 list (see Davies, 1963), include (1) the physical needs for food, clothing, shelter, health, and physical safety; (2) the social-affectional needs for love: for getting, being, and staying together (including the need for perpetuating the species); (3) the self-esteem or dignity needs for achieving a sense of one's distinct and worthy individual existence; (4) the self-actualization needs for finding and pursuing those activities that are most suited to each individual's unique innate potential, as this potential develops in a complex environment offering a wide range of activity choices.

The first need to appear in a human being does so at conception and continues throughout life: the physical need to survive. The fertilized egg, the zygote, needs nourishment; the fetus, as it moves through its intrauterine life, needs nourishment; the newborn baby needs nourishment; and so do people at all other stages of life. The other physical needs—for clothing, shelter, health, and physical safety—become more or less active at birth. They are manifest, for example, in the cries of an infant when it is cold and in an adult's discomfort with inadequate clothing and buildings that are too cold or too hot. The lifelong need for health commences with the cries of an infant when it is sick and ends decades later with the final breath of an ailing, dying person. Similarly, the lifelong need for physical safety is first manifest in an infant's cries of fright when it experiences a sudden loss of physical support (as when it is dropped, even onto its bed, or when it is suspended by its hands), is later manifest in the fear of aggressive childhood peers, and still later in the fear of being mugged, raped, or killed in combat or by nuclear holocaust.

The three other sets of basic substantive needs beyond the physical also generally emerge in sequence, the second of the four coming into prominence after the physical needs are secured, the third after the first and second are adequately secured, and the fourth after the prior three have been at least minimally well cared for.

The second set of needs—the social-affectional or love needs for getting, being, and staying together—emerge at or not long after birth. The close kinship between the physical and the love needs is epitomized in the child nursing at its mother's breast. At once it is getting a healthy dose of food and of affection—so simultaneously and conjointly that we have to abstract one need from the other to say that the act of nursing satisfies two needs of the neonate. If the distinction between these two needs is not easily recognizable, we need only recall the experimental work of Harlow with his mother-deprived monkeys (Harlow, 1953; Harlow and Suomi, 1971; Harlow and Mears, 1979) to note the catastrophic consequences for primates that are physically well provided for but emotionally deprived. We can confirm the effects of emotional deprivation for humans in the clinical research of Spitz (1949, 1965) and Bowlby (1969, 1973). And in Geber's field research on *kwashiorkor* (the African "weaning disease"), we can note the catastrophic effects of the practice of simultaneously weaning small children and removing them from their mothers (Geber, 1973; Geber and Dean, 1955). In adults we can note the sequential, priority relationship between the physical and the social-affectional needs in a couple of ways: (1) When people are physically mal-nourished, ill, or threatened with bodily harm, they are usually much less inter-ested in sex than when they are well fed, healthy, and physically secure. (2) Marriages between a food-providing and brutal husband and a compliant housewife are less likely to endure as women, especially since World War II and especially in advanced industrial societies, have been able to get jobs and provide for their own physical needs. If the physical needs did not have higher priority than the social-affectional or love needs, perhaps women would have divorced their husbands at much higher rates *before* the beginning of their economic eman-cipation rather than *after*.

The third set of substantive needs are the self-esteem or dignity or equality needs. The dignity needs emerge in infancy out of the love needs, as the child gradually becomes aware of the separateness of its being and relates this emergent self to others. The infant begins to enjoy not simply being fed, cuddled, and kissed but also being responded to and recognized as a now distinct entity who is smiled at and praised when it can successfully play the earliest games. These self-esteem, dignity needs, like the physical and the love needs, continue throughout life. In children they take the form of seeking recognition for their uniqueness and their self-generated accomplishments. In adults they take a wider variety of forms, ranging from the person who is proud of being told by his boss that he has done a job well, to the carpenter or contractor who is proud of the house he has con-structed, to the composer who is proud of her musical creation. In politics the self-esteem or dignity needs take the form of the expectation and then the demand that all people be recognized as equal. These basic, organic needs have, as we shall see, tremendous portent for the emergence of democratic, popularly responsible polit-ical institutions.

The self-actualization needs are the last to emerge from their genetically innate but dormant state in the human organism. They are first evident in the form of play among very young children—play in which children enjoy smearing mud or paint on almost anything, graduate to piling stones or blocks together, and then begin to form more structured objects and images. Self-actualization—fulfillment—needs also are evident in children's simple and then complex vocal-izations, verbalizations, and other expressions of their distinct, unique interests and their individual interactions with parts of the environment. In adults self-actualization takes as many different forms as there are individual human beings, because no two human beings are exactly alike in either their heredity or their environment since conception.

In preindustrial societies, however, the range of opportunities for self-actu-alization is severely restricted because most people spend most of their time trying to stay alive and well. Although individuals may be able to express food prefer-ences, and to work not simply with skill but also with unique style as they harvest grain or prepare meals, their choice of occupations is limited by their highest-priority need: their nearly constant preoccupation with securing only the minimal means of survival. In industrial societies, with their increasingly intricate division of labor and specialization of function, the opportunities for self-fulfillment sometimes seem almost infinite. The kinds of paying work available should, it would seem, allow an individual to find an occupation that is both challenging and remunerative. If the work is or becomes monotonous, an individual can change jobs or at least seek relief and fulfillment in after-work activity. Nevertheless, repetitive work remains a major problem, particularly in a highly task-differentiated industry but also in routinized service industries, where most of the office work is machinelike and monotonous. Only relatively, then, can one say that the opportunities for self-fulfillment are better in industrial than in agrarian society.

Those who are living a full and satisfying life become unconscious of the regular manner in which all their higher-priority basic needs have to be fulfilled before they can continue their uniquely self-fulfilling activity. All they need do to be reminded of them is to get hungry for more than a day or so, to get ill, or to get mugged, raped, or otherwise assaulted. Suddenly such people experience the profoundest trauma: physical deprivation. This loss requires them consciously or unconsciously to turn away from whatever else they have been doing to a frank and almost total concern with restoring their health, comfort, and physical safety. They can no longer act very much like civilized beings of the sort that we casually call human. A writer or a senator who is hospitalized with a serious illness, for example, is for the duration of the illness primarily a patient, perhaps impatiently enduring the illness before returning to the self-fulfilling activity.

Physical needs are well secured only where people are living in the most developed, integrated, prosperous, interdependent, and nonviolent industrialized societies—and only among perhaps 10 to 20 percent of the people living in these advanced and emancipating societies. It has taken more than four hundred years—from the wars of the Reformation to the second generation after World War II—to secure the good life for what remains a minority in the most orderly and open conditions.

The ways in which physical deprivation (the highest-priority need) can override the self-actualization needs (the most distinctly human but the lowest-priority needs) are easy to see and appreciate. There is a comparable reassertion of the other basic needs—those for affiliation and self-esteem or dignity. Generally, if one is by circumstances required to choose between self-fulfilling activity and avoiding depreciation and degradation, the individual will attend to his dignity needs before reverting to self-fulfilling activity. However much an artist may love to paint, a composer to write music, a ball player to play ball, these individuals will make major efforts to arrange a show or a concert or to get into a game, so that their artistic creativity and skill can be appreciated. People need social recognition in order to confirm that the work they enjoy for its own sake is regarded by others as worthy. The nineteenth-century abolitionist William Lloyd Garrison was indeed fulfilling himself in a highly moral cause, but he could not fulfill himself in a closet. He said in 1831 when he founded the antislavery journal *The Liberator*: "I will not equivocate—I will not excuse—I will not retreat a single inch—and *I will be heard.*" Garrison was demanding not only freedom for slaves but also recognition for himself. A few decades earlier, Beethoven, although almost totally deaf, undertook to direct the performance of his Ninth Symphony—before an appreciative, adoring audience (Solomon, 1977, pp. 269–270). Beethoven needed to be held in high esteem as well as to create music.

Correlatively, the relationship between the self-actualization needs and the love needs is evident in the difficulty that people have in pursuing their particular self-fulfilling work when they lose a beloved through death or separation. Political people often will take enormous risk in their careers because of an affair that might wreck their political life if made public. A few years after he was married, Lyndon Johnson was willing to abandon politics because of his love for his mistress (Caro, 1982, chap. 25), although he did not actually do so. Franklin Roosevelt had a similar love affair while he was assistant secretary of the navy during World War I. He was willing to risk his career by divorcing his wife and marrying his beloved. In Roosevelt's case at least, career needs were not the only ones leading to a breakup of the romantic affair; there was also the sense that it would be hard on the children and the fear that his wealthy, widowed mother would disinherit her only son if he married the woman. Material and love needs relating to family overrode romantic love needs and ironically made it possible for Roosevelt to fulfill himself politically. A divorce in the 1920s would very likely have ended his political career (Lash, 1973, chap. 21).

The relationship between the dignity needs and those having generally higher priority is implicit in some of what has been said above, but other examples may help explain it. Married people often will take frequent and even public humiliation rather than abandon their spouses, which would deprive them of not only the physical but also the mental rewards for being together. Humiliating relationships are endured because people find it better to stick with a spouse who is providing food, sex, and some companionship than to be alone and perhaps hungry. As mentioned, a fundamental explanation for the increase in divorces in advanced industrial societies is that both of the parties to the marriage have careers and incomes and no longer have the material necessity for staying together; often they can find more affectionate, dignifying, and interesting successors to their spouses.

The priority relationship between the love needs and the physical needs is such an elemental one that its political portent is typically ignored. When people are physically deprived, basic social ties often are weakened or destroyed. As noted earlier, Aronoff (1967) found striking differences in the stability of marital relationships in a very poor community of cane cutters and in a physically much healthier village of fishermen. The fishermen not only had more stable marriages but also had family histories reflecting marital stability.

Instrumental Needs. The second set of needs, the instrumental needs, are also regarded as innate. They include (1) the need for security, (2) the need for knowledge, and (3) the need for power. These needs are conceived here as bearing a means-end relationship to the substantive needs. That is, people want to have security typically not for its own sake but to be secure in the provision of each of their substantive needs: they want to be secure about their food, their health, their physical safety. They want to be secure about being loved, esteemed, and self-actualized. Similarly, people pursue knowledge typically not for its own sake but as a means for satisfying each of their substantive needs. They want to know how to provide food, to gain love, to find dignity, and to fulfill themselves. Similarly, people pursue power typically and normally not for its own sake but as a means for satisfying each of their substantive needs.

The instrumental needs are hard to distinguish from one another. The aphorism "Knowledge is power" could as readily be rephrased "Security is power," or "Knowledge is security." And they do not seem to bear any priority or sequential relationship to one another. It is not more important, for instance, to know than to be secure or to have power.

Conceiving the instrumental and substantive basic needs in a means-end relationship helps us understand human and, therefore, political motivation more clearly. Instead of concluding that a person or a society is pursuing power for its own sake, we can ask "For what purpose do people want power?" And then we can look psychologically for the object of the search for power. Did the peasants and farmers who composed the armies of Cromwell, of the American Revolution, of the French Revolution, or of the Chinese Revolution want to shoot and kill and to be victorious just for fun, *or were they seeking to enlarge their control over the political means* relating to their material wants, their social cohesiveness against divisive forces, and their dignity? Similarly, were the leaders of these revolutionary armies pursuing power for its own sake or as a means of fulfilling (in addition to the indicated substantive needs of their troops) their desire to self-actualize as leaders?

To make power an object that is pursued for its own sake omits any of what we call ethical considerations as factors motivating both general publics and elites. Justice becomes, as Plato said, the interest of the stronger, and we are left with an explanation for the Puritan Revolution that omits all but the Hobbesian motivation. Such an explanation tells us simply that soldiers and generals, citizens and their leaders engage in conflict for its own sake and not to produce even a somewhat more equal—more just—society in which every individual is somewhat more equally dignified and has a slightly more equal share of power. And what was true during these earlier revolutions is true in the 1980s vintage in Latin America and the Middle East; people are using violence as a *means* to gain, among other things, dignity.

Causally Plural Complex of Basic Needs. Every overt act of every human being is a product of more than one basic need. And so any analysis asserting, for example, that an overt action of either one individual or of a society can be explained as motivated by survival or dignity or even power is not a fundamental but, rather, a reductionist analysis. It is as reductionist as a chemical analysis would be in asserting that it is hydrogen that produces water or a proton that produces hydrogen.

We have already noted that both physical and love needs are being satisfied when an infant is breast feeding. We may also note that the American revolutionists in 1775 were commencing a war for independence not just for the principle that all men are created equal but also for the improvement of their material circumstances. That is, both physical and dignity needs were involved. And for revolutionary leaders, not only these needs but also their self-fulfilling activity as leaders of the revolution were involved.

So three things need to be borne in mind when we examine overt political action: (1) Which of the basic needs are involved? (2) Which one or more of them are most prominent? (3) Which of them is being asserted for the first time among most people in a society? In the American Revolution, the physical, social, and dignity needs all seem to have been active among most of the public; the physical and dignity needs seem to have been most prominent; and the dignity needs were evidently the *newly* asserted needs. Among American campus rebels in the 1960s, the threat of being drafted for the Vietnamese war activated a variety of needs. They ranged from the threat of bodily harm to the loss of dignity (as individuals whom the government regarded as useful instruments of national policy) to the loss of self-fulfilling activity (as their career preparations in college were to be interrupted by military service). Of course, in *every* political act, the effort to exercise power is an ingredient.

Stages of Political Development

Earlier I said that there is an orderly, nonrandom relationship between the stages of individual and of political development. Before considering the political stages, we need to be rather specific about what political entities are involved in development and, therefore, what entities are at which stage of development. To take some extreme cases, we may say that in a very narrow sense Diogenes was politically autonomous, even anarchic, when in his brief meeting with Alexander he asked the great leader not to stand between him and the sun. Or we may say that two rather civilized anarchists, Tolstoi and Kropotkin, were at an ultimate stage of political development when they wrote so potently during the twilight of the autocratic czarist gods. Or we may say that Ortega y Gasset—in his disdain for grubby, materialistic, mass market, modern societies—was also a universal and free spirit writing in a Spain that was oscillating politically between a parochial feudal oligarchy and a populist anarchy.

These influential individuals, from Diogenes to Ortega y Gasset, were remarkably free as individuals. But neither Alexander's empire, nor the Russian empire, nor Spain in the 1920s much resembled the "good society" that these men symbolically represented. To understand the relationship between individual and political development, we must ascertain (1) the specific circumstances that prevail in a particular society—not those that prevail for a small minority; and (2) the political position of the most advanced groups in that society. We must then determine whether the position of these advanced groups characterizes—not wholly but predominantly—the society of which they are part,

Let us consider an American example. Late in the nineteenth century, a small number of women became the leaders of a somewhat smaller group of followers. These feminists, as they were then called, were functioning in the face of passive, and in some instances active, opposition among most of their contemporary fellow women. The latter, if not content, were resigned to the overt domination of men in the family, church, schools, business, and politics. Late in the twentieth century, after numerous and mostly nonviolent struggles, the principle of nondiscrimination prevails and the practice of sex discrimination is steadily diminishing—at least for middle-class women. Two major events had to occur before women could even ask for greater equality: (1) Women had to become economically—that is, materially—independent. (2) They had to establish a community—that is, a sense of their togetherness. In other words, their social, *and before their social their physical*, needs had to be fairly well secured.

Let us consider another American example. In 1863, by executive proclamation, slavery was abolished. The principle was thereby denied that there could be a category of people who could lawfully be owned. The real-life concomitants of this principle of inequality took the form of lynching; tenant farming; and racial segregation, which persisted a century after Lincoln proclaimed the principle of equality. Nevertheless, late in the twentieth century, black people are approaching equality. But before black people could effectively demand equality, they had to establish a community of shared identity; and before that, they had to have a sufficiently independent economic base not to be continuously and perilously dependent on white people for their very survival.

Now let me define the stages of political development, which then will be briefly related to stages of individual development.

1. *Primitive Anarchy.* The basic characteristics of this form of government are these: The political rules have been internalized, and there are very few rules to be internalized. Rules about making decisions that affect everyone have become firmly established over centuries and have become second nature to everyone. Primitive anarchy is the polity (almost the apolity) that typically prevails in hunting and gathering societies and in established feudalities—for example, on manors in medieval Europe and on estates (haciendas and fazendas) in contemporary Latin America. The conditions are quite static, and the main preoccupation is survival.

2. *Anomic Anarchy.* This is the transition polity that is common when an internalized polity of tradition is breaking down as a result of intrusive modernizing influences. When medieval and contemporary landed estates are breaking up as a result of agricultural specialization and marketing of farm commodities, serfs and peasants are typically unable to subsist. Individuals, usually young family members, migrate to cities to work for wages. This is the Hobbesian society, wherein the fierce struggle to survive erodes traditional habits and values; there is a lawless, egocentric "individualism" and the devil or robbers take the hindmost. Anomic anarchy in full or somewhat attenuated form prevails in the ghettos and slums of big cities in even modern, relatively well-integrated nations.

3. *Oligarchy.* This is the polity resulting when people who are passing painfully through anomic anarchy no longer feel able to cope with the threat and the reality of thievery, robbery, assault, rape, and murder. They surrender the control of their own lives to a strong, institutionally irresponsible government and its often brutal police and army. People in such conditions regard the war of each against all as worse than the harsh but somewhat less arbitrary force of "law." Oligarchy is the form of polity that prevails in developing nations, including some nations with a high degree of surface order and stability. The popular acceptance of oligarchy broke down in Hungary in 1956 and in Poland in 1981, but in both instances oligarchy was reestablished. Similarly, in France oligarchy was briefly replaced with more popular government in 1789 but was then reestablished in 1801, when Napoleon declared himself emperor. Portugal, until the death of Antonio Salazar in 1970 and the 1974 popular military coup ("the Revolution of the Flowers"), was in the oligarchy stage. And so was Spain until the death of Francisco Franco in 1975. In the 1970s and 1980s, both countries were making the first significant steps beyond oligarchy toward democracy.

4. *Democracy.* This is the stage that develops, both violently and peacefully, out of oligarchy. In the first efforts to make government responsible to the general public, groups within the society that have the political (and military) power to confront the government gradually put checks on it. In perhaps all cases, starting with ancient Athens, the politically potent antagonists of oligarchical rule are at least initially a minority. In the name of equality, they typically reestablish oligarchy, but in a less publicly irresponsible form. In Athens at its most democratic,

both women and slaves were effectively kept out of political power. In the German Protestant Reformation and in the English Puritan Revolution, the overwhelming majority of the population—peasants in a still mainly agrarian society—were excluded from power. In the American Revolution and the French Revolution, the commercial, manufacturing, and plantationing high bourgeoisie effectively dominated the democratic government during most of the first two hundred years.

However, the power conflicts between various elite groups (colonial overlords versus indigenous lords, industrial entrepreneurs versus slaveholders, "big business" versus "big labor") and power conflicts between rulers and ruled commence the process of making government responsible to the entire citizenry. Early in the process of democratization, government is made responsible to one or more groups—usually possessing substantial wealth. These groups, often competing with each other for control of the government, develop an adversary relationship to government. This adversary relationship gets institutionalized, the number of groups demanding power increases, and gradually the government becomes responsible to the general public.

5. *Civilized Anarchy.* This is the stage that emerges somewhat more peacefully out of democracy—somewhat more peacefully, that is, than democracy emerges out of oligarchy. It is the stage that was envisioned by Marx and Engels ([1932] 1976), various Utopian socialists, and the explicit anarchist Kropotkin ([1892] 1968). In this stage there is a return to the internalized condition of self-regulation that prevails in primitive anarchy. Now, however, internalization is not simple but very complex, involving a host of rules governing interactions between different kinds of people in a complexly integrated, industrialized society.

Civilized anarchy is indeed based on some age-old rules (for example, prohibitions against the arbitrary taking of life and property), but it is also based on rules that have accumulated in modern societies—rules relating not simply to physical needs to survive and accumulate goods but also to needs that loosely solidify citizens with each other, dignify them equally, and provide the equal opportunity for all citizens to fulfill their individual potential. That is, individual fulfillment is not to remain the inheritance of the rich and well born but is to become a common expectation of everyone.

Some symptoms of the gradual appearance of civilized anarchy already exist: the willingness of most people to abide by traffic rules that need to be enforced against a small fraction of drivers, the concern for the quality of the natural environment, the recognition of the right of everyone to pursue education not just for trade but for esthetic reasons, and the campaigns to get government off people's backs. Communities of students in colleges and universities also are vanguard civil anarchies; very little coercive power is needed to maintain the peaceful community in which students prepare themselves to enter self-fulfilling careers. Utopian communities, religious and otherwise, are similarly vanguard civil anarchies, though they tend not to endure, perhaps partly because they are too intense, too all-consuming of the community members' energies, too directive of their interests, and too intrusive into their individual privacy.

Of course, civilized anarchy can never prevail everywhere and for all human beings, because in at least some people there are genetic antisocial factors. And, practically, civilized anarchy is many centuries in the future. As the previous paragraphs indicate, however, some portents of civilized anarchy are already dimly visible.

The Developmental Connection

The relationship between the development of individuals and of polities has been implied here and occasionally made explicit. But a few more things need saying, to indicate not only what kinds and degrees of individual and political development are being linked but also what is not being linked.

First, there is a ratchet-like quality to the interaction. As more people in a society become more mature, they demand change in public institutions and in the power structure. When they replace the struggle of each against all for survival with some kind of community commitment, they can form solidarity groups that demand limits on the arbitrary power of government. This demand becomes possible because of the solidification of an inarticulate body of survivalists. Post-survivalists see—with the often brutal help of an irresponsible oligarchy—the futility of continuing the anarchic struggle. They become unified as a growth process, and this growth puts pressure on government to change. Once people start to limit government, their natural demand for equality and for dignity emerges; and they direct their natural need for power toward achieving greater equality. So oligarchy is gradually replaced by democracy; and, as the areas spread in which equality is recognized, government gradually becomes more democratic. The more equally people share political power, the more responsible they become. And the more responsible they become, the more they are able to internalize the rules necessary for people to have equal opportunity and to diminish the ability of particular groups (like the military-industrial complex, as President Eisenhower called it) to regain control over the public. The more the internalization, the more self-confident are people of their own ability to govern themselves. And this heads people in the direction of the autonomy that leads to civilized anarchy.

Second, no polity can unequivocally be categorized as at a single stage of political development. If a society is composed of people who are mainly in either a feudal or a hunting, fishing, and gathering economy, then that society very likely is in the stage of primitive anarchy, even if a tiny fraction of the population is highly advanced. An example would be a tribal area or a rural area in a Third World nation where the landlord sends his sons to school in the country's big city or to Europe or America. When such a rural society is breaking down and there is a large migration from country to city, those who stay in the country remain in a stage of primitive anarchy while those who go to the city enter a stage of anomic anarchy. The same applies to the transition from anomic anarchy to oligarchy, from oligarchy to democracy, and from democracy to civilized anarchy: a society, a nation, is best characterized as being at that stage of political development where most of its citizens are located.

Third, there is no one-to-one relationship between an individual's development as a private person and as a citizen. It would be unrealistic to say that all people in primitive anarchy are self-contained laws unto themselves, whether in their private or their public lives. It would be unrealistic to say that all people in a democracy demand or even want equality of opportunity and of power or that all citizens equally demand dignity. But if equality is at least a consensual expectation—if the citizens generally are not passively content to be ruled by an oligarchy—then, even though substantial portions of the population are irresponsible, compliant, or even indifferent, democracy is probably a more appropriate term for the stage of development than oligarchy.

Fourth, there is little if any likelihood that a nation can bypass a stage of political development, any more than an individual can bypass a stage of development from infancy, childhood, and adolescence to maturity. Individuals do swing back and forth within a limited range as they mature: Adolescents sometimes act like children and sometimes like adults. Nations that are in an oligarchical stage sometimes act with anomic anarchy and sometimes with real responsibility, as India has done since its 1947 independence. France went through such oscillations in the period that started with the 1789 revolution, continued through the First Republic and the empires, and probably ceased when Charles de Gaulle ended his constitutional monarchy. Germany similarly oscillated from the late-nineteenth-century empire to the Weimar Republic and the Nazi dictatorship, the oscillations not really stopping until the end of Konrad Adenauer's constitutional monarchy.

However, with all such oscillations, corresponding to the "mood" swings of individual adolescents, no nation seems to have moved from primitive or anomic anarchy to democracy, bypassing oligarchy. Marx and Lenin to the contrary, none of the socialist nations have bypassed the socialist stage and moved from early capitalistic to mature "communistic" society; in fact, all the nations that adopted a socialist ideology after World Wars I and II remain oligarchies and have not yet achieved institutionalized responsibility of rulers to ruled. They have yet to achieve either democracy or socialism.

The epoch of the socialist states began at the end of World War I, went dormant for three decades, and then emerged in great force after World War II. In these young nations, there has been a universal contradiction between egalitarian, democratic ideology and regimes that have enjoyed the same bourgeois corruption that the new regimes swore to end. This has been true in perhaps unbroken succession in the mother country of socialism, the Soviet Union, and in the Eastern European, Indian, African, and Asian socialist states. In each of them, the elite have not understood either themselves or their citizens, as products of their own historical past, as a people who became a nation. They have not seen themselves as products of the old regimes and the old societies they have overthrown. They have not been able to act as their vision demanded. They have been class conscious but not self-conscious. There was nothing particularly wrong about their dreams. What failed was the ability of human beings to distinguish their dreams from their own behavior. More fundamentally, people have assumed either that they are totally enslaved (or determined by broad social forces) or totally free. The process of diminishing the enslavement or the determinism is not understood psychologically.

In sum, contrary to the action-oriented Marxists at the start of the 1917 revolution in Russia, I do not see how it is possible for any individual or any people to bypass history—to move speedily from miserable to ideal circumstances and to fulfillment of self and of all others. That is, every individual and every people must go through each stage of individual development, just as they must go through each stage of political development. So each individual as a citizen— that is, each individual in his or her political role—must move from primitive anarchy, through anomic anarchy, oligarchy, and democracy *before* moving to civilized anarchy. Where the institutions of a society are sufficiently developed that all individuals in the first two decades of life can go through primitive anarchy, anomic anarchy, and oligarchy in the development of their patterns of interaction with others—in family, school, and community groups—then the society is ready for democracy. But where children are socialized to obey parents and teachers blindly and where such institutions as churches and economic organizations are similarly authoritarian, then individuals who reach maturity in these circumstances are not ready for democracy. And even individuals who feel that they are beyond such blind obedience and authoritarianism—because they had permissive parents and went to liberal schools—are not ready for democracy if they are unable to relate to others in their society who are not so socialized. They remain, like Ortega y Gasset, detached adherents of a detached, perhaps liberal, elite.

The road to civilized anarchy is even longer and rockier. For one thing, it must be paved: The society must be wealthy enough for each individual to have free access to the training and the education that will draw out each individual's full potential. For another thing, there must be a broad measure of empathy, so that individuals do not need to ask for whom the bell tolls and do understand that at times everyone needs the welfare state—whether as a new or an established entrepreneur, a farmer facing not the ups but the downs of a worldwide commodity market, a gifted student who cannot afford to go to college, or a nearly illiterate guest worker.

Even if one can say that street and highway traffic moves with sufficient smoothness to indicate internalization of the rules of the road, it is a long way to add that all other rules necessary for cooperative interaction are internalized. Nowhere in the world is there yet evidence that enough people within any nation have the empathy for others, the sense of social responsibility, and the ability to see themselves as others see them that are prerequisites for a movement out of democracy and toward civilized anarchy.

There has been progress since the anomic anarchy of seventeenth-century England that Hobbes called the frightful state of nature. There has been progress since the oligarchical epochs that produced Napoleon in France and Hitler in Germany. There has been progress toward democracy. But if we say that achievement of democracy will be the final political achievement, we have no ability to discover the causes for the discontents within democracy and no ability to foresee the future.

References

Aronoff, J. *Psychological Needs and Cultural Systems.* New York: Van Nostrand Reinhold, 1967.

Bowlby, J. *Attachment.* New York: Basic Books, 1969.

Bowlby, J. *Separation.* New York: Basic Books, 1973.

Caro, R. *The Years of Lyndon Johnson: The Path to Glory.* Vol. 1. New York: Knopf, 1982.

Davies, J. C. *Human Nature in Politics.* New York: Wiley, 1963.

Durkheim, E. *The Division of Labor in Society.* New York: Free Press, 1933. (Originally published 1893.)

Durkheim, E. *Suicide.* New York: Free Press, 1951. (Originally published 1897.)

Durkheim, E. *Moral Education: A Study in the Theory and Application of the Sociology of Education.* New York: Free Press, 1961. (Originally published 1902.)

Einstein, A., and Freud, S. *Why War?* Paris: International Institute of Intellectual Cooperation, 1932.

Engels, F. *The Peasant War in Germany.* In L. Krieger (ed.), *Friedrich Engels: The German Revolutions.* Chicago: University of Chicago Press, 1967. (Originally published 1850.)

Freud, S. *Group Psychology and the Analysis of the Ego.* London: Hogarth Press, 1922.

Geber, M. "L'Environnement et le développement des enfants africains" [The environment and development of African children]. *Enfance*, 1973, *3-4*, 145-174.

Geber, M., and Dean, R. F. A. "Psychological Factors in the Etiology of Kwashiorkor." *Bulletin of the World Health Organization*, 1955, *12*, 471-475.

Harlow, H. F. "Mice, Monkeys, Men, and Motives." *Psychological Review*, 1953, *60*, 23-32.

Harlow, H. F., and Mears, C. *The Human Model: Primate Perspectives.* New York: Wiley, 1979.

Harlow, H. F., and Suomi, S. J. "Social Recovery by Isolation-Reared Monkeys." *Proceedings of the National Academy of Sciences*, 1971, *68*, 1534-1538.

Hobbes, T. *Leviathan.* (M. Oakeshott, ed.) New York: Macmillan, 1962. (Originally published 1651).

James, W. *The Principles of Psychology.* 2 vols. Mineola, N.Y.: Dover, 1950. (Originally published 1890.)

Jones, E. *The Life and Work of Sigmund Freud.* Vol. 1. New York: Basic Books, 1953.

Jones, E. *The Life and Work of Sigmund Freud.* Vol. 2. New York: Basic Books, 1955.

Kropotkin, P. *The Conquest of Bread.* New York: Blom, 1968. (Originally published 1892.)

Lash, J. P. *Eleanor and Franklin.* New York: New American Library, 1973.

McDougall, W. *Introduction to Social Psychology.* Boston: Luce, 1921. (Originally published 1908.)

MacLean, P. "On the Evolution of Three Mentalities." In S. Arieti and G. Chrzanowski (eds.), *New Dimensions in Psychiatry: A World View.* Vol. 2. New York: Wiley-Interscience, 1975.

Mannheim, K. *Ideology and Utopia: An Introduction to the Sociology of Knowledge.* San Diego: Harcourt Brace Jovanovich, 1954. (Originally published 1929.)

Marx, K. *Capital.* (F. Engels, ed.) 3 vols. New York: International Publishers, 1967. (Originally published 1867.)

Marx, K., and Engels, F. *The German Ideology.* Chicago: Imported Publications, 1976. (Originally published 1932.)

Maslow, A. H. "A Theory of Motivation." *Psychological Review*, 1943, *50*, 370-396.

Murray, H. A. *Explorations in Personality.* New York: Oxford University Press, 1938.

Ortega y Gasset, J. *The Revolt of the Masses.* New York: Norton, 1957. (Originally published 1930.)

Rousseau, J. J. *Émile.* (A. Bloom, trans.) New York: Basic Books, 1979. (Originally published 1762.)

Solomon, M. *Beethoven.* New York: Associated Music Publishers (Schirmer), 1977.

Sorokin, P. *The Sociology of Revolution.* Philadelphia: Lippincott, 1925.

Spitz, R. "The Role of Ecological Factors in Emotional Development in Infancy." *Child Development*, 1949, *20*, 145–155.

Spitz, R. *The First Year of Life: A Psychoanalytic Study of Normal and Deviant Development of Object Relationships.* New York: International Universities Press, 1965.

Spitz, R. *The First Year of Life: A Psychoanalytic Study of Normal and Deviant Development of Object Relationships.* New York: International Universities Press, 1965.

Thomas, W. I. *The Unadjusted Girl.* Excerpted in M. Janowitz (ed.), *W. I. Thomas on Social Organization and Social Personality.* Chicago: University of Chicago Press, 1966. (Originally published 1923.)

Tucker, R. C. *The Marx-Engels Reader.* New York: Norton, 1972.

THREE

Interrelationship
of Political Ideology
and Public Opinion

Paul M. Sniderman
Philip E. Tetlock

A phenomenon may be hard to grasp not because we know too little about it but
because we know too much. So it is with ideology and public opinion. Much has
been learned. More remarkably, much of what has been learned has subsequently
been confirmed. Yet it remains true that analyzing public opinion, in Key's (1961,
p. 8) words, is "not unlike coming to grips with the Holy Ghost." A chief reason
for this difficulty is that the more we learn about public opinion, the less apparent
is its basis of organization. The nub of the problem is simply put. There is strong
evidence that members of the general public pay little attention to politics and
know little about it. Their ideas about politics, moreover, tend to be loosely tied
together. They do not seem to make use of ideological categories, such as liberalism
or conservatism, to organize their responses to candidates or political parties. Nor
do many of them, given a chance to define liberalism and conservatism in their
own words, appear to understand what these terms mean, except in a superficial
way. And so the better we have come to understand public opinion, the more
obscure has become the notion of ideology, at least as applied to the public at large.

One response has been to draw back from quantitative studies of public

Note: We wish to acknowledge the helpful comments of Henry Brady, Richard A.
Brody, James H. Kuklinski, and Michael Hagen on earlier versions of this chapter.
Preparation of this chapter was assisted by funds from the Survey Research Center at the
University of California, Berkeley.

opinion and instead look at politics from the perspective of individuals, one by one. The object here is to see what sense each individual makes of politics, in his or her own terms. To those taking this perspective, ideology gives the impression of being garbled by the average citizen because the individuals who make up the general public, with their individual concerns and distinctive points of view, are treated as though they were essentially alike and shared a common point of view. But listen to one person at a time, and the responses will make a great deal more sense; they take on coherence when judged within the context of each individual's overall belief system.[1]

This approach has much to recommend it. It does, however, have the drawback of taking care of the problem of ideology by conceding it. For the question, at bottom, is not whether members of the general public can make sense of politics but, rather, whether they can make sense of the terms in which politics is actually carried on. And these terms are, inescapably, ideological: liberal versus conservative, left versus right. Elite politics is not wholly a matter of ideology, but we cannot fully comprehend the one without also comprehending the other.

A useful step to take is to ask, again, what it means to speak of ideology among the mass public. Again, this is a question that is difficult to respond to, not because of the obscurity of the answer but because of its very clarity. So ideology might mean an ability, and a willingness, to explicate the history of liberalism and conservatism or to lay out the principal policies associated with each. But if it means either, the mass public, one must conclude, is innocent of ideology (see Kinder and Sears, 1985). But perhaps ideology means something quite different, an outlook both less cerebral in character and, because simpler, more common in occurrence. So at least we shall suggest. Ideology, in our view, involves definite and politically relevant preferences—liking liberals and disliking conservatives, or the other way around—at any rate, for the general public. From this angle, ideology is better understood as a set of root likes and dislikes rather than an assemblage of abstractions. And these likes and dislikes, if coherent, provide people with the means they need to figure out a relatively coherent set of opinions, covering many of the major issues of the day.

When we consider belief systems as systems, two questions are especially important. The first concerns the degree of organization of mass belief systems; the second, the mechanisms of their organization. The first question is descriptive, the second, causal. Accordingly, we shall proceed in two sections: the first descriptive, the second causal. The first section takes up the question of the connectedness of mass belief systems. In this respect the balance of evidence favors Converse's (1964) classic analysis of public opinion, with its stress on the minimal connectedness of mass belief systems. At the same time, there is evidence also of a substantial measure of connectedness, or organization, in mass belief systems. The second section takes up the problem of dynamics; its concern is not whether mass belief systems are organized but, rather, how they come to be organized.[2]

A basic key to understanding this organization, we believe, is the idea of consistency. The notion of consistency has been much measured, less often analyzed. Its meaning appears obvious, another example of how familiarity breeds misunderstanding. We think it useful to distinguish two principal forms of consistency. People may strive to maximize consistency between beliefs—that is, cognitive consistency. Or they may strive to maximize consistency between their beliefs and their likes and dislikes—that is, affective consistency. The first form of consistency is more familiar; all the same, the second is the more fundamental, at least in the political domain.[3]

In brief, we shall suggest that a substantial part of the mass public is able to work through to a coherent view of politics; the reason that people are able, and willing, to do so has less to do with a wide knowledge of politics and political ideas than with a politically coherent set of personal likes and dislikes.

The Minimalist-Maximalist Controversy

Systematic research on public opinion and ideology, in the last decade, has had two programmatic objectives: to reject Converse's (1964) now classic argument concerning the lack of structural coherence in public opinion; or, alternatively, to reject such rejections. This debate has, understandably, prompted an impression of a field tugged in two opposing directions—of a lack, in equal measure, of consistency and progress in research (see Bennett, 1977). This impression is somewhat misleading. To be sure, two distinct interpretations of public opinion—one we shall call minimalist; the other, maximalist—have emerged; and it is customarily supposed that if one of them is right, the other must be wrong. This conclusion is itself wrong. The two models of public opinion, far from being mutually exclusive, are mutually complementary.

In saying that both minimalist and maximalist models hold, we might mean one of three things: (1) that the same individual approximates both models, but at different points in time; (2) that some individuals are better described by one model, others by the other; or (3) that the same individual, at the same point in time, is well described by both models, depending on the region of his or her belief system under examination. The first alternative is almost certainly true. The linkages in a person's belief system should tighten markedly if that person could be induced merely to think about the issues at hand (McGuire, 1985; Tesser, 1978), certainly if his interest in politics could be aroused (Judd, Krosnick, and Milburn, 1981; Nie and Andersen, 1974). True or not, however, there is a dearth of systematic evidence, bearing directly on political belief systems, on the variability of the same person in different situations. It is, accordingly, the second two possibilities we shall concentrate on, and more on the second than the third, again because of the uneven coverage of research.

It is, however, not enough to focus on what belief systems look like; it is necessary to consider as well how they work. Unfortunately, research on public opinion is frequently descriptive and nearly always cross-sectional. Experimental treatment, apart from a glittering exception here and there (for example, Sullivan, Pierson, and Marcus, 1978), is conspicuous by its absence. And longitudinal analysis, again apart from the honorable exception (for example, Converse and Markus, 1979; Markus, 1979), is a similar rarity. As a consequence, we shall surely get some important things wrong, or at any rate greatly simplify complex and subtle processes of opinion formation and organization.[4] We shall take our chances all the same.

Concretely, our starting point is a swirl of studies surrounding the central tenets of a minimalist model of public opinion and ideology. The heart of the model is simply put: (1) The average citizen's knowledge of politics—whether of abstract ideas or of details of the political process—is very limited. (2) In interpreting politics the general public does not, with few exceptions, consider general political principles or ideological perspectives, preferring instead to evaluate politicians and their parties by a simpler calculus—for instance, group benefits or, more simply still, the "nature of the times." (3) The average citizen's preferences on some arguably basic political issues are remarkably transient—so much so as to give the impression that many have never formed a real opinion in the first place. (4) The average citizen's views on one issue are only loosely, or minimally, connected to his views on other issues. The balance of evidence favors at least three of the four propositions; the outcome of the stability/lability dispute remains obscure. But it is well to consider research on these propositions in some detail, to make plain the force and consistency of the evidence supporting the minimalist model.

This overview of the evidence is all the more necessary as we shall go on to suggest a second, and quite different, interpretation of public opinion—a maximalist model as against a minimalist one. A maximalist interpretation can assume two forms. In the first, and weak, version, emphasis falls on the solidity and connectedness of elements of mass belief systems *within* particular regions of the system. This version is clearly correct. It has always been understood that even the mass public has quite definite, and well-organized, ideas on some subjects. An especially notorious example is racial attitudes. No one supposes that prejudice is a nonattitude. In the second, and strong, version of the maximalist position, emphasis falls on the connectedness of elements of mass belief systems *across* particular regions of the system. Very briefly, the strong version holds that there are not only "packages of beliefs" but also "packages of packages." It is the strong, not the weak, version on which we shall focus.

A maximalist interpretation emphasizes the connectedness and consistency of belief systems; a minimalist, their lack of connectedness. But the two offer complementary, not conflicting, models of public opinion. Either maximalist or minimalist interpretation may apply, depending on whose beliefs about what (or toward whom) are considered. The difference between maximalist and minimalist models is a matter of emphasis—a difference of degree, not kind. Nonetheless, the two inspire quite different perspectives. Only if one believes that public opinion is, in some nontrivial sense, connected and coherent does it make sense to think in terms of ideology (or, more broadly still, of political culture) at the level of the general public. Moreover, only on the presumption that mass belief systems are organized does it make sense to ask what the expression "An idea system is consistent" means and, more fundamentally, what forces are responsible for producing consistency.

The idea of consistency has been a central one in research on belief systems, and researchers customarily conclude that there is precious little consistency in mass belief systems. But this conclusion is partly a function of a failing in the customary approach to the analysis of consistency. That failing, we believe, is the effort to assess consistency descriptively, without attempting to analyze it causally. Or, to put the point more generally, the structure of a belief system cannot be rightly understood in isolation from its dynamics. What does it mean to say this? We shall make an attempt at explaining by concentrating on the internal workings of belief systems. What are some of the different forms that consistency may take? May some kinds of inconsistency—for instance, between principle and policy—

reflect consistency at another level? Or, to reason the other way around, is one source of connectedness in belief systems the very need to cope with inconsistency? And, last, how exactly do pressures to consistency operate in mass belief systems?

These questions are all of interest to us, but none more than the last. For if the concept of ideology is to have any utility in the analysis of mass preferences, we must face a simple, yet fundamental, question: How are citizens able to form a coherent outlook on politics—a political ideology—when characteristically they know little about it?

The Minimalist Model. The minimalist model rests on four assumptions: (1) that citizens lack political knowledge, (2) that they do not use (or understand) abstract political ideas, (3) that their political preferences are unstable, and (4) that their political preferences are inconsistent with one another.

All four assumptions continue to enjoy empirical support, none more than the first. By and large, citizens pay little attention to politics; not surprisingly, they know little about it. For example, two out of every three are ignorant of the term of office for United States senators; one out of every two does not know which party controls Congress, if it is not controlled by the president's party (Wolfinger, Shapiro, and Greenstein, 1980). Ignorance in the foreign policy domain is even more profound. Converse (1975) reports that almost half of a national survey sample were unaware—at the height of the Berlin Wall crisis of 1961—that the city was encircled in depth by enemy troops; McGuire (1985) reports that nearly 40 percent of one survey sample believed that Israel is an Arab nation.

Lacking information, citizens tend to lack opinions, even on highly publicized issues. So, between one fifth and one third are without any opinion whatever on specific issues, such as government-guaranteed jobs, Medicare, trade with Communist countries, and foreign trade in general (Erikson, Luttbeg, and Tedin, 1980, p. 22). And a still larger number are ignorant of where they stand in ideological terms. For example, in the 1976 National Election Study, one third of the respondents (from a general population sample), when asked to place themselves on a seven-point liberal-conservative scale, declined to do so, on the grounds that they had not given the question any thought (Erikson, Luttbeg, and Tedin, 1980, p. 22).

Equally disconcerting, when people do express opinions, their opinions often appear to be inventions of the moment. Substantial percentages (generally, about one third) of subjects are prepared to advance opinions on extremely obscure or even fictitious legislative proposals (see, for example, Bishop, Oldendick, Tuchfarber, and Bennett, 1980; Schuman and Presser, 1977). Opinions expressed are also very sensitive to trivial changes in question wording (Turner and Krauss, 1978; Schuman and Presser, 1977, 1981) and to the order in which questions are asked (Schuman and Presser, 1981). It is tempting to conclude that many survey respondents simply give "top-of-the-head" responses (Fischhoff, Slovic, and Lichtenstein, 1980; Fiske and Taylor, 1984) designed to extricate themselves quickly from a potentially embarrassing social confrontation with the interviewer.

This portrait of the mass public, first painted in the 1950s, has gone unchanged in the last three decades, save for touching up a feature here and there. One of these alterations concerns people's knowledge of their congressman. Initially, investigators estimated it as quite low (see Campbell, Converse, Miller, and Stokes, 1960); it was thought that only about half of all citizens know who their congressman is. But, as Tedin and Murray (1979) have pointed out, recalling a person's name, unaided, is a hard task; a fairer one is being able to recognize it. And, in fact, name recognition of congressional candidates is fairly commonplace, according to Mann and Wolfinger (1980). But, such details aside, it is invariably argued—or conceded—that the mass public has only minimal knowledge of the details of politics.

The second assumption in the minimalist model—concerning the average citizen's use, or understanding, of political abstractions—is also solid, notwithstanding a recent impression of shakiness. The fundamental point of interest here is not what an individual believes but, rather, how he thinks about politics. What analytical categories does he deploy to make sense of politics? At least since *The American Voter* (Campbell and others, 1960), the professional consensus has been that only a handful of citizens—between two and five percent—make effective use of abstract constructs such as liberalism and conservatism to organize their evaluations of candidates or political parties. The great bulk of citizens make sense of political choices in concrete rather than abstract terms. Their judgments tend to be made on the basis of "group benefits," favoring (or opposing) a candidate who is judged to be helpful (or harmful) to particular groups, or (relying on a still more rudimentary calculus) on the basis of "the nature of the times,"—that is, supporting incumbents in good years and opposing them in bad ones.

The electorate, presumably, can be sorted out according to level of conceptualization. This presumption has undergone friendly amendment, first by Field and Anderson (1969), then more vigorously by Nie, Verba, and Petrocik (1979). The number of Americans, it was argued, who make use of abstract categories such as liberalism and conservatism depends not only on their own characteristics—for instance, their level of schooling—but also on the character of politics itself. Specifically, more citizens will view an election in ideological terms if it is openly fought on liberal-conservative lines (for example, Johnson-Goldwater) than if the election focuses on personal qualities of presidential candidates (for example, Eisenhower-Stevenson). And, indeed, the number of voters viewing politics in ideological or near-ideological terms did increase from 9 percent in 1956 to 24 percent in 1976. This change has been touted as evidence that the American voter is more capable of ideological judgment than commonly supposed. Unhappily for this interpretation, Smith (1980) has used panel data to examine the over-time reliability of individual respondents for two of the schemes for coding levels of conceptualization: Field and Anderson's (1969) and Nie, Verba, and Petrocik's (1979). An individual's level of conceptualization should not oscillate from election to election (1) if there are, in fact, such levels and (2) if the measure of levels of conceptualization dependably assesses them. But analyzing the 1956–1960 panel, Smith found that the reliability coefficients were exceedingly low: at the highest, .35 (tau-beta); at the lowest, zero. Moreover, change in levels of conceptualization was not tied to conceptually plausible sources of change, such as interest in politics, attention to politics in the media, and political activity.

From one point of view, Smith's finding is clear-cut; from another, equivocal. His results persuasively show that measures of levels of conceptualization are not dependable; or, alternatively, that the idea of levels of conceptualization (and not merely a particular measure of it) is not useful; or both. However that may be, it seems reasonable to infer that a sizable fraction of the citizens interviewed (of the small fraction who putatively are ideologues or near ideologues) are using phrases borrowed from the media. The very unreliability of responses from one election to another underlines how small is the number of citizens *in the habit* of analyzing politics in ideological terms.[5]

Smith's result, then, vindicates the spirit of the original minimalist claim on levels of conceptualization. It is perhaps worth adding that qualitative analysis of open-ended interviews, in which respondents are free to talk about politics in their own words, reinforces the conclusion of more quantitative content analyses. If one has listened to citizens struggle to explain what the terms "liberal" and "conservative" mean, it is hard to credit suggestions that a sizable number of them have the power to discuss these abstract concepts in any degree of depth or detail— at any rate as abstract concepts.

In contrast, research on the stability of preferences, the third assumption in the minimalist model, is in a muddled state. It would seem a straightforward matter to calculate whether people tend to take the same side of an issue at successive points in time. Not so. On one side are Converse and his colleagues (Converse, 1964, 1970; Converse and Markus, 1979) and Jennings and Niemi (1981). According to their calculations, change in issue preferences, over two-year intervals, is exceedingly high among mass publics. Generally, less than two thirds endorsed the same sides of policy controversies that they had endorsed two years earlier (chance alone would lead to half of the respondents answering in the same way). Moreover, the pattern (as against the incidence) of change suggests that many respondents—perhaps most—are expressing "nonattitudes." On the other side are Achen (1975) and Erikson (1979). They contend that, far from there being massive volatility in public preferences, there is actually little true attitude change, once corrections for measurement error have been made (see also Judd and Milburn, 1980; Judd, Krosnick, and Milburn, 1981).

Which of these two positions is the correct one? Unfortunately, it is not at all clear how to decide. The answer that one winds up with depends, wholly it seems, on the assumptions that one makes at the outset. The most critical of these assumptions is the proper treatment of "measurement error." On the one side is the traditional psychometric position that (1) instability is the result of methodological failings (such as imprecise questions or interviewer mistakes) and (2) instability should be removed before one calculates the stability of preferences. On the other side is the objection that this procedure, sensible as it sounds, discards as error variance the very wobbliness in response which is evidence of instability.

This debate has a worrisomely categorical quality. Temporal instability of response can obviously stem from *both* inadequate measures and labile, poorly defined respondent preferences. It is unnecessarily extreme to attribute all measurement error to only one underlying source. The role of individual differences also remains to be fully resolved. On the one side is Converse's celebrated "black-and-white" model. According to this model, the general population is divided into two subsets, one consisting of respondents whose attitudes are perfectly stable, the other of respondents whose attitudes are perfectly random. On the other side, both Achen and Erikson, though making use of different measures, converge on the conclusion that political sophistication and stability of preferences are *not* related. This, it should be said, seems curious. One would suppose that persons who are uncommonly knowledgeable and sophisticated about politics would, other things being equal, be more stable, more rooted, in their preferences than persons who are neither knowledgeable nor well educated (for supporting evidence, see Judd, Krosnick, and Milburn, 1981; Putnam, Leonardi, and Nanetti, 1979; Schuman and Presser, 1981). Or, to put the point more generally, as yet the stability/lability problem has not been reducible to individual differences; and it is hard, at any rate for us, to conceive of a genuinely theoretical resolution to the controversy that cannot, at some level, be expressed in terms of individual differences.

But it is the question of constraint, the fourth part of the minimalist model, that has excited the most attention. Constraint is a direct measure of connectedness or consistency among individuals' opinions; for it is defined, operationally, as the predictability of an individual's opinion on one issue given knowledge of his position on another. Converse (1964) showed, persuasively, the minimal constraint among the average citizen's issue preferences, at least in the 1950s. In all, four issues in domestic politics were examined (employment, aid to education, federal housing, and the Federal Electric Power Corporation) and three in international politics (economic aid, military aid, and isolationism). The mean correlation (tau-gamma) within domestic issues was .23; within foreign issues, .23; and between the two, .11—suggesting that what the average citizen thinks about one issue has little connection with what he thinks about any other. This lack of constraint could not, moreover, be attributed to question wording or selection. For example, substantial constraint existed among the domestic issue preferences of Converse's elite sample—congressional candidates (average tau-gamma = .53).

The minimalist view has been subject to strong criticism. In particular, Nie, Verba, and Petrocik (1979) have maintained that issue constraint rose substantially in the mid-1960s, so much so that the belief systems of mass publics became as constrained in the 1970s as those of political elites had been in the 1950s. The Nie criticism of Converse has itself run into criticism, particularly by Sullivan, Piereson, and Marcus (1978, 1979). By experimentally manipulating the types of questions asked of respondents in a single survey (pre- versus post-1964 Survey Research Center formats), these investigators demonstrated, persuasively in our opinion, that changes in levels of constraint between the 1950s and 1960s resulted primarily from changes in the wording of questions and response options, not from changes in the political consciousness of citizens at large (see also Bishop, Oldendick, Tuchfarber, and Bennett, 1978; Bishop, Tuchfarber, and Oldendick, 1978).

In short, the minimalist model of public opinion continues to demand support, notwithstanding the many efforts in recent years to undermine it. And, in our opinion, a minimalist model of public opinion is the most useful baseline model—one's best guess as to what public opinion is like, other things being equal. Even so, it needs to be supplemented by a maximalist interpretation as well. But can one emphasize both the lack of connectedness in mass belief systems and their coherence? We believe that one can. And in setting out how a maximalist interpretation offers useful perspectives on mass belief systems, we shall focus on two questions: (1) What evidence of a systematic kind is there for a maximalist interpretation in addition to—not instead of—a minimalist one? (2) What are the bases for coherence in mass belief systems, given how little the mass public actually knows about politics?

Structure: Evidence for a More Maximalist Interpretation. There has always been good reason to suppose that—at some level—the general public has coherent attitudes or "packages of beliefs"; isolationism is an example, as are attitudes toward civil liberties and civil rights, or even some forms of conservatism (McClosky, 1958, 1964, 1967). But there is evidence, now, of a second order of organization: of "packages of packages of beliefs." The same (or very similar) sets of ideas go together, it seems, in the general public as well as among opinion leaders. So McClosky and Brill (1983) found, among the former as well as the latter, an organized and inclusive orientation toward democracy, encompassing beliefs about the right of the media to employ radicals; toward the range of ideas to which children may properly be exposed; toward the use of federal agents to spy on radical organizations; toward the use of town halls by politically deviant groups, such as the American Nazi party; toward provision of lawyers to indigent defendants accused of a crime, at public expense if necessary; toward prayer in the public schools; toward obscenity and censorship; toward equal rights for homosexuals; toward police searches of homes or cars without a warrant; toward racially restricted covenants; even toward the Miranda rule. Each was an array of issues with connections among them; the issues were put together in a coherent form, suggesting organization of political thought.

In addition, there seem to be webs of beliefs, stretching across different domains of concern; these webs are similarly spun for the mass public as for political elites. Thus, McClosky (1967) has shown that an isolationist outlook on foreign affairs is embedded in a family of aggressive and judgmental attitudes identically (or at least very similarly) organized among the general population and political leaders. And Nunn, Crockett, and Williams (1978), replicating Stouffer's (1955) analysis, have demonstrated the persistence of a definite, and internally coherent, outlook on the rights of admitted or suspected Communists to free speech, written expression of opinion, and employment in the mass media, in universities and high schools, and even in defense plants. A person who is tolerant in one of these respects is likely to be tolerant in the others. The *pattern* of covariation of ideas about civil liberties and civil rights is much the same for the mass public as for opinion leaders.

One might suppose that the consistency, at any rate on the part of the general population, is spurious, a function not of what people think about civil liberties and civil rights but, rather, of how they feel toward groups whose rights are being challenged. To a degree this is so. People tend to take a consistent stand on whether a particular group is entitled to civil liberties as civil rights, not only because of their position on civil liberties and civil rights but also because of their feelings toward particular groups (Sullivan, Marcus, Feldman, and Piereson, 1981). The coherence of citizens' ideas about tolerance, nonetheless, is impressive. Not only is the person who is tolerant of Communists' rights in one respect likely to be tolerant of them in general. He is also likely to be tolerant on issues that have nothing to do with Communists, or even with the issue of political tolerance itself, narrowly or customarily defined. Thus, the person tolerant of Communists' civil liberties is likely to be tolerant, too, of showing X-rated movies and of teaching about sex in schools (Nunn, Crockett, and Williams, 1978, p. 49).

But evidence of this kind is qualitative (suggesting that there is organization among mass belief systems) rather than quantitative (that is, establishing *how much* organization there is). A useful step in the quantitative direction has been taken by Stimson (1975). Rather than making a comparison *between* mass public and political elites, Stimson focuses on differences *within* the mass public.

Following Converse, Stimson suggests that the connectedness of belief systems should vary systematically with "cognitive capacity": The more adept people are at abstract reasoning, and the larger their fund of knowledge, the more likely their beliefs are to be well organized. To convert this suggestion into a testable hypothesis, Stimson developed a measure of cognitive ability: an index (divided into quartiles) combining education and political information. Then he showed convincingly that, for the two highest "ability" groups, the (self-identification) liberal-conservative scale correlated markedly with specific issues, such as busing, Medicare, and even withdrawal from Vietnam. By contrast, the correlations were far smaller, and more irregular, for the two lowest groups. In addition, Stimson used factor analysis to demonstrate that the higher the cognitive ability group, the more organized their political ideas—as evidenced, on the one side, by fewer factors extracted and, on the other, by the increased variance accounted for by extracted factors (see also Judd, Krosnick, and Milburn, 1981).

Chong, McClosky, and Zaller (1983) have taken a further step, documenting constraint in mass belief systems at the level of values. Their data (see Table 1) are drawn from parallel surveys, conducted between 1975 and 1977, one on a cross-sectional general population sample and two on "elite" samples. They draw two conclusions; one we agree with, one we do not. Consistency levels for political tolerance, they emphasize, though they vary with a person's degree of awareness, are not much lower for the least aware than for the most aware. Most members of the general public organize their opinions about tolerance-related issues on the same basis—and nearly as coherently—as opinion leaders do. Chong, McClosky, and Zaller argue, and we agree, that this finding is evidence of structure on the part of the mass public. They go on, however, to remark that, among the unaware, beliefs on issues other than tolerance are only "weakly correlated"—"an indication that their opinions are superficial, or, in effect, nonattitudes" (pp. 429–430). This seems a curious emphasis, given their findings. The general public is divided into arithmetic thirds, according to level of political awareness. And what stands out is not that the consistency levels of the least aware third are low but, rather, that

Table 1. Average Interitem Gammas for Survey Questions
Relating to Capitalism and Democracy.

| | Political Awareness | | | | |
| | General Public | | | Elites | |
	Low	Middle	High	Opinion Leaders	Ideological Elite
Democratic Values					
Tolerance-related issues	0.54[a]	0.65	0.79	.071	0.82
Non-tolerance-related issues	0.36	0.52	0.60	0.81	0.87
All democracy issues	0.37	0.45	0.62	0.65	0.80
Capitalist Values	0.23	0.46	0.71	0.74	0.88
(Number in Sample)	(309)	(310)	(310)	(533)	(1,426)

Source: Adapted from Chong, McClosky, and Zaller, 1983.

[a]Each cell entry is an average interitem gamma for the issue domain and subpopulation specified.

the consistency levels of the most aware third are high. Perhaps this is a matter of a half-empty, half-full glass. All the same, the comparison of the most aware third and opinion leaders is striking: With respect to tolerance-related issues, all issues of democratic values, and even all measures of capitalist values, the beliefs of the most aware third are every bit as consistent as those of opinion leaders.

We are not arguing that the general public is as consistent as opinion leaders are. Our point rather is that the belief systems of at least one third of the mass public are impressively organized—even by comparison with those of opinion leaders. Also well organized are the idea systems of the middle third of the general public, again as far as the values of democracy and capitalism are concerned. These correlations, moreover, are for individual items. But a single item is a more imperfect measure than a multi-indicator scale. Using such a scale, Chong, McClosky, and Zaller found that the same attitudes, similarly organized, appear among the general public as among the elites. It takes more effort (that is, longer and more reliable scales) to locate political attitudes among the mass public; they are there all the same.

These findings in support of the maximalist model speak to the question of degree of connectedness in mass belief systems— but descriptively, not causally. They do not address the issue of how political ideas come to be organized. It is these processes of organization that need to be considered.

The Idea of Consistency

How do mass belief systems work? How are they organized? What holds them together? These are the questions that we shall address. And the largest part of their answer, we shall suggest, turns around the idea of consistency.

The idea of consistency has not been a central one in theoretical analyses of mass belief systems, perhaps partly because consistency theories are no longer fashionable (McGuire, 1985) but more likely because severely minimalist models have been in the ascendancy. Nonetheless, consistency seems to us a pivotal notion, indispensable if we are to understand the causal workings of idea systems. Accordingly, we shall sketch an approach to the dynamics of mass belief systems centered around the idea of consistency. There are three sets of questions we particularly wish to consider. First, when is a consistency approach to idea systems likely to be especially useful? Second, supposing there is a tendency to consistency, with respect to what do people strive to be consistent? Third, how can a sizable number of citizens put together a coherent outlook on politics, given that they typically know little about it?

Consistency, though hardly a ruling passion, is nevertheless a noticeable tendency. Even when people are not being consistent, they like to seem so; and they wish to appear consistent not only in others' eyes (Tedeschi and Rosenfeld, 1981) but, perhaps as importantly, in their own (Aronson, 1968). Even so, it is not helpful to exaggerate the strength of the tendency to consistency. People only occasionally pay attention to politics. And though their ideas about it may be organized, they tend to be only loosely so. Indeed, if it were only a matter of strictly logical consistency, their ideas about politics might well be a hodge-podge. But though pressure to logical consistency may be weak, pressure toward affective consistency is not. Or, more exactly, if people's likes and dislikes of strategic groups in politics are organized and coherent, then they will be under pressure to bring their beliefs into conformity with their feelings. So, at least, we shall argue.

Limitations and Strengths of a Consistency Approach. The average person's low level of attention to, and knowledge of, politics would seem to argue against the importance of consistency as a force organizing his belief system. In general, one might suppose that a pressure to consistency will be stronger when people attend closely to an area of interest, weaker when they give it little attention or lack much knowledge of it. But, paradoxically, it is partly because the general public's level of political attention and awareness tends to be low that a consistency approach is useful. Consider, for example, the resistance of mass belief systems to change. To what extent, one may ask, do the political preferences of ordinary citizens register changes in political eras, perhaps not immediately or in detail but over the longer haul and in general terms? In this connection the pioneering work of Page and his colleagues is most helpful. They have examined all opinion poll questions on public policy issues, repeated with identical wording, in surveys between 1935 and 1979 conducted by the National Opinion Research Center, Gallup, or the Center for Political Studies (Page and Shapiro, 1982). The stability of policy preferences, Page and Shapiro show, is impressive. A shift of six percentage points (or more) constituted the standard of change. This is scarcely a severe standard—indeed, no more than the minimum for statistical significance. Even so, more than half of the responses to the policy questions showed no change whatever. And most of the changes that did occur were quite small, typically less than ten percentage points. To be sure, this is stability at the aggregate level and no doubt masks movement at the individual level. Nonetheless, a "limited effects" model seems to be in order.

This finding may seem puzzling at first, less so on reflection. The general public's political preferences appear vulnerable to change, both because mass belief systems are not tightly organized and because they are not strongly buttressed with knowledge; in contrast, highly organized, well-buttressed belief systems would seem most resistant to change (see McGuire, 1964). Yet the very factor that makes mass belief systems appear vulnerable to change helps immunize them against it. Mass belief systems tend to be loosely organized because the general public's levels of attention to politics tend to be low; but it is precisely because most citizens pay little attention to politics that their policy preferences are difficult to change. Efforts to influence political attitudes are not likely to succeed if people are unmotivated to attend to or think about political communications (see Petty and Cacioppo, 1981).[6]

Consistency, certainly, is not the only process of importance. Few of us think up our own ideology; most of us accept one or another of the leading alternatives, with some personal embellishment. Therefore, an approach focusing not on consistency but on learning political norms and positions is clearly useful. But is it as useful as one focusing on consistency? Or, more exactly, when is a consistency approach likely to be more useful? When is a learning approach likely to be more profitable? A handle on this question is offered by Gamson and Modigliani (1966). Their concern is with the interplay between knowledge of politics and acquisition of opinions on foreign policy issues. Of the three models they develop, two are of particular interest. The first is a social learning, or conformity, model. Very briefly, this line of explanation asserts that the more knowledgeable people are about politics, the more likely they are to support the government's position. The key to conformity, in this view, is awareness. On the one side, people are not likely to adopt a new idea, however motivated they are to accept it, unless they are aware of it; on the other, they are motivated to accept it if they are aware that it is official government policy.[7] This is a classic example of a social learning model, much like Sniderman's (1975) analysis of commitment to democratic values. But on empirical examination it comes in second best. A superior model, Gamson and Modigliani report, is a cognitive consistency one. Foreign policy preferences, according to a consistency interpretation, are a function of one's general political orientation or ideology. Or, more precisely, the more politically aware and knowledgeable one is, the tighter or more consistent should be the connection between one's overall outlook and one's specific policy opinions.

It is useful, therefore, to distinguish two processes underlying the acquisition of opinions—one driven by a consistency strain, the other by a normative strain. When is the one more likely to predominate, and when the other? On some issues—for example, freedom of speech—there is an effective consensus, particularly among the elite, about what is right and proper. And this consensus tends to exert pressure on citizens generally to support the norm of freedom of speech. But on other issues the most salient fact is that there is no elite consensus, no predominating agreement on what course of action is right and effective. Indeed, just the opposite: Elite and informed opinion is sharply divided, not infrequently along liberal versus conservative lines. If so, the pressure toward conformity with a norm is likely to be replaced by pressure toward consistency with a salient attitude or principle, such as liberalism-conservatism (at least among the more politically aware of the general public).

In short, a consistency model works better in the analysis of opinions on policy issues; a social learning model works better in the analysis of commitment to democratic values. Consensual issues are likely to be dominated by a normative strain; contested ones, by a consistency strain. Thus, on the one side, McClosky (1964) and others have demonstrated that greater sophistication promotes convergence, for liberals and for conservatives, on democratic values. And, on the other, Zaller (1983) has shown that greater sophistication promotes divergence between liberals and conservatives on contested issues—the war in Vietnam, for example, or gay rights. In sum, on consensual issues, the greater the political awareness, the stronger the strain to adopt normatively dominant values; on contested issues, the greater the political sophistication and awareness, the stronger the strain to maximize consistency between ideological outlook and issue preferences. The study of ideology tends to be concerned more with contested issues than consensual ones, perhaps because conflict is a focal point of interest in politics. To this extent, a consistency approach is likely to be more useful than a social learning one.

Consistency with Respect to What? The idea of consistency seems straightforward, perhaps because it is so familiar. But consider: It is one thing to suppose a tendency to consistency—but consistency with regard to what? After all, maximizing consistency with respect to one element of a belief system not infrequently has the effect of maximizing inconsistency with respect to some other element. This is an obvious possibility, even more obvious given the loose linkages among mass belief systems. A less obvious possibility is that members of the mass public, in maximizing consistency, *systematically* differ in the elements of their belief systems that they choose to make consistent (Lane, 1973).

The question is how the different parts of belief systems fit together—or, more exactly, how the various parts fit together differently for different individuals.

Suppose that two people are making a judgment on a certain issue. Each may seek to maximize consistency. But each holds a variety of beliefs, only loosely connected. Will both strive to maximize consistency with the same idea-element? And if not, on which element will they focus? The findings of Kuklinski, Metcalf, and Kay (1982) provide an instructive clue. Analyzing an anti-nuclear initiative in California, they explored the acquisition of new opinions rather than the amendment of established ones. Specifically, they found that opinions are acquired through instrumental means, from reference groups, and as a result of one's values—the third of particular interest to us. People's values, obviously, can help organize their reactions to a new issue, such as the establishment of nuclear power plants. But people have more than one value at least potentially relevant to an issue like nuclear power. Will they focus on the same one? If not, why will some focus on one, others on another? With respect to the anti-nuclear initiative, Kuklinski and his colleagues found that less knowledgeable citizens connected their views on the initiative to their orientations toward technology; in contrast, more knowledgeable citizens anchored their position to their overall ideologic outlook.

Elements of a belief system, this finding suggests, may be ranged along a continuum. At one extreme are elements relevant to an issue in the most immediate—and immediately obvious—way, just as orientations to technology are immediately relevant to opinions about nuclear power plants. At the other extreme are elements more distant and more abstract—for example, ideology. Whether people tend to connect their policy preferences with ideas that are proximal or distal varies systematically with their political awareness and sophistication. The less aware they are, the more likely a connection is to be made with an immediately relevant and relatively specific idea; the more aware they are, the more likely it is to be made with a relatively removed, and comparatively abstract, idea.

It is worth thinking about what this finding suggests about the nature of consistency in mass belief systems. Either people's general orientations toward technology or, alternatively, their overall ideological views provide a basis for judgment in the case of nuclear technology. As there is more than one point of reference, so there is more than one meaning of consistency. Conventional estimates of constraint, it follows, are likely to be underestimates of the consistency of belief systems—underestimates, certainly, if people differ in the idea-elements with respect to which they are maximizing consistency.[8]

How shall we get a handle on consistency, given that the point of reference can vary? Causal analysis of the organization of idea systems is necessary; otherwise, one cannot tell what is being put together with what. An especially useful example of this issue is the well-known problem of the mismatch between support for democratic values in the abstract and commitment to them in specific controversies.

There is strong evidence that the general public is more likely to support democratic values in the abstract than in specific cases (see, for example, McClosky, 1964; Prothro and Grigg, 1960; McClosky and Brill, 1983). This "inconsistency" between general principles and specific application is customarily taken as evidence for a minimalist model; for it seems to illustrate the wispiness of cognitive connections in mass belief systems. Indeed, perhaps the most popular explanation of this lack of consistency between abstract and specific is precisely the average citizen's lack of political knowledge (McClosky and Brill, 1983). Lacking knowledge, citizens fail to understand the policy implications of abstract ideas. They support, say, the principle of free speech but fail to see its relevance to the issue of whether a Communist should be permitted to speak at a local high school.

According to a second interpretation, people mismatch principle and policy not because they do not know any better but precisely because they do. For instance, Jackman (1978, 1981) argues that the better educated are more likely to *say* they favor the principle of racial equality—people, after all, learn the right, the socially desirable, thing to say in school; however, actually doing something to realize racial equality is another matter. So the better educated, though more likely to support the principle of racial equality, are not more likely to support government policies to realize the principle, or so Jackman argues.

There is a third possibility, more consistent with a maximalist interpretation. The "inconsistency" between favoring racial equality at the level of principle and not favoring it at the level of policy may reflect consistency at another level. Sniderman, Brody, and Kuklinski (1984) have made this argument, taking as an example the mismatch between principle and policy discovered by Jackman. As against her emphasis on social desirability, they focus on the structure of policy reasoning, identifying two of its dimensions as differentiation and integration. Differentiation refers to the number of separate considerations brought to bear in deriving a policy preference. Integration refers to the extent to which these antecedent considerations are understood to be interrelated.

Following Stimson's (1975) lead, Sniderman, Brody, and Kuklinski examined the structure of policy reasoning at varying levels of cognitive ability (indexed by education). In brief, they found that the higher the level of cognitive ability, the more likely people were to be aware of connections among antecedent considerations—for example, between their political outlook in general terms and their attitude toward specific policy. In addition, the lower the level of cognitive ability, the narrower and more immediate the range of factors people took into account in deriving a policy preference on the issue of equality.

Taken together, these findings throw a somewhat paradoxical light on the idea of consistency. First, the less well educated need *not* be less consistent than the well educated—if by consistency one means purely an ability to predict, for example, the stand they take on policy given their attitude toward the principle of racial equality; for the more factors that a person takes into account, the less impact any one of them is likely to have on a particular preference. In the case of racial equality, the less well educated and less politically sophisticated can achieve a measure of consistency precisely because, in deriving a preference on policy, they weigh so heavily the most immediately obvious consideration—namely, their attitude toward the principle of racial equality. Second, it is often supposed that the more coherent, or connected, a person's belief system, the more consistent it is likely to be. But it is only when people become aware of the connections among the various elements in their belief systems that they can become aware of inconsistencies or conflicts between their ideas. It is the well-educated (not the poorly educated) conservative who is more likely to be aware of the conflict between being on the political right and favoring an activist federal government on behalf of racial equality. An increase in ideological consistency, in this case, comes at the expense of an increase in "inconsistency" between principle and policy.

It is useful to take this consistency analysis a step further. Otherwise, there is a danger of supposing that we are giving an explanation of the dynamics of mass belief systems when we are only giving a name to them. At least two questions need attention. First, who is more likely, and who less, to experience inconsistency in the policy implications of basic values? Second, what are the different ways in which people cope with inconsistency? Actually, there may be some connection between how much inconsistency a person experiences and how that person resolves it, or so the value pluralism model of ideological reasoning suggests (Tetlock, 1983, 1984a).

The key claims of the value pluralism model can be summarized in two general sets of propositions:

1. A person is likely to think about an issue domain in a differentiated and integrated fashion to the degree that the issue domain activates conflicting values of approximately equal strength. Value conflicts can, of course, take many forms. One classic example is the often-cited tension between the values of freedom and equality (Hofstadter, 1948; Lipset, 1963; Pole, 1978)—tension that becomes manifest in debates over issues such as redistributive income policies and national health insurance. Other examples of value conflict include the tension between national security versus freedom (for example, debates over the military draft or domestic CIA activities), national security versus fiscal conservatism (debates over defense spending), or protection of natural beauty versus economic prosperity (debates over mining and drilling in public parklands).[9]

2. When an issue domain activates conflicting values of very unequal strength, there is little psychological pressure to think about the issue domain in differentiated or integrated terms. Here the value pluralism model draws on Abelson's (1959) analysis of modes of resolving cognitive-affective inconsistency. When two idea-elements of unequal strength come into conflict, the least-effort solution to the conflict (people are assumed to be "cognitive misers" unless forced to be otherwise) is to *deny* the importance of the less important idea-element and to bolster the importance of the more important idea-element. The net effect is to make the dominant idea-element all the more dominant (what Festinger, 1964, termed "spreading of the alternatives"). By contrast, when two idea-elements of approximately equal strength come into conflict, denial and bolstering are much less plausible modes of inconsistency resolution. People must turn to more effort-demanding, "integratively complex" strategies, such as differentiation (distinguishing the impact of policy options on more than one value) and integration (developing rules or schemata for coping with tradeoffs between important values).

The value pluralism model has been used to explain a number of empirical findings. First, it helps to explain why, in general, centrists and advocates of moderate left-wing political causes tend to think about policy issues in more complex and flexible ways than do advocates of right-wing political causes—a pattern that is observable in general population samples (for a review, see Stone, 1980) but is especially pronounced in elite samples, such as members of the United States Senate and the British House of Commons (Tetlock, 1983, 1984a). The work of Rokeach (1973, 1979) suggests that centrists and moderate leftists attach high priority to more contradictory values (in particular, freedom-equality) than do advocates of right-wing causes.

Second, the value pluralism model helps to explain why—as Tetlock (1984a) found in his content analysis of the Putnam (1971) interviews with British parliamentarians—complexity of thought tends to fall off as one moves from the moderate left ("social democrat" faction of the British Labour party) to the extreme left (radical socialist members of the British Labour party). Extreme egalitarians presumably value equality so highly that it enables them to avoid many difficult value tradeoffs that moderate egalitarians must confront (for example, nationalization of all major modes of production might reduce concentration of wealth in private hands but would be very expensive and probably result in considerable economic dislocation and inefficiency).

Third, the value pluralism model is well positioned to explain ideology-by-issue interactions that arise in the differentiation and integration of people's thinking in policy domains. For example, Tetlock, Bernzweig, and Gallant (forthcoming) found that Supreme Court justices with liberal and moderate voting records associated themselves with more integratively complex judicial opinions than did conservative justices (replicating the pattern found in the Senate and the general public). The trend was, however, significantly more pronounced on economic issues (cases involving labor versus management and business versus government conflicts) than on civil liberties issues (cases involving due process, First Amendment, and discrimination issues). According to Tetlock, Bernzweig, and Gallant, liberals and moderates experience much more intense value conflict than do conservatives on economic issues, but only somewhat more intense conflict than do conservatives on civil liberties issues. (A post hoc but plausible interpretation is that the civil liberties issues were more likely to evoke shared elite values concerning constitutional protections for free speech, tolerance of deviant viewpoints, and due process; see McClosky and Brill, 1983.)

Recent data (Tetlock, 1984b) give even more direct support to the hypothesized role of value conflict in promoting differentiated and integrated political thought. In this study two types of information were collected from a nonelite (college student) sample: (1) subjects' rank-order evaluations of the importance of each of eighteen "terminal values" from the Rokeach Value Survey (values included national security, natural beauty, economic prosperity, equality, and freedom); (2) subjects' support for six public policy positions and their thoughts on each issue (for example, redistributive income policies, domestic CIA surveillance, defense spending). Each of the public policy positions had been selected on the basis of pretest scaling data which indicated that the issue brought at least two values from the Rokeach Value Survey into conflict (for example, the defense spending question was phrased in such a way as to activate tension between the values of national security and economic prosperity). On each of the six issues, people tended to report more differentiated and integrated thoughts when the issue domain activated conflicting values that were equally or almost equally important in their value hierarchy. This study provides the most direct evidence yet that the degree of conflict between basic political values exerts an important influence on the complexity of thought in that domain.

The value pluralism model, then, is an approach to the causal analysis of inconsistency—to understanding who are most likely to experience it, when they are likely to experience it, and how they cope with it. But this analysis of inconsistency presupposes a backdrop of stable values underlying political belief systems. It supposes people to be committed to definite ideological outlooks and attempts to explain how they resolve inconsistencies arising within the context of these relatively coherent ideological orientations. Such maximalist assumptions may be tenable in analyzing the policy reasoning of elites, but they appear much less plausible when applied to mass belief systems in general. After all, as we observed earlier, ordinary citizens hardly have a compendious knowledge of politics. And their understanding of abstract concepts such as liberalism or conservatism is, to be generous, thin. Given this fact, is not an approach to mass belief systems that focuses on consistently organized ideological constructs simply too rationalistic? In short, the question still remains: How is it possible for ordinary citizens to put together a consistent outlook on politics, given that they know so little about it?

Possible Determinants of Consistency

In the remainder of this chapter, we consider particular causal mechanisms responsible for consistency of structure in mass belief systems. However, rather than set out an exhaustive laundry list of hypotheses, we shall concentrate on three: the syllogistic, the associationist, and the affective. We shall explore each mechanism in turn, although the three are not mutually exclusive; each may, and very likely does, play an important role in integrating mass belief systems. We also must admit to the partiality of our own theoretical stance. Affective processes, we believe, play an especially crucial role in giving mass belief systems what structure they do possess. The building blocks of political coherence, we shall propose, are personal likes and dislikes of politically strategic small groups. Even citizens who know little about political ideas or the political process can put together a consistent political outlook, provided they at least know whom they like and, perhaps more important, whom they dislike.

Syllogism as Organizing Principle. Ideological reasoning, from this point of view, is syllogistic in structure. People's ideological identification—their perception of themselves as liberal or conservative—serves as their major premise. And the test of ideological reasoning is their ability and willingness to arrive at a conclusion on a specific issue consonant with their overall outlook (Holm and Robinson, 1978).

According to the syllogistic thesis, ideological reasoning is a matter of deduction. The syllogism is a causal metaphor for political reasoning generally, including reasoning about democratic values (see McClosky and Brill, 1983). In this view the decisive question is whether or not a citizen will recognize that a particular issue "falls under" a larger principle. So one may ask whether or not citizens understand that the specific question of a Communist's speaking at a public school is "covered by" the general principle of free speech. At issue, then, is whether or not citizens can logically connect general and specific, principle and policy. To speak of the structure of belief systems is to speak of their logical structure.

A syllogism is a natural metaphor for idea systems (for a particularly elegant development of the syllogistic metaphor, see McGuire's, 1981, probabilogical model of attitude structure). The syllogism does not seem, however, an especially fitting metaphor for mass belief systems, at any rate as far as politics is concerned. Purely as an empirical matter, it is not plausible to suggest that sizable numbers of the mass public infer their stands on specific issues, relying only (or even primarily) on their ideological identification. As Levitin and Miller (1979) have shown, the correlation between ideological location and issue preference is far from strong— even among the well educated.

Domain hypotheses represent a more interesting variant of the syllogistic position. Consistency, in this approach, takes the form of subject matter. For example, it has repeatedly been observed that beliefs about guaranteed jobs and aid for minorities "go together"—that is to say, preferences on these issues are more highly correlated with one another than either is correlated with, say, attitudes toward abortion (see, for example, Beck, 1982; Knoke, 1979).

Domains are often thought of as collections of issues that activate similar underlying values (Dawson, 1979)—values that can serve as major premises in policy reasoning. For instance, one domain, usually the most prominent, has a "New Deal" flavor; key issues that define it are guaranteed standard of living and jobs and government aid for blacks and other minorities. The "logic" here seems a political one—activist government versus individual responsibility. Issues in this domain are, characteristically, framed in terms of group benefits—assistance to the jobless, for example, or to blacks. When no group is explicitly named, these issues usually involve some aspect of a national policy on behalf of the disadvantaged (Beck, 1982). This first domain captures the essence of liberalism-conservatism, as popularly understood, which is perhaps a warning against labeling a "group interests" approach to politics as oversimplified or unideological.

A second domain consists of beliefs about moral issues—the Equal Rights Amendment, abortion, school prayer. It is not clear how to characterize the "logic" of this domain. Beck (1982) contrasts its "pure logic" with the "political logic" of the first domain, though one would seem as much the vehicle of the cultural packaging of ideas as the other.

It is not easy to evaluate the utility of a domain approach to consistency. One problem is figuring out what it means to say that belief systems have domains. Clearly, this is a way of saying that belief systems are multi- rather than unidimensional; and the question of whether they are multidimensional or not would seem to be a straightforward matter of fact, to be settled by quantitative analysis. But the choice between uni- or multidimensional is a false choice. No leading analyst, to our knowledge, contends that mass or elite belief systems are unidimensional. It is sometimes supposed that this is Converse's position—quite wrongly, in our view. Belief systems, he implies, tend to have a *primary* dimension, at any rate to the extent that they are ideological in character. But to say that there is a primary dimension is quite different from saying that there is only one dimension. And, as a moment's reflection suggests, a unidimensionalist position must be wrong, unless one is willing to make the implausible assumption that mass belief systems are governed by a single, omnipotent value.

The choice between uni- and multidimensional is a false choice for a second reason, a reason that becomes obvious once one considers the relation between political sophistication and the structural complexity of belief systems. In general, the number of dimensions that emerges from factor analyses of policy preferences varies inversely with cognitive ability. As Stimson (1975) has shown, the better educated and more informed about politics people are, the simpler the dimensional structure of their issue preferences; the less well educated and well informed, the larger the number of dimensions underlying their issue preferences.[10] This relationship between the dimensionality of issue preferences and cognitive ability has come to be commonly accepted. All the same, its implication is not widely appreciated. If there is indeed such a relationship, it makes little sense to ask whether there are "really" two domains, or three, or possibly more—as though there were one correct number. At a minimum, the number of domains varies with the political sophistication and knowledge of respondents.

However that may be, the domain approach tends to be descriptive. It seems to us wrong, or at any rate risky, to attempt to describe how elements of a belief system go together empirically without showing how they go together causally. In this connection, the correlation between political sophistication and structural complexity of issue preferences is especially intriguing. The more sophisticated tend to put together more issues, despite differences among issues in manifest content. What sort of a rule, to establish what goes with what, might they be using? A deductive rule seems unlikely, given the adventitious links between many of the issues. So we shall consider two alternative causal mechanisms for organizing belief systems.

External Events as Determinants of Structure. The presumption guiding a domain hypothesis is that "content," a logic of ideas, is the organizational principle of belief systems. A second, quite different, approach is associationist: Ideas in belief systems go together not because, in some substantive sense, they belong together but, rather, because they have been put together by the course of events. The core of mass belief systems, according to one such associationist view, consists of racial attitudes, at any rate since the mid-1960s. Several, including Converse (1964), have hinted at this possibility; but the most thorough, and original, presentation has been made by Carmines and Stimson (1982). Analyzing the 1972 National Election Study, they make three key points: (1) principal components analysis of issue preferences has revealed substantial constraint (connectedness or consistency) in the belief systems of better-educated and better-informed citizens; (2) however, levels of constraint plunge if attitudes toward racial issues (specifically toward desegregation and toward black activists) are controlled, whereas (3) constraint persists if other issues (specifically, government-guaranteed standard of living or Vietnam) are controlled. In consequence, Carmines and Stimson deduce that racial attitudes form the core of mass belief systems.

This result is unexpected, even puzzling, as Carmines and Stimson themselves point out. No doubt, race is a central issue in American politics. But that is far from saying that it is *the* issue, by itself; responsible for coherence of public opinion. Moreover, it is one thing to note that racial attitudes are correlated with liberal and conservative self-identification; it is another to conclude that racial attitudes very largely define liberalism or conservatism.

Why should racial attitudes be the glue that holds mass belief systems together? What are the causal mechanisms responsible for constraint? To address these questions, Carmines and Stimson advance the "time-bundling" hypothesis. This is, admittedly, a post hoc hypothesis; nonetheless, it is an intriguing idea and worth consideration. In brief, Carmines and Stimson argue that attitudinal constraint has a distinctively electoral source. Citizens pay most attention to politics during presidential elections; political learning is for this reason episodic. Moreover, the campaign issues that candidates bring into public awareness are partly adventitious, intelligible within the context of a particular campaign but by no means predictable before it. Candidates, in short, bundle together new issues and old. Thus, in 1964 Barry Goldwater linked opposition to desegregation with conservatism; in 1964 and 1968, Lyndon Johnson and George Wallace linked support for civil rights with liberalism.

The hypothesis, however, is not compelling as an explanation of the putatively central role of race in integrating mass belief systems, on at least two grounds—one methodological, the other logical. The methodological problem is this. The pool of issues that Carmines and Stimson analyze has two distinct parts. The first consists of an assortment of concerns: government-guaranteed jobs, tax reform, legalization of marijuana, Medicare, women's rights. Many of these issues are only loosely related to one another, and each is measured by only one question. In contrast, the second part of the pool consists of one issue only—race. Although the area of racial attitudes has, it seems (Carmines and Stimson, 1982), two dimensions—attitudes toward desegregation and attitudes toward protest—each is measured by factor scales, each scale comprising multiple indicators. Thus, the Carmines-Stimson test of comparative partial correlations pits racial attitudes (taken together) against opinion about government-guaranteed jobs and about Vietnam (taken separately). That is hardly a fair competition: on the one side, two well-measured and complementary scales; on the other, a single issue indexed by a single question.

The logical difficulty involves the "rise" thesis. Carmines and Stimson, among others, argue that mass belief systems became more constrained (connected or consistent) in the 1960s than they had been in the 1950s. But the balance of evidence, as we observed, suggests that the apparent rise in constraint resulted primarily from changes in question wording and format. Two positions, then, are possible. One can argue that idea systems lack constraint now, just as they did earlier, or, alternatively, that idea systems possessed a fair measure of constraint then, just as they do now. In either case the time-bundling hypothesis must fail, whether for suggesting that there is marked constraint after the mid-1960s when in fact there is not (the first alternative) or for suggesting that there was not constraint before the mid-1960s when in fact there was (the second). To put the point differently, the time-bundling hypothesis requires a showing of change in constraint; but the most plausible view is that there was no change—either because constraint remained low or because it was always high.

These problems notwithstanding, Carmines and Stimson have made an important contribution in laying out an associationist analysis of the core of mass belief systems. This approach must surely have a kernel of truth in it—if the last fifty years of research on learning and memory have anything to tell us about how people think. Beyond this, Carmines and Stimson's formulation gives valuable warning on two points. First, the "coherence" of political ideologies owes much to the chance conjunction of ideas, brought together under the pressure of elections. And, consequently, one must be wary of an excessively cognitive approach to belief systems, a concentration on the immanent "logic" of ideas.

Political Affect as Organizing Principle. A third approach suggests that the source of structure in mass belief systems is affective. This approach has two versions, one familiar, one perhaps less so. The familiar version focuses on differences in personality or temperament between conservatives and liberals (see, for example, McClosky, 1958; Wilson, 1973). Conservatives are more likely to be anxious, lacking in self-esteem, hostile, and psychologically inflexible—all factors that impede the development of a tolerant, open mind and encourage instead a punitive and intolerant stance (Adorno, Frenkel-Brunswik, Levinson, and Sanford, 1950; Sniderman, 1975; Stone, 1980; Wilson, 1973).

Analysis of the structure of mass belief systems, focusing on the imprint of personality characteristics, has much to recommend it. A compelling example of this approach is McClosky's (1967) classic analysis of isolationism. Isolationist attitudes, he demonstrates, are a small part of a larger network of political and social attitudes. This network stretches across domains, including (in addition to foreign policy issues) a susceptibility to extremist ideas (both on the left and on the right) and such basic social and psychological orientations as ethnocentrism and intolerance of ambiguity. And holding this network together, so it seems, is a fundamentally aversive psychological temper, a disposition to reject, to punish, to eliminate, and to control what is unfamiliar, foreign, unusual, or threatening (see also Tetlock, 1981).

Belief systems, plainly, may owe some of their coherence to deep-seated feelings. "World views" can be shaped by anxiety, hostility, or frustration. Yet this is probably not a complete explanation of the connectedness of belief systems, particularly at the level of the mass public, partly because the average citizen is not likely to attach special importance to politics and is therefore not likely to invest deep feelings in political ideas. Then, too, the correlation between people's psychological makeup and their political outlook is far from perfect. Accordingly, it is useful to consider a second version of affective consistency—one that is both less "deep" and more common.

The second (more sociological) version of affective consistency focuses on feelings toward strategic political groups—above all, on personal likes and dislikes of liberals and conservatives. Levitin and Miller (1979) and Conover and Feldman (1981) have both elaborated models of ideology incorporating such an affective component. The two models are graphically represented in Figure 1. The Levitin-Miller model treats ideology—in their term, "ideological location"—as a compound of two elements, one cognitive, the other affective. The cognitive is indexed by people's ideological identification (whether they label themselves as liberal or conservative and, additionally, how liberal or conservative they perceive themselves to be). The affective is represented by people's feeling about liberals and conservatives (how much they like the one, as opposed to the other). The actual mechanics of how these two elements are combined to form a composite measure of ideology are not important here, though it is worth noting that the measure of ideological location is modeled after that of party identification. What is important is the theoretical conception of ideology that lies behind the Levitin-Miller model. The heart of this conception can be stated simply: Both identification and affect are causal determinants of political behavior, on a more or less equal footing; their influence is additive, and, as a consequence, liberalism-conservatism tends to unidimensionality, even among the mass public.

The Conover-Feldman model offers a radically different conception of the role of affect in mass belief systems. Theirs is an affect-driven conception. A person's ideological identification is a function, they believe, of his ideological likes and dislikes. These likes and dislikes, in turn, derive from likes and dislikes for an array of "symbolic" political groups (such as labor unions and blacks) and, in addition, from policy preferences (regarding, for example, taxation or guaranteed

Figure 1. Schematic Models of Political Ideology.

Levitin-Miller Model of Ideological Location

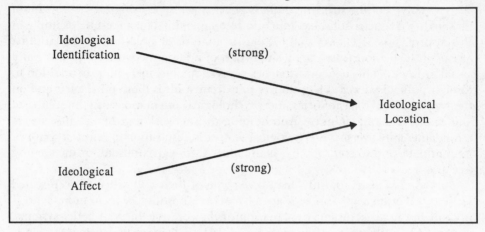

Conover-Feldman Model of Ideological Identification

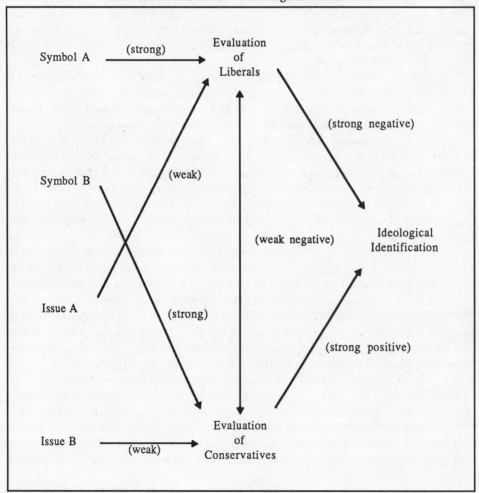

jobs), though far more strongly from the former than the latter. According to this model, people's ideological identifications originate in their feelings toward politically strategic groups—most notably, liberals and conservatives.

A second feature of the Conover-Feldman model is arguably more fundamental and certainly more innovative: the denial of bipolarity. We are accustomed to assuming that someone who favors the liberal side opposes the conservative one, or the other way around. Not so, according to Conover and Feldman; favoring one side does not mean opposing the other, at any rate not among the mass public. A chief piece of evidence, they suggest, is the (zero-order) correlation between feelings toward liberals and feelings toward conservatives. It is exceedingly modest in size, about .17. Evidently, liking liberals does not imply, or is not generally understood to imply, disliking conservatives, or the other way around.

The Levitin-Miller and the Conover-Feldman models offer valuable clues in understanding how substantial numbers of citizens construct a more or less coherent outlook on politics, even though they know little about it. The answer must turn around some causal mechanism, some simplifying rule of thumb. What might such a mechanism be? One possibility is a likability heuristic (Brady and Sniderman, forthcoming; Chubb, Hagen, and Sniderman, 1984). If people know which side they like—and, perhaps more important, which they dislike—their views of politics are likely to take on a consistent, even ideological character. Two points are of particular importance here—one in criticism of the Conover-Feldman model, the other in criticism of the Levitin-Miller model.

The first point concerns the bipolarity of mass belief systems. The weakness of the zero-order correlation between feelings toward liberals and feelings toward conservatives is misleading. The better educated the individual, the better he understands that liking the one implies disliking the other. Thus, the correlation between liberal and conservative "feeling thermometers" for college graduates is substantial: approximately -.60 in the National Election Study of 1976 (Chubb, Hagen, and Sniderman, 1984). It is quite wrong, then, to conclude that mass belief systems are not bipolar; or, rather, the mistake lies in speaking as though belief systems either are or are not bipolar. Some are markedly so, some less so; and the extent to which they are varies systematically and strongly with education. It is misleading to rely on the average when the variance is high—a point worth remembering for research on mass belief systems generally.

The second point concerns the linkage between ideology and issue preference. The Levitin-Miller model underestimates this linkage because, in representing ideology, it lumps together ideological identification (self-perception) and ideological affect (feelings toward liberals and toward conservatives). But these two components must be taken apart before they can be put together properly. The nub of the issue is affective consistency. As Chubb, Hagen, and Sniderman (1984) show, there is a formidable linkage between ideological identification and issue preference, provided only that people know which ideological side they like and which they dislike.

The likability heuristic focuses on personal feelings toward politically strategic groups. Therefore, it fits with other ongoing work, perhaps the outstanding example of which is the research of Sullivan, Marcus, Feldman, and Piereson (1981) on the nature of tolerance. Their work is worth considering, partly to underline the importance now attached to the organizing role of groups, even more to distinguish two quite different versions of how this organization is effected.

According to Sullivan and his colleagues, whether or not we are prepared to tolerate a particular group—whether, for instance, we believe that it should be outlawed or that its members should be permitted to make a speech—depends on how we feel about the group. Quite simply, the more a person dislikes a group, the less likely he is to put up with it. From this point of view, liberals have appeared more tolerant politically than conservatives, principally because it is groups on the left—Communists, socialists, atheists—that have borne the brunt of controversy. But ask liberals to tolerate groups on the right—that is, groups they intensely dislike—and they are much less likely to comply.

It is the logic, not the validity, of the hypothesis that is of interest here. Coherence, from this point of view, is a function of group affect. People adopt beliefs to conform to their feelings about a *particular* group, supporting its rights if they like it, opposing them if they dislike it. This theoretical position closely matches earlier speculation on the role of groups as a source of organization of mass belief systems (see, for example, Berelson, Lazarsfeld, and McPhee, 1954; Converse, 1964). Thus, Converse (1964) has argued that, at least in the case of blacks, affect provides a basis for a coherent policy response. It is not necessary to know that favoring one "liberal" policy entails favoring others; it suffices to know that one dislikes blacks and so "should" consistently oppose policies intended to assist them.

This is a useful hypothesis, one form of affective consistency, but all the same not the one we are proposing. The consistency that this hypothesis can account for is confined to one particular group. Liking (or disliking) a group may provide a basis for a consistent response to policies affecting *that* particular group, but not to a broad range of policies concerning different groups. In contrast, our concern is with feelings toward ideologically opposite groups. The most obvious example of this, of course, is liking (or disliking) liberals and conservatives. And the crucial point is not how people feel toward either one of them but, rather, how they feel toward both. The crucial elements in ideological reasoning, we are suggesting, are people's ideological affect (that is, their feelings toward liberals and toward conservatives) and their ideological identification (that is, their perception of themselves as liberal or conservative). These two elements, put together in the right way, serve as a rule of thumb, a calculus for figuring out what stand to take on a wide array of major issues. How, more exactly, does this calculus work? How can a likability heuristic provide a basis for ideological reasoning? We assume that people, in figuring out what they believe about an issue (or, for that matter, what others believe about it, too), proceed as though there were three factors, two major and one minor, to be taken into account. The major factors are people's overall ideological position and the difference between their feelings about liberals and about conservatives. The first factor is familiar (ideological self-identification); the second less so, and thus worth comment. The basis for cognitive consistency, we suspect, is affective consistency. It is the coherence of a person's likes and dislikes that counts. Thus, liking liberals is not a guide to inferring policy preferences— not at least if one also likes conservatives. The key is liking one side and disliking the other.[11]

According to the likability heuristic, the more liberal (or conservative) people's overall outlook, and the larger the difference in their feelings about liberals and conservatives, the further to the left (or right) they will place themselves on a specific issue, such as Medicare or government assistance for blacks and other minorities. What does such a heuristic imply about mass belief systems? In research on mass belief systems, there is sometimes a tendency to conceive of citizens as warehouses of opinion. In this view, when people are asked their opinion on an issue, they search through their stock to find a preformed belief. As against this "warehouse" view, we suspect that people often must figure out what they think, and must do so on the spot. And though it is implausible to suppose that average citizens would efficiently organize and store opinions on a large number of issues, it is much less implausible to suppose that a substantial number of them can follow a simple heuristic, or rule of thumb, to estimate their position on many issues.

Confronted with an issue, people must pick a side. In addition, they must decide how far to one or the other side they are. The likability heuristic combines a cognitive element (ideological self-identification) and an affective one (ideological affect). It is tempting to attribute the direction of an opinion to the one and its degree to the other. The temptation should be resisted. There does not seem to be a neat division of labor between the cognitive and affective. Rather the reverse: The two elements interact, the one depending on the other. It is as if people infer their position on an issue by calculating how far to the left (or right) they stand overall, multiplied by how differently they feel toward liberals as compared to conservatives.

This heuristic, it should be emphasized, is a general one. People make the same calculation whether the issue is guaranteed jobs or aid to minorities and whether it is the policy preferences of, say, liberals or indeed of themselves they are estimating. In a word, people can figure out a lot of things because they are, essentially, figuring out the same thing; that is, after all, what it means to say that ideology is a simplifying calculus. And simplifying or not, the likability heuristic is explicitly ideological. In estimating preferences, according to the heuristic, people consult their view of how liberal (or conservative) they are and how they feel about liberals and conservatives.

One point about the workings of the likability heuristic perhaps deserves special emphasis: the nature of the relationship between ideological affect and ideological identification. The relationship is one of interaction—in mathematical terms, multiplicative rather than additive. People weight their estimates of where liberals and conservatives stand on issues in proportion to the differences in their feelings toward them. So, the more they like the one and dislike the other, the further from the center they perceive *both* to be. Accentuation, in a word, is the mark of ideological inference. The ideologue sees politics in heightened colors: The left and the right stand for different policies—very different policies. Contrariwise, the nonideologue sees liberals and conservatives as much alike; that is, as close to the center. One might say, therefore, that the trademark of ideological reasoning is exaggeration. Indeed, it may make more sense to distinguish the ideologue not by the accuracy of his perception of liberalism and conservatism but, instead, by the types of mistakes he tends to make. Thus, the ideologically sophisticated tend to overestimate, the unsophisticated to underestimate, issue differences between liberals and conservatives (Brady and Sniderman, forthcoming).

One qualification to the previous argument is, however, in order. Much common sense and some systematic data suggest that a process other than accen-

88   **Political Psychology**

tuation is also at work; for people probably do not accentuate the differences between liberals and conservatives perfectly evenhandedly. Other things equal, people will tend to move their side (or themselves) closer to the center, or middle of the road (see Ross, Greene, and House, 1977, on the false consensus effect). A fairly widespread perceptual predisposition exists to see one's own attitudinal positions as reasonable and, therefore, widely shared by others.

This qualification notwithstanding, the engine driving ideological reasoning, according to the likability heuristic, is affect—feelings toward liberals and conservatives.[12] Curiously enough, however, the likability heuristic—cognitively economical though it is—may itself place a major limit on ideological reasoning. For there is a bias to positivity (Sears, 1982). In many circles it is not thought proper to dislike a candidate or even a political party. The more socially desirable response (and one that many people may internalize) is to express positive affect— relatively indiscriminately—toward a broad range of political stimuli. People have to care a fair amount about political issues to go, so to speak, to the trouble of disliking one side or the other. To be sure, more are prepared to do so than are able, or willing, to discuss politics in abstract terms. Even so, there seems a limit— say, a quarter to a third of the mass public.[13]

However that may be, it is the willingness to dislike the other side that allows many people to make sense of politics. And, in this respect, there is a profound difference between liberals and conservatives in the general public: Conservatives dislike liberals much more than liberals dislike conservatives. It is by no means clear why this is so. One possibility is that the greater propensity of conservatives to dislike liberals is rooted in personality differences between the two groups. According to McClosky (1958) and others (for example, Stone, 1980; Wilson, 1973), conservatives are more likely than liberals to score high on measures of hostility, intolerance of ambiguity and diversity, and anxiety, among other aversive personality characteristics. But whatever the ultimate psychological causes of the difference between conservatives and liberals in their feelings toward each other, the political consequences need to be considered.

One of these concerns what people think others think. To what extent is the public at large able to estimate preferences of liberals and conservatives (or men and women, or blacks and whites)? In brief, there is evidence of a systematic error: The general public overestimates how liberal liberals are, while at the same time underestimating how conservative conservatives are (Brady and Sniderman, forthcoming). And the reason for this, quite simply, is that conservatives tend to accentuate how far from the political center liberals are, whereas liberals tend to minimize how far from the extreme conservatives are. Conservatives would seem to have the better of it. Their opponents, if they misperceive their beliefs, do so by perceiving them as centrist. In contrast, conservatives, if they misperceive liberals, do so by perceiving them as extremist.

There is a second implication, also worth noting. According to the likability heuristic, a person who knows that he dislikes one ideological alternative can figure out where he stands on a particular issue. And if conservatives dislike liberals more than liberals dislike them, then conservatives should be better able (or more willing) to translate with fidelity their ideological identification into consistent stands on concrete issues. And, indeed, conservatives are more likely to be consistent in taking issue stands consonant with their overall political outlook than liberals are (Chubb, Hagen, and Sniderman, 1984).

In sum, if the likability heuristic is valid, there is reason to suspect an ideological asymmetry: Conservatives are more likely to have well-defined conceptions of what they should think, and what others think, about major issues than liberals are. In addition, if the heuristic is valid, it is somewhat clearer how many citizens can put together a relatively coherent outlook on politics, even though they may know relatively little about it.

A Concluding Note

The question of ideology and the mass public is a bedrock issue, perhaps as much for normative as for empirical reasons. For the issue, at bottom, is the rationality of citizens. To what extent can the general public be counted on to understand politics in the same terms as the politically influential or the politically sophisticated? People who take a large part in politics tend to see events that take place, and choices that have to be made, at least partly in terms of left and right, liberal and conservative. And if they could not think of politics in these terms, it would not make nearly as much sense to them. But are these terms meaningful to the public at large? Or is much of politics conducted in a language foreign to the general public? Note that the question is not whether the public at large is capable of rationality, in some sense or other. A number of recent efforts have spelled out various ways in which citizens may be said to make informed and competent political choices—for example, by relying on retrospective judgments (Fiorina, 1981). The question is, rather, whether elite politics tends to be conducted according to a conception of rationality more or less incomprehensible to the general body of citizens.

Thoughtful analysts of public opinion have concluded that citizens are innocent of ideology (see, for example, Kinder and Sears, 1985). Public opinion, in their view, must be understood in other terms—as an expression of values, social pressure, personality needs, and the like. This view has much merit. All the same, it is also worthwhile to ask whether a substantial number of citizens do, in fact, find the language of "high" politics comprehensible. We can answer this question only if we can acquire a causal understanding of the inner workings of mass belief systems. Unfortunately, much of our understanding to date consists of "negative knowledge"—we know what the answer is not. It cannot be argued, for example, that the mass public has a firm grip on liberalism and conservatism as complex political philosophies. Yet a substantial portion of the public may have a clear preference for one and against the other. We believe that these ideological preferences are psychologically rooted in the widespread reliance on simple, easy-to-execute rules of thumb, such as the likability heuristic, in policy reasoning. People's likes and dislikes of strategic political groups provide them with the clues they need in order to understand politics in terms of liberal versus conservative. The likability heuristic allows citizens who are unable or unmotivated to master a political ideology to mimic it. To be sure, the resultant ideological understanding of mass publics may be a crude and simplified one; but so are most effective ways of understanding a complex world.

Notes

1. Possibly the most influential, certainly the most thoughtful, exposition of this point of view is offered by Lane (1962, 1973). For a more recent expression

of this perspective, see Hochschild (1981). For an innovative and fascinating attempt at bridging qualitative and quantitative approaches to the study of belief systems, see Elkins (1982).

2. The term "dynamics," as used here, refers to a substantive concern, not a methodological approach—that is, to an understanding of the forces responsible for the workings of belief systems, not necessarily to their analysis over time.

3. This distinction between cognitive and affective consistency is not without its problems. Much controversy exists in psychology over the relative utility of explanations that assign primacy to cognitive versus affective processes (see Lazarus, 1984; Tetlock and Levi, 1982; Zajonc, 1984). We use the term "belief" to refer to people's perceptions of the likelihood that particular objects of thought are associated with particular attributes or consequences (subjective probability judgments, such as "The president's policies certainly caused the recession" or "American industry may be losing its competitive edge"); we use the term "affect" to refer to people's liking or disliking of particular objects of thought ("I admire the president," "I detest greedy unions"). Obviously, cognitive and affective judgments are closely intertwined, and causality can flow in both directions (our beliefs may both shape our feelings about events and serve to justify those feelings).

4. An even more fundamental cautionary caveat must be noted. Most of the available evidence comes from the study of one particular political system (the United States) during one particular historical period (post–World War II). The generalizability of our conclusions to other political systems and periods of history is largely an open empirical question. For interesting theoretical discussions of the cross-cultural and transhistorical stability of social psychological findings in general, see Gergen (1973), Schlenker (1974), and Triandis (1978).

5. We should note that both measures examined by Smith relied on the so-called master codes, not the original, detailed codes developed and analyzed by Campbell and his colleagues (1960). Analysis of the original codes (Klingemann, 1979; Miller and Miller, 1976) supports the impression of a modest increase in ideological content; though, following Smith (1980), it seems more prudent to interpret this finding as a change in styles of speech rather than in patterns of thought. For a recent review of the level-of-conceptualization controversy, see Cassell (1984).

6. This point is at the root of the paradox of conformists and conformity. In general, the lower people's self-esteem (to pick just one personality characteristic related to conformity), the more inclined they are to conform to a persuasive communication that they receive and comprehend (McGuire, 1985). But the lower people's self-esteem, the more likely they are to deviate from, not to conform to, the prevailing norms of the larger society. Conformists, in a word, tend not to conform in the real world; they tend to deviate not because they wish to do so but because they are less exposed to, and less appreciative of, the political norms of a liberal society (Sniderman, 1975).

7. Government, this model assumes, is perceived as a positively valenced source (possessing both expertise and trustworthiness)—an assumption perhaps more persuasive in the early 1960s than subsequently. Sigelman and Conover (1981) have updated the Gamson and Modigliani analysis, reporting quite different results, perhaps because of the passage of time, more likely in our view because of their focus on the Iranian crisis.

8. The conventional approach for assessing constraint, it should be recalled, calculates the correlation between opinions on two issues—the same two issues for everyone. Not surprisingly, advocates of idiographic or case study approaches to the study of political belief systems are also highly critical of this method of assessing constraint (Lane, 1973).

9. Value conflict need not, moreover, be thought of as a purely theoretical construct; systematic methods for assessing the intensity of value conflict can be developed (Dawson, 1979; Rokeach, 1973; Rosenberg, 1968; Tetlock, 1984b).

10. This finding may have the sound of a paradox, treating simplicity as a sign of complexity. However, the simpler dimensional structure of well-educated respondents does not reflect their inability to differentiate issue preferences but, rather, their ability to integrate issue preferences in terms of superordinate constructs such as liberalism-conservatism. The more people recognize the interrelationships among their stands on issues, the higher the covariation among their stands on issues, and the simpler the dimensional structure revealed by factor analysis of those issue stands.

11. We say "liberals and conservatives" given our interest in ideology; further study may well show that affect toward other cognate pairs of groups (for example, Democrats and Republicans, business and labor, blacks and whites) similarly structures political perception.

12. Other writers have advanced similar hypotheses (see especially Putnam, 1971). The analysis advanced here is also very compatible with social judgment theory (Sherif, Sherif, and Nebergall, 1965), if one is willing to make the reasonable assumption that high differential affect toward liberals and conservatives is a sign of greater ego involvement.

13. This limit, it should be noted, is relatively malleable. Should political conflict become more salient, more citizens will respond with differential affect toward ideologically opposing groups.

References

Abelson, R. P. "Modes of Resolution of Belief Dilemmas." Journal of Conflict Resolution, 1959, 3, 342–352.

Achen, C. H. "Mass Political Attitudes and the Survey Response." *American Political Science Review*, 1975, 69, 1218–1231.

Adorno, T., Frenkel-Brunswik, E., Levinson, D., and Sanford, N. *The Authoritarian Personality.* New York: Harper & Row, 1950.

Aronson, E. "Dissonance Theory: Progress and Problems." In R. P. Abelson and others (eds.), *Theories of Cognitive Consistency: A Sourcebook.* Skokie, Ill.: Rand McNally, 1968.

Beck, P. A. "Politics and the Structure of Policy Thinking." Paper presented at annual meeting of the American Political Science Association, Denver, 1982.

Bennett, W. L. "The Growth of Knowledge in Mass Belief Systems: An Epistemological Critique." *American Journal of Political Science,* 1977, 21, 465–500.

Berelson, B. R., Lazarsfeld, P. F., and McPhee, W. N. *Voting: A Study of Opinion Formation in a Presidential Campaign.* Chicago: University of Chicago Press, 1954.

Bishop, G. F., Oldendick, R. W., Tuchfarber, A. J., and Bennett, S. E. "The Changing Structures of Mass Belief Systems: Fact or Artifact?" *Journal of Politics,* 1978, 40, 781–787.

Bishop, G. F., Oldendick, R. W., Tuchfarber, A. J., and Bennett, S. E. "Pseudo-Opinions on Public Affairs." *Public Opinion Quarterly*, 1980, *44*, 198-209.

Bishop, G. F., Tuchfarber, A. J., and Oldendick, R. W. "Change in the Structure of American Political Attitudes: The Nagging Question of Question Wording." *American Journal of Political Science*, 1978, *22*, 250-269.

Brady, H., and Sniderman, P. "Ideological Maps of Politics." *American Political Science Review*, forthcoming.

Campbell, A., Converse, P. E., Miller, W. E., and Stokes, D. E. *The American Voter*. New York: Wiley, 1960.

Carmines, E. G., and Stimson, J. A. "The Two Faces of Issue Voting." *American Political Science Review*, 1980, *74*, 78-91.

Carmines, E. G., and Stimson, J. A. "Racial Issues and the Structure of Mass Belief Systems." *Journal of Politics*, 1982, *44*, 2-20.

Cassell, C. A. "Issues in Measurement: The 'Levels of Conceptualization' Index of Ideological Sophistication." *American Journal of Political Science*, 1984, *28*, 418-429.

Chong, D., McClosky, H., and Zaller, J. "Patterns of Support for Democratic and Capitalist Values in the United States." *British Journal of Political Science*, 1983, *13*, 401-440.

Chubb, J. E., Hagen, M. G., and Sniderman, P. M. "A Two-Dimensional Theory of Ideology." Working paper no. P-84-2, Hoover Institution, Stanford University, 1984.

Conover, P. J., and Feldman, S. "The Origins and Meaning of Liberal/Conservative Self-Identifications." *American Journal of Political Science*, 1981, *25*, 617-645.

Converse, P. E. "The Nature of Belief Systems in Mass Publics." In D. E. Apter (ed.), *Ideology and Discontent*. New York: Free Press, 1964.

Converse, P. E. "Attitudes and Non-Attitudes: Continuation of a Dialogue." In E. R. Tufte (ed.), *The Quantitative Analysis of Social Problems*. Reading, Mass.: Addison-Wesley, 1970.

Converse, P. E. "Public Opinion and Voting Behavior." In F. Greenstein and N. Polsby (eds.), *Handbook of Political Science*. Vol. 4. Reading, Mass.: Addison-Wesley, 1975.

Converse, P. E. "Rejoinder to Abramson." *American Journal of Political Science*, 1979, *23*, 97-100.

Converse, P. E., and Markus, G. B. "Plus ça change . . . The New CPS Election Study Panel." *American Political Science Review*, 1979, *73*, 32-49.

Dawson, P. A. "The Formation and Structure of Political Belief Systems." *Political Behavior*, 1979, *1*, 99-122.

Elkins, D. J. "The Nature of Belief Systems in Issue Politics." Paper presented at annual meeting of the Canadian Political Science Association, Ottawa, 1982.

Erikson, R. S. "The SRC Panel Data and Mass Political Attitudes." *British Journal of Political Science*, 1979, *9*, 89-114.

Erikson, R. S., Luttbeg, N. R., and Tedin, K. L. *American Public Opinion: Its Origins, Content, and Impact*. (2nd ed.) New York: Wiley, 1980.

Festinger, L. *Conflict, Decision, and Dissonance*. Stanford, Calif.: Stanford University Press, 1964.

Field, J. O., and Anderson, R. E. "Ideology in the Public's Conceptualization of the 1964 Election." *Public Opinion Quarterly*, 1969, *33*, 380-398.

Fiorina, M. P. *Retrospective Voting in American National Elections.* New Haven, Conn.: Yale University Press, 1981.

Fischhoff, B., Slovic, P., and Lichtenstein, S. "Knowing What You Want: Measuring Labile Values." In T. Wallsten (ed.), *Cognitive Processes in Choice and Decision Behavior.* Hillsdale, N.J.: Erlbaum, 1980.

Fiske, S. T., and Taylor, S. E. *Social Cognition.* Reading, Mass.: Addison-Wesley, 1984.

Gamson, W. A., and Modigliani, A. "Knowledge and Foreign Policy Opinions: Some Models for Consideration." *Public Opinion Quarterly,* 1966, *30,* 187-199.

Gergen, K. J. "Social Psychology as History." *Journal of Personality and Social Psychology,* 1973, *26,* 309-320.

Hochschild, J. L. *What's Fair? American Beliefs About Distributive Justice.* Cambridge, Mass.: Harvard University Press, 1981.

Hofstadter, R. *The American Political Tradition.* New York: Vintage Books, 1948.

Holm, J. D., and Robinson, J. P. "Ideological Identification and the American Voter." *Public Opinion Quarterly,* 1978, *42,* 235-246.

Jackman, M. R. "General and Applied Tolerance: Does Education Increase Commitment to Racial Integration?" *American Journal of Political Science,* 1978, *22,* 302-324.

Jackman, M. R. "Education and Policy Commitment to Racial Integration." *American Journal of Political Science,* 1981, *25,* 256-269.

Jennings, M. K., and Niemi, R. G. *Generations and Politics.* Princeton, N.J.: Princeton University Press, 1981.

Judd, C. M., Krosnick, J. A., and Milburn, M. A. "Political Involvement and Attitude Structure in the General Public." *American Sociological Review,* 1981, *46,* 660-669.

Judd, C. M., and Milburn, M. A. "The Structure of Attitude Systems in the General Public: Comparisons of a Structural Equation Model." *American Sociological Review,* 1980, *45,* 627-643.

Key, V. O. *Public Opinion and American Democracy.* New York: Knopf, 1961.

Kinder, D. R., and Sears, D. O. "Public Opinion and Political Action." In G. Lindzey and E. Aronson (eds.), *Handbook of Social Psychology.* (3rd ed.) Reading, Mass.: Addison-Wesley, 1985.

Klingemann, H. D. "Measuring Ideological Conceptualizations." In S. H. Barnes and M. Kaase (eds.), *Political Action: Mass Participation in Five Western Democracies.* Beverly Hills, Calif.: Sage, 1979.

Knoke, D. "Stratification and the Dimensions of American Political Orientations." *American Journal of Political Science,* 1979, *23,* 772-791.

Kuklinski, J. H., Metcalf, D. S., and Kay, A. J. "Citizen Knowledge and Choices on the Complex Issue of Nuclear Energy." *American Journal of Political Science,* 1982, *26,* 615-642.

Lane, R. E. *Political Ideology.* New York: Free Press, 1962.

Lane, R. E. "Patterns of Political Belief." In J. N. Knutson (ed.), *Handbook of Political Psychology.* San Francisco: Jossey-Bass, 1973.

Lazarus, R. S. "On the Primacy of Cognition." *American Psychologist,* 1984, *39,* 124-129.

Levitin, T. E., and Miller, W. E. "Ideological Interpretations of Presidential Elections." *American Political Science Review,* 1979, *73,* 751-771.

Lipset, S. M. *The First New Nation.* New York: Basic Books, 1963.

McClosky, H. "Conservatism and Personality." *American Political Science Review*, 1958, *52*, 27-45.

McClosky, H. "Consensus and Ideology in American Politics." *American Political Science Review*, 1964, *58*, 361-382.

McClosky, H. "Personality and Attitude Correlates of Foreign Policy Orientations." In J. Rosenau (ed.), *Domestic Sources of Foreign Policy*. New York: Free Press, 1967.

McClosky, H., and Brill, A. *Dimensions of Tolerance: What Americans Believe About Civil Liberties*. New York: Russell Sage Foundation, 1983.

McGuire, W. J. "Inducing Resistance to Persuasion: Some Contemporary Approaches." In L. Berkowitz (ed.), *Advances in Experimental Social Psychology*. Vol. 1. Orlando, Fla.: Academic Press, 1964.

McGuire, W. J. "The Probabilogical Model of Cognitive Structure and Attitude Change." In R. E. Petty, T. M. Ostrom, and T. C. Brock (eds.), *Cognitive Responses to Persuasion*. Hillsdale, N.J.: Erlbaum, 1981.

McGuire, W. J. "The Nature of Attitudes and Attitude Change." In G. Lindzey and E. Aronson (eds.), *Handbook of Social Psychology*. (3rd ed.) Reading, Mass.: Addison-Wesley, 1985.

Mann, T. E., and Wolfinger, R. E. "Candidates and Parties in Congressional Elections." *American Political Science Review*, 1980, *74*, 617-632.

Markus, G. B. "The Political Environment and the Dynamics of Public Attitudes: A Panel Study." *American Journal of Political Science*, 1979, *23*, 338-359.

Miller, A. H., and Miller, W. E. "Ideology in the 1972 Election: Myth or Reality?" *American Political Science Review*, 1976, *70*, 832-849.

Nie, N. H., and Andersen, K. "Mass Belief Systems Revisited: Political Change and Attitude Structure." *Journal of Politics*, 1974, *36*, 540-591.

Nie, N. H., Verba, S., and Petrocik, J. R. *The Changing American Voter*. Cambridge, Mass.: Harvard University Press, 1979.

Nunn, C. Z., Crockett, H. J., Jr., and Williams, J. A., Jr. *Tolerance for Nonconformity: A National Survey of Americans' Changing Attitudes to Civil Liberties*. San Francisco: Jossey-Bass, 1978.

Page, B. I., and Shapiro, R. W. "Changes in America's Policy Preferences." *Public Opinion Quarterly*, 1982, *46*, 24-42.

Petty, R. E., and Cacioppo, J. T. *Attitudes and Influence Processes*. Dubuque, Iowa: Brown, 1981.

Pole, J. R. *The Pursuit of Equality in American History*. Berkeley: University of California Press, 1978.

Prothro, J. W., and Grigg, C. M. "Fundamental Principles of Democracy: Bases of Agreement and Disagreement." *Journal of Politics*, 1960, *22*, 276-294.

Putnam, R. D. "Studying Elite Culture: The Case of Ideology." *American Political Science Review*, 1971, *65*, 651-681.

Putnam, R. D., Leonardi, R., and Nanetti, R. V. "Attitude Stability Among Political Elites." *American Journal of Political Science*, 1979, *23*, 463-494.

Rokeach, M. *The Nature of Human Values*. New York: Free Press, 1973.

Rokeach, M. *Understanding Human Values: Individual and Social*. New York: Free Press, 1979.

Rosenberg, M. J. "Hedonism, Inauthenticity, and Other Goads Toward Expansion of a Consistency Theory." In R. P. Abelson and others (eds.), *Theories of Cognitive Consistency: A Sourcebook*. Skokie, Ill.: Rand McNally, 1968.

Ross, L. E., Greene, D., and House, P. "The False Consensus Effect: An Attributional Bias in Self-Perception and Social Perception Processes." *Journal of Experimental Social Psychology,* 1977, *13,* 279–301.

Schlenker, B. R. "Social Psychology and Science." *Journal of Personality and Social Psychology,* 1974, *29,* 1-15.

Schuman, H., and Presser, S. "Public Opinion and Public Ignorance: The Fine Line Between Attitude and Non-Attitude." *American Journal of Sociology,* 1977, *85,* 1214–1225.

Schuman, H., and Presser, S. "Public Opinion and Public Ignorance: The Fine Line Between Attitude and Non-Attitude." *American Journal of Sociology,* 1977, *85,* 1214–1225.

Schuman, H., and Presser, S. *Questions and Answers in Attitude Surveys: Experiments on Question Form, Wording, and Context.* Orlando, Fla.: Academic Press, 1981.

Sherif, C. W., Sherif, M., and Nebergall, R. E. *Attitude and Attitude Change: The Social Judgment Approach.* Philadelphia: Saunders, 1965.

Sigelman, L., and Conover, P. J. "Knowledge and Opinions About the Iranian Crisis: A Reconsideration of Three Models." *Public Opinion Quarterly,* 1981, *45,* 477–491.

Smith, E. R. "The Levels of Conceptualization: False Measures of Ideological Sophistication." *American Political Science Review,* 1980, *74,* 685–696.

Sniderman, P. M. *Personality and Democratic Politics.* Berkeley: University of California Press, 1975.

Sniderman, P. M., Brody, R. A., and Kuklinski, J. H. "Policy Reasoning in Political Issues: The Problem of Racial Equality." *American Journal of Political Science,* 1984, *28,* 75–94.

Stimson, J. A. "Belief Systems: Constraint, Complexity, and the 1972 Election." *American Journal of Political Science,* 1975, *19,* 393–418.

Stone, W. F. "The Myth of Left-Wing Authoritarianism." *Political Psychology,* 1980, *2,* 3–20.

Stouffer, S. A. *Communism, Conformity and Civil Liberties.* New York: Doubleday, 1955.

Sullivan, J. L., Marcus, G. E., Feldman, S., and Piereson, J. E. "The Sources of Political Tolerance: A Multivariate Analysis." *American Political Science Review,* 1981, *75,* 92-106.

Sullivan, J. L., Piereson, J. E., and Marcus, G. E. "Ideological Constraint in the Mass Public: A Methodological Critique and Some New Findings." *American Journal of Political Science,* 1978, *22,* 233–249.

Sullivan, J. L., Piereson, J. E., and Marcus, G. E. "An Alternative Conceptualization of Political Tolerance: Illusory Increases 1950s–1970s." *American Political Science Review,* 1979, *73,* 781–794.

Sullivan, J. L., Piereson, J. E., Marcus, G. E., and Feldman, S. "The More Things Change, the More They Stay the Same: The Stability of Mass Belief Systems." *American Journal of Political Science,* 1979, *23,* 176–186.

Tedeschi, J. T., and Rosenfeld, P. "Impression Management and the Forced Compliance Situation." In J. T. Tedeschi (ed.), *Impression Management Theory and Social Psychological Research.* Orlando, Fla.: Academic Press, 1981.

Tedin, K. L., and Murray, R. W. "Public Awareness of Congressional Representatives." *American Politics Quarterly,* 1979, *6,* 509–513.

Tesser, A. "Self-Generated Attitude Change." In L. Berkowitz (ed.), *Advances in Experimental Social Psychology.* Vol. 2. Orlando, Fla.: Academic Press, 1978.

Tetlock, P. E. "Personality and Isolationism: Content Analysis of Senatorial Speeches." *Journal of Personality and Social Psychology*, 1981, *41*, 737–743.

Tetlock, P. E. "Cognitive Style and Political Ideology." *Journal of Personality and Social Psychology*, 1983, *45*, 118–126.

Tetlock, P. E. "Cognitive Style and Political Belief Systems in the British House of Commons." *Journal of Personality and Social Psychology*, 1984a, *46*, 365–375.

Tetlock, P. E. "A Value Pluralism Model of Ideological Reasoning." Paper presented at annual meeting of the American Psychological Association, Toronto, 1984b.

Tetlock, P. E., Bernzweig, J., and Gallant, J. "Supreme Court Decision Making: Cognitive Style as a Predictor of Ideological Consistency of Voting." *Journal of Personality and Social Psychology*, forthcoming.

Tetlock, P. E., and Levi, A. "Attribution Bias: On the Inconclusiveness of the Cognition-Motivation Debate." *Journal of Experimental Social Psychology*, 1982, *18*, 68–88.

Triandis, H. C. "Some Universals of Social Behavior." *Personality and Social Psychology Bulletin*, 1978, *4*, 1–16.

Turner, C. F., and Krauss, E. "Fallible Indicators of the Subjective State of the Nation." *American Psychologist*, 1978, *33*, 456–470.

Wilson, G. D. *The Psychology of Conservatism*. Orlando, Fla.: Academic Press, 1973.

Wolfinger, R. E., Shapiro, M., and Greenstein, F. I. *Dynamics of American Politics*. Englewood Cliffs, N.J.: Prentice-Hall, 1980.

Zajonc, R. B. "On the Primacy of Affect." *American Psychologist*, 1984, *39*, 117–123.

Zaller, J. "The Role of Elites in Shaping Public Opinion." Working Paper no. 63, Survey Research Center, University of California, Berkeley, 1983.

FOUR

༄༄༄༄༄༄༄༄༄༄༄༄༄༄༄༄༄༄༄

Environmental Beliefs
and Values

Lester W. Milbrath

Humans have always pondered the environment because it is the very foundation
of life. The way that they choose to relate to it becomes their lifestyle. At first, as
the human species struggled to maintain its existence on the planet, environments
often were seen as harsh and demanding as well as sometimes comforting and
supporting. But, as humans became more and more successful in winning out
over other species and establishing an increasingly dominant position on the
planet, they became more inclined to look on the environment as a resource base
that could be exploited to enhance their domination. Schnaiberg (1980, pp. 10–11)
contrasts the people who perceive the environment mainly as the "home for mankind" with those who look on the environment as a "sustenance base." For some
the environment has a semireligious mystical quality; it is an object of wonder
and beauty, a thing to be loved and cherished for its own sake. This love of nature
is an important belief and value for modern-day environmentalists; it is one of the
most strongly differentiating characteristics between environmentalists and nonenvironmentalists (Milbrath, 1979, 1981c). Our research has shown that, in addition
to this strong love for nature, environmentalists are distinctive in their level of

Note: This chapter was prepared with the advice and assistance of Barbara Fisher
and Martha Cornwell. Researchers from the International Institute for Environment and
Society in the Science Center in Berlin, the Department of Sociology at the University of
Bath in England, and the Environmental Studies Center at the State University of New
York at Buffalo designed and carried out the three-nation comparative study discussed in
the section headed "Vanguard Versus Rearguard." Information about the questionnaires
used and the sampling procedures is available in Milbrath (1984). Credit for developing the
typology and the data displayed in Tables 7, 8, and 9 should be shared with two members
of the German team, Hans Joachim Fietkau and Hans Kessel, and another member of the
American team, Jeffrey Coopersmith.

caring and compassion for others. Their sense of compassion, which springs from a highly developed sense of empathy, extends not only to those near and dear but also to people in other countries, to other species, and to future generations (Milbrath, 1979).

The modern industrial societies that have developed over the past 400 years are supported by a different belief about the relationship between humans and their environment—the belief that humans are destined to dominate nature. Nature is seen as a resource base to which humans can apply their science and technology in order to extract material goods, not simply to support life but to create a life of ease and comfort (Catton, 1980). As humans have taken this increasingly exuberant attitude toward nature, they have tended to equate a high quality of life with the acquisition of more and more material goods. Economic values and ever increasing levels of wealth have become the dominant objects of public policy in most modern industrial societies. As a result, a psychological distance has been created between many humans and their natural environment. They have become preoccupied with man-made environments and the technological manipulation of things (Anderson and Lipsey, 1978), most recently with computers. For these people the natural environment has faded into the background and typically is taken for granted; it is thoughtlessly used for the disposal of wastes.

The environmentalist critique of modern industrial societies goes much deeper than a concern about the despoilation of nature. Man's genius in using science and technology to conquer diseases and dramatically prolong human life, coupled with extraordinary success in extracting more wealth from nature, has produced an explosion in human population. World population doubling, which used to take many centuries, now takes only thirty-five years. If present trends continue, a young child could experience two doublings of population within his lifetime; the present world population of approximately 6 billion could double twice to become 20 billion before he dies. Unfortunately, much of this growth will occur in the less developed parts of the world, where there is the weakest resource base to support this kind of increase.

The inhabitants of the developed countries use their wealth and technology to take an even more exuberant attitude toward nature. It has been estimated that the average modern American consumes sixty times as many resources as the average citizen of India (Catton, 1980, p. 205). The modern human is not simply *Homo sapiens* but has turned into *"Homo colossus."* This "new species" is withdrawing resources from the earth's crust, particularly energy, at such a prodigious rate that natural processes have no hope of renewing them in any reasonable time span. Catton (1980, p. 46) says that "we are living on four parts phantom carrying capacity for every one part of permanent (real) carrying capacity." That is, modern society is supported largely by resources that cannot be renewed fast enough to sustain its present ways. In Catton's judgment, and in that of many others, the human species already has gone into "overshoot." There is no way that present population and resource consumption growth rates can continue. Our destiny will be to die back to a level that can be sustained by the natural carrying capacity of the environment. This physical necessity to die back will force profound changes on humans—changes in their beliefs, values, economic structure, social structure, and political system.

Some environmentalists, then, foresee deep and lasting social change; many are calling for a completely new society. They believe that the transition to this new society will be smoother and less painful if it can be approached with thoughtful recognition of what must be done to make human society sustainable over the long run. They fear the pain, suffering, and death that are likely to occur if we go on as we are, destroying the capability of the natural environment to support our economic, social, and political institutions. The environmentalists sharing this cluster of beliefs and values have formed themselves into a social movement; they have become a vanguard using education, persuasion, and politics to try to lead humans to their vision of a new, better, and more sustainable society.

As might be expected, this new vanguard is opposed by a rearguard, composed of those who believe that modern industrial societies are working quite well and should continue on their present trajectory. These people primarily value material wealth and look on nature as a resource to be exploited in order to extract more wealth. They are so confident of the ingenuity of humans that they regard economic growth as limitless (Simon, 1981). They believe that science and technology have been a great boon to humans and that the present structure of industrial society, with its emphasis on aggressive competitiveness in a market framework, produces the most wealth and the best society. They have a strong faith in the merit of modern society's beliefs and values as well as its current economic, social, and political arrangements.

These contrasting beliefs and values separate into two "world views"; in a very real sense, they are political ideologies. A number of research studies (Constantini and Hanf, 1972; Cotgrove, 1982; Cotgrove and Duff, 1980; Dunlap, 1980; Dunlap and Van Liere, 1978b; Milbrath, 1981a, 1984; Van Liere and Dunlap, 1981a, 1981b; Weigel, 1977; Yankelovich, 1972, 1981; Yankelovich and Lefkowitz, 1980a, 1980b) have shown that beliefs and values about the environment form into clusters that constitute highly contrasting world views or political ideologies. These contrasting views are parsimoniously set forth in Table 1. The outstanding characteristics found in the world view of vanguard environmentalists are their high valuation on nature; their sense of empathy, which generalizes to compassion toward other species, other peoples, and other generations; their desire to plan carefully and to act so as to avoid risks to humans and nature; their recognition that there are limits to growth and that we humans must adapt to those limits; and their desire for a completely new society that incorporates new ways to conduct our economic and political affairs. On each of these points, they are opposed by the defenders of the present system.

Environmentalists, as well as the researchers who study environmental beliefs and values, often refer to these contrasting world views as competing paradigms. The set of beliefs and values currently in vogue in modern industrial society can be called the dominant social paradigm (DSP) and is defended by a rearguard convinced that the system should be retained. As noted in Table 1, the environmentalist vanguard is advocating a new set of beliefs and values—a "new environmental paradigm" (NEP) (Dunlap and Van Liere, 1978b). Cotgrove (1982, pp. 26–27, 88) has done some of the clearest thinking about paradigms:

> Paradigms . . . provide maps of what the world is believed to be like. They constitute guidelines for getting about and for identifying and solving problems. Above all, paradigms provide the frame-

Table 1. Contrast Between Competing Paradigms.

New Environmental Paradigm (NEP)

I. High valuation on nature
   A. Nature for its own sake (worshipful love of nature)
   B. Humans harmonious with nature
   C. Environmental protection over economic growth

II. Generalized compassion toward:
   A. Other species
   B. Other peoples
   C. Other generations

III. Carefully plan and act to avoid risk
   A. Science and technology not always good
   B. Stop further development of nuclear power
   C. Develop and use soft technology
   D. Use regulation to protect nature and humans—government responsibility

IV. Limits to growth
   A. Resource shortages
   B. Population explosion—limits needed
   C. Conservation

V. Completely new society needed (new paradigm)
   A. Humans seriously damaging nature and themselves
   B. Openness and participation
   C. Emphasis on public goods
   D. Cooperation
   E. Postmaterialism
   F. Simple lifestyles
   G. Emphasis on worker satisfaction in jobs

VI. New politics
   A. Consultative and participatory
   B. Partisan dispute over human relationship to nature
   C. Willingness to use direct action
   D. Emphasis on foresight and planning

Dominant Social Paradigm (DSP)

I. Lower valuation on nature
   A. Nature to produce goods
   B. Human domination of nature
   C. Economic growth over environmental protection

II. Compassion for only those near and dear
   A. Exploit other species for human needs
   B. Unconcern for other people
   C. Concern for this generation only

III. Accept risk to maximize wealth
   A. Science and technology great boon to humans
   B. Proceed swiftly to develop nuclear power
   C. Emphasize hard technology
   D. Deemphasize regulation—individual responsibility

IV. No limits to growth
   A. No resource shortages
   B. No problem with population
   C. Production and consumption

V. Present society working well (keep DSP)
   A. Humans not seriously damaging nature
   B. Hierarchy and efficiency
   C. Emphasis on market
   D. Competition
   E. Materialism
   F. Complex and fast lifestyles
   G. Emphasis on jobs for economic need

VI. Old politics
   A. Determination by experts
   B. Partisan dispute over management of the economy
   C. Opposition to direct action
   D. Emphasis on market control

work of meaning within which "facts" and experiences acquire significance and can be interpreted.

Paradigms are not only beliefs about what the world is like and guides to action; they also serve the purpose of legitimating or justifying courses of action. That is to say, they function as ideologies. Hence, conflicts over what constitutes the paradigm by which action should be guided and judged to be reasonable is itself a part of the political process. The struggle to universalize a paradigm is part of a struggle for power.

[A paradigm] is dominant not in the statistical sense of being held by most people, but in the sense that it is the paradigm held by dominant groups in industrial societies and in the sense that it serves to legitimate and justify the institutions and practices of a market economy. . . . It is the taken-for-granted commonsensical view which usually determines the outcome of debates on environmental issues.

As Table 1 shows, these competing paradigms are highly contrastive:

The protagonists face each other in a spirit of exasperation, talking past each other with mutual incomprehension. It is a dialogue of the blind talking to the deaf. Nor can the debate be settled by appeals to the facts. We need to grasp the implicit cultural meanings which underlie the dialogue. . . .

It is because protagonists to the debate approach issues from different cultural contexts, which generate different and conflicting implicit meanings, that there is mutual exasperation and charges and countercharges of irrationality and unreason. What is sensible from one point of view is nonsense from another. It is the implicit, self-evident, taken-for-granted character of paradigms which clogs the channels of communication [Cotgrove, 1982, pp. 33, 82].

So far, we have spoken of the competing paradigms as pure types. A number of studies (Cotgrove, 1982; Milbrath, 1981a, 1984; Schwartz and Ogilvy, 1979; Yankelovich and Lefkowitz, 1980a, 1980b) have shown that many people hold beliefs that partake of both paradigms. In order to portray the main clusterings of relevant beliefs, I have arrayed them in a two-dimensional space in Figure 1. The horizontal dimension of that space differentiates persons who resist social change from persons who strongly advocate social change to deal with environmental problems. The resisters to social change generally believe that manageable technical adjustments will suffice to deal with these problems. In a deeper sense, the resisters to social change believe that our present socioeconomic system, with its emphasis on human domination of nature, is satisfactory, whereas the advocates of social change want a new socioeconomic system with a more harmonious relationship between humans and nature. The vertical dimension of the space contrasts people who highly value a safe, clean, and beautiful environment with those who highly value material wealth and deemphasize environmental protection.

The rearguard, which defends the DSP, is positioned in the lower-right

Figure 1. Spatial Representation of Postures Toward the Environment.

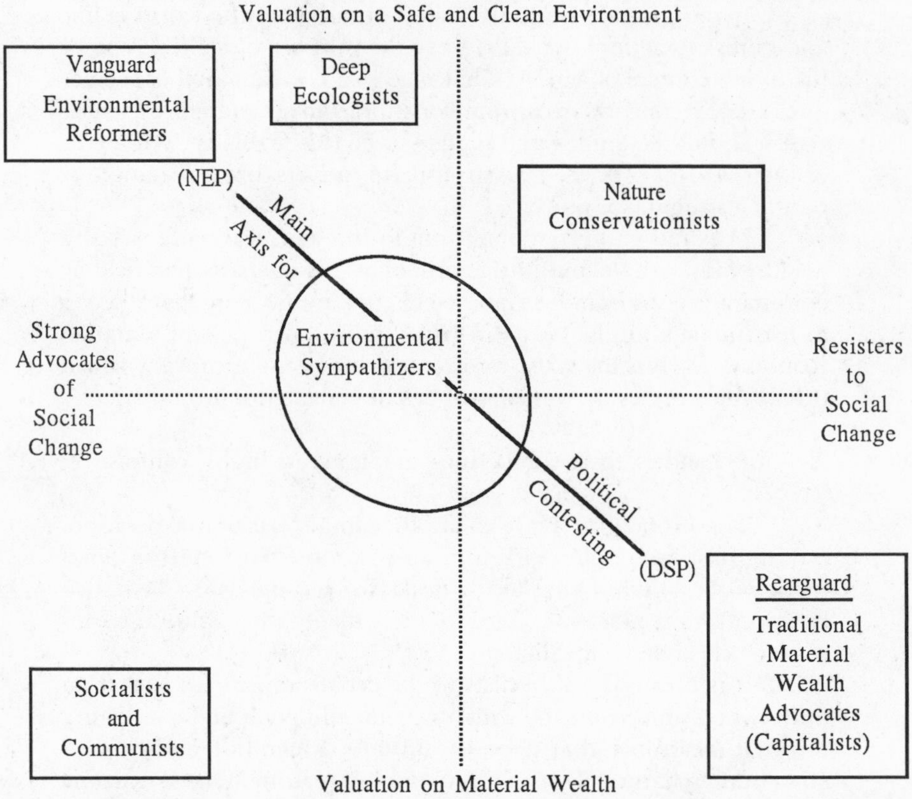

Valuation on a Safe and Clean Environment

Valuation on Material Wealth

corner, indicating the high valuation it places on material wealth and its resistance to social change. At the opposite upper-left corner are the environmental reformers in the vanguard, who place a high valuation on a safe and clean environment and are strong advocates of social change. Many of these people have organized into vigorous groups that strive for public education about environmental problems and use electoral activity and pressure-group tactics to bring about social change. Most of them eschew violence as a valid way to pursue their ends, but many of them are willing to use direct actions—such as protests, demonstrations, boycotts, and sit-ins—to communicate their views. It is fair to say that they are the major social force working for fundamental change in the relationship between humans and nature active in American society today.

The labels "rearguard" and "vanguard" are, of course, my own. I do not intend these labels to be pejorative. The outstanding characteristic of those in the rearguard is that they are defenders of the DSP, and the outstanding characteristic of those in the vanguard is that they are trying to bring about a new society. The people in the rearguard and the vanguard may not perceive themselves as such; that is beside the point. The social change that we are examining is so fundamental, and moves so slowly, that many of the actors participating in the change process, or resisting it, may not recognize the cumulative significance for the society as a whole of the changes that are occurring in their own beliefs and values as well as in the beliefs and values of others. Both sets of actors are trying to make a better world. It is up to us to understand the ways in which these worlds would be similar and the ways in which they would be different.

As indicated, the mass of people in the United States, and in most other advanced industrial countries, partake of the beliefs of both paradigms and thus can be plotted near the center of the space in Figure 1. They are sympathetic toward environmental values but also hold aspirations for material wealth. On the other dimension, they have gone some distance in recognizing a need for basic social change but have not yet learned what a new, more satisfactory, social paradigm will be. They are labeled on the figure as "environmental sympathizers" because most people, in fact, do sympathize with the environmental movement. Table 2 reports the percentage of the United States public that agrees with or accepts the environmental perspective on twelve items that were included in the United States component of a three-nation study of environmental beliefs and values (to be discussed more fully later in this chapter). As Table 2 shows, three-fourths or more supported the environmental perspective on most items. These percentages, as well as those from several other studies (Dunlap and Van Liere, 1978b; Mitchell, 1978, 1980c; Utrup, 1978; Yankelovich, 1981; Yankelovich and Lefkowitz, 1980a, 1980b), show that within the United States public there is substantial departure from the beliefs and values of the old DSP; this departure is significant in other advanced industrial countries as well (Cotgrove, 1982; Milbrath, 1984). Repeated studies over the years since Earth Day 1970 show that the level of support for environmentalism continues to be quite high despite the public's overwhelming preoccupation with economic woes in the worldwide recession of the early 1980s. A *New York Times*/CBS news poll in April 1983 showed a *rise* in support for environmental protection over the levels reported in September 1981.

Those in the lower-left quadrant in Figure 1, labeled "Socialists and Communists," have long been advocates of major social change in "Western" societies, but they are similar to the business/industrial sector of society in their strong emphasis on economic values and material wealth. Their main difference from the capitalists is their preference for planning and public ownership of the means of production rather than private ownership that relies on the market system to allocate goods and services. Despite struggling for many years to win adherents to their point of view, the Socialists and Communists have not had much success in the United States. They do not, presently, constitute a strong force for social change there.

The "left-right" dimension that has been in vogue for many decades in characterizing political differences has less relevance for beliefs concerning the relationship between humans and nature. Both left and right endorse a strong valuation on material wealth; therefore, the left-right dimension should be placed along the bottom of the diagram. Many people, especially the young people in modern industrial societies, find that "left versus right" is not very relevant for characterizing their political beliefs. Interpreters and consumers of public opinion should be cautious, therefore, about using the left-right dimension to characterize politics and political stances in modern industrial societies. Even though the environmental reformers are placed in the upper-left quadrant of the figure, that should not be taken to mean they are favorable to socialism or antagonistic to

Table 2. Levels of Support for Environmental Values in the U.S. Public in 1980–1982.

Item	% Disagreeing/Rejecting Environmental Perspective		% Agreeing/Accepting Environmental Perspective	
	1980	1982	1980	1982
1. There are likely to be serious and disruptive shortages of essential raw materials if things go on as they are.	10	18	88	69
2. The storage of nuclear wastes is too dangerous.	24	23	66	66
3. Humans must live in harmony with nature in order to survive.	6	8	92	87
4. Mankind is severely abusing the environment.	14	17	80	76
5. A society that emphasizes environmental protection over economic growth.	19	21	62	59
6. A society that saves its resources to benefit future generations rather than using them for the present generation.	16	14	73	73
7. Nature is OK but other things are more important vs. I cherish nature and preserve it as one of the most precious things in life.	16	14	73	76
8. Generally speaking, how strongly do you favor or oppose the environmental movement?	17	19	67	53
9. I perceive the condition of the world environment to be a large problem.	15	8	62	76
10. A country that encourages people to remake their environment to suit their needs vs. a country that encourages people to adapt to their natural environment.	17	15	73	71
11. A country that gets the energy it needs by better insulating its homes, driving cars that use less gasoline, and conserving more energy vs. a country that gets the energy it needs by digging more coal mines and drilling more oil wells, building more power plants, and producing more energy.	19	12	71	77
12. Environmental problems are urgent (an average across ten problems).	14	15	70	72

Note: Persons taking a neutral position on these questions are not reported in the table; hence, the percentages will not add to 100. Data are drawn from a study of environmental beliefs and values (see Milbrath, 1984).

capitalism. Most of these reformers find considerable fault with both systems, particularly their dominating emphasis on economic values.

A number of people think of themselves as environmentalists although they do not share the strong desire for social change evident in the vanguard (Buttel and Johnson, 1977). We have identified these people in the diagram as "nature conservationists." They place a high valuation on a safe and clean environment but tend also to adhere to many of the beliefs, values, and social structures of modern industrial society. Many of them are politically conservative, believing that our economic and political forms are working well and should be continued (Duff and Cotgrove, 1980). Many of them have high confidence in science and technology to resolve most environmental problems (Cotgrove, 1982; Milbrath, 1981a, 1984). They are willing, however, to accept strong laws and regulations for protection of the environment. Many of the people in the American business community (even many labor leaders) fall in this category (Milbrath, 1981a, 1981c); they often call for a "balance" of environmental values and material wealth values (Continental Group, 1982). That leaves undefined, of course, the relative weights persons would assign to environmental values and economic values.

The "deep ecologists" are immersed in nature emotionally and philosophically (Devall, 1979, 1980, 1982; Mitchell, 1980a; Naess, 1973). While many "reform environmentalists" have these same deep feelings, those singled out here as deep ecologists typically are not very involved in politics and political reform. Many of them live in counterculture communities that are close to nature and minimally disturb the biosphere as they interact with nature to provide their life needs; in this sense they are both radical and conservative. In philosophy and consciousness, deep ecology is spiritual and deeply attuned to the "organic community" (Bookchin, 1982). "Earth First" is an organization that leads the deep ecology movement; many of its members perceive themselves as the true vanguard leading to a new society. Although society may eventually learn important lessons from the experiences of the deep ecologists, they presently do not constitute a strong political force for near-term social change.

Now that we have examined the important belief and value differences that shape the environmental attitudes of the major actors in the contemporary political arena, we should direct our attention to assessing environmentalism as a social movement.

The Environmental Movement

Environmentalism has, indeed, become a social movement—a social movement of some consequence, as will be demonstrated later in this chapter. It already has had considerable impact on the way that we do things in modern society (new laws, new processes, new concepts) and, in my judgment, it is destined to have an even greater impact in the future.

As with most social movements (Banks, 1972; Ryan, 1969), the environmental movement has undergone some transformation with time (Faich and Gale, 1971; Humphrey and Buttel, 1982; McConnell, 1971; Mitchell, 1979b, 1980a; O'Riordan, 1971, 1979; Sandbach, 1980). The modern-day environmental movement has its roots in a conservation movement that achieved prominence in the late nineteenth and early twentieth centuries in the United States (Fox, 1981; McConnell,

1954). The plentiful supply of cheap land in the New World led many immigrant settlers to exploit land ruthlessly, with little concern for future generations. Land was treated as a commodity, enabling some people to get rich quickly; as a result, widespread speculation in land ownership took place. This exploitive mentality toward land was carried to such an extreme that it created a reaction in the form of the conservation movement. One prominent object of the movement was to set aside certain beautiful tracts of public land as national parks to avoid their being purchased and exploited for private gain. Yellowstone National Park, established in 1872, was the first national park in the world and set a model for park development in the United States as well as in many other countries. The conservation movement, led by such famous leaders as Theodore Roosevelt and Gifford Pinchot, had the preservation of beautiful nature as its most prominent objective; this objective continues to be central to the environmental movement today (Pierce, 1979).

At about this same time, conservation movements were getting under way in other countries, most prominently in England, with an emphasis on the preservation of unspoiled nature (O'Riordan, 1979; Zetterberg, 1978). Cotgrove (1982, p. 2) has listed twelve British organizations with this objective that were founded either in the last half of the nineteenth century or the first half of the twentieth century. These groups were interested in the preservation of commons, open spaces, footpaths, birds, forests, ancient buildings and monuments, and soils.

A second emphasis for many of the conservationists was efficiency; they perceived waste and despoilation as inefficient and detracting from the ability of society to create wealth (Hays, 1959; O'Riordan, 1971; Schnaiberg, 1980, pp. 378–389). According to Schnaiberg, the efficiency emphasis of the conservation movement was strongly supportive of industrial capitalism and the upper middle class. In fact, many scholars regarded the movement as upper middle class (Devall, 1970a; Harry, Gale, and Hendee, 1969). Most of the people in the conservation movement accepted the existing economic-social-political arrangements of the society; they had excellent access to major economic and political decision makers and did not question the belief and value structure and societal arrangements that dominated this industrially oriented and market-controlled society. Most of them saw no conflict between conservation and economic growth. Some scholars refer to this group as "wise multiple-use progressives" (Hays, 1959; Nash, 1973).

Another early conservation leader, John Muir, had a different vision of the relationship between humans and nature. He saw man as immersed in nature rather than the lord over nature (Devall, 1982; Fox, 1981; Nash, 1973): "Everything is flowing into everything else." His philosophy was deeply spiritual, and he became spiritual godfather to such later leaders as Aldo Leopold, Rachel Carson, David Brower, and David Ehrenfeld. He is also godfather to today's "deep ecologists."

As the conservation movement grew, it was joined by many people who were interested in such outdoor sports as hunting and fishing. These activities had, and continue to have, attraction for working-class as well as middle-class persons. Such American groups as the National Rifle Association and the National Wildlife Federation have hundreds of thousands of members, even millions, and are able to wield considerable influence in public affairs and legislation. Their base has become so broad that the movement no longer can be called middle class.

As human degradation of the environment advanced to what many began to believe was an alarming level, the movement began transforming from a conservation movement to an environmental protection movement (Bartell and St. George, 1974; Morrison, 1972). Frightening increases in air and water pollution appeared in the 1960s and were the most visible mobilizing factors (Dillman and Christenson, 1975; Kromm, Probald, and Wall, 1973); media attention, such as the focus on the Santa Barbara oil spill of 1968, was particularly significant in making the public aware of these problems (Murch, 1971). The public health movement and the consumer movement strengthened concern for the environment. Awareness of pollution dangers grew swiftly in all classes but was further advanced in the middle class (Buttel and Flinn, 1974). Residents in urban areas, where the degradation was greater, became aware faster; and the awareness in urban areas was more widespread than in rural areas (Erskine, 1972a, 1972b; Tremblay and Dunlap, 1978; Zuiches, 1976). Earth Day 1970 was the high point of public consciousness and clamor for environmental cleanup.

Many commentators during the 1960s also were successful in focusing public attention on problems of population growth; people began to see the connection between increasingly dense population and increasing levels of pollution (Barnett, 1973, 1974; Simon, 1971; Smith, Scheuneman, and Zeidberg, 1964). Curiously, there was little public understanding during the 1960s of the possibility of resource depletion and the energy shortage that would confront them with a jolt in the 1970s (Milbrath, 1975). Not only were people largely uninformed about possible resource shortages, but they resisted accepting information about them (Anderson and Lipsey, 1978; Bartell, 1976; Jackson, 1980), possibly because a recognition of resource shortages would be likely to require acknowledgment that there could be limits to growth. The undeniable existence of shortages in the 1970s slowly eroded that resistance in the United States. In the latter part of the 1970s, the horrors of toxic waste poisoning began to emerge in a variety of places, and a sense of urgency to control toxic wastes soon took a prominent place on the agenda of concerns of the environmental movement.

Beginning in the late 1960s, and continuing into the present, the environmental vanguard has urged people to question proposed technological "advances," since technology can bring evil as well as good and ever higher levels of technology can be counterproductive and even dangerous. This charge was particularly salient for exports of Western technology to less developed countries. Highly sophisticated technology may displace workers instead of producing jobs; it is likely to be highly consumptive of energy and other resources; and it is vulnerable to breakdown due to lack of parts and skilled technicians. The environmental vanguard urged the use of "appropriate" technology, that which is suited to the socioeconomic and political realities of a setting. This thrust became something of a mini social movement with its own networks of interested people and its own literature (Lovins, 1977; Morrison, 1980, Schumacher, 1973). Appropriate technology became one of the important components of the belief structure of environmentalists (Mitchell, 1980a).

Fear of nuclear power intensified and spread widely through the population of industrial societies over the dacade of the 1970s and has continued to increase in the 1980s (Milbrath, 1984; Mitchell, 1980b, 1981, 1982). It has become the most emotional and divisive of the environmental concerns. Believers in industrial capitalism could accept the fact that there is air and water pollution and that vigorous technological efforts must be made to clean it up; they could recognize that population growth is a problem; they could recognize resource shortages and pledge vigorous efforts to find new sources of energy and materials; they could not deny the clamor of the public to be free from toxic poisons and accepted stiff regulations as well as cleanup campaigns. But the demand of noisy environmentalists to stop further growth and development of nuclear power seemed to strike at the very heart of modern industrial capitalism. Environmental activists who had found the doors of public offices open to them when they complained about pollution or toxics found a deaf ear and a vigorous determination to plunge ahead when they complained about nuclear power (Nelkin and Pollak, 1980, 1982; Slovic, Fischhoff, and Lichtenstein, 1982). Feeling that all other avenues were being closed to them, some environmentalists took to the streets and demonstrated their convictions about nuclear power by throwing their bodies before bulldozers and trucks or chaining themselves to fences, in eloquent evidence of the depth of their feelings.

Fear of nuclear power seems to be linked to fear of nuclear war and fear of technology running wild. People who admire and have faith in technology are much more likely to accept nuclear power (Benedict, Bone, Leavel, and Rice, 1980). There is, at present, in most advanced industrial societies a linkage between the environmental movement and the peace movement. In Germany, for instance, over half of the population favors both movements and more than 80 percent of environmentalists regard themselves as strong supporters of the peace movement (Milbrath, 1984). In 1982 several important environmental organizations in the United States announced that they were initiating studies and campaigns for the purpose of avoiding nuclear war, because such a war would be the most devastating of environmental catastrophes.

Throughout the 1960s and 1970s, awareness developed that environmental problems could not be solved by technological fixes, that solving these problems would require basic changes in society (Milbrath, 1975, 1981a, 1981c, 1981d). Awareness of continued population growth, and increasing shortages of raw materials and energy, led many people to conclude that there are limits to growth (Bowman, 1977; Cotgrove, 1982; Milbrath, 1981a). Increasing numbers of the environmental vanguard began to recognize that, in order to deal effectively with the problems they saw, they had to challenge the very foundations of modern industrial society: "The environmentalist movement has been forced to change from a consensual to a conflictual movement, from a concern with reform within a framework of consensual values to a radical challenge to societal values" (Cotgrove, 1982, p. 10).

In the Federal Republic of Germany, the environmentalists could not get adequate recognition of their views within the traditional party structure and have formed new "Green Parties," which have successfully obtained representation in state parliaments and approximately twenty-five seats in the national parliament. In the United States, most environmental organizations have thus far tried to appeal simultaneously to nature conservationists and to reform environmentalists; these two basic kinds of environmentalists have worked together for many common goals. The determination of the Reagan administration to turn the nation away from environmentalism and refocus it on economic values has galvanized many national environmental organizations to take overt political action and try to get candidates elected to public office who are favorable to their perspective. Several of these organizations set up political action committees and were happy to report to their members that approximately 70 percent of the candidates that they supported were successful in winning election in 1982. During 1983 Ann Burford and James Watt, who headed the most environmentally relevant agencies in the Reagan administration, were both forced to resign; public opinion forced a change in Reagan's environmental policies (Mitchell, 1984). It is fair to say that, as of today, the environmental reform movement in the United States, England, and West Germany constitutes a vanguard leading a thrust for major social reform, which most of its members perceive as essential for achieving the values they hold dear (Milbrath, 1984).

Members of the environmental movement, then, while agreed on the importance of protecting the natural environment, are split on whether or not major socioeconomic-political change is required in order to have a good society. The reform environmentalists, the vanguard, are proposing a new environmentally oriented societal paradigm that challenges the old dominant social paradigm defended by the rearguard. The nature conservationists seem to be less certain about their social purpose and partake of both sets of values (paradigms).

It is often asserted that environmentalism is on the decline, that the movement peaked with Earth Day 1970 and has diminished in importance as economic concerns have become increasingly urgent (Dunlap and Dillman, 1976; Dunlap and Van Liere, 1977; Honnold and Nelson, 1981; Schnaiberg, 1980). Is this true? It is helpful to examine this question from several perspectives.

Economic concerns clearly have become more urgent since 1970; even environmentalists give them first rank in urgency (Milbrath, 1981c). The people who claim the primacy of economic values over environmental values, the "rearguard," captured the United States presidency in 1980. The politicians devote less attention to the environment, and this depresses media coverage; recently, however, media coverage of environmental degradation has been extensive in the United States. Many environmental laws have been passed, and many people feel they are working well (Mitchell, 1980c); this diminishes the clamor for change. On the other hand, concern about environmental protection and values continues as high as ever (Althoff and Greig, 1977; Bowman, 1977; Milbrath, 1981b, 1981c, 1984; Mitchell, 1978, 1979a, 1980c; Utrup, 1978; Table 2 in this chapter). The range of environmental matters to be concerned about keeps growing (energy, toxics, nuclear power, land use, resource depletion). Fear of nuclear energy is growing (Milbrath, 1984; Mitchell, 1980b, 1981, 1982). The deemphasis of environmental values and proposed weakening of environmental laws by the Reagan administration have raised a public outcry and swelled memberships in environmental organizations. Both the Harris poll and a *New York Times*/CBS poll in early 1983 showed a significant increase from 1981 in the percentage of Americans desiring to *strengthen* environmental protection. The new values and concerns of environmentalism seem to have taken root to become a permanent aspect of public life in modern industrial societies (Milbrath, 1984).

I recently presented a graduate seminar on "Environmentalism as a Social Movement." Our study group examined numerous articles and books on the environmental movement (in particular the April 1980 issue of the *Natural Resources*

Journal, which has a symposium on "Whither Environmentalism?"). At the conclusion of our deliberations, we were able to arrive at the following generalizations about the environmental movement:

1. It is a value-oriented reformist movement, but we must make a distinction between environmentalists who wish to retain the present socioeconomic-political system and those who wish to change it drastically. Environmental organizations typically try to appeal to both types.
2. The movement is viewed sympathetically by a high percentage of the general public (in the range of 60 to 80 percent) in most developed industrial countries of the West. There is less awareness and fewer sympathizers in Eastern European countries and in less developed countries.
3. The movement is well institutionalized in the West and has been sufficiently successful to generate considerable opposition (mostly by defenders of the DSP). There are many voluntary organizations that make up the movement, with formal memberships running into hundreds of thousands, even millions. In West Germany more people belong to environmental organizations than to political parties (Milbrath, 1984). These organizations are large enough to have their own bureaucracies and lobbyists and are able to have significant impact on legislation as well as on the decisions in public bureaucracies.
4. Most of the organizations that make up the movement have a democratic system for selecting leadership; as with most organizations, leadership tends to be oligarchic, with some rotation of leadership over the years (Devall, 1970b).
5. The leadership seems exceptionally dedicated to its cause, with many of the leaders working for low salaries; they tend to be well educated, not charismatic or fanatic. The leadership tends to be drawn from the upper-middle and upper classes (as is true of most organizations), but general membership of the organizations spreads across the full spectrum of socioeconomic status.
6. Members are recruited either by direct mail or by proselytizing from person to person. Perception of environmental threat is a prominent motive for joining, as is the desire to be out in nature together with others with similar interests.
7. Perception of dire threat from an environmental insult, such as the discovery of toxic waste in a neighborhood, can galvanize previously unaware and inactive persons to form a new organization and to take many kinds of political action. Most of these groups are local, focusing on their immediate problem. Many hundreds of such groups have been formed in the past few years. Some of the participants have become permanent environmental activists (Shaw and Milbrath, 1983).
8. About 10 percent of the broad public in the United States belong to an environmental organization, but a much smaller percentage (perhaps around 1 percent) are active (Milbrath, 1981c; Mitchell, 1980a). The members of this active group tend to be well educated and middle class.
9. We have already indicated that the movement is opposed by defenders of the DSP, but it is significant that no broad antienvironmental movement has been generated. Environmentalism is perceived as valuable by most people; therefore, those who might wish to oppose the movement do not feel that they can be openly antienvironmental. Even Ronald Reagan and James Watt claim that they are environmentalists.

10. At the levels of the state and federal governments, there is a great deal of co-operation among environmental groups in supporting or opposing legislation and in transmitting messages to public bureaucracies. Although local groups also are willing to cooperate, most of these groups act independently. The various groups rarely compete for members, although they sometimes compete for recognition. Since there already is considerable diversity within the move-ment, there has been little pressure toward splintering. Many people belong to several environmental organizations, and this cross-cutting of memberships is likely to reduce any tendency toward splintering.

11. Most groups are supported primarily by membership dues; they also hold money-raising events and receive a few grants from foundations and from private individuals.

12. Direct-action tactics, such as marches, demonstrations, and boycotts, are used by the environmental vanguard but not frequently. Most of the actions are peaceful and within channels. There seems to be no disposition whatsoever for the movement to become violently revolutionary, at least not so far.

13. The emotional component of the environmental movement is very important. It is based on values that are cherished dearly by most members.

14. The beliefs of the movement are slowly being articulated into an ideology, a new environmental paradigm. This emerging paradigm seems to be widely shared at the elite level, but there still is considerable belief diversity among the rank and file (Stallings, 1973; Utrup, 1979).

15. Because of belief similarities, the movement has important linkages to the antinuclear movement, the peace movement, the women's movement, and the consumer movement. Environmental beliefs and values also are similar to what Inglehart (1971, 1977, 1981, 1982) conceptualizes as "postmaterialism" (Watts and Wandesforde-Smith, 1981). Inglehart theorizes that contemporary young adults, raised in an era of material affluence, have downplayed material values while elevating values such as participation, self-realization, environ-mental protection, and quality of life.

Correlates of Environmentalism

Why is it that some people become environmentalists and others do not? Writers for the popular media and scholars often try to answer such questions by using demographic categories, such as sex, age, and social class. Normally these categories are instructive, since they stand for certain types of background and learning experiences. However, demographic categories explain very little of the difference between environmentalists and nonenvironmentalists; Van Liere and Dunlap (1980) reviewed a number of studies to arrive at this conclusion. Belief and value variables explain much more of the difference (Milbrath, 1979, 1981b, 1984); however, since a great deal of the research in this area has used demographic categories, it still will be useful to begin our inquiry by looking at those factors.

Environmentalism has been measured in a variety of ways in these studies. Usually an expression of a belief in or support for environmental protection is a central aspect of the measure. The choice of measure may affect the strength of the observed relationship (Van Liere and Dunlap, 1981b) but seldom the direction. The generalizations that follow hold across many specific studies using many

Table 3. Example of an Environmental Scale.

1. Generally speaking, how strongly do you favor or oppose the environmental movement?

   strongly oppose   -3   -2   -1   0   1+   2+   3+   strongly favor

2. If the government planned to clean up pollution in your community, how strongly would you favor or oppose raising taxes for these projects, knowing that your own taxes would go up?

   strongly oppose   -3   -2   -1   0   1+   2+   3+   strongly favor

3. I perceive the condition of the environment as:

   no problem   1   2   3   4   5   6   7   a large problem

4. How concerned are you about the environment?

   not at all   1   2   3   4   5   6   7   extremely
   concerned   concerned

5. Some people have suggested that protecting the environment could result in some people losing their jobs. Assuming that we have to settle for somewhat higher unemployment in order to protect the environment, is it more important to protect jobs or to protect the environment?

   more important to   3   2   1   0   1   2   3   more important to
   protect jobs   protect
                                                            environment

specific measures. (An environmentalism scale that I have found useful is presented in Table 3; see Weigel and Weigel, 1978, for another example.)

    Demographic Indicators. First let us look at age as a correlate of environmentalism. Many studies have shown that younger persons are more environmentally oriented than older persons (Buttel, 1979; Buttel and Flinn, 1977, 1978b; Dillman and Christenson, 1975; Eastman, Hoffer, and Randall, 1974; Honnold, 1981; Hornback, 1974; Jackson, 1980; McTeer, 1978; Milbrath, 1981c; Mitchell, 1978, 1980c; Rathbun and Lindner, 1980; Uyeki, 1980). Simple self-interest helps to explain some of this relationship; undertaking several years of effort to clean up the environment can hardly be as important to someone who expects to live only another eight or ten years as it is to a person who is looking forward to sixty or more years of continued life. Additionally, vigorous physical contact with the natural environment, such as hiking, is likely to be much more attractive to a young person than an older person. Furthermore, environmental topics are likely to have been part of the curriculum for persons passing through the schools in the past ten years, whereas those topics were largely unknown to people who went to school forty or fifty years ago. While the relationship between age and environmentalism typically is statistically significant, the correlations usually are fairly low (in the .20 to .30 range).

    Studies using gender as a variable show that females typically are more environmentally oriented than males (Honnold, 1981; Jackson, 1980; McStay and Dunlap, 1982; Merchant, 1980; Rathbun and Lindner, 1980; Ray, 1975; Uyeki, 1980; Zuiches, 1976). As mentioned earlier, environmentalists tend to have a stronger and more generalized sense of compassion than nonenvironmentalists do.

In modern society females are socialized to be more compassionate than males. Women are expected to be nurturing and protective, whereas males are expected to be aggressive and competitive. This nurturing and protective posture of females shows up particularly strongly in their opposition to nuclear power (Brody, 1981; Passino and Lounsbury, 1976; Reed and Wilkes, 1980), in desires for strong regulation against polluters, and in vigorous actions to protect people against the dangers of toxic wastes. For example, most of the indigenous leaders among the homeowners mobilized by the toxic waste crisis at Love Canal in Niagara Falls, New York, were women (Levine, 1982; Shaw and Milbrath, 1983).

The relationship between environmentalism and social class is quite complex and difficult to summarize in a few sentences. We noted earlier that many of the members, and particularly the leaders, of environmental organizations come from the middle or upper-middle class. It is often charged in polemical antienvironmental essays that the environmental movement is an upper-class movement. Tucker (1977, 1982a, 1982b) assumes that economic self-interest is the major basis on which people choose their postures toward environmentalism. Since the people in the upper-middle class already have a good job and a sufficient supply of goods, they selfishly now would like to slow down economic growth so that they can continue to enjoy pristine nature. Poorer people, however, need more material goods and desire continued economic growth much more highly than they desire environmental protection. Tucker implies that environmentalism is a selfish action by a privileged class seeking to suppress the aspirations of those who are not so privileged. Is this portrait accurate?

Empirical studies of the relationship between environmentally protective beliefs and social class do not support the portrait. Socioeconomic status is weakly related to expressions of environmental concern and to support of environmental protection; there is contradictory evidence on the direction of the relationship. In some studies status and concern are positively related, while in other studies they are negatively related (Buttel and Flinn, 1974, 1978b; Cutler, 1981; Devall, 1970a; Eastman, Hoffer, and Randall, 1974; Grossman and Potter, 1977; Jackson, 1980; Koenig, 1975; Tognacci, Weigel, Wideen, and Vernon, 1972; Uyeki, 1980). In thinking about this mystery, we should remember that, while environmental concern is strong at all ranks of socioeconomic status, the people who are active in environmental organizations come mainly from the middle class (Mitchell, 1980a); nearly all organizations with a broad base are led by people from the middle class. The implication that working-class people have little interest in beautiful nature or in being free from pollution simply is not borne out by the facts. As pointed out above, working-class people have a strong desire for intimate interaction with nature, and recent studies investigating concern for a clean environment show no difference by social class (Milbrath, 1981c; Mitchell, 1980c; Utrup, 1978).

One of the reasons that summary measures of socioeconomic status do not show clear-cut relationships to environmentalism is that the components of what is normally thought of as class measurement (education, income, and occupation) do not relate to environmentalism in the same way. Many studies have shown a small but significant positive relationship between education and awareness of the environment and levels of environmental concern (Buttel, 1979; Buttel and Flinn, 1977, 1978a, 1978b; Cauley and Groves, 1975; Cohen, 1973; Devall, 1970a; Dillman and Christenson, 1975; Hornback, 1974; Mitchell, 1980a; Rathbun and Lindner,

1980; Simon, 1971; Strand, 1981; Tognacci, Weigel, Wideen, and Vernon, 1972; Watkins, 1974, 1975; Weigel, 1977; Wohlwill, 1979; Zuiches, 1976). Over the last two decades, entire national populations have learned about the existence of environmental problems. It is impossible for a person to become concerned about something of which he is not aware. Education and even IQ (Horvat and Voelker, 1976) are significant influences speeding up the process of becoming aware. Environmental knowledge is complex and integrative; education and interest in learning help people to grasp its meaning.

Income is correlated with education, but, as a social influence on environmentalism, it acts quite differently from education. Economic self-interest seems to mediate much of the relationship between income and environmentalism (Rathbun and Lindner, 1980). What little relationship there is seems to be curvilinear; persons who are the highest and lowest in income tend to be a little less environmentally oriented than people in the middle (Buttel and Flinn, 1978b; Milbrath, 1984; Mitchell, 1978, 1980c; Watkins, 1975). Persons of very high income tend to be employed in business, and business people tend to hold economic values more highly than environmental values. Very poor people also strongly desire a better economic situation. Persons of middle income tend to be highly educated and more environmentally aware, as we just noted. In regression analyses income tends to wash out as an explanatory variable for environmental concern.

We unravel the mystery a little further when we turn to an examination of occupation. Many studies have used occupational status as a measure, but the findings have been very equivocal; that is because it is the wrong kind of occupational measure to apply. It is much more relevant to categorize people according to their sector of employment. Persons who are primarily engaged in the production and sale of material goods (Cotgrove, 1982, calls it the market sector) tend to be less environmentally oriented than persons who primarily provide services (the nonmarket sector) (Cotgrove, 1982; Cotgrove and Duff, 1980; Milbrath, 1984; Sewell, 1971). Governmental regulations in many countries inhibit persons engaged in extraction and manufacturing from discharging their wastes into the environment. These regulations are a bothersome burden, consuming both time and money, and are resented by many people in the production sector; they claim that the regulations inhibit their ability to make money. Persons in the service sector also bear some cost of environmental protection, but these costs are camouflaged, whereas the benefits of a safe and clean environment are visible and highly valued. There are clear value differences with respect to the environment between these groups; persons in the production sector tend to value material goods more highly, whereas persons in the service sector tend to value a clean environment more highly (Cotgrove, 1982; Milbrath, 1981a, 1981c). The direction of causation is not clear. Are there initial differences in values that lead young people to choose careers in either the production sector or the service sector (Duff and Cotgrove, 1982); or, once people are on the job, are these values strongly taught and reinforced in each of these sectors? It is probable that both kinds of influences are at work to produce this difference. Simple measures of class status cannot capture the richness of the relationships just discussed; that is why they do a poor job of explaining environmentalism.

Cotgrove (1982, pp. 95–96) is the most prominent proponent of using sector of employment to explain environmentalism:

Our own data point to some tentative conclusions on the class location of environmentalists. At the level of ideology, the majority reject the ideology of market capitalism. . . . Their second main difference is in their lack of commitment to material and economic goals compared with the traditional left. Unlike the trade union officials, environmentalists share the dominant paradigm view that material and nonmaterial values are antagonistic. But they plump for nonmaterial goals and values. . . . Our analysis suggests that environmentalism is an expression of the interests of those whose class position in the "nonproductive" sector locates them at the periphery of the institutions and processes of industrial capitalist societies. . . . It is a protest against alienation from the processes of decision making, and the depoliticization of issues through the usurpation of policy decisions by experts, operating within the dominant economic values. . . . Their attack is not simply rooted in their subordinate position. It is also a challenge to the goals and values of the dominant class, and the structures and institutions through which these are realized. Environmentalists' rejection of beliefs in the efficacy of the market, risk taking, and reward for achievement, and of the overriding goal of economic growth and of economic criteria, is a challenge to the hegemonic ideology which legitimates the institutions and politics of industrial capitalism. . . . What we are suggesting then is that any understanding of the quite different values and beliefs of environmentalists and industrialists is to be found in part in their relations to the core economic institutions of society. Environmentalists are drawn predominantly from a specific fraction of the middle class, whose interests and values diverge markedly from other groups in industrial societies.

Most studies that have examined the relationship between race and environmentalism have shown that blacks are less environmentally oriented than whites (Hershey and Hill, 1977-78; Rathbun and Lindner, 1980). The major economic-political preoccupation of American blacks has been to improve their economic situation and to achieve equal rights. Since many blacks still have not attained these goals, they are unlikely to take on a new cause that they regard as lower in priority (Kreger, 1973). There is little evidence that blacks actively oppose environmentalism; many of them are concerned about pollution and toxics (Cutler, 1981; Mitchell, 1978; United Auto Workers, 1973). An April 1983 *New York Times*/CBS poll showed that blacks were as concerned as whites about maintaining high environmentally protective standards. However, there are apparently very few messages and very few reinforcements in the black culture to encourage participation in the environmental movement.

Using Beliefs and Values to Explain Environmentalism. Measures of beliefs and values are much more highly correlated with environmentalism than demographic measures are. Most of the belief and value differences between the environmental vanguard and the DSP defenders in the rearguard have already been set forth in Table 1. It should be reemphasized that these beliefs and values cluster into structures that constitute ideologies. The better educated and more sophisticated a person is, the more tightly organized this ideological structure becomes. Existing research would make it possible to elaborate these world views much more thoroughly than the formulation shown in Table 1, but that is a tortuous inquiry that not only would be likely to bore the reader, and would be difficult to remember, but also would inordinately lengthen this chapter.

Even though one can specify important belief and value differences between environmentalists and nonenvironmentalists, it still begs the question "Why do some people become environmentalists whereas others do not?" While self-interest explanations frequently are proffered, it often is not clear what one's self-interest truly is. Is it in the best interest of a wealthy businessman to acquire even more wealth, or would his quality of life be more significantly improved if he had a clean and beautiful environment in which to live and recreate? Is it in the best interest of a poor laborer to emphasize economic values and jobs while he is required to breathe polluted air, fish and swim in polluted water, and be exposed to toxic poisons?

Early childhood experiences are probably quite important. Persons who learn early in life to love and cherish nature are likely to retain that value; it is likely to influence later decisions with respect to training and career choice. Similarly, persons who develop compassionate personalities learn how to empathize with and feel the suffering of other peoples, other species, and other generations. This ability to empathize naturally leads them to take a wider range of factors into consideration and to take a longer time perspective; such persons are much more likely to see the importance of environmental protection (Borden and Francis, 1978; Milbrath, 1975, 1979, 1984).

An explanatory factor that is not often considered, but is vitally important for understanding environmentalism, is social learning. People are slowly being forced to recognize that they are injuring their environment. Most persons who have become environmentalists have gone through the experience called "consciousness raising." Consciousness raising is stimulated and reinforced by societal institutions; it is a necessary ingredient in social learning (Arbuthnot and Lingg, 1975; Milbrath, 1975). We mentioned earlier that most people in the United States became aware of pollution problems in the 1960s but did not become aware of resource depletion and toxic waste problems until the late 1970s; social learning was taking place in both instances. In social learning, nature is the most powerful teacher. When people begin to hurt seriously or when their world no longer works the way it is supposed to, they become motivated to learn about this new environmental condition with which they must come to terms. Our studies show numerous instances where people have learned to become environmentalists (Milbrath, 1975, 1984); interestingly, there are almost no instances of people learning to become nonenvironmentalists or antienvironmentalists.

Vanguard Versus Rearguard: Postures Toward Social Change

The vanguard and the rearguard (identified in Figure 1) both strive to have their belief paradigm dominate the thought patterns and the decisional processes of modern industrial societies. Social learning is the main social process providing hope that the new environmental paradigm (NEP) of the vanguard can become the dominant social paradigm (DSP). How far has that social learning progressed?

What are the possible consequences of this learning process for politics and social change in the near future? The best evidence that we can bring to bear on these questions derives from a three-nation (England, West Germany, and the United States) comparative study of environmental beliefs and values. In this study information was gathered not only from a random sample of the public but also from samples of the following elites: environmentalists, business leaders, labor leaders, and elected and appointed officials. The study was conducted in the three nations by means of mail questionnaires (approximately 50 percent response rate) in 1980 and was repeated in 1982. The questions were crafted through extensive pretests and were as close to identical as possible in each of the three countries as well as across study years.

The heart of the difference between adherents of the old dominant social paradigm and the advocates of a new environmental paradigm is the conception each group has of the relationship between humans and nature. Humans have always drawn their sustenance from nature, but people differ in their beliefs about the extent to which humans should manipulate and control nature. In essence, it comes down to a value question: Which do we value more highly—keeping nature healthy or amassing material wealth? One section of the questionnaire was introduced by this statement: "The following are contrasting statements on emphases or directions our society should be taking. Please mark the box with the number indicating the extent of your preference for one or the other emphasis." The contrasting emphases were separated by a seven-point semantic differential scale. Table 4 shows the contrasting emphases people gave to preserving nature for its own sake as opposed to using nature to produce goods. Frequency distributions and mean scores are shown for the general public and for various leadership groups in the United States in 1980 and 1982 and in England and Germany in 1982 (this question was not asked in England and Germany in 1980).

One powerful impression from Table 4 is the broad distribution of people across all seven categories; this was true not only for the public in each country but also for the leaders. The mean score for the public in the United States and England is very close to the middle category. Germans are somewhat more likely than Americans and English to believe that we should preserve nature for its own sake, but there are many Germans who believe the opposite. We should not infer from the table that individuals are experiencing severe inner conflict between these two values; if that were the case, there would be high percentages in the middle categories (as, for example, United States officials in 1980 and English officials in 1982). The more valid inference is that people hold widely differing beliefs about the proper relationship between humans and nature. Environmentalists and business leaders in all three countries, but especially in the United States, exemplify these wide differences. Nearly all the environmentalists believe that nature should be preserved for its own sake, while business leaders are more likely to emphasize using nature to produce material goods. The people in modern industrial societies are in such disagreement about the proper relationship between humans and nature that this value difference is likely to be a major area of contention for many years to come. Note, finally, that there is very little change from 1980 to 1982.

It is rare for humans to destroy nature wantonly; instead, they usually destroy nature as they pursue other goals, which they perceive to be overriding. People in modern industrial societies have quite different perceptions about

Table 4. Beliefs About the Proper Relationship Between Humans and Nature in Three Nations (Percentage in Each Response Category).

	Preserving Nature for Its Own Sake					Using Nature to Produce the Goods We Use		
	1	2	3	4	5	6	7	Mean
United States, 1980								
General Public	12	12	16	14	19	12	14	4.15
Environmentalists	32	28	18	12	5	1	2	2.40
Business Leaders	3	5	16	12	27	21	14	4.74
Labor Leaders	11	12	10	19	19	12	17	4.27
Elected Officials	3	7	25	24	18	19	4	4.17
Appointed Officials	5	10	22	15	29	16	3	3.98
United States, 1982								
General Public	17	15	13	11	11	15	18	4.01
Environmentalists	30	26	14	10	6	7	5	2.77
Business Leaders	5	7	10	14	22	24	18	4.85
Labor Leaders	14	19	11	11	16	14	15	3.98
Elected Officials	7	13	29	13	13	11	13	4.34
Appointed Officials	6	18	17	11	23	16	9	3.84
Federal Republic of Germany, 1982								
General Public	32	16	9	6	8	14	16	3.43
Environmentalists	34	23	12	10	8	7	6	2.79
Business Leaders	15	10	12	5	20	23	15	4.34
Members of Parliament	7	17	19	11	17	19	10	4.12
England, 1982								
General Public	23	12	10	9	12	15	19	3.94
Environmentalists	28	19	18	12	8	9	6	3.02
Business Leaders	9	15	10	14	17	21	14	4.32
Public Officials	12	13	12	24	16	12	11	4.01

whether nature is being seriously damaged. Most of the people in the rearguard perceive that there is environmental damage, but they believe that it is moderate and that it can readily be corrected by technological development and legal constraints. These people typically have a strong faith in the efficacy of science and technology for solving most problems. The word "faith" seems appropriate here, since this strong belief has an almost religious character. People on the other side, the vanguard, perceive the damage to nature as much more threatening, virtually undermining society's ability to survive. These people typically have much less faith in science and technology and believe that nothing short of a basic social change will suffice to resolve environmental problems. As Cotgrove (1982) has noted, the difference between these world views is so great that the protagonists talk past each other in frustrating incomprehension. The "nature conservationists" are likely to side with the vanguard in believing that environmental damage is serious; but they also are likely to side with the rearguard in believing that most environmental problems can be solved by technological fixes. In our study we asked people which kind of change was most needed to solve environmental problems. The percentages of the people choosing between these contrasting viewpoints are reported in Table 5.

As the table shows, people in modern industrial societies are quite divided on this issue as well. Note that there is greater polarization here than in the previous table, with only a few taking a neutral position. Environmentalists very strongly believe that a basic change in society is needed, while business leaders almost equally strongly declare that better scientific and technical development is the answer. The division between these two groups is even sharper in Germany than it is in the United States. As a matter of fact, all the groups in Germany are more sharply divided on this issue. English respondents, from all four groups, were inclined more toward basic change than their counterparts in Germany or the United States, where faith in technology is exceptionally strong. So strong is this belief in technology, especially among business leaders and public officials, that many still refuse to believe that it cannot solve the problem of shortages in natural resources.

A valuation on economic growth is a key belief of the industrial DSP; it is a dominant policy aspiration in nearly all industrialized countries. When people are simply asked whether or not economic growth is a valuable thing, a high proportion typically assert that it is. People in industrialized countries also value a safe and clean environment. Since the vigorous pursuit of one of these values may diminish the realization of the other, trading off the two values in an item will help us discern more clearly whether we are in a transition phase between abandonment of the old paradigm and acceptance of a new one. Data on this item are presented in Table 6. This item was one of the most revealing in our study, so Table 6 displays the full distribution and the mean for each group, in each country, and for each year for which we have data. A great deal of information is presented in Table 6; it warrants careful study.

One would suppose from attending to the media and listening to political discourse that nearly everyone prefers economic growth over environmental protection; that is what the old DSP advocates, and the idea is constantly reinforced by leaders of the "establishment." The data from our studies show, however, that people in the United States chose environmental protection over economic growth

Table 5. Beliefs About the Kind of Change Most Needed to Solve Environmental Problems (Percentage in Each Response Category).

	Greater Scientific and Technical Development					Basic Change in Nature of Society		Mean
	1	2	3	4	5	6	7	
United States, 1980								
General Public	18	10	9	11	13	13	25	4.47
Environmentalists	5	3	6	14	14	19	39	5.42
Business Leaders	40	23	7	7	8	6	7	2.46
Labor Leaders	40	13	1	8	8	10	19	3.37
Elected Officials	15	13	13	11	25	11	11	4.11
Appointed Officials	16	18	12	13	20	11	11	3.79
United States, 1982								
General Public	12	9	9	11	14	19	26	4.85
Environmentalists	7	8	5	10	13	23	35	5.21
Business Leaders	33	21	13	9	8	8	8	2.94
Labor Leaders	22	13	11	8	12	16	18	3.99
Elected Officials	15	24	4	13	13	20	11	3.89
Appointed Officials	17	24	10	10	11	19	8	3.64
Federal Republic of Germany, 1982								
General Public	29	13	6	9	6	13	25	3.88
Environmentalists	14	5	3	7	6	19	46	5.27
Business Leaders	52	21	6	6	4	6	5	2.27
Members of Parliament	32	16	7	10	11	12	12	3.36
England, 1982								
General Public	8	11	6	9	11	17	37	5.04
Environmentalists	3	2	4	6	13	22	50	5.88
Business Leaders	15	16	12	10	16	17	15	4.06
Public Officials	7	21	9	13	16	13	21	4.34

Table 6. Preferences of Different Types of Respondents in Three Nations for a Societal Emphasis on Economic Growth vs. Environmental Protection (Percentage in Each Response Category).

	Environmental protection over economic growth									Economic growth over environmental protection						Mean	
	1		2		3		4		5		6		7			Mean	
	80	82	80	82	80	82	80	82	80	82	80	82	80	82	80	82	
United States																	
General Public	26	21	18	21	18	17	19	20	8	9	5	7	6	5	2.99	3.17	
Environmentalists	52	45	24	27	8	12	12	12	1	1	1	3	2	1	1.97	2.12	
Business Leaders	8	5	5	7	16	8	30	30	28	29	6	14	8	7	4.16	4.40	
Labor Leaders	20	23	18	14	13	17	29	26	5	12	8	3	6	5	3.26	3.16	
Appointed Officials	12	5	15	19	21	17	34	34	11	17	7	8	1	0	3.45	3.62	
Elected Officials	5	13	19	17	23	17	32	36	12	9	5	4	4	4	3.58	3.40	
England																	
General Public	29	28	19	24	18	11	22	16	6	8	2	6	4	7	2.80	2.955	
Conservation Society	66	57	25	27	3	9	5	4	1	2	0	1	0	0	1.48	1.70	
(same as Environmentalists in 82)																	
Nature Conservationists	44	—	23	—	15	—	13	—	2	—	2	—	2	—	2.18	—	
Business Leaders	13	10	15	18	20	17	37	35	10	12	3	6	3	3	3.38	3.49	
Labor Leaders	28	—	14	—	19	—	26	—	5	—	4	—	4	—	2.95	—	
Public Officials	13	14	19	19	25	22	27	29	11	8	3	6	3	1	3.23	3.22	
Federal Republic of Germany																	
General Public	38	31	13	13	9	11	18	13	6	8	5	12	11	12	2.99	3.38	
Environmentalists	56	61	20	14	5	5	6	5	4	3	3	7	6	5	2.16	2.14	
Business Leaders	17	7	14	14	11	14	31	29	15	19	9	15	4	2	3.55	3.92	
Public Officials	26	13	22	22	9	18	28	28	9	10	4	6	1	3	2.88	3.28	

by a ratio of 3 to 1 in both 1980 and 1982. The public in Germany also selected environmental protection over economic growth by a ratio of 3 to 1 in 1980 and 2 to 1 in 1982; in England the ratio was nearly 5 to 1. These high ratios in favor of environmental protection were not simply an artifact of question wording or of the use of a mail questionnaire. In the fall of 1981, the Minnesota poll used a similar question in a personal interview and found the public there selecting environmental protection over economic growth by a ratio of 2.5 to 1. In the fall of 1979, the Harris survey used a nearly identical question in a personal interview study with 7,010 respondents; it found a 2-to-1 ratio in favor of environmental protection.

This question much more strongly differentiates groups within countries than it shows differences across countries. Environmentalists in all three countries were nearly unanimously in favor of environmental protection over economic growth. It might be supposed that business leaders would be nearly unanimous in the opposite direction, but that was not the case. Business leaders in all three countries, and in both waves of the study, tended to be undecided when they attempted to choose between these two values; high percentages took the neutral or near neutral position. This tradeoff seems to be somewhat more divisive among the public in Germany than in England and the United States. The large differences between groups within countries signals that this will be an issue of strong political contention for many years to come.

As was pointed out previously, environmentally related beliefs and values form into structures that we call paradigms. The following analysis most clearly portrays the differences in these belief structures between the vanguard and the rearguard. For this analysis we use the whole file, including the elites as well as the public, and utilize three variables to divide the samples into eight types. The first variable divides the people in the sample by whether they perceive the condition of the environment as a large problem or a small problem. At the next stage, each of these groups is divided between those who believe that environmental problems can be solved by better technology and those who believe that a basic change in society is required (the same items as in Table 5). The resulting four groups are divided once more between those who believe that there are limits to growth and those who deny such limits. These divisions are sketched out graphically at the top of Tables 7, 8, and 9. (Tables 8 and 9 for Germany and England report data only for 1982; the item contrasting technological development with basic social change was not administered in those two countries in 1980.)

The persons in Type 1, on the left side of the tables, believe that the environmental problem is a small problem that can be fixed by technological development and that there are no limits to growth. These are typical central beliefs within the dominant social paradigm (DSP), and it seemed appropriate to label this type as "rearguard." The persons with the opposite set of beliefs (Type 8)— those who say that there is a large environmental problem that can be solved only by basic social change and that there are limits to growth—can appropriately be labeled as the "vanguard." Persons who believe that there is a large environmental problem but that it can be solved by better technology rather than by basic social change, and that there are limits to growth, have been labeled "nature conservationists" (Type 6). Each of the eight types has a somewhat distinctive belief structure, but the rearguard and the vanguard have the most tightly organized

Table 7. Types of Actors in Social Change (Portrait of a Revolution in Process), U.S. Sample 1980 and 1982.

	SMALL PROBLEM								LARGE PROBLEM							
Perceived Condition of Environment																
Change Most Needed to Solve Environmental Problems	Better Technology				Basic Change in Society				Better Technology				Basic Change in Society			
Are There Limits to Growth?	no limits		yes, limits		no limits		yes, limits		no limits		yes, limits		no limits		yes, limits	
Type Name and No.	1 Reargard		2 Establishment		3 Weakly Active Est. Followers		4 Undecided Middle		5 Nat. Cons. Est. Followers		6 Nature Conservationists		7 Young, Lower-Class Env. Sympathizers		8 Vanguard	
Year	80	82	80	82	80	82	80	82	80	82	80	82	80	82	80	82
Number of People in Sample:	348	203	229	105	165	103	260	183	78	49	112	69	108	58	351	250
Percent of Whole File	21	20	14	10	10	10	16	18	5	5	7	7	7	6	21	24
Percent of Public	18	17	14	9	11	14	19	26	5	4	8	6	8	5	18	19
Postures Toward Social Change:																
(Percent) Probably Change Parties	9	15	8	14	4	11	12	18	6	33	10	50	8	46	43	68
(Mean) Support Direct Action	2.29	2.24	2.53	2.34	2.71	2.99	3.29	3.20	3.24	3.61	3.92	4.15	4.01	4.57	4.56	5.11
(Mean) Support Peace Movement		2.52		2.70		3.07		3.44		3.98		4.16		4.60		5.41
(Percent) Join Environmental Groups	17	23	22	31	24	22	24	35	25	41	35	56	37	46	54	72
(Percent-Mean) Active on Env. Issues[a]	17	2.85	22	2.61	17	2.31	27	2.75	30	2.90	28	3.77	31	3.29	48	3.79
(Percent) Complained About Env. Problem		41		41		38		48		47		71		57		78
(Mean) Need for Nuclear Power	6.10	5.81	5.90	5.26	5.37	5.09	5.18	4.34	5.76	4.56	5.00	4.21	4.54	3.55	3.79	2.61
(Mean) Planning vs. Market	3.83	4.61	3.52	4.61	3.20	4.19	3.02	3.93	3.06	3.73	2.56	3.34	2.31	3.23	2.41	2.82
(Mean) Preserve Nature vs. Produce Goods	4.82	5.13	4.56	4.27	4.38	4.27	4.06	3.98	3.97	3.65	4.04	3.51	3.59	3.31	2.71	2.74
(Mean) Avoid vs. Accept Risks		4.52		4.36		3.70		3.53		3.27		3.52		2.65		2.56
(Mean) Env. Protection vs. Economic Growth	4.12	4.45	3.76	4.11	3.57	3.76	3.03	3.02	2.87	3.00	2.56	2.34	2.30	2.36	1.94	1.87
Demographics:																
Percent in Service Sector	29	30	32	38	48	39	46	57	47	37	45	64	54	54	59	76
Percent Male	81	89	78	79	66	67	59	60	71	75	74	77	50	55	57	59
Education	high		high		medium		low		medium		medium		low		high	
Income	high		high		medium		low		medium		medium		low		medium high	
Age	medium		older		medium		medium		older		older		younger		young	

[a] 1980 figures show percentages; 1982 figures show means.

Table 8. Types of Actors in Social Change (Portrait of a Revolution in Process), German Sample 1982.

Perceived Condition of Environment	SMALL PROBLEM				LARGE PROBLEM			
Change Most Needed to Solve Environmental Problems	Better Technology		Basic Change in Society		Better Technology		Basic Change in Society	
Are There Limits to Growth?	no limits	yes, limits	no limits	yes, limits	no limits	yes, limits	no limits	yes, limits
	1	2	3	4	5	6	7	8
Type Name and No.	Rearguard	Establishment	Weakly Active Est. Followers	Undecided Middle	Nat. Cons. Est. Followers	Nature Conservationists	Young, Lower-Class Env. Sympathizers	Vanguard
Number of People in Sample	85	307	17	165	34	242	29	458
Percent of Whole File	6	23	1	12	3	18	2	34
Percent of Public	5	24	1	15	3	20	2	29
Postures Toward Social Change:								
(Percent) Probably Change Parties	8	9	6	15	13	34	29	50
(Mean) Support Direct Action	1.95	2.47	3.12	3.41	3.74	4.37	4.83	5.63
(Mean) Support Peace Movement	2.44	3.14	3.75	4.05	4.15	4.89	5.52	6.01
(Percent) Join Environmental Groups	19	15	12	13	24	31	38	47
(Mean) Active on Env. Issues	3.38	3.49	3.29	3.25	4.41	4.16	4.38	4.68
(Percent) Complained About Env. Problem	18	23	29	22	33	38	36	54
(Mean) Need for Nuclear Power	6.39	5.90	5.47	4.98	5.47	4.67	3.31	2.81
(Mean) Planning vs. Market	6.42	5.68	4.24	4.99	4.71	5.44	4.76	4.56
(Mean) Preserve Nature vs. Produce Goods	4.51	3.98	4.24	3.51	3.41	3.26	3.86	2.99
(Mean) Avoid vs. Accept Risks	4.15	3.36	3.94	3.45	2.85	3.02	3.07	2.56
(Mean) Env. Protection vs. Economic Growth	4.36	3.74	3.76	3.25	3.16	3.10	4.03	2.48
Demographics:								
Percent in Service Sector	22	33	33	51	33	44	58	56
Percent Male	81	71	59	53	76	65	72	62
Education	high	medium	medium	low	medium	low	medium	high
Income	high	high	high	medium	medium	low	low	low
Mean Age	42	47	46	41	36	46	36	38

Table 9. Types of Actors in Social Change (Portrait of a Revolution in Process), English Sample 1982.

Perceived Condition of Environment	SMALL PROBLEM				LARGE PROBLEM			
Change Most Needed to Solve Environmental Problems	Better Technology	Basic Change in Society			Better Technology		Basic Change in Society	
Are There Limits to Growth?	no limits	yes, limits	no limits	yes, limits	no limits	yes, limits	no limits	yes, limits
	1	2	3	4	5	6	7	8
Type Name and No.	Rearguard	Establishment	Weakly Active Est. Followers	Undecided Middle	Nat. Cons. Est. Followers	Nature Conservationists	Young, Lower-Class Env. Sympathizers	Vanguard
Number of People in Sample	101	99	96	185	12	31	43	310
Percent of Whole File	12	11	11	21	1	4	5	35
Percent of Public	9	14	19	25	2	3	5	24
Postures Toward Social Change:								
(Percent) Probably Change Parties	4	8	7	18	25	24	26	53
(Mean) Support Direct Action	2.67	3.00	3.01	3.17	3.58	3.90	3.72	5.10
(Mean) Support Peace Movement	2.73	2.95	3.40	3.62	3.58	4.29	4.42	5.37
(Percent) Join Environmental Groups	22	25	18	34	33	57	49	77
(Mean) Active on Env. Issues	2.31	2.22	2.22	2.37	3.08	2.74	2.92	3.62
(Percent) Complained About Env. Problem	42	43	40	46	75	53	56	88
(Mean) Need for Nuclear Power	5.55	5.42	4.75	4.59	5.42	4.81	4.00	2.84
(Mean) Planning vs. Market	4.53	3.64	3.57	3.21	3.33	2.74	3.24	2.50
(Mean) Preserve Nature vs. Produce Goods	4.97	4.25	4.12	4.01	3.25	3.48	3.17	2.84
(Mean) Avoid vs. Accept Risks	4.55	3.86	3.63	3.63	2.58	3.10	2.93	2.49
(Mean) Env. Protection vs. Economic Growth	4.30	3.49	3.16	2.81	2.83	2.48	2.19	1.62
Demographics:								
Percent in Service Sector	34	27	35	43	27	73	47	62
Percent Male	87	63	69	75	83	73	77	60
Education	high	medium	low	medium/high	low	high	low	high
Income	high	high	low	med./high	medium	medium	med./high	low
Mean Age	47	49	47	48	52	48	46	49

structures; they also are more likely to attract the elites. When these eight types were distributed as a dimension, in the manner shown in the three tables, we discovered that many other variables in the study distributed linearly along the dimension. This point can be substantiated most clearly by an examination of the findings for the items dealing with posture toward social change, as reported in Tables 7, 8, and 9.

Change Parties. Let us begin the analysis by examining the probability that a respondent would be influenced in his choice of party at the next election by its policy on environmental questions. The percentage of people reporting that they would probably change parties ascends in a nearly linear fashion as we scan across all three tables from Type 1 to Type 8. In 1980, in the United States, only 8 or 9 percent of the people in the rearguard indicated that they would probably change parties based on environmental concerns, but 43 percent of the vanguard indicated that they would probably do so. By 1982 these percentages had risen dramatically in each of the types; 68 percent of Type 8 claimed that they would change parties. The near-linear pattern holds for both years. The Germans and English in 1982 showed a similar pattern of ascendancy across types.

Support Direct Action. Direct action—such as protests, demonstrations, and boycotts—has become common in modern industrial societies (Barnes and Kaase, 1979; Marsh, 1977) and has frequently been used by environmentalists; Germany especially had an upsurge of such actions in the late 1970s and early 1980s. Generally, the established leadership (which already has good access) opposes the use of direct action, whereas groups lacking normal channels for influence tend to favor the use of direct action. In all three of the countries, people were quite divided over whether or not it is good for society when groups use direct action. Scanning across Tables 7, 8, and 9, we see that support for direct action ascends nearly linearly from Type 1 to Type 8 in all three countries. The linear pattern from Type 1 to Type 8 occurred so frequently that we began to treat the pattern as a variable that we correlated with other variables. The Pearson correlation of this variable with support for direct action in the United States data rose from .43 in 1980 to .54 in 1982. This finding constitutes one of several indicators that, on these issues, conflict is sharpening in the United States between the rearguard and the vanguard. The German data showed a similarly sharply ascending order from rearguard to vanguard (Pearson $r = .59$). The ascendancy in the English data was less dramatic, with a correlation of .44.

Support Peace Movement. The peace movement has been active throughout the decades since World War II, but it blossomed forth with considerable strength in Europe in the late 1970s and in the United States in 1982, enlisting hundreds of thousands in public demonstrations in favor of peace, disarmament, a nuclear weapons freeze, and so forth. Many environmentalists have also been active in the peace movement; both movements constitute a strong thrust toward social change. Support for the peace movement rises linearly as one reads across the tables from the rearguard to the vanguard. The Pearson correlation of this variable with the rearguard-vanguard dimension for the United States is .52, .54 in Germany, and .46 in England.

Join Environmental Groups. Joining a group generally has been recognized as an effective way to help ensure that one's voice is heard on public issues. In all three countries, as might be expected, there is a clear rise from rearguard to vanguard in the percentages of people reporting that they belong to environmental groups. Group participation is higher in the United States than in Germany, with England falling between the two. Since group activity is a more common form of political participation in the United States than in Germany, this finding may reflect a cultural difference between these two countries. Despite this cultural inhibition, about 60 percent of the German respondents indicated that they were interested in becoming members of environmental groups. The environmental issues seem to have special mobilizing power; as mentioned previously, more Germans now belong to environmental groups than to political parties.

Active on Environmental Issues. One item asked respondents how active they were on environmental issues. It did not ask about the direction of the activity, so some may have been trying to dilute environmental protection while others were striving to strengthen it. The most active people tended to be found toward the extremes of the rearguard-vanguard dimension (remember that most of the elites fall toward the extremes), with the higher activity levels toward the vanguard end.

Complain About Environmental Problems. Substantial percentages of respondents in the United States and England, and slightly lower percentages in Germany, reported that they had complained about environmental problems. This finding suggests that people from all walks of life have experienced annoying environmental problems, since there was not a clear linear progression from rearguard to vanguard as we noticed earlier for other variables; still, it is clear that people on the vanguard end of the dimension are much more likely to lodge such complaints.

Support Nuclear Power. As was pointed out earlier, the wisdom of developing nuclear power has been an especially divisive issue between rearguard and vanguard for many years. Scanning across the three tables, we see a decline in support for nuclear power that is almost linear from Type 1 to Type 8. The one exception, which holds for all three national samples, is the Type 5 individual, who recognizes that the environment is a large problem, would solve it through better technology, and denies limits to growth. Persons with this belief structure understandably favor nuclear power. Note in Table 7 that there was less support in the United States in 1982 than in 1980 for nuclear power within all eight types. Other items in the study also disclosed that a decline in support for nuclear power took place in the first two years of the decade.

Favor Planning Versus Market. The rearguard defenders of the DSP believe in relying heavily on the supply-and-demand market to allocate goods and services; this belief is a central article of faith within the DSP, which presumes that the market maximizes the public good. Persons who challenge this belief contend that foresight and planning are needed to ensure that the public good is adequately provided for. The means for the item "Planning versus Market," which are reported in the three tables, show that the rearguard is clearly more in favor of using the market to ensure the public good, whereas the vanguard is more in favor of using foresight and planning. It was to be expected as part of their ideology that persons who are in favor of better technology to solve environmental problems and who perceive no limits to growth are more likely to favor the use of the market.

View Regarding Use of Nature. We saw in Table 4 that people hold quite different views on the appropriate relationship between humans and nature. When this item is related to the eight types in Tables 7, 8, and 9, we see that the emphasis on using nature to produce goods declines nearly linearly from rearguard to vanguard in the United States. There was a similar decline in England and Germany.

Acceptability of Risk. Persons who are willing to use science and technology to exploit nature for the production of goods are generally more willing to accept physical risks in order to produce greater wealth. As Table 7 shows, the willingness to accept physical risks declined nearly linearly from rearguard to vanguard in the United States in 1982. A similar decline also was observable in the German and English samples, but it was not quite as linear as in the United States. The decline was not quite as steep on this issue as on some of those previously discussed, because environmentalists themselves are divided on this issue. This division is atypical in that environmentalists are nearly unanimous in holding the same positions on many other items.

Favor Environmental Protection over Economic Growth. This item, which was discussed in connection with Table 6, shows a near-linear decline in preference for economic growth as one scans across from rearguard to vanguard on all three tables. In the United States, the Pearson correlation, expressing the strength of the relationship of scores on this item with scores on the rearguard-vanguard dimension, was .45 in 1980 and .55 in 1982; this is another indication that conflict is sharpening between the rearguard and the vanguard.

What Kinds of People Are in the Rearguard and Vanguard?

If one reads down the columns of Tables 7, 8, and 9, one can obtain a descriptive portrait for each of the types. Such a discussion, however, would take us too far afield; interested readers are invited to study the tables and to arrive at their own portrait. Readers desiring a discussion of these types, as well as more discussion on the points above, should consult Milbrath (1984). Our purpose in examining these tables in this chapter is to show the extent to which people have accepted the NEP of the vanguard, to demonstrate the significant belief differences between rearguard and vanguard, and to suggest how those differences are likely to affect politics and governance in the near-term future in modern industrial societies.

The data for the percent of the public in the rearguard and vanguard categories in the three tables show that in the United States the vanguard and the rearguard currently attract approximately the same proportion of the public in support of their views, whereas in Germany and England there is more public support for the vanguard than for the rearguard. The most significant demographic difference between the rearguard and the vanguard is the tendency for the rearguard to be employed in the production sector and for the vanguard to be employed in service sector. This relationship suggests which special interests are likely to be served should the rearguard or the vanguard win the battle to determine who will shape the future direction of modern society. Assuming that modern industrial society will continue its transformation from an emphasis on production to a greater emphasis on service, we can anticipate further growth in the vanguard, since that is where those in service occupations are more likely to be found.

The tables also show that the rearguard has a high percentage of males, whereas females are more likely to be found in some of the middle categories (where more of the public is found) and in the vanguard. This finding is further empirical evidence of the modest tendency, mentioned previously, for women to be more attracted to environmentalism than men are.

Both the rearguard and the vanguard tend to be highly educated, but in all three countries those in the rearguard have more income than those in the vanguard. There was a clear tendency in the United States and Germany for the vanguard to be younger than the rearguard; age showed no clear relationship to the types in England.

It is important to keep in mind that most of the public in all three countries are found in the middle categories, sharing some of the beliefs of the vanguard and some of the beliefs of the rearguard. People are uncomfortable when they are faced with a social condition that makes them feel unsure about what they really believe. When confronted by puzzling, unsatisfactory, and painful social and economic conditions, they are likely to feel pressure toward some kind of resolution. Under such conditions people will be tempted to retrogress to an earlier vision of the "good society" with its "tried-and-true values." The Reagan victories in 1980 and 1984 may be examples of that phenomenon. But if the paradigm that is retreated to continues to be based on false premises about how the world works, the policies that are adopted will fail, and the people are likely to turn to yet another leader promising another panacea.

Conclusion

The data shown here, plus other data that could not be reported within the space limitations of this chapter, clearly indicate that the social learning process is well under way in several advanced industrial countries (Arbuthnot and Lingg, 1975; Milbrath, 1981a), although a new basic consensus that will constitute the new DSP may not fully evolve for at least a couple of decades. The "establishment" in business and government can be expected to resist change as long as possible. As of this writing, the old DSP still holds sway over public policy despite strong clamorings from the environmental vanguard and other minorities. While this social learning process is taking place, it will be difficult for any leader to get the people to agree on basic values. There will be insufficient consensus on the kind of society we would like to live in for the government to be able to take effective action. If this lack of consensus is coupled with more frequent and more widespread resource shortages, it is virtually certain that there will be high rates of inflation and a lowering of material standards; these losses will be felt most strongly by the poor and disadvantaged. People will perceive that their socioeconomic system is no longer working; the pressure to rethink basic beliefs about how the world works will be intense.

As people struggle to find ways to express politically the new beliefs that they are developing, they are likely to find that the party structures of modern governments do not provide them with an effective channel for their views. The strong showing of Senator Gary Hart in the 1984 Democratic primaries seemed to be based, at least partly, on a frustration with traditional party structures. The traditional left-right dimension, which we are so familiar with in discussions of modern government, incorporates and institutionalizes a conflict over the ownership and management of the means of production and over the obligation of government to look after disadvantaged people. Where do environmentalists fit

on that dimension? They perceive that all the parties are striving to maximize
wealth and are taking an exploitive, extractive, and dominating role toward nature.
There is no natural home on the old left-right party dimension for the belief that
humans should live in a more harmonious relationship with nature (and the
subsidiary policy perspectives that flow from that belief). Feeling "at sea," these
NEP supporters may adhere to no party. Hart drew heavily from independents.
The three-nation study shows that, as these NEP supporters seek political expression, they are more likely than others to turn to direct action (protests, demonstrations, and so forth); they also are likely to seek expression through special-interest
groups or through citizen participation in bureaucratic decision making. Some
of them will drop out of the system and simply become indifferent to politics.

If the vanguard gains adherents and becomes more cohesive, the rearguard
defenders of the DSP are likely to organize more strongly. The basic dispute
between these two groups *may* become the dominant dimension along which
political parties become oriented. If that happens, the defenders of the DSP—the
rearguard—are likely to attract supporters from either the old left or the old right;
but these supporters are more likely to come from the right, since that is the
position the right currently defends (Dunlap and Gale, 1974; Milbrath, 1981d,
1984). At the opposite end of the new dimension, we already find that the people
in the NEP vanguard are somewhat "left-leaning" (Buttel, 1979; Buttel and Flinn,
1976; Dunlap and Allen, 1976; Dunlap and Gale, 1974; Koenig, 1975; Mazmanian
and Sabatier, 1981; Milbrath, 1984; Mitchell, 1980a; Ray, 1975; Tognacci, Weigel,
Wideen, and Vernon, 1972; Zuiches, 1976), although a few may also come over
from the right. Some of the current adherents of the left will continue to be strong
defenders of the DSP and will join the rearguard in opposing the NEP.

Cotgrove (1982, p. 92) found that the belief structure of the traditional left
is much more similar to that of the NEP than it is to the belief structure of the
DSP. The major differences between the traditional left and the NEP are that the
traditional left places more emphasis on material goods and has higher confidence
in science and technology. The traditional left is curiously silent about the proper
relationship between humans and nature; Marx and Engels gave very little attention to this relationship. Some of the neo-Marxists are trying to fill this gap by
placing environmental values in a central place in their belief and value structures
(Agger, 1979).

Environmentalists, especially the reform environmentalists, have learned
over the past decade that they must carry their battle to the political sphere in
order to realize the values that they hold dear. In Germany, where the traditional
party structure was inhospitable to their views, they have formed new "Green
Parties" that are beginning to contest successfully for public office; similar movements are under way in France. Environmentalists in England and the United
States have not come so far. Up to this point, environmental groups in the United
States have tried to appeal to both the nature conservationists and the environmental reformers. They also have tried to engender and maintain support for
environmental beliefs and values within both major political parties. Recent political and governmental actions against environmental beliefs and values have stimulated many environmental groups to become more active politically. As
mentioned earlier, they had a modicum of success in the United States in the 1982
national, state, and local elections. As of this writing, there is still little discussion

among environmentalists in the United States of the possibility of forming a new political party. Barry Commoner, a nationally recognized environmental leader, ran for president in 1980, but he was so unsuccessful in attracting media attention that most of the people never knew he was running. The data shown in this chapter suggest that there is considerable latent support for environmental beliefs and values that could be mobilized into a strong political force. Given the frustrating failures of third-party leaders attempting to build strong parties in the past in the United States, a mobilization of environmental sympathizers is more likely to occur if the central beliefs and the values of the environmental vanguard are taken up as a major thrust by one of the already established political parties.

Whether environmentalism eventually wins a strong political following is not likely to be determined by the relative attractiveness of what the two paradigms promise to do. A life of ease, luxury, and excitement as promised by the DSP has a superficial attraction compared to the NEP's admonitions to husband resources, to share, and to adopt subdued lifestyles. If attractiveness were to be the main criterion, the current DSP would be likely to continue its dominance. Continued dominance assumes, however, that the type of society produced by the DSP is sustainable. It is central to the argument of the environmental vanguard that a society based on the DSP is unsustainable. If this argument is correct, and it may well be, people will abandon the DSP because they will discover that it is no longer workable. Ultimately, the belief structure that encourages a sustainable society is the structure that will attract the political support necessary for it to become dominant. From the environmentalists' point of view, the more rapidly they can elaborate and articulate their new paradigm so as to attract followers and gain political power, the easier will be the social transition to the new society they hope to create.

References

Agger, B. *Western Marxism: An Introduction*. Santa Monica, Calif.: Goodyear, 1979.

Althoff, P., and Greig, W. H. "Environmental Pollution Control: Two Views from the General Population." *Environment and Behavior*, 1977, *9*, 441–456.

Anderson, R. W., and Lipsey, M. A. "Energy Conservation and Attitudes Toward Technology." *Public Opinion Quarterly*, 1978, *42* (1), 17–30.

Arbuthnot, J., and Lingg, S. "A Comparison of French and American Environmental Behaviors, Knowledge and Attitudes." *International Journal of Psychology*, 1975, *10*, 275–281.

Banks, J. A. *The Sociology of Social Movements*. London: Macmillan, 1972.

Barnes, S. H., and Kaase, M. (eds.). *Political Action: Mass Participation in Five Western Democracies*. Beverly Hills, Calif.: Sage, 1979.

Barnett, L. D. "A Study of the Relationship Between Attitudes Towards World Population Growth and U.S.A. Population Growth." *Journal of Bio-Social Science*, 1973, *5*, 61–69.

Barnett, L. D. "Zero Population Growth, Inc.: A Second Study." *Journal of Bio-Social Science*, 1974, *6*, 1–22.

Bartell, T. "Political Orientations and Public Response to the Energy Crisis." *Social Science Quarterly*, 1976, *57* (2), 430–436.

Bartell, T., and St. George, A. "A Trend Analysis of Environmentalists' Organizational Commitment, Tactic Advocacy, and Perceptions of Government." *Journal of Voluntary Action Research*, 1974, *3*, 41–46.

Benedict, R., Bone, H., Leavel, W., and Rice, R. "The Voters' Attitudes Toward Nuclear Power: A Comparative Study of Nuclear Moratorium Initiatives." *Western Political Quarterly*, 1980, *33* (1), 7–23.

Bookchin, M. *The Ecology of Freedom: The Emergence and Dissolution of Hierarchy.* Palo Alto, Calif.: Cheshire Books, 1982.

Borden, R. J., and Francis, J. L. "Who Cares About Ecology?: Personality and Sex Difference in Environmental Concern." *Journal of Personality*, 1978, *46*, 196–203.

Bowman, F. H. "Public Opinion and the Environment: Post-Earth Day Attitudes Among College Students." *Environment and Behavior*, 1977, *9*, 385–416.

Brody, C. J. "Nuclear Power: Sex Differences in Public Opinion." Unpublished doctoral dissertation, Department of Sociology, University of Arizona, 1981.

Buttel, F. H. "Age and Environmental Concern: A Multivariate Analysis." *Youth and Society*, 1979, *10* (3), 237–256.

Buttel, F. H., and Flinn, W. L. "The Structure of Support for the Environmental Movement, 1968–70." *Rural Sociology*, 1974, *39*, 56–69.

Buttel, F. H., and Flinn, W. L. "Environmental Politics: The Structuring of Partisan and Ideological Cleavages in Mass Environmental Attitudes." *Sociological Quarterly*, 1976, *17*, 477–490.

Buttel, F. H., and Flinn, W. L. "Conceptions of Rural Life and Environmental Concern." *Rural Sociology*, 1977, *42*, 544–555.

Buttel, F. H., and Flinn, W. L. "The Politics of Environmental Concern: The Impacts of Party Identification and Political Ideology on Environmental Attitudes." *Environment and Behavior*, 1978a, *10*, 17–36.

Buttel, F. H., and Flinn, W. L. "Social Class and Mass Environmental Beliefs: A Reconsideration." *Environment and Behavior*, 1978b, *10*, 433–450.

Buttel, F. H., and Johnson, D. E. "Dimensions of Environmental Concern: Factor Structure, Correlates, and Implications for Research." *Journal of Environmental Education*, 1977, *9* (2), 49–64.

Catton, W. R., Jr. *Overshoot: The Ecological Basis of Revolutionary Change.* Urbana: University of Illinois Press, 1980.

Cauley, V. B., Jr., and Groves, D. L. "Some Important Variables Related to Conservation Knowledge and Interest." *Journal of Youth and Adolescence*, 1975, *4* (1), 67–72.

Cohen, M. R. "Environmental Information Versus Environmental Attitudes." *Journal of Environmental Education*, 1973, *5* (2), 5–8.

Constantini, E., and Hanf, K. "Environmental Concern and Lake Tahoe: A Study of Elite Perceptions, Backgrounds and Attitudes." *Environment and Behavior*, 1972, *4* (2), 209–242.

Continental Group. *Toward Responsible Growth: Economic and Environmental Concern in the Balance.* Stamford, Conn.: Continental Group, 1982.

Cotgrove, S. F. *Catastrophe or Cornucopia: The Environment, Politics and the Future.* New York: Wiley, 1982.

Cotgrove, S.F., and Duff, A. "Environmentalism, Middle Class Radicalism and Politics." *Sociological Review*, 1980, *28* (2), 333–351.

Cutler, S.C. "Community Concern for Pollution." *Environment and Behavior*, 1981, *13* (1), 105–124.

Devall, W. B. "Conservation: An Upper-Middle Class Social Movement. A Replication." *Journal of Leisure Research*, 1970a, *2*, 123-126.

Devall, W. B. "The Governing of a Voluntary Organization: Oligarchy and Democracy in the Sierra Club." Unpublished doctoral dissertation, Department of Sociology, University of Oregon, 1970b.

Devall, W. B. "Reformist Environmentalism." *Humboldt Journal of Social Relations*, 1979, *6* (2), 129-158.

Devall, W. B. "The Deep Ecology Movement." *Natural Resources Journal*, 1980, *20*, 299-322.

Devall, W. B. "John Muir as Deep Ecologist." *Environmental Review*, 1982, *6*, 63-86.

Dillman, D. A., and Christenson, J. A. "The Public Value for Air Pollution Control: A Needed Change of Emphasis in Opinion Structures." *Cornell Journal of Social Relations*, 1975, *10* (1), 73-95.

Duff, A. G., and Cotgrove, S. F. "Types of Environmental Protest in Britain." School of Humanities and Social Sciences, University of Bath, England, 1980. (Mimeographed.)

Duff, A. G., and Cotgrove, S. F. "Social Values and the Choice of Careers in Industry." *Journal of Occupational Psychology*, 1982, *55*, 97-107.

Dunlap, R. E. (ed.). "Ecology and the Social Sciences: An Emerging Paradigm." *American Behavioral Scientist* (special issue), 1980, *24* (1).

Dunlap, R. E., and Allen, M. P. "Partisan Differences on Environmental Issues: A Congressional Rollcall Analysis." *Western Political Quarterly*, 1976, *29*, 384-397.

Dunlap, R. E., and Dillman, D. A. "Decline in Public Support for Environmental Protection: Evidence from a 1970-74 Panel Study." *Rural Sociology*, 1976, *41*, 382-390.

Dunlap, R. E., and Gale, R. P. "Party Membership and Environmental Politics: A Legislative Rollcall Analysis." *Social Science Quarterly*, 1974, *55*, 670-690.

Dunlap, R. E., and Van Liere, K. "Further Evidence of Declining Public Concern with Environmental Problems: A Research Note." *Western Sociological Review*, 1977, *8*, 108-112.

Dunlap, R. E., and Van Liere, K. *Environmental Concern: A Bibliography of Empirical Studies and a Brief Appraisal of the Literature.* Monticello, Ill.: Vance Bibliographies, 1978a.

Dunlap, R. E., and Van Liere, K. "The New Environmental Paradigm." *Journal of Environmental Education*, 1978b, *9* (4), 10-19.

Eastman, C., Hoffer, P., and Randall, A. *A Socio-Economic Analysis of Environmental Concern: Case of the Four Corners Electrical Power Complex.* Bulletin 626. Las Cruces: Agricultural Experiment Station, New Mexico State University, 1974.

Erskine, H. "The Polls: Pollution and Industry." *Public Opinion Quarterly*, 1972a, *36*, 263-280.

Erskine, H. "The Polls: Pollution and Its Costs." *Public Opinion Quarterly*, 1972b, *36*, 120-135.

Faich, R. G., and Gale, R. P. "The Environmental Movement from Recreation to Politics." *Pacific Sociological Review*, 1971, *14* (3), 270-287.

Fox, S. *John Muir and His Legacy: The American Conservation Movement.* Boston: Little, Brown, 1981.

Grossman, G. M., and Potter, H. R. "A Longitudinal Analysis of Environmental Concern: Evidence from the National Surveys." Paper presented at annual meeting of the American Sociological Association, Chicago, 1977.

Harry, J., Gale, R., and Hendee, J. "Conservation: An Upper Middle Class Social Movement." *Journal of Leisure Research,* 1969, *1,* 246-254.

Hays, S. P. *Conservation and the Gospel of Efficiency.* Cambridge, Mass.: Harvard University Press, 1959.

Hershey, M. R., and Hill, P. B. "Is Pollution a White Thing? Racial Differences in Pre-Adult Attitudes." *Public Opinion Quarterly,* 1977-78, *41* (4), 439-458.

Honnold, J. "Predictors of Public Environmental Concern in the 1970's." In D. Mann (ed.), *Environmental Policy Formation.* Lexington, Mass.: Heath, 1981.

Honnold, J., and Nelson, L. D. "Age and Environmental Concern: Some Specification of Effects." Paper presented at annual meeting of the American Sociological Association, Toronto, 1981.

Hornback, K. E. "Orbits of Opinion: The Role of Age in the Environmental Movement's Attentive Public, 1968-1972." Unpublished doctoral dissertation, Department of Sociology, Michigan State University, 1974.

Horvat, R. E., and Voelker, A. M. "Using a Likert Scale to Measure 'Environmental Responsibility.' " *Journal of Environmental Education,* 1976, *8* (1), 36-47.

Humphrey, C. R., and Buttel, F. R. *Environment, Energy, and Society.* Belmont, Calif.: Wadsworth, 1982.

Inglehart, R. "The Silent Revolution in Europe: Intergenerational Change in Post-Industrial Societies." *American Political Science Review,* 1971, *65,* 991-1017.

Inglehart, R. *The Silent Revolution: Changing Values and Political Styles Among Western Publics.* Princeton, N.J.: Princeton University Press, 1977.

Inglehart, R. "Post-Materialism in an Environment of Insecurity." *American Political Science Review,* 1981, *75* (4), 880-900.

Inglehart, R. "Value Change in Japan and the West." *Comparative Political Studies,* 1982, *14,* 445-479.

Jackson, E. L. "Perceptions of Energy Problems and the Adoption of Conservation Practices in Edmonton and Calgary." *Canadian Geographer,* 1980, *24* (2), 114-130.

Koenig, D. J. "Additional Research on Environmental Activism." *Environment and Behavior,* 1975, *7,* 472-485.

Kreger, J. "Ecology and Black Student Opinion." *Journal of Environmental Education,* 1973, *4* (3), 30-34.

Kromm, D. E., Probald, E., and Wall, G. "An International Comparison of Response to Air Pollution." *Journal of Environmental Management,* 1973, *1,* 363-375.

Levine, A. G. *Love Canal: Science, Politics, and People.* Lexington, Mass.: Heath, 1982.

Lovins, A. *Soft Energy Paths Toward a Durable Peace.* New York: Harper & Row, 1977.

McConnell, G. "The Conservation Movement: Past and Present." *Western Political Quarterly,* 1954, *7,* 463-478.

McConnell, G. "The Environmental Movement: Ambiguities and Meanings." *Natural Resources Journal,* 1971, *11,* 427-436.

McStay, J., and Dunlap, R. "Male-Female Differences in Concern for Environmental Quality: A Research Note." Scientific paper, Agricultural Research Center, Washington State University, Pullman, 1982.

McTeer, J. H. "Teenage-Adult Differences in Concern for Environmental Problems." *Journal of Environmental Education*, 1978, *9* (2), 20–23.

Marsh, A. *Protest and Political Consciousness*. Beverly Hills, Calif.: Sage, 1977.

Mazmanian, D., and Sabatier, P. "Liberalism, Environmentalism, and Partisanship in Public Policy Making: The California Coastal Commissions." *Environment and Behavior*, 1981, *13* (3), 361–384.

Merchant, C. *The Death of Nature: Women, Ecology, and the Scientific Revolution*. New York: Harper & Row, 1980.

Milbrath, L. W. "Environmental Beliefs: A Tale of Two Counties." Environmental Studies Center, State University of New York at Buffalo, 1975. (Mimeographed.)

Milbrath, L. W. "Values and Beliefs That Distinguish Environmentalists from Non-Environmentalists." Paper presented at annual meeting of the International Society for Political Psychology, Washington, D.C., 1979.

Milbrath, L. W. "Beliefs About Our Social Paradigm: Are We Moving to a New Paradigm?" Paper presented at 22nd annual convention of the International Studies Association, Philadelphia, 1981a.

Milbrath, L. W. "Environmental Values and Beliefs of the General Public and Leaders in the United States, England, Germany. In D. Mann (ed.), *Environmental Policy Formation*. Lexington, Mass.: Heath, 1981b.

Milbrath, L. W. "General Report: U.S. Component of a Comparative Study of Environmental Beliefs and Values." Occasional Paper Series, Environmental Studies Center, State University of New York at Buffalo, 1981c. (Mimeographed.)

Milbrath, L. W. "The Relationship of Environmental Beliefs and Values to Politics and Government." Paper presented at 4th annual conference of the International Society for Political Psychology, Mannheim, Germany, 1981d.

Milbrath, L. W. *Environmentalists: Vanguard for a New Society*. Albany: State University of New York Press, 1984.

Mitchell, R. C. "The Public Speaks Again: A New Environmental Survey." *Resources*, 1978, *60*, 1–6.

Mitchell, R. C. "Silent Spring/Solid Majorities." *Public Opinion*, 1979a, *2*, 16–20, 55.

Mitchell, R. C. "Since Silent Spring: Science, Technology and the Environmental Movement in the United States." In *Scientific Expertise and the Public: Conference Proceedings*. Oslo: Norwegian Research Council, Institute for Studies in Higher Education, 1979b.

Mitchell, R. C. "How 'Soft,' 'Deep,' or 'Left'? Present Constituencies in the Environmental Movement for Certain World Views." *Natural Resources Journal*, 1980a, *20*, 345–358.

Mitchell, R. C. "Polling on Nuclear Power: A Critique of the Polls After Three Mile Island." In A. Cantril (ed.), *Polling on the Issues*. Cabin John, Md.: Seven Locks Press, 1980b.

Mitchell, R. C. *Public Opinion on Environmental Issues: Results of a National Survey*. Report for the Council on Environmental Quality. Washington, D.C.: U.S. Government Printing Office, 1980c.

Mitchell, R. C. "From Elite Quarrel to Mass Movement." *Transaction/Society*, 1981, *18* (5), 76–84.

Mitchell, R. C. "Rationality and Irrationality in the Public's Perception of Nuclear Power." Paper presented at annual meeting of the American Association for the Advancement of Science, Washington, D.C., 1982.

Mitchell, R. C. "Public Opinion and Environmental Politics in the 1970s and 1980s." In N. J. Vig and M. E. Kraft (eds.), *Environmental Policy in the 1980s: The Impact of the Reagan Administration*. Washington, D.C.: Congressional Quarterly Press, 1984.

Morrison, D. E. "The Environmental Movement Moves On—and Changes." Paper presented at Purdue University Water Resources Seminar, 1972.

Morrison, D. E. "The Soft Cutting Edge of Environmentalism: Why and How the Appropriate Technology Notion is Changing the Movement." *Natural Resources Journal*, 1980, *20*, 275-298.

Murch, A. W. "Public Concern for Environmental Pollution." *Public Opinion Quarterly*, 1971, *35*, 100-106.

Naess, A. "The Shallow and the Deep, Long Range Ecology Movement." *Inquiry*, 1973, *16*, 95-100.

Nash, R. *Wilderness and the American Mind*. (Rev. ed.) New Haven, Conn.: Yale University Press, 1973.

Nelkin, D., and Pollak, M. "Political Parties and the Nuclear Energy Debate in France and Germany." *Comparative Politics*, 1980, *12* (2), 127-141.

Nelkin, D., and Pollak, M. *The Atom Besieged: Extraparliamentary Dissent in France and Germany*. Cambridge, Mass.: MIT Press, 1982.

O'Riordan, T. "The Third American Conservation Movement: New Implications for Public Policy." *Journal of American Studies*, 1971, *5*, 155-171.

O'Riordan, T. "Public Interest Environmental Groups in the United States and Britain." *American Studies*, 1979, *13*, 409-438.

Passino, E. M., and Lounsbury, J. W. "Sex Differences in Opposition to and Support for Construction of a Proposed Nuclear Power Plant." In L. M. Ward, S. Coren, A. Gruft, and J. B. Collins (eds.), *The Behavioral Basis of Design*. Vol. 1. Stroudsbourg, Pa.: Dowden, Hutchinson & Ross, 1976.

Pierce, J. C. "Water Resource Preservation: Personal Values and Public Support." *Environment and Behavior*, 1979, *11* (2), 147-161.

Rathbun, P. F., and Lindner, G. "Energy Needs vs. Environmental Values: Balancing of Competing Interests." Paper presented at annual meeting of the American Sociological Association, New York, 1980.

Ray, J. R. "Measuring Environmentalist Attitudes." *Australian and New Zealand Journal of Sociology*, 1975, *11* (2), 70-71.

Reed, J. H., and Wilkes, J. M. "Sex and Attitudes Toward Nuclear Power." Paper presented at annual meeting of the American Sociological Association, New York, 1980.

Ryan, B. F. *Social and Cultural Change*. New York: Ronald Press, 1969.

Sandbach, E. *Environment, Ideology and Policy*. Montclair, N.J.: Allanheld, Osmun, 1980.

Schnaiberg, A. *The Environment: From Surplus to Scarcity*. New York: Oxford University Press, 1980.

Schumacher, E.F. *Small Is Beautiful: Economics as If People Mattered*. New York: Harper & Row, 1973.

Schwartz, P., and Ogilvy, J. *The Emergent Paradigm: Changing Patterns of Thought and Belief*. Menlo Park, Calif.: Stanford Research International, 1979.

Sewell, W. R. D. "Environmental Perceptions and Attitudes of Engineers and Public Health Officials." *Environment and Behavior*, 1971, *3*, 23-59.

Shaw, L. G., and Milbrath, L. W. "Citizen Participation in Governmental Decision Making: The Toxic Waste Threat at Love Canal, Niagara Falls, New York." Working Paper Series, Rockefeller Institute, Albany, N.Y., 1983.

Simon, J. *The Ultimate Resource*. Princeton, N.J.: Princeton University Press, 1981.

Simon, R. J. "Public Attitudes Toward Population and Pollution." *Public Opinion Quarterly*, 1971, *35*, 93–99.

Slovic, P., Fischhoff, B., and Lichtenstein, S. "Facts vs. Fears: Perceived Risk and Opposition to Nuclear Energy." Paper presented at annual meeting of the American Association for the Advancement of Science, Washington, D.C., 1982.

Smith, W. S., Scheuneman, J. J., and Zeidberg, L. D. "Public Reaction to Air Pollution in Nashville, Tennessee." *Journal of the Air Pollution Control Association*, 1964, *14*, 445–448.

Stallings, R. A. "Patterns of Belief in Social Movements: Clarifications from an Analysis of Environmental Groups." *Sociological Quarterly*, 1973, *14*, 465–480.

Strand, P. J., "The Energy Issue, Partisan Characteristics." *Environment and Behavior*, 1981, *13* (4), 509–519.

Tognacci, L. R., Weigel, R. H., Wideen, M. F., and Vernon, D. T. A. "Environmental Quality: How Universal is Public Concern?" *Environment and Behavior*, 1972, *4*, 73–86.

Tremblay, K. R., Jr., and Dunlap, R. E. "Rural-Urban Residence and Concern with Environmental Quality: A Replication and Extension." *Rural Sociology*, 1978, *43* (3), 474–491.

Tucker, W. "Environmentalism and the Leisure Class." *Harper's*, 1977, *255*, 49–56.

Tucker, W. "The Environmental Era." *Public Opinion*, 1982a, *5* (1), 41–47.

Tucker, W. *Progress and Privilege: America in the Age of Environmentalism*. New York: Doubleday, 1982b.

United Auto Workers. *Pollution Is Not a "White Thing."* Detroit: Conservation and Resource Development Department, United Auto Workers, 1973.

Utrup, K. "Environmental Public Opinion: Trends and Tradeoffs, 1969–1978." Resources for the Future, Washington, D.C., 1978. (Mimeographed.)

Utrup, K. "How Sierra Club Members See Environmental Issues." *Sierra*, 1979, *64*, 14–18.

Uyeki, E. S. "Steps to Spaceship Earth." Paper presented at annual meeting of the American Sociological Association, New York, 1980.

Van Liere, K. D., and Dunlap, R. E. "The Social Bases of Environmental Concern: A Review of Hypotheses, Explanations and Empirical Evidence." *Public Opinion Quarterly*, 1980, *44* (2), 181–197.

Van Liere, K. D., and Dunlap, R. E. "Cognitive Integration of Social and Environmental Beliefs." Paper presented at annual meeting of the American Sociological Association, Toronto, 1981a.

Van Liere, K. D., and Dunlap, R. E. "Environmental Concern: Does It Make a Difference How It's Measured?" *Environment and Behavior*, 1981b, *13* (6), 651–676.

Watkins, G. A. "Developing a 'Water Concern' Scale." *Journal of Environmental Education*, 1974, *5* (4), 54–58.

Watkins, G. A. "Scaling of Attitudes Toward Population Problems." *Journal of Environmental Education*, 1975, *7* (1), 14–26.

Watts, N., and Wandesforde-Smith, G. "Postmaterial Values and Environmental Policy Change." In D. Mann (ed.), *Environmental Policy Formation*. Lexington, Mass.: Heath, 1981.

Weigel, R. H. "Ideological and Demographic Correlates of Pro-Ecology Behavior." *Journal of Social Psychology*, 1977, *103*, 39–47.

Weigel, R. H., and Weigel, J. "Environmental Concern: The Development of a Measure." *Environment and Behavior*, 1978, *10*, 3–15.

Wohlwill, J. F. "Social and Political Matrix of Environmental Attitudes: An Analysis of the Vote on the California Coastal Zone Regulation Act." *Environment and Behavior*, 1979, *11*, 71–85.

Yankelovich, D. *The Changing Values on Campus: Political and Personal Attitudes of Today's College Students*. New York: Washington Square Press, 1972.

Yankelovich, D. "New Rules in American Life: Searching for Self-Fulfillment in a World Turned Upside Down." *Psychology Today*, April 1981, *15*, passim.

Yankelovich, D., and Lefkowitz, B. "National Growth: The Question of the 80's." *Public Opinion*, 1980a, (3), 44–57.

Yankelovich, D., and Lefkowitz, B. "The New American Dream: The U.S. in the 1980's." *The Futurist*, 1980b, *14* (4), 3–15.

Zetterberg, H. L. "Environmental Awareness and Political Change in Sweden." Paper prepared for a conference on Environmental Awareness and Political Change, sponsored by the International Institute for Environment and Society (Berlin) and the Conservation Foundation (Washington, D.C.), in Berlin, Jan. 1978.

Zuiches, J. J. *Acceptability of Energy Policies to Mid-Michigan Families*. Research Report no. 298. East Lansing: Agriculture Experiment Station, Michigan State University, 1976.

FIVE

ᘓᘓᘓᘓᘓᘓᘓᘓᘓᘓᘓᘓᘓᘓᘓᘓᘓᘓᘓ

Contributions
of Psychohistory
to Understanding Politics

Geoffrey Cocks

Modern psychohistory came to professional consciousness in 1957 in a speech in New York to the American Historical Association by its outgoing president, William Langer. Langer (1958), whose brother Walter was a psychoanalyst, declared that if he were a young historian just starting out he would devote his career to the application of psychoanalytic insights to history. Langer then proceeded to sketch an analysis of the irrational dynamics of the human response to the Black Death, which scourged medieval Europe in the fourteenth century. Against the backdrop of the "black death" visited upon twentieth-century Europe by the Nazis, Langer's call to his colleagues to turn to a systematic study of the irrational in history was possessed of undeniable urgency, especially in the realm of political history. No doubt the influence of his brother, who during the war had produced a psychoanalytic study of Hitler for the American Office of Strategic Services, was significant (see Loewenberg, 1983).

This professional appeal, while not falling on deaf ears, nevertheless faced several problems in the way of its acceptance by historians. First, many of Langer's colleagues in their professional conservatism did not like to be told, in effect, that for some time they had been missing the point. Second, Freudian concepts, while not unknown to historians, involved in their application a somewhat daunting degree of intellectual retooling and, even more significantly, the personally threatening prospect of confession upon the couch. Finally, the enthusiastic claim for the utility of psychoanalytic theory in historical inquiry had to overcome the legacy of clumsy attempts at historical psychobiography made by psychoanalysts and other amateur historians during the height of Freudian fashion in the United States during the 1920s. Many of these works were caricatures of history and reinforced the belief of most historians that they had nothing worthwhile to learn from the psychoanalytic school.

On the other hand, Langer's arguments for the historical exploitation of psychoanalytic theory could draw on some advantageous dispositions within the field. First, the twentieth century had witnessed spectacular growth in the social sciences, areas of newly sophisticated human knowledge that offered historians intriguing new perspectives on their material. The Marxist interpretation and some of the work of the *Annales* school in France are only two examples of the many fruitful interactions along the lines of interdisciplinary collaboration. Thus, there was valuable precedent for interdisciplinary work in the field of history. Second, the American cultural and intellectual interest in Freud had remained strong, and historians themselves had not remained unaffected by this interest in the psychoanalytic perspective. Third, and most important, was the fact that historians in their work had of necessity run across and dealt with what in Freudian parlance was called the unconscious. Indeed, the traditional bent within the discipline toward studying leaders and "great men" made the psychoanalytic concern for the total dynamic mental life of the individual a fundamentally appealing one.

During the next several decades, therefore, some noted historians sought to explore and establish the lines of the overlapping boundaries of history and psychoanalysis. Hans Meyerhoff, a philosopher of history, was one of the first colonizers of this new methodological territory. In a paper presented at a Los Angeles symposium in November 1961, he went carefully over the common ground shared by the two disciplines. Meyerhoff (1962, p. 4) concluded that psychoanalysis and history have much in common because "historical method is an integral part of psychoanalytic theory and therapy" and because "psychoanalysis cannot be divorced from a study of society and history." Citing the historigraphical work of Wilhelm Dilthey, R. G. Collingwood, Benedetto Croce, and E. H. Carr, Meyerhoff (1962, p. 16) argued that the contemporary historian re-creates the "thought of the past" in order to "discover the inner and hidden 'meaning' behind the overt sequence of events." The historian involves himself emotionally and intellectually in the totality of the individual and collective past, whereby, to paraphrase Pirandello, he fills the limp sack of facts with interpretation. This process leads to "understanding" or "insight" into the special cases with which history, in its concern for the particular, is exclusively filled. Anticipating the criticism of, among others, psychologist Hans Eysenck, Meyerhoff declared that psychoanalysis, like history, is actually empirical in its concern with the individual case study. Science, more strictly defined, strives toward the general and abstract, while history and psychoanalysis in their application eschew this nomothetic quest in favor of idiographic wandering—a characteristic in form and content of the work of psychoanalyst Erik Erikson, whom Meyerhoff cites and who, by his publication in 1958 of *Young Man Luther: A Study in Psychoanalysis and History,* produced the first work of modern psychohistory. Some years later, in 1977, Peter Loewenberg, like Meyerhoff from the University of California at Los Angeles, was to argue that twentieth-century revelations about the nature of human scientific inquiry rendered the smug scientific dismissal of psychoanalysis as science in the broad sense substantially hollow. Indeed, according to Loewenberg, the idiographic rigor demanded by history was an important strengthening of psychoanalysis's own emphasis on the unique and a strong check against any overindulged tendency toward theoretical abstraction.

H. Stuart Hughes, one of the grand masters of European intellectual history, also addressed himself during this period to the question of the use of psychoanalysis in history. In his *History as Art and as Science,* Hughes (1964) devoted a chapter to the historian's search for motive, the "prime quest" for both disciplines, and at the outset wondered why it had taken so long for history and psychoanalysis to find each other. The answer, of course, lay in their history: a mutual misunderstanding stemming from the nineteenth-century traditions surrounding both disciplines, the dry search for facts on the one hand and the mechanistic tradition on the other. Their commonalities appear self-evident now: the stress on plural explanations, the importance of ostensibly trivial detail, the regular confrontation with the irrational in human affairs, the inevitable and indispensable subjective involvement of the investigator in the life of his subjects, and a shared concern for the logical and emotional coherence of an account in place of correspondence to general laws (see Friedländer, 1978).

Writing out of the French psychoanalytic tradition, Alain Besançon also noted the common concerns and methods of psychoanalysts and historians. Besançon (1968, p. 155) emphasized the "echo awakened in [the historian] by the various texts" as a means of understanding a culture or a period through the self-aware study of documents left us by the great and small actors in the human drama of history. Besançon further asserted that the Oedipus complex is crucial for understanding man's social reality, since it is this conflict through which every individual must pass in order to enter the larger society, and, thus, every culture must have historically revealing ways of dealing with it.

The strength of psychohistory as it has evolved is its careful detection of the mix of rational and irrational in political affairs and the intriguing and disturbing combination of inflexibility and flexibility, dysfunction and function, in political leaders as varied as Adolf Hitler and Woodrow Wilson (Greenstein, 1969). Psychohistorical studies, while reminding us of the influence of the past on the present, also provide us with the most complete case studies of the motives and actions of individual policy makers as well as insight into the emotional forces behind specific political movements as a whole.

This chapter will attempt to show how psychohistory, with its concern for the emotional content of human thoughts and actions at particular times and places in history, can illuminate the psychological dimensions of political life. It is from history, with its trove of rich detail of human activity, that political psychology can draw its most complete and instructive examples, confirming, enriching, and correcting models drawn from contemporary observation and theory.

Issues in Psychohistory

Psychohistorical Paradigms. Psychiatrist and psychohistorian Robert Jay Lifton (1970) has outlined four paradigms serving the evolution of psychohistory, the first two stemming from Freud's own work. Starting with *Totem and Taboo,* Freud ([1913] 1955) hypothesized what Lifton calls a "prehistorical paradigm" based on the "Oedipal Event." This macrohistorical metaphysic sees all human history as repetition of an original crime (and the attendant guilt) of the sons against the father of the hypothesized "primal horde," in essence leaving nothing important for the historian to do. Freud's other model, closely connected with his role as a pioneer in medical psychology, views individual psychopathology stemming from childhood experiences and fantasies as the key to unlocking the secrets of history. In Lifton's view, both models are insufficient as a basis for genuine psychohistorical inquiry, since they are united in the assumption that history is simply the larger story of the intrapsychic struggles of the individual. Lifton sees partial amelioration of this problem in Erikson's (1958, 1969) studies of Luther and Gandhi as "great men" who, in the coincident realms of ego and society, wrestled with the Freudian instinctual in themselves but in a way that involved and resolved a central historical problem shared by the people and culture of the time. Lifton himself has advanced a fourth paradigm: that of "shared psychohistorical themes." For Lifton the crucial element in understanding human history is an appreciation for collective historical experience that operates not on an instinctual, intrapsychic level but in the cultural realm of the "symbolic" and the "formative." Lifton rejects the causal preoccupations of classical psychoanalysis and emphasizes the interactions over time between personal and cultural predispositions and historical events.

Whatever paradigm is used, however, psychohistory is based firmly, and by and large exclusively, on Freudian psychoanalysis. Although nonpsychoanalytic models have been of some use (Raack, 1970: Crosby and Crosby, 1981), the strength of psychohistory lies in its rigorous, historical concern with the detailed psychological antecedents of individual actions and events. Such a concern has been evinced by psychoanalysis since its inception as a movement in medical psychology directed against a positivist and physicalist psychiatry (Decker, 1977; Cocks, 1985). Psychoanalysis and psychohistory are both idiographic (rather than nomothetic) in nature, wishing to know the motivational details arising from the organism's interaction with the environment in particular cases. The inductive emphasis on evidence, rather than an exclusive deductive reliance on a generalizing theory, was actually an anticipation of a current widespread skepticism about systems in social science. There is a significant contemporary trend, as exemplified by humanistic psychology and "sociology of the everyday," toward a typically historical balance between material and theory. Thus, Barzun (1972) is inaccurate when he claims that psychohistory lies far from history because psychohistory is committed to scientific generalization and jargon. Barzun's further assertion—that historians have gotten along quite well with their intuitive and literary psychological insight—only strengthens Rolle's (1980) counterargument—namely, that the historical profession has been chiefly concerned with rational explanations for events and that the insight into unconscious factors in history displayed by its best practitioners has been enriched by the primarily Freudian twentieth-century advances in the study of the human psyche. (See also Crosby, 1979.)

Psychoanalysis: Artifact or Tool? But whatever its basic orientation, is psychoanalysis in fact a useful mode of inquiry? It has been charged, first of all, that psychoanalysis is outdated, culture bound, and, thus, scientifically worthless. Crews (1980) is one who has turned from an enthusiastic espousal of psychoanalytic theory to vigorous apostatic criticism. Viewing psychoanalysis as an artifact of a dead era, Crews goes on to cite the large amounts of plain bad work done in the various fields of applied psychoanalysis, especially psychohistory. Charging that psychoanalysis is empirically nonsensical, he calls for a more rigorously scientific approach to human behavior. Whatever the failings of psychoanalysis and psychohistory (and there have been many), Crews's gravamina are not so much destroying the psychoanalytic and psychohistorical claim to insight as they are illustrating the tremendously elusive nature of the human mind in historical action. The very controversy among psychoanalysts and psychohistorians over systems, theories, and techniques is a sign not of rigor mortis or decomposition but of further fruitful fermentation in that most difficult realm of thought and inquiry concerned with the human mind and body. Freud's thought is anything but culture bound in its rigorous pursuit of the emotional, the ambiguous, *and the historical* in what people think and do, based as it is on penetrating insights into everyday human behavior. Moreover, the Freudian concepts of the dynamic unconscious, of conflict, and of ambivalence are vital and insightful metaphors for use in the study of human history. No other psychological theory or system has been nearly so useful to the historian.

It will not do, therefore, to maintain that psychoanalysis must be discarded and a fresh start made. Echoing Crews, Stannard (1980) has called for just such a new beginning on a behavioral basis that would dispense with the archaic notion of the unconscious. Stannard declares that psychohistory has failed, but he leaves unanswered the question of what it is at which psychohistory has allegedly failed. Stannard, also an apostate, obviously once expected too much from psychohistory, a common misapprehension that has led in the opposite directions of overenthusiasm and disillusionment.

Psychohistory, properly understood and applied, does not offer a "Freudian" view of history in the sense of an external metaphysical construct that seeks to define the nature and direction of history as a whole. Rather, psychohistory offers a number of means for unlocking an understanding of what Loewenberg (1982) has termed "feeling states." Freud's thought itself was not a monolith. Initially, his concept of the mind was economic and topographical—its functioning the result of energies coursing through the conscious, preconscious, and unconscious. Later, however, he developed a structural model of the mind, conceiving of the agencies of the ego, superego, and id in tension between the inner and outer world (see Yankelovich and Barrett, 1970).

Early Freudian drive, or libido, theory, as Loewenberg (1982) points out, has been helpful in detailing patterns of behavior beholden to past traumata. Subsequent psychoanalytic models, however, offer more time-specific ways of understanding the dynamics of human behavior. Instead of concentrating on an essentially static model based on a pattern of repetition of behavior stemming from experiences in childhood, ego psychology, along with pre-Oedipal object relations theory (see Cocks, 1977a; Hughes, 1977, 1983), emphasizes the individual's functioning in response to situations and other human beings at specific points during a lifetime. Loewenberg (1982, p. 4) uses Brodie's (1981) study of Richard Nixon as an example of the differences between the earlier and later models: "Her emphasis on the theme of Nixon the liar from boyhood to maturity, from parental home to the White House, is unsatisfactory in its neglect of Nixon's many ego strengths and adaptations in a long political career." History, properly done, sees human beings acting out of a complex combination of rational and irrational impulses formed by memory and environment.

The whole trend in psychoanalytic thought toward a more holistic investigation of "character"—which really began with Freud's ([1916] 1957) ruminations on "Those Wrecked by Success"—has drawn psychoanalytic theory closer and closer to history in a mutual concern with the ego—where the internal world of drive, wish, and fantasy collides and conjoins with the cognitive, rational, and external world of objects and aims. Reich's (1949) notion of "character armor" constituted another notable step in this direction through its concern with the phenomenological exterior—"the readily observable and explicitly reported externals of appearance, bearing, manner, conduct, behavior, and personal style" (Loewenberg, 1982, p. 46). Pflanze (1972) used this Reichian model to good effect in his study of Bismarck.

The psychoanalytic basis for psychohistory has also been criticized for a masculine bias inherited from Freud and Viennese culture. This bias is congenial with the traditional historical concern with men, an orientation only recently challenged by the twin twentieth-century forces of social history and feminism. Even though his work helped free women (and men) from some of the more nonsensical constraints imposed by Victorian views on sexuality, Freud in some frustration finally asked "Was will das Weib?" Psychohistory itself has, thus, had to wrestle in particular seriousness with the issues involved in the historical study of women. Wellman (1978) has argued that the traditional male bias in psychoanalysis has been exaggerated in most psychohistorical works because of the traditional concern with the almost exclusively male world of political leaders and movements.

At the same time, Wellman's arguments do call up the evolution within psychoanalysis away from libido theory, which, according to Wellman, regarded reproduction (and hence the achievement of genitality) as the chief function of human beings. This notion helped put women in their domestic place, fully equipped only for a reproductive role in society. Wellman contends that humanistic psychology regards a sexually neutral self-realization as the ultimate aim of the human organism. The trend within psychoanalysis itself toward ego psychology left behind the strict sexual determinism of early psychoanalytic theory. Thus, psychohistory draws from a psychoanalytic tradition that is now more generally appropriate for understanding women in history as well as men.

The rise of social history has also contributed to the growing psychohistorical study of women (Smith-Rosenberg, 1975). The natural concern of psychohistorians for matters of family, child rearing, and socialization—as exemplified in the group studies by Demos (1970a, 1970b, 1971, 1982) and Greven (1970, 1978) and the research of Hunt (1970) into the childhood of Louis XIII of France— forges a strong link, according to Smith-Rosenberg (1975), between psychohistory and the historical study of women. Most important, perhaps, psychohistorical works on women are beginning to become a prominent part of the literature, notably with Strouse's (1980) biography of Alice James and a forthcoming biography of Emma Goldman by Wexler (1980).

Prescription in Psychohistory. Another issue in psychohistory centers around the prescriptive tradition inherited from psychoanalysis. Lifton, for example, has come to see himself in the tradition of Freud, the psychoanalyst, rather than of

Erikson, the psychohistorian. Prescription, as Lifton (1979, pp. 290-291) himself expresses it, is a concern with "ultimate or immortalizing issues" that manifest themselves most clearly in the human symbolic response to traumatic events such as medieval plagues or the atomic bombing of Hiroshima:

> In the important sequence from Freud to Erikson in great man theorizing, Erikson moved from the instinctual to the more genuinely historical, but in the process might have lost some of Freud's suprapersonal (in our terms, ultimate) theoretical emphasis. Perhaps that loss was inevitable, given Erikson's formidable task of integrating psychoanalytic and historical imagination. But at least some of the difficulty may derive from Erikson's simultaneous attempt to hold to and depart from Freud's basic paradigm as applied to history—holding to instinct while simultaneously substituting identity for it—and in the process perhaps conceptually neglecting that transcendent area of concern Freud sought so valiantly and (from the standpoint of subsequent theorists) frustratingly within the instinctual idiom.

We may discern in Lifton's thought here an interesting mix of urgency and hope. The urgency comes from what we can appropriately call a shared concern of modern civilization: the nuclear destruction of the world—in Freudian terms, the potential victory of Thanatos over Eros (Freud, [1930] 1961). Lifton's hope, on the other hand, springs from his medical background—the ancient impulse to cure—and from the modern social and natural scientific faith in progress. Freud's own turn from medical practice toward philosophy late in life resulted as much from his dispositional rejection of these implicit traditions in medicine and science as from his desire to round out his *Weltanschauung*.

Erikson's psychohistory also displays some strong marks of the prescriptive tradition in psychoanalysis. Erikson seeks to prescribe a cure for the ills of civilization, and the cure revolves around his beloved concept of identity. This desire is apparent in the almost demonic portrait he draws of Martin Luther's father and in his embracing of Mohandas Gandhi's perceived struggle against "pseudospeciation" (Erikson, 1969). As Erikson (1958) notes with penetrating insight, he himself has constantly searched for his own identity after a childhood disrupted by national tensions. It is no wonder, therefore, that in his work Erikson seeks an amelioration among nations of what Freud called "the narcissism of small differences." Erikson's ideals, however, impart a certain vagueness to his concept of identity and substitute a measure of moral exhortation for hardheaded, critical, and objective analysis (Fitzpatrick, 1977; Kovel, 1974).

This prescriptive tradition is crucially related to the dynamics of psychohistory as an emergent subdiscipline of history. Indeed, the major topic of debate in psychohistory as it moved during the 1970s toward an autonomous articulation of its theory, method, and practice has been whether psychohistory is a scientific rather than a historical discipline. According to DeMause (1974), the chief advocate of psychohistory as a predictive science, the history of childhood reveals progressive stages of development from ancient times to the present. This progress has laid the foundation for the elimination of human conflict through enlightened parenting. There is nothing wrong with DeMause's ethical intent, but here good wishes get in the way of good history. The reductionism contained in this pre-scriptive historiography has led DeMause to see war and military organizations purely in terms of the infant's experience of the maternal heartbeat. It also brought about his inaccurate prediction that the early relationship between Jimmy Carter and his mother would lead the United States into war in 1979. Conflicting evidence or interpretations are dismissed.

Such uncritical fiddling with the realms of objective and subjective analysis, as well as the exuberant but careless mixing of scientific and historical method, distorts history. Distortion is an omnipresent danger in the application of models to history: Generalizations come to command the exercise, producing caricatures and stereotypes. Whatever use the historian makes of social scientific theories and models, he must respect the reality of change and development in human history; the complexities of history break the bounds of any single theory or model. Although useful work has been done by "culturalists" such as Kardiner (1949) in an anthropological search for "basic personalities" within human groups, the historian, like the psychoanalyst, should tend to look after the unique. One need only recall the limitations of the "national character" studies that were in vogue during the 1940s and early 1950s.

Freud himself built psychoanalysis on the basis of a concern for human disability, a preoccupation that wove together the gloomy strands that came to darken his final philosophical musings. The psychoanalytic movement in general, taking a cue from its founder's own post–World War I turn to a greater appreci-ation for the functioning of the ego, pursued a course more consistent with the basic medical urge to cure. Under the leadership of neo-Freudians such as Erich Fromm, Karen Horney, and Harry Stack Sullivan, among others, the movement came to expect the healthy human psyche to be able to adjust to, and become productive within, society at large.

Our concern, however, is with the value of various psychoanalytic models for the historical enterprise. Just as Freud's final setting of his philosophical house in order drew his thought away from history by reducing it to the repetition of a prehistorical primal event, the neo-Freudian and medical tendency toward prescription displays the limitations of moral and medical insistence as an ade-quate approach to historical understanding. To return to Lifton, whose chief source of psychoanalytic inspiration is the work of Otto Rank, we find an empha-sis on the sledgehammer events of history that allegedly produce dramatic expres-sions of the human desire for symbolic—or, as in Lifton's (1968) view of Mao, "revolutionary"—immortality. For Lifton it is the *pathos* of the situation that produces inspirational human action and hence historical meaning. Freud, by contrast (and here we are following Rieff's 1979 analysis of Freud's philosophy), emphasized the *ethos* of man's existence, the (ultimately) macrohistorical predis-position that submerges subsequent actions in a sea of past conditions.

It is a thesis of this chapter that Freud's basic orientation to the past is congenial to the historian's task. The value of psychoanalysis to the historian is its careful detailing of the continuous balance of tension within the individual, who is constantly dealing with the personal realities of physical and mental life. Every historical event, every social structure, interacts with a complex sense of existence and identity, which, though malleable to a degree, is already established on an individual basis. What the historian sees (or should see) is the product of the interaction between the self, as significantly formed by early experiences, and the later events of life and processes of rational choice and action. The careful historian wants to know about the dynamics of the past as it affects the present. Event and structure are crucial, but less so than the *continuous lived experience* of human beings as individuals and in groups. There is, after all, very much more past in the human condition than present.

The virtues of history are found in the careful detailing of its subject matter by means of the unparalleled insight won by perspective, its sober rigor striving to provide a comprehensive and coherent view of a particular period, event, or phenomenon. History is supposed to provide an understanding of the past for its own sake. The problem is that the present century—and the prescriptive tradition in psychoanalysis and psychohistory reflects this—presses for solutions to multiplying and accelerating problems. Given this prescriptive tendency, it is vital that balance and thoughtful eclecticism obtain in the new avenues explored by historians. This caveat means, first of all, that psychohistory be regarded as one tool among many that can be grasped by the historian and not as any sort of fully autonomous science, as DeMause would have it. An insistence, however, on breadth and balance in the historian's approach to his work must also include the recognition that the historian will and should have a philosophical point of view. The crucial point for us is that psychoanalysis and psychohistory have an inherent tendency toward prescription, which—in combination with, or in place of, a more general philosophical or moral commitment—can partially or completely distort the historian's findings.

This critique does not mean to imply that there is no value in the work of those such as Fromm, Reich, and Lifton. It means only that the historian, and especially the psychohistorian, must employ a broader view. It is the virtue of the historicist tradition, for example, that it demands an eye, an ear, and a mind for the unique in time, place, and tradition: the historian opening himself up to the myriad voices in which history speaks.

Problems of Evidence. The availability and suitability of evidence is another especially significant issue for psychohistorians. Evidence from the childhoods of most figures in history, especially for those far in the past, is often unavailable, sketchy, or unreliable. A historian wishing to understand the actions of an adult by questing for the childhood experiences informing them must combine close analysis of the subject's own words, observations by contemporaries, and any discernible patterns of behavior with psychoanalytic theory to extrapolate the nature of early influences. In the process the psychohistorian must take care that the hypothesized quality of small bits of evidence does not become simply a device to compensate for lack of quantity of solid evidence.

A further consequence of what some traditional historians see as the psychohistorian's desperate search for evidence and argument is the problem of circularity. The use of psychoanalytic case studies so common in psychohistorical research has the potential to overwhelm historical material through the scientific virtuosity and clinical confidence of its combination of cause and effect. As one example out of the historical literature on Hitler discussed in extended fashion later in this chapter, we will consider an aspect of the debate over Hitler's sexual constitution. Bromberg (1971, 1974; Bromberg and Small, 1982) and, subsequently,

Waite (1977) have argued that Hitler suffered from either monorchism, the congenital lack of a testicle, or cryptorchism, an undescended testicle, and that the symptomatology of monorchid and cryptorchid boys recorded in psychoanalytic case studies matches up with Hitler's behavior throughout his life. Binion (1973, p. 253) rejects this hypothesis by challenging the evidence for Hitler's missing a testicle and by asserting that Bromberg's thesis is circular: "For Bromberg, the alleged aftereffects evidence the supposed formative influences, which then explain the alleged aftereffects, with a circularity that rolls right by the bulk of the records."

Reductionism. The danger of circular reasoning in the reconstruction of the past is a variety of an even larger issue, that of reductionism. A shiny new theory can be intoxicating as it slashes through the thickets of history, revealing the true ground beneath. Such a threat to careful historical research is not unique to psychohistory, but the use of psychoanalytic theory can contribute to the real danger of methodological slash-and-burn. In psychohistory reductionism has taken two forms. The first, more traditional and more common, involves the reduction of a subject's motives (or an era's events or a group's actions) to a single root cause, such as the Oedipus complex. This was the marked tendency of the secret wartime report prepared on Hitler for the Office of Strategic Services by psychoanalyst Walter Langer (1972). The second, and more recent, form of reductionism in psychohistory is exemplified by Binion's (1973, 1976) study of Hitler. Binion's approach, associated with the DeMause school of psychohistorical thought, represents not reductionism *within* the psychohistorical model, as manifest in Langer, but the reduction *of* history *to* psychohistory. For Binion the key to Hitler's adult behavior is not an Oedipus complex but an interlocking complex of psychohistorical states, ranging from Klara Hitler's "maternal trauma" through Adolf's "gas trauma" to Germany's collective "November trauma," which in the end was the cause of Auschwitz and Stalingrad. This latter reductionistic tendency of contemporary psychohistory, while based on valuable research into the history of childhood (DeMause, 1974) and illuminated by Binion's intellectual fireworks, is the greater threat to balanced historical study of the individual and society in history.

In a review of Langer's study of Hitler, Orlow (1974) has wisely and concisely pointed out the dangers of reductionism. First of all, Orlow calls attention to the "ahistorical" bias of Freudian psychoanalysis, which holds that the phenomena of mental life elucidated by Freud apply equally to all times and places. Orlow (p. 135) then notes that this generalizing tendency in psychoanalysis is also manifest in Langer's tendency to characterize the German masses as "feminine-masochistic" and to ignore the "time-and-class-specific aspects of [Hitler]." Finally, Orlow (p. 137), citing Binion (1973), notes that psychoanalysts and psychohistorians regard "societal abstractions as extensions of personal relations." They believe that they can see behind their subjects' words and deeds what unconsciously was "really meant."

Subjectivity in Psychohistory. History is, as Dilthey (1962) put it, a "human science," in which the subjective—or, as Freud put it, affective—link between historian and subject is as indispensable as it is unavoidable. The role of subjectivity, especially in the psychohistorical study of political figures, constitutes an important aspect of any discussion of the weaknesses and strengths of psychohistory. This discussion divides neatly into three sections. The first includes those works of psychological analysis scarred by the author's conscious or unconscious antagonism for his subject. Fortunately, such works are rare, and they are usually written not by historians but by political or personal enemies—an infamous example being Bullitt's (Freud and Bullitt, 1967) attack on Woodrow Wilson.

The second mode of subjectivity is that of identification in both the general and specific sense. Hughes (1964) has argued that the historian must have some sort of emotional tie to a historical subject if he is to acquire the degree of interest, commitment, and empathy required to understand the past. This is particularly the case with historical biography, the historical encounter most like that of psychoanalyst and patient. In noting this similarity, Klauber (1968, p. 85) has recalled the work of the great historian Collingwood (1946): "It remains a great advance in philosophical insight to perceive that an act of intuition by identification with the thoughts and feelings of another human being is a creative act which deserves to be distinguished from an act of creative intuition which does not depend upon identification." But we must also assume that between a historian and his subject there most likely exists and grows a web of specific points of psychological contact, a network of shared concerns that opens up one life, or portions of a life, more fully to one historian than to another. The more intense and genuine these concerns, all other things being equal, the greater the insight that most likely will be manifest in the final product. Erikson's psychohistorical work is a good example of what Strozier (1977) calls "disciplined subjectivity." As a psychoanalyst, Erikson (1958) has emphasized the need for the historian to respond to the emotions the historical subject matter awakens in him and rightly sees history and psychoanalysis as kindred disciplines—both seeking multiple explanations for specific events and striving for a coherent understanding of the past.

The third area of historical subjectivity emerges from an often criticized tendency within psychoanalysis toward debunking. In the atmosphere of frantic disillusionment following World War I, Strachey (1918)—with his sketches in *Eminent Victorians*—began the tradition of stripping away the friendly masques produced by the phalanx of official biographies of the Victorian era. This was a necessary corrective, but—especially with the "discovery" of psychoanalysis in the 1920s—it soon led to the substitution of chic diagnosis for factual analysis (Mack, 1971). This tradition, when embraced by historians, flourished responsibly with the historian's traditional emphasis on the careful and comprehensive search for documentation and interpretive balance. The cataclysms of the new century also spurred responsible and concerned interest in the personal dynamics of political leaders who held the lives of millions of people in their hands and in their heads. A healthy skepticism, even cynicism, grew up over the allegedly rational process of politics and leadership—in fact, a liberal dream already frayed and tattered by the violent and demagogic turn of the new century.

Critics of psychohistory, however, have often found the genre guilty of debunking to the point of distortion. Coles (1973) has denounced Clinch's (1973) group portrait of the Kennedy brothers as nothing more than a heavy-handed hatchet job on some prominent achievers by an envious little scholar. Coles prefers the grace of a Freud on Leonardo da Vinci—so much so that Mazlish (1973), who wrote the introduction to the Clinch book, has accused Coles of reserving the role of critic of the high, mighty, and talented to those blessed by the "gift of grace." Clinch's analysis is, in fact, marred by the too often one-dimensional application of psychopathological labels, but Mazlish's response has merit. It is easy to idealize, even etherealize, political leaders, especially charismatic ones, and Coles's defense of the Kennedys has about it the injured sensibility of a Boston liberal Brahmin. Wills (1982), no enemy of liberalism and no friend of psychohistory, is the most recent to lay bare some of the less flattering dimensions of the keepers of the American Camelot. Apart from the difficulties, regularly cited by critics, of forging psychohistorical links between leader and led, analyzing American presidents in the face of national veneration is in general no easy task: easier with Nixon (Mazlish, 1970, 1972; Mazon, 1978; Brodie, 1981) and Johnson (Kearns, 1976), harder with Jefferson (Brodie, 1971, 1974) and Jackson (Rogin, 1976). Lincoln (Strozier, 1982) and Wilson (George and George, 1956) fall somewhere in between, since admiration for them is often mixed with puzzled sympathy.

The virtue of these attempts, whatever their individual faults or merits, lies in the corrective they bring to the image of a president as national leader beyond flesh and blood. American presidents—like the ironsided Bismarck, whose vulnerabilities and defenses have been skillfully revealed by Pflanze (1972; see also Sempell, 1974)—were, are, and always will be human beings with emotions. Although presidents are not the only proper and popular subjects for such study (see Brodie, 1959; Rogow, 1963; Glad, 1966; Mazlish, 1976), given their tremendous power, it seems not only desirable but prudent that we understand their characters. This is the chief justification, even with the genre's limits on perspective and evidence, for the fast psychobiographical sketches of sitting presidents, such as those on Nixon (Mazlish, 1970, 1972) and Carter (DeMause and Ebel, 1977; Mazlish and Diamond, 1980), and for Barber's (1972) continuing attempt to describe and define the "presidential character."

Psychoanalysis and Group Phenomena. How can the psychoanalytic model, with its focus on the individual, help to explain the group phenomena that compose much of the historian's concern? Building on Freud's ([1921] 1955) own attempt, the psychohistorical answers to this question include DeMause's (1981, p. 181) bold conviction that the "science" of psychohistory can, through the empathic analysis of "group fantasy," plumb the "psychology of the largest group." Most other psychohistorians have been much more restrained in their approach to this problem. Mazlish (1968) has pointed out that the psychological characteristics of groups are dynamic, not static, and that regional, ethnic, social, and cultural differences must not be ignored, as, for example, they tended to be in the national character studies of the 1940s and 1950s. Mazlish's (1975) own subsequent study of the lives of James and John Stuart Mill attempts to attack this problem from another direction. Mazlish sees the relationship between Mill *père et fils* as revealing of the social and economic changes of the nineteenth century, which within the family brought Oedipal conflict to the fore—a human dynamic that caught the genial attention of Freud in *fin de siècle* Vienna. Such an approach, similar to Erikson's notion of the "great man" as embodiment of the chief concerns of his era, is a valid way of bridging the gap between the psychoanalyst's essential concern with the individual and the historian's natural interest in the group. The group can also be approached directly, however, as in Loewenberg's (1971a) deft motivational analysis of the youthful supporters of national socialism. Combining social history and psychoanalytic insights into the lives of infants and children disrupted by separation and undernourishment, Loewenberg connects the childhood experiences of the members of the generational "cohort" of 1902–1915 in Germany before, during, and immediately after World War I to their later enthusiasm for Hitler and the Nazis.

Yet within the ranks of psychohistorians themselves grave doubts about the success of efforts to bridge the gap "between a psychology of repressed instinctual strivings and a complex and multidimensional historical reality" (Wurgraft, 1975, p. 491) have continued to be expressed. Historian Fred Weinstein and sociologist Gerald Platt have together been at the forefront of a campaign to adapt and change psychoanalytic concepts to explain collective phenomena. In their first collaborative venture (Weinstein and Platt, 1969), they attempted to explain social change by adopting a Freudian instinctual model as modified by ego psychologist Heinz Hartmann and by sociologist Talcott Parsons. Since then, however, Weinstein and Platt (1973) have turned to an ego psychological model, emphasizing the ego's functioning within the social and cultural context at all stages of life. This new model, they (1972, 1975) argue, allows for fruitful new insight into history not offered by more traditional psychoanalytic concerns. The emphasis on the structural, however, has led Weinstein (1980) to produce an analysis of the German response to nazism in which the individual portraits are unsatisfyingly flat and abstract.

Psychohistorians must strive toward a greater understanding of the individual psyche (especially of the leader), political culture, and social collectivities. It is a most difficult task, and at present the primary contribution of psychohistory to history and to political psychology has been an elucidation of the unconscious motives of various individual figures of the past. At the other end of the human polity, it has offered some limited insight into cultural and social concerns through the study of the family and childhood. But the meeting ground of individual leader and group following in politics has remained shrouded, most likely because intervening structural, social, economic, and political factors play a major role in the construction of mass constituencies for individual leaders.

Hitler as Psychohistorical Case Study

Most psychohistorical work has taken the form of biography (Glad, 1973; Prisco, 1980; Runyan, 1982; Shore, 1981); the best works of psychohistorical biography offer insights into their subjects' times by drawing on political, social, economic, and cultural contexts and by evoking a feeling for the times as reflected in the subjects' lives and careers. Writing such psychohistorical biographies requires what Wright (1981, p. 109), in a sketch of the career of Pierre Laval, has termed a "temperamental interpretation of history": "One can rarely predict on the basis of some statistical analysis, or class origin, or age or condition, how individual human beings are going to behave in crisis circumstances. In our era, as in any age, crisis behavior is likely to spring from impulses deep in the personality structure or even the subconscious, impulses that combine differently from one individual to the next." Wright reforges the link to the past that is lost in Lifton's studies of crises and makes clear that history is a stream with cataracts and splashes, not composed of isolated pools of stimulus and response. Wright's conclusion that Laval is not to be understood in purely rational terms also underlines Kennan's (1961, p. 203) earlier observation that "the mysterious life of the feelings and attitudes of men . . . is all that really counts in politics." (See also Loewenberg, 1971b, 1971c, 1975a.) This truth has not always been recognized. Tucker (1982) has recalled how his own opinion, from his embassy post in Moscow, that the personality of Stalin determined the nature of the Soviet system was rejected outright by his superiors. The thaw after Stalin's death in 1953 and Khrushchev's revelations three years later confirmed in Tucker a view since exhaustively developed in his biography of Stalin (Tucker, 1973).

The historical record also allows us to reflect on European statesmen such as Josef Beck and Neville Chamberlain, who were utterly convinced that Hitler was, like them, a rational "realist." No other twentieth-century figure has attracted as much historical attention as Adolf Hitler, and the large number of psychohistorical studies in the ever expanding historical subgenre of "Hitlerature" (Cocks, 1979, p. 67) offer the best possible material for a more intensive concluding look at some fundamental issues of historical method crucial to the application of psychoanalysis to history: the balance between objectivity and subjectivity and between history and theory, the question of causes versus conditions, the relationship between psychobiography and psychohistory, and the importance of coherence in historical explanations versus the nomothetic insistence on correspondence to an established corpus of "facts."

Treatments of Hitler and the Nazis still too often invoke the occult or any one of many other popular, spectacular, and nonsensical diagnoses. Probably the sorry standard for this type of work was set by Krueger (1943, p. 41), who falsely claimed to have been Hitler's psychiatrist and privy to the spectacular psychopathological mayhem of the brown cult: "I began to suspect a murder-complex in my patient when he confessed to me that he had used an SS Guard bayonet-knife in an orgiastic ritual of a *Blut und Ehre* (Blood and Honor) cult born in the imagination of a Nazi sadist who combined Oriental eroticism with Aryan mythology in a concoction of terror, lust, and unspeakable cruelty with credulous Hitler youth as the willing victims. He had made use of the bayonet-knife to cut a bleeding swastika between the breasts of a female cultist, and then, in a moment of erotic madness, he had made a homicidal attack upon the young blonde girl, whom he had rushed to me for treatment." Recent psychohistorical works, by contrast, have done much to clear away such debris and provide a revealing portrait of Hitler's motivations.

The Psychopathological Model. Waite's (1971a, 1971b, 1977) responsible historical approach to studying Hitler is based on a psychopathological model. Although Glad (1973, p. 320), among others, has stressed the need "to go beyond the usual concern with the idiosyncratic, the pathological, and the therapeutic," any serious appreciation of a man like Hitler must begin with the material presented and analyzed by Waite. Beyond this congruence of method and subject matter, psychoanalysis itself, as we have already noted, has steadily evolved along the lines of a more general ego psychology (Loewenberg, 1982) rather than remaining what it, in fact, never was: a means for studying psychopathological states qualitatively distinct from normal mental functioning. Psychoanalytic theory, although founded on insights concerning adults and children in a family setting, is also an especially appropriate model for the study of a young Austrian careening out of precisely the same family structure that spawned the cases on which Freud in nearby Vienna was to build psychoanalysis. Drawing from this tradition and

exploiting the mass of documentary evidence on Hitler's life—from his own ruminations, the testimony of associates, and the official data on his regime—Waite
(1977), following Bromberg (1971), characterizes Hitler as a "borderline personality" (between neurosis and psychosis) with a sado-masochistic guilt complex
arising from an intensified Oedipus complex surrounding his authoritarian father
and overindulgent mother. This condition, coupled with an array of compensatory
attitudes stemming from cryptorchism and overdetermined castration anxiety, led
to massive projection onto the Jews, sexual masochism, and an urge for self-
destruction.

Waite's book, while inclusive and psychoanalytically informed, tends to be
somewhat loose-jointed through its use of numerous psychoanalytic case studies
and models to characterize various aspects of Hitler's character and development.
The result, while revealing in many respects, is patchwork; what is lacking is a
unified perspective on Hitler's life and career as a whole. Waite relies rather too
heavily on Langer's (1972) theory about Hitler's masochistic sexual perversion,
the evidence for which was fourthhand when Langer assembled it during the war.
Moreover, in his effort to add to the cumulative effect of evidence, Waite sometimes
strains the data to fit a speculation (see, for example, Waite, 1977, p. 68) or relies
too heavily on questionable sources, such as Hanfstaengle (1957) and Hoffmann
(1955). Waite also tends to list pathological syndromes, to speak in drive-theory
terms of static obsessions, and to eschew a more dynamic explanation of the
balance between Hitler's psychological strengths and weaknesses. This tendency
leads him to distort German history and culture as a whole by seeing it, through
Hitler, in pathological terms.

A helpful critique of Waite (1977) can be constructed along the lines of a
dynamic "hierarchy of motives." Waite, while listing other motives, maintains,
for example, that certain crucial actions taken by Hitler indicate an unconscious
urge for self-destruction. The general patterns of failure in Hitler's life, previously
explored by McRandle (1965), must, however, as Loewenberg (1982) has argued,
be set against his tremendous successes in order to ask the proper historical question: "Why now?" We must go even further, though, and ask what hierarchy of
motives lay behind any given decision. Why, for instance, did Hitler order his
tanks to stop short of Dunkirk on May 24, 1940? Waite (1977) suggests that self-
destructive urges prompted Hitler to let the British escape, a supposition that fits
the composition of Waite's overall psychopathological portrait of Hitler from
"primal scene trauma" to suicide (see Waite, 1977, p. 162). But surely other considerations at the time were more significant—for example, von Rundstedt's concern over the refitting of the panzers for the campaign in southern France, which
worked on Hitler's occasional panic at pivotal military junctures; and Hitler's
sentimental, ideological, and strategic receptiveness to Göring's plea to let the
more nazified Luftwaffe, fresh from victories over Warsaw and Rotterdam, finish
off the British Expeditionary Force (BEF). Hitler's strategic motive here may have
been his desire to show the British that the English Channel was no defense in an
age of air power. This possible rational motive, however, links up with the thesis
that Hitler, on psychological as well as practical grounds, did not want to invade
England and thus hoped that "sparing" the BEF would convince the English to
make peace, perhaps even to ally with Germany (Cocks, 1977b).

Binion's (1977) reaction to this discussion is revealingly simplistic: Hitler wanted to save his panzers for the rest of the French campaign. Binion, in likewise attempting to save a monocausal thesis that will tolerate no elements of psychological multicausality (see below), has been painfully and ironically forced to adopt a simplistic rational explanation for a psychologically complex and significant action. The (psycho)historian must, in fact, deal with and detail the broader rational and irrational elements of the mind in life. This broader and more synthetic approach to Hitler biography transcends Binion's notion of trauma critiqued below, Waite's suggestive but limited emphasis on psychopathology, and Lasswell's (1931) notion of displacement of personal problems onto politics. An early model of a more synthetic approach was Erikson's (1950) analysis, first published during the war (Erikson, 1942), of the mixture of propaganda and neurotic complaint in the compelled and self-styled adolescent Führer, who mobilized and articulated some of the central psychological concerns of German society and culture generated by a collective historical experience. Erikson never expanded on his brief study (see Erikson, 1958), and few psychohistorians (see Cocks, 1977b, 1979) have followed up on it.

A diagnosis of pure psychopathology, even if neurotic or borderline rather than psychotic, has a tendency to separate the subject from the rest of society. A vital question for historians, especially in the case of Hitler, is how an appeal to the masses was generated and sustained. One cannot answer this question by adopting an unsatisfactory "mechanical" point of view—that is, by regarding this appeal as merely the result of a carefully staged and orchestrated set of devices by which psychological effects were produced. The historian wishes to discover the overdetermined motivational *content* of a historical phenomenon. In the case of Hitler and the Germans, the historian must carefully delineate *all* points of contact and appeal, an interaction involving a combination of the rational, the psychopathological, and the "traumatic." The first step in this process can be taken by means of a careful analysis of the leader's character and motivations.

Waite's use of the psychoanalytic notion of guilt-induced, self-destructive impulses, while appropriate and useful, can thus tend to reduce a complex phenomenon almost to the dimensions of label. There is, it is true, a likelihood that self-destructive impulses played a role in Hitler's decision to invade Russia, as Waite (1977) maintains; the more important reason for Hitler's launching of Barbarossa, however, was the desire to realize, by means of another *Blitzkrieg*, his irrational racial dream of *Lebensraum*. The timing of the invasion most likely came as a result of his disappointment with England (a rational response to failure but also retaining irrational elements of desire and hope for *rapprochement*), a rational anxiety over the strengthening of Russian defenses, and a rational and an irrational concern that time was on the side of his enemies (number, size) and working against him (fear of personal decline and death). The chief means used to defend the idea that Hitler was seeking his own destruction in his move East on June 22, 1941, is that the German invasion was bound to fail and that Hitler subconsciously knew this while unconsciously wishing it. Yet most military experts in the West at the time, albeit with some biased anticipation, agreed that the Russians would collapse. It has been convincingly argued (Stolfi, 1982), moreover, that Guderian's Second Panzer Army was ready to take Moscow and end the campaign victoriously in August 1941 when Hitler ordered it south to help encircle and destroy huge Russian armies in the Ukraine. A late freeze subsequently left the German motorized columns in the mud west of the Soviet capital. It might be argued that Hitler's decision for the Ukraine instead of Moscow contained elements of self-destructiveness, but the decision was also composed of rational consider-ations (for example, not to let large Russian forces escape into the vast hinterland as they had against Napoleon); Hitler's overconfident desire for another spectacular encirclement, which would also remove the last threat to his flank when he moved against Moscow; and the general Nazi conviction that the subhuman Russians were beaten and the way to Moscow would remain open.

Loewenberg (1982, pp. 29–31) offers an explanation based on object rela-tions theory: that by 1941, with the "neutralization" of the Jews and as a defense against the "inner badness" increasingly manifest in various physical ailments, Hitler developed a full-blown megalomania, declaring that he could take on the whole world. The result was a paranoid turning against the Soviet Union on June 22, an unnecessary and disastrous declaration of war on the United States on December 11, and the assumption of direct control over German armies in the field on December 19. Self-destruction could well have been a motive for Hitler's declaration of war on America, but this act is even more suggestive as part of the behavioral pattern outlined by Loewenberg. Indeed, the incumbent military crises may have also strengthened Hitler's determination in late 1941 and early 1942 finally to exterminate the Jews so as to exercise this newly mobilized megalomania, which was being frustrated in Russia and only briefly satisfied by words of war against America.

No one answer to these questions is satisfactory, but we may presume that some significant and even spectacular synthesis, based on an ordering of motiva-tional factors, will arise over time out of this rich reservoir of research and analysis. Perspective on a historical figure or epoch is not just a matter of time and distance, but of variety and quality of work done. The important matter to keep in mind is that, at every stage and in every era of historical research, care must be taken to consider the complex conditions of historical experience. In Hitler's case, it is also necessary, for example, to consider the role that drugs played in his documented physical and mental deterioration after 1942. This is an issue that not coinciden-tally raises additional questions of theory and method in history. A new "biopsy-chiatry," as it is sometimes called, has arisen of late—especially in America—to challenge the psychodynamic basis of the psychiatry that was pioneered by Freud. Freud himself once said that all mental phenomena would one day be explained by chemistry, but it is unlikely that chemistry will ever become a mean-ingful way of explaining motive in history. With regard to Hitler, Heston and Heston (1979) have concluded that from 1942 on he was suffering from acute amphetamine poisoning. This, according to their study of Hitler's medical records, explains his increasingly erratic and self-defeating behavior during the last three years of his life. But such a thesis has nothing to say about Hitler's behavior before 1942 or about the basic motives for his actions. Heston and Heston acknowledge this, and they themselves also avoid the darker tendency, popular among some Hitler apologists, to separate the "good" pre-1940s Hitler, who only wanted to secure Germany's rightful place in Europe, from the "bad" Hitler, who was driven to massive misdeeds by disease and drugs.

This ahistorical tendency of better exculpation through chemistry has, however, recently surfaced in the literature on Woodrow Wilson. Weinstein (1981) attributes Wilson's problems at the end of World War I to a series of strokes. In contrast, George and George (1956), taking a psychodynamic approach, had viewed Wilson's thoughts and actions as psychological responses to the strict Calvinist family environment presided over by his father. Weinstein's evidence is shaky, but more important for our purposes is the fact that Weinstein's book has been published by Princeton University Press as part of the papers of Woodrow Wilson edited by Wilson biographer Arthur Link. Link, a traditionally minded historian and unabashed admirer of Wilson, has sought to meet criticism and psychological analysis of Wilson with evidence of a discrete medical syndrome that explains his subject's greatest failure and, thus, saves the rest of Wilson's career from psychoanalytic scrutiny.

Beyond the specifics of the Wilson and Hitler cases, however, it must be asked whether such biological inquiry in general serves the historian's cause. To be sure, physiological states and disorders exist and must be taken into historical account (as with, for example, George III: see Macalpine and Hunter, 1969). But what exactly is the relationship between the hypothesized presence of, say, strokes and Wilson's subjective state? Or between Hitler's subjective state and his hypothesized Parkinsonism (Recktenwald, 1963)? The historian must look to the complex interactions of physical, mental, and environmental conditions over time and not be seduced, either for specific reasons or out of a general desire for the too certain and concrete, into embracing a scientific system that will eliminate his reason for being: the search for, and explication of, motive and the detailing of human desire and conflict. In this respect, as we have seen, psychoanalysis—unlike chemical analysis or pure physiological diagnosis—is compatible with history in method and aim.

The Traumatic Model. Binion (1973, 1976), in his psychohistorical study of Hitler, takes a completely different tack from that of Waite. Binion's thesis is that Hitler's anti-Semitism was the product of a traumatic reliving of his mother's death from iodoform poisoning in the course of treatment for breast cancer by Dr. Eduard Bloch in 1907, a trauma whose effects were released by his own mustard gas poisoning in 1918. Hitler unconsciously wished to overcome this trauma by reliving it, for he felt guilt at having prompted the fatal ministrations of iodoform (which, like mustard gas, eats into the flesh). He projected this guilt onto the Jews and derived the image of his victimized mother from Germany (which he idiosyncratically called "Motherland"). The Hitler who emerged from the military hospital at Pasewalk was newly dynamic, charismatic, and sensitized to Germany's longing for *Lebensraum* in the East through oral aggression exaggerated by Klara's solicitude, drawn from her own maternal trauma toward infant Adolf as a "replacement child." The German people, in turn, Binion (1976, p. xi) argues, were "susceptible to Hitler at a key psychic sore spot: the German trauma of defeat suffered in 1918." Hitler's career, then, was a "double track." One track led to Auschwitz, as he revenged himself on the Jew poisoner and sought to undo his mother's death. The other track led to Stalingrad, as he aligned his oral demands with Germany's own reexperiencing of Ludendorff's defeat. Finally, Hitler willed utter catastrophe as "punishment due." Fusing the early traumatic model of psychoanalysis with a notion of the mind drawn from the pre-Socratic philosopher Anaxagoras, Binion (1978a) has created a method of historical inquiry that rests on the almost unrestricted investigative power of empathy. For Binion case studies and psychopathological models are of no use in understanding a historical figure, for they employ circular reasoning and label what they should investigate.

A critique of Binion's (1973, 1976) work on Hitler must begin with an acknowledgment of his contributions to psychohistory in general, as noted above, and to Hitler research in specific. Binion has contributed new knowledge about events in Hitler's life (the treatment of his mother's cancer), has demonstrated the psychological importance of later stages in Hitler's life (for example, at the end of World War I), and has illuminated what we might call the peculiar "density" of any one individual's experience. Binion's two great historical ideals are causality and empathy, the latter discovering the former. According to Binion, the historian's empathic communion with his subject must not be cluttered with extrinsic models and theories; instead, immersion in the documents themselves will reveal the causes of a historical figure's actions. There is justice in this approach. Hitler's life in particular has often been buried in models and theories. Because he was such a malevolently spectacular figure, those who write about him are often irresistibly tempted to "prove" a theory about human behavior while at the same time satisfying the urge to cure by a therapeutic exorcism of history (Brink, 1975). Thus, while Binion agrees with Stierlin (1977) about the psychological importance for Hitler of his mother's "maternal trauma" over the loss of previous children, psychoanalyst Stierlin goes one way with his treatment and historian Binion another with his history.

Binion insists that Hitler suffered from a "Bloch complex" arising from the 1907 death of his mother, allegedly from iodoform poisoning in the course of treatment for breast cancer. Langer (1972) and Waite (1971b, 1977), on the other hand, have stressed Hitler's reawakened Oedipal fantasies regarding Eduard Bloch's treatment of Klara Hitler. A bitter debate has exploded over the matter, but it is clear that some sort of balance must be struck between the role played by Hitler's reaction to Bloch's actions and the role of Hitler's fantasy life as fed by antecedent experiences. The division here rests in great measure on the issue of the use of models in history: Binion, through hermitic study of the documents, *senses* the trauma Hitler suffered, while Waite gives structure and meaning to the event by applying a traditional psychoanalytic model. Whatever the limitations of Waite's approach, models and theories cannot be dispensed with, as Binion would have it; much good work continues to come out of their use, as shown in Loewenberg's (1983) study of the Austrian socialist father and son Viktor and Friedrich Adler and colleague Otto Bauer, and in Mack's (1976) psychobiography of T. E. Lawrence. Good history can be neither all material nor all model.

Binion (1978b, p. 295) sees Hitler as a "demonic nobody" who was raised to the role of historical actor by a series of traumata that linked up with the trauma suffered by Germany at the close of World War I. For Binion the traditional historical emphasis on conditions (Bloch, 1964) is valueless, interfering with his desire to make simple linear sense out of the complexities of human motivation and meaning in history. But Hitler properly understood was a man who, like everyone else, emerged from the myriad daily and continuous "events" of specific psychological, familial, social, cultural, and temporal contexts. Admittedly, some passages in his life may have been more crucial and determinative than others, but a broader view of the conditions that produced and sustained Hitler must be preferred over Binion's narrower approach. What Binion has, in fact, done is to establish a tyranny of history (through the "event") and the historian (through "empathy") over his subject. Indeed, the whole notion of traumatic reliving as the engine of personal history in its linkage of the past and its re-creation in the present seems suspiciously close to the historian's own professional activity and, thus, a reflection not of history but of the interpreter. In reality, however, any historical subject inhabits a world of tension, choice, compulsion, influence, and opportunity. Out of these total experiences in Hitler's case arose a monstrous passion and the basis for his appeal to a larger audience.

The second part of Binion's equation, the linking up in 1918 of Hitler's relived trauma with that allegedly suffered by the German people over defeat in World War I, is a well-known metaphor; but, when it is given exclusive explanatory status, it is unfortunately reductionistic. Binion's insistence on simple cause and effect and on the methodological and metaphysical efficacy of empathy distorts his original and valuable, if undocumented, insight into widespread German frustration over the loss of the Eastern imperium won at Brest Litovsk. The psychohistorian must be especially careful when attempting to understand the reasons for the behavior of groups. According to Binion, Hitler's ideal of *Lebensraum* drew on Erich von Ludendorff's "expansive principles" (Hillgruber, 1981, p. 52) and exploited German disenchantment over the loss of captured Russian territory in November 1918. But, like the "Bloch complex," this link between Hitler and the Germans was contributory and not causal; it was part of a larger and more complex interactive process of social and psychological factors. Not all, perhaps not even most, Germans were "traumatized" by the loss of the Eastern territories, and even those who were responded individually to Hitler for a number of historically meaningful reasons. But Binion's notion of a "link" here assumes a mechanical nature, which obscures the actual flow of events and influences. Binion must resort to such an artifice because he has already knocked Hitler out of his larger psychological, social, and cultural orbit by the adoption of a traumatic scheme. Therefore, to explain why atypical and isolated Adolf Hitler reached the Germans with his peculiar yet familiar brew of *Schwärmerei* and *Schweinerei*, Binion must, in turn, knock the Germans out of their historical context so that the two can meet on common "psychohistorical" ground. He thereby blows single issues out of all proportion. According to Dilthey (1962), an individual's history reveals and reflects those human institutions and traditions of which he is a part; this is one vital component of historical meaning. To understand the German "trauma," then, one must use a number of tools and analyze a wealth of different data, not flee into metaphor and psychological reductionism. Binion's (1969) earlier essay on Leopold III of Belgium—using the same traumatic model, it must be said— is more convincing because the evidence for reinforcing traumatic events in Leopold's life is stronger. But even so, do we have the full story on Leopold and his historical significance? Are there other aspects of his life that should be investigated or other approaches that might reveal more about his character, the motives for his actions, and, through him, his society, his culture, his times?

Binion's findings on Hitler are at best contributory, neither the only answer nor the proof of his theory of history. His certainty, however, about the exclusive validity of his interpretation rests on confidence in his own special brand of insight. Although Binion himself relies on an early version of psychoanalytic theory and practice, the self-proclaimed core of his method is the empathic insight wrested from the material by the historian (Binion, 1977, p. xi): "To probe Hitler's politics I immersed myself in his words and deeds until I could feel out the motive forces behind them. Each successive insight led me to validating material previously unknown or overlooked." Even more problematically, as we have seen, Binion (1978a, p. 321) claims special insight not only into Hitler but into his mass audience as well, here referring to a Hitler speech of May 3, 1921, on the lost territories in the East: "That documentary find confirmed for me my intuition of the German trauma. . . . The insight had been won through self-projection into his national public. This opened mass phenomena to direct psychohistorical inquiry." Beyond the special difficulties in defining a mass psyche, such a lonely and exalted empathy means that Binion rejects not only the intrusion of models and theories (except his own) but the use of anything but the purest primary source for his subject's words (see Binion, 1968). For Binion primary and secondary works not reporting his subject's actual words are useful only in confirming his own empathic interpretation of the words themselves, as exemplified by his selective use of the recollections of Hitler's friend August Kubizek.

Binion (1977) has claimed, in effect, that he knows Hitler through his words better than did an early colleague of, and standard source on, Hitler, Hermann Rauschning (1940). Rauschning's arguments and conclusions have rightly been challenged by historians, but there is no doubt that he was there and that his reporting of Hitler's remarks is accurate. This accuracy has been confirmed by other sources on Hitler's utterings, which show a consistency of theme and expression. Stenographic accuracy, in any case, is not always necessary to convey what the psychohistorian in particular wants to know. The same considerations apply, to cite two further examples, to the publication of Otto Wagener's recollections from close range (see Turner, 1978) and the earlier memoirs of German England expert Fritz Hesse (1954). Such sources are ignored by Binion, since his historical method demands a communion, not a discussion (see Binion, 1981). And since his interpretation is based completely on conviction, there is little hope of an objective discussion or confirmation of it. In contrast, those who use a variety of sources and models—as, for instance, Waite has done—offer not only a breadth of vision and information, conducive to refutation, augmentation, emendation, and further inquiry, but also a degree of control over the distortion inherent in too subjective an involvement in the material.

The phenomenon of countertransference—that is, the subjective response of the psychoanalyst to the patient—was originally regarded by Freud as an impediment to analysis (Loewenberg, 1982). It has since been recognized within the psychoanalytic community that this phenomenon is not only unavoidable but desirable and effective in gaining insight into the patient. Historians, among others, have long known the same thing (Loewenberg, 1977), and proper psychohistorical method calls for the careful use of subjective as well as objective analysis. Nonetheless, a historian must be aware of his own biases and subjective concerns, so that they will not distort his view of the past. The best work in history expresses the emotional link between historian and subject as insight and understanding. The key is finding the proper balance between objectivity and subjectivity. Binion (1978a, p. 314) himself, in speaking of the tendency of historical records to provide just what the psychohistorian needs, inadvertently admits the dangers of too much subjectivity: "My own odd experience has been that the key pieces always survive, however little else does." In finding exactly what he is looking for, Binion, in the blunt words of Loewenberg (1975b, p. 23), has in the last analysis produced a work on Hitler "based on Binion's fantasies and not Hitler's."

Conclusion

We have seen how psychohistory, spurred by the charismatic mass movements of the twentieth century, has grappled in new ways with political history by applying the knowledge of the human psyche gained by psychoanalysis. The psychoanalytic tradition, as we have noted, lies between art and science in such a way as to be a peculiarly appropriate mode of inquiry for historians seeking out the motives behind particular words and deeds of the past. Different approaches and models based on this tradition, with their various advantages and shortcomings, have been of tremendous value in helping to make sense of the historical record. We have also seen how the prescriptive tendency inherited from psychoanalysis as a medical discipline and philosophical system, while offering some, often impassioned, insights, runs counter to the historian's aim, also embodied by the Freudian paradigm, of subjecting theory to experience. In the end, patient historical rigor, rather than impatient political or cultural remedy, will provide for temperate and informed, if no less earnest, prescription. Psychohistory, in its contribution to the psychological understanding of political man, will help moderate impatient inflation of present conviction and instill proper humility in the face of human experience. It is, after all, the role of history, as of all art, to show by means of both the unique and the common the poverty of the conceit that other lives have nothing to tell us.

References

Barber, J. *The Presidential Character: Predicting Performance in the White House.* (2nd ed.) Englewood Cliffs; N.J.: Prentice-Hall, 1972.

Barzun, J. "The Muse and Her Doctors." *American Historical Review*, 1972, 77, 36–64.

Besançon, A. "Psychoanalysis: Auxiliary Science or Historical Method?" *Journal of Contemporary History*, 1968, 3, 149–162.

Binion, R. *Frau Lou: Nietzsche's Wayward Disciple.* Princeton, N.J.: Princeton University Press, 1968.

Binion, R. "Repeat Performance: A Psychohistorical Study of Leopold III and Belgian Neutrality." *History and Theory*, 1969, 8, 214–259.

Binion, R. "Hitler's Concept of *Lebensraum:* The Psychological Basis." *History of Childhood Quarterly*, 1973, 2, 187–258.

Binion, R. *Hitler Among the Germans.* New York: Elsevier, 1976.

Binion, R. "Reply." *Psychohistory Review*, 1977, 6 (1), 71–72.

Binion, R. "Doing Psychohistory." *Journal of Psychohistory*, 1978a, 5, 313–323.

Binion, R. Review of Waite (1977). *Journal of Psychohistory*, 1978b, 5, 295–301.

Binion, R. *Soundings: Psychohistorical and Psycholiterary.* New York: Psychohistory Press, 1981.

Bloch, M. *The Historian's Craft.* (P. Putnam, trans.) New York: Random House, 1964.

Brink, T. "The Case of Hitler: An Adlerian Perspective on Psychohistory." *Journal of Individual Psychology*, 1975, *31*, 23–31.

Brodie, F. *Thaddeus Stevens: Scourge of the South.* New York: Norton, 1959.

Brodie, F. "Jefferson Biographers and the Psychology of Canonization." *Journal of Interdisciplinary History*, 1971, *2*, 155–171.

Brodie, F. *Thomas Jefferson: An Intimate History.* New York: Norton, 1974.

Brodie, F. *Richard Nixon: The Shaping of His Character.* New York: Norton, 1981.

Bromberg, N. "Hitler's Character and Its Development: Further Observations." *American Imago*, 1971, *28*, 289–303.

Bromberg, N. "Hitler's Childhood." *International Review of Psycho-Analysis*, 1974, *1*, 227–244.

Bromberg, N., and Small, V. *Hitler's Psychopathology.* New York: International Universities Press, 1982.

Clinch, N. *The Kennedy Neurosis: A Psychological Portrait of an American Dynasty.* New York: Grossett & Dunlap, 1973.

Cocks, G. "A. A. Milne: Sources of His Creativity." *American Imago*, 1977a, *34*, 313–326.

Cocks, G. " 'Cowardice, Thy Name Is Bourgeoisie!' Hitler as Rankian Hero." Unpublished manuscript, 1977b.

Cocks, G. "The Hitler Controversy." *Political Psychology*, 1979, *1* (2), 67–81.

Cocks, G. *Psychotherapy in the Third Reich: The Göring Institute.* New York: Oxford University Press, 1985.

Coles, R. "Shrinking History." *New York Review of Books*, Feb. 22, 1973, pp. 15–21; March 8, 1973, pp. 25–29.

Collingwood, R. *The Idea of History.* Oxford, England: Clarendon Press, 1946.

Crews, R. "Analysis Terminable." *Commentary*, 1980, *70* (1), 25–34.

Crosby, F. "Evaluating Psychohistorical Explanations." *Psychohistory Review*, 1979, 7 (4), 6–16.

Crosby, F., and Crosby, T. "Psychobiography and Psychohistory." In S. Long (ed.), *The Handbook of Political Behavior.* New York: Plenum, 1981.

Decker, H. *Freud in Germany: Revolution and Reaction in Science 1893–1907.* Psychological Issues Monograph 41. New York: International Universities Press, 1977.

DeMause, L. "The Evolution of Childhood." *History of Childhood Quarterly*, 1974, *1*, 503–575.

DeMause, L. "What Is Psychohistory?" *Journal of Psychohistory*, 1981, *9*, 179–184.

DeMause, L., and Ebel, H. (eds.). *Jimmy Carter and American Fantasy.* New York: Psychohistory Press, 1977.

Demos, J. *A Little Commonwealth: Family Life in Plymouth Colony.* New York: Oxford University Press, 1970a.

Demos, J. "Underlying Themes in the Witchcraft of Seventeenth-Century New England." *American Historical Review*, 1970b, *75*, 1311–1326.

Demos, J. "Developmental Perspectives on the History of Childhood." *Journal of Interdisciplinary History*, 1971, *2*, 315–328.

Demos, J. *Entertaining Satan: Witchcraft and the Culture of Early New England.* New York: Oxford University Press, 1982.

Dilthey, W. *Pattern and Meaning in History: Thoughts on History and Society.* (H. Rickman, ed.) New York: Harper & Row, 1962.

Erikson, E. "Hitler's Imagery and German Youth." *Psychiatry*, 1942, 5, 475–493.

Erikson, E. "The Legend of Hitler's Childhood." In *Childhood and Society*. New York: Norton, 1950.

Erikson, E. *Young Man Luther: A Study in Psychoanalysis and History*. New York: Norton, 1958.

Erikson, E. *Gandhi's Truth: On the Origins of Militant Nonviolence*. New York: Norton, 1969.

Eysenck, H. "What Is Wrong with Psychoanalysis?" In *Uses and Abuses of Psychology*. New York: Viking Penguin, 1953.

Fitzpatrick, J. "Some Problematic Features of Erik H. Erikson's Psychohistory." *Psychohistory Review*, 1977, 5 (3), 16–27.

Freud, S. *Totem and Taboo*. In J. Strachey (ed.), *The Complete Psychological Works of Sigmund Freud*. Vol. 13. London: Hogarth Press, 1955. (Originally published 1913.)

Freud, S. *Some Character-Types Met with in Psycho-Analytic Work*. Chap. 2: "Those Wrecked by Success." In J. Strachey (ed.), *The Complete Psychological Works of Sigmund Freud*. Vol. 14. London: Hogarth Press, 1957. (Originally published 1916.)

Freud, S. *Group Psychology and the Analysis of the Ego*. In J. Strachey (ed.), *The Complete Psychological Works of Sigmund Freud*. Vol. 18. London: Hogarth Press, 1955. (Originally published 1921.)

Freud, S. *Civilization and Its Discontents*. In J. Strachey (ed.), *The Complete Psychological Works of Sigmund Freud*. Vol. 21. London: Hogarth Press, 1961. (Originally published 1930.)

Freud, S., and Bullitt, W. *Thomas Woodrow Wilson: A Psychological Study*. Boston: Houghton Mifflin, 1967.

Friedländer, S. *History and Psychoanalysis: An Inquiry into the Possibilities and Limits of Psychohistory*. (S. Suleiman, trans.) New York: Holmes & Meier, 1978.

George, A., and George, J. *Woodrow Wilson and Colonel House: A Personality Study*. Don Mills, Ontario: Longman Canada, 1956.

Glad, B. *Charles Evans Hughes and the Illusions of Innocence*. Urbana: University of Illinois Press, 1966.

Glad, B. "Contributions of Psychobiography." In J. N. Knutson (ed.), *Handbook of Political Psychology*. San Francisco: Jossey-Bass, 1973.

Greenstein, F. *Personality and Politics: Problems of Evidence, Inference, and Conceptualization*. Chicago: Markham, 1969.

Greven, P. *Four Generations: Population, Land and Family in Colonial Andover, Massachusetts*. Ithaca, N.Y.: Cornell University Press, 1970.

Greven, P. *The Protestant Temperament: Patterns of Child Rearing, Religious Experience and Self in Early America*. New York: Knopf, 1978.

Hanfstaengle, E. *Hitler: The Missing Years*. London: Eyre & Spottiswoode, 1957.

Hesse, F. *Hitler and the English*. (F. A. Voigt, ed. and trans.) London: Wingate, 1954.

Heston, L., and Heston, R. *The Medical Casebook of Adolf Hitler: His Illnesses, Doctors and Drugs*. Briarcliff Manor, N.Y.: Stein & Day, 1979.

Hillgruber, A. *Germany and the Two World Wars*. (W. Kirby, trans.) Cambridge, Mass.: Harvard University Press, 1981.

Hoffmann, H. *Hitler Was My Friend*. (R. Stevens, trans.) London: Burke, 1955.

Hughes, H. "History and Psychoanalysis: The Explanation of Motive." In *History as Art and as Science*. New York: Harper & Row, 1964.

Hughes, J. "Toward the Psychological Drama of High Politics: The Case of Bismarck." *Central European History*, 1977, *10*, 271–285.

Hughes, J. *Emotion and High Politics: Personal Relations at the Summit in Late Nineteenth-Century Britain and Germany*. Berkeley: University of California Press, 1983.

Hunt, D. *Parents and Children in History: The Psychology of Family Life in Early Modern France*. New York: Basic Books, 1970.

Kardiner, A. *The Psychological Frontiers of Society*. New York: Columbia University Press, 1949.

Kearns, D. *Lyndon Johnson and the American Dream*. New York: Harper & Row, 1976.

Kennan, G. *Russia and the West Under Lenin and Stalin*. Boston: Little, Brown, 1961.

Klauber, J. "On the Dual Use of Historical and Subjective Method in Psychoanalysis." *International Journal of Psycho-Analysis*, 1968, *49*, 80–88.

Kovel, J. "Erik Erikson's Psychohistory." *Social Policy*, 1974, *4* (5), 60–66.

Krueger, K. *I Was Hitler's Doctor: His Intimate Life*. New York: Biltmore, 1943.

Langer, W(alter). *The Mind of Adolf Hitler: The Secret Wartime Report*. New York: Basic Books, 1972.

Langer, W(illiam). "The Next Assignment." *American Historical Review*, 1958, *63*, 283–304.

Lasswell, H. *Psychopathology and Politics*. Chicago: University of Chicago Press, 1931.

Lifton, R. *Death in Life: The Survivors of Hiroshima*. New York: Basic Books, 1967.

Lifton, R. *Revolutionary Immortality: Mao Tse-tung and the Chinese Cultural Revolution*. New York: Random House, 1968.

Lifton, R. "Psychohistory." *Partisan Review*, 1970, *37*, 11–32.

Lifton, R. *The Broken Connection: On Death and the Continuity of Life*. New York: Simon & Schuster, 1979.

Loewenberg, P. "The Psychohistorical Origins of the Nazi Youth Cohort." *American Historical Review*, 1971a, *76*, 1457–1502.

Loewenberg, P. "Theodor Herzl: A Psychoanalytic Study in Charismatic Political Leadership." In B. Wolman (ed.), *The Psychoanalytic Interpretation of History*. New York: Basic Books, 1971b.

Loewenberg, P. "The Unsuccessful Adolescence of Heinrich Himmler." *American Historical Review*, 1971c, *76*, 612–641.

Loewenberg, P. "Psychohistorical Perspectives on Modern German History." *Journal of Modern History*, 1975a, *47*, 229–279.

Loewenberg, P. "Recent Trends of Hitler Biographies." Paper presented at Georgetown History Forum Conference on German History, Oct. 1975b.

Loewenberg, P. "Why Psychoanalysis Needs the Social Scientist and the Historian." *International Review of Psycho-Analysis*, 1977, *4*, 305–315.

Loewenberg, P. "Psychoanalytic Models of History: Freud and After." Paper presented at conference on "History and Psychology: Recent Studies in the Family, Biography and Theory," Stanford University, May 1982.

Loewenberg, P. *Decoding the Past: The Psychohistorical Approach*. New York: Knopf, 1983.

Macalpine, I., and Hunter, R. *George III and the Mad Business.* New York: Pantheon Books, 1969.

Mack, J. "Psychoanalysis and Historical Biography." *Journal of the American Psychoanalytic Association,* 1971, *10,* 143–179.

Mack, J. *A Prince of Our Disorder: The Life of T. E. Lawrence.* Boston: Little, Brown, 1976.

McRandle, J. "The Suicide." In *The Track of the Wolf: Essays on National Socialism and Its Leader, Adolf Hitler.* Evanston, Ill.: Northwestern University Press, 1965.

Mazlish, B. "Group Psychology and Problems of Contemporary History." *Journal of Contemporary History,* 1968, *3,* 163–177.

Mazlish, B. "Toward a Psychohistorical Inquiry: The 'Real' Richard Nixon." *Journal of Interdisciplinary History,* 1970, *1,* 49–105.

Mazlish, B. *In Search of Nixon: A Psychohistorical Portrait.* New York: Basic Books, 1972.

Mazlish, B. Letter to the Editor. *New York Review of Books,* May 3, 1973, p. 36.

Mazlish, B. *James and John Stuart Mill: Father and Son in the Nineteenth Century.* New York: Basic Books, 1975.

Mazlish, B. *Kissinger: The European Mind in American Policy.* New York: Basic Books, 1976.

Mazlish, B., and Diamond, E. *Jimmy Carter: A Character Portrait.* New York: Simon & Schuster, 1980.

Mazon, M. "Young Richard Nixon: A Study in Political Precocity." *The Historian,* 1978, *41,* 21–40.

Meyerhoff, H. "On Psychoanalysis as History." *Psychoanalysis and the Psychoanalytic Review,* 1962, *49,* 3–20.

Orlow, D. "The Significance of Time and Place in Psychohistory." *Journal of Interdisciplinary History,* 1974, *5,* 131–138.

Pflanze, O. "Toward a Psychoanalytic Interpretation of Bismarck." *American Historical Review,* 1972, 77, 419–444.

Prisco, S. *An Introduction to Psychohistory: Theories and Case Studies.* Frederick, Md.: University Publications of America, 1980.

Raack, R. "When Plans Fail: Small Group Behavior and Decision-Making in the Conspiracy of 1808 in Germany." *Journal of Conflict Resolution,* 1970, *14,* 3–19.

Rauschning, H. *The Voice of Destruction.* New York: Putnam, 1940.

Recktenwald, J. *Woran hat Adolf Hitler gelitten? Eine neuropsychiatrische Deutung* [From what did Adolf Hitler suffer? A neuropsychiatric interpretation]. Munich: Reinhardt, 1963.

Reich, W. *Character Analysis.* (2nd ed.) (T. Wolfe, trans.) New York: Orgone Institute Press, 1949.

Rieff, P. *Freud: The Mind of the Moralist.* (3rd ed.) Chicago: University of Chicago Press, 1979.

Rockwood, D., and Cocks, G. "The Use and Abuse of Psychohistory." *Journal of Psychohistory,* 1977, *5,* 131–138.

Rogin, M. *Fathers and Children: Andrew Jackson and the Subjugation of the American Indian.* New York: Random House, 1976.

Rogow, A. *James Forrestal: A Study of Personality, Politics and Policy.* New York: Macmillan, 1963.

Rolle, A. "The Historic Past of the Unconscious." In H. Lasswell, D. Lerner, and H. Speier (eds.), *Propaganda and Communication in World History*. Vol. 3. Honolulu: University of Hawaii Press, 1980.

Runyan, W. *Life Histories and Psychobiography: Explorations in Theory and Method*. New York: Oxford University Press, 1982.

Sempell, C. "Bismarck's Childhood: A Psychohistorical Study." *History of Childhood Quarterly*, 1974, *2*, 107–124.

Shore, M. "Biography in the 1980s: A Psychoanalytic Perspective." *Journal of Interdisciplinary History*, 1981, *12*, 89–113.

Smith-Rosenberg, C. "The New Woman and the Psycho-Historian: A Modest Proposal." *Group for the Use of Psychology in History Newsletter*, 1975, *4* (3), 4–11.

Stannard, D. *Shrinking History: On Freud and the Failure of Psychohistory*. New York: Oxford University Press, 1980.

Stierlin, H. *Adolf Hitler: A Family Perspective*. New York: Psychohistory Press, 1977.

Stolfi, R. "Barbarossa Revisited: A Critical Reappraisal of the Opening Stages of the Russo-German Campaign (June–December 1941)." *Journal of Modern History*, 1982, *54*, 27–46.

Strachey, L. *Eminent Victorians*. New York: Putnam, 1918.

Strouse, J. *Alice James: A Biography*. Boston: Houghton Mifflin, 1980.

Strozier, C. "Disciplined Subjectivity and the Psychohistorian: A Critical Look at the Work of Erik H. Erikson." *Psychohistory Review*, 1977, *5* (3), 28–31.

Strozier, C. *Lincoln's Quest for Union: Public and Private Meanings*. New York: Basic Books, 1982.

Tucker, R. *Stalin as Revolutionary, 1879–1929: A Study in History and Personality*. New York: Norton, 1973.

Tucker, R. "A Stalin Biographer's Memoir." Paper presented at conference on "History and Psychology: Recent Studies in the Family, Biography and Theory," Stanford University, May 1982.

Turner, H. (ed.). *Hitler aus nächster Nähe: Aufzeichnungen eines Vertrauten 1929-1932* [At Hitler's elbow: Notes of a confidant, 1929-1932]. Frankfurt on Main: Ullstein, 1978.

Waite, R. "Adolf Hitler's Anti-Semitism: A Study in History and Psychoanalysis." In B. Wolman (ed.), *The Psychoanalytic Interpretation of History*. New York: Basic Books, 1971a.

Waite, R. "Adolf Hitler's Guilt Feelings: A Problem in History and Psychology." *Journal of Interdisciplinary History*, 1971b, *1*, 229–249.

Waite, R. *The Psychopathic God: Adolf Hitler*. New York: Basic Books, 1977.

Weinstein, F. *The Dynamics of Nazism: Leadership, Ideology and the Holocaust*. Orlando, Fla.: Academic Press, 1980.

Weinstein, F. *Woodrow Wilson: A Medical and Psychological Biography*. Princeton, N.J.: Princeton University Press, 1981.

Weinstein, F., and Platt, G. *The Wish to Be Free: Society, Psyche, and Value Change*. Berkeley: University of California Press, 1969.

Weinstein, F., and Platt, G. "History and Theory: The Question of Psychoanalysis." *Journal of Interdisciplinary History*, 1972, *2*, 419–434.

Weinstein, F., and Platt, G. *Psychoanalytic Sociology: An Essay on the Interpretation of Historical Data and the Phenomena of Collective Behavior*. Baltimore: Johns Hopkins University Press, 1973.

Weinstein, F., and Platt, G. "The Coming Crisis in Psychohistory." *Journal of Modern History*, 1975, *47*, 202–228.

Wellman, J. "Some Thoughts on the Psychohistorical Study of Women." *Psychohistory Review*, 1978, 7 (2), 20–24.

Wexler, A. "The Early Life of Emma Goldman." *Psychohistory Review*, 1980, 7 (4), 7–21.

Wills, G. *The Kennedy Imprisonment: A Meditation on Power*. Boston: Little, Brown, 1982.

Wright, G. *Insiders and Outliers: The Individual in History*. New York: W. H. Freeman, 1981.

Wurgraft, L. Review of Weinstein and Platt (1973). *Journal of Interdisciplinary History*, 1975, *5*, 491–496.

Yankelovich, D., and Barrett, W. *Ego and Instinct: The Psychoanalytic View of Human Nature—Revised*. New York: Random House, 1970.

SIX

Ingredients of Leadership

Margaret G. Hermann

Leaders and leadership have held a place of importance in considerations of politics since time immemorial. Guides have been written indicating how a person can achieve and retain a position of political leadership; biographies of political leaders are commonplace; media archives contain voluminous records of what political leaders have said and done; some analysts try to forecast what certain leaders will do, while others try to explain what and why these same leaders have behaved in a particular way; leaders' names become attached to policies, and they are held accountable for their consequences. And yet the systematic study of political leadership remains in its infancy. As Burns (1978, p. 2) has observed, political "leadership is one of the most observed and least understood phenomena on earth." Part of the problem is the lack of agreement on what political leadership is and on what is involved in exercising such leadership. Differences exist because those studying political leadership often are looking at leaders and leadership from different vantage points and with different purposes in mind. Like the proverbial blind men feeling the elephant, each thinks that his focus and purpose connotes the whole.

Note: Support for writing this chapter was received from the Leadership Development Program of the Mershon Center at Ohio State University. The chapter benefited from the exchange of ideas on leadership with members of the Mershon Faculty Leadership Seminar—in particular, Virgil Blanke, Lila Carol, Luvern Cunningham, Frederick Cyphert, Charles Hermann, Richard Herrmann, David Lampton, Thomas Milburn, Philip Stewart, Donn Vickers, and Robert Woyach.

Throughout this chapter the terms "group" and "organization" are used as generic terms to cover the variety of institutions and units in which political leaders function; "follower" and "constituent" are used as synonyms for those being led. Where "he" is used, "she" could equally as well have been used. The discussion in this chapter assumes that there is a leader and one or more sets of followers in a somewhat organized political setting. The focus is not on how an individual becomes a political leader or on the establishment of a political unit.

The intent of the present chapter is to examine the various ways of looking at leadership and to propose a framework for the study of political leadership that incorporates the important pieces of these other conceptualizations. The framework will be amplified by illustrations from research and writing on political leadership.

The Leadership Dilemma

Reviews of the many ways in which leadership has been defined (see, for example, Bass, 1981; Broedling, 1981; Burns, 1978; Cronin, 1980; Hunt and Larson, 1975, 1977, 1979; Hunt, Sekaran, and Schreisheim, 1982; Kellerman, 1984; McCall and Lombardo, 1978; Mintzberg, 1973; Paige, 1977; Stogdill, 1974; Vroom, 1976) suggest four images of leadership. The first might be called the "pied piper of Hamelin" image of leadership. Like the pied piper, who led the mice out of Hamelin, the leader sets the goals and directions for his followers and with promises charms them into following him. The leader is in charge of what happens and how it happens. In this image of leadership, the leader and his characteristics are the focus of attention. By knowing what the leader is like and what his goals and strategies are, we will be able to describe leadership. The "great man" and trait approaches to leadership grow out of this image.

A second image of leadership is that of the leader as salesman. Leadership involves being sensitive to what people want and offering to help them get it. Responsiveness to people's needs and desires is important as is being able to persuade people that you can help them. According to this view, what happens will depend on the relationship between leaders and followers. Transactional and exchange theory approaches to leadership revolve around this image.

A third image of leadership focuses on the leader as puppet. In this image of leadership, the leader is given direction and strength by his followers, who pull the strings and make him move. The leader is the agent of the group, reflecting the goals of the group and working in its behalf. To understand leadership one needs to learn about the expectations and goals of the followers. In this image leadership is "in the eye of the beholder." Many of the attributional approaches to leadership have this focus.

The fire-fighting view of leadership provides a fourth image. In this image leadership occurs in response to what is happening in the environment. Therefore, by learning about the context in which leadership is occurring, we can understand the nature of the leadership. The environment provides demands, constraints, and choices for leaders and followers. Contingency theories of leadership build on this image.

The dilemma for those studying political leadership is that illustrations of all four images of leadership are readily available. Moreover, a poll of the "man-on-the-street" variety would probably reveal the expectation that a strong political leader would inculcate all four images. Such a leader would have vision but at the same time would be responsive to his followers' wishes and able to persuade them to work for their convictions while considering when the time is right for action. One way of dealing with this dilemma is to consider leadership as an umbrella concept, containing under it a number of different types of variables that combine to determine the nature of the leadership at any point in time.

Figure 1 suggests some possible ingredients of leadership based on the

Figure 1. The Ingredients of Leadership.

Context or Setting

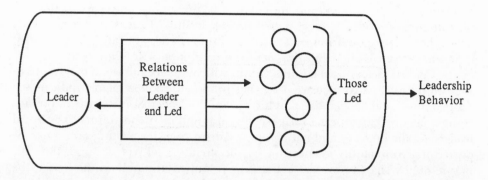

images described above. To understand leadership we need to know something about (1) the leader's personality and background, as well as the recruitment process by which he became a leader; (2) the characteristics of the groups and individuals whom the leader is leading; (3) the nature of the relationship between the leader and those he leads; (4) the context or setting in which the leadership is taking place; and (5) the outcome of interactions between the leader and those led in specific situations. What kind of leadership we have depends on the nature and combination of these five ingredients. As in a recipe for food, these basic ingredients can be combined in different ways to produce a variety of results.

In the rest of this chapter, we will examine these various ingredients of leadership in more detail, in an attempt to specify what aspects of each are critical to understanding leadership. Because the focus of this chapter is political leadership, the particular factors we will study in our examination of each ingredient will be those that have been found or proposed as relevant to the exercise of political leadership. To delimit more carefully what the "political" in political leadership refers to, let us look at the context ingredient first.

Context Factors

"Context" is used here to refer to the setting in which leadership is occurring or is sought. In thinking about the context of leadership, we need to consider the situation in which the leader and led find themselves. When leadership of a political nature is exercised, the situation generally calls for a decision regarding the allocation of resources or rewards for a group or organization or a decision regarding what a group or organization's goals and strategies should be (see, for example, Katz, 1973; Kellerman, 1984; Tucker, 1981). These are decisions in which all those involved generally have a stake and in which there are often "winners" and "losers." Moreover, these are decisions around which explicit value conflicts can develop over what is "right" and "wrong" and over what kind of outcome is desirable.

Although there is a tendency to limit political leadership to what happens in a governmental setting, the above consideration of the types of decisions political leaders must confront suggests that political leadership can occur in a broader context. The principal or headmaster of a school, a general in the army, the head of a local Chamber of Commerce, the chairman of the board of a corporation, the organizer of a citizen's action group, the head of a clinic or hospital, the minister of a church, the head of a union, the curator of a museum, a university president— all can, and often do, engage in political leadership. That is, they often must decide how an organization's resources and rewards are allocated, or they must determine the goals and strategies that the organization will follow.

Context factors set the limits within which leaders and those they are leading can operate. As R. Stewart (1982) has proposed, context factors indicate the "constraints" and "demands" that are put on the leader. Some of the important context factors that appear to trigger demands and offer constraints to political leaders are the presence and nature of formalized rules for making decisions, the degree of accountability to constituents, the strength and type of opposition, the nature of any shared political beliefs, the resources available to the leader, the organizational layering between leader and led, and the general tenor of the times. Each of these context factors helps to define the situation in which political leadership can take place.

By learning whether there are formalized rules for making decisions and the nature of such rules, we can begin to understand under what circumstances a leader can exercise leadership and the limits on leadership behavior. For example, the checks and balances built into the American democratic system allow leaders (presidents, governors, mayors) to indicate their dislike or impatience with what is happening in the legislative system through use of the veto. The legislators can indicate their concerns and preferences through the manner in which they deal with the leader's appropriations requests. The system is designed to keep each party sensitive to the other; the effects of decreases in this sensitivity have led to accusations such as "imperial presidency" (Schlesinger, 1973) or "tethered presidency" (Franck, 1981) or to titles such as "Boss" (Royko, 1971). The vote of "no confidence" plays a similar role in parliamentary systems.

By learning to whom a leader is accountable, we ascertain what followers he will need to pay attention to. The more accountable the leader is to certain followers, the more attention the leader will direct toward them. If leaders are elected by a specific group, the leaders must be concerned—at least around election time—with how they are viewed by these followers. The more frequently such elections are held, the more influence the followers have over the leader. If the leader wants to retain his position, he will be responsive to the interests and expectations of these followers. Members of the U.S. House of Representatives, for example, who must stand for reelection every two years, tend to spend more time in their home districts and maintain closer ties with their home district constituents than United States senators, whose terms are six years.

If leaders are appointed, they are generally required to display loyalty to and support for those who appointed them (see, for example, Bennis, 1973; Destler, 1983). Such leaders often must walk a fine line between doing their job and pleasing those who put them in their positions. Appointed leaders, however, can employ several strategies to achieve some latitude for molding the groups they lead: (1) They can differentiate within their role between issues and problems of concern to those who appointed them and issues and problems of little concern.

Latitude increases over those issues/problems of little concern. (2) They can develop an independent power base as a counter to those who appointed them. (3) They can become indispensable to those who appointed them, so that any attempt at dismissal will reflect poorly on those doing the appointing. School superintendents often employ all three of these techniques to ensure keeping their jobs and to allow them to be more than an agent of the school board (see, for example, Cunningham and Hentges, 1983).

As with accountability, the strength and nature of opposition indicate whom a political leader must pay attention to and under what circumstances. The most pressing problem for a political leader occurs when his opposition is located within a constituency to which he is responsible, seeks to remove him as leader, and has a wide base of support. In such cases a political leader is forced to deal with the opposition if he is to retain his leadership position. If there are established rules for handling such situations—as, for example, votes or mediation/arbitration—these mechanisms are invoked. But if these means of resolving differences are not in place, the leader often must save his position by engaging in compromise or coalition-building behavior. Hagan (1980), studying the effects of such cases at the top levels of government in thirty-six countries around the world, found that most aspects of government came to a standstill while the leaders tried to salvage their positions.

Opposition within a political leader's constituencies can also be based on differences over policy or over the choice of a particular response to a problem. These circumstances provide the leader with opportunities to become a salesman for his point of view by highlighting the differences betwen what he believes and the beliefs of the opposition, by redefining or reinterpreting his position so that there is little difference, or by coopting people from the opposition and having them urge change on their fellows. In seeking ratification in the United States Senate for the test ban treaty in 1963, President Kennedy was confronted with a Senate substantially opposed to the treaty. By using each of these strategies, Kennedy was able to get the treaty passed (see Lepper, 1971).

Political leaders also are constrained to work within the belief systems and norms of their constituencies. Do the people perceive that there is an enemy? Are there some well-defined ways of dealing with the enemy? Is there a particular religious belief system that most follow? Do the people expect to participate in policy making and have their opinions sought after? Is there a preference for centralized or decentralized control? Are resources perceived to be abundant or scarce? The more generally shared a particular belief or norm among the leader's constituents, the more the leader has to pay attention to and work within the parameters of that belief or norm. In recent discussions of leadership in America, Maccoby (1981) and Naisbett (1984) have noted that Americans increasingly are demanding to participate in policy making, particularly when the policy in question affects them. "The new leader is a facilitator, not an order giver" (Naisbett, 1984, p. 209). Kellerman (1984, pp. 65–66) suggests that Americans have always shown "ambivalence and resistance" to strong political leadership: "Americans do not ordinarily grant anyone the right to lead them anywhere for very long." To function effectively in this American political culture, leaders and would-be leaders must be sensitive to this belief in the importance of input, if not participation, in decision making.

These shared norms and beliefs can vary across time, across cultures, and even within a culture across ethnic groups. Thus, we find different patterns of political leadership through time, around the world, and within the same country as leaders try to cope with the belief systems and norms of their followers. One of the major problems that leaders of newly independent nations have faced is bringing together groups with tribal, linguistic, and racial differences, in an attempt to forge national shared orientations and perspectives that often go against the grain of deeply entrenched group norms and beliefs (see, for example, Jackson and Rosberg, 1984; Rosberg and Jackson, 1982; Roth, 1968; Wriggins, 1969). Leaders who are not sensitive to changes in these shared norms and beliefs can lose their positions. As Nixon (1982, p. 36) has observed, one of the reasons Churchill and de Gaulle lost their leadership positions after World War II may have been that "the qualities that make a man a great leader in war are not necessarily those that the people want in peace."

Also of concern in considering the context factors affecting political leadership are the resources immediately under the control of the leader. Can the leader mobilize the resources for leadership, or must he seek authorization from or cooperate with other groups or individuals to gain access to resources? Such political leaders as school superintendents, mayors, governors, generals, and union presidents can propose agendas for action but can implement what they want to do only with resources authorized by groups of coequals: school boards, city councils, state legislatures, prime ministers/presidents, and management. These situations call for different leadership strategies than when the resources are under the leader's immediate control. Negotiation, consensus seeking, coalition building, compromise, and other conflict resolution techniques become important to gaining access to the resources. Leaders who can directly mobilize the resources necessary for leadership can be more demanding, prescriptive, and inflexible.

Some political leadership settings permit fact-to-face interaction between the leader and the led; others involve mediated interaction, the leader's constituencies knowing him only through the media or through representatives of the leader. Many political leaders must operate in both types of settings. Thus, a president or prime minister interacts face to face with his cabinet and leaders of any parliament or legislature, but his leadership is mediated to the people at large and to the bureaucracy. Whereas he has control over his actions with those he sees personally, the president/prime minister must rely on others to create the appropriate image for those where leadership is mediated. What the leader seeks from these two types of constituencies often differs as well. Policy generation and decision making are frequently the functions of the face-to-face groups, while building support and implementation are generally the foci of the "at-a-distance" leadership. What is required of the leaders and followers in each of these settings differs. The vast literature on leaders in small groups has relevance for face-to-face political leadership (see, for example, C. Hermann, 1978; Hollander, 1978; Janis, 1972; Verba, 1961; Vroom and Yetton, 1973); the literature on leaders in organizations is more applicable to "at-a-distance" political leadership (see Bennis, 1978; Buck and Korb, 1981; Destler, 1972; George, 1980; Maccoby, 1976; Mintzberg, 1973; Peters and Waterman, 1982).

Political leaders must also be attuned to the general tenor of the times in which they are operating. Is the period one of relatively little change, turmoil, or crisis or one of rapid change, much turbulence, and many crises? L. Stewart (1977) notes that different styles of leadership are required as times move from the relatively peaceful to the more turbulent. Compare the problems that faced big-city local officials in the United States during the 1960s as marches, demonstrations, and riots over civil rights and Vietnam became almost commonplace with the less dramatic problems these same officials had to deal with in the 1970s. Jackson and Rosberg (1984) have likened the political leader to the commander of a ship, arguing that under certain circumstances the leader is involved in political navigation—guiding and steering the political unit toward its goals—while at other times the leader is engaged in political seamanship, trying to keep the political unit afloat with some stability and order. In turbulent times followers frequently become more demanding, coordination among activities and groups becomes more difficult, and the leader's legitimacy and position are often under attack.

Another aspect of the times that can provide information about the context of leadership is whether the period is one in which resources are plentiful or one in which resources are scarce. As one university president (Enarson, 1981) has observed, it requires different skills and motivation to lead an institution when things must be continuously cut back than when one has the luxury of starting new programs and of going in new directions. As resources become scarcer, competition among constituents can become exaggerated, as can criticism of the leader. The leader always appears to be favoring one side over another, whether or not such is indeed the case. The values of equality and "fair play" can develop into rallying cries for groups of constituents. The leader is "damned if he does and damned if he doesn't."

As this discussion suggests, the context begins to define the parameters within which political leadership can take place. The context indicates which constituents the leader will want to pay attention to and delimits any constraints on how the leader can interact with those he is trying to lead. Moreover, the context puts bounds on the procedures/processes the leader can use in engaging in leadership. In effect, the context determines how effective political leadership will be defined and by whom.

Leader Characteristics

A second ingredient of leadership is the leader—the individual who has been given authority to make decisions for a set of individuals, a group, an organization, or a government and is held accountable (by these individuals or this group, organization, or government) for the consequences of any decisions. We are interested here in what the political leader is like. Specifically, what characteristics may influence the way in which the leader exercises political leadership?

A search of journalistic and scholarly writing on political leaders suggests that the following seven characteristics can influence political leadership: (1) the leader's basic political beliefs, (2) the leader's political style, (3) the leader's motivation for seeking a political leadership position, (4) the leader's reactions to stress and pressure, (5) the manner in which the leader was first recruited into a political leadership position, (6) the leader's previous political experience, and (7) the political climate when the leader was starting out. Information about beliefs, style, motivation, and reaction to stress tells us something about the leader's personality;

data on the other items provide informaton about the leader's background and base of experience. The reader will note a similarity between these seven characteristics and the kind of information President Carter sought about Prime Ministers Sadat and Begin in preparation for the Egyptian-Israeli negotiations in the fall of 1978 (see Carter, 1982, p. 320).

Political Beliefs. One of the most direct ways of understanding the relationship between what a political leader is like and what he is likely to urge on his followers comes through learning about the leader's basic political beliefs. Beliefs determine how leaders interpret the political environment and help leaders chart and map the political terrain in which they are operating. Beliefs imply goals and strategies. Thus, for example, a union president's belief about the usefulness of a strike as a means of gaining leverage in bargaining with management can affect the way in which he leads the union during a period of negotiation. A legislative leader's belief in the importance of holding the party line can influence his relationship with other legislators and the issues he brings to a vote. And a school board president's belief that curriculum as well as financial decisions are part of the board's responsibility can affect the agenda for all the board members.

Recently some scholars have attempted systematically to study the belief systems of political leaders and to suggest the implications of beliefs for leadership behavior. Using the "operational code" concept developed by Leites (1951) and George (1969, 1979), a number of researchers have examined the political beliefs of American presidents, secretaries of state, and senators (see, for example, Holsti, 1970; Johnson, 1977; Stuart and Starr, 1982; Walker, 1977). The operational code provides a tool by which to assess both the philosophical and the instrumental beliefs that guide a political leader's policy positions. Holsti (1977) and Walker (1983) have distinguished four types of operational codes and have proposed the kinds of political behavior that leaders with these operational codes are likely to advocate and urge on their followers.

In addition to learning what a leader believes, we need to learn how strongly he holds these beliefs. How important are the beliefs to the leader? Is the leader so persuaded of his beliefs that they are a dominant force in his life, acting as a lens through which all external events are interpreted; or is the leader more responsive to the environment, letting events shape and change his beliefs? The more resistant a leader's beliefs are to outside influences, the more likely those beliefs are to affect his leadership activity. Like the crusader of old, the leader with strong political beliefs seeks to convince others of his position and is likely to see much of what is happening politically as relevant to his cause. Leaders whose views are less firmly entrenched are more pragmatic. The particular situation will generally determine how firmly—and whether—such leaders will press their case. Stoessinger (1979) has argued that the strength of leaders' beliefs is a critical dimension in assessing the effectiveness of those responsible for making American foreign policy in the twentieth century and that recent American presidents and secretaries of state can be divided into "crusaders" and "pragmatists." Tetlock (1984) has observed similar divisions among members of the British House of Commons based on the strength of the parliamentarians' ideological positions.

Political Style. A leader's political style can also influence those he leads. The influence, though, is more indirect than that of beliefs. Whereas political beliefs directly influence policy, political style sets the tone and pattern of leadership: how the leader interacts with those he is leading and how he acts when representing his followers. For example, does the leader emphasize personal diplomacy and face-to-face meetings, or does he prefer to work through intermediaries? Does he tend to work with other people, or does he prefer to "go it alone"? Is there an emphasis on political rhetoric and propaganda? Does the leader have a flair for the dramatic? Is the leader interested in studying problems in detail, or does he seek more general information? Is secrecy essential during the policy-making process? Each of these questions focuses on an element of political style. Kotter and Lawrence (1974) have identified five types of mayors based on political style factors: the caretaker, the ceremonial, the personality/individualist, the executive, and the program entrepreneur.

The political style of a leader can have limiting effects on those working with the leader, in at least two ways. First, those around the leader tend to cater to his stylistic preferences in order to keep open access to him. Second, there is the doppelgänger effect (Bennis, 1973); that is, political leaders tend to surround themselves with people who are their doubles—people with similar stylistic preferences or complementary styles. The leader selects advisers and staff with whom he feels "comfortable" and "compatible." As observed about President Nixon and his special assistant for national security affairs, Henry Kissinger, both acted as if "centralized authority was a prerequisite for flexibility; both men were critical of ad hoc styles of decision making . . . [and both] were distrustful of bureaucracies" (Eldridge, 1976, p. 20). Through his doubles, the leader's style can permeate the political unit.

Motivation for Position. What are the leader's reasons for seeking a leadership position? Among the motives attributed to political leaders are the need for power, a cause (a problem they want to see addressed, a philosophy they want adopted, a crisis), a sense of obligation, the need for approval and esteem from others, the challenge of the position, the need for status and recognition, and the need to compensate for personal problems (see Burns, 1978; M. Hermann, 1977; Knutson, 1973; Lasswell, 1930, 1948; Rejai, 1979; Wriggins, 1969). These motives have implications for what political leaders will do. Barber (1965), studying Connecticut legislators, found that different motives for becoming a member of the state legislature were associated with different kinds of legislative behavior. The names Barber attached to the four types of legislators he discovered as a result of this analysis give some flavor of the relationship between motivation and behavior: advertiser, spectator, reluctant, and lawmaker. The advertiser was interested in status and recognition and used the legislature as a forum for self-advancement; the spectator was motivated by the need for approval and was essentially submissive in the legislative process; the reluctant, drawn into the legislative arena out of a sense of obligation, became involved with moral and ethical issues in the legislature; the lawmaker was challenged by the position and became actively involved in initiating legislation and in committee work. Rejai (1979; Rejai and Phillips, 1983) has observed a similar relationship between motivation for leadership and political behavior in revolutionaries.

In addition to influencing what they will do, leaders' motives will drive them to seek political leadership positions that provide the opportunity for satisfying their needs. "Leadership is fired in the forge of ambition and opportunity" (Burns, 1978, p. 126). Browning and Jacob (1964) have reported a match between local political leaders' motivation and the demands of the leadership role they occupied; moreover, those with the strongest motivation sought leadership positions with the greatest likelihood of satisfying their needs. The author (M. Hermann, 1979b, 1980) has observed a similar phenomenon among heads of government around the world. There often appears to be a fit between what the leadership position will enable a leader to do and what the leader wants to do.

It is tempting at this point to suggest that political leaders fail or leave office at least partly because their motives are no longer compatible with the leadership position. The leader may have misperceived the opportunity, the situation may have changed with time, the needs and interests of those being led may have changed, or the leader's own needs may be different. In his biography of the post–World War II German leader Kurt Schumacher, Edinger (1965) has provided an interesting study of a person whose motives at points in his career were compatible with the leadership role he sought and at other times were incompatible. Where there was a match between his motives and the demands of the position, Schumacher appears to have been more successful at both acquiring and holding leadership than when there was a mismatch.

Reactions to Stress. Political leadership positions are stressful because the situations the leader faces are often marked by uncertainty, involve high stakes, depend on the cooperation of multiple groups and organizations, and involve conflicts of values. To achieve such positions, political leaders have had to learn to deal with stress. In this section we are interested in what political leaders do when stress becomes higher than usual and in the situations where political leaders become particularly vulnerable to stress.

A rather large literature has now developed on political leaders' reactions to stress (see George, 1974, 1980; M. Hermann, 1979a; Holsti, 1972; Janis, 1972). As stress increases, leaders tend to become more rigid; to reach conclusions more quickly; to focus less on the consequences of actions; to see the present in terms of the past; to rely only on close associates, whose opinions and support can be counted on; and to take direct control of the decision-making process. These changes reduce the number of options, as well as the amount and kinds of information considered, and enable the leaders to focus more on searching for support than on dealing with the situation; that is, they permit the leader to deal with the stress by avoiding facing all the ramifications of the problem.

Not all leaders react in this fashion. As Robert Kennedy (1969, p. 31) observed about the policy makers who participated in the United States decision making during the Cuban missile crisis, the quality of the performance of those involved was quite varied. Some were highly creative and resourceful, while others were erratic and "even appeared to lose their judgment and stability." As Kennedy's comment suggests, some leaders find stressful situations motivating and rise to the challenge; others experience some distress in such situations and respond as the literature indicates; a few become debilitated and unable to act. All these responses have implications for the leadership that the individual leader will provide. Thus, it is important to ascertain how a leader usually responds to stress.

How a leader responds to stress becomes particularly important in explaining his behavior in those situations where the stress is no longer something that threatens only the group, organization, or government but also the leader personally—that is, where the leader's own self-esteem becomes involved. Some of the problems and situations that can lead to internalization of stress are those that pose a threat to the leader's position as leader or to a policy in which he has invested much time and effort; that are likely to lead to failure and consequent loss of status for the political unit; that threaten the leader or those immediately around him with physical harm; or that the leader has little control over but for which he will be held accountable. Watergate, Vietnam, and the Iranian hostage crisis were such situations for American presidents Nixon, Johnson, and Carter, respectively. The student riots in the late 1960s posed such problems for college and university presidents, as did the Vietnam protests and civil rights protests for city mayors and state governors. Integration mandates have posed such situations for school superintendents.

These situations and problems, when internalized, can become all-consuming for the leader. Other issues are forgotten or set aside, and attention becomes riveted on dealing with the "life-and-death" issue facing the leader. All resources are directed toward coping with the problem. Political leadership becomes focused, drawing the attention of all in the political unit to what is now the leader's problem. By studying how a leader has handled other potentially stressful situations and problems, we may be able to predict which of these types of situations he will internalize and how he will deal with the problem once it is internalized. A brief examination of President Wilson's behavior during the ratification process of the Treaty of Versailles illustrates this point.

Getting the Treaty of Versailles ratified by the U.S. Senate became a stressful situation for Woodrow Wilson as he saw this treaty, which he had worked so hard and long to get, going down to defeat. The treaty had become *his* treaty and the centerpiece of his plan for a better world. Not only the treaty but Wilson's own self-esteem was on the line. George (1971) suggests that Wilson's behavior during the Senate ratification vote mirrored other occasions when he also was threatened with defeat to policies or positions with which he himself identified during his term as governor of New Jersey and as president of Princeton University. In these instances Wilson "could tolerate no ambiguity and could recognize no legitimate intermediate position. He tended to lump together all of his opponents. . . . Instead of modest concessions to win a sufficient number of moderates over, he stubbornly insisted upon his own position and rudely rebuffed their overtures, thus driving them into the arms of his most bitter and extreme opponents. . . . He seems to have experienced opposition to his will in such situations as an unbearable threat to his self-esteem" (George, 1971, p. 94). "A political obeserver, had he studied carefully Wilson's career as president of Princeton University, might have forecast accurately the shape of things to come during the period when Wilson was president of the United States" (Link, 1947, pp. 90–91).

Background Factors. As just suggested for Wilson, information on a leader's background can provide insights into the kind of leadership he will exercise. In particular, information on the leader's first political position, on the nature of his political experiences, and on the political climate into which he was socialized can help in understanding what the leader will do.

Barber (1972) has argued that knowledge about a political leader's first political position provides clues about later leadership behavior. The nature of the position, the means by which it was acquired, and the ways in which the leader behaved have implications for future leadership activities. A leader will tend

on future occasions to fall back on the rhetoric and practices that helped him
succeed the first time. Because it was the first, this experience is often given added
significance in memory and remains especially vivid. Glad (1980, p. 92) observes
that Jimmy Carter, in his successful race to become a Georgia state senator, his
entry position into politics, "exhibited many of the qualities that would help him
in his later political quests": a singleminded pursuit of his goal, "an ability to
dramatize the righteousness of his cause," and an ability to develop "an enthusiastic and dedicated following" of people in the right places. And Ronald Reagan,
as Cannon (1982, p. 35) has noted, "can recount the saga of the strike committee's
daily maneuvers with a detail that eludes him on many presidential issues." Working with the strike committee, made up of faculty and fellow students at Eureka
College in Illinois in the autumn of 1928, was the experience that "first thrust
Reagan into the limelight . . . and was Reagan's first venture into politics"
(pp. 35–36). Reagan became a spokesman for the committee after one meeting at
which he discovered that "an audience has a feel to it and, in the parlance of the
theater, that audience and I were together" (Reagan, 1965, p. 37). "Always, and
it is no small measure of his effectiveness in public life, Reagan would think of
speech making as a way of binding himself and the audience together" (Cannon,
1982, p. 36).

   What kind of experience has the political leader had in the kind of position
he now holds? How similar is the present position to others he has held? How
long a tenure does the leader have in his present position? The answers to these
questions provide us with some ideas about the repertoire of behaviors the leader
will have; how concerned the leader will need to be with consolidating and legitimating his position, as opposed to getting on with the task at hand; how much
influence the leader can probably have over policy; and how much the leader will
have to learn on the job. With experience the leader gains a sense of what will
work and not work, and he also learns which cues in the environment must be
taken into account and which are superfluous in specific situations. Manchester
(1978) has proposed that General Douglas MacArthur's long experience in the Far
East aided him in his post as supreme commander for the allied powers for the
reconstruction of Japan—in knowing how far he could go, in trying to fit what
was done within the Japanese sense of tradition.

   There is a growing debate over whether the skills learned in one type of
political position transfer to another (see Burns, 1984; Cronin, 1980; C. Hermann,
1983; Moore, 1983; National Governors' Association, 1978, 1981; Rejai, 1984; Woronoff, 1972). Are the skills needed to run a political campaign the same as the skills
needed to govern? Are the skills developed as a revolutionary similar to those
needed to form and maintain a government? How easily can those holding leadership positions in the private sector move into leadership positions in the public
sector? The author (M. Hermann, 1983) has found that the very skills that enabled
certain African leaders to be good revolutionaries in the struggle for independence
often hindered them in their attempts to govern their new countries. The more
responsive and sensitive these African revolutionaries were to contextual cues, the
easier their transition was. Those with a plan, which they were determined to
implement regardless of its appropriateness, and those who had difficulty moving
from an adversarial posture to one of conciliation and compromise had problems
with the transition.

It also becomes important to ascertain how the leader acquired his present position and why. Did he work his way through the system, was he advanced by a patron, was he coopted because of certain expertise or a particular characteristic? This information can tell us how much the leader knows about the individuals, groups, and organizations with which he must work; how likely he is to be imbued with their norms and goals; how dependent the leader is on certain other individuals and groups and how responsive he must be to them; and how broad a mandate the leader has to institute change. Carlson (1972) and Dusek (1982) have reported very different kinds of experiences and characteristics for "place-bound" and "career-bound" school superintendents. The place-bound superintendents—those who came up through the ranks in one school district to assume their position—are not expected to "rock the boat," whereas the career-bound superintendents—those who move from one place and superintendency to another place and new superintendency—are often brought in to do a particular task or to tackle a specific problem. Examining Regional First Party secretaries in the Soviet Union, P. Stewart (1977) found that different types of attitudes were associated with different recruitment patterns.

In addition to their experiences, leaders are also products of their times. What was going on when the leader was growing up, seeking his first job, and assuming responsibility? What were the events and ideas shaping young people during the time the leader was moving from adolescence through early adulthood, often the time when political socialization is occurring most rapidly? What were the problems and issues that people were having to cope with? Surveying America's future leaders, Broder (1981, p. 11) has commented: "America is changing hands. In the 1980s the custody of the nation's leadership will be transferred from the World War II veterans, who have held sway for a generation, to a new set of men and women. These newcomers . . . do not carry the memories or the scars of the Great Depression. They were not part of the victory over totalitarianism in Italy, Germany, and Japan. . . . Theirs has been a time of affluence and inflation, of extraordinary education advance, and of wrenching social change and domestic discord. . . . Their wars were fought in Korea and Vietnam, and if fewer of them returned as casualties, none returned as victors." Broder's observations suggest the common generational experiences that can have an effect on those who become leaders. These common experiences help to shape the norms and beliefs of the leaders and their constituents about the political environment. If not completely imbued themselves with the ideas that have shaped their generation, leaders will have to deal with these ideas in their constituents to retain their positions of leadership.

In Summary. To understand the impact the leader will have on political leadership, we need to learn about seven characteristics of the leader. Knowledge about a leader's beliefs and how strongly they are held suggests the kinds of goals and strategies the leader will urge on his political unit and how hard he will push for his views. Information about a leader's political style indicates something about how the political unit will be structured and will function. The leader's motivation is often reflected in the type of political unit he seeks to lead and in the general focus of attention of the leader's behavior. Learning how the leader reacts to stress provides insight into what issues are likely to cause problems for the leader and how detrimental and pervasive stress is likely to be. Knowledge about the leader's political background indicates how experienced he is at his position, how free of political debts and obligations he is, and what strategies and styles have paid off for the leader across time. In effect, in examining these characteristics, we learn how principled, how flexible and responsive, how driven, how stress resistant, and how experienced the leader is, as well as some of the implications of these traits for what the leader is likely to do in a position of political leadership.

Leaders' Constituencies

Leaders are leaders because they have followers—people who have granted them authority and to whom they are accountable, their constituents. Political leaders often have more than one constituency for whom they are providing leadership. A mayor's constituencies, for instance, are the people who elected him, as well as the members of the party he represents, the city bureaucracy, the city council, and the local interest groups that petition the city for aid. A school board president's constituencies are the members of the school board, the parents of children in the schools, the tax-paying citizens of the community, the teachers and administrators, and the students in the schools. In examining political leadership, we need to recognize who the leader's various constituencies are in order to understand to whom the leader must be responsive and the demands, expectations, and images (the implicit evaluations of the leader by his followers) that are helping to determine the leader's behavior.

Constituents who have face-to-face contact on a regular basis with a leader can communicate their desires directly, and their images of the leader are based on these experiences. In many political leadership situations, however, constituents have never had the chance to meet their leaders face to face but know them only through others or through the media. Expectations and images are translated and retranslated, shaped and molded. Constituents must rely on others to learn about the leader, and leaders must rely on others to learn what their constituents want. The possibility for misperceptions and misunderstandings increases; the possibility for manipulation also increases (see, for example, Barber, 1980; Dubin, 1979; Iyengar and others, 1984). Chapter Seven of this volume describes some of the factors that can influence the expectations and images of constituents who do not have face-to-face contact with their political leaders.

In addition to knowing what constituents expect, we need to learn what motivates them to follow this particular leader. Why is he their leader? Why are they members of this group? Some people become constituents simply because they live in the leader's political jurisdiction. Others may have an issue that they want to receive attention, a cause they wish to see pursued. Some may idealize the leader; some may regard him as a mentor or patron. Others may be following their friends' or associates' lead or acting out of a sense of civic duty. These different reasons present the leader with different kinds of leadership tasks.

Answers to two other questions are relevant to understanding the importance of knowledge about constituents for political leadership. How mobilizable are the various constituent groups? And how dependent is the leader on the constituents for his position? Responses to these two questons suggest which set or sets of constituents leaders may show preferences to and may focus attention on when conflicts arise among constituencies or when their positions are threatened. The answers to these questions help to determine which constituents the leader will want to monitor.

To some extent, the issue of mobilizability among constituents hinges on the attention, interest, and motivation of a leader's various followers. Are the constituents attuned enough to what is happening that a simple appeal can activate them, or must there be a crisis involving them to catch their attention and activity? Is there a particular cause or program that the constituents want enacted or achieved and for which they are willing to work, at times regardless of cost? Is there personal rapport between leader and led that can be turned into active support when it is needed? As well as knowing where a leader's potential supporters are, by considering mobilizability we learn where the leader's potential opponents are as well and how quickly they are likely to surface. Wriggins (1969) has stressed that only by constantly mapping the constituent terrain for mobilizable proponents and opponents and acting on this information can leaders in Third World countries survive.

Although political leaders may have several constituencies, often they are more dependent for their position on certain of these groups or individuals than others. The congressman who indicates there is no way he could have supported party leadership and voted against a bill that meant jobs for people in his district has noted his differential dependence on two types of constituents. We are asking here which groups of constituents have the ability to remove leaders from their positions. The answer may depend on the issue, who is interested in the issue, and the particular point in time. Elected officials become much more tied to those who elected them during a campaign period; single-interest groups have more of an effect when their issue is being debated or discussed. Knowing what the constituencies on whom a leader is dependent will and will not tolerate in his leadership suggests the boundaries likely to be visible in that leader's activity.

McCall and Lombardo (1978, p. 154) have observed: "Maybe the real essence of leadership lies in the leader's ability to deal with nonfollowers—the countless peers, colleagues, bosses, associates, and key people who occupy positions in other units or outside organizations that directly influence the group's ability to do its job." Constituents' views of how well a political leader interacts with other leaders or coequals, of their leader's effectiveness with other leaders, can affect their own sense of confidence and well-being. Followers want their leader to appear to be in charge and to be having some influence in such relationships. Thus, the local media are quick to highlight what happens between city council president and mayor; union members observe carefully the negotiations between union leadership and management; people observe what their head of state does when he goes abroad or to an international meeting. Judgments of how effective a political leader is emerge from such observations, as do the seeds of discontent. Ascertaining constituents' views on their leader's skill in dealing with other leaders can provide insight into how satisfied the constituents are with the leader.

As with information about the political context and leaders, knowledge about who a leader's constituents are and what they want and expect from their leaders provides us with insight into the nature of political leadership. In learning about a political leader's constituents, we can begin to see to whom the leader is responding and why, to ascertain the degree of support the leader is likely to have for various kinds of activities and from whom, and to determine the degree of confidence, authority, and esteem invested in the leader.

Relations Between Leader and Constituents

How do political leaders relate to those they are trying to lead? With multiple constituencies and their often varying expectations, needs, and interests, political leaders, if they want to retain their positions, are faced with building relationships that foster convergence, or at least minimize conflict, among those individuals and groups to whom they are accountable. Eric Jonsson, a former mayor of Dallas, has likened this process to "walking on a moving belt while juggling," with people throwing things at one and an end of the belt on fire (quoted in Kotter and Lawrence, 1974, p. 175). The leader becomes involved in what Thompson (1967) has called the coalignment process (see also Kotter and Lawrence, 1974). The leader works on maintaining a "fit" ("match," "congruence," "compatibility") between the expectations and needs of his various groups of followers, his own goals and interests, and those of the political unit he is leading. Political leaders perform the following functions in striving to coalign and relate to their constituents: (1) build networks and coalitions, (2) set the agenda and shape policy, (3) inspire enthusiasm, (4) shape and maintain an image, (5) select and develop an effective staff, (6) gather information, and (7) accomplish tasks. In effect, in relating to his constituents, the political leader becomes a consensus builder, a policy advocate, a motivator, an advertiser, a recruiter, a listener, and a manager.

Neustadt (1960) has defined the major tools of a political leader as those of persuasion and bargaining. These tools are particularly important to the political leader as he works to build networks and coalitions among his constituencies to support specific policies and programs. Patronage, tradeoffs, negative sanctions, appeals to reference-group loyalties and friendship, cooptation, and compromise all become ways of persuading followers to be supportive and enable the leader to develop consensus among diverse constituencies. "Reward the faithful and the susceptible; intimidate the opponent and the wavering ally" (Wriggins, 1969, p. x). Through such consensus-building activities, the leader begins to make sure that he can mobilize his constituencies when he needs their support.

To ensure that their own goals and their constituents' goals receive attention and policy consideration, political leaders try to set the agenda for their groups. For issues that they perceive are important to a number of their constituent groups, they become policy advocates in an attempt to have the issue addressed or to work for a specific position. In such instances political leaders become active in a particular area, putting their prestige and power on the line in an attempt to resolve the issue. If the leader is successful, there is a certain bonding of leader to followers. The agenda-setting/policy-shaping function also can involve educating constituents to realize that there is a need for certain kinds of policies. Action rhetoric, highlighting certain statistics and poignant case studies, and constant publicity are ways of increasing constituents' awareness and of convincing other leaders that a problem exists (see Cobb and Elder, 1972).

Journalist James Reston has observed that in the United States the White House is the "pulpit of the nation and the president the chaplain." As chaplain, the president provides inspiration for the people, builds morale, and gives the nation a sense of mission. One way for political leaders to relate to their various constituents is by getting them enthusiastic and excited about what is happening in their political unit. This inspiration can come from espousing an ideology that promises improvement in the lot of all people. It can also come from emphasizing the strengths and positive qualities of a group as well as from suggesting that there is an external threat to the survival of the group. The political leader counts on the increased morale and enthusiasm of his constituents to improve their perceptions of his leadership abilities and their willingness to follow him. Some charismatic theories of leadership have been built around this motivating function (see, for example, House, 1977).

Because many constituents of political leaders know their leaders only indirectly, through others' eyes or through the media, leaders' relationships with their followers are often based on the image that results. Shaping and tailoring that image so that it represents what the leader wants to convey and matches the needs and expectations of the constituents can become a preoccupation of political leaders. Leaders try to arrange for opportunities to present themselves in the best light or to accentuate their leadership skills. They seek press secretaries (or their equivalents) and public opinion specialists to guide their activities. As Lehnen (1972, p. 268) observed in studying United States governors, "Public opinion is the governor's wealthy, jealous mistress—demanding his attention, critical of his shortcomings, potentially dangerous to his position, but a necessary component for achieving many of his objectives." Image management permits the political leader some control over this "mistress."

In addition to the at-a-distance quality of much political leadership, Seligman (1968) has noted the corporate character of such leadership. Political leadership is a collective product of many individuals acting on behalf of and in consultation with the leader. By carefully selecting, developing, and configuring these other key players, the leader can indirectly build relationships with various kinds of constituents. Kotter and Lawrence (1974, pp. 163-164), in their discussion of the relatively successful administration of Mayor Ivan Allen of Atlanta, note: "He created a small but important mayor's office" by hiring two assistants "who played roles . . . that Allen himself could not assume. [One assistant] was central to Allen's creating, maintaining, and using a relationship with the city bureaucracy and the city council. He was a politically sophisticated and nurturing type of person with historical ties [to these two political bodies] that Allen did not have. [The other assistant] had the technical skills to deal with Washington and the sensitivity to deal with young blacks, which again Allen himself did not seem to have." Selective recruiting improved the relationship between leader and constituents.

In order to know what his various constituencies want, to begin to anticipate problems, and to cope with constituents' expectations, the political leader learns to monitor the environment in which he is operating—to be aware of his constituents' views of what he is doing and advocating. The leader becomes a listener, reaching out "as widely as he can for every scrap of fact, opinion, gossip, bearing on his interests and relationships [as leader]. . . . He becomes his own director of his own central intelligence" (Neustadt, 1960, p. 154). The very act of showing interest in learning about constituents' wants and opinions can improve

rapport, as Hentges (1983) found for public school superintendents and as Kotter
and Lawrence (1974) observed in mayors. There is an increased sense of importance
and of efficacy on the part of the constituents from whom informaton is sought.
In effect, in the information-gathering process, the leader keeps in close touch
with his various constituents while increasing their sense of participation in policy
making.

Accomplishing something—making decisions, implementing policies—
also helps in developing the relationship between political leader and constituents,
since such accomplishments indicate an interest in constituents' problems. Leaders
walk a tightrope with respect to working toward their group goals. They must
show some movement toward the goals without unrealistically raising the expectations of their various constituents; they must demonstrate short-term gains without jeopardizing long-term solutions; and they must deal with high-priority
collective needs and problems when such priorities may be low for certain important constituencies. In choosing problems to work on, many leaders engage in a
political calculus regarding the effort and risk involved in tackling the issue
relative to its impact on constituent support. Wriggins (1969, pp. 191–206) has
provided an example of such a calculation for Third World leaders in dealing
with the goal of developing their countries' economies. On the positive side,
economic development activities "may provide short-run gains in the quality of
life"; "may provide an integrative goal after independence is achieved"; "may help
to counteract tribal, regional, or other disharmonies"; and "may permit the government to provide additional resources to large groups in the society which it
fears otherwise may become disaffected." On the negative side, economic development activities may necessitate austerity measures, may not "spread advantages
equally," and may increase expectations and, in turn, opposition when development is not rapid enough. Thus, any activity regarding development has both
positive and negative aspects that must be weighed when one is making a choice.
Wriggins notes that one way for leaders to deal with this dilemma is to find a
problem to work on that cuts across a leader's constituencies and for which incremental success is possible. Incremental success helps to build confidence in the
leader's ability to do some things that are meaningful for his constituents.

We have been discussing functions that political leaders perform to develop
relationships with followers. Followers also engage in activities that facilitate the
relationship for political leaders. One such activity occurs for a short period of
time after a political leader assumes his position. For most political leaders, there
is a "honeymoon period" during which constituents refrain from criticism and
lend support; in effect, they withhold judgment and let the leader have time to set
the tone for his administration. If they are organized and have ideas or a plan of
action, leaders have more opportunity during this period to shape policy and the
group's agenda than at any other time. This "honeymoon period" generally lasts
only a brief time—often only a hundred days. It ends when some set of constituents
perceives that the leader is charting a wrong course or when there is a general
perception that the leader has had enough time to start.

Most constituents are not, of course, concerned about the leader's behavior
all the time. Only when decisions begin to impinge on things they hold dear or
when they have problems that are not being addressed do many constituents focus
their attention on the leader. For problems and decisions within their "zone of

indifference" (Barnard, 1938; Dubin, 1979), the constituents are accepting, compliant, and supportive of the leader, because what happens is of little consequence to them. Dubin has observed that leaders can build on this zone of indifference by adopting a "divide-and-conquer" strategy. If leaders can define the zone of indifference for their various constituencies, they can differentially target and time behavior so that no one group is affected all the time and so that there are enough indifferent groups to provide support for the action.

Constituents also engage in a "silent conspiracy for good" (Dubin, 1979, p. 231). Once leaders are accepted by certain groups of followers, these followers want to make the leader look good—even if they must rationalize his errors and inactivity. Hollander (1958, 1961, 1964, 1978) has proposed that, in the process of attaining leadership positions, leaders earn "idiosyncrasy credits," which they can expend in nonconforming behavior without losing esteem in the eyes of their followers. This phenomenon is particularly evident in the constituents of elected leaders; the followers "have a sense of investment in the leader that makes them feel greater responsibility for the leader's performance" (Hollander, 1978, p. 42).

Followers perceive their role in the relationship with leaders in different ways. Some want to be led, some want to be partners, some want to be inspired, some want to lead. Blanke (1983) has referred to these various ways of structuring the leader-follower relationship as power over, power through, power with, and power against. Little (1984) suggests that followers look for leaders who are predisposed to certain kinds of relationships with them. How the followers structure their other social arrangements influences their choice of and relationship with leaders. If the followers see themselves generally in opposition or competition with others, they will relate to a strong leader; if they see themselves as partners with others, they will seek a coequal as leader; if they see themselves as dependent on others, they will seek a leader on whom they can depend. Followers with these different relational orientations will be looking for leaders to emphasize certain of the functions described at the beginning of this section and to deemphasize others. Their evaluation of the leader will depend on the fit between their orientation and the leader's behavior.

In sum, political leaders relate to their various constituents through processes that are intended to increase the convergence or compatibility among the constituents' expectations, needs, and interests. Leaders can count on support from their constituents (1) if they are just beginning their tenure in a position, (2) if the followers are relatively indifferent to the problem or issue being addressed, (3) if they have built up some good will with their followers, and (4) if the followers' relationship with the leader matches their image of what the nature of the relationship should be.

Leadership Behavior

Leadership behavior is the action that results when a leader and those he is leading interact in a specific situation. Of all the ingredients of political leadership, behavior has received the least attention. One of the major reasons for this neglect is the difficulty we have in defining what kind of behavior indicates leadership behavior. There are many ways of allocating resources and rewards and of arriving at goals and strategies for a political unit—the focus of political leadership stipulated early in this chapter. Behavior that assures survival of the political unit is probably the bottom line, but what other kinds of behavior indicate political leadership? Among some possible behaviors are building consensus on priorities for action, maintaining the status quo, balancing the budget, changing programs or priorities, avoiding conflict, improving the quality of life of constituents, and institutionalizing processes and procedures. Tucker (1981) has proposed that the behaviors of importance to political leadership are definition of the situation for the political unit, design of a plan of action, and mobilization of constituents in support of the plan. Differentiating between transforming and transactional political leadership, Burns (1978) believes that the behaviors we should be examining are responsiveness to the needs, aspirations, and values of followers as well as the shaping (elevating) of these needs, aspirations, and values and the institutionalization of processes and procedures for continued responsiveness and change.

Another reason for the dearth of research on leadership behavior is its dependence on the other ingredients of leadership for specification. If we are interested in being descriptive regarding leadership behavior, instead of prescriptive in the manner of Burns and Tucker, often—in order to determine what behaviors are relevant—we need information about the context, the leader, the leader's constituents, and the relationship between the leader and led. The context in which leadership is taking place and the expectations and desires of the leader's constituents suggest the nature of the problem the political unit is facing and the kind of leadership behavior that is needed. The characteristics of the leader and the relations the leader has with his constituents indicate whether the leader is likely to be responsive to either the context or his constituents and, thus, whether the behavior the leader is engaging in matches that implied by an analysis of the context and constituents. Fiedler (1967; Fiedler and Chemers, 1976) has shown how the mix of these ingredients of leadership can affect behavior in groups. Groups differed in their levels of productivity and degree of cohesiveness, depending on the motivation of the leader, the amount of structure in the task, the degree of control the leader had over the group, and the amount of support group members gave to the leader. Examining the effectiveness of United States presidents, Wrightsman (1982) has shown that how much a president emphasizes such behaviors as identifying goals and priorities, getting legislation passed, and crisis decision making depends on the interaction of his characteristics with contextual and constituent factors.

As this discussion suggests, there is a need for more careful consideration about what behaviors characterize political leadership. The discussion also indicates that we may learn more about what behaviors are relevant as we move beyond focusing on one of the ingredients of leadership to exploring how the ingredients interact.

Conclusion

To understand political leadership, one must learn not only about the leaders involved but also about the individuals and groups whom the leaders are attempting to lead, about the nature of the relationship between the leaders and those they are leading, about the context or situation in which the leadership is taking place, and about the nature of the behavior being undertaken. Political leadership results from the interaction of these various ingredients of leadership; it is an umbrella concept that can be understood only if one examines all the ingredients and their combination. Much of the research on political leadership to date has focused on one of the ingredients. Thus, we have the four images of political leadership described at the outset of this chapter—the pied piper (with emphasis on the leader), the puppet (with emphasis on the followers), the salesman (with emphasis on the relationship between leader and led), and the fire fighter (with emphasis on the context). The challenge to those working in the political leadership area is to begin to combine the ingredients of leadership, in order to specify under what conditions, for what kinds of leaders and constituents, with what types of relationships, and for what behaviors these images hold. We have begun to delineate the factors that seem to have an impact for each of the ingredients of political leadership; now it is time to examine how each ingredient impinges on the others.

Consider the following kinds of questions. Under what contextual conditions can a leader's characteristics have an effect on political leadership; under what conditions are leaders fairly constrained in the effect they themselves can have on what happens? Do certain types of political leaders emphasize one way of relating to their constituents over others? What is the effect of such an emphasis on leadership behavior and on constituents' images? Does the nature of the context determine the ways political leaders need to relate to their constituents to garner their support? In answering questions like these, we can begin to understand how the various ingredients of leadership combine to affect one another.

Because political leadership involves decisions regarding allocation of resources and designation of goals and strategies, it often has a profound effect on events and at times on the direction of history. Political leadership makes a difference in all our lives. We can ill afford to continue focusing primarily on aspects of it and not understand the whole.

References

Barber, J. D. *The Lawmakers*. New Haven, Conn.: Yale University Press, 1965.

Barber, J. D. *The Presidential Character: Predicting Performance in the White House*. Englewood Cliffs, N.J.: Prentice-Hall, 1972.

Barber, J. D. *The Pulse of Politics: Electing Presidents in the Media Age*. New York: Norton, 1980.

Barnard, C. I. *The Functions of the Executive*. Cambridge, Mass.: Harvard University Press, 1938.

Bass, B. *Stogdill's Handbook of Leadership*. New York: Free Press, 1981.

Bennis, W. "The Doppelgänger Effect." *Newsweek*, Sept. 17, 1973, p. 13.

Bennis, W. *The Unconscious Conspiracy: Why Leaders Can't Lead*. New York: AMACOM (division of American Management Association), 1978.

Blanke, V. "Power." Unpublished manuscript, Department of Educational Administration, Ohio State University, 1983.

Broder, D. S. *Changing of the Guard: Power and Leadership in America*. New York: Viking Penguin, 1981.

Broedling, L. A. "The Psychology of Leadership." In J. H. Buck and L. J. Korb (eds.), *Military Leadership*. Beverly Hills, Calif.: Sage, 1981.

Browning, R. P., and Jacob, H. "Power Motivation and the Political Personality." *Public Opinion Quarterly,* 1964, *28,* 75–90.

Buck, J. H., and Korb, L. J. (eds.). *Military Leadership.* Beverly Hills, Calif.: Sage, 1981.

Burns, J. M. *Leadership.* New York: Harper & Row, 1978.

Burns, J. M. *The Power to Lead: The Crisis of the American Presidency.* New York: Simon & Schuster, 1984.

Cannon, L. *Reagan.* New York: Putnam, 1982.

Carlson, R. O. *School Superintendents: Careers and Performance.* Westerville, Ohio: Merrill, 1972.

Carter, J. *Keeping Faith: Memoirs of a President.* New York: Bantam Books, 1982.

Cobb, R., and Elder, C. *Participation in American Politics: The Dynamics of Agenda-Building.* Baltimore: Johns Hopkins University Press, 1972.

Cronin, T. E. *The State of the Presidency.* (2nd ed.) Boston: Little, Brown, 1980.

Cunningham, L. L., and Hentges, J. T. (eds.). *The American School Superintendency, 1982: A Full Report.* Arlington, Va.: American Association of School Administrators, 1983.

Destler, I. M. *Presidents, Bureaucrats, and Foreign Policy.* Princeton, N.J.: Princeton University Press, 1972.

Destler, I. M. "The Rise of the National Security Assistant, 1961–1981." In C. W. Kegley, Jr., and E. R. Wittkopf (eds.), *Perspectives on American Foreign Policy.* New York: St. Martin's Press, 1983.

Dubin, R. "Metaphors of Leadership: An Overview." In J. G. Hunt and L. L. Larson (eds.), *Crosscurrents in Leadership.* Carbondale: Southern Illinois University Press, 1979.

Dusek, C. A. "A Reexamination of the Differences Between Career-Bound and Place-Bound School Superintendents." Unpublished doctoral dissertation, Department of Educational Administration, Ohio State University, 1982.

Edinger, L. J. *Kurt Schumacher: A Study in Personality and Political Behavior.* Stanford, Calif.: Stanford University Press, 1965.

Eldridge, A. F. "The Crisis of Authority: The President, Kissinger, and Congress (1969–1974)." Paper presented at annual meeting of the International Studies Association, Toronto, March 1976.

Enarson, H. "Reflections of a University President." Paper presented at the Mershon Leadership Seminar, Ohio State University, May 1981.

Fiedler, F. E. *A Theory of Leadership Effectiveness.* New York: McGraw-Hill, 1967.

Fiedler, F. E., and Chemers, M. M. *Improving Leadership Effectiveness: The Leader Match Concept.* New York: Wiley, 1976.

Franck, T. M. (ed.). *The Tethered Presidency: Congressional Restraint on Executive Power.* New York: New York University Press, 1981.

George, A. L. "The 'Operational Code': A Neglected Approach to the Study of Political Leaders and Decision-Making." *International Studies Quarterly,* 1969, *13,* 190–222.

George, A. L. "Some Uses of Dynamic Psychology in Political Biography: Case Materials on Woodrow Wilson." In F. I. Greenstein and M. Lerner (eds.), *A Source Book for the Study of Personality and Politics.* Chicago: Markham, 1971.

George, A. L. "Adaptation to Stress in Political Decision-Making." In G. V. Coelho, D. A. Hamburg, and J. E. Adams (eds.), *Coping and Adaptation.* New York: Basic Books, 1974.

George, A. L. "The Causal Nexus Between Cognitive Beliefs and Decision-Making Behavior: The 'Operational Code.' " In L. S. Falkowski (ed.), *Psychological Models in International Politics*. Boulder, Colo.: Westview Press, 1979.

George, A. L. *Presidential Decision Making in Foreign Policy: The Effective Use of Information and Advice*. Boulder, Colo.: Westview Press, 1980.

Glad, B. *Jimmy Carter: In Search of the Big White House*. New York: Norton, 1980.

Hagan, J. D. "Regimes, Opposition, and Foreign Policy: A Cross-National Analysis of the Impact of Domestic Politics on Foreign Policy Behavior." Unpublished doctoral dissertation, Department of Political Science, University of Kentucky, 1980.

Hentges, J. T. "Superintendent–School Board Relations." In L. L. Cunningham and J. T. Hentges (eds.), *The American School Superintendency, 1982: A Full Report*. Arlington, Va.: American Association of School Administrators, 1983.

Hermann, C. F. "Decision Structure and Process Influences on Foreign Policy." In M. A. East, S. A. Salmore, and C. F. Hermann (eds), *Why Nations Act*. Beverly Hills, Calif.: Sage, 1978.

Hermann, C. F. "Public Leadership Qualities in Micro and Macro Situations." Paper presented to the Columbus Area Leadership Program, Nov. 10, 1983.

Hermann, M. G. (ed.). *A Psychological Examination of Political Leaders*. New York: Free Press, 1977.

Hermann, M. G. "Indicators of Stress in Policy Makers During Foreign Policy Crises." *Political Psychology*, 1979a, *1*, 27–46.

Hermann, M. G. "Who Becomes a Political Leader? Some Societal and Regime Influences on Selection of a Head of State." In L. S. Falkowski (ed.), *Psychological Models in International Politics*. Boulder, Colo.: Westview Press, 1979b.

Hermann, M. G. "Assessing the Personalities of Members of the Soviet Politburo." *Personality and Social Psychology Bulletin*, 1980, *6*, 332–352.

Hermann, M. G. "Leadership and Nation Building." Paper presented at annual meeting of the International Society of Political Psychology, St. Catherine's College, Oxford University, July 1983.

Hollander, E. P. "Conformity, Status, and Idiosyncrasy Credit." *Psychological Review*, 1958, *65*, 117–127.

Hollander, E. P. "Some Effects of Perceived Status on Responses to Innovative Behavior." *Journal of Abnormal and Social Psychology*, 1961, *63*, 247–250.

Hollander, E. P. *Leaders, Groups, and Influence*. New York: Oxford University Press, 1964.

Hollander, E. P. *Leadership Dynamics: A Practical Guide to Effective Relationships*. New York: Free Press, 1978.

Holsti, O. R. "The 'Operational Code' Approach to the Study of Political Leaders: John Foster Dulles' Philosophical and Instrumental Beliefs." *Canadian Journal of Political Science*, 1970, *3*, 123–155.

Holsti, O. R. *Crisis, Escalation and War*. Montreal: McGill-Queen's University Press, 1972.

Holsti, O. R. "The 'Operational Code' as an Approach to the Analysis of Belief Systems." Final Report to the National Science Foundation, Grant SOC75-15-368, Duke University, 1977.

House, R. "A 1976 Theory of Charismatic Leadership." In J. G. Hunt and L. Larson (eds.), *Leadership: The Cutting Edge*. Carbondale: Southern Illinois University Press, 1977.

Hunt, J. G., and Larson, L. (eds.). *Leadership Frontiers.* Carbondale: Southern Illinois University Press, 1975.

Hunt, J. G., and Larson, L. (eds.). *Leadership: The Cutting Edge.* Carbondale: Southern Illinois University Press, 1977.

Hunt, J. G., and Larson, L. (eds.). *Crosscurrents in Leadership.* Carbondale: Southern Illinois University Press, 1979.

Hunt, J. G., Sekaran, U., and Schreisheim, C. (eds.). *Leadership: Beyond Establishment Views.* Carbondale: Southern Illinois University Press, 1982.

Iyengar, S., and others. "The Evening News and Presidential Evaluations." *Journal of Personality and Social Psychology,* 1984, *46,* 778–787.

Jackson, R. H., and Rosberg, C. G. "Personal Rule: Theory and Practice in Africa." *Comparative Politics,* 1984, *16,* 421–442.

Janis, I. L. *Victims of Groupthink.* Boston: Houghton Mifflin, 1972.

Johnson, L. K. "Operational Codes and the Prediction of Leadership Behavior: Frank Church at Midcareer." In M. G. Hermann (ed.), *A Psychological Examination of Political Leaders.* New York: Free Press, 1977.

Katz, D. "Patterns of Leadership." In J. N. Knutson (ed.), *Handbook of Political Psychology.* San Francisco: Jossey-Bass, 1973.

Kellerman, B. (ed.). *Leadership: Multidisciplinary Perspectives.* Englewood Cliffs, N.J.: Prentice-Hall, 1984.

Kennedy, R. F. *Thirteen Days.* New York: Norton, 1969.

Knutson, J. N. "Personality in the Study of Politics." In J. N. Knutson (ed.), *Handbook of Political Psychology.* San Francisco: Jossey-Bass, 1973.

Kotter, J. P., and Lawrence, P. R. *Mayors in Action: Five Approaches to Urban Governance.* New York: Wiley, 1974.

Lasswell, H. D. *Psychology and Politics.* Chicago: University of Chicago Press, 1930.

Lasswell, H. D. *Power and Personality.* New York: Viking Penguin, 1948.

Lehnen, R. G. "Public Views of State Governors." In T. Beyle and J. O. Williams (eds.), *The American Governor in Behavioral Perspective.* New York: Harper & Row, 1972.

Leites, N. *The Operational Code of the Politburo.* New York: McGraw-Hill, 1951.

Lepper, M. M. *Foreign Policy Formulation: A Case Study of the Nuclear Test Ban Treaty of 1963.* Westerville, Ohio: Merrill, 1971.

Link, A. S. *Wilson: The Road to the White House.* Princeton, N.J.: Princeton University Press, 1947.

Little, G. *Political Ensembles.* Melbourne Politics Monograph. Parkville, Victoria, Australia: University of Melbourne, 1984.

McCall, M. W., Jr., and Lombardo, M. (eds.). *Leadership: Where Else Can We Go?* Durham, N.C.: Duke University Press, 1978.

Maccoby, M. *The Gamesman.* New York: Simon & Schuster, 1976.

Maccoby, M. *The Leader: A New Face for American Management.* New York: Simon & Schuster, 1981.

Manchester, W. *American Caesar: Douglas MacArthur, 1880–1964.* Boston: Little, Brown, 1978.

Mintzberg, H. *The Nature of Managerial Work.* Englewood Cliffs, N.J.: Prentice-Hall, 1973.

Moore, A. H. "High-Level Leadership: An Exploratory Study of the Dynamics of the Job of Presidents of Public Two-Year Colleges in the State of Ohio." Unpublished doctoral dissertation, Department of Educational Administration, Ohio State University, 1983.

Naisbett, J. *Megatrends: Ten New Directions Transforming Our Lives.* New York: Warner Books, 1984.

National Governors' Association. *Governing the American States: A Handbook for New Governors.* Washington, D.C.: Center for Policy Research, National Governors' Association, 1978.

National Governors' Association. *Reflections on Being Governor.* Washington, D.C.: Center for Policy Research, National Governors' Association, 1981.

Neustadt, R. E. *Presidential Power: The Politics of Leadership.* New York: Wiley, 1960.

Nixon, R. M. *Leaders.* New York: Warner Books, 1982.

Paige, G. D. *The Scientific Study of Political Leadership.* New York: Free Press, 1977.

Peters, T. J., and Waterman, R. H., Jr. *In Search of Excellence: Lessons from America's Best-Run Companies.* New York: Harper & Row, 1982.

Reagan, R., with R. G. Hubler. *Where's the Rest of Me?* New York: Duell, Sloan, Pearce, 1965.

Rejai, M. *Leaders of Revolution.* Beverly Hills, Calif.: Sage, 1979.

Rejai, M. "Revolutionary Leaders and Their Oppositions." Paper presented at annual meeting of the International Society of Political Psychology, Toronto, June 1984.

Rejai, M., and Phillips, K. *World Revolutionary Leaders.* New Brunswick, N.J.: Rutgers University Press, 1983.

Rosberg, C. G., and Jackson, R. H. *Personal Rule in Black Africa: Prince, Autocrat, Prophet, Tyrant.* Berkeley: University of California Press, 1982.

Roth, G. "Personal Rulership, Patrimonialism, Empire-Building in New States." *World Politics,* 1968, *20,* 194–206.

Royko, M. *Boss: Richard J. Daley of Chicago.* New York: New American Library, 1971.

Schlesinger, A. M., Jr. *The Imperial Presidency.* Boston: Houghton Mifflin, 1973.

Seligman, L. G. "Leadership: Political Aspects." In D. Sills (ed.), *International Encyclopedia of the Social Sciences.* Vol. 9. New York: Macmillan, 1968.

Stewart, L. H. "Birth Order and Political Leadership." In M. G. Hermann (ed.), *A Psychological Examination of Political Leaders.* New York: Free Press, 1977.

Stewart. P. D. "Attitudes of Regional Soviet Political Leaders: Toward Understanding Political Change." In M. G. Hermann (ed.), *A Psychological Examination of Political Leaders.* New York: Free Press, 1977.

Stewart, R. *Choices for the Manager.* Englewood Cliffs, N.J.: Prentice-Hall, 1982.

Stoessinger, J. G. *Crusaders and Pragmatists: Movers of Modern American Foreign Policy.* New York: Norton, 1979.

Stogdill, R. M. *Handbook of Leadership Research.* New York: Free Press, 1974.

Stuart, D., and Starr, H. "The 'Inherent Bad Faith Model' Reconsidered: Dulles, Kennedy, and Kissinger." *Political Psychology,* 1982, *3,* 1–33.

Tetlock, P. E. "Cognitive Style and Political Belief Systems in the British House of Commons." *Journal of Personality and Social Psychology,* 1984, *46,* 365–375.

Thompson, J. *Organizations in Action*. New York: McGraw-Hill, 1967.

Tucker, R. C. *Politics as Leadership*. Columbia: University of Missouri Press, 1981.

Verba, S. *Small Groups and Political Behavior: A Study of Leadership*. Princeton, N.J.: Princeton University Press, 1961.

Vroom, V. H. "Leadership." In M. Dunnette (ed.), *Handbook of Industrial and Organizational Psychology*. Skokie, Ill.: Rand McNally, 1976.

Vroom, V. H., and Yetton, P. W. *Leadership and Decision-Making*. Pittsburgh: University of Pittsburgh Press, 1973.

Walker, S. G. "The Interface Between Beliefs and Behavior: Henry A. Kissinger's Operational Code and the Vietnam War." *Journal of Conflict Resolution*, 1977, *21*, 129–168.

Walker, S. G. "The Motivational Foundations of Political Belief Systems: A Re-Analysis of the Operational Code Construct." *International Studies Quarterly*, 1983, *27*, 179–202.

Woronoff, J. *West African Wager: Houphouet Versus Nkrumah*. Metuchen, N.J.: Scarecrow Press, 1972.

Wriggins, W. H. *The Ruler's Imperative: Strategies for Political Survival in Asia and Africa*. New York: Columbia University Press, 1969.

Wrightsman, L. S. "The Social Psychology of U.S. Presidential Effectiveness." Robert I. Watson Memorial Lecture, University of New Hampshire, April 13, 1982.

SEVEN

Presidents in the Public Mind

Donald R. Kinder
Susan T. Fiske

Presidents create and convey identities that are to some degree uniquely their own. Particularly in periods such as the present, marked by candidate-centered campaigns, weak party organizations, and independent-minded voters, presidents are understood and judged increasingly on their own terms. Our chapter grapples with the appraisal process that connects presidents to their publics. It is about presidential leadership from that fabled perspective of the average American.

The social science literature pertinent to political leadership defined in this way is both vast and unruly. It is anchored at one end by case studies of charismatic figures (see, for example, Converse and Dupeax, 1966; Hyman and Sheatsley, 1953; Kavanaugh, 1974) and at the other by broad essays on the meaning and possibilities of leadership (see Burns, 1978; Edelman, 1964; Greenstein, 1965). At its center, to the degree that the literature can be said to possess a center, stands research on voting: entangled in controversy and promiscuously expanding (Converse, 1975; Kinder and Sears, 1985). Our essential problem is not that the literature provides no answers to our question but that it offers too many.

To try to order this jumble, we rely eclectically on ideas developed in social psychology. Social psychology has problems of its own: vigorous internal debates, formidable conceptual difficulties, unreplicable findings. There is, nevertheless,

Note: Portions of this chapter were originally prepared for the conference on Mass Response to Political Leadership, sponsored by the Center for Political Studies of the University of Michigan and held in New Haven, Connecticut, May 22-23, 1978. Randolph Wagner contributed substantially to that effort. For their thoughtful reactions, we thank conference coparticipants Robert Abelson, Heinz Eulau, Robert Lane, Warren Miller, David Sears, and Shelley Taylor. Shanto Iyengar, Richard Lau, David Mayhew, Steven Rosenstone, and Janet Weiss offered valuable comments on an earlier draft.

a natural bridge between the two: between social psychological theory and research, on the one hand, and the process of presidential appraisal, on the other. Although we cannot and do not promise a single grand theory, we do hope to deliver a set of general principles put to double use: both to organize the fragmented literature that bears on appraisal and to provide an account of how Americans make sense of and ultimately come to judge their president.

For heuristic purposes we have imagined that the appraisal process can be neatly divided into two tasks: understanding and judgment. This is a drastic but convenient fiction; as we will see soon enough, processes of comprehension and judgment are implicated in one another. In this chapter, however, we adopt this distinction, with separate sections devoted to each task.

Understanding Presidents

We take as our point of departure Lippmann's (1922) observation, offered more than a half century ago, that the trials and tribulations of daily life are compelling in a way that politics can rarely be. To expect ordinary Americans to become absorbed in affairs of state, wrote Lippmann, would be to demand of them an appetite for political knowledge quite peculiar, if not pathological. Countless surveys undertaken since have certainly sustained Lippmann's claim: Americans are indeed indifferent to much that transpires in politics, hazy about many of its principal players, lackadaisical regarding debates that preoccupy officialdom, oblivious to essential facts that the politically well informed take for granted, and unsure or just plain wrong about the policies advanced by presidents and presidential hopefuls (Kinder and Sears, 1985). A share of this confusion, of course, is not the citizen's own doing but must be traced instead to the real complexity of political life and the ambiguity that governments and leaders often cultivate (see Bennett, 1976; Page, 1978). And virtually all Americans express concern about some feature of public life; under extraordinary circumstances political events may capture the attention of the entire public. Still, for most Americans, most of the time, politics constitutes a remote and curious sideshow, well subordinate to the demands and obligations of day-to-day living. Consequently, in developing a psychological account of the presidential appraisal process in the pages ahead, we will be deeply suspicious of proposals that presume on the public's part a voracious hunger for the political. We have assumed the reverse.

Although typically not preoccupied by political matters, Americans nevertheless achieve some understanding of political life in general and the part played by the president in that life in particular. Our business here is to suggest how such accomplishments are won. For this purpose we rely on two complementary and quite general perspectives in social and cognitive psychology. The first is predicated on the assumption that people make sense of events partly by understanding their causes. Take, for example, the fact that the consumer price index rose at an annual rate of nearly 18 percent in the first quarter of 1980. Why? Because of a president's inability to control run-away federal spending? Because of escalating oil prices demanded by OPEC? Or was the enemy us—our unwillingness to curtail the purchase of products that we did not really need? The point here is that meaning is ascribed to rising prices, as to other political events, through the attribution of cause. It is one thing to understand inflation in terms of moral collapse on the part of American consumers, quite another to attribute rising prices to failure in the White House. The public understands political events partly by identifying their causes.

The second type of understanding is schema-based understanding—a process in which new information is interpreted on the basis of prior knowledge. People achieve understanding by recognizing that new information represents a particular instance of a more general type. The news that the president is stepping up military assistance to El Salvador may be interpreted by many as the initial move leading inevitably to another Vietnam. Understanding the particular event comes about through the elicitation of a general interpretative framework, or schema.

Understanding Through the Attribution of Cause

Attribution theory aspires to provide a systematic account of how ordinary people explain social events. Defined most grandly, the subject matter of attribution theory is epistemology: "the processes by which man 'knows' his world and, more importantly, *knows that he knows*" (Kelley, 1973, p. 107). In practice, attribution theory has been applied to mundane puzzles of everyday life. "If a person is aggressively competitive in his behavior, is he this kind of person, or is he reacting to situational pressures? . . . If a person fails on a test, does he have low ability, or is the test difficult" (Kelley, 1973, p. 107)? Attribution theory describes the implicit rules by which people answer such questions.

"Rational" Attribution. Although the writings of Heider (1958) continue to be the richest single source of ideas about attribution processes, Kelley, Jones, and others systematized Heider's ideas—and went well beyond them—in a series of influential theoretical papers (Jones and Davis, 1965; Jones and McGillis, 1976; Kelley, 1967, 1971, 1972, 1973). These latter-day attribution theorists sustained Heider's claim that the most important distinction made by observers in their explanations of social acts is between *internal* causes—the traits, abilities, intentions, and so on, of the actor—and *external* causes—the incentives, pressures, demands, and so on, of the situation. Suppose, for example, that the president rails against the dangers of big government. Is this to be taken as a reflection of the president's beliefs (internal cause) or as a strategic response to political pressure (external cause)?

Kelley developed two general principles to describe how observers go about answering such causal questions.[1] The first, covariation, assumes that the would-be attributor has in hand relatively extensive information. Under such circumstances the attributor should be likened to a naive scientist, who detects patterns of covariation and attributes causality accordingly. A number of experiments have shown that everyday explanations can take the form predicted by the covariation principle, though the fit is far from perfect (McArthur, 1972, 1976; Orvis, Cunningham, and Kelley, 1975). Problems arise mainly because attributors rarely have complete information and never have unlimited time.

Causal analysis nevertheless proceeds, but in a way that Kelley attempts to describe with the configurational principle. Underinformed and pressed for time, attributors draw on their assumptions about what classes of causal forces, in what combination, could have produced the observed effect. According to Kelley (1972,

p. 2), "the mature individual has a repertoire of such abstract ideas about the operation and interaction of causal factors. These conceptions enable him to make economical and fast attributional analysis, by providing a framework within which bits and pieces of relevant information can be fitted in order to draw reasonably good causal inferences."

The simplest of these abstract ideas is multiple sufficiency: the assumption that an observed effect could have been produced by *either* of several plausible causes. Under this assumption the role of any particular cause in producing an observed effect will be discounted if other plausible causes are also present. It is one thing for Edward Kennedy to give a strongly worded speech in favor of desegregation to an NAACP convention on the occasion of Martin Luther King's birthday; our attributor will presumably discount somewhat Kennedy's own beliefs as a cause for his action, attributing it instead to situational, strategic incentives. It is quite another matter for Kennedy to give the same speech before a hostile antibusing rally gathered on the Boston Common; here our attributor will have far less difficulty figuring out what Kennedy's true beliefs are (see Mills and Jellison, 1967, for an experimental analogue).

Extreme or unusual effects demand more than a single cause; they evoke the assumption of multiple necessity (Cunningham and Kelley, 1975; Kun and Weiner, 1973). Conspiracy theories may owe at least some of their substantial popular appeal to the disjuncture between the gravity of the event to be explained and the single-factor explanations often promoted by official reports. The assassination of John Kennedy is utterly incommensurate, in attribution terms, with the Warren Commission's conclusion that Lee Harvey Oswald acted alone (see McCauley and Jacques, 1979).

Attribution Error. Attribution research has recently relinquished Kelley's rational construction of the attribution process—a move forced in part by demonstrations that, even under pristine laboratory conditions, people make a mess of simple covariation tasks (Crocker, 1981; Kelley, 1973; Nisbett and Ross, 1980). In the current wave of research, error has replaced rationality; but, unfortunately, no coherent alternative to Kelley's theory has yet emerged. We have, instead, a miscellaneous catalogue of imperfections—"curious kinks in a pure logic of causal attribution" (Abelson, 1976, p. 75). Here we emphasize the three shortcomings that bear especially on the presidential appraisal process (for a complete roster of attribution pitfalls, see Fiske and Taylor, 1984).

Self-serving attribution, defined as causal analysis in the service of "subjective forces of needs and wishes" (Heider, 1958, p. 121), is the first. It shows up most clearly in experimental research on achievement. People explain their own success as caused by effort and ability, while failure is written off to bad luck or impossible tasks. As Stevens and Jones (1976, p. 818) put it: "Attributions for a failing performance are heavily influenced by the apparent need to defend self-esteem. . . . Subjects confronting the worse circumstances are the most defensive." (For reviews of the experimental evidence, see Bradley, 1978; Miller and Ross, 1975.)[2]

Attributing cause self-servingly—in ways that preserve and reinforce prior attitudes—takes on a special plausibility in the context of the murky world of national politics. That world is far removed from the average citizen, complicated and difficult to fathom, yet enormously important. It is the stage where good and evil collide, where life-and-death decisions are made. Looking at that world, the ordinary citizen may often resort to self-serving causal analysis. Consider the case of a presidential campaign in particular. Presidential candidates spend a great deal of their time talking about their own successes along with their opponents' many failures (Page, 1978). From the citizen's point of view, such campaigns reduce almost inevitably to arguments about responsibility. Who is to blame for a sputtering economy, for crime in the streets, for a missile gap, for the decline of morality? Campaigns are laced with attribution puzzles. By the evidence on self-serving attribution, it should come as no surprise that, in solving these puzzles, Americans will be influenced by their prior wishes—by judgments of "what ought to be" and "what one would like to be," as well as by "what is."

A second attribution shortcoming of political consequence is that people account for the conduct of another typically by focusing too much on the other's qualities and dispositions, too little on situational features (Jones and Nisbett, 1971). Instead of interpreting the activities of the Watergate underlings as due at least in part to monstrous social pressure (external cause), for example, most of us gravitate naturally to explanations that stress ambition, weakness, obsequiousness, or other dispositional failings (internal cause). The bias toward actor-based explanations at the expense of situation-based explanations, suggested first by Heider some thirty years ago, is by now sufficiently well established by experimental research that Ross (1977) has declared it "the fundamental attribution error." (For a review of the extensive evidence supporting this declaration, see Fiske and Taylor, 1984.)

One explanation for this error emphasizes the perceptual vantage point taken by observers of social conduct. For observers the action is figural; the situation, background. An observer's attention is drawn naturally to the action itself—and therefore to the actor—rather than to the situation. Extending this point, Taylor and Fiske (1978) have proposed that the fundamental attribution error is but one manifestation of a more general mistake: to settle too readily on causes that happen to be salient (also see McArthur, 1980).

In the political realm, no one happens to be more salient than the president (Gans, 1979; Grossman and Kumar, 1981). And Americans do demand a lot of their chief executive; since Franklin Roosevelt they have seemed to expect prosperity, peace, order, justice, and more (Brody and Page, 1975; Greenstein, 1978). Because of the president's extraordinary visibility, and the public's inclination toward person-centered explanations, the responsibilities assigned a president may invariably surpass what a president can do. Perhaps the fundamental *political* attribution error is embodied in the extravagant assumptions Americans make regarding presidential power.

Although people may be capable of complex causal analysis, they seem rarely to rise to such heights. Our third, and most general, shortcoming is attributional "satisficing": "Individuals may be primarily motivated to seek a single sufficient or satisfactory explanation, rather than one that is the best of all possible explanations" (Kanouse, 1971, p. 11; also see Axelrod, 1976; Jones and Davis, 1965; Taylor and Fiske, 1978). Satisficing seems especially apt for everyday political causal analysis. A sustained and sophisticated analysis of political cause and effect seems largely out of reach of most Americans. As Brody and Page (1975, p. 146) put it: "The ordinary citizen cannot hope to know fully the web of political causation and cannot hope to answer the slippery arguments of politicians." In the face of formidable complexity, ordinary people should perhaps be forgiven for their tendency to latch onto simple causal conclusions.

Understanding Through Schema Elicitation

Another general approach to understanding presumes that events are understood when they are recognized as instances of something already known. Understanding requires the elicitation of a good-fitting prior theory, or "schema" (Bartlett, 1932; Fiske and Linville, 1980: Hastie, 1981; Rummelhart and Ortony, 1977; Taylor and Crocker, 1981). Social schemas are the informal, tacit theories that people hold about the social world—about what it is and how it works. Schemas pertaining to persons are often referred to as "prototypes" (Cantor and Mischel, 1979; Rosch, 1977). In the political realm, for example, we suspect that Americans possess prototypical conceptions of what presidents should be and do. The assumptions that people make about social groups are called "stereotypes" (Hamilton, 1979; Miller, 1982). Pronouncements about the "black vote," the "union vote," or the "woman's vote" all traffic in social stereotypes. "Scripts" refer to people's expectations about event sequences (Abelson, 1981; Schank and Abelson, 1977). During presidential campaigns many Americans develop scripts that have the campaign begin in New Hampshire, move through a series of caucuses and primaries that winnow the pack of contenders and test the front-runners, and culminate in the nomination of a single candidate at the summer convention. While schemas vary enormously in content—since they contain what people know about the world—they all serve the identical function: providing the contextual frameworks within which actors, groups, and events are understood.

In principle, schemas do so efficiently, if not always accurately. Costs associated with becoming informed about a newly declared presidential candidate, for example, can be substantially reduced if the candidate is categorized as one instance of a well-understood prototype. Suppose Dan Rather introduces a story on the evening news about an obscure senator from Montana, say, who has just announced his intention to capture the Democratic party's presidential nomination. Suppose further that, in due course, the senator wins an astonishing victory in the New Hampshire primary. Should voters pause to consider just who this audacious outsider might be, they will draw, in part, on their prototypical knowledge about such candidates. They will then notice those features of news presentations that are implied by their prototypes; they will make use of their prototypes to embellish their impression of the candidate, naturally and automatically assuming that the particular senator resembles in personal qualities and political positions their general prototype; and, finally, in their tentative evaluation of the senator, they may rely as much on their prototypes, which are thoroughly value laden, as on the particular details provided about the senator from Montana.

This example illustrates that schemas provide several efficiencies in the processing of information. They tell us what to expect. They provide guidelines for distinguishing relevant details from irrelevant. They clear up ambiguities. They help us to remember. And they supply criteria to guide our judgment. Experimental evidence bearing on each of these allegations is accumulating at a feverish clip (Fiske and Taylor, 1984; Markus and Zajonc, 1985).

The considerable efficiencies of schema-based understanding come with a price, however. The darker side of schematic understanding has two aspects. The first is that the informal, tacit theories people hold about the social (and political) world may seriously misrepresent the way things really are. The ordinary person's sometimes extraordinary notions about how the economy works, what constitutes a Communist system of government, or what a Democratic presidential candidate is likely to believe about federal spending may be utterly and demonstrably wrong. The second aspect of error is derived from the simplification inherent in schema-based understanding. Citizens forgo the subtle and textured appreciation of a particular case for the economies that come from categorizing the case as a general type. For example, in a series of experiments, Cantor and Mischel (1979) found that, when an individual is described in terms that evoke a prototype, people confidently remember attributes associated with the prototype, whether such attributes were in fact presented or not. Similarly, Taylor and her colleagues (1978) have demonstrated that culturally shared knowledge about social groups—in this case, stereotypes about women and blacks—distorts people's understanding of particular women and blacks, and in ways that reinforce the stereotype. And in his analysis of foreign policy decision makers, Jervis (1976) argues that international relations scripts held by diplomats and other experts derive from cataclysmic historical events (for instance, what happened as a result of the Munich pact gives rise to a "Munich script") and are applied rather indiscriminately. In their interpretation of events, foreign policy decision makers honor their scripts too much and give too little consideration to evidence about the events themselves (Gilovich, 1981; for further discussion of these points, see Taylor and Crocker, 1981).

These results should apply to presidential appraisal as well. Instead of examining the nuances of a particular candidate's proposals on domestic spending, Americans may be quite content to assume that the particular candidate is simply another one of those Democrats with their expensive social programs. This does indeed appear to happen (Feldman and Conover, 1983). Such understanding is certainly efficient and, given the peripheral place of politics for most people, perhaps even rational. But with too ready a reliance on prototypes, stereotypes, and scripts, citizens will necessarily end up slighting the particular qualities of particular cases.[3]

Judgments About Presidents

As they go about their day, Americans naturally come into contact with pictures and stories about the president, many of which they never notice or else quickly forget. They make sense of political events that involve the president partly through causal analysis, partly by treating such events as instances of something they already understand. They may also, on occasion, deliver judgments about the president's performance.

Judgments for What?

A first question is *why* they do so. Why, when interviewers gently inquire, are upward of 90 percent of the American public prepared to deliver an opinion regarding how well the incumbent is managing (Mueller, 1973)? To understand why requires investigation into the psychological *functions* such opinions perform. Following Katz (1960), we assume that opinions about the president may perform four functions in particular. To some degree, judgments of the president serve instrumental needs. That is, presidential opinions reflect to a certain extent the tangible rewards and punishments the president has delivered (or has appeared to deliver). The logic here, nakedly utilitarian, was emphasized by Neustadt (1960, p. 95) in his influential analysis of presidential power: "What a president should be is something most men see by light of what is happening to *them*. Their notions of the part a president should play, their satisfaction with the way he plays it, are affected by their private hopes and fears. Behind their judgments of performance lie the consequences in their lives."

Judgments of the president also serve a value-expressive function. Presidents propose and criticize policies, participate in and preside over custom and ritual, stand for and against certain groups, embrace and rail against treasured values. Judgments of the president, therefore, come to reflect not only material calculations but also affirmations of identity (Edelman, 1964).

Opinions about the president no doubt also play a knowledge function. "People need standards or frames of reference for understanding their world, and attitudes help to supply such standards" (Katz, 1960, p. 175). Attitudes toward the president in particular seem especially likely to play this role. Americans may reduce the complexity of political affairs to manageable proportions by placing the president in the center of things, a tendency no doubt encouraged both by their own tendencies toward person-centered explanations (Ross, 1977) and by the media's extraordinary fascination with the president (Gans, 1979; Robinson and Sheehan, 1983). Keeping track of international and national events then reduces to the simpler task of keeping track of the president.

Finally, under unusual circumstances, opinions about the president may also serve a darker purpose, the externalization of inner troubles. "Externalization occurs when an individual, often responding unconsciously, senses an analogy between a perceived environmental event and some unresolved inner problem. He adopts an attitude toward the event in question which is a transformed version of his way of dealing with his inner difficulty. By doing so, he may succeed in reducing some of the anxiety which his own difficulty has been producing" (Smith, Bruner, and White, 1956, p. 43). For example, in his discussion of working-class men coping with the burdens of freedom, Lane (1962) suggests that those who felt most troubled by freedom—who could not fully enjoy it themselves, who thought freedom dangerous, who worried extravagantly about its extension—were also those most uneasy about their own impulses (also see Sullivan, Marcus, Feldman, and Piereson, 1981).

In short, Americans hold and express opinions about the president because such opinions provide valuable services. They reflect the tangible benefits and costs the president has brought about in the past and may deliver in the future (the instrumental function). They represent a particularly powerful way to express those values and beliefs that define political identity (the value-expressive function). They offer a device by which the complicated world of politics can be understood (the knowledge function). And they may even provide a partial solution to inner conflicts (the ego-defensive function). This list constitutes a general answer to *why* Americans form judgments of the president, but it does not of course tell us anything about *how* such judgments are formed.

Dynamics of Judgment

One general possibility is defined by the "Olympian ideal of full rationality" (Simon, 1983). That is, in forming judgments of the president, the typical American might carefully, dispassionately, and exhaustively survey all that she knows about the president; map such knowledge against a complete set of stable values; reconcile whatever conflicts exist among her values; and finally, taking all this into account, calculate an overall judgment. While original and illuminating conclusions can sometimes be derived from such idealized assumptions (see, for example, Downs, 1957; Olson, 1965), we find it more useful to begin with the more modest assumptions about human judgment typically made in psychological theory and corroborated in psychological research.

Abandoning the extravagant demands of full rationality, we suppose instead that judgments of the president reflect rough-and-ready comparisons Americans make between what they know about a particular president and what they expect of an ideal (or at least an acceptable) one. Presidents are measured against a set of normative standards. Such standards no doubt have multiple sources. They might be provided by a conception of the ideal, represented either as a set of abstract features that any president must possess—vision, honesty, strength—or as particularly heroic examples of presidents past—perhaps incumbents still operate in the shadow of Franklin Roosevelt. Standards applied to the present incumbent might also be established by the most conspicuous failures of the immediate predecessor: Nixon's scandal may have elevated the significance of honesty in the public's presidential appraisals; Carter's ineffectiveness may have quickened the public's interest in presidential competence. The point is that judgment results from comparing the incumbent president against a normative one.

In making such comparisons, Americans do not exhaustively survey everything they know. Instead, they consider just a sample of what they know—and, as we will see later, it is a sample of convenience at that. Which considerations are paid attention to and which ignored depends on their accessibility, which may be momentary and fleeting. Fischhoff, Slovic, and Lichtenstein (1980, p. 127) put the general point well: "People solve problems, including the determination of their own values, with what comes to mind. The more detailed, exacting, and creative their inferential process, the more likely they are to think of all they know about the problem. The briefer that process becomes, the more they will be controlled by the relative accessibility of various considerations." We assume that, under ordinary circumstances, judgments about the president are offered rather casually; that the process is seldom "detailed, exacting, and creative." As a consequence, judgments depend not on what people know in an absolute sense but on what happens to come to mind (also see Kahneman and Tversky, 1979; Taylor and Fiske, 1978; Tversky and Kahneman, 1981).

We assume further that, in assembling what they know, Americans are not merely passive observers of the political scene. Rather, they are active participants in the entire process, contributing to the creation of what they know about a president in at least two major respects. First, in Bruner's (1957) famous phrase, "They go beyond the information given." Knowing one central element about a president will lead naturally and automatically to inferences about others. The announcement that Governor Balderdash is seeking the Republican party's presidential nomination may tell citizens a good deal, insofar as their concept of Republican is inferentially complex. They will then effortlessly and automatically "know" which groups Balderdash favors, what policies he advocates, and so on (Feldman and Conover, 1983). Second, new developments involving the president will get interpreted as evaluatively consistent with previous judgments. Confronted with evidence that challenges prior views of the president, many citizens may resort to denial, bolstering, rationalization, or some such cognitive maneuver (Abelson, 1968). For example, although the president's critics and supporters peer at the same national economy, they may reach quite different conclusions about its vitality (Kinder, 1981). In short, what comes to mind about a particular president originates partly in inference (particularly early in the appraisal process) and is partly the result of inconsistency reduction (especially later on, as people develop firmer presidential impressions).

Defining Presidential Standards

If judgment entails measuring the incumbent against a set of normative standards, then our next move must be to reveal, to the degree possible, just what those standards are. Which presidential characteristics do Americans pay attention to? By what standards are presidents judged? We take up a number of possibilities, some familiar, some exotic: Perhaps presidents are judged by the party they represent, the ideology they embody, the policies they promote, the groups they stand for, the successes and failures they preside over, the sorts of people they seem to be, the particular affects they evoke, and, finally, the appearances they convey.

Party Identification. In *The Voter Decides,* Campbell, Gurin, and Miller (1954) defined party identification as an individual's sense of personal attachment to a political party. It soon became apparent that Americans take such attachments rather seriously. According to panel observations, they almost never abandon one party for the other (Converse, 1964; Converse and Markus, 1979). Moreover, their judgments of prominent political figures seem to reflect their underlying commitment to party most of all. For example, shortly after General Eisenhower declared himself to be a Republican, the American public divided along party lines: Republicans loved Ike; Democrats, suddenly, were not so sure (Converse and Dupeax, 1966; Hyman and Sheatsley, 1953).

The implications of such results were developed in grand style in *The American Voter.* There Campbell, Converse, Miller, and Stokes (1960) treated party identification as causally antecedent to the voters' opinions about the candidates, issues, and events that give each election its unique character. While leaving open the possibility that such opinions might influence attachments to party at occasional critical junctures, Campbell and his associates maintained that the path of influence is preponderantly the other way. In their view, party identification is a standing commitment, a "persistent adherence," which gives aid and comfort to American citizens confronting a murky political world: "To the average person the affairs of government are remote and complex, and yet the average citizen is asked periodically to formulate opinions about these affairs. At the very least he has to decide how he will vote, what choice he will make between candidates offering different programs and very different versions of contemporary political events. In this dilemma, having the party symbol stamped on certain candidates, certain issue positions, certain interpretations of political reality is a great psychological convenience" (Stokes, 1966a, pp. 125-127).[4]

While our account so far seems to establish the central place of party in the presidential appraisal process, it has a decidedly old-fashioned ring. In recent years revisionists in increasing numbers have argued that party identification should be regarded not as a standing decision but as a "running balance sheet on the two parties" (Fiorina, 1977, p. 618).

Revisionists are partly right. Party identification is not the immovable force behind the ordinary person's political judgments that it was portrayed to be in *The American Voter* (and elsewhere, with less care). Party identification both influences and is influenced by a variety of political judgments: most conspicuously, by the performance of government (Fiorina, 1981; Kinder and Kiewiet, 1981; Rivers, 1981), by policy disagreements (Markus, 1979; Franklin and Jackson, 1983), and by the emergence of new candidates (Markus and Converse, 1979). But although party identification does change in response to what parties (and governments) do and what they fail to do, it does so sluggishly. In this respect the "running balance sheet" metaphor is quite misleading. Indeed, in looking over this evidence, we find the stronger message to be how difficult it is to budge Americans from their commitment to party. Party identification *is* central to the standards Americans apply in judging their president.[5]

Ideology. Presidents might also be held up to ideological standards, alternately venerated or despised for embodying the abstract principles of liberalism, conservatism, or some other "ism." There is a serious problem with this proposition, however, and it is simply this: The vast majority of Americans appear quite innocent of ideology (Converse, 1964; Kinder, 1983). Americans' political ideas are evidently not deduced from sweeping master principles about government and society. If ideological reasoning requires manipulation of abstract political principles, then it is clear that few Americans operate ideologically.[6]

Opinions on Policy. Another and related aspect of the American public's conception of a presidential ideal has to do with policy. Presidents might be judged according to the policies they promote and oppose. In *The American Voter,* however, Campbell and associates (1960) concluded that opinions on specific matters of policy ordinarily play a modest role in the presidential appraisal process, a conclusion that provoked a strong reaction. Beginning with Key's (1966) posthumously published volume *The Responsible Electorate,* a major preoccupation of research on voting over the past twenty years has been to rehabilitate the political reputation of the ordinary American, and to do so by demonstrating that policy-based judgment is more widespread than was originally alleged in *The American Voter.* At this point the general consensus is that presidents (and presidential hopefuls) are, indeed, judged partly by the policies they recommend (Brody and Page, 1972; Jackson, 1975; Markus and Converse, 1979; Page and Jones, 1979).[7] The strength of this relationship depends both on the particular and ideographic interests of voters (Rabinowitz, Prothro, and Jacoby, 1982) and especially on the political context, a point we will return to later.

Performance. Presidents may be judged not only by the policies they promote but also, and quite separately, by the outcomes such policies seem to have brought about. That a president's support does indeed hinge at least partly on performance has been argued most forcefully by Downs (1957) in his formal analysis of democratic politics and by Key (1966) in his final ruminations on the prospects for a responsible electorate, and has since been amply sustained, particularly by aggregate investigations into the dynamics of presidential popularity over time.

Provoked by Mueller's (1970, 1973) pioneering research, many analysts have wrestled with the question of how presidents go about gaining and—more commonly—losing public support. We now know that dramatic, sharply focused international crises involving the president typically boost support. Jimmy Carter was a beneficiary of this phenomenon when his popularity ratings nearly doubled following the seizure of the American embassy in Tehran and the almost simultaneous Soviet invasion of Afghanistan. We know also that a president's support depends heavily on the vitality of the nation's economy; high unemployment, rising prices, slow growth in real disposable income—all eat away at a president's support. So do costly misadventures in foreign lands; as the number of Americans killed in Vietnam grew, public support for Johnson and Nixon deteriorated. So, too, do scandals in high places; with each new incriminating revelation during the Watergate period, Nixon's support diminished. Considered together, economic conditions, war, scandal, and international crises explain much of the over-time variation in presidential support (Hibbs, Rivers, and Vasilatos, 1982a, 1982b; Kernell, 1978; Kernell and Hibbs, 1981).

Although these aggregate results go a long way toward substantiating the political significance of performance, they necessarily disclose little about individual voters. That case is better made by analysis at the individual level and has been done most comprehensively by Fiorina (1981; though see Kramer, 1983). Across the entire span of the Survey Research Center's National Election Studies, Fiorina found that assessments of government performance—most notably, on peace and war, economics, and civil rights—correlate consistently and occasionally substantially with evaluations of the incumbent president (which, in turn, are strongly associated with the vote; see also Converse and others, 1969; Kinder and Kiewiet, 1981; Page, 1978, chap. 7; Popkin and others, 1976).[8]

If a president's support depends on performance, how do people gauge performance itself? How do they know whether an incumbent has succeeded or failed? For economic performance one obvious possibility is that people simply examine their own circumstances and then judge the president accordingly (Popkin and others, 1976). But "pocketbook voters" have proved difficult to find. Americans seem to pay rather little attention to their own economic circumstances when judging the president. Those who directly experience the ravages of unemployment, whose family financial condition has seriously eroded, or who are discouraged about their family's economic futures are generally little more critical of the incumbent president than are their economically secure neighbors (Kinder, 1981; Kinder and Kiewiet, 1981; Kinder and Mebane, 1983; Schlozman and Verba, 1979; Sears and Lau, 1983). In reaching judgments of the president, Americans seem to pay primary attention instead to the economic problems and achievements of the country. Thus, a president's support declines when prices and unemployment rise, not so much because citizens blame the president for their private hardships but because they hold the president accountable for the American society's hardships. This result is generally consistent with the instrumental function played by presidential judgments noted earlier, but with a twist. What Americans seem to ask their president is not so much "What have you done for *me* lately?" but more "What have you done for the *country* lately?"[9]

Group Identification. The decline of the concept of group in studies of public opinion and voting over the last two decades is an intriguing puzzle, for which we have no explanation, only a lament. Not so very long ago, voting was regarded as a group experience. Campaigns reinforced or activated predispositions rooted in group membership (Lazarsfeld, Berelson, and Gaudet, 1944; Berelson, Lazarsfeld, and McPhee, 1954; see also Converse and Campbell, 1968). In little more than a decade, this emphasis virtually disappeared. Apart from the loyalties Americans develop to the political parties, group identification is given little place in contemporary accounts of presidential appraisal.

There is one exception to this—Stokes's (1966b) six-factor model—and it is a powerful one. Stokes coded voters' open-ended commentaries on the candidates and parties into one of six categories: references to the Republican candidate, the Democratic candidate, domestic policy, foreign policy, government performance, and, most pertinent here, the groups involved in politics and the questions of group interest affecting them. For each category, voters were then assigned a score corresponding to the difference between the number of pro-Republican remarks and the number of pro-Democratic remarks. When presidential vote was regressed against all six, the group benefits factor turned out to be important, and in *all* the presidential elections so far examined (see, for example, Kagay and Caldeira, 1980: Popkin and others, 1976).

A more general demonstration of the prominent role played by group identification in political reasoning is given by the persistent citation citizens make of social groups in their appraisals of parties and presidential candidates. In Converse's (1964) coding of open-ended replies in the Survey Research Center's 1956 national survey, citizens who enlisted social groups in their comments comprised by far the largest single category—42 percent of the entire public. Such citizens typically named benefits and deprivations that parties and candidates had visited upon social groups in the past or might deliver in the future. These findings seem quite representative. References to groups continue to occupy a central place in citizens' appraisals of parties and candidates (Kagay and Caldeira, 1980) and not only in the United States (see Klingemann, 1979).

Although the concept of group has been largely neglected in contemporary studies, voters have, no doubt, continued undaunted. Voters know and judge presidents by the groups they champion and oppose (for theoretical stirrings in this direction, see Conover and Feldman, 1983b; Klein, 1984; Miller and others, 1981).

Personality. Whenever Americans have been asked what they like and dislike about major presidential candidates (and national samples have been asked such questions on a regular basis since 1952), many have responded by referring to the candidates' personal qualities. Roughly one fourth do so, alluding not to domestic or foreign policy, nor to past political performance, but to intelligence, honesty, warmth, or some other personal trait. From Eisenhower to the present, such personalizing has been a sizable and stable part of the images created by presidential candidates (Nimmo and Savage, 1976, summarize much of this evidence; also see Kagay and Caldeira, 1975; Miller and Miller, 1976, 1977; Page, 1978; Shabad and Andersen, 1979). This finding suggests that presidents and would-be presidents are appraised in terms of the traits they exemplify—or, better, traits they *appear* to exemplify.[10]

Not just any trait will do. Impressions of presidents seem to be dominated by a few central characteristics. By cataloguing the answers citizens offered to the standard open-ended questions about presidential candidates included in the SRC/CPS election studies, Miller and Miller (1976, 1977) identified four such characteristics: competence, leadership, trust, and reliability (see also Miller, Wattenberg, and

Malanchuk, 1982; Page, 1978). Different techniques have produced comparable results (Kinder, 1984; Kinder and Abelson, 1981; Kinder, Abelson, and Fiske, 1979). Such regularities suggest that Americans may hold "implicit personality theories" (Bruner and Tagiuri, 1954; Schneider, 1973) about presidents, as they evidently do about their friends and neighbors. Thus, information bearing on the personal qualities of presidents gets assimilated to a few central traits. Such traits appear to constitute powerful judgmental standards. Studies show that presidents and would-be presidents must at least convey competence and integrity or suffer grievous consequences (Kinder, 1984; Kinder and Abelson, 1981; Markus, 1982).

Affect. Among their many other obligations, presidents may also be expected to deliver emotional benefits. For the presidency, Barber (1972, p. 4) reminds us, is more than an institution. It "is the focus for the most intense and persistent emotions in the American polity. The president is a symbolic leader, the one figure who draws together the people's hopes and fears for the political future." And surely one thing that presidential campaigns try to do is mobilize the electorate's emotions. Success at the polls would seem to depend in no small measure on the candidate's ability both to evoke positive feelings from potential voters (hope and pride) and, perhaps especially, to avoid stirring up negative feelings (fear and anger). This claim is supported both by current thinking in social psychology (see, for example, Leventhal, 1980; Mandler, 1975; Zajonc, 1980) and by results from several recent national surveys. Presidents and presidential hopefuls do, in fact, evoke strong feelings. Moreover, particular candidates elicit distinctive profiles of affective response. In 1980, for example, Edward Kennedy elicited mainly anger and sadness, while Jimmy Carter elicited mainly frustration and unease. Such feelings are separate from the more cognitive elements of ideal presidential standards reviewed so far. They contribute independently and powerfully to overall support (Abelson and others, 1982; Kinder and Abelson, 1981; on the last point, for parallel results in different domains, see Conover and Feldman, 1983a; Tyler, 1980).

Appearance. Finally, popular appeal may also depend partly on a president's appearance. While such an allegation may be scandalous from the perspective of democratic theory, it is, in fact, a quite reasonable generalization to draw from experimental findings in social psychology. By the verdict of dozens of experiments, the good-looking lead more fulfilling, more effective lives. They are "seen as more responsible for good deeds and less responsible for bad ones; their evaluations of others have more potent impact; their performances are upgraded; others are more socially responsive to them, more ready to provide them with help, and more willing to work hard to please them" (Huston and Levinger, 1978, p. 122; see also Berscheid and Walster, 1974). Such effects show up, it is important to note, even when experimental subjects are provided with extensive information about the person under appraisal. Under such informationally rich circumstances, people nevertheless continue to see the physically attractive as smarter, judge their work as more competent, and are more willing to follow where they lead.

Perhaps appearance counts in politics, too. If the appearance of presidents and presidential candidates does indeed influence their appeal, such effects no doubt occur nonconsciously. Most would agree that good looks have nothing to do with leadership, that a winning smile has no place in the selection of the leader of the Free World. It is precisely because appearance affects judgments outside awareness that such influence is possible at all (Nisbett and Bellows, 1977).

Judgment, Diversity, and Context

Implicit in what we have said so far is that normative conceptions of the presidency are widely shared and very stable. We have spoken of the typical American's presidential standards as if there existed typical Americans whose conceptions of a normative president, moreover, were permanently fixed. This is not entirely caricature; to a certain extent, what comes to mind in presidential judgments reflects standards that *are* shared and stable. But in this final section, we want to explore variations around central tendencies of two types: Presidential standards vary both from one citizen to the other, as a reflection of individual diversity, and from one historical period to the next, as a reflection of alterations in context.

Individual Diversity. Which standards are honored and which ignored is to some degree a matter of personal taste. For example, Americans who differ in their conception of an ideal president's personal qualities also differ in the standards they employ in judging the incumbent. Those whose ideal embodies competence above other qualities tend to form judgments dominated by how well the president measures up against a standard of competence; those whose ideal embodies integrity tend to form judgments dominated by how well the president measures up against a standard of integrity (Kinder and others, 1980).

Or consider the surprisingly weak empirical returns from research on pocketbook voting. These results are entirely consistent with the *typical* American's remarkably apolitical understanding of personal economic life. While people nowadays seldom blame themselves for their own economic predicaments (an apparent change from the Great Depression; see Garraty, 1978), neither do they blame government. Nor do they look to government for assistance in solving their problems. Instead, they see their problems as caused by proximal, particularistic forces (an unsympathetic boss, a local factory closing), and they rely on their own resources in seeking solutions (Kinder and Mebane, 1983; Schlozman and Verba, 1979; Sniderman and Brody, 1977). Such a view is, of course, consistent with the finding that most Americans do not judge the president by the condition of their own pocketbook. But not every American subscribes to such an apolitical theory. For those Americans who cite collective causes and political solutions for their family's economic predicament, the consequences are substantial: They see politics and economics as deeply intertwined; they assess the course of national economic events in terms of their own family's improvements and possibilities; and their judgments of the president are influenced by their own economic experiences (Feldman, 1982; Kinder and Mebane, 1983).

Political Context. Which standards are honored and which ignored in presidential judgments also varies with alterations in context. When the political context changes, what comes to mind will also change. Consider, as one example, the great commotion over whether Americans judge presidents, and choose between presidential candidates, on the basis of the policies they recommend. Sometimes they do, sometimes not. Policy-based voting in presidential elections waxes and wanes according to the clarity and aggressiveness by which the rival candidates promote policies that really differ (Converse and others, 1969; Page and Brody, 1972; Petrocik, 1980).

A similar relationship holds for the personal qualities that presidents convey. Although competence and integrity may always be available, the relative importance Americans attach to each in particular cases varies enormously. Partly this variation has to do with the special qualities of the candidates themselves. McGovern's celebrated campaign fiascoes in 1972, for example, seemed to direct voters' attention to competence. Popkin and associates (1976) argue convincingly that McGovern's downfall had less to do with his leftist policy proposals than with his apparent inability to manage a campaign. More generally, assessments of competence seem to carry greater weight in political judgment than do considerations of integrity—but with occasional and revealing exceptions. In the 1980 primary season, apparently by virtue of their special histories, Edward Kennedy and John Connally managed to reverse the public's customary priorities. For Kennedy and Connally alone among a set of 1980 presidential hopefuls, judgments of integrity—preponderantly pejorative—were most important in determining overall judgment (Kinder and Abelson, 1981). The general point is that the distinctive and conspicuous qualities of particular candidates may alter the relative importance the public assigns to competence and integrity.

So, in a more general sense, may the distinctive and conspicuous qualities of the times (Barber, 1980; Page, 1978). The "long national nightmare" of Watergate, culminating in Nixon's resignation, may have enhanced the importance of integrity for the 1976 campaign and may have contributed as well to the success of the Carter candidacy, with its unrelenting emphasis on decency and trust. The Carter White House experience, as popularly interpreted, appeared to shift the public's priorities. The central characterological question of the 1980 campaign seemed to be: Who is *capable* of governing (Kinder and Abelson, 1981; Markus, 1982)?

A final illustration concerns the standards Americans apply to presidential performance. While there may be general agreement that the president should be held accountable for providing peace, prosperity, defense, justice, tranquility (and perhaps more), the relative importance of each may vary sharply with alterations in context. This hunch is supported by a series of experiments that, by systematically varying the content of television news programs, created alternative contexts. The experiments demonstrated that viewers' judgments of the president are influenced by which problems network news programs pay attention to and which problems they ignore. Judgments of the president by people exposed to news about inflation were influenced especially by their sense of how well the president was controlling prices; judgments of the president by those exposed to stories focusing on the nation's defense were influenced especially by their ratings of the president's performance on defense; and so on. Moreover, when the president is portrayed as responsible either for causing a problem or for failing to solve it, the consequences for overall judgment are especially great (Iyengar and Kinder, 1985a, 1985b; Iyengar, Peters, and Kinder, 1982; Iyengar and others, 1984).

These examples could be multiplied and extended, but the general point should be apparent. Presidential judgments reflect both the diverse ways Americans regard the political world and the way that world changes.

Conclusion

By assembling evidence bearing on the way in which the public appraises presidents and those who seek the presidency, and by providing a common language derived from psychology for understanding the appraisal process, we have tried to define an appraisal literature and promote its development. In so doing, we have often been haunted by the ghost of V. O. Key. In the preface to his magnificent *Public Opinion and American Democracy*, Key (1961) offered the complaint, well justified at the time, that the study of public opinion had been taken over by social psychologists. The result, according to Key, was "a large body of research findings characterized often by methodological virtuosity and on occasion even by theoretical felicity, [but] whose relevance for the workings of government is not always apparent" (p. vii). Key returned to this theme at the very end of the book, arguing that, while public opinion studies "may excite human curiosity," they "are bootless unless the findings about the preferences, aspirations, and prejudices of the public can be connected with the workings of the governmental system" (p. 535). What, Key might ask us here, are the implications of our account of the presidential appraisal process for the possibilities and shortcomings of democratic politics?

Good question. It has motivated much of the work reviewed here, including our own. But to answer it satisfactorily requires both methodological virtuosity and theoretical felicity. We need a fully adequate description of what Americans are doing when they appraise their president, something we are groping toward but have not yet attained. We hope our chapter may serve as a useful way station toward such a description.

Notes

1. We concentrate here exclusively on Kelley's version of attribution theory because it is in Kelley's writings that the theory reaches its fullest development. We encourage interested readers to pursue other theoretical variations on the attribution theme (Fiske and Taylor, 1984).

2. How the results on defensive attribution should be interpreted is subject to debate. Some emphasize motivational explanations, as Stevens and Jones (1976) do; others (for example, Ross and Sicoly, 1979) argue for an informational account.

3. To speak of *the* citizen's prototype implies a uniformity to knowledge that is quite unreal. Some find intrigue and high drama in even minor political developments, but many others—out of cynicism, apathy, or a preoccupation with other activities—could scarcely care less. Prototypes about presidents and would-be presidents held by the politically expert are likely to be more elaborate, more easily invoked, and put to more sensitive use than are those held by citizens less enchanted by politics (Converse, 1975; Fiske and Kinder, 1981).

4. The privileged position of party identification was consolidated in Converse's (1966) development of the normal vote and richly illustrated in the Survey Research Center (SRC) team's reports on the presidential elections of 1960, 1964, and 1968 (Converse, Clausen, and Miller, 1965; Converse and others, 1961, 1969).

5. Much has also been made in recent years of the decline if not demise of party identification. Beginning in 1965, more and more Americans began to call themselves Independents; fewer and fewer claimed to be strong partisans of either party. This decline continued through 1974 but seems now to have plateaued. While neither party has been disadvantaged—the *balance* of partisanship over the past twenty-five years has remained essentially stationary—the change is, nevertheless, one of massive proportions. To Burnham (1970) this meant further evidence of the onward and irreversible march of party decomposition. We think, however, that reports of the demise of party identification have been exaggerated. It is

incontestable that fewer Americans now than in the 1950s define themselves in party terms. But many Independents, in fact, remain covert party supporters (Keith and others, 1977). Moreover, while voters honored party less in selecting a president in 1968 and 1972 than in previous elections, the power of party rebounded sharply in 1976 and 1980 (Kinder and Sears, 1985). Party identification *has* weakened, but nothing in the evidence so far suggests that our theory of presidential appraisal should abandon it.

6. We are moving quickly over treacherous ground. For a detailed recounting of the literature on the ideology question, see Kinder (1983) and Chapter Three in this volume; for a convincing account of an abbreviated ideology at work in American political thinking, see Conover and Feldman (1981).

7. We have glossed over the formidable identification and estimation problems associated with the policy-judgment connection. Correlations between policy positions and candidate evaluations may reflect any one of three underlying processes (Brody and Page, 1972): "policy-based evaluation," in which citizens support candidates to the degree that their views on policy resemble their own; "projection," in which citizens favorably inclined toward a candidate will project their own opinions onto the candidate; and "persuasion," in which citizens adjust their policy opinions in the direction of agreement with an admired candidate. Estimating the impact of policy on judgment thus requires simultaneously taking into account projection and persuasion. Most empirical work ignores this problem; research by Jackson (1975), Markus and Converse (1979), and Page and Jones (1979) does not, and each reports sizable effects of policy on judgment.

8. Assessments of performance may also influence evaluations of an incumbent president's challenger, though in a different way (Downs, 1957). While a significant share of the president's campaign will be given to glorifying his administration's record (Page, 1978), the challenger has no comparably conspicuous history. As a consequence, voters may rely on their expectations of how well the challenger would perform if elected. And such expectations, in turn, may be based substantially on voters' general sense of the ability of the party the challenger represents to manage national problems. These predictions were neatly borne out for economic performance in the 1972 and 1976 presidential elections (Kinder and Kiewiet, 1981).

9. Preliminary indications suggest that judgments of the president may reflect assessments of *group* economic predicaments as well (Conover, 1984; Kinder, Rosenstone, and Hansen, forthcoming).

10. It is often difficult to separate the personal from the political in citizens' descriptions of candidates. References to personality are typically made within a context that is explicitly political. To complain that the president is bargaining ineffectively with a recalcitrant Congress over defense policy may be interpreted as an assertion about the president's personal qualities (about his incompetence, say), as an assertion about policy, or, most properly, as an assertion about both.

References

Abelson, R. P. "Psychological Implication." In R. P. Abelson and others (eds.), *Theories of Cognition Consistency: A Sourcebook.* Skokie, Ill.: Rand McNally, 1968.

Abelson, R. P. "Social Psychology's Rational Man." In S. Benn and G. Mortimore (eds.), *Rationality and the Social Sciences*. London: Routledge & Kegan Paul, 1976.

Abelson, R. P. "The Psychological Status of the Script Concept." *American Psychologist*, 1981, *36*, 715-729.

Abelson, R. P., and others. "Affective and Semantic Components in Political Person Perception." *Journal of Personality and Social Psychology*, 1982, *42*, 619-630.

Axelrod, R. (ed.). *The Structure of Decision: The Cognitive Maps of Political Elites*. Princeton, N.J.: Princeton University Press, 1976.

Barber, J. D. *The Presidential Character*. Englewood Cliffs, N.J.: Prentice-Hall, 1972.

Barber, J. D. *The Pulse of Politics*. New York: Norton, 1980.

Bartlett, F. C. *Remembering*. Cambridge, England: Cambridge University Press, 1932.

Bennett, W. L. *The Political Mind and the Political Environment*. Lexington, Mass.: Lexington Books, 1976.

Berelson, B. R., Lazarsfeld, P. F., and McPhee, W. N. *Voting: A Study of Opinion Formation in a Presidential Campaign*. Chicago: University of Chicago Press, 1954.

Berscheid, E., and Walster, E. "Physical Attractiveness," In L. Berkowitz (ed.), *Advances in Experimental Social Psychology*. Vol. 7. Orlando, Fla.: Academic Press, 1974.

Bradley, G. W. "Self-Serving Biases in the Attribution Process: A Reexamination of the Fact or Fiction Question." *Journal of Personality and Social Psychology*, 1978, *36*, 56-71.

Brody, R. A., and Page, B. I. "Comment: The Assessment of Issue Voting." *American Political Science Review*, 1972, *66*, 450-458.

Brody, R. A., and Page, B. I. "The Impact of Events on Presidential Popularity: The Johnson and Nixon Administrations." In A. Wildavsky (ed.), *Perspectives on the Presidency*. Boston: Little, Brown, 1975.

Bruner, J. S. "Going Beyond the Information Given." In J. S. Bruner and others (eds.), *Contemporary Approaches to Cognition*. Cambridge, Mass.: Harvard University Press, 1957.

Bruner, J. S., and Tagiuri, R. "Person Perception." In G. Lindzey (ed.), *Handbook of Social Psychology*. Vol. 2. Reading, Mass.: Addison-Wesley, 1954

Burnham, W. D. *Critical Elections and the Mainsprings of American Politics*. New York: Norton, 1970.

Burns, J. M. *Leadership*. New York: Harper & Row, 1978.

Campbell, A., Converse, P. E., Miller, W. E., and Stokes, D. E. *The American Voter*. New York: Wiley, 1960.

Campbell, A., Gurin, G., and Miller, W. E. *The Voter Decides*. New York: Harper & Row, 1954.

Cantor, N., and Mischel, W. "Categorization Processes in the Perception of People." In L. Berkowitz (ed.), *Advances in Experimental Social Psychology*. Vol. 12. Orlando, Fla.: Academic Press, 1979.

Conover, P. J. "The Impact of Group Economic Interests on Political Evaluations." Unpublished manuscript, Department of Political Science, University of Kentucky, 1984.

Conover, P. J., and Feldman, S. "The Origins and Meaning of Liberal/Conservative Self-Identifications." *American Journal of Political Science,* 1981, *25,* 617–645.

Conover, P. J., and Feldman, S. "Emotional Reactions to the Economy." Paper delivered at annual meeting of the American Political Science Association, Chicago, Sept. 1983a.

Conover, P. J., and Feldman, S. "Group Identification, Values, and the Organization of Political Beliefs." Paper presented at annual meeting of the Midwest Political Science Association, Chicago, April 1983b.

Converse, P. E. "The Nature of Belief Systems in Mass Publics." In D. E. Apter (ed.), *Ideology and Discontent.* New York: Free Press, 1964.

Converse, P. E. "The Concept of a Normal Vote." In A. Campbell and others (eds.), *Elections and the Political Order.* New York: Wiley, 1966.

Converse, P. E. "Public Opinion and Voting Behavior." In F. Greenstein and N. Polsby (eds.), *Handbook of Political Science.* Vol. 4. Reading, Mass.: Addison-Wesley, 1975.

Converse, P. E., and Campbell, A. "Political Standards in Secondary Groups." In D. Cartwright and A. Zander (eds.), *Group Dynamics.* (3rd ed.) New York: Harper & Row, 1968.

Converse, P. E., Clausen, A. R., and Miller, W. E. "Electoral Myth and Reality: The 1964 Election." *American Political Science Review,* 1965, *59,* 321–336.

Converse, P. E., and Dupeax, G. "De Gaulle and Eisenhower: The Public Image of the Victorious General." In A. Campbell, P. E. Converse, W. E. Miller, and D. E. Stokes (eds.), *Elections and the Political Order.* New York: Wiley, 1966.

Converse, P. E., and Markus, G. B. "Plus ça change . . . The New CPS Election Study Panel." *American Political Science Review,* 1979, *73,* 32–49.

Converse, P. E., and others. "Stability and Change in 1960: A Reinstating Election." *American Political Science Review,* 1961, *55,* 209–280.

Converse, P. E., and others. "Continuity and Change in American Politics: Parties and Issues in the 1968 Election." *American Political Science Review,* 1969, *63,* 1083–1105.

Crocker, J. "Judgment of Covariation by Social Perceivers." *Psychological Bulletin,* 1981, *90,* 272–292.

Cunningham, J. D., and Kelley, H. H. "Causal Attribution for Interpersonal Events of Varying Magnitude." *Journal of Personality and Social Psychology,* 1975, *43,* 74–93.

Downs, A. *An Economic Theory of Democracy.* New York: Harper & Row, 1957.

Edelman, M. *The Symbolic Uses of Politics.* Urbana: University of Illinois Press, 1964.

Feldman, S. "Economic Self-Interest and Political Behavior." *American Journal of Political Science,* 1982, *26,* 446–466.

Feldman, S., and Conover, P. J. "Candidates, Issues and Voters: The Role of Inference in Political Perception." *Journal of Politics,* 1983, *45,* 810–839.

Fiorina, M. P. "An Outline for a Model of Party Choice." *American Political Science Review,* 1977, *21,* 601–626.

Fiorina, M. P. *Retrospective Voting in American National Elections.* New Haven, Conn.: Yale University Press, 1981.

Fischhoff, B., Slovic, P., and Lichtenstein, S. "Knowing What You Want: Measuring Labile Values." In T. Wallsten (ed.), *Cognitive Processes in Choice and Decision Behavior*. Hillsdale, N.J.: Erlbaum, 1980.

Fiske, S. T., and Kinder, D. R. "Involvement, Expertise, and Schema Use: Evidence from Political Cognition." In N. Cantor and J. Kihlstrom (eds.), *Cognition, Social Interaction, and Personality*. Hillsdale, N.J.: Erlbaum, 1981.

Fiske, S. T., and Linville, P. W. "What Does the Schema Concept Buy Us?" *Personality and Social Psychology Bulletin*, 1980, *6*, 543–557.

Fiske, S. T., and Taylor, S. E. *Social Cognition*. Reading, Mass.: Addison-Wesley, 1984.

Franklin, C. H., and Jackson, J. E. "The Dynamics of Party Identification." *American Political Science Review*, 1983, *77*, 957–973.

Gans, H. J. *Deciding What's News*. New York: Pantheon Books, 1979.

Garraty, J. A. *Unemployment in History*. New York: Harper & Row, 1978.

Gilovich, T. "Seeing the Past in the Present: The Effect of Associations to Familiar Events on Judgments and Decisions." *Journal of Personality and Social Psychology*, 1981, *40*, 797–806.

Greenstein, F. I. "Popular Images of the President." *American Journal of Psychiatry*, 1965, *122*, 523–529.

Greenstein, F. I. "Change and Continuity in the Modern Presidency." In A. King (ed.), *The New American Political System*. Washington, D.C.: American Enterprise Institute, 1978.

Grossman, M. B., and Kumar, M. J. *Portraying the President*. Baltimore: Johns Hopkins University Press, 1981.

Hamilton, D. L. "A Cognitive-Attributional Analysis of Stereotyping." In L. Berkowitz (ed.), *Advances in Experimental Social Psychology*. Vol. 12. Orlando, Fla.: Academic Press, 1979.

Hastie, R. "Schematic Principles in Human Memory." In E. T. Higgens, C. P. Herman, and M. P. Zanna (eds.), *Social Cognition*. Hillsdale, N.J.: Erlbaum, 1981.

Heider, F. *The Psychology of Interpersonal Relations*. New York: Wiley, 1958.

Hibbs, D. A., Jr., Rivers, R. D., and Vasilatos, N. "The Dynamics of Political Support for American Presidents Among Occupational and Partisan Groups." *American Journal of Political Science*, 1982a, *26*, 312–332.

Hibbs, D. A., Jr., Rivers, R. D., and Vasilatos, N. "On the Demand for Economic Outcomes: Macroeconomic Performance and Mass Political Support in the United States, Great Britain, and Europe." *Journal of Politics*, 1982b, *44*, 426–462.

Huston, T. L., and Levinger, G. "Interpersonal Attraction and Relationships." In M. R. Rosenzweig and L. W. Porter (eds.), *Annual Review of Psychology*, 1978, *29*, 115–156.

Hyman, H. H., and Sheatsley, P. B. "The Political Appeal of President Eisenhower." *Public Opinion Quarterly*, 1953, *17*, 443–460.

Iyengar, S., and Kinder, D. R. "More Than Meets the Eye: TV News, Priming, and Public Evaluation of the President." In G. Comstock (ed.), *Public Communication and Behavior*. Vol. 1. Orlando, Fla.: Academic Press, 1985a.

Iyengar, S., and Kinder, D. R. "Society, Image, Mind: Television News and the Making of American Opinion." Unpublished manuscript, Center for Political Studies, University of Michigan, 1985b.

Iyengar, S., Peters, M. D., and Kinder, D. R. "Experimental Demonstrations of the 'Not-So-Minimal' Consequences of Television News Programs." *American Political Science Review*, 1982, *76*, 848-858.

Iyengar, S., and others. "The Evening News and Presidential Evaluations." *Journal of Personality and Social Psychology*, 1984, *46*, 778-787.

Jackson, J. E. "Issues, Party Choices, and Presidential Votes." *American Journal of Political Science*, 1975, *19*, 161-185.

Jervis, R. *Perception and Misperception in International Politics*. Princeton, N.J.: Princeton University Press, 1976.

Jones, E. E., and Davis, K. E. "From Acts to Dispositions: The Attribution Process in Person Perception." In L. Berkowitz (ed.), *Advances in Experimental Social Psychology*. Vol. 2. Orlando, Fla.: Academic Press, 1965.

Jones, E. E., and McGillis, D. "Correspondent Inferences and the Attribution Cube: A Comparative Reappraisal." In J. H. Harvey and others (eds.), *New Directions in Attribution Research*. Vol. 1. Hillsdale, N.J.: Erlbaum, 1976.

Jones, E. E., and Nisbett, R. "The Actor and the Observer: Divergent Perceptions of the Causes of Behavior." In E. E. Jones and others (eds.), *Attribution: Perceiving the Causes of Behavior*. Morristown, N.J.: Silver Burdett, 1971.

Kagay, M. R., and Caldeira, G. A. "I Like the Looks of His Face: Elements of Electoral Choice, 1952-1972." Paper presented at annual meeting of the American Political Science Association, San Francisco, Sept. 2-5, 1975.

Kagay, M. R., and Caldeira, G. A. "A 'Reformed' Electorate? Well, at Least a Changed Electorate, 1952-1976." In W. J. Crotty (ed.), *Paths to Political Reform*. Lexington, Mass.: Heath, 1980.

Kahneman, D., and Tversky, A. "Prospect Theory: An Analysis of Decision Under Risk." *Econometrica*, 1979, *47*, 263-291.

Kanouse, D. F. "Language, Labelling and Attribution." In E. E. Jones and others (eds.), *Attribution: Perceiving the Causes of Behavior*. Morristown, N.J.: Silver Burdett, 1971.

Katz, D. "The Functional Approach to the Study of Attitudes." *Public Opinion Quarterly*, 1960, *24*, 163-204.

Kavanaugh, D. *Crisis Charisma and British Political Leadership: Winston Churchill as the Outsider*. Sage Professional Paper in Contemporary Political Sociology, Vol. 1, No. 06-001. Beverly Hills, Calif.: Sage, 1974.

Keith, B. E., and others, "The Myth of the Independent Voter." Paper presented at annual meeting of the American Political Science Association, Washington, D.C., Sept. 1977.

Kelley, H. H. "Attribution Theory in Social Psychology." In D. Levine (ed.), *Nebraska Symposium on Motivation*. Vol. 15. Lincoln: University of Nebraska Press, 1967.

Kelley, H. H. *Attribution in Social Interaction*. Morristown, N.J.: Silver Burdett, 1971.

Kelley, H. H. *Causal Schemata and the Attribution Process*. Morristown, N.J.: Silver Burdett, 1972.

Kelley, H. H. "The Processes of Causal Attribution." *American Psychologist*, 1973, *28*, 107-128.

Kernell, S. "Explaining Presidential Popularity." *American Political Science Review*, 1978, *72*, 506-522.

Kernell, S., and Hibbs, D. A., Jr. "A Critical Threshold Model of Presidential Popularity." In D. A. Hibbs, Jr., and H. Fassbender (eds.), *Contemporary Political Economy*. Amsterdam: North-Holland, 1981.

Key, V. O., Jr. *Public Opinion and American Democracy*. New York: Knopf, 1961.

Key, V. O., Jr. *The Responsible Electorate*. Cambridge, Mass.: Harvard University Press, 1966.

Kinder, D. R. "Presidents, Prosperity, and Public Opinion." *Public Opinion Quarterly*, 1981, *45*, 1–21.

Kinder, D. R. "Diversity and Complexity in American Public Opinion." In A. Finifter (ed.), *The State of the Discipline*. Washington, D.C.: American Political Science Association, 1983.

Kinder, D. R. "Presidential Character Revisited." Paper presented at 19th annual Carnegie Symposium on Cognition, Carnegie Mellon University, Pittsburgh, May 1984.

Kinder, D. R., and Abelson, R. P. "Appraising Presidential Candidates: Personality and Affect in the 1980 Campaign." Paper presented at annual meeting of the American Political Science Association, New York, Sept. 1981.

Kinder, D. R., Abelson, R. P., and Fiske, S. T. "Developmental Research on Candidate Instrumentation: Results and Recommendations." Unpublished paper, Center for Political Studies, University of Michigan, 1979.

Kinder, D. R., and Kiewiet, D. R. "Sociotropic Politics: The American Case." *British Journal of Political Science*, 1981, *11*, 129–161.

Kinder, D. R., and Mebane, W. R. "Politics and Economics in Everyday Life." In K. Monroe (ed.), *The Political Process and Economic Change*. New York: Agathon Press, 1983.

Kinder, D. R., Rosenstone, S. J., and Hansen, J. M. "Group Economic Well-Being and Political Choice." *Journal of Social Issues*, forthcoming.

Kinder, D. R., and Sears, D. O. "Public Opinion and Political Action." In G. Lindzey and E. Aronson (eds.), *Handbook of Social Psychology*. (3rd ed.) Reading, Mass.: Addison-Wesley, 1985.

Kinder, D. R., and others. "Presidential Prototypes." *Political Behavior*, 1980, *2*, 315–338.

Klein, E. D. *Consciousness and Group Politics: The Rise of the Contemporary Feminist Movement*. Cambridge, Mass.: Harvard University Press, 1984.

Klingemann, H. D. "Measuring Ideological Conceptualizations." In S. H. Barnes and M. Kaase (eds.), *Political Action: Mass Participation in Five Western Democracies*. Beverly Hills, Calif.: Sage, 1979.

Kramer, G. H. "The Ecological Fallacy Revisited: Aggregate- Versus Individual-Level Findings on Economics and Elections and Sociotropic Voting." *American Political Science Review*, 1983, 77, 92–111.

Kun, A., and Weiner, B. "Necessary Versus Sufficient Causal Schemata for Success and Failure." *Journal of Research in Personality*, 1973, 7, 197–207.

Lane, R. E. *Political Ideology*. New York: Free Press, 1962.

Lazarsfeld, P. F., Berelson, B., and Gaudet, H. *The People's Choice*. New York: Columbia University Press, 1944.

Leventhal, H. "Toward a Comprehensive Theory of Emotion." In L. Berkowitz (ed.), *Advances in Experimental Social Psychology*. Vol. 13. Orlando, Fla.: Academic Press, 1980.

Lippmann, W. *Public Opinion.* New York: Macmillan, 1922.

McArthur, L. Z. "The How and What of Why: Some Determinants and Conse-quences of Causal Attribution." *Journal of Personality and Social Psychology,* 1972, *22,* 171-193.

McArthur, L. Z. "The Lesser Influence of Consensus Than Distinctiveness Infor-mation on Causal Attributions: A Test of the Person-Thing Hypothesis." *Jour-nal of Personality and Social Psychology,* 1976, *33,* 733-742.

McArthur, L. Z. "What Grabs You? The Role of Attention in Impression Forma-tion and Causal Attribution." In E. T. Higgins and others (eds.), *Social Cog-nition.* Hillsdale, N.J.: Erlbaum, 1980.

McCauley, C., and Jacques, S. "The Popularity of Conspiracy Theories of Pres-idential Assassination: A Bayesian Analysis." *Journal of Personality and Social Psychology,* 1979, *37,* 637-644.

Mandler, G. *Mind and Emotion.* New York: Wiley, 1975.

Markus, G. B. "The Political Environment and the Dynamics of Public Attitudes: A Panel Study." *American Journal of Political Science,* 1979, *23,* 338-359.

Markus, G. B. "Political Attitudes During an Election Year: A Report on the 1980 NES Panel Study." *American Political Science Review,* 1982, *76,* 538-560.

Markus, G. B., and Converse, P. E. "A Dynamic Simultaneous Equation Model of Electoral Choice." *American Political Science Review,* 1979, *73,* 1055-1070.

Markus, H., and Zajonc, R. B. "The Cognitive Perspective in Social Psychology." In G. Lindzey and E. Aronson (eds.), *Handbook of Social Psychology.* (3rd ed.) Reading, Mass.: Addison-Wesley, 1985.

Miller, A. G. (ed.). *In the Eye of the Beholder: Contemporary Issues in Stereotyping.* New York: Praeger, 1982.

Miller, A. H., and Miller, W. E. "Ideology in the 1972 Election: Myth or Reality?" *American Political Science Review,* 1976, *70,* 832-849.

Miller, A. H., and Miller, W. E. "Partisanship and Performance: 'Rational' Choice in the 1976 Presidential Election." Paper presented at annual meeting of the American Political Science Association, Washington, D.C., Sept. 1977.

Miller, A. H., Wattenberg, M. P., and Malanchuk, O. "Cognitive Representations of Candidate Assessments." Paper presented at annual meeting of the American Political Science Association, Denver, Sept. 1982.

Miller, A. H., and others. "Group Consciousness and Political Participation." *American Journal of Political Science,* 1981, *25,* 494-511.

Miller, D. T., and Ross, M. "Self-Serving Biases in the Attribution of Causality: Fact or Fiction?" *Psychological Bulletin,* 1975, *82,* 213-225.

Mills, J., and Jellison, J. M. "Effect on Opinion Change of How Desirable the Communication Is to the Audience the Communicator Addressed." *Journal of Personality and Social Psychology,* 1967, *6,* 98-101.

Mueller, J. E. "Presidential Popularity from Truman to Johnson." *American Political Science Review,* 1970, *64,* 18-34.

Mueller, J. E. *War, Presidents, and Public Opinion.* New York: Wiley, 1973.

Neustadt, R. E. *Presidential Power: The Politics of Leadership.* New York: Wiley, 1960.

Nimmo, D., and Savage, R. L. *Candidates and Their Images.* Pacific Palisades, Calif.: Goodyear, 1976.

Nisbett, R. E., and Bellows, N. "Verbal Reports About Causal Influences on Social Judgments: Private Access Versus Public Theories." *Journal of Personality and Social Psychology,* 1977, *35,* 613–624.

Nisbett, R. E., and Ross, L. *Human Inference: Strategies and Shortcomings in Social Judgment.* Englewood Cliffs, N.J.: Prentice-Hall, 1980.

Olson, M. *The Logic of Collective Action: Public Goods and the Theory of Groups.* Cambridge, Mass.: Harvard University Press, 1965.

Orvis, B. R., Cunningham, J. D., and Kelley, H. H. "A Closer Examination of Causal Inference: The Roles of Consensus, Distinctiveness, and Consistency Information." *Journal of Personality and Social Psychology,* 1975, *32,* 605–616.

Page, B. I. *Choices and Echoes in Presidential Elections.* Chicago: University of Chicago Press, 1978.

Page, B. I., and Brody, R. A. "Policy Voting and the Electoral Process: The Vietnam War Issue." *American Political Science Review,* 1972, *66,* 979–995.

Page, B. I., and Jones, C. C. "Reciprocal Effects of Policy Preference, Party Loyalties, and the Vote." *American Political Science Review,* 1979, *73,* 1071–1089.

Petrocik, J. R. "Contextual Sources of Voting Behavior: The Changeable American Voter." In J. C. Pierce and J. L. Sullivan (eds.), *The Electorate Reconsidered.* Beverly Hills, Calif.: Sage, 1980.

Popkin, S., and others. "Comment: What Have You Done for Me Lately? Toward an Investment Theory of Voting." *American Political Science Review,* 1976, *70,* 779–805.

Rabinowitz, G., Prothro, J. W., and Jacoby, W. "Salience as a Factor in the Impact of Issues on Candidate Evaluation." *Journal of Politics,* 1982, *42,* 41–63.

Rivers, R. D. "The Dynamics of Party Support in the American Electorate, 1952–1976." Paper presented at annual meeting of the American Political Science Association, New York, Sept. 1981.

Robinson, M. J., and Sheehan, M. A. *Over the Wire and on TV.* New York: Russell Sage Foundation, 1983.

Rosch, E. "Classification of Real-World Objects: Origins and Representations in Cognition." In P. N. Johnson-Laird and P. C. Wason (eds.), *Thinking.* Cambridge, England: Cambridge University Press, 1977.

Rosenstone, S. J., Hansen, J. M., and Kinder, D. R. "Measuring Change in Personal Economic Well-Being." Unpublished manuscript, Department of Political Science, Yale University, 1984.

Ross, L. "The Intuitive Psychologist and His Shortcomings." In L. Berkowitz (ed.), *Advances in Experimental Social Psychology.* Vol. 10. Orlando, Fla.: Academic Press, 1977.

Ross, M., and Sicoly, F. "Egocentric Biases in Availability and Attribution." *Journal of Personality and Social Psychology,* 1979, *37,* 322–336.

Rummelhart, D. E., and Ortony, A. "The Representation of Knowledge in Memory." In R. C. Anderson, R. J. Spiro, and W. E. Montague (eds.), *Schooling and the Acquisition of Knowledge.* Hillsdale, N.J.: Erlbaum, 1977.

Schank, R. C., and Abelson, R. P. *Scripts, Plans, Goals and Understanding.* Hillsdale, N.J.: Erlbaum, 1977.

Schlozman, K. L., and Verba, S. *Injury to Insult.* Cambridge, Mass.: Harvard University Press, 1979.

Schneider, D. J. "Implicit Personality Theory." *Psychological Bulletin*, 1973, *79*, 294-309.

Sears, D. O., and Lau, R. R. "Inducing Apparently Self-Interested Political Preferences." *American Journal of Political Science*, 1983, *27*, 223-252.

Shabad, G., and Andersen, K. "Candidate Evaluations by Men and Women." *Public Opinion Quarterly*, 1979, *43*, 18-35.

Simon, H. A. *Reason in Human Affairs*. Stanford, Calif.: Stanford University Press, 1983.

Smith, M. B., Bruner, J. S., and White, R. W. *Opinions and Personality*. New York: Wiley, 1956.

Sniderman, P. M., and Brody, R. A. "Coping: The Ethic of Self-Reliance." *American Journal of Political Science*, 1977, *21*, 501-522.

Stevens, L., and Jones, E. E. "Defensive Attribution and the Kelley Cube." *Journal of Personality and Social Psychology*, 1976, *34*, 809-820.

Stokes, D. E. "Party Loyalty and the Likelihood of Deviating Elections." In A. Campbell and others (eds.), *Elections and the Political Order*. New York: Wiley, 1966a.

Stokes, D. E. "Some Dynamic Elements of Contests for the Presidency." *American Political Science Review*, 1966b, *60*, 19-28.

Sullivan, J. L., Marcus, G. E., Feldman, S., and Piereson, J. E. "The Sources of Political Tolerance: A Multivariate Analysis." *American Political Science Review*, 1981, *75*, 92-106.

Taylor, S. E., and Crocker, J. "Schematic Bases of Social Information Processing." In E. T. Higgins, C. A. Herman, and M. P. Zanna (eds.), *Social Cognition*. Hillsdale, N.J.: Erlbaum, 1981.

Taylor, S. E., and Fiske, S. T. "Salience, Attention, and Attribution: Top of the Head Phenomena." In L. Berkowitz (ed.), *Advances in Experimental Social Psychology*. Vol. 11. Orlando, Fla.: Academic Press, 1978.

Taylor, S. E., and others. "Categorical and Contextual Bases of Person Memory and Stereotyping." *Journal of Personality and Social Psychology*, 1978, *36*, 778-793.

Tversky, A., and Kahneman, D. "The Framing of Decisions and the Psychology of Choice." *Science*, 1981, *211*, 453-458.

Tyler, T. "Impact of Directly and Indirectly Experienced Events." *Journal of Personality and Social Psychology*, 1980, *39*, 13-28.

Zajonc, R. B. "Feeling and Thinking: Preferences Need No Inferences." *American Psychologist*, 1980, *39*, 151-175.

EIGHT

𝕫𝕫𝕫𝕫𝕫𝕫𝕫𝕫𝕫𝕫𝕫𝕫𝕫𝕫𝕫𝕫𝕫𝕫𝕫

Conflict: A Social Psychological Perspective

Morton Deutsch
Shula Shichman

We live in a period of history where conflicts over natural resources are likely to increase markedly and where hydrogen bombs and other weapons of mass destruction can destroy civilized life. The social need for better ways of managing conflict is urgent. In response to this need, a relatively small number of social scientists—still too few—have been working to provide the knowledge that will lead to more constructive conflict resolution.

In this chapter we seek to provide an overview of the research and theoretical knowledge that have been accumulating about conflict. We believe that the scientific work in this area is contributing to the emergence of a new mode of thinking about conflict, with an array of concepts that highlight some of the central processes involved in disputes and that provide a coherent basis for organizing the details of such processes. As a result, the mystical aura of the inevitability of destructiveness often associated with conflict has been reduced, and new insights about how to manage conflicts more productively at the interpersonal, intergroup, and international levels have emerged.

Our approach to conflict in this chapter is social psychological. We are brash enough to advance the view that the social psychological perspective provides a useful framework for considering the processes involved in conflict, whether the conflict is interpersonal, intergroup, or international. We even go so far as to suggest that what one can study in the social psychology laboratory has conceptual

Note: The writing of this chapter was supported in part from a National Science Foundation Grant (BNS-77-16017).

relevance for the understanding of large-scale conflict processes. We make the scientifically optimistic assumption of a correspondence in social processes across different types of social units. We hope our assumption is a valid one. We are in much the same position as the astronomers. It seems unlikely that we shall ever be able to conduct true experiments with large-scale social events. However, if we are able to identify the conceptual similarities between the large scale and the small, as the astronomers have between the planets and Newton's apple, we may be able to understand, predict, and possibly control what happens in large-scale sociohistorical processes by investigating what occurs in interpersonal and intergroup situations with which we can experiment. In short, we believe that the games people play as subjects in laboratory experiments may have relevance to such important social concerns as war, peace, and social justice.

The social psychological study of conflict is characterized not so much by the nature of the conflicting units it studies (although interpersonal and intergroup conflict are investigated most commonly) as by its approach to conflict. This approach is distinguished by its focus on the interplay between psychological and social processes. It is concerned with the perceptions, beliefs, and values of the conflicting units as well as their actualities; these may or may not correspond. It is concerned with how the social realities of the parties in conflict affect their perceived and experienced realities and how the psychological realities of the conflicting parties affect the development of their social realities.

The social psychological perspective on conflict highlights the possibility of discrepancy between the objective and the perceived state of affairs. Recognition of this possibility suggests a typology of conflicts (Deutsch, 1973) that emphasizes the relationship between the two. Such an emphasis leads to specification of the types of distortion that can occur, including the nonrecognition of real conflicts of interest as well as their displacement and misattribution. This emphasis, in turn, leads to a consideration of what activates the sense of injustice and what turns a latent into a veridical conflict (Deutsch, 1974, 1985). This focus also suggests examination of the social and psychological determinants of the readiness to cope with real conflicts in an undistorted way. The power, internal cohesion, and structure of the parties, as they affect and are affected by the course of conflict between them, are inherent concerns in this perspective.

Social psychological research on conflict during the past twenty-five years or so has largely taken the form of experimental gaming and has mostly been identified as research on bargaining and negotiation. Research in this area has primarily addressed three major, overlapping questions: (1) What are the conditions that give rise to a constructive or destructive process of conflict resolution? In a sense, this question arises from a focus on the cooperative potential inherent in conflict. (2) What are the circumstances, strategies, and tactics that lead one party to do better than another in a conflict situation? This question emerges from a focus on the competitive features of a conflict situation. (3) What determines the nature of the agreement between the conflicting parties, if they are able to reach an agreement? This question is a relatively recent one and has been addressed under the heading of research on the social psychology of equity and justice. In the next three sections, we shall attempt to describe the tentative answers that social psychological research has given to the foregoing questions.

Conditions Determining the Constructiveness of Conflict

In social psychology the question "What are the conditions that give rise to a constructive or destructive process of conflict resolution?" has been most directly addressed in research conducted in our laboratory, which is summarized by Deutsch (1973). This research has employed a variety of experimental games: the Prisoner's Dilemma, the Acme-Bolt trucking game, the Allocation game, the Siegel-Fouraker buyer-seller game, and several intergroup situations. In addition, exploratory field research has been done on the mediation process in labor-management conflict (Kressel, 1971) and in divorcing (Kressel, Morillas, Weinglass, and Deutsch, 1978) as well as on marital conflict (Shichman, 1982).

Our research started with the assumption that the parties involved in a conflict would be more likely to engage in a constructive process of conflict resolution if they had a cooperative rather than a competitive orientation toward one another. Earlier research (Deutsch, 1949a) had demonstrated that a cooperative process is a more productive way of dealing with a problem facing a group than a competitive process. We reasoned that the same would be true in a mixed-motive situation, where conflict could be viewed as a mutual problem facing the conflicting parties. Initial research on trust and suspicion employing the Prisoner's Dilemma game strongly supported this reasoning, as did subsequent research employing other experimental formats. This finding is very important and has considerable theoretical and practical significance.

At a theoretical level, it permitted linkage between a prior characterization of cooperative and competitive social processes (Deutsch, 1949b) and the processes of conflict resolution that would typically give rise to constructive or destructive outcomes. That is, a way was found to characterize the central features of constructive and destructive *processes* of conflict resolution. This finding—which represented a major advance beyond the characterization of *outcomes* as constructive or destructive—was not only important in itself but opened up a new possibility: the very significant possibility that we would be able to develop insight into the conditions that initiated or stimulated the development of cooperative-constructive versus competitive-destructive processes of conflict. Much of the research done in our laboratory has been addressed to developing this insight.

Nature of the Issue in Conflict

The likelihood that a conflict will take a constructive or a destructive course depends on the nature of the issue: its size, its rigidity, its centrality, its relationship to other issues, and the level of consciousness of the issue.

Size. As Fisher (1964) has pointed out, conflict size increases as the size of the conflicting units increases. He notes also that conflict size is increased to the extent that (1) the conflict is over principles, rights, and personalities; (2) the resolution of conflict establishes important precedents; (3) the conflict is perceived in win-lose terms; (4) the views and interests of the conflicting parties are discordant; and (5) the conflict is unfocused, nonspecific, and ill defined.

In an experiment on the effects of conflict size, Deutsch, Canavan, and Rubin (1971), using the Acme-Bolt trucking game, found that, as conflict size increased,

cooperation became more difficult, the joint payoffs decreased, and improvement in the joint payoffs over trials increased. The results clearly show that a cooperative process of conflict resolution and the attainment of a mutually satisfying agreement are more likely when conflict size is small. Nevertheless, under certain conditions a large conflict may seem so potentially dangerous that it exerts a strong pressure to reach agreement. To reduce the size of conflict, one may diminish the perceived opposition between the parties in values and interests through emphasizing common superordinate goals (Sherif, 1966) and through the techniques of controlled communication (Burton, 1969), role reversal (Cohen, 1950; Rapoport, 1960), and encounter group exercises (Schutz, 1967). These techniques essentially assume that perceived opposition can be reduced if the conflicting parties can be led to see how much they have in common, if their differences can be seen in the context of their similarities and agreements. They also commonly assume that perceived differences will decrease if misunderstandings are eliminated through improved, open, full, direct communication between the parties. Sometimes, however, the removal of misunderstanding sharpens the awareness of conflicting interests or beliefs, an awareness that had been beclouded by benevolent misunderstandings (Johnson, 1967).

It is somewhat surprising that, in the literature dealing with the management of conflict, there has been relatively little focus on what Fisher (1964) calls *issue control*. Controlling the importance of what is perceived to be at stake in a conflict may prevent the conflict from taking a destructive course. Many conflicts may be defined in a way that either magnifies or minimizes the size of the disputed issues. In general, "here-now-this" conflicts, which are localized in terms of particular, delimited actions and their consequences, are much easier to resolve constructively than conflicts that are defined in terms of principles, precedents, or rights, where the issues transcend time and space and are generalized beyond the specific action to personalities, groups, races, or other large social units or categories. Thus, when a quarrel starts to center on personalities or group membership rather than on specific actions, it usually takes a nonproductive turn. Similarly, when a discussion focuses on rights or principles rather than on what is specifically taking place at a given time and locale, it is not likely to be fruitful. Thus, in the Cuban missile crisis, neither the United States nor the Soviet Union would have been ready to negotiate about a fundamental principle such as "freedom" or "communism." Notwithstanding, they were able to negotiate about the much smaller, more focused, and specific issue of the location of seventy-two weapon systems.

Issue Rigidity. Issue rigidity may be determined by the nature of the issue as well as by the parties' attitudes. Certain issues (such as power or status) are more conducive to rigid definition than others. When the parties perceive no alternatives or substitutes for their expected outcomes or for the methods of achieving them, the conflict becomes rigidly defined. Issue rigidity is, of course, increased when the conflicting parties freeze themselves into positions (Fisher and Ury, 1981), through cognitive rigidity or the lack of cognitive resources for conceiving of alternatives, and by self-definitions that a change in one's position is a humiliation or loss of honor.

Centrality of the Issue. The more an issue threatens one's well-being, self-esteem, image, honor, reputation, position, or power, the more central and intense the conflict is, the more intangible the issues it creates, and the more irreconcilable the conflict becomes (Rubin and Brown, 1975). The Israeli-Arab conflict, for exam-

ple, is over highly central, rigidly defined issues around rights and principles, determined by political, historical, economic, and psychological causes. The resulting difficulty of achieving a solution that is satisfactory to both parties has culminated in five wars in the Middle East, with the prospect of still more to come (Bar-Tal, 1983).

The Number of Issues. A larger number of issues are more difficult to resolve—other factors held constant—than a smaller number. Consider, for example, the negotiation of a civil aviation agreement between the United States and the Soviet Union. In 1961 the United States refused to sign the agreement, treating it as a part of the then pending Berlin confrontation. In 1968 both the United States and the Soviet Union were ready to treat the aviation agreement as a separate issue, unrelated to Berlin; consequently, they signed the agreement (Fisher, 1969).

When multiple issues are involved, a constructive resolution is more likely if the issues are considered simultaneously rather than sequentially (Pruitt, 1981). Kelley (1966) found that dealing with the issues singly or on a subset basis made it more difficult to reach an agreement over all the issues. Reaching agreement on one item before settling the others declined over sessions, while reaching a total agreement on all items in their entirety increased over sessions and was preferred by most bargainers. Kelley concludes that treating the issues as a package rather than on a one-by-one basis allows the generation of more alternatives and increases the number of options to reach an overall agreement. Similarly, Froman and Cohen (1970) found that bargaining over multiple issues at one time led to more equitable and higher joint outcomes and required fewer steps. They conclude that negotiating each issue separately raises the level of conflict in the system and is less efficient than negotiating the issues as one set. Others (for example, Fisher, 1969), on the other hand, advocate fractioning the objectives into smaller components and dealing with them one at a time rather than in an overall confrontation. Dividing up a problem increases the likelihood of reaching an agreement, limits disagreement to specific issues, increases the chances of achieving the objectives, and reduces the risks of war in international conflicts.

Rubin and Brown (1975) suggest that the effectiveness of the two opposing approaches may depend on the number of issues. When the number of issues under dispute grows from few to many, formulating subsets of issues or breaking down the conflict into a number of issues may facilitate a constructive course of conflict and reaching agreement. As the number of issues in contention increases, the pressures toward differentiating them are likely to increase as well, and the fractioning of the issues so that they are smaller and specific—"issue control" (Fisher, 1964) or into "package deals" (Ikle, 1964)—promotes the resolution of conflict.

A question related to the number of issues refers to the order of dealing with multiple issues and is answered by two opposing viewpoints. One advocates considering the more important issues first, assuming that reaching agreement on the major issues will promote agreement on more trivial ones. The other approach advocates considering the less important issues first, assuming that the cooperation and recognition of common interests will facilitate the resolution of more major issues. It seems likely that both approaches have merit, each being more appropriate under certain conditions but not under other conditions. Empirical assessment of the circumstances leading to greater effectiveness of one or another approach is lacking, so that the question is left open for investigation.

Consciousness of the Issue. Conflict that is denied or unacknowledged may be either displaced or repressed and thus be more difficult to resolve. Acknowledgment of a conflict does not automatically lead to engagement in an attempt to resolve it, since the conflict may still be avoided for various reasons. Avoidance serves as a defense against confrontation with the other party; and it precludes a mutually satisfying resolution, inhibits the development of the relationship, and reduces the possibility of learning more about and understanding the other party. Avoidance may also lead to displacement of the issue to other areas (Coser, 1956), which, in turn, may decrease the likelihood of resolving the other conflicts and may impair the relationship between the parties.

Motivational Orientation

Motivational orientation refers to one's attitudinal disposition toward another. Deutsch (1973) distinguishes among three basic types of motivational orientations: cooperative—the person has a positive interest in the welfare of the others as well as in his own welfare; individualistic—the person has an interest in doing as well as he can for himself and is unconcerned about the welfare of the others; and competitive—the person has an interest in doing better than the others and in doing as well as he can for himself.

The effects of cooperative, individualistic, and competitive orientations—induced by experimental instructions—on the development of trust or suspicion were investigated in a Prisoner's Dilemma game (Deutsch, 1958, 1960a). In addition to motivational orientation, the influence of psychological simultaneity of choice and of communication availability was explored. The data indicate that in all experimental conditions a cooperative orientation leads to cooperative choices and expectations that result in mutual gain, whereas a competitive orientation leads to competitive choices and expectations that result in mutual loss. The choice-expectation patterns of the individualistically oriented subjects are much more influenced by the specific experimental treatments, so that, under conditions of full psychological simultaneity and of opportunity for two-way communication, the tendency of individualistically oriented subjects to choose cooperatively is increased. It can be concluded that a cooperative orientation will produce trusting and trustworthy behavior even when the situational facilities do not encourage it—for example, when no communication is permitted and when one has to choose without knowledge of the other person's choice. On the other hand, even when situational facilities are encouraging, a competitive orientation will result in suspicious and/or untrustworthy behavior. Trusting relationships can be developed under an individualistic orientation if external circumstances provide support for mutual trust—for instance, if the individual is given an opportunity to commit himself to a cooperative agreement through communication and an opportunity to know what the other person chooses.

The effects of motivational orientation on bargaining have been studied in several ways: varying the experimental instructions (Crawford and Sidowski, 1964; Deutsch and Lewicki, 1970; Griesinger and Livingston, 1973; Summers, 1968; Willis and Hale, 1963), manipulating the reward structure (Crombag, 1966; Gallo and Dale, 1968; Jones and Vroom, 1964; Krauss, 1966; Raven and Eachus, 1963; Rubin, 1971b; Shapira and Madsen, 1969; Wallace and Rothans, 1969), measuring the subjects' attitudes before the bargaining sessions begin (Benton and others, 1969; Kelley and Stahelski, 1970a, 1970b), and introducing varied payoff matrices (Aranoff and Tedeschi, 1968; Horai and others, 1969; Komorita and Mechling, 1967; Lindskold, Bonoma, and Tedeschi, 1969). After reviewing this research evidence, Rubin and Brown (1975, p. 213) conclude that "regardless of the particular method by which motivational orientation has been varied, it appears that a cooperative motivational orientation leads to more effective bargaining than an individualistic, and especially than a competitive motivational orientation."

Kennan (1983) suggests altering the dangerous Soviet-American relations by reducing the intense competitive orientation of the two nations through fostering cooperative activities. The collaborative approach includes courses of action such as restoring the full confidentiality and civility of communication between the two governments, gradually approaching the elimination of nuclear weapons, and, finally, taking advantage of those areas where possibilities for collaboration and mutuality of interests between the two nations exist, such as in the scientific and cultural fields or in the area of environmental problems.

Communication Process

The communication process is another of the factors determining whether the conflict will take a cooperative or a competitive course; the cooperativeness or competitiveness of the bargaining process influences, in turn, the use and characteristics of the communication. A competitive process tends to produce ineffective and impoverished communication, characterized by misleading, deceptive, and unreliable information; lack of verbalization of relevant thoughts and feelings; use of espionage to obtain information that the other is unwilling to give; little trust in information provided by the other; and increased likelihood of misunderstandings and misinterpretations. A cooperative process, on the other hand, is characterized by open and honest exchange of relevant information, where each participant is interested in informing and being informed by the other. The sharing of information enables the parties to get to the core of their knowledge and resources. The communication process between Japan and the United States during 1941 provides an example of a deceptive, misleading, and unreliable exchange of information between competing powers (Goldston, 1978), as does the process between the Soviet Union and the United States at the start of the Cuban missile crisis.

Some investigators report increased cooperation and bargaining effectiveness when there is availability of communication as opposed to its total absence (Bixenstein and Douglas, 1967; Bixenstein, Levitt, and Wilson, 1966; Deutsch, 1958; Scodel and others, 1959; Shure, Meeker, and Hansford, 1965; Terhune, 1968; Wandell, 1968). Krauss and Deutsch (1966), however, did not find that merely providing bargainers with the opportunity to communicate improved their bargaining effectiveness, and they suggest that the use of communication channels will be determined by other factors—for instance, the bargainers' motivational orientation, the personalities of the participants, and situational factors such as the availability or nonavailability of threat and the induction of trust or suspicion (Rubin and Brown, 1975).

In a study of the conditions of communication (that is, instances where communication was permitted and where communication was not permitted),

Deutsch (1958) found that, in contrast to both the cooperative and the competitive orientations, the behavior resulting from an individualistic orientation is very much influenced by situational determinants. The opportunity to commit oneself to a cooperative agreement through communication and the opportunity to know what the other is doing as one decides what to do facilitate considerably the development of mutual cooperation between individualistically oriented subjects.

How can communication opportunities be used to elicit mutual trust between the parties and, thus, facilitate a cooperative process of conflict resolution? A study designed to answer this question (Loomis, 1959) revealed that communication is likely to be effective in inducing trust in individualistically oriented people to the extent that the following basic features of cooperation are explicitly communicated: expression of one's cooperative intention, expression of one's cooperative expectations, expression of one's planned reaction to violations of one's expectations, and expression of a means of restoring cooperation after a violation of one's expectations has occurred. Thus, explicit communication of a cooperative system that specifies mutual responsibilities and procedures for handling violation and restoring cooperation may facilitate the development of trust.

The effects of both threat potential and the availability of communication (permissive communication) were investigated in a series of studies (Deutsch and Krauss, 1960, 1962; Krauss and Deutsch, 1966). In one study the Acme-Bolt trucking game paradigm was employed to test the effects of bilateral communication (both parties permitted to talk) combined with three levels of threat ("no threat," "unilateral threat," and "bilateral threat"). The results indicated that only threat had a significant effect and that the permission to communicate had no effect on the ability to reach agreement. It seems, then, that the opportunity to communicate does not necessarily result in an amelioration of conflict; indeed, the opportunity to communicate does not necessarily result in communication at all. Actually, little communication occurred; most subjects did not utilize their opportunity to communicate. Apparently, "the competitive orientation induced by the threat potential . . . was sufficiently strong to overcome any possible amelioration effects of communication. In the no-threat condition, where competitiveness is at a minimum, the advantage gained by the use of communication to coordinate effort was offset by the time consumed by talking" (Deutsch, 1973, p. 232). Thus, in a highly competitive situation, communication was infrequent and often failed to ameliorate conflict. A similar finding is reported by Scodel and his associates (1959) and by Wandell (1968), and such a finding is consistent with Kee's (1970) conclusion that communication is more deceptive and threatening when bargainers are induced to be suspicious rather than trusting.

Testing the effect of compulsory communication, Krauss and Deutsch (1966) found that only in the unilateral-threat condition (where only one of the bargainers had a weapon that could be used as the basis of threats) did the communication produce better outcomes. In the bilateral-threat condition (where both bargainers had weapons), the compulsory communication could not overcome the competitive orientation and thus did not have an ameliorating effect. In the no-threat condition (where neither bargainer had a weapon), the communication produced no effect.

As the results of these experiments indicate, the effects of communication must be considered in conjunction with motivational orientation. Thus, communication may be employed to coordinate effort or to intensify the competitive process through threats and insults. How, then, can communication be structured to increase bargaining effectiveness? Structuring may be introduced through a third party, through the experimenter's instructions, or through the development of rules that regulate the bargaining behavior. Krauss and Deutsch (1966) investigated the effects of the researcher's instructions on bargaining effectiveness. They compared the effects of untutored communication (where the researcher stressed the importance of communicating but did not specify the content of the communication) and of tutored communication (where the researcher instructed the subjects to negotiate a fair solution under a bilateral-threat condition). The investigators found that tutored communication facilitated better payoffs, whereas untutored communication did not improve the bargaining outcomes. The instructions induced more cooperation among the tutored subjects by providing them with an authoritative direction to utilize communication to reach a fair solution that would be acceptable to both sides.

Another way of structuring communication is through prescribing the manner in which communication is to occur (including the timing and the content of communication) during the bargaining. As to the timing of communication, Krauss and Deutsch found that postdeadlock communication was more effective than predeadlock communication. Evidence related to the structure of the content of communication is provided by Loomis's (1959) finding that the more complete the communication, the more likely it is to induce cooperative bargaining. A similar result is reported by Radlow and Weidner (1966), who found more cooperation in a message condition (where the message's content prompted a cooperative definition of the situation) than in a no-message condition. Other studies (Cheney, 1969; Gumpert, 1967; Hornstein, 1965) suggest that the availability and use of competitive messages, such as warnings, threats, or punishments, is likely to introduce elements that may reduce bargaining effectiveness (Rubin and Brown, 1975).

In sum, the availability of communication channels does not guarantee their usage or the improvement of bargaining outcomes. Factors such as motivational orientation and the influence of third parties determine whether or not communication takes place and the way it is utilized. Burton and his associates (Burton, 1969, 1979) and Kelman and his co-workers (Kelman, 1972, 1976, 1979; Kelman and Cohen, 1979; Cohen and Azar, 1981; Cohen and others, 1979) have developed "problem-solving workshops" to foster effective communication between people from nations that are involved in international conflict. The workshops seem well based in social psychology, but little evidence for their effectiveness exists as yet.

The Crude Law of Social Relations

Most of the results of the studies described in the preceding pages seem explainable by "Deutsch's crude law of social relations," which states that the characteristic processes and effects elicited by a given type of interdependence of social relationship (cooperative or competitive) tend also to elicit that type of social relationship. Thus, cooperation induces and is induced by a perceived similarity in beliefs and attitudes, a readiness to be helpful, openness in communication, trusting and friendly attitudes, sensitivity to common interests and deemphasis of opposed interests, and orientation toward enhancing mutual power rather than power differences. Similarly, competition induces and is induced by suspicious and hostile attitudes; the use of tactics of coercion, threat, or deception; attempts to enhance the power differences between oneself and the other; poor communication; lack of awareness of similarities in values; and increased sensitivity to opposed interests.

In other words, if one has systematic knowledge of the effects of cooperative and competitive processes, one will have systematic knowledge of the conditions that typically give rise to such processes and, by extension, to the conditions that determine whether a conflict will take a constructive or destructive course. Deutsch's (1949a, 1949b) theory of cooperation and competition is a theory of the *effects* of cooperative and competitive processes; hence, from the crude law of social relations, it follows that this theory provides insight into the conditions that give rise to cooperative and competitive processes.

The crude law is *crude*. It expresses surface similarities between "effects" and "causes"; the basic relationships are genotypical rather than phenotypical. The surface effects of cooperation and competition depend on the underlying type of interdependence ("positive" and "negative") and type of action ("effective" or "bungling"), the basic social psychological processes involved in the theory ("substitutability," "cathexis," and "inducibility"), and the social medium and social context through which these processes are expressed. Thus, the manner in which "positive cathexis" is expressed in an effective, positive interdependent relationship will depend on what is appropriate to the social medium and context; that is, presumably one would not seek to express it in such a way that one's partner would be humiliated or embarrassed as a result. Similarly, the effectiveness of either cooperation or competition as an initiating or inducing condition of a cooperative or competitive process depends not on its "phenotype" but rather on the inferred "genotype" of type of interdependence and type of action. Thus, in most social media and social contexts, "perceived similarity in basic values" suggests the possibility of positive linkage between oneself and the other. However, this same "similarity in basic values" may induce a negative relationship if we both seek something that is in scarce supply and available only to one of us. Also, although threats are mostly perceived in a way that suggests a negative linkage, a threat that seems intended to compel a person to do something that is good for him or that he feels he should do can suggest a positive linkage.

Although the crude law is crude, it is a synthesizing principle that integrates and summarizes a wide range of social psychological phenomena. Not only do the typical effects of a given relationship tend to induce that relationship, but any of the typical effects of a given relationship tend to induce the other typical effects of that relationship. For example, among the typical effects of a cooperative relationship are positive attitudes, perception of similarities, open communication, and an orientation toward mutual enhancement. One can integrate much of the literature on the determinants of positive and negative attitudes in terms of the other associated effects of cooperation and competition. Thus, positive attitudes result from perceptions of similarity, open communication, and so on. Similarly, many of the determinants of "effectiveness of communication" can be linked to other typical effects of cooperation or competition. And so on.

The crude law is crude, so it can be improved. Its improvement requires a linkage with other areas in social psychology, particularly social cognition and social perception. Such a linkage would enable us to view phenotypes in their social environments in such a way as to lead us to perceive correctly the underlying genotypes. We would then be able to know under what conditions "perceived similarity" or "threat" will be experienced as having an underlying genotype different from the one that is usually associated with its phenotype.

Finally, from the crude law, one would expect that any relationship would normally intensify. For example, if a relationship were more cooperative than competitive, it would move increasingly in a cooperative direction, and the intensity of cooperation would increase. Undoubtedly, this intensification does occur to some extent, but it tends to be limited. What are the influences restricting such a process? It seems likely that there are both external and internal constraining factors. Externally, the involvement and pull of other simultaneous relationships and overlapping situations tend to prevent and contain what might be termed an obsessive intensification of any particular relationship. Internally, there seem to be normal pathologies that develop in most types of relationships; these appear to curb the unceasing intensification of the relationship.

Malignant Social Conflicts

In the preceding pages, we have sought to provide theoretical and research insights into the conditions that give rise to a constructive or destructive process of conflict resolution. In this section we consider a particular form of destructive conflict, one characterized by a "malignant social process" (Deutsch, 1983). In a malignant conflict, the participants become enmeshed in a web of interactions and defensive-offensive maneuvers that worsen instead of improve their situations, making them more insecure, vulnerable, and burdened. Pathological disputes have a tendency to expand and escalate so that they become independent of their initiating causes. In such a dispute, the conflict processes themselves serve to perpetuate and intensify the conflict.

Deutsch (1983) has described a number of key elements (all of them evidenced in the relations between the United States and the Soviet Union) that contribute to the development and perpetuation of a malignant process: (1) an anarchic social situation, (2) a win-lose or competitive orientation, (3) internal conflicts (within each of the parties) that express themselves through external conflicts, (4) cognitive rigidity, (5) misjudgments and misperceptions, (6) unwitting commitments, (7) self-fulfilling prophecies, (8) vicious escalating spirals, and (9) a gamesmanship orientation, which turns the conflict away from issues of what in real life is being won or lost to an abstract conflict over images of power. Several of these are described below.

Anarchic Social Situation. There is a kind of situation that does not allow the possibility of "rational" behavior because the conditions for social order or mutual trust do not exist. The current security dilemmas facing the superpowers particularly result from their being in such a situation. In such "nonrational situations," an individual or a nation often will attempt to increase its own welfare or security without regard to the security or welfare of others, and the attempt will prove to be self-defeating. Consider, for example, the United States decision to develop and test the hydrogen bomb, in order to maintain military superiority over the Soviet Union, rather than to work for an agreement to ban testing of the H-bomb and thus prevent a spiraling arms race involving this monstrous weapon

(Bundy, 1982). This decision led the Soviet Union to attempt to catch up. Soon both superpowers were stockpiling H-bombs in a nuclear arms race that still continues in different forms.

United States leaders believe that if the Soviets had been the first to develop the H-bomb, they would have tested it and sought to reap the advantages from doing so. They were probably right. Both sides are aware of the temptations for each to increase security "by getting ahead." The fear of "falling behind," as well as the temptation to "get ahead," leads to a pattern of interactions that increases insecurity for both sides. Such situations, which are captured by the Prisoner's Dilemma game, have been extensively studied by social scientists (see Alker and Hurwitz, 1981, for a comprehensive discussion). When confronted with such social dilemmas, an individual or a nation can avoid being trapped in mutually reinforcing, self-defeating cycles only if it attempts to change the situation so that a basis of social order or mutual trust can be developed.

Competitive Orientation. If the participants in a conflict see it as a win-lose, competitive struggle, the resulting social process will tend to perpetuate and escalate the conflict. Communication between the parties will be unreliable and impoverished, enhancing the possibility of error and misinformation and reinforcing pre-existing stereotypes and expectations toward the other. It will appear that the solution of the conflict can be imposed by one side or the other only by means of superior force, deception, or cleverness; the attempts to create and maintain a power superiority will change the focus from the immediate issue in dispute to the more abstract issue of power for its own sake. A suspicious, hostile attitude will develop, which increases the sensitivity to differences and threats while minimizing the awareness of similarities. Behavior will be permitted that would be considered outrageous if directed toward someone like oneself. Since neither side will be likely to grant moral superiority to the other, the conflict will escalate as one side or the other engages in behavior morally outrageous to the other.

Internal Conflicts. Although competition is a necessary condition for malignant conflict, it is not a sufficient one. Malignant conflict persists because internal needs require the competitive process between the conflicting parties. There are many kinds of internal needs for which a hostile external relationship can be an outlet: It may provide an acceptable excuse for internal problems, which can be seen as caused by the adversary or by the need to defend against the adversary; it may provide a distraction, so that internal problems appear less salient; it can provide an opportunity to express pent-up hostility arising from internal conflict through combat with the external adversary; it may enable one to project disapproved aspects of oneself (which are not consciously recognized) onto the adversary and to attack them through attack on the adversary; it may permit important parts of one's self—including attitudes, skills, and defenses developed during conflictual relations in one's formative stages—to be expressed and valued because the relations with the present adversary resemble earlier conflictual relations. When an external conflict serves internal needs, it is difficult to give it up until other means of satisfying these needs are developed. There is little doubt that the conflict between the superpowers has served important internal functions for the ruling establishments in the United States and the Soviet Union.

Misjudgments and Misperceptions. Impoverished communication, hostile attitudes, and oversensitivity to differences—typical effects of competition—lead to distorted views that may intensify and perpetuate conflict; other distortions and egoistic biases commonly occur in the course of interaction. Many of these misperceptions function to transform a conflict into a competitive struggle—even if the conflict did not emerge from a competitive relationship. (See Jervis, 1976, for an excellent discussion of misperception in international relations.)

Unwitting Commitments. In a malignant social process, the parties not only become overcommitted to rigid positions but also become committed, unwittingly, to the beliefs, defenses, and investments involved in carrying out their conflictual activities. The conflict then is maintained and perpetuated by the commitments and investments given rise to by the malignant process itself. Thus, for example, in explaining his opposition to an American proposal shortly before Pearl Harbor, Prime Minister Tojo said that the demand that Japan withdraw its troops from China was unacceptable. As quoted in Jervis (1976, p. 398): "We sent a large force of one million men [to China] and it has cost us well over 100,000 dead and wounded, [the grief of] their bereaved families, hardships for four years, and a national expenditure of several tens of billions of yen. We must by all means get satisfactory results from this."

Self-Fulfilling Prophecies. Merton (1957), in his classic paper "The Self-Fulfilling Prophecy," has pointed out that distortions are often perpetuated because they may evoke new behavior that makes the originally false conception come true. The specious validity of the self-fulfilling prophecy perpetuates a reign of error. The prophet will cite the actual course of events as proof that he was right from the very beginning. The dynamics of the self-fulfilling prophecy help to explain individual pathology (for example, the anxious student who, afraid that he might fail, worries so much that he cannot study, with the consequence that he does fail). It also contributes to our understanding of social pathology (prejudice and discrimination against blacks, for example, keeps them in a position that seems to justify the prejudice and discrimination).

So, too, in international relations. If the policy makers of East and West believe that war is likely, and either side attempts to increase its military security vis-à-vis the other, the other side's response will justify the initial move. The dynamics of an arms race has the inherent quality of *folie à deux*, wherein the self-fulfilling prophecies mutually reinforce one another. As a result, both sides are right to think that the other is provocative, dangerous, and malevolent. Each side, however, fails to recognize that its own policies and behavior have contributed to the development of the other's hostility. If each superpower could recognize its own part in maintaining the malignant relations, that recognition could lead to a reduction of mutual recrimination and an increase in mutual problem solving.

The United States and the Soviet Union are entrapped in the pathological social process described here, giving rise to a web of interactions and defensive maneuvers, which, instead of improving their situations, make them both feel less secure, more vulnerable, more burdened, and a threat to each other and to the world at large. This pernicious process is fostered and maintained by anachronistic competition for world leadership; security dilemmas created for both superpowers by competitive orientations and the lack of a strong world community; cognitive rigidities arising from archaic, oversimplified, black-and-white, mutually antagonistic ideologies; misperceptions, unwitting commitments, self-fulfilling prophecies, and vicious escalating spirals, which typically arise during the course of competitive conflict; gamesmanship orientations to security dilemmas, which turn a conflict from what in real life is being won or lost to an abstract conflict over images of power, in which nuclear missiles become the pawns for enacting the game of power; and by internal problems and conflicts that can be managed more easily because of external conflicts.

Deescalating Conflict

One of the techniques that can be employed to deescalate conflict and reestablish trust, once an impass or a deadlock has been reached, is Osgood's (1962) Graduated and Reciprocated Initiatives in Tension Reduction (GRIT). This procedure consists of a graduated series of announced deescalation steps, action, and reciprocation. One party begins the GRIT process by announcing some steps it is going to take to reduce tension and destructiveness; it then takes the step and explicitly states its expectation that the other party is also interested in replacing escalation with constructive strategies. If the other reciprocates in response to the tension-reducing initiative(s), then the first party starts another round of such initiatives, and so on. Reviewing the literature, Lindskold (1978) concludes that the GRIT strategy has much research support.

Another approach to preventing destructive conflict is the method of principled negotiation, developed by Fisher and Ury (1981). This method of deciding issues on their merits may serve as an alternative to hard or soft positional bargaining, which involves successive taking and giving up of a sequence of positions. Principled negotiation consists of four elements: separating the people from the problem, focusing on interests rather than positions, generating a variety of options for mutual gain, and basing the outcomes on some objective criteria independent of the parties' positions. Although, as yet, there has been little research on the method of principled negotiation, it seems entirely consistent with the existing theoretical and research literature.

Third parties may also serve to limit the escalation of conflict. Rubin and Brown (1975, p. 56) indicate that third parties generate pressures toward agreement, which "may emanate from the mere knowledge of their present and/or future involvement, from their specific attributes (such as personality and reputation), and, most directly, from the interventions which they initiate. These pressures push bargainers in two primary directions: toward deference to norms of fairness, social responsibility, reciprocity, and equity of exchange; and toward the search for alternatives to their preferred positions." For third-party interventions to be effective, however, the bargainers must have sufficient trust and confidence in the third party's ability to function in his role as mediator (Kressel, 1971; Rubin and Brown, 1975).

The mere knowledge of the availability of a trusted third party as a factor facilitating the bargaining process deserves a special note. Whereas a concession initiated by the bargainer may be perceived as a sign of weakness to be exploited by the adversary, a concession suggested by a third party may reduce a bargainer's accountability for the concession and, thereby, ameliorate negative evaluations of him by the opposing party as well as by his own constituency (Johnson and Tullar, 1972; Kerr, 1954; Pruitt, 1971; Rubin and Brown, 1975; Stevens, 1963; Tedeschi, Schlenker, and Bonoma, 1973; Walton, 1969; Walton and McKersie, 1965).

Psychological research, as well as everyday phenomena, indicates that third-party interventions are often helpful in reaching an effective conflict resolution. Pruitt and Johnson (1970) found that intervention by a mediator enabled bargainers to make larger and more frequent concessions without viewing themselves as weak for having conceded. Pruitt and Johnson attribute the results to the face-saving function of the mediator. The above findings are corroborated by Podell and Knapp (1969), who report that subjects perceived their programmed robot opponent as being more willing to make concessions and as less weak when the concessions were preceded by an intervention from a mediator than when a mediator was not present. Both Pruitt and Johnson's and Podell and Knapp's results indicate that concessions initiated by oneself are interpreted more as a signal of weakness than concessions initiated by a third party.

Third parties can serve many functions when intervening in a resolution of conflict: (1) focusing the attention of the parties on the objective issue in contention, rather than on their personal feelings, by separating the people from the problem; (2) clarifying the parties' intentions and expected gains and costs; (3) exploring alternative solutions through directing the discussion to interests as well as through facilitating a creative generation of options; (4) allowing all or both parties to save face; (5) facilitating communication between opposing parties; (6) regulating the costs of conflict; (7) regulating public intervention or interference; (8) identifying and promoting the use of additional resources; (9) establishing and reinforcing norms of equity, fairness, and justice in the bargaining situation; and (10) legitimizing one's position when one's request reflects the view of an impartial third party (Deutsch, 1973; Fisher and Ury, 1981; Kerr, 1954; Kressel, 1971; Rubin and Brown, 1975; Tedeschi, Schlenker, and Bonoma, 1973). Walton (1969) categorizes the interventions of third parties as (1) those affecting the structure of the confrontation (for example, the site, time constraints, and audiences) and (2) those affecting the dialogue process (for example, the agenda and communication channels).

Summary of Findings

We have presented a survey of some of the experimental research and theorizing bearing on the important question of what determines whether a conflict will take a constructive or destructive course. In our view, significant progress has been made in providing a preliminary answer to this fundamental query. First of all, constructive and destructive processes of conflict resolution have been equated with cooperative and competitive processes, respectively; and, second, investigators have demonstrated that the typical effects of a cooperative (competitive) process tend to induce a cooperative-constructive (competitive-destructive) process of conflict resolution. Since we have well-established theoretical and research knowledge of the typical effects of cooperative and competitive processes, we have an answer to the question heading this section.

Thus, if one wants to create the conditions for a destructive process of conflict resolution, one would introduce into the conflict the typical characteristics and effects of a competitive process: poor communication, coercive tactics, suspicion, the perception of basic differences in values, an orientation to increasing power differences, challenge to the legitimacy of the parties, and so on. On the other hand, if one wants to create the conditions for a constructive process of conflict resolution, one would introduce into the conflict the typical effects of a cooperative process:

good communication, the perception of similarity in beliefs and values, problem-centered negotiations, mutual trust and confidence, informal friendly contacts, information sharing, and so on. Moreover, if one examines the roles of mediators and conciliators and similar third parties, one can describe their essential functions as seeking to produce constructive conflict resolution by creating the conditions that characterize an effective, cooperative problem-solving process. Knowledge of these conditions, in effect, provides an intellectual framework for third-party interventions.

Methods of Securing Advantage over Adversaries

Most of the important theoretical work by social scientists in relation to the question "What are the circumstances, strategies, and tactics that lead one party to do better than another in a conflict situation?" has been done not by social psychologists but by economists, political scientists, and those concerned with collective bargaining. Notable contributions have been made by Chamberlain (1951), Schelling (1960, 1966), Stevens (1963), Walton and McKersie (1965), Kahn (1965), Jervis (1970, 1976), and Snyder and Diesing (1977). Earlier, Machiavelli ([1513] 1950) and Potter ([1948] 1965) had described useful strategies and tactics for winning conflicts. Machiavelli emphasized methods of using one's power most effectively so as to intimidate or overwhelm one's adversary; Potter showed his readers how to play on the good will, cooperativeness, and politeness of an opponent so as to upset him and make him lose his "cool." More recently Alinsky (1971) has described a "jujitsu" strategy that the "have-nots" can employ against the "haves" and outlined various tactics of harassing and ensnarling the "haves" in their own red tape by exerting pressure on them to live up to their own formally stated rules and procedures.

Social psychologists have just barely begun to tap and test the rich array of ideas about strategies and tactics for winning conflicts, or for increasing one's bargaining power and effectiveness, that exist in the common folklore as well as in the social and political science literatures. Summaries of the relevant social psychological research on bargaining and negotiation can be found in Deutsch (1973); Druckman (1973, 1977); Tedeschi, Schlenker, and Bonoma (1973); Krivohlavy (1974); Rubin and Brown (1975); Chertkoff and Esser (1976); Morley and Stephenson (1977); Magenau and Pruitt (1978); and Pruitt (1981). This research has provided some support and some qualification of preexisting ideas about bargaining strategy and tactics. We shall briefly discuss research relating to "being ignorant," "being tough," "threats and promises," and "bargaining power."

"Being Ignorant"

Common sense suggests that one is better off if one is informed rather than ignorant. However, Schelling (1960) has advanced the interesting idea that in bargaining it is sometimes advantageous to be in a position where one is or appears to be ignorant of his opponent's preferences. Research (Cummings and Harnett, 1969; Harnett and Cummings, 1968; Harnett, Cummings, and Hughes, 1968) provides experimental support for Schelling's idea. In several different bargaining situations, a bargainer who did not have complete information about his opponent's bargaining schedule began bargaining with higher initial bids, made fewer concessions, and earned higher profits than bargainers with complete information. When a bargainer is ignorant of what the other wants, or appears so, he may justify to himself and to the other a relative neglect of the other's interests; neglecting the other's interests when they are known is a more obvious and flagrant affront. During World War II, the Allies' claimed ignorance of the genocide of the Jewish population of Europe saved them the cost involved in an attempt to stop the holocaust.

The bargaining tactic of "ignorance," as well as other such tactics as "brinksmanship" or "appearing to be irrational," can be characterized in terms of the bargaining doctrine of "the last clear chance." The basic notion here is that a bargainer will gain an advantage if he can appear to commit himself irrevocably, so that the last clear chance of avoiding mutual disaster rests with his opponent. A child who works himself up to the point that he will have a temper tantrum if his parents refuse to let him sit where he wants in the restaurant is employing this doctrine. So is the driver who cuts in front of someone on a highway while appearing to be deaf to the insistent blasts of the other's horn. Such tactics do not always work; they seem most likely to do so when the situation is asymmetrical (one party can use the tactic but the other cannot) and when the opponent does not have a strong need to improve or uphold his reputation for "resolve" or "toughness."

"Being Tough"

"Bargaining toughness" has been defined experimentally as setting a high level of aspiration, making high demands, and offering fewer and smaller concessions than one's opponent. Those who advocate a tough approach reason that offering few concessions reduces the opponent's aspiration level and, consequently, increases the payoff of the tough bargainer. Those who oppose the tough strategy argue that toughness induces one's opponent to be tough as well. Thus, Kennedy could not appear soft on Vietnam because of Khrushchev's toughness toward China at the time. In contrast, making concessions decreases mistrust and increases the likelihood of reaching agreement. For example, through conceding to the United States around the turn of the century, Britain succeeded in strengthening its friendship with the United States (Jervis, 1982).

While some experiments support the effectiveness of the tough strategy (Benton, Kelley, and Liebling, 1972; Chertkoff and Conley, 1967; Komorita and Brenner, 1968; Pilisuk and Skolnick, 1968; Pruitt and Johnson, 1970), the overall literature (see Magenau and Pruitt, 1978) points to a more complex conclusion: Lower initial demands and high concession rates facilitate reaching an agreement (Bartos, 1974; Benton, Kelley, and Liebling, 1972; Hamner, 1974; Harnett and Vincelette, 1978); however, extremely low initial demands and fast concessions may impede agreement because they may lead the other to expect more than the concession maker is ultimately willing to yield. Using the American course of action during the Cuban missile crisis, Jervis (1982) illustrates how a state that acts in a risk-taking manner in a situation where toughness is not anticipated can be expected to act even more boldly in less constrained situations. By the same token, if a state makes concessions on issues that are more important to it than to its adversary and/or in situations in which it has power advantages, it can be expected to be even more appeasing in situations that are less conducive to the state's being tough.

Pruitt (1981) proposes an inverted U-shaped relationship between a bargainer's demands and his gains. Bargainers with low demands will reach agreement but will achieve low profits; bargainers with high demands will fail to reach agreement; and bargainers with moderate demands will achieve agreement at a good level of payoff. Thus, "toughness plays a dual role and has contradictory consequences. On the one hand, toughness decreases the likelihood of an agreement, while, on the other hand, it increases the payoffs of those who survive this possibility of a failure" (Bartos, 1970, p. 62). Evidence for this conclusion comes from three studies (Bartos, 1974; Benton, Kelley, and Liebling, 1972; Chertkoff and Conley, 1967).

Similar to the distinction between tough and soft approaches to bargaining is Walton's (1964) differentiation between two strategies of social change, one involving power tactics and the other focusing on attitude change through the establishment of friendliness and trust. Walton suggests that the two seemingly contradictory strategies can be integrated into a broader strategy of social change through alternating between the two strategies, carrying out the two strategies by different subgroups, selecting power tactics with the least negative impact on attitudes, or selecting attitudinal tactics that detract least from the power strategy.

Threats and Promises

Threats and promises are means of social influence that affect the other's behavior through linking an externally imposed incentive (negative or positive) to the relevant alternatives. Thus, threats offer punishments and promises offer rewards as a basis for social influence (Deutsch, 1973; Kelley, 1965; Rubin and Brown, 1975; Sawyer and Guetzkow, 1965; Schelling, 1960). Research evidence shows that the use of promises tends to increase the likelihood of reaching a mutually satisfying agreement, while the use of threats tends to reduce this likelihood. Thus, bargainers who use promises tend to behave more cooperatively and more effectively (Cheney, Harford, and Solomon, 1972; Radlow and Weidner, 1966), achieve higher joint profits (Lewicki and Rubin, 1974), and have higher earnings (Rubin, Lewicki, and Dunn, 1973) than bargainers who use threats (Cheney, Harford, and Solomon, 1972; Deutsch, 1960b; Deutsch and Solomon, 1959; Lewicki and Rubin, 1971). Furthermore, promisers are viewed more favorably than threateners (Dunn, 1972; Evans, 1964; Heilman, 1972; Lewicki and Rubin, 1971), and threateners tend to evoke hostility in the other (Gumpert, 1967; Smith and Anderson, 1972). Threats are more likely to be perceived as hostile and coercive and to produce negative reaction when they are compellent (that is, when they specify what the target should do) rather than deterrent (when they specify what the target should not do)(Schelling, 1966) and when they are illegitimate rather than legitimate (Hover and others, 1972).

The main advantage of a high magnitude of threat or reward is that it may produce immediate overt compliance (Tedeschi, Schlenker, and Bonoma, 1973). The main disadvantage is that it may alienate those subjected to it. A tendency to alienation is affected by the type of power used and by the legitimacy of its use. Illegitimate use of threat or reward is most likely to elicit resistance and alienation because it may be experienced as a violation of one's rights to autonomy and self-respect. Alienation reduces one's trust and thus makes one less receptive to noncoercive forms of influence. Coercive power may produce immediate compliance; nevertheless, in the long run, it is costly and consumes the user's resources.

Rubin and Brown (1975) assume that promises and threats are likely to be used to the extent that a bargainer believes he cannot successfully exert influence otherwise (Kelley, Beckman, and Fischer, 1967; Rubin, 1971a; Shomer, Davis, and Kelley, 1966; Smith and Anderson, 1972). Threat is most likely to occur when the threatener is either individualistically or competitively oriented and, thus, has no positive interest in the other person's welfare; when the threatener expects the threat to be effective; or when the threatener expects not to be worse off as a result of the use of threat.

In spite of the negative effects that threats may have on bargaining (Borah, 1963; Deutsch and Krauss, 1960; Deutsch and Lewicki, 1970; Gallo, 1966; Gumpert, 1967; Hornstein, 1965; Kelley, 1966; Shomer, Davis, and Kelley, 1966), threats do not inevitably lead to a reaction of hostility and counterthreat. The use of and the response to threat depend on its following major characteristics: legitimacy, credibility, magnitude, clarity and precision of contingencies involved, and costs and benefits to the user (Deutsch, 1973).

Legitimacy. One's influence is more likely to be seen as legitimate when promises rather than threats are used, because threats are viewed more as an infringement on one's rights to autonomy and independence. However, under certain circumstances threats may be perceived as legitimate: when the threatened individual makes no claim to the rights of free choice and self-determination and grants the other the right to set the terms of the relationship; when the threat is directed at an illegitimate action; when the threat derives from justified needs or claims; and when the threat is consistent with the adversary's values and principles (Deutsch, 1973). President Kennedy's demand that the missiles be withdrawn from Cuba looked legitimate for several reasons. First, it sought to restore the balance of force in the hemisphere, which had been violated by Russia's actions. Second, the demand was unanimously supported by Latin American countries. This legitimization facilitated the Soviets' compliance with the demand. From an individual, group, or nation who seeks to establish or maintain an image of legitimacy, more legitimate threat is likely to be more credible and, consequently, more effective. Making a threat legitimate may be accomplished through legitimizing both the content and the process of implementing the threat. A good strategy for legitimizing threat is to relate it closely in time, place, and theme to the demand when the demand is clearly a legitimate one (Fisher, 1969).

Credibility. A threat or promise made by a source will be credible as a function of the perceived strength and reliability of the source's desire to influence, the perceived capability of the source to implement his threat or promise at an acceptable level to himself, his perceived commitment to implement it, and its appropriateness to what he desires. In other words, the determination, capability, intentions, and appropriateness of the source of influence are important in building his credibility and prestige. An example of a credibility problem goes back to World War II. Having adopted a policy of appeasement, Britain and France did not come across as credible in their threat to Hitler that they would not only go to war over Poland but also fight to the end (Jervis, 1976). Another factor that affects credibility is the degree to which the source's actions have matched his words in the past. Tedeschi, Schlenker, and Bonoma (1973, p. 239) define threat credibility operationally as "the proportion of times a source backs up his threats by punishing target's noncompliant acts over all those occasions when such noncompliance occurs," and summarize research that reveals that immediate compliance varies as a direct function of threat credibility or of both threat credibility and magnitude.

Magnitude. The magnitude of a threat or promise affects not only the degree of compliance but also the perception of the credibility and legitimacy of the attempted influence. Thus, a threat or a promise that is perceived as credible or legitimate will have a stronger influence the greater its magnitude. However, the credibility of a threat or a promise will decrease as its magnitude increases, particularly if a less costly incentive would be sufficient. Threats or promises that are disproportionate in magnitude may be viewed as illegitimate or inappropriate even if credible and, consequently, elicit resistance to comply.

The influence of the magnitude of promises or threats on their affective consequences was investigated by Raven and Kruglanski (1970). They contend that a larger as opposed to a smaller threat may seem a sign of respect for one's opponent. As to promises, a small promise may convey some degree of liking for the other, while too large a promise may be seen as a bribe (Rubin and Brown, 1975).

Clarity and Precision of the Contingencies Involved. The communication of a threat or a promise may be either explicit or tacit. An explicit communication precisely states the contingencies involved and takes the form of "If you do/don't Y, I will do/not do X" while a tacit communication does not spell out the contingencies and takes the form of "I will do/not do X" (Tedeschi, Schlenker, and Bonoma, 1973). The likelihood of influencing the other is greater when the contingencies involved in the threat or a promise are clearly and specifically designated (Fisher, 1969). A general and ambiguous statement of the contingencies involved impairs the credibility and legitimacy of the message, creates the impression that one has little power to implement it, and decreases the effectiveness of the threat or the promise. However, when the source is not certain of his own intentions or when he doesn't really want to implement his threat or promise, he may prefer to communicate tacitly rather than explicitly (Tedeschi, Schlenker, and Bonoma, 1973).

Costs and Benefits to the User. Generally, the costs of carrying out a threat— including the other's resistance and counterpunitive action—are higher than those involved in making one. Thus, carrying out a threat incurs costs to both parties. The disadvantages of implementing a threat are usually not fully considered or precisely estimated before the threat is made, but the source is tempted to implement the threat—while attempting to justify it—in order to maintain his credibility. The bombing of North Vietnam from mid-1965 to mid-1967 cost the United States more than the monetary value of destruction inflicted on North Vietnam during that period. Had the Americans considered the North Vietnamese perception of the bombing—that it was costing the United States more than it was costing them— they might have better understood why the bombing failed to exert its intended influence (Fisher, 1969).

The tendency to respond with resistance or counterthreat to a threat derives, in part, from an attempt to save face on the part of the threatened party. Face-saving behaviors are most likely to occur during aggressive or competitive encounters in which the target has suffered a *public* loss of self-esteem and status. In an attempt to restore its self-esteem and social esteem, the target may take costly retaliatory actions, motivated by the desire to deter the current threatener as well as future opponents, who are likely to use threat if the target does not alter its image as weak and compliant (Tedeschi, Schlenker, and Bonoma, 1973).

Tedeschi and his associates (1973, p. 141) have summarized the results of the research on threats and promises as follows: "Threats seldom improve and almost always decrease a bargainer's outcomes if his adversary is similarly armed and the values are important to both parties. Yet, when threats are available, bargainers are tempted to use them."

Bargaining Power

Power, or the ability to influence, has been experimentally defined in the context of bargaining in the following ways: (1) the relative dependence of the bargainers, (2) the relative power of each party to elicit concessions from the other party or to inflict harm upon the other, (3) the relative desirability of the alternatives to bargaining that are available to each of the bargainers, and (4) the relative time pressure on each bargainer to reach an agreement.

Common sense would suggest that a bargainer is likely to be better off if he has more power than his adversary. The results of social psychological research indicate that the situation is more complex than it seems at first impression. The research evidence (Magenau and Pruitt, 1978; Rubin and Brown, 1975) indicates that agreement is relatively easy to reach and the outcomes to the parties are high when bargaining power is equal (Aranoff and Tedeschi, 1968; Baranowski and Summers, 1972; Borah, 1963; Deignan, 1970; Faley and Tedeschi, 1971; Kelley, Beckman, and Fischer, 1967; Komorita and Barnes, 1969; McClintock and others, 1973; Pepitone and others, 1970; Sheposh and Gallo, 1973; Solomon, 1960; Swingle, 1970; Swingle and MacLean, 1971). When bargaining power is somewhat unequal, a power struggle often ensues as the bargainer with more power tries to assert superior claims and as these are resisted by the bargainer with lesser power; the result of this struggle is that agreement is difficult to reach and the bargainers have low outcomes. When bargaining power is markedly unequal, the differences in bargaining power are more likely to be accepted as legitimate and lead to quick agreement, with the advantage going to the more powerful bargainer (Hornstein, 1965; Rubin, 1971a). However, if the less powerful bargainer does not believe that the differences in power provide a legitimization of relatively low outcomes to him, he will resist what he considers to be greed and exploitation; agreement here also will be less likely and outcomes will be low.

Summary of Findings

From this brief and very incomplete survey of some of the experimental research bearing on the strategy and tactics of waging conflict, it is evident that social psychological research has given some support to rather surprising tactics (such as "being ignorant") and has raised some doubts about common assumptions regarding the advantages obtained from "toughness" as a strategy, from "coercive tactics," and from "superior bargaining power." Although the experimental research on bargaining has produced interesting results, social psychologists have not yet developed a systematic theory of social influence. Our descriptive categories for classifying the various strategies and tactics employed in competitive bargaining have not gone beyond the excellent early work of Walton and McKersie (1965). We have not developed miniature theories of seduction, coercion, blackmail, or bluffing, and we lack sufficient empirical knowledge of these "black arts" to provide a curriculum for a school for scoundrels. Partly, our deficiency in these respects reflects a tendency to neglect theorizing and to favor research—a tendency that is characteristic of much of social psychology. Partly, it results from our insular tendency to ignore related work in other areas of social psychology—for example, Jones's (1964) work on ingratiation, Freedman's (1966) work on "the foot-in-the-door" technique, and Moscovici's (1976) approach to social influence and social change.

Nature of Agreements

In addition to the types of factors discussed in the preceding section, two compatible ideas have been advanced in answer to the question "What determines the nature of the agreement between conflicting parties if they are able to reach an agreement?" One of these ideas is related to "perceptual prominence"; the other, to "distributive justice."

Schelling (1960) has suggested that perceptually prominent alternatives serve a key function in permitting bargainers to come to an agreement. These alternatives acquire their salience because of their perceptual uniqueness, simplicity, or "good form." Schelling (1960, p. 70) has pointed out: "Most bargaining situations ultimately involve some range of possible outcomes within which each party would rather make a concession than fail to reach agreement at all. . . . The final outcome must be a point from which neither expects the other to retreat; yet the main ingredient of this expectation is what one thinks the other expects the first to expect, and so on. . . . These infinitely reflexive expectations must somehow converge on a single point, at which each expects the other not to expect to be expected to retreat." A perceptually prominent agreement—for example, "a 50-50 split," "equal concessions"—provides an obvious place to converge and to stop making or expecting further concessions. Research has provided some support for Schelling's idea (see Pruitt, 1981, for a summary).

Homans (1961, 1974) has suggested that the principle of distributive justice plays a role in determining how people will decide to allocate the rewards and costs to be distributed between them. Although Homans was not primarily concerned with conflict or bargaining, it is evident that his conception of distributive justice does not exclude them. He has emphasized one particular canon or rule of distributive justice, that of "proportionality" or "equity": In a just distribution, rewards will be distributed among individuals in proportion to their contributions. "Equity theorists," such as Adams (1963, 1965; Adams and Freedman, 1976) and Walster (Walster, Walster, and Berscheid, 1978) have continued Homans's emphasis on the rule of proportionality and have elaborated a theory and stimulated much research to support the view that psychological resistance and emotional distress will be encountered if the rule of proportionality is violated. Other social psychologists—Deutsch (1974, 1975), Lerner (1975), Leventhal (1976), and Sampson (1969)—have stressed that "proportionality" is only one of many common canons of distributive justice. Amplifying Rescher's (1966) list of principles, Deutsch (1979) has described eleven rules of distributive justice that are widely used in different contexts; others have listed even more.

Among the many possible distribution rules, several have been particularly prominent and have been the foci of political ideologies:

1. *Need* ("to each according to need")—the utopian idea of distributive justice advocated by Communist theorists. This principle is commonly invoked in relation to the goods that are requisites for physical survival: food, shelter, medical care, and responsible parenting of children.

2. *Equality* ("to each equal shares")—the egalitarian value of democratic theorists. Sometimes the stress is on "equal opportunity" (each should have equal access to resources), and sometimes it is on "equal outcomes" (each should have the resources necessary to overcome whatever handicaps would prevent equal outcomes). This principle is often invoked in relation to liberties and rights in the political and socialization-education spheres and is commonly expected in solidarity-communal relations.

3. *Contribution* ("to each according to contribution")—the value appealed to by meritocratic theorists as well as by Marxists ("from each according to his ability, to each according to his work") during the socialist transition period from capitalism to communism. This principle is frequently employed in the economic sphere for the allocation of honors, resources, and consumer goods.

4. *Effort* ("to each according to effort or sacrifice")—the principle espoused by the Puritan ethic. It is commonly applied in the socialization and religious spheres for the allocation of praise and recognition.

5. *Justified self-interest* ("to each according to what can be legally obtained"). Power, position, one's market value, and the like, can be used to take as much as possible for oneself as long as one does not act illegally. This principle underlies the ideology of the competitive, free-enterprise system and is usually invoked in political and economic spheres.

We are beginning to know a little about what makes a given rule of justice stand out as saliently appropriate in a given situation of conflict. A number of social psychologists (Deutsch, 1975; Lamm and Kayser, 1978; Lerner, 1975; Leventhal, 1976; Mikula and Schwinger, 1978; Sampson, 1975) have articulated hypotheses about factors favoring the selection of one or another rule, and have begun to do related experiments. Deutsch (1985), for example, has applied and elaborated his crude hypothesis of social relations (the typical consequences of a given type of social relation tend to elicit that relation) so that it is relevant to the question of what rule of justice will predominate in a group or social system. Specifically, economically oriented groups will tend to use the principle of equity (contribution); solidarity-oriented groups, the principle of equality; and caring-oriented groups, the principle of need. He has then characterized typical effects of economically oriented relations, solidarity-oriented relations, and caring relations and has hypothesized that these different kinds of typical effects will elicit different principles of distributive justice.

Thus, among the typical consequences of an economic orientation (Diesing, 1962) are (1) the development of a set of values including maximization, a means-end scheme, neutrality or impartiality with regard to means, and competition; (2) the turning of man and everything associated with him into commodities—including labor, time, land, capital, personality, social relations, ideas, art, and enjoyment; (3) the development of measurement procedures that enable the value of different amounts and types of commodities to be compared; and (4) the tendency for economic activities to expand in scope and size. The crude hypothesis advanced above would imply that if a social situation is characterized by impersonality, competition, maximization, an emphasis on comparability rather than uniqueness, and largeness in size or scope, then an economic orientation and the principle of equity are likely to be dominant in the group or social system. Specific experimental hypotheses could readily be elaborated: The more competitive the people are in a group, the more likely they are to use equity, rather than equality or need, as the principle of distributive justice; the more impersonal the relations of the members of a group are, the more likely they are to use equity; and so forth. Results in our laboratory as well as in the laboratories of other investigators (for example, Mikula, 1981) are consistent with the crude hypothesis.

Summary of Findings

We have briefly considered two types of factors that influence the nature of the agreement conflicting parties are likely to reach: factors affecting the perceptual prominence of alternative possibilities of agreement and factors influencing whether the agreement will be perceived as just. Our discussion has not been extensive because there has not yet been much relevant research. It should be apparent, however, that if a conflict is experienced as having been resolved unjustly, it is not likely that the conflict has been adequately resolved.

Conclusion

In this chapter our objective was to provide a social psychological perspective on conflict. We believe that this perspective has relevance to intergroup and international disputes, as well as to interpersonal conflicts created in the experimental laboratory. A number of key conclusions emerging from this orientation have general relevance to conflict.

1. Few conflicts are intrinsically and inevitably win-lose conflicts. A common tendency is to misperceive conflicts of interest, as well as other conflicts in which the parties have become invested in their positions, as being "win-lose" in nature.

2. If the conflict is not by its nature a win-lose conflict, one should develop and maintain a cooperative problem-solving orientation, which focuses on the interests of different parties (and not their positions) and seeks a solution that is responsive to the legitimate interests of both sides. Various procedures for fostering the development of such an orientation have been described by Johnson and Johnson (1982), Fisher and Ury (1981), and many others.

3. A full, open, honest, and mutually respectful communication process should be encouraged, so that the parties can clearly express and comprehend one another's interest with empathetic understanding; such a process will discourage the misunderstandings that lead to defensive commitments and to a win-lose orientation. In recent years a highly developed social psychology technology has emerged for fostering such a communication process and for reducing the misunderstandings and provocations that often characterize the communications between parties in conflict (see Burton, 1969, 1979; Kelman, 1972, 1979).

4. A wide range of options for potentially solving the problem of the diverging interests of conflicting parties should be developed. Many techniques and procedures—such as "brainstorming" and "synectics"—are now available to help people increase the variety, novelty, and range of alternative possibilities available

to them as they attempt to solve problems. (For a discussion of procedures for stimulating creativity, see Stein, 1974, 1975.)

5. A sophisticated awareness should be developed of the norms, rules, procedures, and tactics—as well as the external resources and facilities—available to support "good-faith" negotiations and deter "dirty tricks," "refusals to negotiate," and "exploitativeness" on the part of any of the negotiators involved in conflict. The point is that there are resources and effective procedures for dealing with many of the common problems and impasses that often lead a conflict to degenerate into a destructive process. There are potentially helpful third parties—counselors, mediators, conciliators, and arbitrators. There are often effective ways of inducing someone to negotiate despite an initial reluctance. And so on.

Let us conclude by stating that, although there has been significant progress in the study of conflict, the progress does not yet begin to match the social need for understanding conflict.

References

Adams, J. S. "Toward an Understanding of Inequity." *Journal of Abnormal and Social Psychology*, 1963, *67*, 422–436.

Adams, J. S. "Inequity in Social Exchange." In L. Berkowitz (ed.), *Advances in Experimental Social Psychology*. Vol. 2. Orlando, Fla.: Academic Press, 1965.

Adams, J. S., and Freedman, S. "Equity Theory Revisited: Comments and Annotated Bibliography." In L. Berkowitz and E. Walster (eds.), *Advances in Experimental Social Psychology*. Vol. 9. Orlando, Fla.: Academic Press, 1976.

Alinsky, S. D. *Rules for Radicals: A Practical Primer for Realistic Radicals*. New York: Random House, 1971.

Alker, H. R., Jr., and Hurwitz, R. *Resolving Prisoner's Dilemmas*. Washington, D.C.: American Political Science Association, 1981.

Aranoff, D., and Tedeschi, J. T. "Original Stakes and Behavior in the Prisoner's Dilemma Game." *Psychonomic Science*, 1968, *12*, 79–80.

Baranowski, T. A., and Summers, D. A. "Perception of Response Alternatives in a Prisoner's Dilemma Game." *Journal of Personality and Social Psychology*, 1972, *21*, 35–40.

Bar-Tal, D. "Israel-Palestinian Conflict: A Cognitive Analysis." Paper presented at the European-Israeli Conference on Group Processes and Intergroup Conflict, Tel-Aviv, Oct. 1983.

Bartos, O. J. "Determinants and Consequences of Toughness." In P. Swingle (ed.), *The Structure of Conflict*. Orlando, Fla.: Academic Press, 1970.

Bartos, O. J. *Process and Outcome in Negotiation*. New York: Columbia University Press, 1974.

Benton, A. A., Kelley, H. H., and Liebling, B. "Effects of Extremity of Offers and Concession Rate on the Outcomes of Bargaining." *Journal of Personality and Social Psychology*, 1972, *24*, 73–83.

Benton, A. A., and others. "Reactions to Various Degrees of Deceit in a Mixed-Motive Relationship." *Journal of Personality and Social Psychology*, 1962, *12*, 170–180.

Bixenstein, V. E., and Douglas, J. "Effect of Psychopathology on Group Consensus and Cooperative Choice in a Six-Person Game." *Journal of Personality and Social Psychology*, 1967, *5*, 32–37.

Bixenstein, V. E., Levitt, C. A., and Wilson, K. V. "Collaboration Among Six Persons in a Prisoner's Dilemma Game." *Journal of Conflict Resolution*, 1966, *10*, 488–496.

Borah, L. A., Jr. "The Effects of Threat in Bargaining: Critical and Experimental Analysis." *Journal of Abnormal and Social Psychology*, 1963, *66*, 37–44.

Bundy, M. "The Missed Chance to Stop the H-Bomb." *New York Review of Books*, May 13, 1982, pp. 13–14.

Burton, J. *Conflict and Communication: The Use of Controlled Communication in International Relations.* London: Macmillan, 1969.

Burton, J. *Deviance, Terrorism, and War: The Process of Solving Unsolved Social and Political Problems.* New York: St. Martin's Press, 1979.

Chamberlain, N. *Collective Bargaining.* New York: McGraw-Hill, 1951.

Cheney, J. H. "The Effects upon the Bargaining Process of Positive and Negative Communication Options in Equal and Unequal Power Relationships." *Dissertation Abstracts*, 1969, *30*, 2146–2147A.

Cheney, J., Harford, T., and Solomon, L. "The Effects of Communicating Threats and Promises upon the Bargaining Process." *Journal of Conflict Resolution*, 1972, *16*, 99–107.

Chertkoff, J. M., and Conley, M. "Opening Offer and Frequency of Concessions as Bargaining Strategies." *Journal of Personality and Social Psychology*, 1967, *7*, 181–185.

Chertkoff, J. M., and Esser, J. K. "A Review of Experiments in Explicit Bargaining." *Journal of Experimental Social Psychology*, 1976, *12*, 464–487.

Cohen, J. "Technique of Role-Reversal: The Study of International Conferences." Paper presented at meeting of the World Federation for Mental Health, Paris, 1950.

Cohen, S. P., and Azar, E. E. "From War to Peace: The Transition Between Egypt and Israel." *Journal of Conflict Resolution*, 1981, *25*, 87–114.

Cohen, S. P., and others. "Evolving Intergroup Techniques for Conflict Resolution: An Israeli-Palestinian Pilot Workshop." *Journal of Social Issues*, 1979, *33* (1), 165–189.

Coser, L. *The Function of Social Conflict.* New York: Free Press, 1956.

Crawford, T., and Sidowski, J. B. "Monetary Incentive and Cooperation/Competition Instructions in a Minimal Social Situation." *Psychological Reports*, 1964, *15*, 233–234.

Crombag, H. F. "Cooperation and Competition in a Means-Interdependent Triad: A Replication." *Journal of Personality and Social Psychology*, 1966, *4*, 692–695.

Cummings, L. L., and Harnett, D. L. "Bargaining Behavior in a Symmetric Bargaining Triad." *Review of Economic Studies*, 1969, *36*, 485–501.

Deignan, G. M. "Perceptual, Interpersonal and Situational Factors in Cooperation and Competition." *Dissertation Abstracts*, 1970, *31*, 1371A.

Deutsch, M. "An Experimental Study of the Effects of Cooperation and Competition upon Group Process." *Human Relations*, 1949a, *2*, 199–232.

Deutsch, M. "A Theory of Cooperation and Competition." *Human Relations*, 1949b, *2*, 129–152.

Deutsch, M. "Trust and Suspicion." *Journal of Conflict Resolution*, 1958, *2*, 265–279.

Deutsch, M. "The Effect of Motivational Orientation upon Trust and Suspicion." *Human Relations*, 1960a, *13*, 123–139.

Deutsch, M. "The Pathetic Fallacy." *Journal of Personality*, 1960b, *28*, 317–332.

Deutsch, M. *The Resolution of Conflict: Constructive and Destructive Processes.* New Haven, Conn.: Yale University Press, 1973.

Deutsch, M. "Awakening the Sense of Injustice." In M. Lerner and M. Ross (eds.), *The Quest for Justice.* Toronto: Holt, Rinehart & Winston of Canada, 1974.

Deutsch, M. "Equity, Equality and Need: What Determines Which Value Will Be Used as the Basis of Distributive Justice?" *Journal of Social Issues*, 1975, *31*, 137–150.

Deutsch, M. "Education and Distributive Justice: Some Reflections on Grading Systems." *American Psychologist*, 1979, *34*, 391–401.

Deutsch, M. "The Prevention of World War III: A Psychological Perspective." *Political Psychology*, 1983, *4*, 3–32.

Deutsch, M. *Distributive Justice: A Social Psychological Perspective.* New Haven, Conn.: Yale University Press, 1985.

Deutsch, M., Canavan, D., and Rubin, J. "The Effects of Size of Conflict and Set of Experimenter upon Interpersonal Bargaining." *Journal of Experimental Social Psychology*, 1971, *7*, 258–267.

Deutsch, M., and Krauss, R. M. "The Effect of Threat upon Interpersonal Bargaining." *Journal of Abnormal and Social Psychology*, 1960, *61*, 181–189.

Deutsch, M., and Krauss, R. M. "Studies of Interpersonal Bargaining." *Journal of Conflict Resolution*, 1962, *6*, 52–76.

Deutsch, M., and Lewicki, R. J. " 'Locking-In' Effects During a Game of Chicken." *Journal of Conflict Resolution*, 1970, *14*, 367–378.

Deutsch, M., and Solomon, L. "Reactions to Evaluations by Others as Influenced by Self-Evaluation." *Sociometry*, 1959, *22*, 93–112.

Diesing, P. *Reason in Society.* Urbana: University of Illinois Press, 1962.

Druckman, D. *Human Factors in International Negotiation: Social-Psychological Aspects of International Conflict.* Beverly Hills, Calif.: Sage, 1973.

Druckman, D. (ed.). *Negotiations: Social-Psychological Perspectives.* Beverly Hills, Calif.: Sage, 1977.

Dunn, L. "Effects of Sex of Transmitter and Sex of Recipient upon the Effectiveness of Promises and Threats." Unpublished manuscript, Tufts University, Medford, Mass., 1972.

Evans, G. "Effects of Unilateral Promise and Value of Rewards upon Cooperation and Trust." *Journal of Abnormal and Social Psychology*, 1964, *69*, 587–590.

Faley, T., and Tedeschi, J. T. "Status and Reactions to Threats." *Journal of Personality and Social Psychology*, 1971, *17*, 192–199.

Fisher, R. "Fractionating Conflict." In R. Fisher (ed.), *International Conflict and Behavioral Science: The Craigville Papers.* New York: Basic Books, 1964.

Fisher, R. *International Conflict for Beginners.* New York: Harper & Row, 1969.

Fisher, R., and Ury, W. *Getting to Yes. Negotiating Agreement Without Giving In.* Boston: Houghton Mifflin, 1981.

Freedman, J. L. "Compliance Without Pressure: The Foot-in-the-Door Technique." *Journal of Personality and Social Psychology*, 1966, *2*, 195–202.

Froman, L. A., Jr., and Cohen, M. D. "Compromise and Logroll: Comparing the Efficiency of Two Bargaining Processes." *Behavioral Sciences*, 1970, *15*, 180–183.

Gallo, P. S., Jr. "Effects of Increased Incentives upon the Use of Threat in Bargaining." *Journal of Personality and Social Psychology*, 1966, *4*, 14–20.

Gallo, P. S., Jr., and Dale, I. A. "Experimenter Bias in the Prisoner's Dilemma Game." *Psychonomic Science,* 1968, *13,* 340.

Goldston, R. *The Road Between Wars: 1918-1941.* New York: Fawcett, 1978.

Griesinger, D. W., and Livingston, J. W. "Toward a Model of Interpersonal Motivation in Experimental Games." *Behavioral Science,* 1973, *18,* 173-188.

Gumpert, P. "Some Antecedents and Consequences of the Use of Punitive Power by Bargainers." Unpublished doctoral dissertation, Teachers College, Columbia University, New York, 1967.

Hamner, W. C. "Effects of Bargaining Strategy and Pressure to Reach Agreement in a Stalemated Negotiation." *Journal of Personality and Social Psychology,* 1974, *30,* 458-467.

Harnett, D. L., and Cummings, L. L. "Bargaining Behavior in an Asymmetric Triad: The Role of Information, Communication, and Risk-Taking Propensity." Unpublished manuscript, University of Indiana, 1968.

Harnett, D. L., Cummings, L. L., and Hughes, C. D. "The Influence of Risk-Taking Propensity on Bargaining Behavior."*Behavioral Science,* 1968, *13,* 91-101.

Harnett, D. L., and Vincelette, J. P. "Strategic Influences on Bargaining Effectiveness." In H. Sauermann (ed.), *Contributions to Experimental Economics.* Vol. 7. Tübingen, Federal Republic of Germany: Mohr, 1978.

Heilman, M. "Attitudes, Expectations and Behavior in Response to Threats and Promises as a Function of the Influencer's Reputation." Unpublished doctoral dissertation, Teachers College, Columbia University, 1972.

Homans, G. C. *Social Behavior: Its Elementary Forms.* San Diego: Harcourt Brace Jovanovich, 1961.

Homans, G. C. *Social Behavior: Its Elementary Forms.* (Rev. ed.) San Diego: Harcourt Brace Jovanovich, 1974.

Horai, J., and others. "The Effects of Contingent Threats upon Target's Behavior." *Journal of Social Psychology,* 1969, *78,* 293-294.

Hornstein, H. A. "The Effects of Different Magnitudes of Threat upon Interpersonal Bargaining." *Journal of Experimental Social Psychology,* 1965, *1,* 282-293.

Hover, J., and others. "The Effects of Threats Which Vary in Their Rationale, Demand and Consequence Components." Unpublished manuscript, Teachers College, Columbia University, 1972.

Ikle, F. C. *How Nations Negotiate.* New York: Harper & Row, 1964.

Jervis, R. *The Logic of Images in International Relations.* Princeton, N.J.: Princeton University Press, 1970.

Jervis, R. *Perception and Misperception in International Politics.* Princeton, N.J.: Princeton University Press, 1976.

Jervis, R. "Perception and Misperception: An Updating of Analysis." Paper presented at annual meeting of the International Society of Political Psychology, Washington, D.C., June 24-27, 1982.

Johnson, D. F., and Tullar, W. L. "Style of Third Party Intervention, Face Saving and Bargaining Behavior." *Journal of Experimental Social Psychology,* 1972, *8,* 319-330.

Johnson, D. W. "Use of Role Reversal in Intergroup Competition." *Journal of Personality and Social Psychology,* 1967, *7,* 135-141.

Johnson, D. W., and Johnson, F. P. *Joining Together.* (2nd ed.) Englewood Cliffs, N.J.: Prentice-Hall, 1982.

Jones, E. E. *Ingratiation*. East Norwalk, Conn.: Appleton-Century-Crofts, 1964.

Jones, S. C., and Vroom, V. H. "Division of Labor and Performance Under Cooperative and Competitive Conditions." *Journal of Abnormal and Social Psychology*, 1964, *68*, 313-320.

Kahn, N. *On Escalation: Metaphors and Scenarios*. New York: Praeger, 1965.

Kee, H. W. "The Development, and the Effects upon Bargaining, of Trust and Suspicion." *Dissertation Abstracts*, 1970, *30*, 4017-4018A.

Kelley, H. H. "Experimental Studies of Threats in Interpersonal Negotiations." *Journal of Conflict Resolution*, 1965, *9*, 79-105.

Kelley, H. H. "A Classroom Study of the Dilemmas in Interpersonal Negotiations." In K. Archibald (ed.), *Strategic Interaction and Conflict: Original Papers and Discussion*. Berkeley, Calif.: Institute of International Studies, 1966.

Kelley, H. H., Beckman, L. L., and Fischer, C. S. "Negotiating the Division of a Reward Under Incomplete Information." *Journal of Experimental Social Psychology*, 1967, *3*, 361-398.

Kelley, H. H., and Stahelski, A. J. "Errors in Perception of Intentions in a Mixed Motive Game." *Journal of Experimental Social Psychology*, 1970a, *6*, 379-400.

Kelley, H. H., and Stahelski, A. J. "The Interference of Intentions from Moves in the Prisoner's Dilemma Game." *Journal of Experimental Social Psychology*, 1970b, *6*, 401-419.

Kelman, H. C. "The Problem-Solving Workshop in Conflict Resolution." In R. L. Merritt (ed.), *Communication in International Politics*. Urbana: University of Illinois Press, 1972.

Kelman, H. C. "The Problem-Solving Workshop: A Social-Psychological Contribution to the Resolution of International Conflicts." *Journal of Peace Research*, 1976, *13*, 79-90.

Kelman, H. C. "An Interactional Approach to Conflict Resolution and Its Application to Israeli-Palestinian Relations." *International Interactions*, 1979, *6*, 99-122.

Kelman, H. C., and Cohen, S. P. "Reduction of International Conflict: An Interactional Approach." In W. G. Austin and J. Worchel (eds.), *The Social Psychology of Intergroup Relations*. Monterey, Calif.: Brooks/Cole, 1979.

Kennan, G. "Reflections: Breaking the Spell." *New Yorker*, Oct. 3, 1983, pp. 44-46.

Kerr, C. "Industrial Conflict and Its Resolution." *American Journal of Sociology*, 1954, *60*, 230-245.

Komorita, S. S., and Barnes, M. "Effects of Pressures to Reach Agreement in Bargaining." *Journal of Personality and Social Psychology*, 1969, *13*, 245-252.

Komorita, S. S., and Brenner, A. R. "Bargaining and Concession Making Under Bilateral Monopoly." *Journal of Personality and Social Psychology*, 1968, *9*, 15-20.

Komorita, S. S., and Mechling, J. "Betrayal and Reconciliation in a Two-Person Game." *Journal of Personality and Social Psychology*, 1967, *6*, 349-353.

Krauss, R. M. "Structural and Attitudinal Factors in Interpersonal Bargaining." *Journal of Experimental Social Psychology*, 1966, *2*, 42-55.

Krauss, R. M., and Deutsch, M. "Communication in Interpersonal Bargaining." *Journal of Personality and Social Psychology*, 1966, *4*, 572-577.

Kressel, K. "Labor Mediation: An Exploratory Survey." Unpublished manuscript, Teachers College, Columbia University, 1971.

Kressel, K., Morillas, M., Weinglass, J., and Deutsch, M. "Professional Intervention in Divorce." *Journal of Divorce*, 1978, *2*, 119-155.

Krivohlavy, J. *Ziveschenminschliche Konflicte und experimentelle Spiels* [Interpersonal conflict and experimental games]. Berne, Switzerland: Hans Huber, 1974.

Lamm, H., and Kayser, E. "The Allocation of Monetary Gain and Loss Following Dyadic Performance." *European Journal of Social Psychology*, 1978, *8*, 275-278.

Lerner, M. J. "The Justice Motive in Social Behavior: Introduction." *Journal of Social Issues*, 1975, *31*, 1-20.

Leventhal, G. S. *Fairness in Social Relationships*. Morristown, N.J.: Silver Burdett, 1976.

Lewicki, R. J., and Rubin, J. "A Model of Promise and Threat Use in Interpersonal Bargaining." Unpublished manuscript, Yale University and Tufts University, 1971.

Lewicki, R. J., and Rubin, J. "The Effects of Motivational Orientation and Relative Power upon the Perception of Interpersonal Influence in a Non-Zero Sum Game." Unpublished manuscript, Dartmouth College, 1974.

Lindskold, S. "Trust Development, the GRIT Proposal, and the Effects of Conciliatory Acts on Conflict and Cooperation." *Psychological Bulletin*, 1978, *85*, 772-793.

Lindskold, S., Bonoma, T., and Tedeschi, J. T. "Relative Costs and Reactions to Threats." *Psychonomic Science*, 1969, *15*, 205-207.

Loomis, J. L. "Communication, the Development of Trust, and Cooperative Behavior." *Human Relations*, 1959, *12*, 305-315.

McClintock, C. G., and others. "Motivational Bases of Choice in Three-Choice Decomposed Games." *Journal of Experimental Social Psychology*, 1973, *9*, 572-590.

Machiavelli, N. *The Prince and the Discourses*. New York: Modern Library, 1950. (Originally published 1513.)

Magenau, J. M., and Pruitt, D. G. "The Social Psychology of Bargaining: A Theoretical Synthesis." In G. M. Stephenson and C. J. Brotherton (eds.), *Industrial Relations: A Social Psychological Approach*. Chichester, England: Wiley, 1978.

Merton, R. K. *Social Theory and Social Structure*. New York: Free Press, 1957.

Mikula, G. "Concepts of Distributive Justice in Allocation Decisions: A Review of Research in German-Speaking Countries." *German Journal of Psychology*, 1981, *5*, 222-236.

Mikula, G., and Schwinger, T. "Intermember Relations and Reward Allocation: Theoretical Considerations of Affects." In H. Brandstatter, J. H. Davis, and H. Schuler (eds.), *Dynamics of Group Decisions*. Beverly Hills, Calif.: Sage, 1978.

Morley, I., and Stephenson, G. *The Social Psychology of Bargaining*. London: Allen & Unwin, 1977.

Moscovici, S. *Social Influence and Social Change*. Orlando, Fla.: Academic Press, 1976.

Osgood, C. E. *An Alternative to War or Surrender*. Urbana: University of Illinois Press, 1962.

Pepitone, A., and others. "Justice in Choice Behavior: A Cross-Cultural Analysis." *International Journal of Psychology*, 1970, *5*, 1-10.

Pilisuk, M., and Skolnick, P. "Inducing Trust: A Test of the Osgood Proposal." *Journal of Personality and Social Psychology*, 1968, *8*, 121-133.

Podell, J. E., and Knapp, W. M. "The Effect of Mediation on the Perceived Firmness of the Opponent." *Journal of Conflict Resolution*, 1969, *13*, 511–520.

Potter, S. *The Theory and Practice of Gamesmanship*. New York: Bantam Books, 1965. (Originally published 1948.)

Pruitt, D. G. "Indirect Communication and the Search for Agreement in Negotiation." *Journal of Applied Social Psychology*, 1971, *1*, 205–239.

Pruitt, D. G. *Negotiation Behavior*. Orlando, Fla.: Academic Press, 1981.

Pruitt, D. G., and Johnson, D. G. "Mediation as an Aid to Face Saving in Negotiation." *Journal of Personality and Social Psychology*, 1970, *14*, 239–246.

Radlow, R., and Weidner, M. F. "Unenforced Commitments in 'Cooperative' and 'Non-Cooperative' Non-Constant-Sum Games." *Journal of Conflict Resolution*, 1966, *10*, 497–505.

Rapoport, A. *Fights, Games, and Debates*. Ann Arbor: University of Michigan Press, 1960.

Raven, B. H., and Eachus, H. T. "Cooperation and Competition in Means-Interdependent Triads." *Journal of Abnormal and Social Psychology*, 1963, *67*, 307–316.

Raven, B. H., and Kruglanski, A. W. "Conflict and Power." In P. Swingle (ed.), *The Structure of Conflict*. Orlando, Fla.: Academic Press, 1970.

Rescher, N. *Distributive Justice*. New York: Bobbs-Merrill, 1966.

Rubin, J. Z. "The Nature and Success of Influence Attempts in a Four-Party Bargaining Relationship." *Journal of Experimental Social Psychology*, 1971a, *7*, 17–35.

Rubin, J. Z. Review of P. Swingle (ed.), *The Structure of Conflict*. *Contemporary Psychology*, 1971b, *16*, 436–437.

Rubin, J. Z., and Brown, B. R. *The Social Psychology of Bargaining and Negotiation*. Orlando, Fla.: Academic Press, 1975.

Rubin, J. Z.; Lewicki, R. J., and Dunn, L. "Perception of Promisors and Threateners." *Proceedings of the 81st Annual Convention of the American Psychological Association*, 1973, *8*, 141–142.

Sampson, E. E. "Studies of Status Congruence." In L. Berkowitz (ed.), *Advances in Experimental Social Psychology*. Vol. 4. Orlando, Fla.: Academic Press, 1969.

Sampson, E. E. "On Justice as Equality." *Journal of Social Issues*, 1975, *31*, 45–65.

Sawyer, J., and Guetzkow, H. "Bargaining and Negotiation in International Relations." In H. C. Kelman (ed.), *International Behavior: A Social-Psychological Analysis*. New York: Holt, Rinehart & Winston, 1965.

Schelling, T. C. *The Strategy of Conflict*. Cambridge, Mass.: Harvard University Press, 1960.

Schelling, T. C. *Arms and Influence*. New Haven, Conn.: Yale University Press, 1966.

Schutz, W. C. *Joy: Expanding Human Awareness*. New York: Grove Press, 1967.

Scodel, A., and others. "Some Descriptive Aspects of Two-Person Non-Zero Sum Games." *International Journal of Conflict Resolution*, 1959, *3*, 114–119.

Shapira, A., and Madsen, M. C. "Cooperative and Competitive Behavior of Kibbutz and Urban Children in Israel." *Child Development*, 1969, *40*, 609–617.

Sheposh, J. P., and Gallo, P. S., Jr. "Asymmetry of Payoff Structure and Cooperative Behavior in the Prisoner's Dilemma Game." *Journal of Conflict Resolution*, 1973, *17*, 321–333.

Sherif, M. *In Common Predicament: Social Psychology of Intergroup Conflict and Cooperation.* Boston: Houghton Mifflin, 1966.

Shichman, S. "Constructive and Destructive Resolution of Conflict in Marriage." Unpublished doctoral dissertation, Teachers College, Columbia University, 1982.

Shomer, R. W., Davis, A. H., and Kelley, H. H. "Threats and the Development of Coordination: Further Studies of the Deutsch and Krauss Trucking Game." *Journal of Personality and Social Psychology,* 1966, *4,* 119–126.

Shure, G. H., Meeker, R. J., and Hansford, E. A. "The Effectiveness of Pacifist Strategies in Bargaining Games." *Journal of Conflict Resolution,* 1965, *9,* 106–117.

Smith, W. P., and Anderson, A. J. "Threats, Communication and Bargaining." Unpublished manuscript, Vanderbilt University, 1972.

Snyder, G. H., and Diesing, P. *Conflict Among Nations.* Princeton, N.J.: Princeton University Press, 1977.

Solomon, L. "The Influence of Some Types of Power Relationships and Game Strategies upon the Development of Interpersonal Trust." *Journal of Abnormal and Social Psychology,* 1960, *61,* 223–230.

Stein, M. I. *Stimulating Creativity.* Vol. 1. Orlando, Fla.: Academic Press, 1974.

Stein, M. I. *Stimulating Creativity.* Vol. 2. Orlando, Fla.: Academic Press, 1975.

Stevens, C. M. *Strategy and Collective Bargaining Negotiation.* New York: McGraw-Hill, 1963.

Summers, O. A. "Conflict, Compromise, and Belief Change in a Decision-Making Task." *Journal of Conflict Resolution,* 1968, *12,* 215–221.

Swingle, P. G. "Exploitative Behavior in Non-Zero-Sum Games." *Journal of Personality and Social Psychology,* 1970, *16,* 121–132.

Swingle, P. G., and MacLean, B. "The Effect of Illusory Power in Non-Zero-Sum Games." *Journal of Conflict Resolution,* 1970, *15,* 513–522.

Tedeschi, J. T., Schlenker, B. R., and Bonoma, T. V. *Conflict, Power and Games.* Hawthorne, N.Y.: Aldine, 1973.

Terhune, K. W. "Motives, Situation, and Interpersonal Conflict Within Prisoner's Dilemma." *Journal of Personality and Social Psychology* (Monograph Supp.), 1968, *8,* 1–24.

Wallace, D., and Rothans, P. "Communication, Group Loyalty, and Trust in the Prisoner's Dilemma Game." *Journal of Conflict Resolution,* 1969, *13,* 370–380.

Walster, E., Walster, G. W., and Berscheid, E. *Equity Theory and Research.* Newton, Mass.: Allyn & Bacon, 1978.

Walton, R. E. "Two Strategies of Social Change and Their Dilemmas." Unpublished manuscript, Purdue University, 1964.

Walton, R. E. *Interpersonal Peacemaking: Confrontations and Third Party Consultation.* Reading, Mass.: Addison-Wesley, 1969.

Walton, R. E., and McKersie, R. B. *A Behavioral Theory of Labor Negotiations: An Analysis of a Social Interaction System.* New York: McGraw-Hill, 1965.

Wandell, W. A. "Group Membership and Communication in a Prisoner's Dilemma Setting." *Dissertation Abstracts,* 1968, *28,* 4767–4768B.

Willis, R. H., and Hale, J. F. "Dyadic Interaction as a Function of Amount of Feedback and Instructional Orientation." *Human Relations,* 1963, *16,* 149–160.

NINE

❧❧❧❧❧❧❧❧❧❧❧❧❧❧❧❧❧❧❧❧❧❧❧❧

Psychological Approaches to International Relations

Robert Mandel

Recently there has been a revolution in the analysis of the human element in international relations. Most scholars of the field no longer believe that states always use the "billiard ball" rational actor approach; no longer treat psychological influences as random accidents or idiosyncratic deviations; and no longer assume that the most subjective aspects of international behavior are inherently unanalyzable. This change in the basic paradigm of process and interaction in the international arena did not develop without resistance. Many political scientists have regarded the psychological studies of world politics as "well intentioned but of dubious realism and relevance" (Holsti, 1976a, p. 15). As one analyst has argued (Pettman, 1975, p. 202), "psycho-political delusions cannot substitute for human mortality, military vulnerability, industrial weakness, a disadvantageous geographic position, or for a society riven by serious divisions, whatever the deluded leader or led might try." Many have exhibited great reluctance to transfer results from the interpersonal to the international level because of the different opportunities and constraints and the methodological problems of generalizing from laboratory experiments or content analysis. But by the early 1970s, these scholars had to cope with numerous studies demonstrating the feasibility, policy relevance, and explanatory power of what psychological analysis had to offer in the international relations field.

Unfortunately, although considerable agreement has emerged that subjective aspects of human behavior frequently follow stable, repeatable, and generalizable patterns, there has been insufficient coordination of paradigms and terminology in the application of psychology to world politics. Of course, the discipline of psychology itself contains much internal dissension over both theory and evidence; but the proliferation of jargon and taxonomies in the application to foreign affairs has been so great that any meaningful and cumulative contribution to knowledge on the subject has been severely undermined. No set of overarching frameworks for analysis has emerged here, and it is often difficult to compare findings.

One of the major problems leading to this conceptual morass is the inherently intertwined nature of the different aspects of the field. Beliefs, perceptions, attitudes, and intentions all seem to mesh together in an indeterminate manner. Group effects, personality effects, physiological effects, bureaucratic role effects, organizational structure effects, cultural effects, and training effects on decision making all seem difficult to separate. Bargaining and conflict models overlap with, and sometimes seem even to duplicate, policy-making models. Isolating one slice of the complex psychological pie seems almost impossible in world politics.

The focus of the existing research on psychological influences in international relations is on distortions introduced from the "ideal" rational model of information processing. This ideal standard, alternatively called the "analytic" or "utility-maximization" model (Steinbruner, 1974, chap. 2; Snyder and Diesing, 1977, chap. 5), is suggestive of a flawless computer and as such is the most subject to challenge from psychological theories emphasizing limited human capabilities. This standard assumes that humans carefully and systematically clarify values and objectives, identify a wide range of alternatives to meet these ends, seek out information and opinions about these alternatives, and then evaluate each of the options in terms of the gains and losses involved.

Psychological approaches deny the widespread feasibility of this rational standard in foreign policy making, and in some cases its desirability as well. This lack of feasibility can be due to a variety of constraining conditions, including time pressure; amount, ambiguity, or inconsistency of information or goals; physiological limitations; idiosyncratic personal traits; organizational structure and the individual's role within it; the societal/cultural environment; or issue salience (Pruitt, 1965; Allison, 1971, chaps. 3 and 4; Axelrod, 1976, p. 241; Etheredge, 1978b, chap. 2; Stein, 1978, p. 336; Mandel, 1979, chap. 7; Mandel, 1984b, pp. 10–11). As Dougherty and Pfaltzgraff (1971, pp. 316–317) note, "For many decades, the Western intellectual's faith in the essential rationality of human behavior (inherited from the Enlightenment) has steadily disintegrated." Those who assert that the rational standard is undesirable are, in effect, questioning whether it always increases effectiveness. Several analysts (Morgan, 1977, chap. 5; Janis and Mann, 1977, p. 45; Stein, 1978, p. 332; George, 1980, pp. 62–63; Mandel, 1984b, pp. 17–25) point out that this standard may inhibit effectiveness by, for example, handcuffing the leadership of a divided pluralistic society; slowing down responses to situations that demand immediate action; promoting an excessive and harmful striving for consistency; and exhibiting dull, uncreative, and even inhumane characteristics. Furthermore, a growing group of analysts (Jervis, 1970; Dror, 1980; Heuer, 1982) show that, by perpetuating and amplifying distortions, one can help achieve foreign policy objectives through deception and manipulation.

For varying reasons and with varying levels of awareness and intentionality, humans distort their view of the world, their analysis of their subjective reality, and their behavioral response to this analysis. These distortions could more specifically occur at a number of different stages: when one is identifying a problem, gathering information, processing information, formulating a decision, implementing an action, or responding to feedback (Mandel, 1984b, pp. 8–9). Individuals could distort their perception of a situation and yet still draw inferences from this perception in accordance with the rational model; or they could have rationally derived images and behave irrationally. Thus, the notion of distortion assesses deviations both in an individual's definition of reality and in the inferences based on that reality.

The causes of these distortions tend to fall into two principal categories—cognitive and affective. Cognitive analysis attributes these distortions to the difficulties a careful and logical person would have in making inferences from an ambiguous environment under trying conditions (Jervis, 1976, p. 3); while affective analysis attributes the distortions to personal emotions, such as insecurity, hostility, and humiliation (Etheredge, 1978b; Janis and Mann, 1977).

Those who apply these psychological theories of distortion in international relations have been much more concerned with adversarial relationships than with those among friends or allies—largely because the distortions appear to be greatest when one is dealing with enemy relationships, and the most critical international events (crises and wars) involve antagonistic relationships. This emphasis, however, neglects the psychology of international cooperation. And by focusing both on distortions from an ideal standard and on hostile relationships, the psychological studies have perhaps unintentionally highlighted the most negative aspects of international behavior.

There seem to be two principal holes in this psychological research on world affairs. First, the findings still need to be put into perspective; more insights are required concerning when each approach is necessary or sufficient to explain human behavior. Some analysts appear to be content simply to develop a new conceptual scheme, and they leave it to others (who never seem to appear on cue) to demonstrate when exactly their scheme best applies in the international arena. Even speculation about this question is not prevalent, and the result is that contending theories about the origins, nature, and consequences of distortion in human behavior continue to coexist without effective synthesis or even juxtaposition. Furthermore, scholars rarely seem to place their theories explicitly in the context of theories from other disciplines—such as economics—that purport to have relevance to world politics; consequently, the psychological theories appear to remain in a conceptual vacuum. Researchers who have made a preliminary attempt to relate psychological and other elements in international relations have approached the task from two differing vantage points: examining the relative potency of psychological components compared to other influences on world affairs (Wilkenfeld and others, 1980, pp. 226-229); and examining the interaction of psychological components with these other influences (East, Salmore, and Hermann, 1978, chap. 10).

The second hole is the almost total lack of meaningful prescription to deal with these prevalent distortions. The policy relevance of the psychological approach depends heavily not only on identifying defects in foreign policy making but also on discovering specific ways of correcting or altering them. An "if-only" mode of analysis seems to dominate here ("if only officials were more intelligent"), and the few solutions offered have appeared weak (Kaplowitz, 1981, p. 23).

This chapter attempts to review and integrate the major recent theories on psychological approaches to international relations, and in the process to create a little order out of chaos. The emphasis here is on the substantive research specifically relating psychology and world politics that has appeared in the last ten years, given the availability of reviews of earlier literature (Kelman, 1965a; Kelman and Bloom, 1973). The psychology of political elites receives most of the attention, rather than such mass-oriented issues as global education, international public opinion, or the formation of international attitudes through transnational experiences. Three major clusters of theories emerge here: (1) perception and personality theories, suggesting how attitudinal and behavioral predispositions guide individuals in interpreting the world; (2) decision-making and bureaucratic politics theories, indicating how attitudinal and behavioral predispositions within national governments affect the way that foreign policy is made; and (3) bargaining and deterrence theories, denoting how attitudinal and behavioral predispositions among national governments influence the ways that interstate tensions are resolved. Within each cluster this chapter examines the general patterns of distortion and the changes under stress, and explores the ways of reducing the distortions. Every attempt is made to standardize terminology and to present findings in a comparative perspective without sacrificing precision and interpretive differences.

Perception and Personality Theories

Theories concerning the attitudinal and behavioral predispositions of individuals in their interpretation of the world deal with the most basic question in exploring human behavior: What distortions occur when people assimilate incoming information about the international system? The perceptual theories stress the cognitive elements, while the personality theories emphasize the affective components.

Perception theorists differ in their definitions of distorted perception in the international arena. Many writers think of misperceptions as those that diverge from reality (Stoessinger, 1964, chap. 14), and they focus on comparing the "facts" about a global situation to the perceptions of the individuals involved. This approach seems inadequate because of the frequent inability, even with the benefit of historical perspective, to describe reality accurately in a field filled with slanted or incomplete information. A more useful notion of distorted perceptions (Kelman, 1965b, p. 7; Jones and Nisbett, 1972; Mandel, 1977, 1979) seems to be that distortions are the differences between an individual's/nation's self-perception (the "actor" perspective) and other individuals'/nations' perceptions of that individual/ nation (the "observer" perspective). Others' perceptions are distorted to the extent that they differ from self-perception. This approach rejects an absolute comparison to reality and, instead, provides a relative referent—self-perception—for any external perceptions. There is no assumption here that anyone's self-perception is the most accurate, but simply that it is the only ascertainable common denominator for gauging distortions in most perceptions in world politics. The tendencies in the literature have been to concentrate on perceptions of others rather than perceptions of self, and on elite rather than mass perceptions.

Perhaps the most widely discussed perceptual distortion is cognitive consistency (Jervis, 1976, chap. 4; Kinder and Weiss, 1978; Mandel, 1979, chap. 3; Lebow, 1981; Mitchell, 1981). This theory indicates that images are temporally balanced, forcing a correspondence between present images and past images of a situation, regardless of changing circumstances. Thus, individuals process information in such a way that it fits neatly into preexisting mental categories and does not challenge strongly held views. Cognitive consistency is maintained through a number of processes, including "selective attention"—that is, ignoring inconsistent information and interpretations (White, 1970); and "cognitive bolstering"— focusing on evidence that directly supports existing views (George, 1980, pp. 38–39; Janis and Mann, 1977, pp. 82–85). One issue debated in this regard is whether individuals/states see what they expect to see (sometimes involving "worst-case" analysis) or what they desire to see ("wishful thinking"). Jervis (1976, chap. 10) argues from a cognitive point of view that, when the two conflict, expectations prevail over desires in world politics, but Snyder and Diesing (1977, chap. 4) empirically tested this notion and did not confirm it. Apparently, sweeping generalizations cannot be made because too many situational variables—such as variations in the strength of desires and expectations, in the level of confidence, and in the past history of coping with undesired outcomes (Mandel, 1979, pp. 16–17)— have a significant influence. Cognitive dissonance theory (Festinger, 1957; Wicklund and Brehm, 1976) serves to explain how postdecisional regret is minimized when desires are not fulfilled: individuals/nations seek strong justifications for their circumstances to reassure themselves that they are right, or in the best possible situation, in the face of contrary evidence (particularly when there is a strong perceived causal link between the individual/nation and the dissonance-arousing event).

Another perceptual distortion has to do with ethnocentrism (LeVine and Campbell, 1972; Mandel, 1979, chap. 4; Eldridge, 1979, pp. 41–45). That is, members of an in-group view an out-group through their own cultural filters, regarding the in-group as superior and virtuous and the out-group as contemptible and inferior. Some consider ethnocentrism "a universal psychosociological syndrome" across cultural and national settings (Druckman, 1968). This syndrome, which exaggerates differences between self and others, results from group socialization, producing conformity in perception through standardized communication systems and similar cultural views of salience and of familiarity (Oskamp, 1972). There is, however, disagreement over whether individuals/nations generally perceive out-groups as weak (in accordance with in-group superiority notions) or as strong (in accordance with xenophobic threat notions) (LeVine and Campbell, 1972, pp. 212–223). My own research (Mandel, 1977) indicates that nations pursuing status quo policies view themselves as significantly less powerful (and hostile) than they appear to other states, and nations pursuing aggressive policies view themselves as significantly more powerful (and hostile) than they appear to other states. One frequent consequence of ethnocentrism is the emergence of group stereotypes (Cauthen and others, 1971; Eldridge, 1979, pp. 22–30; Mitchell, 1981, pp. 85–118), psychological constructs that assign certain characteristics to individuals solely on the basis of group membership.

Two bodies of theory closely linked to ethnocentrism are the actor-observer distinction and black-and-white thinking. According to actor-observer theory (Jones and Nisbett, 1972), a branch of attribution theory, an individual/nation attributes its own behavior to external stimuli, whereas it attributes the behavior of others to their internal "stable dispositions." This tendency, which results from the more detailed knowledge and concern about one's own history and motives, causes individuals/nations to overestimate (relative to the judgment of outsiders) the appropriateness of their own behavior and their responsibility for positive outcomes. Black-and-white thinking (White, 1970, chap. 8, 1984; Mitchell, 1981, chap. 5) is a distortion whereby individuals/states reduce social reality into dichotomous categories, such as good-bad and friend-foe (George, 1980, p. 72), with the moral self-image as the white part and the diabolical enemy image as the black part.

The personality theories provide a different explanation of the ways in which individuals interpret the world; at the same time, these theories provide a fuller understanding of the roots of the patterns of perceptual distortion on the international level. Etheredge (1978a, 1978b), for example, has examined the effects of personality on foreign policy. He shows that various personality traits—reflecting such tendencies as the level of self-esteem, cognitive complexity, intolerance of ambiguity, neurotic conflict, projection of fantasy goals, distrust, interpersonal dominance, and introversion—can simultaneously affect policy preferences and perceptions of other nations. Among his specific conclusions, for example, is that individuals who are high in dominance are more supportive of military measures than those who are low in dominance and that extroverts are more interested in better relations with Communist nations than introverts are. He identifies the sources of personality-related error in decision making as the proclivity (1) to express personal motives, behavioral patterns, and fears in decisions without flexibly assessing the value of this self-expression; (2) to use this expression to shape beliefs about external reality; and (3) to employ these first two processes to deceive oneself and to believe one's decisions are correct and rational.

Margaret Hermann has done perhaps the most extensive research on the role of personality in foreign policy. In a recent study, she identifies six clusters of personality characteristics (nationalism, belief in one's own ability to control events, need for power, need for affiliation, conceptual complexity, and distrust of others) and links them to foreign policy behavior (professed orientation to change, independence/interdependence of action, level of commitment, hostility-friendliness, and type of environmental feedback) (Hermann, 1980). In evaluating these relationships, she examines the level of interest and training in foreign affairs of the decision elites. Her results indicate that need for affiliation correlates positively with professed orientation to change, particularly for leaders with a great deal of interest in foreign affairs; that need for power correlates negatively with interdependence, particularly for leaders with little interest in foreign affairs; and that distrust of others correlates negatively with level of commitment, particularly for leaders with little training in foreign affairs. This type of research has helped us answer the critical question originally posed by Verba (1969, p. 220): When do decision makers choose international relations as the outlet for their personal emotional needs? Another study by Hermann (1979) reveals what kinds of personalities individuals who become political leaders are likely to have. For example, heads of state who are high in nationalism, in need for power, and in distrust of others are more prevalent in nations with lower levels of modernization. In other research Hermann (1974, 1980) shows that a composite leader personality of low nationalism, high cognitive complexity, low close-mindedness, and high belief in ability to control events tends to be the most cooperative internationally.

Aside from these major studies, a few more isolated results have emerged on the role of personality in international relations. Falkowski (1979), in a study of flexibility in foreign policy making, found that more flexible officials tended to use present foreign policy points of reference, whereas less flexible officials tended to use a greater number of past points of reference. Explicitly examining perceptual distortions in international images, Scott (1965) found that individuals with high "image complexity" (with multifaceted bases for their perceptions) exhibited less cognitive consistency. Personality can also associate with a specific foreign policy role. A number of studies (Russett and Hanson, 1975; Mandel, 1977; Etheredge, 1978b) show that military elites are particularly hawkish because of their higher emotional involvement and greater perceived hostility and competitiveness.

Personality may affect not only an individual decision maker's foreign policy behavior but also the international stance of an entire government. This broader effect of personality seems most likely to occur (M. Hermann, 1976, pp. 328-331; Holsti, 1976b, p. 30) when a situation is nonroutine, stressful, unanticipated, or ambiguous; when the policy-making process is not differentiated or developed; or when a decision maker is free of bureaucratic constraints, is charismatic, or had a dramatic rise to power.

When an individual is under stress, the general perception and personality patterns undergo significant deterioration. Stress can include high levels of perceived time pressure, outside threat, uncertainty or surprise, emotional and physical fatigue, and a high probability of military hostilities (C. Hermann, 1972; Brecher, 1979; George, 1980; Lebow, 1981). As Janis and Mann (1977, p. 50) more generally state, "A 'stressful' event is any change in the environment that typically induces a high degree of unpleasant emotion (such as anxiety, guilt, or shame) and affects normal patterns of information processing." These conditions often define a crisis in international relations.

The findings in this area are scattered but consistent. Rosenblatt (1964) and Schwartz (1972) indicate that high levels of perceived threat are likely to increase ethnocentrism on the international level. Pruitt (1965) notes that ambiguity of evidence and predispositions to perceive international threat lead to systematic distortions in the perception of evidence, causing "possibilistic thinking," in which future possibilities are viewed as probabilities. Holsti (1972, chap. 5) contends that time pressure causes an impairment of judgment during crises, and this impaired judgment leads nations to overemphasize the adversary's military capabilities and to overlook conditions that would limit the adversary's ability or willingness to attack. Etheredge (1978b, p. 104) claims that the ambiguity of the international situation enhances the projection of individual personality into the process. Snyder and Diesing (1977, p. 329) point out that background images usually do not change during the course of a crisis. Janis and Mann (1977, p. 50) assert that stress often leads to "defensive avoidance": heightened selective inattention, selective forgetting, distortion of the meaning of warning messages, and construction of rationalizations that minimize negative consequences. If the decision maker cannot find adequate means of escaping serious losses and faces sufficiently high time pressure and threat, then, Janis and Mann argue, that official experiences "hypervigilance": cognitive constriction, reduction of memory, disruption and simplification of thought processes, and—in its most extreme form—panic. According to George (1980, p. 49), stress impairs perception in foreign policy making by causing decision makers to overlook important aspects of a crisis and to rely more heavily on past experience. Finally, Holsti (1970, p. 305) concludes that crisis conditions have a greater impact on variations in perception (of hostility) than do individual personality distinctions.

In light of this section's discussion, perceptual theories reveal the general human tendencies to overstate (1) the influence of the past on present situations and (2) the differences between oneself and others, whereas personality theories show (1) how individual traits affect foreign policy orientations and (2) when these traits have their most significant impact. Cognitive study of perception seems more likely to generate universal patterns than affective study of personality, so it is not surprising that there is more foreign policy research in the first area than in the second. The two areas of research need much more cross-fertilization of ideas, for their interrelationship poses many interesting questions. When and how does cognitive consistency reduce or expand personality distortions? What kinds of personality traits are most susceptible or resistant to perceptual distortions? When does each group of theories have a greater impact on foreign policy making? This chapter's juxtaposition of findings from the two areas shows their parallels but also some potential inconsistencies, such as the tendency for perceptual theories to focus on expectations while personality theories emphasize desires and fears.

Decision-Making and Bureaucratic Politics Theories

In a sense, studies in the area of attitudinal and behavioral predispositions of national governments move our understanding of the psychology of international relations one step further, by placing the perception and personality theories in an explicit context (the bureaucratic environment) for a particular purpose (the formulation and implementation of foreign policy decisions). The basic question asked here is "What distortions occur when foreign policy officials with certain images make decisions within their bureaucratic environment?" Decision-making theories relate more to each individual official, while bureaucratic politics theories stress the impact of the organizational setting. Although it may seem difficult to distinguish decision-making theories from the perceptual and personality theories presented earlier, there is a critical difference: Here an external influence (an organization's decision-making context) is generally the primary determinant of distortions in the decision process, whereas in the earlier section an internal influence (an individual's interpretive filters) was generally the main determinant of distortions in personal political orientations.

The deviations (in organizational decision making) from the ideal rational decision-making model cannot be subsumed under a single heading. Instead, what emerges are four different dimensions of distortion, or irrationality, in policy making (Mandel, 1984b, p. 645): (1) incompatibility of a decision with policy goals, prevailing consensus, or preferred outcomes; (2) incomplete search for and evaluation of possible outcomes; (3) logical inconsistency among statements and/or actions regarding a decision; and (4) nondispassionate style of decision making. Concerning the first dimension, George (1980, p. 2) discusses the frequent tradeoff between the "quality" and the "acceptability" of a decision, and Howard (1971, p. 6) has shown that a decision rarely conforms to preferred outcomes. In the second dimension, there is a tradeoff between the comprehensiveness and the efficiency of the process, and some scholars (Lindblom, 1959; Mandel, 1979, p. 8; Stein and Tanter, 1980, p. 13) are skeptical of the policy maker's ability to be totally systematic. As to the third dimension, the ideal of logical consistency has too many forms that vary across cultures, time, and policy issues (Stein, 1978, p. 329), and the initial beliefs preserved may not be well grounded (George, 1980, pp. 62–63). The last dimension reflects Janis and Mann's (1977, p. 45) emphasis on the emotional "hot cognition" syndrome in decision making and officials' inescapable human frailties. Through these four dimensions, decision makers may deviate from the ideal rational model by being either too sluggish and stagnant—"stick-in-the-mud" irrationality—or too rash and reckless—"daredevil" irrationality (Mandel, 1984b, p. 647).

The most widely discussed individual cognitive distortions in decision making are distorted incrementalism and satisficing, which are related to perceptual cognitive consistency. "Disjointed incrementalism" (Lindblom, 1959) refers to a bureaucrat who "muddles through" the decision-making process, failing to consider a wide range of policy alternatives or to relate means to ends, and thus produces policies only incrementally different from those that preceded them. Satisficing (Simon, 1955) refers to a bureaucrat who acts on the first "acceptable" alternative thought rather than attempting a comprehensive survey of all available alternatives, thus perpetuating inertia because the first available options tend to be those used in the past or those currently in operation. Both of these distortions are implicit in K. Deutsch's (1978, pp. 88–90) "pinball machine" model of foreign policy making, in which the exact path of foreign policy is unpredictable and almost haphazard, but the range of directions is narrowly constrained. In all these approaches, each individual decision maker exhibits "bounded rationality": premature closure to innovation and to a wide variety of policy alternatives, and exaggeration of the order and certainty in his environment (Kinder and Weiss, 1978, p. 723), in order to deal with what George (1980, chap. 2) describes as two key difficulties—value complexity and inadequate information—facing foreign policy makers.

A parallel cognitive approach is Steinbruner's (1974) cybernetic model of individual decision making. In this approach the policy maker simplifies decisions by reducing variety, ignoring elaborate calculations, and following a few basic feedback channels. Officials see no need for a careful assessment of probable outcomes, and they avoid value tradeoffs through an almost intuitive approach to policy making.

Two approaches that systematically attempt to represent this simplified belief structure of individual decision makers are cognitive mapping (Axelrod, 1976; Shapiro and Bonham, 1973, 1982) and the operational code (Walker, 1977; Hoagland and Walker, 1979; George, 1979; Holsti, 1982; Starr, 1983, chap. 3). Cognitive maps display a decision maker's images of the causal linkages operating in the policy domain. Axelrod (1976, pp. 243–244) asserts that even sophisticated decision makers use unsophisticated cognitive maps, which, like the cybernetic model, ignore key tradeoffs: "The picture of a decision maker that emerges from the analysis of cognitive maps is of one who has more beliefs than he can handle, who employs a simplified image of the policy environment that is structurally easy to operate with, and who acts rationally within the context of his simplified image." Operational codes refer to policy makers' beliefs about strategy and tactics; these beliefs serve as filters for analyzing political situations and as norms to guide choices. The operational code taps bureaucrats' attitudes toward the "essential" nature of political life; the prospects of fulfilling one's political aspirations; the predictability and controllability of political trends; and the optimal approaches for selecting and pursuing goals, dealing with risks and timing, and advancing self-interests. As George (1980, p. 45) notes, the function of the operational code for the policy maker is to simplify and channel the tasks of processing information, inventing and appraising options, and choosing the best action.

Janis and Mann's (1977) model of individual decision-making distortions includes more emotional or affective influences. They describe the patterns of unconflicted adherence, unconflicted change, defensive avoidance, hypervigilance, and vigilance, of which only the last (thoughtful weighing of costs and benefits) represents effective decision making. Unconflicted adherence and unconflicted change are ineffective because the official lacks interest in the issue; defensive avoidance fails completely because the official avoids exposure to disturbing information and engages in wishful thinking; and hypervigilance produces errors because officials engage in frantic search and appraisal in a state of high emotional arousal. One can see the applicability of this affective approach to foreign policy making through Etheredge's (1978b, p. 46) comment that the degree of emotional involvement by career diplomats in the international realm is at least as great as that of domestic policy professionals in their programs.

Representing the bureaucratic politics perspective is Allison's (1971) pioneering work on structural constraints on foreign policy making. Finding the "rational actor" model of limited explanatory value, he introduces the "organizational process" model and the "bureaucratic politics" model. In the organizational process model, foreign policy is determined primarily by standard operating procedures that follow the general direction of incrementalism and satisficing; in the bureaucratic politics model, foreign policy results from the intensive political in-fighting among the decisional units (agencies) in the bureaucracy. The aphorism "where you stand depends on where you sit," noting the central importance of an official's specific bureaucratic position, is exemplified by Halperin's (1974) study of American foreign policy making. He emphasizes individuals'/organizations' use of issues to maintain or increase influence in the bureaucracy; the strong resistance to efforts to reduce functions viewed as part of the "essence" of an agency; and the distorted reporting of information by decision makers to support their own stands so as to enhance their positions and to suit their superiors' preconceived biases.

George (1980, pp. 112-113) summarizes the major distortions in foreign policy making emerging from this bureaucratic politics perspective. Each decisional unit acquires information about an issue that advances its own interests or its own view of the national interest, identifies and evaluates policy options on the basis of its own parochial interests, resorts to oversimplification and rhetorical exaggeration in policy debates, uses its bargaining advantages to manipulate the flow of advice, relies on standard operating procedures developed earlier, and thus is generally unable to deal incisively with foreign policy. He further points out two consequences of bureaucratic politics (pp. 114-115): (1) Foreign policy decisions may be more responsive to the internal dynamics of the policy process than to the requirements of the foreign policy problem. (2) Because of the internal complexity, policy makers have more difficulty understanding and communicating with other governments.

Janis's (1972) groupthink syndrome looks at neither individual nor structural-organizational inducements to distorted decisions but, rather, at group conformity effects. It basically specifies that the strivings for unanimity among members of a foreign policy-making group override their motivations to realistically appraise alternative courses of action. The result is overoptimism, blind group loyalty, lack of vigilance to external change and threats, and sloganistic thinking about the inferiority of other policy-making groups and nations. In this last respect, groupthink is parallel to perceptual theories of ethnocentrism. However, other analysts of small-group behavior (Gaenslen, 1980) believe that striving for unanimity under some conditions is a constructive rather than a distortion-enhancing aspect of collective policy making.

A number of closely related studies (Semmel and Minix, 1979; Semmel, 1982; Minix, 1982) examine the "risky-shift" phenomenon—that groups tend to opt for decision alternatives that may be more risky than the average preference of individual members—in the foreign policy setting. This research points out that the risky-shift behavior of decision-making groups has both a cognitive dimension, in that the choice shift results from the immediate situation rather than from broad conditions surrounding the decision, and an affective dimension, in that the shift results from one's having to decide in the presence of others and to share responsibility with them. Military decision makers, in particular, are more likely to shift to risk when they are in groups than when they are acting alone, and this shift is larger for the military than for civilians. C. Hermann (1978, p. 98) notes more specifically that the tendency for foreign policy groups to opt for innovative (and therefore usually more risky) decision alternatives is greater among "leader-autonomous" groups (with authoritative leaders and relatively independent members) using advocacy processes than among delegate groups (with all members of equal power and responsible to someone else) using persuasion or bloc voting. All these findings indirectly show from a small-group perspective where the greatest resistance exists to conservative incrementalism and satisficing tendencies.

Scholars have paid a great deal of attention to the effects of stress (or crisis) on foreign policy decision making and bureaucratic politics, and they have discovered both positive and negative consequences. As Kinder and Weiss (1978, pp. 722–723) contend, stress can lead to a diminished focus of attention, reduced ability to discriminate the important from the trivial, reduced tolerance of ambiguity, and inability to see essential aspects of the situation; but this tension can also lead to vigilant and systematic information processing. There is growing agreement (Pruitt, 1965, p. 395; De Rivera, 1968, pp. 150–151; Milburn, 1972, p. 264; Mandel, 1979, p. 54; George, 1980, pp. 48–49) that a curvilinear "inverted U-shaped" relationship exists between stress and decision-making performance, with mild stress causing performance to improve (given the necessary time and resources) and severe stress causing performance to worsen.

Regarding the more specific effects of stress on decision making and bureaucratic politics, Janis (1972, chap. 8) notes that the greater the threats perceived by a cohesive decision-making body, the greater the chances that it will resort to concurrence seeking rather than critical thinking. C. Hermann (1969, p. 155) similarly shows that the frequency of consensus among policy makers rises under crisis conditions. Lentner (1972, p. 130) and C. Hermann (1972, p. 197) conclude that crisis decision making becomes increasingly centralized, with fewer outsiders consulted. Moving from these group effects of stress to the effects of stress on incrementalism and satisficing, Snyder and Diesing (1977, p. 406) directly assert that bounded rationality is the most pervasive form of policy making in international crises. George (1980, p. 49) and Holsti (1972, pp. 15, 19, 21) conclude that stress increases cognitive rigidity, with lower creativity in perceiving alternatives and reduced receptivity to discrepant information; shortens and narrows the policy-making perspective, with less attention to long-range consequences or side effects of options; and shifts the burden of preventing disaster to the opponent. Brecher (1979, pp. 469–471) notes a greater disposition toward affective-based decisions and toward ad hoc forms of consultation during periods of high stress. According to Wiegele (1973, 1982), biological limitations—ill health, fatigue, advanced age, jet lag, and the absence of the usual secretion of adrenalin to deal with stress—may inhibit decision-making performance in international crises. In comparing the various explanations of the effects of crises on decision making, Lebow (1981, p. 200) concludes that "the responsiveness of policy makers to developments within their operating environment is a far more important determinant of crisis performance than the pace [time pressure] of these developments."

In summary, decision-making theory shows the inertia and conservatism inherent in the foreign policy context, while bureaucratic politics theory shows the narrow organizational self-interest inherent in the constituent parts of the foreign policy-making bureaucracy. In either case, analysts seem to focus their criticism on the inability of officials to adapt constructively to changing circumstances, rather than on the inappropriateness of the foreign policy context in terms of organizational structure, roles, incentives, or recruitment and indoctrination patterns. The avenues for future research here are many: When does the self-interest of bureaucratic units coincide with and diverge from the national interest? When is decision-making inertia most likely to contribute to and detract from sound foreign policy? How do group effects and organizational effects interact with each other and with individual effects in creating policy distortions? How do these decision-making and bureaucratic politics distortions differ across nations and within national bureaucracies? How do these differences affect intergovernmental and intragovernmental understanding/communication? Juxtaposing the two sets of theories reveals a great deal of interconnectedness but also shows that each may differ in its way of assessing a quality policy context. Decision-making theory stresses more the importance of the comprehensiveness of search-and-evaluation procedures, while bureaucratic politics theory emphasizes the compatibility with prevailing suborganizational consensus.

Bargaining and Deterrence Theories

Theories concerning the effects of attitudinal and behavioral predispositions among national governments on the ways that interstate tensions are resolved provide the last logical piece in the overall puzzle of the psychology of international relations. These theories highlight the distortions in the way that states relate to one another—partially at least as a result of the aforementioned perceptual, personality, decision-making, and bureaucratic politics distortions. A key question thus emerges: What are the distorting impediments in the global pattern of interaction among nations, given the individual and organizational constraints under which foreign policy makers operate? Bargaining theories refer more to behavior at the cooperative end of the scale, while deterrence theories refer more to behavior at the competitive/coercive end. The two sets of theories are closely related. Deterrence often links to bargaining failure or to bargaining strategies that mutually stress the use of (or threatened use of) high levels of force. Unlike the earlier areas discussed in this chapter, the bulk of the literature on bargaining and deterrence is not based on psychological perspectives, and so the review here is even more selective. However, several writers (Steinbruner, 1976; Druckman, 1977; Spector, 1977; J. Snyder, 1978) have noted the critical importance of psychological analysis of these two topics.

Identifying distortions in a meaningful way is as tricky in the fields of bargaining and deterrence as in the areas of perception and decision making, for there is no identifiable norm or referent in interstate behavior. A distortion in the bargaining process between two nations is usually considered to be anything that unnecessarily leads the bargainers involved toward "intractability"—unwillingness or inability to achieve a compromise solution, to make concessions in the negotiations, and/or to resolve any disagreements (Mandel and Clarke, 1981, p. 25). Distortions in deterrence are generally regarded as tendencies that unnecessarily lead to a breakdown of the stability built on the mutually perceived coercive threat, usually resulting in war. Of course, these notions of distortion are highly controversial, for key distortions could easily lead to bargaining compromise, concession making, and resolution (rather than intractability) and to deterrence stability (rather than instability). Furthermore, there is much ambiguity in the idea of "unnecessarily" producing undesired outcomes. Nonetheless, given their prevalence, these definitions appear functional for organizing a review of this literature and for paralleling the notions of distortion presented earlier.

Much of the work on bargaining, particularly that employing game theory, has assumed rationality and complete information on the part of the bargainers. But the psychological approaches to negotiations have avoided that assumption and have examined variations in the characteristics of the bargainers, in the information conditions, in the opportunities for communication, and in the strategy choice (Lockhart, 1979, chap. 2). The three major areas leading to distortions in the international bargaining process are (1) the influence relationships among the bargaining sides, which can range from rigidly opposing interests through a mutually antagonizing structure of payoffs, bargaining power, and strategies; (2) the external environment of the bargaining sides, which can include adverse interference from domestic or global pressures; and (3) the coping abilities of the bargaining sides, which can involve ineffectiveness in understanding, processing, and responding to information about the negotiating situation (Mandel and Clarke, 1981, pp. 5-6).

Specific distortions emerge from this bargaining literature. In the area of influence relationships, payoffs that present difficulties (including time and costs involved) in splitting up benefits and/or in generating minimally acceptable benefits often impede bargaining settlement, especially when each side perceives the benefits as zero-sum (Schelling, 1963, pp. 31-32, 163). Equality or "symmetry" in bargaining power also links to intractability (Snyder and Diesing, 1977, p. 262) by promoting deadlock, despite limited findings that disparity in bargaining power can lead to condescension toward the adversary (Lall, 1966, p. 133) and that equal power can facilitate negotiations "in good faith" (Druckman, 1973, p. 22). International bargaining power includes not only traditional military-industrial capabilities but also subjective elements such as willingness to use power (involving level of interests at stake) and initial advantage in the situation ("who holds all the cards"); thus, circumstances such as "asymmetry in motivation" (George, Hall, and Simons, 1971, p. 216)) can eclipse objective power rankings in the negotiating setting. Coercive strategies, involving the use of fear through the threat of negative sanctions, tend to be more likely to inhibit bargaining than accommodative strategies (Hamner and Yukl, 1977, p. 155; Hopmann, 1974). M. Deutsch (1973, p. 365) explains that coercive strategies are likely to be reciprocated; this tendency can be especially dangerous if the adversary perceives the approach as capricious or vindictive (Lockhart, 1979, p. 119), if competition in risk taking and a test of nerve results (Williams, 1976, p. 141), or if both sides rely on irrevocable commitments to demonstrate their resolve (Druckman, 1973, p. 33).

Regarding the external environment of the bargaining sides, bargaining breakdown often occurs when bargainers are subject to a meaningful veto of their strategies and goals from domestic or global forces, and these forces oppose or severely constrain the negotiators' positions. Lockhart (1979, pp. 70–71) shows that domestic constraints often conflict with global exigencies and prevent quick adjustment among bargaining nations; and Lall (1966, p. 246) reports that global concern can similarly produce inflexibility, especially if a powerful outside actor becomes perturbed.

Finally, the coping abilities of the bargainers themselves are critical. Negotiators who lack creativity or responsiveness—who do not search through a wide range of alternatives or develop new options to cope with changing circumstances or failure—tend to be unsuccessful (Sawyer and Guetzkow, 1965, p. 485). A complex bargaining situation with a large number of bargaining nations (Midgaard and Underdal, 1977) or an issue with broad scope (Druckman, 1973, p. 18) pose special problems for bargainers with these cognitive limitations. Turning to affective elements in negotiations, Bartos (1967) notes that highly xenophobic bargainers seem to have difficulty achieving compromises, and Lall (1966, p. 133) asserts that emotionalism—when it surfaces in forms such as pride, anger, or vanity—impedes bargaining success. Openness, too, can inhibit bargaining settlements (Druckman, 1973, p. 47; Snyder and Diesing, 1977, pp. 251–252; Jönsson, 1978, p. 384) because it promotes affective aspects of negotiation—such as prestige and propaganda considerations, inflammatory warnings, and face saving—among the bargainers. Negotiators with impaired coping abilities along these cognitive or affective lines seem to gain credibility at the expense of the critically needed flexibility (Mandel and Clarke, 1981, p. 14).

Switching from bargaining theories to deterrence theories involves moving from notions of cooperative or coercive diplomacy to notions of the threat of the raw use of force outside of a negotiating context. Deterrence generally means the use of threats by one nation to prevent another from taking undesired actions (Morgan, 1977, p. 17). A major debate has emerged on deterrence. Some believe that it is primarily a cognitive process (Rosi, 1973, p. 96), working through a dispassionate cost-benefit analysis; others contend that it is primarily an affective process (Brodie, 1973, pp. 430–431), working through emotional fear. Psychological approaches to deterrence concentrate on both cognitive and affective distortions that lead to its breakdown.

A number of scholars have recently analyzed the instances when deterrence fails. Of course, many argue that it fails simply because the amount of deterrence and coercion is less than required (Burton, 1979, p. 87), but there are also analyses of more fundamental limitations.

Jervis (1976, chap. 3) shows that, given the condition of international anarchy, deterrence may break down and lead to a spiraling arms race, due to paranoia about implausible threats and the drive for security among nations. Because offensive and defensive weapons are generally indistinguishable, it is hard to perceive the difference between status quo and aggressive nations. Existing hostility leads states to distort their information processing and to be too prone to perceive active enemies. In particular, Jervis notes, deterrence fails if a threat is not credible, if the costs of war are too low and one side prefers war to retreat, or if threats reveal a large and genuine conflict of interests. In a later work, Jervis (1979, pp. 305–310) adds that deterrence may fail because a state may misunderstand the other's values, the way the other sees the world, the other's strength and options, or the other's basic intentions.

Morgan (1977) goes further in elaborating the limits of deterrence. He suggests that deterrence is hard to sustain when low-level challenges emerge from nations seen as unimportant over matters viewed as not vital to national security. Particular types of "irrational" personalities of national leaders can lead to a breakdown: if a decision maker is willing to take high risks; if the threats trigger in the leader rage, suspicion, or hostility; or if the official's pride, honor, or ego makes retreat impossible. Turning to the bureaucratic setting, Morgan asserts that deterrence is less likely to work when normal processes of recruitment and socialization break down, especially when there has just been a revolution or coup or extremely high levels of internal turmoil in one of the nations involved.

George and Smoke (1974) and George (1980, chap. 14) point out that deterrence runs into trouble when one is operating beneath the strategic level, at the levels of limited and "sublimited" conflict, because here deterrence is dependent on a mutiplicity of subjective elements that fluctuate over time and are highly dependent on context. They cite three distinct patterns to the failure of deterrence: (1) If an initiator perceives a defender as having no commitment, then the initiator can respond with a "quick, decisive" move. (2) If the initiator perceives the defender as uncertain in its commitment, then the initiator can respond with a "limited probe." (3) If an initiator perceives a defender as "unequivocal but soft" in its commitment, then the initiator can respond with "controlled pressure." All these patterns can lead to war. Deterrence may also backfire by enhancing a "devil image" of the deterrer or by hardening an opponent's conviction that a deterrer is not responsive to legitimate interests, both of which can lead to more belligerent action later on by the deterred nation. Several of these arguments support George and Smoke's conclusion that deterrence is just a time-buying strategy, having negative effects in the long run because it frustrates adversaries who desire to alter the status quo in their favor.

This last point brings up the important idea that certain types of dissatisfactions in the international system are so fundamental that they do not seem susceptible in the long run to stable deterrence through threat of the use of force. For example, ethnically based territorial disputes appear to be "the most intractable, most emotional, and most violence prone" of all international conflicts (Mandel, 1980b, p. 435), and they do not seem resolvable through balance-of-

power logic. A prominent cluster of psychosocial theories of international conflict—rank-disequilibrium theories—help to explain the frequent resistance to
deterrence-based stability. Rank-disequilibrium theory, developed by Galtung
(1964), indirectly applies Gurr's (1970) relative deprivation theory—specifying a
conflict-producing gap between expectations and achievements—on the international level. The condition of rank disequilibrium occurs when a nation perceives
that it has some "topdog" (high) and some "underdog" (low) rankings on the
international status pecking order. This situation is most likely to lead to conflict
if the nation perceives itself to be topdog in achieved status (military-industrial
capabilities) yet underdog in ascribed status (prestige or recognition from other
states). Wallace (1973) and Midlarsky (1975) have done major follow-up studies of
Galtung's notion, which they call status inconsistency, and Wallace explicitly
explains the underpinnings of this theory: Rank disequilibrium creates dissatisfaction because it violates the crucial system norm that nations receive rewards in
proportion to their position on the power pecking order. Threatening to deprive
rewards or inflict punishment through deterrence strategies would not seem to be
effective in the long run against nations already feeling illegitimately deprived of
status by an unjust international hierarchy.

Under stressful conditions bargaining and deterrence distortions generally
expand. Highly uncertain situations and high time pressure generally inhibit
bargaining effectiveness (Druckman, 1973, pp. 28, 54; Jönsson, 1978, p. 385)
because it is difficult to learn anything about the adversary's positions. Snyder and
Diesing (1977, p. 503) conclude that faulty information processing, high interdependence among allies, preemptive compulsions, highly incompatible interests,
and underestimates of the costs of conflict cause bargaining to degenerate into war
during international crises. As to deterrence, R. Snyder (1961, p. 141) points out
that time pressure increases the chances that decision makers convert false alarms
into war. Morgan (1977, pp. 174–186) notes that crisis conditions create some
advantages for deterrence but can hurt its effectiveness by creating overconfidence
about certain success; by causing each side to exaggerate the rationality of others;
and by promoting groupthink, the "risky shift," and cognitive bolstering.

This section's review of the literature on bargaining and deterrence demonstrates (1) the ways in which the distortions identified by perceptual, personality,
decision-making, and bureaucratic politics theories can inhibit interstate relations;
(2) the severe limitations, in particular, on the utility of threat or coercive strategies;
and (3) the types of international disagreements least susceptible to stable settlement. Psychological distortions have a much more tangible and devastating consequence here than in earlier sections—the possibility of war. Bargaining analysts
seem to focus too much on the influence relationships among the bargaining sides
to the neglect of their external environment; and deterrence analysts appear to
concentrate too heavily on bilateral nuclear superpower confrontations to the
virtual exclusion of consideration of multilateral or conventional deterrence among
developing nations. Both theories nicely incorporate each other's findings but are
not sufficiently cognizant of the parallels between interstate and intrastate (intragovernmental) relations. There needs to be more research on the similarities and
differences between a sound foreign policy decision and a sound international
bargain. Furthermore, appeasement and conciliation strategies need more careful
study from a psychological vantage point; too often they seem to be either super-

ficially dismissed as unworkable in a power politics world or idealistically welcomed as the optimal across-the-board solution. What is most ironic in juxtaposing bargaining and deterrence theories is that bargaining theory views rigidly opposing interests through a mutually antagonizing structure of payoffs and power as leading to intractability, whereas deterrence theory views the identical situation as being the most stable in preventing war.

Ways of Reducing Psychological Distortions

As mentioned earlier in this chapter, the literature on psychological approaches to international relations is far more concerned with identifying distorting influences on attitudinal and behavioral predispositions than with finding effective solutions for reducing these distortions. A number of specific ideas have nonetheless emerged, albeit fragmented and untested, and this brief survey mentions a few of the major notions. In this review of distortion-reducing mechanisms, there is, of course, no necessary presumption that the distortions addressed are undesirable.

To reduce distortions related to perception and personality, self-awareness is often advocated. Jervis (1976, chap. 12) claims that awareness of perceptual errors may lead to avoidance of them. Personally administered "safeguards," based on this increased awareness, can decrease confidence in prevailing beliefs, increase sensitivity to alternative explanations and images, and thereby decrease the amount of discrepant information needed to induce individuals to reexamine their views. Jervis asserts that individuals should make their values and beliefs more explicit and should not permit their tasks, prospects for the future, and identities to be tied to specific images of others. Etheredge (1978b, pp. 106-108) similarly advocates greater psychological self-understanding by policy makers about their inherent mental processes and their biased and overconfident functioning. Such increased self-awareness "might enlarge their capacity to use their personal predispositions more modestly and their intuitive resources more flexibly in the service of accurate empathy and successful policy." He contends that understanding one's own personality leads to a deeper sense of one's values and an inner freedom to have one's ideas challenged without feeling threatened. Finally, Axelrod (1976, pp. 244-248) suggests that distortions can diminish if a decision maker "externalizes his implicit cognitive map" or analyzes for himself his own causal inferences about the environment. This approach, he argues, would eliminate the need to consult with outside experts for guidance on cognitive mapping, and it allows policy makers to use their own concepts and values in an easy-to-understand manner. But Kinder and Weiss (1978, p. 729) criticize these suggestions: "There is no reason to believe that *knowing* about the unconscious tendency to order or structure a decision problem according to prior expectation enables a decision maker to behave any differently. Because so much of the cognitive and emotional work of decision proceeds unconsciously, it is difficult to assess and understand, and particularly difficult to control."

Most of the prescriptions emerge in the context of distortions related to decision making and bureaucratic politics. Each idea attempts in a slightly different manner—some focusing on cognitive dimensions and others on affective dimensions, some on structure and others on function—to improve the quality of decision making.

In recent years the use of a "devil's advocate" has become popular among high executives in government, especially when they are dealing with foreign policy issues. The purpose of this individual is to guarantee the surfacing and defense of unpopular viewpoints, in order to ensure fuller consideration of a wide range of policy alternatives. But this technique—regardless of its particular mode of implementation—has severe drawbacks. As George (1980, p. 170) contends, a devil's advocate, who must consciously role-play a position that nobody else would support, is severely limited in his ability to persist in a challenge or to develop a coalition within the policy group. Janis (1972, p. 215) asserts that devil's advocates often become domesticated and can speak up only as long as they remain within the bounds of what leading members of a group consider to be acceptable dissent. This institutionalized devil's advocate, rather than generating the much-needed turbulence among decision makers, may simply create the comfortable feeling that they have considered all sides of the issue, and thus the technique becomes tokenized (Mandel, 1979, pp. 120–121).

Other writers on this subject urge that changes be made in the structure of the policy-making process. George (1972; 1980, chap. 11) suggests a "multiple advocacy" system, which requires the executive to (1) structure and manage the policy-making system so as to ensure that there are advocates to cover the range of interesting policy options on a given issue; (2) equalize or compensate for disparities among the actors and resources needed for effective advocacy; and (3) identify and correct possible "malfunctions" in the policy-making process before they have a harmful effect on the executive's choice of policy. But George himself (1980, pp. 203–206) admits that some leaders may not be receptive to multiple advocacy, that it might be difficult to recruit able officials with the ability to use the intellectual and bureaucratic resources needed to become effective advocates, that the time required for the interchange among advocates may impose undue delays on decision making, and that it may be hard to find the appropriate person to monitor and manage the multiple advocacy system. Furthermore, Janis and Mann (1977, p. 398) argue that the system might have problems if information were available from only one channel or if the advisers were to thrash out their disagreements privately and confront the chief executive with a unanimous recommendation. Janis (1972, chap. 9) has similarly suggested that, to reduce groupthink distortions, (1) the leader of a policy-making group should assign the role of critical evaluator to each member and accept criticism; (2) the leader should be impartial and not state preferences and expectations at the outset; (3) several independent policy-planning and evaluation groups should be formed at the outset; (4) each policy-making group should occasionally divide into subgroups that meet separately; (5) each member of the group should discuss the issue with trusted associates and report back their reactions; (6) outside experts should attend meetings on a staggered basis; (7) each group should periodically resurvey all warning signals from rival nations or organizations; and (8) policy makers should meet after making a decision to rethink the issue. These suggestions again seem constructive but also seem subject to limitations similar to those mentioned earlier with regard to multiple advocacy.

My own research (Mandel, 1977) indicates that political games are an effective means of increasing the imagination, flexibility, and responsiveness of policy makers. Specifically, human gaming seems to increase the number of policy alternatives considered, the variety of differing approaches to the resolution of policy problems, and the number of stated projected reactions to other actors. Political games are exercises in which teams representing the governments of various nations meet and discuss crisis situations presented in scenarios. During each "period" of a game, each team separately decides on a team "move," which incorporates a written statement of goals, policies to be undertaken, and contingencies in response to the scenarios and the moves of the other teams in the previous game period. The primary basis for the effectiveness of these exercises is their use of role playing, which Janis and Mann (1977, pp. 348-365, 379-388) have found to be quite powerful in causing attitude change among subjects by releasing them from preconceived biases and opening them up to outside opinions. For two decades these games have been played by top-level decision makers at the U.S. Pentagon and by middle-level bureaucrats at RAND, MIT, and the U.S. Central Intelligence Agency. The major drawbacks of these exercises (Mandel, 1980a, p. 372) are that they are mainly useful for short-term planning and they rely heavily on the skill of the scenario writers and game directors for their effectiveness.

Thanks principally to the efforts of Argyris (1970), there has been considerable research on the effects of the T group (or sensitivity session) in government. In a T group, participants throw away all sense of internal and external structure in order to discover their "real" selves. In the government T-group exercises, an attempt was made to induce participants to ignore their bureaucratic roles and positions so as to consider more honestly and openly issues whose discussions were normally impeded by hierarchy and deference. Participants are supposed to become aware of "inhibiting loops" and to trust the intervenor to provide help if they behave in a manner upsetting to others in the group. But, as Campbell and Dunnette (1968) contend, there is growing consensus that, although T groups produce observable changes in behavior, the utility of these changes for participants' performance in organizational roles remains to be demonstrated. This conclusion emerges at least partially because specifying the nature of the behavioral changes generated by T groups is problematic and because their carryover effects for organizational change are fairly limited.

White (1970) and Janis and Mann (1977) suggest the possibility of using the "balance sheet" approach as a means of improving policy making. Using this approach, decision makers carefully and systematically specify, in writing, the alternatives they are considering, along with the associated values of these alternatives, before reaching a decision. But Janis and Mann (1977, p. 379) admit that—when there is defensive avoidance—the balance sheet procedure may often fail to overcome psychological resistance to exploring all the major consequences of the alternative courses of action under consideration. Furthermore, there are no real incentives here for decision makers to alter their behavior, and use of the balance sheet may simply provide them with a format for cloaking their own biases (Mandel, 1979, p. 121). Kinder and Weiss (1978, p. 730) assert that the formidable array of procrastination, denial, and avoidance tactics outlined by Janis and Mann casts doubt on the efficacy of cognitive, rational interventions such as the balance sheet.

Lastly, there are some prescriptions for reducing the distortions associated with bargaining and deterrence. Some of the prescriptions such as fostering accommodative rather than coercive strategies and increasing the credibility of threats and the costs of war—seem obvious from the preceding discussion, but others need more elaboration. Out of the myriad suggestions available, only those specific ideas with direct psychological overtones appear in this discussion.

Perhaps the most frequently mentioned cure for both bargaining and deterrence difficulties is third-party intervention. This suggestion includes intervention by an outside individual, group, nation, or international organization that is usually more powerful than the contending parties. M. Deutsch (1973, p. 376) explains that "third parties who are prestigious, powerful, and skillful may deliberately facilitate a constructive resolution of a conflict by using their prestige and power to encourage such a resolution and by helping provide the problem-solving resources (institutions, facilities, personnel, social norms, and procedures) to expedite discovery of a mutually satisfactory solution." In an empirical assessment of conflict-controlling measures on the international level, Bloomfield and Leiss (1969) conclude that this form of intervention has been the most common means of reducing violence in the small wars since 1945. This intervention can be either coercive or noncoercive, though the coercive form is much more prevalent in world politics. Fisher and Ury (1978), Burton (1979, pp. 116–122), and Mitchell (1981, chap. 12) present numerous specific and seemingly implementable suggestions on how to use noncoercive mediation to help in a conflict situation. But there is insufficient research on when various types of third-party intervention are most effective, and the costs of failure are truly dire for all parties involved.

Another closely related approach to resolving tensions internationally is the problem-solving workshop (Doob, 1970, 1974; Kelman, 1972; Doob and Foltz, 1973). These workshops use "controlled communication," bringing together minor government officials unofficially representing disputing governments in order to discuss their disagreements freely in an open atmosphere. This approach has been applied in the Somalia-Ethiopia-Kenya dispute, the Cyprus conflict, and the turmoil in Northern Ireland. Looking back over these efforts, Doob (1981, p. 236) contends that the approach remains promising because of the soundness of the psychological theory of attitude change that underlies it. But even he admits that "the participants themselves have been affected, but no international dispute has thereby been settled" (p. 235).

A third approach to reducing the pernicious distortions in both bargaining and deterrence is Osgood's (1962) Graduated and Reciprocated Initiatives in Tension Reduction (GRIT), in which great powers locked into an escalating spiral of hostility can break out of that pattern if one power unilaterally reduces tension as a signal to the other side. Specifically, a superpower could openly announce a minor but relatively significant reduction in its nuclear arms levels without jeopardizing its own security, then wait until its opponent makes a corresponding reduction, and then reduce some more. Ideally, trust could grow under this system. Etzioni (1967) exemplifies this approach in his analysis of the "Kennedy experiment": President Kennedy's "Strategy for Peace" talk in June 1963 initiated a conciliatory and cooperative series of steps between the United States and the Soviet Union in the area of strategic weaponry. However, the criteria needed for this approach to work have not yet been systematically tested (Sullivan, 1976, p. 286) or sufficiently specified.

Finally, some more wide-ranging suggestions have emerged that could indirectly serve to resolve tensions related to bargaining and deterrence. For example,

Holsti (1972, pp. 221–227) asserts that during international crises policy makers should have sensitivity to an adversary's frame of reference, avoid steps that seal off escape routes, use incentives to reduce the possibility of escalation by the adversary, try to slow the pace of crisis events, and pay attention to implementation as well as broad strategic issues. But, to be potentially effective, these ideas clearly need much more specificity regarding techniques and context.

Obviously, none of the prescriptions in any category of attitudinal and behavioral predispositions can alone or together eliminate the psychological distortions discussed in this chapter. But at least they exhibit a postbehavioralist willingness on the part of recent writers in the field to grapple more directly with policy implications and solutions that emerge from their often trenchant critiques of the defective behavior of foreign policy makers. There is a need for more research here, not so much on new solutions as on the comparative effectiveness of existing suggestions for reducing distortions. More specification and testing outside of the artificial confines of the experimental laboratory might help in this regard, and might also improve receptivity among skeptical elite recipients, but, because virtually all the approaches contain the dual dangers of tokenization and unforeseen side effects, there is a need for safeguards against the use of insufficiently tested strategies in critical foreign policy situations. Lastly, each prescription needs to have a clearer goal, target group, time frame, and rationale—especially in terms of explicit linkages to existing theories of pernicious distortions—to promote sound evaluation of the strategies.

Conclusion

The findings of this survey of the literature on psychological approaches to international relations convincingly demonstrate that certain patterns of deterioration are prevalent in human interpretation of the environment, problem solving, and resulting action. These patterns involve significant errors in perception, judgment, and reaction—errors resulting largely from the limited ability of the individuals involved to deal with confusion and complexity or on their personal emotional needs. Stressful conditions—as in international crises—generally exacerbate these patterns just when there is a great need for improved performance. And many of these patterns seem almost inescapable, despite the variety of psychological intervention techniques available.

In international relations there appears at the moment to be a far greater comprehension of the cognitive aspects of human interaction—often involving lazy, stick-in-the-mud, overcautious attitudes and behavior—than of the affective aspects of human interaction—often involving reckless, daredevil, and passionate attitudes and behavior. This imbalance reflects a greater understanding of the psychology of reactionary great powers content with the status quo than that of radical Third World states intent on overthrowing the global pecking order. Scholars and policy makers alike should realize that acting emotionally on the basis of fears or desires is just as pervasive and significant as simplifying the environment through reliance on the inertia of past experience or expectations. But both the cognitive and the affective approaches highlight critically inadequate consideration of tradeoffs and long-range consequences; and both point to a desperate need for more creativity and responsiveness among world leaders and for a richer array of means of promoting these traits.

Psychological perspectives seem most essential in high-stake situations where an individual or a small group controls a nation (Hopple, 1980, p. 163); the potential for cognitive incompetence and emotional arousal seems greatest in situations involving significant change and novelty. But these conditions are much too general; there is a need for considerably more elaboration and differentiation of the relative importance and interrelationships among psychological approaches with respect to other contending explanations of international relations. When does each distortion have its greatest impact on foreign policy? When are these distortions the greatest? What kinds of individuals or groups are prone to the greatest distortions? Which distortions seem inevitable given their context, and which not? There is a general need for more normative inquiry in these areas, with clearer identification of ideal desired conditions; and cross-cultural norms, in particular, need more explicit introduction here, for a distortion in one society may be "rational" in another (Japan may view groupthink as optimal). The distortions manifested by a society's elite can no longer simply be lumped together or restricted to those of official bureaucrats. Recent studies (Russett and Hanson, 1975; Mandel, 1984a) point the way toward significant psychological distinctions between different kinds of elites—government and business—in the United States. Analysts need to move beyond the focus of existing psychological research on war-peace issues relating to the East-West split and deal more with emerging global issues such as interdependence and resource scarcity relating to the North-South split.

The general processes and patterns of psychological distortion may often be quite intuitive, but their application can be surprisingly counterintuitive. New explorations of the field need convey no longer the defensive tone used by proponents of novel and unaccepted fields; but it still needs to be emphasized that the inherent subjectivity and intangibility of psychological interpretations of international relations do not inescapably detract from their potential for systematic evaluation and widespread application. The opportunity for dramatic and enlightening insights here is enormous.

References

Allison, G. T. *Essence of Decision.* Boston: Little, Brown, 1971.

Argyris, C. *Intervention Theory and Method: A Behavioral Science View.* Reading, Mass.: Addison-Wesley, 1970.

Axelrod, R. (ed.). *Structure of Decision.* Princeton, N.J.: Princeton University Press, 1976.

Bartos, O. J. "How Predictable Are Negotiations?" *Journal of Conflict Resolution,* 1967, *11,* 48-96.

Bloomfield, L. P., and Leiss, A. *Controlling Small Wars: A Strategy for the 1970s.* New York: Knopf, 1969.

Brecher, M. "State Behavior in International Crisis." *Journal of Conflict Resolution,* 1979, *23,* 446-480.

Brodie, B. *War and Politics.* New York: Macmillan, 1973.

Burton, J. *Deviance, Terrorism and War.* New York: St. Martin's Press, 1979.

Campbell, J. P., and Dunnette, M. D. "Effectiveness of T-Group Experiences in Managerial Training and Development." *Psychological Bulletin,* 1968, *70,* 73-104.

Cauthen, N. R., and others. "Stereotypes: A Review of the Literature." *Journal of Social Psychology,* 1971, *84,* 103-125.

De Rivera, J. *The Psychological Dimension of Foreign Policy*. Westerville, Ohio: Merrill, 1968.

Deutsch, K. W. *The Analysis of International Relations*. (2nd ed.) Englewood Cliffs, N.J.: Prentice-Hall, 1978.

Deutsch, M. *The Resolution of Conflict*. New Haven, Conn.: Yale University Press, 1973.

Doob, L. W. (ed.). *Resolving Conflict in Africa*. New Haven, Conn.: Yale University Press, 1970.

Doob, L. W. "A Cyprus Workshop." *Journal of Social Psychology*, 1974, *94*, 161–178.

Doob, L. W. *The Pursuit of Peace*. Westport, Conn.: Greenwood Press, 1981.

Doob, L. W., and Foltz, W. J. "The Belfast Workshop." *Journal of Conflict Resolution*, 1973, *17*, 489–512.

Dougherty, J. E., and Pfaltzgraff, R. L. *Contending Theories of International Relations*. Philadelphia: Lippincott, 1971.

Dror, Y. *Crazy States*. Millwood, N.Y.: Kraus, 1980.

Druckman, D. "Ethnocentrism and the Inter-Nation Simulation." *Journal of Conflict Resolution*, 1968, *12*, 45–68.

Druckman, D. *Human Factors in International Negotiation: Social-Psychological Aspects of International Conflict*. Beverly Hills, Calif.: Sage, 1973.

Druckman, D. (ed.). *Negotiations: Social-Psychological Perspectives*. Beverly Hills, Calif.: Sage, 1977.

East, M. A., Salmore, S. A., and Hermann, C. F. (eds.). *Why Nations Act*. Beverly Hills, Calif.: Sage, 1978.

Eldridge, A. F. *Images of Conflict*. New York: St. Martin's Press, 1979.

Etheredge, L. S. "Personality Effects on American Foreign Policy, 1898–1968: A Test of Interpersonal Generalization Theory." *American Political Science Review*, 1978a, 72, 434–451.

Etheredge, L. S. *A World of Men: The Private Sources of American Foreign Policy*. Cambridge, Mass.: MIT Press, 1978b.

Etzioni, A. "The Kennedy Experiment." *Western Political Quarterly*, 1967, *20*, 361–380.

Falkowski, L. S. "Predicting Flexibility with Memory Profiles." In L. S. Falkowski (ed.), *Psychological Models in International Politics*. Boulder, Colo.: Westview Press, 1979.

Festinger, L. *A Theory of Cognitive Dissonance*. New York: Harper & Row, 1957.

Fisher, R., and Ury, W. *International Mediation*. New York: International Peace Academy, 1978.

Gaenslen, F. "Democracy vs. Efficiency: Some Arguments from the Small Group." *Political Psychology*, 1980, *2*, 15–29.

Galtung, J. "A Structural Theory of Aggression." *Journal of Peace Research*, 1964, *2*, 95–119.

George, A. L. "The Case for Multiple Advocacy in Making Foreign Policy." *American Political Science Review*, 1972, *66*, 751–785.

George, A. L. "The Causal Nexus Between Cognitive Beliefs and Decision-Making Behavior: The 'Operational Code' Belief System." In L. S. Falkowski (ed.), *Psychological Models in International Politics*. Boulder, Colo.: Westview Press, 1979.

George, A. L. *Presidential Decision Making in Foreign Policy: The Effective Use of Information and Advice.* Boulder, Colo.: Westview Press, 1980.

George, A. L., Hall, D. K., and Simons, W. E. *The Limits of Coercive Diplomacy.* Boston: Little, Brown, 1971.

George, A. L., and Smoke, R. *Deterrence in American Foreign Policy: Theory and Practice.* New York: Columbia University Press, 1974.

Gurr, T. *Why Men Rebel.* Princeton, N.J.: Princeton University Press, 1970.

Halperin, M. *Bureaucratic Politics and Foreign Policy.* Washington, D.C.: Brookings Institution, 1974.

Hamner, W. C., and Yukl, G. A. "The Effectiveness of Different Offer Strategies in Bargaining." In D. Druckman (ed.), *Negotiations: Social-Psychological Perspectives.* Beverly Hills, Calif.: Sage, 1977.

Hermann, C. F. *Crises in Foreign Policy: A Simulation Analysis.* New York: Bobbs-Merrill, 1969.

Hermann, C. F. "Time, Threat and Surprise: A Simulation of International Crisis." In C. F. Hermann (ed.), *International Crises: Insights from Behavioral Research.* New York: Free Press, 1972.

Hermann, C. F. "Decision Structure and Process Influences on Foreign Policy." In M. A. East, S. A. Salmore, and C. F. Hermann (eds.), *Why Nations Act.* Beverly Hills, Calif.: Sage, 1978.

Hermann, M. G. "Leader Personality and Foreign Policy Behavior." In J. N. Rosenau (ed.), *Comparing Foreign Policies: Theories, Findings, and Methods.* New York: Halsted Press, 1974.

Hermann, M. G. "When Leader Personality Will Affect Foreign Policy: Some Propositions." In J. N. Rosenau (ed.), *In Search of Global Patterns.* New York: Free Press, 1976.

Hermann, M. G. "Who Becomes a Political Leader? Some Societal and Regime Influences on Selection of a Head of State." In L. S. Falkowski (ed.), *Psychological Models in International Politics.* Boulder, Colo.: Westview Press, 1979.

Hermann, M. G. "Explaining Foreign Policy Behavior Using the Personality Characteristics of Political Leaders." *International Studies Quarterly,* 1980, *24,* 7–46.

Heuer, R. J., Jr. "Cognitive Factors in Deception and Counterdeception." In D. C. Daniel and K. C. Herbig (eds.), *Strategic Military Deception.* Elmsford, N.Y.: Pergamon Press, 1982.

Hoagland, S. W., and Walker, S. G. "Operational Codes and Crisis Outcomes." In L. S. Falkowski (ed.), *Psychological Models in International Politics.* Boulder, Colo.: Westview Press, 1979.

Holsti, O. R. "Individual Differences in 'Definition of the Situation.'" *Journal of Conflict Resolution,* 1970, *14,* 303–310.

Holsti, O. R. *Crisis Escalation War.* Montreal: McGill–Queens University Press, 1972.

Holsti, O. R. "Cognitive Process Approaches to Decision-Making: Foreign Policy Actors Viewed Psychologically." *American Behavioral Scientist,* 1976a, *20,* 11–32.

Holsti, O. R. "Foreign Policy Formation Viewed Cognitively." In R. Axelrod (ed.), *Structure of Decision.* Princeton, N.J.: Princeton University Press, 1976b.

Holsti, O. R. "The Operational Code Approach: Problems and Some Solutions." In C. Jönsson (ed.), *Cognitive Dynamics and International Politics.* New York: St. Martin's Press, 1982.

Hopmann, P. T. "Bargaining in Arms Control Negotiations: The Seabeds De-nuclearization Treaty." *International Organization*, 1974, *28*, 313–343.

Hopple, G. W. *Political Psychology and Biopolitics: Assessing and Predicting Elite Behavior in Foreign Policy Crises.* Boulder, Colo.: Westview Press, 1980.

Howard, N. *Paradoxes of Rationality.* Cambridge, Mass.: MIT Press, 1971.

Janis, I. L. *Victims of Groupthink.* Boston: Houghton Mifflin, 1972.

Janis, I. L., and Mann, L. *Decision Making: A Psychological Analysis of Conflict, Choice, and Commitment.* New York: Free Press, 1977.

Jervis, R. *The Logic of Images in International Relations.* Princeton, N.J.: Princeton University Press, 1970.

Jervis, R. *Perception and Misperception in International Politics.* Princeton, N.J.: Princeton University Press, 1976.

Jervis, R. "Deterrence Theory Revisited." *World Politics*, 1979, *31*, 289–324.

Jones, E. E., and Nisbett, R. E. "The Actor and the Observer: Divergent Perceptions on the Causes of Behavior." In E. E. Jones and others (eds.), *Attribution: Perceiving the Causes of Behavior.* Morristown, N.J.: Silver Burdett, 1972.

Jönsson, C. "Situation-Specific Versus Actor-Specific Approaches to International Bargaining." *European Journal of Political Research*, 1978, *6*, 381–398.

Kaplowitz, N. "Psychopolitical Dimensions of International Relations. I: Self-Images, Perceptions of Enemies, and Conflict Orientations." Unpublished manuscript, Mills College, 1981.

Kelman, H. C. (ed.). *International Behavior: A Social-Psychological Analysis.* New York: Holt, Rinehart & Winston, 1965a.

Kelman, H. C. "Social-Psychological Approaches to the Study of International Relations." In H. C. Kelman (ed.), *International Behavior: A Social-Psychological Analysis.* New York: Holt, Rinehart & Winston, 1965b.

Kelman, H. C. "The Problem-Solving Workshop in Conflict Resolution." In R. L. Merritt (ed.), *Communication in International Politics.* Urbana: University of Illinois Press, 1972.

Kelman, H. C., and Bloom, A. H. "Assumptive Frameworks in International Politics." In J. N. Knutson (ed.), *Handbook of Political Psychology.* San Francisco: Jossey-Bass, 1973.

Kinder, D. R., and Weiss, J. A. "In Lieu of Rationality: Psychological Perspectives on Foreign Policy Decision Making." *Journal of Conflict Resolution*, 1978, *22*, 707–735.

Lall, A. *Modern International Negotiations.* New York: Columbia University Press, 1966.

Lebow, R. N. *Between War and Peace.* Baltimore: Johns Hopkins University Press, 1981.

Lentner, H. H. "The Concept of Crisis as Viewed by the United States Department of State." In C. F. Hermann (ed.), *International Crises: Insights from Behavioral Research.* New York: Free Press, 1972.

LeVine, R. A., and Campbell, D. T. *Ethnocentrism: Theories of Conflict, Ethnic Attitudes, and Behavior.* New York: Wiley, 1972.

Lindblom, C. E. "The Science of 'Muddling Through.' " *Public Administration Review*, 1959, *19*, 79–88.

Lockhart, C. *Bargaining in International Conflicts.* New York: Columbia University Press, 1979.

Mandel, R. "Political Gaming and Foreign Policy Making During Crises." *World Politics*, 1977, *29*, 610–625.

Mandel, R. *Perception, Decision Making, and Conflict.* Lanham, Md.: University Press of America, 1979.

Mandel, R. "Policy-Making Perspectives on War Simulations." *Journal of Conflict Resolution*, 1980a, *24*, 359–375.

Mandel, R. "Roots of the Modern Interstate Border Dispute." *Journal of Conflict Resolution*, 1980b, *24*, 427–451.

Mandel, R. "Contending Public-Private Perspectives on the Consequences of the World Oil Glut." Paper presented at 25th annual meeting of the International Studies Association, Atlanta, March 1984a.

Mandel, R. "The Desirability of Irrationality in Foreign Policy Making: A Preliminary Theoretical Analysis." *Political Psychology*, 1984b, *5*, 643–660.

Mandel, R., and Clarke, S. "Intractability in International Bargaining." Paper presented at 22nd annual meeting of the International Studies Association, Philadelphia, March 1981.

Midgaard, K., and Underdal, A. "Multiparty Conferences." In D. Druckman (ed.), *Negotiations: Social-Psychological Perspectives.* Beverly Hills, Calif.: Sage, 1977.

Midlarsky, M. *On War: Political Violence in the International System.* New York: Free Press, 1975.

Milburn, T. W. "The Management of Crisis." In C. F. Hermann (ed.), *International Crises: Insights from Behavioral Research.* New York: Free Press, 1972.

Minix, D. A. *Small Groups and Foreign Policy Decision-Making.* Lanham, Md.: University Press of America, 1982.

Mitchell, C. R. *The Structure of International Conflict.* New York: St. Martin's Press, 1981.

Morgan, P. M. *Deterrence: A Conceptual Analysis.* Beverly Hills, Calif.: Sage, 1977.

Osgood, C. E. *An Alternative to War or Surrender.* Urbana: University of Illinois Press, 1962.

Oskamp, S. "Social Perception." In L. S. Wrightsman and others (eds.), *Social Psychology in the Seventies.* Monterey, Calif.: Brooks/Cole, 1972.

Pettman, R. *Human Behavior and World Politics.* New York: St. Martin's Press, 1975.

Pruitt, D. G. "Definition of the Situation as a Determinant of International Action." In H. C. Kelman (ed.), *International Behavior: A Social-Psychological Analysis.* New York: Holt, Rinehart & Winston, 1965.

Rosenblatt, P. "Origins and Effects of Group Ethnocentrism and Nationalism." *Journal of Conflict Resolution*, 1964, *7*, 131–146.

Rosi, E. (ed.). *American Defense and Detente.* New York: Dodd, Mead, 1973.

Russett, B. M., and Hanson, E. C. *Interest and Ideology: The Foreign Policy Beliefs of American Businessmen.* New York: W. H. Freeman, 1975.

Sawyer, J., and Guetzkow, H. "Bargaining and Negotiation in International Relations." In H. C. Kelman (ed.), *International Behavior: A Social-Psychological Analysis.* New York: Holt, Rinehart & Winston, 1965.

Schelling, T. C. *The Strategy of Conflict.* New York: Oxford University Press, 1963.

Schwartz, D. C. "Decision Making in Historical and Simulated Crises." In C. F. Hermann (ed.), *International Crises: Insights from Behavioral Research.* New York: Free Press, 1972.

Scott, W. A. "Psychological and Social Correlates of International Images." In H. C. Kelman (ed.), *International Behavior: A Social-Psychological Analysis.* New York: Holt, Rinehart & Winston, 1965.

Semmel, A. K. "Small Group Dynamics in Foreign Policymaking." In G. W. Hopple (ed.), *Biopolitics, Political Psychology, and International Politics.* New York: St. Martin's Press, 1982.

Semmel, A. K., and Minix, D. "Small-Group Dynamics and Foreign Policy Decision-Making: An Experimental Approach." In L. S. Falkowski (ed.), *Psychological Models in International Politics.* Boulder, Colo.: Westview Press, 1979.

Shapiro, M. J., and Bonham, G. M. "Cognitive Processing and Foreign Policy Decision-Making." *International Studies Quarterly,* 1973, *17,* 147–174.

Shapiro, M. J., and Bonham, G. M. "A Cognitive Process Approach to Collective Decision Making." In C. Jönsson, (ed.), *Cognitive Dynamics and International Politics.* New York: St. Martin's Press, 1982.

Simon, H. "A Behavioral Model of Rational Choice." *Quarterly Journal of Economics,* 1955, *69,* 99–118.

Snyder, G. H., and Diesing, P. *Conflict Among Nations.* Princeton, N.J.: Princeton University Press, 1977.

Snyder, J. L. "Rationality at the Brink: The Role of Cognitive Processes in Failures of Deterrence." *World Politics,* 1978, *30,* 345–365.

Snyder, R. C. *Deterrence, Weapons, and Decision Making.* China Lake, Calif.: U.S. Naval Ordnance Test Station, 1961.

Spector, B. I. "Negotiation as a Psychological Process." *Journal of Conflict Resolution,* 1977, *21,* 607–618.

Starr, H. *Henry Kissinger: Perceptions of International Politics.* Lexington: University Press of Kentucky, 1983.

Stein, J. G. "Can Decision-Makers Be Rational and Should They Be? Evaluating the Quality of Decisions." In M. Brecher (ed.), *Studies in Crisis Behavior.* New Brunswick, N.J.: Transaction Books, 1978.

Stein, J. G., and Tanter, R. *Rational Decision Making: Israel's Security Choices, 1967.* Columbus: Ohio State University Press, 1980.

Steinbruner, J. D. *The Cybernetic Theory of Decision.* Princeton, N.J.: Princeton University Press, 1974.

Steinbruner, J. D. "Beyond Rational Deterrence: The Struggle for New Conceptions." *World Politics,* 1976, *28,* 223–245.

Stoessinger, J. G. *The Might of Nations.* New York: Random House, 1964.

Sullivan, M. P. *International Relations: Theories and Evidence.* Englewood Cliffs, N.J.: Prentice-Hall, 1976.

Verba, S. "Assumptions of Rationality and Nonrationality in Models of the International System." In J. N. Rosenau (ed.), *International Politics and Foreign Policy.* New York: Free Press, 1969.

Walker, S. G. "The Interface Between Beliefs and Behavior: Henry Kissinger's Operational Code and the Vietnam War." *Journal of Conflict Resolution,* 1977, *21,* 129–168.

Wallace, M. D. *War and Rank Among Nations.* Lexington, Mass.: Lexington Books, 1973.

White, R. K. *Nobody Wanted War: Misperception in Vietnam and Other Wars.* New York: Doubleday, 1970.

White, R. K. *Fearful Warriors: A Psychological Profile of U.S.-Soviet Relations.* New York: Free Press, 1984.

Wicklund, R. A., and Brehm, J. W. *Perspectives on Cognitive Dissonance.* Hillsdale, N.J.: Erlbaum, 1976.

Wiegele, T. C. "Decision-Making in an International Crisis: Some Biological Factors." *International Studies Quarterly,* 1973, *17,* 295–335.

Wiegele, T. C. "The Case for a Biological Perspective in the Study of International Relations." In G. W. Hopple (ed.), *Biopolitics, Political Psychology, and International Politics.* New York: St. Martin's Press, 1982.

Wilkenfeld, J., and others. *Foreign Policy Behavior.* Beverly Hills, Calif.: Sage, 1980.

Williams, P. *Crisis Management: Confrontation and Diplomacy in the Nuclear Age.* New York: Wiley, 1976.

TEN

乞乞乞乞乞乞乞乞乞乞乞乞乞乞乞乞乞乞

Revitalizing
Political Socialization

Richard M. Merelman

Political socialization is the process by which people acquire relatively enduring orientations toward politics in general and toward their own particular political systems. Throughout much of the postwar period into the early 1970s, research on political socialization was heralded for its potential contribution to an understanding of political statics and dynamics. Today, however, this halcyon period has clearly passed. Although research on political socialization continues to mount in volume, the theoretical impetus for the enterprise seems increasingly suspect. While it would be too much to declare the field moribund, it does resemble uncomfortably closely the twitchings of a still-quickened corpse. It is our task to see whether this image is apt or whether, instead, the field of political socialization can be rescued from premature burial.

The image of stagnation stems from a widely held belief that as a research enterprise political socialization lacks either a convincing theoretical rationale or a convincing practical rationale (Marsh, 1971; Searing, Wright, and Rabinowitz, 1976; Dowse and Hughes, 1977; Dowse, 1978). I believe, however, that political socialization is of considerable importance both to theory and to practice. Therefore, in this chapter I will attempt to provide a new theoretical rationale for socialization research. To do so, I will review the recent socialization literature through a simple conceptual framework that, strangely enough, has never been applied to this field (for other approaches, see Niemi, 1973; Sears, 1975; Renshon, 1977; Cundy, 1979a). I will also argue that political socialization is actually of *greater* political importance today than at perhaps any other time in political history. Indeed, one of the chief ironies of contemporary social science is that our

Note: I should like to thank Jon Olson for bibliographical assistance in the preparation of this chapter.

image of socialization has blurred at precisely that moment when the actual processes of socialization have taken on unique political significance. One wonders
whether the two developments are connected, so that, as is so often the case in
human affairs, we suddenly find ourselves most confused about those things we
most need to comprehend.

Contemporary Importance of Political Socialization

Why is political socialization of such enhanced contemporary importance?
The reason is simple: *Other* means of controlling a people have increasingly failed
or been declared illegitimate. Consider, for example, two traditional forms of
political control: force and economic affluence. As is well known, Weber ([1919]
1947, p. 78) defined the state as that institution of society which enjoys a monopoly
of legitimate force. Yet the legitimacy of forceful suppression has become extremely
fragile because a pervasive democratic ideology in theory grants mass publics the
right to shape in crucial ways their own futures. Thus, coercing a population is
no longer protected by myths that allocate to governing elites a right to rule. In
every social institution, democratic pressures challenge coercive techniques of
control—from prohibitions against corporal punishment in the classroom to police
review boards and open-files laws in communities. Moreover, despite the enormous
array of physical force at its command, the state finds itself vulnerable to small
groups of terrorists, to the occasional deranged assassin, or to the poisoner of
Tylenol tablets. Paradoxically, the concentration of coercion in the state has been
accompanied by functional dispersion and interdependency across the whole of
society, so that the throw of a single switch can now plunge an entire community
into darkness. For these reasons, even the most sophisticated machines of centralized coercion are often frustrated in their search for effective employment.

Or consider social control and political domination via the instrument of
economic well-being. For much of the postwar period, students of democracy
argued that advanced industrialization had finally mastered human want. The
result was a modern era of unprecedented political peace—an "end of ideology"
(Bell, 1961). Some theorists of modernization even extended this analysis to the
Third World, arguing that processes of industrial mobilization common to the
West would inevitably emerge elsewhere, permitting indigenous bourgeois forces
to consolidate strong, progressive, bourgeois states. Today, however, few are unqual-
ifiedly optimistic about the economic futures either of industrialized democracies
or of developing Third World nations. Economic stagnation in industrialized
democracies along with massive external debts and economic dependency in the
Third World: this is our current economic lot. The world economy can no longer
assure political stability.

With the decline of legitimate force and reliable economic affluence, political socialization must play a larger role in the struggle for political stability. The
study of political socialization is, therefore, of greater importance today than at
any other recent time.

Possible Theoretical Frameworks

All this may be very well, of course, but what theoretical framework can we
use to help us in our effort? In the early period of political socialization research,

the theoretical frameworks of choice were systems theory and functional analysis (Almond and Verba, 1980; Dawson and Prewitt, 1969), with traces of pluralism occasionally thrown in. But as these particular theories of politics came under attack in the 1960s, the energy and coherence they once supplied socialization research gradually declined. It was then that the study of political socialization began its journey into the wilderness. Of course, interesting theoretical questions have never wholly eluded socialization research (Haan, 1972), but in recent years such questions have assumed an ad hoc quality, alternating unpredictably from one piece of research to another and yielding little in the way of cumulativeness or a vital body of integrated research findings.

The two primary reactions to this theoretical vacuum are "country" approaches and "learning" approaches. Country approaches usually dispense with discussions of general socialization theories, contending only that socialization research can help us understand the politics of a particular nation. It is here that the dominant stream of American socialization research flows, as evidenced recently by Jennings and Niemi (1974, 1981) as well as by Iyengar (1979) and Sigel and Hoskin (1981). This stream of research occasionally touches "democratic theory," but it is mainly concerned with illuminating political processes—such as partisan identification or political participation—presumably most characteristic of a single country or group of countries (Abramson, 1975). This research has helped us understand the politics of individual countries but has yielded no consistent theoretical rationale for the study of political socialization itself, because processes of socialization vary across societies in ways that demand a larger theoretical rationale than country studies can themselves generate. In consequence, country studies yield a laundry list of findings but no impetus for the study of socialization as an integrated, self-contained field.

The second approach, which focuses directly on the process of learning, follows upon and may be seen as a reaction to the flaws of country studies. The learning approach proceeds from the obvious observation that, whatever other differences they possess, all studies of political socialization have at least one thing in common—namely, that they are inquiries into a species of *learning*. Upon this premise the learning rationale has deliberately chosen to construe the process of political socialization *microscopically;* that is, as derived from more universal processes of cognitive growth, emotive development, and moral judgment. Investigators who have accepted the learning rationale have thus busied themselves in an attempt to find an appropriate model of learning to apply to the political socialization process (Merelman, 1969; Landes, 1976; Campbell, 1979; Wilson, 1981).

The learning approach has not entirely ignored important questions about the consequences of political learning for the performance of political systems. Indeed, there are some within the learning tradition who argue that their approach alone promises answers to these questions. But it is hard to credit their argument very far; the problem is an absence of correlation between different forms of learning and different models of politics. For example, a classical conditioning model of political learning fits as easily into a pluralist theory of cost-benefit politics as it does into a hegemonic model of class-based politics. Moreover, the learning approach reveals as much diversity in socialization as have country-based studies. Some aspects of political learning—such as the acquisition of partisanship—fit readily into social psychological or classical behaviorist models of learning; other aspects of political learning—such as enduring orientations toward political participation—fit most easily into Maslowian or neo-Freudian constructs (Knutson, 1972); still others—such as the learning of values relevant to justice, equality, and fairness—fit best into the developmental models of Piaget and Kohlberg (Mladenka and Hill, 1975; Kohlberg, 1981). Because of the plethora of useful learning models, the learning approach has merely complicated the search for a theoretical rationale to support socialization research. It has not supplied such a rationale itself.

The present chapter, therefore, is an exercise in regeneration, inasmuch as it returns us directly to the pursuit of a general theoretical rationale for undertaking political socialization research. I believe such a rationale can emerge only if we first employ existing socialization research to help illuminate four of the "grand theories" of politics: systems theory, hegemonic theory, pluralist theory, and conflict theory. Each of these theories has a long and illustrious history in discussions of politics; more important, each makes either explicit or implicit arguments about political socialization. I will then reverse the process of my inquiry by seeing whether these grand theories can be reconstructed so as to yield a general theoretical rationale for future socialization research. I must confess to feeling negative on this score, and so I try to sketch an alternative fifth paradigm— a slightly more adequate framework to confront the enhanced role of political socialization in contemporary political systems as well as to correct the flaws discovered in looking at the four traditional theories.

The four models of politics which generate the four approaches to socialization that I intend to examine yield quite different conceptions of the socialization process. Table 1 describes these models and a fifth model, which is discussed in the section headed "Need for a New Paradigm." The table summarizes the differences among these approaches by reference to actors in the socialization process, the forces that hold society together and that socialization is designed to support, the primary purposes or concerns of the socialization process, and the psychological outcomes of that process in young people. The table may be used as a point of reference for the work to follow. Let us briefly review each of the four approaches, following the organization the table provides.

The first approach I will consider is systems analysis (Easton, 1965). Systems analysis emerges from the functionalist tradition in sociology (Buckley, 1967). It presents a picture of socialization in which responsible, benevolent, but authoritative political leaders and their loyal subjects are central actors. According to this approach, positive attitudes toward authority emerge in the socialization process through psychologically normal tendencies to respect authority among the young, and also through the provision of positive models of authority at home and school. The result is a harmonious system held together by feelings of deference on the part of followers to leaders, and obligation on the part of leaders to followers. There emerges a political system with high levels of diffuse support, in which young people are, above all else, respectful of political authority, legal order, traditional institutions, and obligations toward participatory citizenship. The primary theorists in this tradition are Émile Durkheim, Talcott Parsons, David Easton, and, to a lesser degree, Harry Eckstein (Parsons, 1951).

As for the hegemonic model, its dominant actors are capitalist owners of consciousness-formation industries and their political allies, on the one hand, and a pliable, latently resentful subordinate class on the other. The relationship

Table 1. Differences Among Approaches to Political Socialization.

Theory	Actors	Forces Holding Society Together	Concern of Political Socialization	Proposed Effects of Political Socialization
Systems Theory	Benevolent leaders and loyal subjects.	Deference, obligation, responsibility.	Provides diffuse support for system.	Positive attitudes toward political authority, law and order, political institutions, and sense of political efficacy.
Hegemonic Theory	Capitalist owners of consciousness-formation industries and their political allies versus pliable, though latently resentful, atomized public.	Manipulation, false consciousness.	Pervasive process of ideological diffusion through multitude of agencies; focus on teaching economic values as central to political action.	Young people should learn message of dominant groups from media, school, and popular culture.
Pluralist Theory	Interest groups and political parties.	Representation within accepted "rules of game."	Creation of public capable of looking after own interests uncowed by authority but tolerant of dissent and knowledgeable about the "rules of the game."	Strong, enduring partisanship identification; learn and employ ideological orientation; learn "rules of game," especially tolerance of dissent; become truly participative.
Conflict Theory	Groups in society in conflict, with enduring antagonisms toward one another (for example, social classes, status groups, cliques within dominant group).	Intragroup solidarity; balance of power among hostile groups; occasional victories for all parties.	Creation of young people who are strongly identified with own group and focused on advancing own group.	Group awareness; learning and employing conflict as a means of conducting everyday politics.
Lateral Theory	Horizontally connected agents of socialization who compete with each other to socialize different models of society.	Choice, egalitarianism, transiency.	Development of rules for choosing among images of society in order to act politically.	Ability to articulate reasons for political interests and/or involvement.

between the dominant and subordinate groups is one of "false consciousness," consisting of superficial and misleading lip service to a manufactured, essentially fraudulent social consensus favoring the economic interests of the dominant groups. Socialization agencies under state control—schools, the mass media, advertising—are instrumental for teaching such economic values as "consumerism" and for creating young people who reject any economic system other than capitalism and are immediately hostile to attacks on the political status quo. The primary theorists in the hegemonic tradition are Karl Marx and Antonio Gramsci (Weiner, 1981).

In the pluralist model, the dominant actors are interest groups and political parties who command the conditional support of active citizens. These citizens are anxious to be represented by competing political organizations so as to have their legitimate aspirations reflected in public policy. They are, therefore, committed but not wedded to particular political groups, and they frequently change allegiances after rational consideration of policy outcomes (Riker and Ordeshook, 1973). The socialization process aims to create a participatory public jealous of its own prerogatives, anxious to participate in ways that permit dissent and choice but rejecting of extreme, destructive forms of mass participation (Hart, 1978). The outcomes of socialization are high levels of citizen efficacy, partisan identification, and interest-group activity organized along a cohesive, left-right political dimension in which all groups abide by norms of free speech, majority rule, and electoral choice. The primary agencies of socialization are schools, parents, the mass media, and competing political organizations. The major theorists in this school are those concerned with the problem of political representation as a cohesive force uniting leaders and followers. These theorists include Jean Jacques Rousseau ([1762] 1953), John Stuart Mill ([1861] 1910), Philip Converse (1964), and Robert Dahl (1982).

Finally, the conflict model describes cohesive groups locked in enduring, inescapable struggle. While a group or stratum may temporarily rule, its hold is always precarious; within groups there is considerable inequality and a tightly authoritarian system of controls, enforced either directly by leaders or indirectly by collective, peer pressures. What holds the fragile fabric of society together under these conditions of constant struggle is intragroup loyalty, brought about in part through socialization. The dominant agencies of socialization are group-based propaganda organs, such as newspapers; focused settings, such as neighborhoods; and organizations representative of group interests. In addition, parents and schools are organized so as to transmit a strong sense of group loyalty. Nevertheless, given conditions of constant struggle, society can endure only because successive groups hold power for short periods, so that, at other times, there is a rough balance of power among groups. The dominant purpose of socialization is the creation of young people loyal to their group and willing to support it against others on a daily basis. The major theorists in this tradition are Gaetano Mosca (1939) and Max Weber (in some aspects of his work; see Weber, [1919] 1947).

Each of these four theories implies that the structure of political socialization resembles in form the structure of contemporary political relations between leaders and led. That is, each of these theories sees socialization as a vertical process, a transaction between people—parents and children, teachers and students, communicators and audiences, leaders and led—of quite different power levels.

Because I believe that each of these models holds only one part of the puzzle of contemporary socialization, an additional paradigm is needed. This additional paradigm must be capable of specifying the range of indeterminacy in the socialization process, because where combinations of the four models actually describe the reality of socialization, or, indeed, where none of the four models applies at all, there must be new considerations. I will therefore discuss a fifth approach, a lateral theory of socialization. This theory argues that the key aspect of contemporary socialization is a wide range of choice among the four traditional models, a range of choice that is continually expanded by lateral connections among equals in the socialization process. Because this lateral approach describes not only contemporary political socialization but also the relations among the four traditional theories, it amounts to a metatheory of political socialization—that is, a theory of theories.

Political Socialization and Systems Theory

In their path-breaking early discussion of the subject, Easton and Dennis (1969) portrayed political socialization as a process by which a political system is provided with "diffuse support," which they described as a reservoir of positive attitudes toward political leaders, toward the regime, toward the political community, and toward specific political institutions. More recently Easton (1975) has moved away from his original conception of diffuse support, conceding that the interaction between short-term reactions to specific policies and long-term attitudes toward the political system as a whole makes problematic any clear demarcation between diffuse and specific support.

Easton's withdrawal from his own concept reveals the difficulties of deciding just what should be included under the rubric of diffuse support. The studies I intend to employ focus on youthful attitudes toward political authority; toward law, order, and convention; toward political institutions; and toward the efficacy of the political self. Positive attitudes in these areas are conducive to a frame of mind that grants to the political system a wide but not limitless margin of maneuver.

Most research on the socialization of diffuse support visualizes an ideal type of citizen, who is generally suspicious of change, marginally active politically, and in most other respects similar to Sniderman's (1982) description of the "committed" citizen. It is questionable whether the "systems-supportive" person is a type consistent with certain elements of a democratic regime. For example, Kohlberg (1980, p. 64) contends that from a moral reasoning perspective the American constitutional system is based on ideas of social contract and individual consent, which are inconsistent with a uniformly supportive mentality of assent to authority. As far as democracies are concerned, therefore, systems theory's bias toward acquiescence and trust in authority is open to dispute (Parry, 1976). These conceptual ambiguities have undoubtedly contributed to the current eclipse of systems analysis.

At this point, however, our task is essentially empirical rather than conceptual. We must judge whether political socialization does, in fact, create trusting, efficacious, conventionally law-and-order-maintaining, proauthority citizens. Let us first focus on research, then range further afield.

Moral Development. One body of research relevant to this question is that on moral development. Research on this subject generally supports the systems theory image of the citizen. The modal stage of moral reasoning among adolescents is resolutely conventional and respectful of law and order, qualities that fit the systems framework (Kohlberg, 1969). The same conclusion applies to youthful perceptions of social structure; for example, Furth (1980) found that youngsters between the ages of six and ten are highly disposed to grant moral authority to their elders throughout the entire range of social roles. The cognitive functions of such role-centered, status quo conceptions may be profound in the young; for example, in an interesting study of playground games, Sluckin (1981) argues that children resort to rituals and verbal formulas to avoid conflict and to protect themselves. They thus become wedded to social order early in life. The resonance between this conclusion and Piaget's ([1932] 1965) conceptions of "heterodox morality" among the young is obvious.

Turiel (1980) has argued that from childhood to adolescence the young develop an increasingly sophisticated appreciation of conventions. The political importance of Turiel's argument is that it visualizes morally advanced justifications among the young for respecting social conventions and the status quo. The perspective is quite different from that of Kohlberg and Piaget, who believe that moral and cognitive advance is inevitably hostile to conventional political morality and systems support. Turiel's argument is quite consistent with studies of adolescent reasoning about distributive issues in politics (Adelson, 1972; Merelman and McCabe, 1974; Connell, 1977; Patterson, 1979), which find no uniform adoption of "postconventional" moral principles that could seriously challenge existing distributions of power, authority, status, or income (Tomlinson, 1975, p. 256).

However, relevant research on moral development is hardly conclusive for systems analysis. Moral reasoning varies considerably in situational application as well as across issue areas (Lickona, 1976). Moreover, the sheer breadth and generality of moral reasoning exceed the scope of attitudes toward specific political authorities and institutions. And, finally, these latter are subject to socialization influences other than moral reasoning. Therefore, we need to examine the strongest argument in favor of the proposition that socialization creates systems support: the benevolent leader hypothesis.

Benevolent Leader Hypothesis. The pioneering research of Greenstein (1965), Easton and Dennis (1969), and Hess (1963) suggested that children generally learn to view political authority favorably. Leaving aside the question of whether favorable attitudes persist in later life, we can examine the current status of the benevolent leader hypothesis as it applies to the American system, where the argument originally emerged. My view is that the existing research creates only slight support for the benevolent leader hypothesis, even among middle-class, white American children. The research, therefore, does not support systems theory.

The strongest recent defense of the benevolent leader hypothesis appears in Greenstein's (1975) cross-national study. Greenstein reports that even in the post-Watergate period American children ten to sixteen years old continued to voice strong support for an idealized presidential figure, although many rejected the actual performance of President Nixon. Greenstein admits that post-Watergate children were more critical than their predecessors in evaluating the president, but he contends that such personal criticism did not disturb the benevolence of their basic presidential images. Moore and his associates (1976) suggest that the cognitive foundation of such benevolent images emerges in early childhood; according to these investigators, almost 25 percent of a sample of children five and six years old believed that presidents take their orders directly from God. Perhaps an early confusion of secular and sacred authority persists as a residue through time, allowing positive attitudes toward political authorities to survive such setbacks as Watergate. (For a full theory, see Eisenstadt, 1981).

Nevertheless, the bulk of relevant contemporary research suggests that children's recent attitudes toward the presidency are much less favorable than they were during the 1960s (Niemi and Sobieszek, 1977). Especially informative in this regard is Arterton (1975), who found that the strongly negative attitudes toward the presidency which had appeared in his earlier research (Arterton, 1974) had not disappeared among children in grades 3-6. A replication of the 1961 Hess/Easton study among seventh and eighth graders in 1973-74 revealed a major decline in positive attitudes (Joslyn, 1977). Indeed, Joslyn argues that this decline extended to institutions other than the presidency itself.

Nevertheless, the benevolent leader hypothesis is not entirely incorrect. Children are always more likely to view the incumbent positively when they are asked to make general attributions, rather than to evaluate specific incumbents or specific personal qualities. My guess is that a tendency to evaluate presidents positively does appear early in youth but that this tendency is open to alteration, depending on political factors or parental influence (Jennings and Niemi, 1981; Tolley, 1973).

Two important recent studies (Jennings and Niemi, 1981; Sigel and Hoskin, 1981) shed indirect light on levels of support for the presidency as well as attitudes toward other political institutions during adolescence. Sigel and Hoskin examined one thousand high school seniors in Pennsylvania during 1974, but they did not specifically ascertain attitudes toward the presidency. Nevertheless, their use of the Survey Research Center's feeling thermometer reveals that positive views among adolescents were essentially symbolic, being reserved primarily for the United States as a nation as well as for the flag. By contrast, these seniors manifested more neutral attitudes toward Congress and the courts, and their attitudes toward the "current government" were predominantly negative. Most of this sample preferred to channel their participatory efforts not toward political organizations but toward local voluntary associations and charitable activities, thereby separating themselves from the corrupting influences they apparently associated with politics.

Like Sigel and Hoskin, Jennings and Niemi do not directly assess attitudes toward the presidency. However, in their panel study of young people (eighteen to twenty-five years old) from 1968 to 1973, they found substantial declines in political trust, both among the youthful cohort and among their parents. Unfortunately, these data do not allow us to draw direct conclusions about the leader imagery of adolescents. Indeed, the fragmentary quality of benevolent leader research suggests the need for new studies over a series of political eras (from periods of calm to periods of turmoil). Facile generalizations based on observations of student disorders in the 1960s or on indirect measures will clearly not do in the long run. On balance, however, the existing literature is not kind to the benevolent leader hypothesis and, thus, does not strengthen the systems paradigm of socialization.

Political Trust. Another dimension of political socialization that is relevant to the systems argument is that of trust in government. Current research indicates that there is an isolable component of political trust that is purely systemic in quality (Abramson and Finifter, 1981) and that persists from adolescence to adulthood (Abramson, 1983). The question, then, is how much political trust is established in the process of socialization.

Jennings and Niemi's (1981) longitudinal data on adolescents from 1968 to 1973 echo other findings on adults during this period. For both age groups, there were sizable declines in political trust. From a 1968 mean of 4.56 on a scale of 6.0, the youthful cohort fell to 3.01 by 1973 (p. 415). Moreover, the decline in trust was steeper for the youthful cohort than for its parents. And Sigel and Hoskin (1981) found only moderate levels of political trust among their Pennsylvania high school seniors in 1974. These students were in fact quite skeptical about authorities, rather than positively supportive.

Declines in political trust among young people appear to be general across most subgroups. Although children from low-income and minority groups may begin life at a relatively low level of trust, their trust levels decline no less precipitously than does the level of trust among more advantaged youngsters. Thus, political reality, as manifested in social inequality, is not alone responsible for the decay of political trust among the young. Instead, it is the way in which political reality filters into the socialization process that is of primary importance.

Significantly, low levels of systems trust do not invariably indicate a limited sense of confidence in the self, or even limited political efficacy. Instead, political distrust among the young may coexist with high levels of personal efficacy as well as with a feeling that the political system may, in fact, be open to change (Phizakalea, 1975; Long, 1976). In such cases socialization creates a pattern of alienation with considerable potential for opposition to the status quo. My interpretation differs markedly from an older "neo-elitist" conception (Wright, 1975, 1976), which views declines in trust and efficacy as productive only of political apathy, rather than of active opposition. Of course, the more important thing is that neither apathy nor opposition is consistent with a systems paradigm.

In all fairness, however, we must note that, as systems theory itself has declined as a popular organizing device for political analysis, so also have inquiries into political trust. There have been few recent studies of political trust among young people; this research lacuna prevents any firm conclusion at this point about the socialization of political trust as an element of systems support.

Evaluations of Political Authority. Comparative research also reveals the fragility and variability of youthful perspectives on political authority. Positive youthful evaluations are not certain but instead depend on a number of contingencies, four of which require discussion. The first is the presence of a forceful and popular incumbent leader. For example, Iyengar (1980–81) discovered that in India adolescent attitudes of system trust turned on attitudes toward Indira Gandhi. Adolescents who favored Mrs. Gandhi altered their levels of system trust as her political fortunes altered. In India—and perhaps elsewhere as well—the "institutionalization" of system support among the young has yet fully to occur (see also Green, 1977).

Second, system trust among the young also depends on general perceptions of political corruption or fairness. This becomes clear in Massey's (1976) study of

Japanese young people, who generally distrust the prime minister, as well as in Kasschau's (1976) study of Mexican children. In both studies perceptions of system corruption erode youthful support. Indeed, Kasschau found that Mexican children (as early as second grade) showed a 50 percent lower rate of support for authorities than their American contemporaries did.

Third, the position of subgroups in the system of social stratification affects support levels among the young. Thus, for example, Landes (1977a, 1977b) reports that support levels are much lower among French Canadian than Anglo-Canadian children. The Anglo-French differences seem clearly to be the result of differential social placement of the two groups. Similar findings have been reported for subgroups within the American context (Lyons, 1970; Abramson, 1977). In a particularly intriguing study, Stevens (1975) found that Japanese American children in a California suburb were far more supportive politically than their Anglo or Chicano counterparts were. These differences can be explained both by culture (traditional Japanese American patterns of deference and successful assimilation) and by social structure (the rapid social mobility of Japanese Americans). In contrast, Chicano students were uniformly low in system support and, unlike Japanese Americans, showed little social-class variation in attitudes. Apparently, Chicanos as a group rank so low in the local stratification system that internal variation becomes unimportant. Moreover, unlike the Japanese Americans, the Chicanos had a persistent clash of cultural and linguistic norms with the dominant white American community (Garcia, 1973; Lamare, 1974; Stevens, 1975). In sum, both class and culture place real limits on socialization to system support in childhood.

Finally, there is some evidence that external threats to a political system may help mobilize the greatest support among children. This possibility emerges from Ichilov and Nave's (1980–81) study of Israeli adolescents, who, more than any other single group surveyed in this chapter, resemble the idealized version of the supportive adolescent. It is doubtful whether so uniformly supportive a set of orientations would have emerged in an Israel with a less traumatic political history; under less turbulent political conditions, the apparently normal processes of adolescent skepticism may well have found their way into Israeli socialization just as they do in other countries. The larger import of these remarks is that the attitudinal patterns which systems theory purports to be *normal* among the young may, in fact, appear only under the most *abnormal*, stressful political circumstances.

Political Socialization and Hegemonic Theory

Ironically, as the appeal of such non-Marxist theories as systems analysis has declined in favor of political economy, Marxists themselves—traditionally very much within the theoretical orbit of political economy—have shown greater interest in the way that ideological "superstructure" "reproduces" both capitalist and state socialist societies. So while non-Marxists have been busy rejecting concepts of "culture," "political culture," "ideology," and "socialization," Marxists have become convinced that *only* such concepts can save their analyses. In particular, only an analysis of ideological superstructure can explain the reluctance of subordinate classes to challenge the declining power of dominant classes in market capitalism (Williams, 1973). Accordingly, a neo-Marxist school of socialization analysis has appeared.

The concept of "hegemony" provides the theoretical focus of the neo-Marxist school. Hegemony is a notoriously complex idea (see Abercrombie, Hill, and Turner, 1980; Weiner, 1981). Nevertheless, the core of the concept resides in Marx and Engels's contention that "the ideas of the ruling class are in every epoch the ruling ideas"; that is, "the class which is the ruling force of society is at the same time its ruling intellectual force" (cited in Abercrombie, Hill, and Turner, 1980, p. 7). Later in this key passage, Marx and Engels argue that the ruling class controls the means of mental production so as to inhibit latent opposition among subordinate classes. As a result, "ruling ideas," which emerge from the hegemonic process, are idealized, morally sanitized versions of the dominant material relationships that structure society. Ultimately, hegemony is maintained by a constantly shifting but politically neutralizing mix of pro- and antisystem attitudes among working-class people (Gramsci, [1948] 1971).

A narrower version of hegemonic theory proves helpful to us. Hegemonic theorists make three arguments about the socialization process, each of which we can investigate with the assistance of the extant literature. These arguments involve *manipulation* in the socialization process, *content* and *quality* of political learning, and the *economic* origins of socialization. Interestingly, we can use these arguments to examine hegemonic theory not only within but also outside capitalist structures. Indeed, ironically enough, hegemonic theory proves exceptionally informative about socialist regimes.

Although systems theory and hegemonic theory generally agree about the supportive consequences of political learning, manipulative elements of political socialization are more central to hegemonic theories than to systems theories. Systems theory usually implies that supportive learning emerges without direct political intervention in the socialization process. By contrast, hegemonic theories contend, in Miliband's (1969, p. 163) words, that hegemony "is not simply something which happens. . . . It is, in very large part, the result of a permanent and pervasive *effort* [italics in the original], conducted through a multitude of agencies and deliberately intended to create what Talcott Parsons calls a 'national supra party consensus' based on 'higher-order solidarity.' "

If Miliband is correct, we must investigate political manipulation of the socialization process. It seems reasonable to expect that such manipulation will be centered in the socialization agencies most open either to state or to corporate control. These include schools and the mass media, two agencies of socialization that are legally open to direct intervention by corporate elites or political leaders and are also thoroughly political in content and purpose.

In addition, this version of hegemonic theory directs our attention beyond "supportive" political values to explicitly economic values. After all, hegemonic theorists claim that the pattern of political rule is constrained by and bound up with economic-class relationships. Therefore, every pattern of political values—whether supportive or not—must be related to the economic structures that determine the pattern of political control.

Finally, hegemonic theory is inviting for its potential application to political socialization in state socialist as well as capitalist societies, because state socialist societies, despite themselves, develop new class bases for political rule. Indeed, hegemonic theory depends heavily on inquiries into state socialist regimes, inasmuch as such regimes—more than those of capitalist societies—undertake as a matter of policy to inculcate a supportive political consciousness among the young. Surely, if a hegemonic theory of socialization is correct about *any* regime, it should be correct about state socialism.

Some mainstream students of political socialization have found hegemonic theory appealing. For example, Dawson, Prewitt, and Dawson outline a hegemonic theory in their 1977 text, and Stacey flirts with such a theory in his 1977 study. Departing from his earlier cognitive developmental framework in 1971, Connell (1977) has since advanced a full-blown hegemonic approach, including original empirical data. There are also critics of the hegemonic approach to socialization—for example, Harman (1980) and Dowse (1978)—who complain that evidence of the working class "playing dead" in the face of hegemonic socialization is sorely lacking.

Let us draw these threads of hegemonic theory together into a series of hypotheses about socialization. We can delineate both a type of socialization and a youthful "product" that conform to the hegemonic model. The hegemonic model predicts that the state and/or large corporations will manipulate schools, the mass media, and popular culture so as to transmit messages favorable to a dominant politicoeconomic class. These messages should "take"—that is, young people should learn from these agencies to support the dominant class.

Schools as Agents. Understandably, hegemonic theorists have paid close attention to schooling (Langeveld, 1981), because schools are most often public institutions directly open to political influence. Hegemonic theorists describe three basic methods by which dominant classes allegedly use schooling to inculcate supportive values. First, curriculum content is slanted in favor of dominant economic, social, and political values. Second, allocating students to different academic tracks and educational fates favors the children of dominant social classes. Children from subordinate classes—though stigmatized—are nevertheless encouraged to believe in the fairness of the social system and in their opportunity to improve themselves without significant collective political action. Third, a "hidden curriculum," consisting of informal school practices (such as teacher domination of discussion, respect for school rules of demeanor and behavior, and competition for "popularity" among peers), reinforces explicit proauthority messages in the curriculum and in the process of academic competition.

Studies of school curricula provide some comfort to the hegemonic perspective. For example, Anyon (1980) and Fitzgerald (1979) document the way in which high school social studies and history textbooks have generally favored American capitalism and the American nation-state. In a quite different context, Martin (1975) carefully demonstrates that elementary school textbooks in Taiwan and in mainland China present starkly different views of the ideal citizen—views generally in line with the capitalist and socialist qualities of the two regimes. Similar findings appear in Canada (Zureik, 1975, p. 40).

There is also evidence that the class-based allocation of students to educational tracks produces a stratification of political ideas among the young. The nature of this stratification generally supports the hegemony argument. Jennings and Niemi (1981), for example, report considerable "political stratification" among their high school seniors, with higher-track, higher-SES students developing more political self-confidence and assertiveness than lower-track students, who adopt the passive role that hegemonic theorists describe. And Morgan (1977) has por-

trayed in detail the social studies milieus that provide effective stratification channels in the socialization process. Morgan's research shows that lower-track students
receive less innovative, more authoritarian political and educational messages
than do upper-class, higher-track students.

At the same time, some people dispute arguments about the hidden curriculum's authoritarian qualities. Merelman (1980a, 1981) argues that American
schools include an *anti*authoritarian hidden curriculum, which students and parents jointly force on teachers and administrators. He claims that the informal
practices of American schools often compromise both economic and political
authority. Even Jennings and Niemi (1974, 1981) point out that between 1965 and
1973 criticisms of administrators and teachers rose dramatically within schools.
And Willis (1977), in an extremely interesting participant observation study of an
English school, concludes that working-class boys do not accept the school's stig-
matization but instead fight back. In fact, they use the very hopelessness of their
social position to test the procedural niceties of school discipline to the limit. They
form their own "legion of the lost" in order to disrupt the pattern of school order.

The question raised by these observations, of course, is how effective the
prohegemonic content and processes of schooling are in producing prohegemonic
attitudes and values among students. Unfortunately, I can find no studies that link
the learning of economic values reliably to school factors. But studies of political
attitudes among young people report little evidence in favor of the hegemonic
approach to schooling. Most such studies find that variations in teacher style and
course content bear little relationship to differences among student political values
(Hawley, 1976). Even when the school itself becomes the unit of analysis, rather
than individual classrooms or teachers, factors such as the formal and the hidden
curriculum appear to have limited influence. As Jennings (1974) sums it up, any
given school characteristic is almost always outweighed by one or more family-
related qualities among students. These observations do not deny the school's
capacity to *confirm* initial class and family differences via certification devices,
such as grading, and thereby to legitimize preexisting power differences among
rising generations. But this process essentially is allocational rather than socializing. To place students according to class background is not necessarily to teach
them "appropriate" values.

Moreover, some aspects of political education are quite inconsistent with
hegemonic theory. Surely one would expect those students who stay in school
longest and who perform best to become most allegiant to the system, which has
already rewarded them handsomely and promises to reward them even more in the
future. Yet, as Grove and his colleagues (1974) and Morgan (1977) point out, the
most advantaged students often become severely critical of schools and other institutions. We must remember that, in advanced industrial societies, schools prepare
their best students for jobs demanding sophisticated reasoning; they can hardly
prevent these same students from applying their reasoning skills to social inequalities and political injustices. The repeated emergence of a skeptical middle-class
intelligentsia may be the price that contemporary hegemonic systems pay for the
economic well-being they so desperately need (Schumpeter, 1950).

It is therefore premature to offer any conclusions about the hegemonic
effects of schooling on the young. Current research on the subject lacks anything

approaching the exhaustive studies of school effects in nonpolitical domains (Coleman and others, 1965; Jencks, 1979; Jencks and others, 1972; Rutter and others, 1979). Until such highly focused, well-financed, methodologically sophisticated studies become available, we can at best conclude that the educational case for hegemony remains to be made.

Media as Agents. More serious problems afflict arguments about the political effects of media on the young. Here again hegemonic theory is strongest at the level of description, in this case descriptions of television's assemblage and themes. For example, Tuchman (1974) and Williams (1975) have shown that elements of television form and news reportage subtly reinforce ruling-class values. Schlesinger (1978) demonstrates that the British Broadcasting Corporation's coverage of Northern Ireland affairs belies the image of impartiality and balance that the corporation professes; instead, such coverage favors the dominant Protestant class over its Catholic opponents. And Gitlin (1980), in an ingenious analysis of television's presentation of the American New Left, identifies a series of processes (for example, derogation) that could well have drained viewer support away from the New Left and delegitimized its position among the young. Finally, Dahlgren (1980) argues that television news suppresses "reflexive" (active) thinking about the citizen's role in politics, instead depicting citizens as helpless objects of government largesse or of political repression.

Again, however, the problem lies in assessing the actual impact of such depictions on the young. Hegemonic theorists rarely investigate children's perceptions of the media, apparently assuming that children see the same things in the media that the theorists themselves see. But various straws in the research wind dispute the hegemonic view of media effects on children.

To begin with, television does not uniformly portray the existing structure of authority in favorable ways. Indeed, Pride and Richards (1975) demonstrate that television news denigrates political authority in its presentation of ecological issues. The same conclusion may apply to other forms of news presentations (Berman and Stookey, 1980). Certainly the growing pattern of subjecting "authoritative" speeches and statements to "instant," often skeptical, analyses can hardly be seen as a way of buttressing authority. Of course, hegemonic theorists often argue that such criticism actually legitimizes the media's appearance of relative balance, a stance that works to the advantage of dominant classes. But this response, too, is mere assertion, not demonstration.

This observation, however, suggests a second criticism of the hegemonic approach to television's effects on the young. Specifically, evidence (Roberts, Pingree, and Hawkins, 1975; Berman and Stookey, 1980) indicates that young people who are attentive to television news and public affairs programs become not only highly informed politically but also more tolerant of political conflict and more hostile to authority than do their less attentive peers. These findings hardly conform to hegemonic expectations.

One of the most serious difficulties with the hegemonic argument is its apparent reluctance to eschew a "mass society" conception of media effects on the young. Ever since Lazarsfeld and Katz (1955), we have become aware that media viewing is not a solitary enterprise, in which vulnerable persons succumb to media domination, but is instead a social process, in which opinion leaders, group memberships, and peer conversations play major roles in determining impact. No recent studies of media effects on youthful political learning have begun to capture these processes in all their complexity, save for that body of studies which examines the role of media effects in influencing youthful attitudes toward violence. But these particular studies are only a bare beginning.

Finally, the hegemonic approach needs to consider evidence that some television depictions stimulate counternormative, antisystem behaviors among the most deprived sectors of society. For example, some studies show that ghetto disorders in the 1960s followed a path of media "contagion," in the sense that television coverage acquainted people with riot techniques and thus encouraged secondary outbreaks (Singer, 1970). Evidence also links television violence to the creation of aggressive tendencies among young viewers. Although youthful violence generally takes private, individual, nonpolitical forms, violence in *any* form constitutes a serious burden for a society and may even create a "crime problem" that strains the resources of dominant classes. Therefore, we would hardly expect secure hegemonic control of the media to stimulate rather than inhibit aggressive forms of youthful viewer response.

Attitudes Toward Social Class and Economic Structures. Perhaps the strongest single piece of evidence in support of the hegemonic model lies in the small body of research on children's attitudes toward social-class and economic structures. In his review of a number of early studies on the subject, Stacey (1977) corroborates hegemonic theory's contentions about early internalization of capitalist images among the young. Searing and Stern (1976) compared British and American high school students and report—contrary perhaps to expectations—that Americans internalize early a conception of steep, unjustified inequality. However, most of those studied believed that, as individuals, they could escape from the snares that would inevitably entrap their peers. More recently, Cummings and Taeble (1978) studied third, sixth, ninth, and twelfth graders in the American Southwest. They report that as students age they become increasingly opposed to unions, state intervention, and welfare, preferring to hold the individual rather than the system responsible for such persistent social problems as poverty. But the location of this study in the Southwest may account in part for these data; by contrast, Merelman (1971a, 1973, 1976) reports that many high school students in Madison, Wisconsin, attribute problems of poverty to social rather than individual conditions (for related cognitive development work, see Crain and Crain, 1976; Furth, 1980). Again, much further inquiry remains to be undertaken.

In a revealing recent study of adult attitudes toward economic stratification in the United States, Hochschild (1981) concludes that Americans develop a bifurcated social consciousness; that is, attitudes toward socialization and customs are highly egalitarian, whereas attitudes toward economics almost uniformly respect differentiation and inequality. Attitudes toward politics straddle the two realms; people apparently hope that liberal democratic political systems can somehow reconcile the tensions between economic inequality and cultural equality. Hochschild (1981, p. 264) sums up her findings by observing: "Thus, what appeared initially to be a paradox—Why do Americans, who pride themselves on legal and political equality, accept so much economic inequality?—becomes perfectly intelligible and even essential in this view. Belief in the necessity and justice of economic differentiation permits political equality to exist; belief in the existence of political equality permits economic differentiation to persist. The disjunction is the very essence of Western liberalism." Certainly, a stronger vindication of hegemonic theory would be hard to imagine; the various pieces of adult cognition reported by Hochschild add up to a delicately balanced portrait of hegemonic "false consciousness." Yet, paradoxically, we cannot trace this consciousness directly to the agencies of socialization that hegemonic theorists normally discuss.

Criticisms of Hegemonic Theory's Treatment of Socialization. Let us now discuss two serious criticisms of hegemonic theory's treatment of socialization. The first involves the apparent failure of state socialist systems—despite their coordinated, overt, governmentally controlled socialization programs—to have a major impact on the young. The second involves reforms in political education.

Certainly, we need not doubt the strength of efforts to create a socialist mentality among youth in such regimes as the Soviet Union, Cuba (Fagen, 1969; Hernandez, 1974; LeoGrande, 1977-78), and China (Whyte, 1977). In the Soviet Union, for example, the regime's socialization aspirations are directly implemented by youth branches of the Communist party, peer group and school-sponsored political education, and children's literature in an extensive library network (O'Dell, 1979). Later on, mandatory on-the-job political education courses take up the same socialization themes. All these Soviet efforts form a web of socialization "hegemony" that is infinitely more intricate and potentially powerful than anything found in liberal democracies.

How effective are these efforts? For obvious reasons it is difficult to answer this question conclusively. Nonetheless, studies of socialization in the Soviet Union cast doubt on the impact of regime efforts. In Cary's (1974) study of Soviet peer groups, most young people claimed that their families, rather than peer groups or party organization, were of primary political importance. Moreover, growing attachment to peer groups in adolescence appparently *alienates* members from the prosystem norms of youth organizations. In short, mechanisms of political socialization among adolescents do not mesh easily in the Soviet Union.

The situation appears to be equally discouraging for political education among adults. White (1977) reviews a number of Soviet government documents that suggest widespread disgust with political education courses. More telling was the sheer ineffectiveness of the education; half of the students questioned could not even define such basic Marxist concepts as "dictatorship of the proletariat." White concludes that there is only spotty acceptance of Marxist-Leninist ideology in the Soviet Union and that sentiments for system reform easily survive the educational efforts of the regime.

Hegemonic theory must also explain why schools have increasingly tried to reform their systems of political education. Curricula that incorporate Kohlberg's (1980) moral development framework and Crick and Heater's (1977) political literacy program attempt to arm students with concepts they can turn against class inequalities. Kohlberg's two advanced stages of moral reasoning are cognitively at odds with the levels of inequality current in industrial societies; efforts to promote moral reasoning, therefore, promise students a secure moral framework for reform efforts (Rawls, 1972). And Crick and Heater's efforts to focus British political education on political participation rather than on the British constitution hold out similar hopes. Of course, as Tapper and Salter (1978), Feldman (1980), and Weissberg (1981) all point out, the reform of political education cannot entirely evade prohegemonic elements of schooling. Still, the diffusion of these two reforms indicates that at least there is a taste for counterhegemonic socialization within institutions supposedly dominated entirely by ruling-class interests.

Political Socialization and Pluralist Theory

Though complex and varied, pluralist theories of politics differ dramatically from hegemonic and systems theories. For example, pluralist theory places less emphasis on attitudes toward authority than does systems analysis. In comparison with hegemonic theory, pluralism shows less interest in economic socialization and in school and media manipulation of the socialization process. What, then, *is* pluralism's focus? Pluralist theory lays primary emphasis on the creation of a public capable of looking after its own political interests, uncowed by authority; however, this public values the political institutions that it attempts to influence. It realizes how vulnerable these institutions are to conflict and how important such institutions are if public demands are to be met effectively. The pluralist model, therefore, envisages a public organized along essentially pragmatic but enduring ideological lines, capable of using the political system to represent, to compromise, and eventually to realize felt interests. Interest representation through flexible, firmly democratic, institutions—this is the heart of the pluralist model.

The major vehicle through which the public works its will in pluralist theory is the political party. Pluralists assert that citizens view political parties not only as extensions of their own durable personal identifications but also as occupants of a left-right (progressive-conservative) political system. The issue position of the party gives citizens the opportunity to realize their own most fundamental dispositions toward political reform or stability, toward expanded or contracted government intervention in the market, or toward generous or restrictive policies regarding individual rights. Again, however, ideological integration of the public via party adherence must always be balanced by consensual beliefs in political tolerance, majority rule, and minority rights. These "rules of the game" prevent necessary ideological and party competition from becoming pathologically conflictual. Of course, this picture requires that citizens develop participatory attitudes; otherwise, the parties cannot function as effective representative mechanisms.

Brief as it is, this overview permits us to portray a third ideal-typical "product" of political socialization. The pluralist model predicts that young people in liberal democracies will (1) develop enduring partisan identifications; (2) learn an ideological orientation to direct their political choice; (3) learn the rules of the game, especially tolerance for dissent; and (4) become truly participatory.

As for socialization agencies, pluralists emphasize the school and the family. The family's political orientations, manifested in both partisanship and ideology, pass from generation to generation, thereby stabilizing the polity as well as providing motivation for new generations to become politically involved. However, because the family is not really a *teaching* institution in the formal sense, it is ill placed to transmit complex rules of the democratic game or to provide specific participatory skills. In these respects it is the school that is most important. To sum up, pluralist theory leads us to examine the family as a major socializer of partisanship, ideology, and participatory motivation (through such psychological channels as self-esteem) and to investigate the school as a socializer of rules of the game and of specific participatory capabilities.

Partisan Identification. No subject has received more attention by political scientists in America than partisan identification. Yet no subject currently suffers greater ambiguity. There are numerous debates about the iterative character of partisanship as conventionally measured (Pierce and Sullivan, 1980), about the interplay between partisanship and other political orientations (Page and Jones, 1979), about the appropriate statistical models to employ in the study of partisanship, and about the number and character of dimensions (intensity, direction) partisanship contains (Dennis, 1981). These problems apply to studies of partisanship in young people as well as adults.

There are also problems that pertain specifically to partisanship among the young. Prominent among these is the sheer instability of youthful partisan identifications. For example, Vaillancourt and Niemi (1974) report that in only a two-month period, from December 1968 to January 1969, 25 percent of their sample of white fourth, sixth, and eighth graders shifted partisan identifications. And lest we assume that widespread short-term instability is confined to the young, Cundy (1980) reports that within only a few *weeks* 14 to 34 percent of the students in a college sociology class shifted their partisan identifications. The dimensions of the problem are clearly serious; in the most reliable and comprehensive study, Jennings and Niemi (1981, p. 49) report that roughly 40 percent of their eighteen-year-olds changed party identification by the time they were twenty-five.

A final difficulty involves the realization that socialization is a *process* as well as a *product* of learning; thus, we must always decide whether measurements taken at any single point in time or even at several time points reflect life-cycle factors general to all age cohorts at different times, generational effects peculiar to a particular age cohort, or period effects common to every age group in the society at the same time. Jennings and Niemi (1981) and Claggett (1981) have made sophisticated attempts to assess these effects.

Venturing conclusions about youthful partisanship is, therefore, a hazardous enterprise. Nevertheless, a review of the literature reveals certain patterns that deserve mention. These patterns essentially divide into two schools of thought, which differ from each other about the role of parental influences and about the sheer incidence of partisanship among the young. The first school of thought argues that partisanship is poorly socialized during the early years, principally because of the failure of the family to play an effective role. The second school agrees about the comparative weakness of partisanship among the young but refuses to blame the family entirely. Instead, it argues that the family's influence on partisanship is stronger than one might suspect from simply examining the low aggregate levels of partisanship among the young.

Estimates of partisan identification in childhood, adolescence, and youth reveal a mixed picture. For example, Jennings and Niemi (1981, p. 153) report an 11 percent increase in the number of Independents from age eighteen in 1965 to age twenty-five in 1973 (37 percent to 48 percent). Converse (1979) has attributed much of this acceleration to transient period effects; however, at least during this particular eight-year span, early socialization did not stabilize strong partisan identifications among most young people.

A dramatic recent study indicates even greater failure to socialize partisanship among the young (Dennis, 1982). Only 26 percent of this sample of ten- to
seventeen-year-olds in Wisconsin reported themselves to be unabashed partisans;
the remainder either vacillated between partisanship and independence or else
totally withdrew from the usual partisan terms of politics. Dennis concludes that
a "norm of independence" has emerged among young people, a norm that encourages young people to vote "for the person, not the party," and therefore to resist
party cues in voting (see also Hess and Torney, 1967). Earlier, Merelman (1971a)
reported that fully half of a sample of sixth, ninth, and twelfth graders in Los
Angeles in 1968 refused to classify themselves as either Republican or Democrat.
Interestingly, this proportion did not decline with age. Finally, there is even some
evidence that the propensity of young people to refuse partisanship is no longer
a purely American phenomenon. Barnes and Kaase (1979, p. 480) report large
numbers of "Independents" among young people in other Western democracies.
Indeed, many were reluctant to be classified even as "fairly close" to the parties
they finally admitted to preferring. Comparably low rates of partisanship in Canadian children are reported by Zureik (1975, p. 45).

Analysts are also in general agreement about the degree of similarity
between parents and youth in partisan identification. Jennings and Niemi (1974)
set the standard by reporting a .48 correlation between eighteen-year-olds and their
parents in 1965, with a decline to .34 by 1973. Other estimates (Niemi, Ross, and
Alexander, 1978; Niemi, Katz, and Newman, 1980; Dennis, 1982) rarely rise above
these correlations, although Styskal and Sullivan (1975) report unusually high
(and perhaps inflated) correlations for social science students at three colleges in
the late 1960s. Nevertheless, most of the pertinent evidence reveals considerable
slippage in the transmission of partisanship from parents to children. Surprisingly
enough, the partisan gap between parents and children is even larger in most
other Western countries, despite the generally stronger party systems in these
countries (Barnes and Kaase, 1979, p. 459).

As we have said, there are two schools of thought about these findings. One
school minimizes them. For example, Tedin (1974, 1980) reports that parents may
enjoy great success in transmitting not only partisan preferences but also issue
attitudes, as long as they communicate freely and easily with their children and
also attribute great salience to politics (see also Kraut and Lewis, 1975). Moreover,
Tedin and others note that slippage usually involves only the intensity of commitment to a parental party rather than conversion to another party. And Cundy
(1979a) argues that, whatever their other liabilities, parents always enjoy a socialization advantage over peers with regard to partisan identification.

Unfortunately, these observations do not take into account recent alterations
in family structure, which may have seriously weakened the family's impact on
partisanship. For example, the traditional image of monolithic parental partisanship now appears mythical; Beck and Jennings (1975) found high (.69), but by no
means total, partisan agreement between parents. Moreover, much recent evidence
(Jennings and Niemi, 1974) suggests that mothers play a larger independent role
in partisan socialization than was once thought to be the case. In situations of
divided parental loyalties, therefore, it should not be automatically assumed that
either parent prevails, thereby establishing a family partisan norm. Instead, the
child may abandon partisanship entirely in order to avoid an unpleasant choice.

Nor are parents themselves as stable in their partisan attachments as perhaps they once were. Finally, the increase of single-parent families obviously weakens the transmission of partisan identification, for such transmission thrives when two parents agree on partisanship. For all these reasons, the pluralist model fares poorly in recent research on partisan identification among children.

Learning of Ideology. If the socialization of partisanship proves somewhat disappointing from the point of view of pluralist theory, we perhaps should expect even less from research into the learning of ideology. After all, few adults spontaneously use a left-right ideological spectrum to analyze politics, as Converse (1964) first noted in a classic article (see also Barnes and Kaase, 1979; Sullivan, Piereson, Marcus, and Feldman, 1979). We would therefore hardly expect to find the socialization process particularly effective as a teacher of ideology. Nevertheless, socialization could play an important role should we discover that what little ideological thinking does emerge develops during the early years. Three or four specific findings make this possibility slim, however.

For one thing young people have trouble connecting partisanship to larger questions of ideology. In the United States, for example, young people see the parties as vehicles for organizing *elections* rather than for expressing ideology. In Britain young people visualize the parties as institutions of governance and social control rather than as articulators of a consistent ideological view (Caldeira and Greenstein, 1978). Only in France do young people connect parties to an ideological perspective (Percheron, 1978).

Nevertheless, the fact is that comparatively few young people possess a consistent ideological view of politics. For example, in Merelman's (1971a) study, only the weakest sort of left-right ideological spectrum had emerged among twelfth-grade students. And Barnes and Kaase (1979), in their comparative study of five Western democracies, found virtually no correlation at all between age and ideological conceptualization.

In addition, there is apparently little parental impact on the ideologies and policy attitudes of young people (Barnes and Kaase, 1979). In 1965 parent-child resemblance on policy opinions was at best moderate, with real strength evident only in those areas (school prayers, racial integration) where parents expressed themselves vigorously to their children. Most telling, however, is the fact that parental opinions on these and other political issues in 1965 were almost entirely unrelated to children's opinions eight years later. Thus, socialization to conservative or liberal ideology does not seem to possess even the durability that socialization to partisan identification possesses.

An important reason for the weakness of early ideological learning lies in the insensitivity of most young people to social-class influences. As Sigel and Hoskin (1981, p. 194) put it in their American study: "Class-based differences [in political attitudes] are relatively small for young people." Class differences in political opinions and ideological preferences do emerge eventually, but only after early socialization has run its course. (But see Berg and Mussen, 1976.) Whether this weakness results from failures in cognitive development, in the weak structuring of social class along neighborhood or familial lines, or from the sheer fuzziness of class in America (Sigel and Hoskin, 1981) is unclear. Nevertheless, a class context for the learning of ideology is not strong among most children.

Development of Tolerance of Dissent. A third area of political socialization research that illuminates pluralist theory focuses on political tolerance. At the outset the key question involves the sheer extent of political tolerance among young people. Merelman (1971b) found unexpectedly slight rates of movement toward greater support for freedom of speech in the adolescent years. Zellman and Sears (1971) found considerable incoherence and contradiction in the tolerance-related attitudes of fifth and sixth graders. They observed that biased attitudes toward groups and situations easily overrode the few general norms of tolerance among the young. In a quite interesting study, Patterson (1979) relates the secure learning of tolerance to accelerated moral development in childhood; that is, tolerance depends on substantial increases in the quality of moral reasoning. Patterson's findings suggest that the conventional levels of moral reasoning in the general public place severe limits on the youthful internalization of tolerance.

But if socialization to tolerance is weak, how can we account for those increases in public tolerance found in Glenn's (1980) recent research? And how can we explain the apparently favorable, enduring impact of higher education on tolerance (Hyman and Wright, 1979)? Some critics (Jackman, 1978; Jackman and Muha, 1983) attribute these optimistic findings to biases in the conceptualization of tolerance. They contend that most of the relevant studies ignore aspects of intolerance that are common among well-educated persons. In the most searching analysis of the subject, Sullivan, Piereson, and Marcus (1982) call recent optimistic findings "illusory." They claim that researchers have been misled by an overconcentration on attitudes toward left-wing groups and inattention to attitudes toward the right. They then conclude that higher education does not increase tolerance of the right, but only tolerance of the left.

Sullivan, Piereson, and Marcus argue that "pluralistic" intolerance best describes public attitudes. Because no particular group is universally condemned, a pluralist polity survives. But pluralistic intolerance represents a considerable dampening of optimism about *increases* in tolerance. In particular, it denies the argument that a strong norm of general tolerance gradually overcomes group-related attitudes during the socialization process. This conclusion gains support from the finding of Glock and associates (1975) that many supposedly well-educated, upper-middle-class adolescents manifest strong racial prejudices. It is also supported by findings that place the learning of religious and racial attitudes earlier in the socialization cycle than the general norm of tolerance itself. Certainly, *early* learning of tolerance would help stabilize the norm.

Political Participation. The last socialization component of the pluralist model that is relevant to our examination is political participation. It is well known that a quite small proportion of the adult public participates in political activities (Milbrath and Goel, 1977). But if we could discover a *high* proportion of politically involved young people, we could perhaps argue that socialization produces "youthful idealism" and, therefore, that the socialization process in this one respect supports the pluralist model. Unfortunately, we can arrive at no such favorable judgment. The proportion of adolescents involved in political activities is minuscule. Even in the early 1970s, despite the stimulation of Vietnam and Watergate, Sigel and Hoskin (1981, p. 142) found only 2 percent of their high school sample involved in political activities. It is obvious that political activity generally ranks extremely low among student priorities.

However, this negative conclusion does not hold up completely once we broaden our conception of political participation. Sigel and Hoskin point out that sizable proportions of their sample were involved regularly in service organizations, in neighborhood organizations, and in church-related activities. In these quasi-political activities, they undoubtedly learn politically useful skills. But they shy away from pluralist-style political organizations. Why should this be so?

In part, of course, the answer lies in the fact that people cannot vote before they become eighteen. But other factors also play a role—chief among them the fact that schools rarely develop effective programs to give young people political experience in the community (Newman, 1981). Such programs may be quite effective as socializers, as Hanks and Eckland (1978) intimate. In addition, there is evidence that participation in politically related school activities, such as student council, inculcates durable norms of political participation (Hanks, 1981). Thus, the school could do more to socialize participatory habits among the young.

In any case, whatever the positive effects of socialization toward participation during the school years, these effects pale next to the impact of adult social-class position on political involvement. As both Acock and Scott (1980) and Verba, Nie, and Kim (1978) report, the more demanding both in visibility and time expenditure the type of political activity one examines, the more powerfully does class position determine participation levels. Class-based advantages massively favor the middle class over the working class in terms of participation. The net result of all these influences, as Verba, Nie, and Kim note, is that political participation in the United States exacerbates social-class inequalities, rather than reducing them in conformity to pluralist theory.

Political Socialization and Conflict Theory

Although Marxism is currently the prominent example of conflict theory in political sociology, Marxism's recent transformation into hegemonic theory has altered its image. In any case, Marxism is not the only form of conflict theory; various other approaches also regard enduring antagonisms between social groups as the norm rather than the exception in politics. In this section we draw on conflict theories outside the Marxist tradition. These theories have in common certain presumptions about the learning of political attitudes, as well as about the relationship between political socialization and the political system.

We can detect two forms of non-Marxist political conflict theory. One form represents an extension of Weberian insights about the antagonistic relations of dominant to subordinate social groups. This tradition locates endemic conflict in the sheer existence of authority, hierarchy, or inequality in any form. The Weberian tradition today is represented by Parkin's (1979) discussion of conflictual status-group practices of exclusion and inclusion, Eckstein's (1975) theory of political authority, Goode's (1978) theory of prestige as a conflict resource, and Blau's (1964) theory of unequal institutionalized exchange. These theories conceive of a stratified society divided hierarchically into conflicting status groups arrayed against each other along one or several noncumulative axes of domination—including prestige, authority, power, occupation, and wealth.

A second variant of conflict theory concentrates on conflicts among equals rather than on conflict between dominants and subordinates. Scholars in this tradition are impressed by defections from group solidarity within, say, a working class (Runciman, 1966), or by the defection of progressive upper-class "intellectuals" from their class "interests" in conservatism. This body of theory argues that fundamental social and political transformations take place only through the decay and fragmentation of ruling groups. A particularly imaginative example of such a theory is that of Bell (1976), who argues that progressive strains in the culture of capitalism render the dominant capitalist class increasingly incapable of governing effectively.

We will discuss both of these variants of conflict theory, first by considering whether research in political socialization illuminates conflict between dominants and subordinates, then by considering recent socialization theory and research relevant to the question of disarray among dominant groups. In both conflict approaches, however, we shall be focusing on essentially the same ideal socialization type, formally comparable to the socialization/personality types we have examined for the three other political theories. Specifically, conflict theories predict that socialization will create young people who are strongly identified with their own status group; who are aware of antagonisms between their group and others; who are willing to circumvent existing normative procedures in order to advance their own group's fortunes; and who are drawn to norms of justice, redistribution, equality, and equity that protect their own group at the expense of others. In short, we look for socialization to create conflicting group consciousness (Giddens, 1975; Jackman and Senter, 1984).

Class Awareness. Research on class awareness in childhood reveals a complex pattern. It does not support the view that children lack class awareness or the view that they always develop class consciousness as a component of learning. Instead, the evidence is mixed. From a purely cognitive standpoint, the evidence suggests (Crain and Crain, 1976; Searing and Stern, 1976; Connell, 1977; Stacey, 1977) that, rather early in the socialization process, young people develop class-based schemas of society. They believe that society is organized in class hierarchies, and they associate class differences with unequal "styles of life" and levels of "respect." But, as Furth (1980) points out, children have trouble connecting abstract concepts, such as inequality, to the concrete class distinctions they perceive. Therefore, they rarely generalize from specific aspects of social class to universal political practices or to directions for remedial action. (See also Damon, 1977.)

From an emotional standpoint, young people seem to be fairly sensitive to examples of injustice, unfairness, and inequity. Sympathetic emotional identification with the underdog appears to grow more rapidly than cognitive capacity; feeling outruns thought. Indeed, some analyses reveal a strong sense of compassion in childhood (Crain and Crain, 1976; Moore and others, 1976), complete with expressions of altruism and care for the distressed and the injured. Thus, some cognitive and affective materials that might prove helpful in constructing class-based ideologies of conflict do emerge early in the socialization cycle. But most authors do not detect such ideologies. For example, Connell (1977, p. 150) argues that "class is not salient as a frame of reference for judging the self"; and Merelman (1974) found that in Britain, where class is traditionally a dominant component of social life, fewer young people identify themselves in class terms than in terms of gender, nationality, or personal interests. And so we confront an interesting question: Why does the young person not typically unite his class awareness, his sympathy for the downtrodden, and his intuition of injustice, and in so doing construct a fully class-conscious identity?

Three factors help explain this puzzling phenomenon. The first is that many young people accept a functionalist explanation for class inequalities; they argue that inequality promotes the productive efficiency of societies. They reason that the price of productivity is some amount of injustice (Simmons and Rosenberg, 1971). Second, many young people from all class backgrounds feel a cognitive pull toward "middle-class" self-identification; this pull encourages them to avoid a starkly dichotomized, conflictual picture of social class. For the young, middle-class self-identification becomes a social half-way house that offers hope for a peaceful, gradual amelioration of class inequalities (see Robinson and Bell, 1978). Finally, many young people accept the reality of class for *others* but deny the relevance of class to themselves. They conceive of class placement for themselves as an *achieved* phenomenon, one they can manipulate through talent, hard work, or simple good fortune. Therefore, they believe that they themselves can succeed without the collective political action that class conflict requires (Searing and Stern, 1976).

The safest conclusion we can offer is that youthful class identification is not by itself strong enough to create a conflict perspective on society. However, socialization to class awareness may combine with other forms of socialization to produce such a perspective. In France, for example, political socialization produces strong ideological cleavages among young people (Percheron, 1978; Caldeira and Greenstein, 1978). Those from high social-class backgrounds often attend elite Catholic schools, where they learn to identify closely with the traditional right in French politics; meanwhile, young people from more modest class backgrounds gravitate toward the secular public schools, where they learn a more leftist political ideology. In France political socialization manages to combine several axes of learning—class, religion, tradition versus modernity—into conflict consciousness in childhood. (See also Schoenfeld, 1976; and, for Canada, Zureik and Pike, 1975, p. 263 ff.)

But socialization cannot itself create true subcultural conflict in the extreme forms of force and violence. Factors other than socialization must also play a role. One such factor appears to be the prior existence of civil conflict via guerrilla forces. Guerrilla conflict affords young people real-life experiences and models. Another factor is the presence of charismatic leaders in conflicting groups. Here we encounter an interesting reversal of the usual "benevolent leader" hypothesis, for in this case identification with the benevolent leader encourages young people to adopt violence and conflict between competing groups as a way of life, rather than, as in the American context, to establish a trusting pattern of identification with people in other social groups.

A primary example of how political socialization can train young people to accept violence may be found in Northern Ireland. Russell (1977) interviewed 3,000 schoolboys aged eight to fourteen and found that majorities among both Protestants and Catholics condoned violence in behalf of their own group's position on Ulster. Moreover, twice as many Protestant as Catholic youths believed that the Ulster government favored "people like them." Thus, the foundations of sectarian conflict appear early in Northern Ireland. Still, there are mitigating factors; Russell reports that religiously mixed friendship groups diminish the tendency among young people to accept violence, and positive attitudes toward teachers are associated with positive attitudes toward the regime. Thus, even the most conflictual socialization processes continue to produce some support for authority, for the status quo, and for political quiescence.

The way in which charismatic leaders help to socialize young people to a conflict perspective is illustrated in a study of the Palestine Liberation Organization (PLO). In the absence of a national entity on which to focus, young Palestinians attach themselves strongly to Yassir Arafat, who, according to Farah (1980, p. 481), serves as a "crucial link between these Palestinian children and the PLO." Trust in the Palestine Liberation Organization among 240 ten- to sixteen-year-old Palestinians depended substantially on positive attitudes toward Arafat. Indeed, research in political socialization could usefully explore many elements of a Weberian perspective on charisma.

Acceptance of Conflict as Means for Conducting Politics. Early socialization research pictured young people as too emotionally and cognitively fragile to accept system-disturbing conflict as a common mode of politics. Even by adolescence, the argument went, most young people would accept only dissent within *existing* system boundaries. But socialization ruled out anything stronger. Today, however, the socialization process in Western democracies has reached out to embrace protest as a legitimate form of political action. Acceptance of protest is found among children from privileged as well as underprivileged backgrounds (Campbell, 1979; Grove and others, 1974). As Sigel and Hoskin (1981, p. 271) put it: "Boycotts and demonstrations formerly considered unconventional are behaviors with which [adolescents] are familiar and which many consider employing when political frustrations reach a certain painful level." Barnes and Kaase (1979), along with Marsh (1975), argue that various extralegal forms of protest now stand alongside more traditional means of political influence, serving to widen the adolescent's repertoire of legitimate action.

However, the more risky or coercive extralegal action becomes, the less support such behavior receives in the socialization process. Moreover, accepting the legitimacy of protest for *others* does not necessarily signify that a person is willing to engage in protest himself. This discrepancy perhaps helps explain why the proportion of young people who actually engaged in protests during the Vietnam War was exaggerated by the media. The media confused a climate of opinion with instances of actual behavior.

Conflict Within Dominant Groups. The formation of an "adversarial" subculture (Wildavsky, 1982) within dominant groups has been a topic of general interest ever since the 1960s, when many affluent students at prestigious universities led protests against policies that appeared to have been in their long-run material interests. Do large numbers of the bourgeois young learn to bite the hand that feeds them?

Certainly, the role of universities in this regard commands our attention. For example, Braungart and Braungart (1975) identify university social science departments as important socializers of antisystem values, and O'Connor (1975) argues that students who possess advanced moral reasoning skills gravitate toward universities which confirm hostility to the status quo. Such phenomena extend even to such unpromising sites as Franco's Spain (Maravall, 1976). Is it possible that, as perceived social-class cleavages decline in advanced industrial societies (Wright and Holub, 1979), conflict consciousness *within* dominant groups may emerge ever more vigorously?

The foremost exponent of this point of view is Inglehart (1977, 1981), who argues that affluence has created a new set of "postindustrial" values favorable to greater equity, fairness, and quality of life. These values appeal to a sizable proportion of middle-class youth, who, once the process of political recruitment carries them into positions of power, implement their values and alter the entire course of public policy (see also Kraus and Fendrich, 1980).

Inglehart's theory, though provocative, presents several problems. Inglehart admits that only a minority of young people ever actually absorb postbourgeois views in advanced industrial societies. Moreover, he is unable to identify the socialization processes by which postbourgeois values develop. "Affluence" itself can provide only the conditions for such values, but the actual socialization mechanisms remain hidden in Inglehart's account. In addition, Inglehart may have overestimated both the intensity of middle-class youth's attachment to postbourgeois values and the strength of conservative countervalues among working-class youth. Marsh (1975) claims that among affluent British youth postbourgeois loyalties are superficial. Meanwhile, in Japan Flanagan (1979) has identified a large segment of working-class youth who are wedded to conservative parties not because of *material* imperatives but, rather, because of a genuine, enduring commitment to traditional *values*. Thus, the postbourgeois sensibility may find itself on the defensive even in "postindustrial" societies.

Moreover, there are contradictory pressures even among the genuinely postbourgeois. As we have seen, a chief agent of postbourgeois values is higher education. But, as Weiner and Eckland (1979, p. 928) point out: "The socializing effects [liberal] of higher education are masked to some extent by the status allocation function [social mobility] of higher education, but more significantly by the fact that going to college is associated with both class origins and the inherited partisan loyalties of one's parents." Thus, the status allocation effects of even a postbourgeois college education may place young people in settings where they become gradually more exposed to conventional pressures. Over time, therefore, the strength of their postbourgeois identifications may erode.

Finally, a permanent conflict between bourgeois and postbourgeois status groups may require structures of mobilization. Although traditional theories of class conflict suffer from many difficulties, they do identify certain foci of organization—such as the shop floor, the union hall, the ethnic neighborhood, the mass movement, and the revolutionary party. But educated postbourgeois people generally disdain the kinds of organized authority necessary to operate such conflict-based institutions. Because the postbourgeois mentality does not gravitate toward such institutions, its conflict consciousness remains essentially individualistic, sectarian, or even romantically utopian (Berger, 1980). The situation is ironic, in that older theories of conflictual socialization excelled at describing conflict strategies and structures—"military campaigns," as it were—but failed to produce soldiers for their campaigns. By contrast, Inglehart's theories describe large armies but produce few viable campaigns. The older view imagines wars without foot soldiers; the newer view imagines foot soldiers who do not go to war. Both views are incomplete.

Need for a New Paradigm

It should be clear from our review of the literature that political socialization does not transmit any single one of our four models to the exclusion of the others. Some young people may accept one of these models of society sometimes, and a few may even cleave to a single model throughout their entire lives. But most people do not hold one of these models unalterably or exclusively; if they did, our survey of the literature would have turned up a more consistent set of conclusions than we have been able to muster. Indeed, it is this very absence of a clear pattern that tempts us to ask one additional question: "Why is there no single, stable socialization pattern to a single model of society?" This is probably the most important question we can now ask about the future of political socialization as a field.

An initial answer to our question involves weaknesses in the political institutions that are the foci of the four models. These institutions have proved to be incapable of retaining the loyalty of older generations and, therefore, of encouraging older generations to socialize loyalty to the institutions.

The systems model considers legitimate authorities (most often heads of state) to be primary recipients of socialized loyalty. Yet in recent years the heads of state in many Western countries have undermined the positive image that the systems model asserts. Scandals such as the Watergate affair obviously give good reason for young people in America to reject the appeals of legitimate authority (Arterton, 1974, 1975). But a less dramatic, though more universal, alteration in the structure of political authority may in the long run be more important: the disappearance of charismatic leaders. The strong leader who epitomizes legitimate authority—a Churchill, De Gaulle, Eisenhower, Adenauer, Nehru, Sukarno, or Nkrumah—is the sort of leader for whom the systems model of socialization works best (Nyomarky, 1967). But contemporary politics does not favor such leaders.

The pluralist model contends that instruments of representation—political parties, interest groups, voluntary associations—are objects of socialized loyalty. But in most parts of the world these institutions have proved increasingly unwieldy as controllers of their societies. Even in England—the citadel of stable two-party politics in the Western world—the politics of party coalition is not beyond the edge of possibility (Crewe and Sarlvik, 1983). Developments such as these weaken the pluralist model in the socialization process.

The conflict model also has suffered, principally because its main actors—unions and working-class political parties—no longer command as much strength as they once enjoyed. Reasons for this decline vary from country to country but seem in most places to involve increased social mobility and the embourgeoisement of the working class (Mann, 1973). Comparable processes of secularization and linguistic assimilation undercut potentially conflictual religious and linguistic loyalties. The result is that the institutions toward which conflictual socialization might be directed are less appealing than they once were.

Finally, the hegemonic model postulates that people will feel loyalty toward the vast economic structures which dominate their lives (Abercrombie, Hill, and Turner, 1980). But the model does not consider the possibility that pervasive cyclical weaknesses both in socialist and capitalist systems might undercut their economic promises and their political viability. Weaknesses in command economies (poor planning, persistent shortages, inefficiencies) and in market systems (inflation, chronic unemployment, severe consumption inequalities) are more visible now than at any time in the past. Moreover, increased dependence of all industrialized economies on expensive materials in uncertain supply has weakened the economic performance of industrialized societies. The objective basis for a hegemonic model in the socialization process, therefore, is perhaps weaker today than it has been at any time since the 1930s.

We have also seen, however, that under some conditions each of these four images of society does get socialized. In other words, we are not dealing with an *absence* of political socialization but, rather, with a new process of socialization, one in which an unprecedented range of social images emerges for young people to choose among. A novel research question thus emerges: How does the socialization process create "rules" for choosing among images of society? This question directs us toward those "deep cognitive structures" of society that structuralists (for example, Leach, 1976) have attempted to describe. Indeed, generalized to the societal level, these patterns of individual choice can be thought of as the meta-culture of a society (Wentworth, 1980, pp. 60-61).

From a Vertical to a Lateral Theory. If new research in socialization is to investigate the development of rules for choosing an image of society, this problem must be connected to alterations in the process of socialization itself. Uncertainty among multiple social models—and the consequent need for rules of choice—develops most easily when socialization loses its vertical or hierarchical character, as embodied in the traditional conception of value transmission from older to younger generations via personal tutelage. These vertical models—typified by the four theories we have just examined—assume that older generations are repositories of wisdom, which they pass intact to the young. And because older people are generally less well educated than the younger generation will eventually *become*, the former are prone to pass on single, simple models rather than several models whose interrelations are complex. It follows, therefore, that alteration in the age grading of society may be a crucial condition for turning a society from vertical to *lateral* forms of socialization. By "lateral socialization" I refer to the development of horizontally connected agents of socialization who compete with one another to reach the young and, in the process, deliver quite varying images of society.

The problem of age as an element of social structure, thus, finally takes a place of importance in our account. One of the features of modern societies, as Eisenstadt (1956) points out, is that age loses its priority as a criterion either for attributing deference or for recruiting people to positions of power. Being older no longer renders a parent automatically worthy of respect, nor a worker worthy of advancement or reward. The same thing is true for kinship. The accident of blood relationship or kinship proximity loses legitimacy as a basis for according respect within families or for recruiting people to occupational and political roles. In the private sphere, age and kinship increasingly take second place to qualities of character and personality (such as compassion, warmth, and kindness), which do not necessarily follow age grades or bloodlines (Schneider, 1968; Merelman, 1980b). In the public world, "merit" as "objectively" (impersonally) measured takes precedence over age and kinship status.

Other factors newly common to industrialized societies have also promoted the movement from vertical to lateral processes of socialization. One such factor is the increased absorption of middle-class women into the world of work. A work life gives such women greater parity with their husbands in the socialization of children (Sapiro, 1983). Therefore, should their political views diverge from their husbands', they may have an independent impact on the political learning of their children. The result is a tendency toward lateral socialization. Young people absorb new social images through a multiplicity of socialization agencies.

A closely related phenomenon is the high levels of social and geographical mobility that characterize most industrialized societies. Although such mobility has little effect on collective inequalities, it does expand the range of stimuli to which individual young persons are exposed. For example, children whose parents move from working-class to middle-class positions are often exposed to conflict models of society in their early years and to pluralist models later on (Form and Huber, 1973). The result, undoubtedly, is some degree of choice and indecision.

A third factor that promotes lateralization and choice is novel forms of political education. Political education has usually served to enhance state domination over the socialization process. Although the fruits of this effort have often been overestimated (as we have seen), state control has usually limited the power of teachers and restricted curricula choice (Bowles and Gintis, 1976). In recent years, however, the range of maneuver afforded educators has broadened, and with this broadening have come conflicts between models of society in the educational process (Tapper and Salter, 1978). In many places teachers have developed professional ideologies and associations that give them some independence from direct state controls. Teacher unions concern themselves mainly with matters of employment and bread-and-butter issues, but they do occasionally contest aspects of curricula and teacher conduct in the classroom. Finally, innovative political educational curricula teach students to consider many different political views (Heater and Gillespie, 1981). All these factors make the classroom less a forum for the inculcation of single models of society and more a forum for the consideration of multiple images.

But underneath these surface alterations that promote a lateralization process lies a more fundamental evolution: the arrival of a new mentality or, indeed, social ethic. This ethic enjoins people to choose their own paths in life, unhindered by traditional loyalties to region, religion, and other primordial groups. As Huntington (1981) has noted, the democratic ethos encourages people not to assume a value simply on the word of others but instead to involve commitment, consent, and free choice in each act of allegiance. Although there are many differences between utilitarian rationalism and existential "leaps of faith," both share a belief that only the individual, alone with his or her conscience, can make authentic choices in politics. The ideological penumbra that in traditional societies grants automatic authority to certain agencies of socialization has dissolved under the impact of democratic individualism. As a result, even quite young children stand as arbiters of their own political fate. They may choose to be like the consumer who makes essentially trivial selections from a menu of advertised items or to be "true believers" for whom choice is an irretrievable commitment. But in either case they must choose.

Qualities of Lateral Socialization. For all these reasons, it is hardly surprising that socialization should increasingly follow a lateral rather than a vertical form. It remains for us briefly to describe some qualities of lateral socialization. Perhaps the most important component of any socialization process is not its manifest content (partisanship, issues, and the like) but the implicit images of power and society that the socialization process itself models. The question thus becomes one of tracing the implicit images of society embedded in the lateral socialization process.

Lateral socialization is a process in which relationships are voluntary, egalitarian, and transient. There is little formal structure, and influence must be won through sentimental attachments. Because there is no center of formal authority in the socialization process, nothing can be assumed from the outset about the consequences of socialization. Instead, sentimental attachments are situated in informal, temporary, though affectively appealing, structures of learning (such as peer groups or mass media viewing). Often the sentimental attachments that dominate the lateral socialization process are tenuous, fragile, subject to fads, and open to unpredictable but disruptive intrusions. It is obvious that this model of socialization diverges significantly from the four frameworks of political socialization that dominated our previous discussion.

The scope of our discussion makes it impossible to describe how a lateralized socialization process produces choices among the four models of society newly available to young people. Research relevant to this question lies in such areas as cognitive psychology, information processing, risk taking, and "script" construction (Schank and Abelson, 1977). This research has yet to make its way into the study of political socialization. Until it does—taking its place alongside Freudian, behaviorist, and cognitive developmental models of learning, which have dominated studies of political learning—elucidation of the rules that structure choice among the four models will remain elusive.

More important for the moment, however, is a matter of theory. Lateral *processes* of socialization are incongruent with the vertical models of society, which are their *content*. Lateral processes are egalitarian, transient, choice making, and individualized. Meanwhile, our models of society view people as subordinate to collectivities, deferential to leaders, and tied to stable hierarchies. Thus, in structural-functional terms, we encounter strain between a lateralized socialization process and the political system psychologically experienced (Smelser, 1962). This strain may prevent the four models, either alone or in combination, from receiving effective diffusion. The political significance of such a lacuna can be only a matter of speculation, but surely alienation, apathy, and even rebellion could be natural consequences (Smelser, 1962).

The question must be addressed from the side of political institutions as well as from the side of the mass public. Customarily, models of socialization place uppermost the question of mass support for political institutions. Such models imply that failures of socialization threaten political institutions. Yet the situation is not one-sided, for complex lateral processes that produce mass indecision or alienation rather than allegiance threaten mass publics as well as their leaders. The reason is that leaders feel threatened when they sense themselves losing the support of rising generations. While this fact has been recognized in previous research, what has not been sufficiently appreciated is that mass support often inhibits leaders in their treatment of followers. Mass support constitutes an implicit moral claim that leaders not abuse their followers' trust. When lateral socialization dissolves trust, the respect of leaders for followers may also vanish, opening followers to forms of manipulation and repression on a scale never before imagined. Why, after all, should leaders feel obligated to refrain from oppressing people who no longer seem to trust them?

We therefore close on a cautionary note for the political process, but a hopeful note for the study of political socialization. The field of political socialization is not at a dead end; rather, it is on the verge of opening new theoretical doors and, therefore, of fulfilling the promise of its pioneering days.

References

Abercrombie, N., Hill, S., and Turner, B. S. *The Dominant Ideology Thesis.* London: Allen & Unwin, 1980.

Abramson, P. R. *Generational Change in American Politics.* Lexington, Mass.: Heath, 1975.

Abramson, P. R. *The Political Socialization of Black Americans.* New York: Free Press, 1977.

Abramson, P. R. *Political Attitudes in America: Formation and Change.* New York: W. H. Freeman, 1983.

Abramson, P. R., and Finifter, A. "On the Meaning of Political Trust: New Evidence from Items Introduced in 1978." *American Journal of Political Science,* 1981, *25,* 297–308.

Acock, A., and Scott, W. "A Model for Predicting Behavior: The Effect of Attitude and Social Class on High and Low Visibility Political Participation." *Social Psychology Quarterly,* 1980, *44,* 59–72.

Adelson, J. "The Political Imagination of the Young Adolescent." In J. Kagan and R. Coles (eds.), *12 to 16: Early Adolescence.* New York: Norton, 1972.

Almond, G., and Verba, S. (eds.). *The Civic Culture Revisited.* Boston: Little, Brown, 1980.

Anyon, J. "Ideology and United States History Textbooks." *Harvard Educational Review,* 1980, *50,* 361–386.

Arterton, F. C. "The Impact of Watergate on Children's Attitudes Toward Authority." *Political Science Quarterly,* 1974, *89,* 269–288.

Arterton, F. C. "Watergate and Children's Attitudes Toward Political Authority Revisited." *Political Science Quarterly,* 1975, *90,* 477–496.

Barnes, S., and Kaase, M. (eds.). *Political Action: Mass Participation in Five Western Democracies.* Beverly Hills, Calif.: Sage, 1979.

Beck, P. A., and Jennings, M. K. "Parents as 'Middlepersons' in Political Socialization." *Journal of Politics,* 1975, *37,* 83–107.

Bell, D. *The End of Ideology.* New York: Macmillan, 1961.

Bell, D. *The Cultural Contradictions of Capitalism.* New York: Basic Books, 1976.

Berg, N. E., and Mussen, P. "Social Class Differences in Adolescents' Sociopolitical Opinions." *Youth and Society,* 1976, *8,* 177–203.

Berger, B. *The Survival of a Counter-Culture.* Berkeley: University of California Press, 1980.

Berman, D., and Stookey, J. A. "Adolescents, Television, and Support for Government." *Public Opinion Quarterly,* 1980, *44,* 33–41.

Blau, P. *Exchange and Power in Social Life.* New York: Wiley, 1964.

Bowles, S., and Gintis, H. *Schooling in Capitalist America.* New York: Basic Books, 1976.

Braungart, R., and Braungart, M. "Family, School, and Personal Political Factors in Student Politics." *Journal of Marriage and the Family,* 1975, *37,* 823–841.

Buckley, W. *Sociology and Modern Systems Theory.* Englewood Cliffs, N.J.: Prentice-Hall, 1967.

Caldeira, G. A., and Greenstein, F. I. "Partisan Orientation and Political Socialization in Britain, France, and the United States." *Political Science Quarterly,* 1978, *93,* 35–51.

Campbell, B. "Theory Building in Political Socialization: Explorations of Political Trust and Social Learning Theory." *American Politics Quarterly,* 1979, *7,* 453–469.

Cary, C. D. "Peer Groups in the Political Socialization of Soviet School Children." *Social Science Quarterly,* 1974, *55,* 451–462.

Claggett, W. "Partisan Acquisition Versus Partisan Intensity: Life-Cycle, Generation, and Period Effects, 1952–1972."*American Journal of Political Science,* 1981, *25,* 193–215.

Coleman, J., and others. *Equal Educational Opportunity.* Washington, D.C.: U.S. Government Printing Office, 1965.

Connell, R. W. *Ruling Class, Ruling Culture.* Cambridge, England: Cambridge University Press, 1977.

Converse, P. E. "The Nature of Belief Systems in Mass Publics." In D. Apter (ed.), *Ideology and Discontent.* New York: Free Press, 1964.

Converse, P. E. "Comment: Rejoinder to Abramson." *American Journal of Political Science,* 1979, *23,* 97–100.

Crain, W., and Crain, E. "Age Trends in Political Thinking: Dissent, Voting, and the Distribution of Wealth." *Journal of Psychology,* 1976, *41,* 179–190.

Crewe, I., and Sarlvik, B. *Decade of Dealignment.* Cambridge, England: Cambridge University Press, 1983.

Crick, B., and Heater, D. *Essays on Political Education.* London: Taylor & Francis, 1977.

Cummings, S., and Taeble, D. "Economic Socialization of Children." *Social Problems,* 1978, *26,* 198–211.

Cundy, D. "Affect, Cue-Giving, and Political Attitude Formation: Survey Evidence in Support of a Social Conditioning Interpretation." *Journal of Politics,* 1979a, *41,* 75–105.

Cundy, D. "Age-Related Trends in Significant Other Partisan Attachments: Some Inferential Findings Concerning Interpersonal Political Communication and Influence." *International Journal of Political Education,* 1979b, *3,* 235–246.

Cundy, D. "Taking Stock: Some Major Difficulties in the Assumptions, Foci, and Conceptual Apparatus of Political Socialization Research." *Georgia Political Science Association Journal,* 1980, *8,* 29–66.

Dahl, R. A. *Dilemmas of Pluralist Democracy.* New Haven, Conn.: Yale University Press, 1982.

Dahlgren, P. "TV News and the Suppression of Reflexivity." *Urban Life,* 1980, *9,* 201–216.

Damon, W. *The Social World of the Child.* San Francisco: Jossey-Bass, 1977.

Dawson, R., and Prewitt, K. *Political Socialization.* Boston: Little, Brown, 1969.

Dawson, R., Prewitt, K., and Dawson, K. *Political Socialization.* (2nd ed.) Boston: Little, Brown, 1977.

Dennis, J. "On Being an Independent Partisan Supporter." Paper presented at annual meeting of the Midwest Political Science Association, Cincinnati, April 15–18, 1981.

Dennis, J. "The Child's Acquisition of Partisanship and Independence." Paper presented at annual meeting of the Western Political Science Association, San Diego, March 25–27, 1982.

Dowse, R. "Some Doubts Concerning the Study of Political Socialization." *Political Studies,* 1978, *26,* 403–410.

Dowse, R., and Hughes, J. A. "Pre-Adult Origins of Adult Political Activity: A Sour Note." In C. Crouch (ed.), *Participation in Politics: British Political Sociology Yearbook.* London: Croom Helm, 1977.

Easton, D. *A Framework for Political Analysis.* Englewood Cliffs, N.J.: Prentice-Hall, 1965.

Easton, D. "The New Revolution in Political Science."*American Political Science Review,* 1969, *63,* 1051–1062.

Easton, D. "A Reassessment of the Concept of Political Support." *British Journal of Political Science,* 1975, *5,* 435–457.

Easton, D., and Dennis, J. *Children in the Political System.* New York: McGraw-Hill, 1969.

Eckstein, H. *Patterns of Authority.* New York: Wiley, 1975.

Eisenstadt, S. N. *From Generation to Generation.* New York: Free Press, 1956.

Eisenstadt, S. N. "Cultural Traditions and Political Dynamics: The Origins and Modes of Ideological Politics." *British Journal of Sociology,* 1981, *32,* 155–182.

Fagen, R. *The Transformation of Political Culture in Cuba.* Stanford, Calif.: Stanford University Press, 1969.

Farah, T. "Learning to Support the PLO: Political Socialization of Palestinian Children in Kuwait." *Comparative Political Studies,* 1980, *13,* 470–484.

Feldman, R. "The Promotion of Moral Development in Prisons and Schools." In R. Wilson and G. Schochet (eds.), *Moral Development and Politics.* New York: Praeger, 1980.

Fitzgerald, F. *America Revised.* Boston: Little, Brown, 1979.

Flanagan, S. "Value Change and Partisan Change in Japan: The Silent Revolution Revisited." *Comparative Politics,* 1979, *12,* 253–279.

Form, W. H., and Huber, J. *Income and Ideology.* New York: Free Press, 1973.

Furth, H. *The World of Grown-Ups.* New York: Elsevier Science, 1980.

Garcia, C. F. *The Political Socialization of Chicano Children.* New York: Praeger, 1973.

Giddens, A. *The Class Structure of the Advanced Societies.* New York: Harper & Row, 1975.

Gitlin, T. *The Whole World is Watching.* Berkeley: University of California Press, 1980.

Glenn, N. D. "Values, Attitudes and Beliefs." In O. G. Brim, Jr., and J. Kagan (eds.), *Constancy and Change in Human Development.* Cambridge, Mass.: Harvard University Press, 1980.

Glock, C., and others. *Adolescent Prejudice.* New York: Harper & Row, 1975.

Goode, W. *The Celebration of Heroes.* Berkeley: University of California Press, 1978.

Gramsci, A. *Selections from the Prison Notebooks.* (G. Hoare and G. N. Smith, eds. and trans.) New York: International Publishers, 1971. (Originally published 1948.)

Green, J. "Children and Politics in the Philippines: Socialization for Stability in a Highly Stratified Society." *Asian Survey,* 1977, *17,* 667–678.

Greenstein, F. I. *Children and Politics.* New Haven, Conn.: Yale University Press, 1965.

Greenstein, F. I. "The Benevolent Leader Revisited: Children's Images of Political Leaders in Three Democracies." *American Political Science Review,* 1975, *69,* 1371–1398.

Grove, J. D., and others. "Political Socialization and Political Ideology as Sources of Educational Discontent." *Social Science Quarterly,* 1974, *55,* 411–424.

Haan, N., "Activism as Moral Protest: Moral Judgment of Hypothetical Dilemmas and an Actual Situation." In L. Kohlberg and E. Turiel (eds.), *The Development of Moral Judgment and Action.* New York: Holt, Rinehart & Winston, 1972.

Hanks, M. "Youth, Voluntary Associations and Political Socialization." *Social Forces,* 1981, *60,* 211–223.

Hanks, M., and Eckland, B. K. "Adult Voluntary Associations and Adolescent Socialization." *Sociological Quarterly,* 1978, *19,* 481–490.

Harman, R. "The State-Conspiracy Model of Political Socialization." *International Journal of Political Education,* 1980, *3,* 309–322.

Hart, V. *Distrust and Democracy.* Cambridge, England: Cambridge University Press, 1978.

Hawley, W. "The Implicit Civics Curriculum: Teacher Behavior and Political Learning." Unpublished manuscript, Duke University, 1976.

Heater, D., and Gillespie, J. (eds.). *Political Education in Flux.* Beverly Hills, Calif.: Sage, 1981.

Hernandez, A. R. "Filmmaking and Politics: The Cuban Experience." *American Behavioral Scientist,* 1974, *18,* 360–392.

Hess, R. "The Socialization of Attitudes Toward Political Authority: Some Cross-National Comparisons." *International Social Science Journal,* 1963, *15,* 542–559.

Hess, R., and Torney, J. *The Development of Political Attitudes in Children.* Hawthorne, N.Y.: Aldine, 1967.

Hochschild, J. *What's Fair?* Cambridge, Mass.: Harvard University Press, 1981.

Huntington, S. *American Politics: The Promise of Disharmony.* Cambridge, Mass.: Harvard University Press, 1981.

Hyman, H., and Wright, C. R. *Education's Lasting Influence on Values.* Chicago: University of Chicago Press, 1979.

Ichilov, O., and Nave, N. "The 'Good Citizen' as Viewed by Israeli Adolescents." *Comparative Politics,* 1980–81, *13,* 361–376.

Inglehart, R. *The Silent Revolution: Changing Values and Political Styles Among Western Publics.* Princeton, N.J.: Princeton University Press, 1977.

Inglehart, R. "Post-Materialism in an Environment of Insecurity." *American Political Science Review,* 1981, *75,* 880–900.

Iyengar, S. "Childhood Political Learning in a New Nation." *Comparative Politics,* 1979, *12,* 205–225.

Iyengar, S. "Trust, Efficacy, and Political Reality: A Longitudinal Analysis of Indian High School Students." *Comparative Politics,* 1980–81, *13,* 37–53.

Jackman, M. "General and Applied Tolerance: Does Education Increase Commitment to Racial Desegregation?" *American Journal of Political Science,* 1978, *22,* 302–324.

Jackman, M., and Muha, M. "Education: Moral Enlightenment or Intellectual Refinement?" Unpublished manuscript, 1983.

Jackman, M., and Senter, M. "Different, Therefore Equal: Beliefs About Trait Differences Between Groups of Unequal Status." In D. J. Treiman and R. V. Robinson (eds.), *Research in Social Stratification and Mobility.* Vol. 2. Greenwich, Conn.: JAI Press, 1984.

Jencks, C. *Who Gets Ahead?* New York: Basic Books, 1979.

Jencks, C., and others. *Inequality.* New York: Basic Books, 1972.

Jennings, M. K. "An Aggregate Analysis of Home and School Effects on Political Socialization." *Social Science Quarterly,* 1974, *55,* 394–410.

Jennings, M. K., and Niemi, R. *The Political Character of Adolescence.* Princeton, N.J.: Princeton University Press, 1974.

Jennings, M. K., and Niemi, R. *Generations and Politics.* Princeton, N.J.: Princeton University Press, 1981.

Joslyn, R. "Adolescent Attitudes Toward the Political Process: Political Learning in the Midst of Turmoil." *Polity,* 1977, *41,* 373–383.

Kasschau, P. "Political Alienation in a Sample of Young Mexican Children." *Sociology and Social Research,* 1976, *30,* 290–314.

Knutson, J. *The Human Basis of the Polity.* Hawthorne, N.Y.: Aldine, 1972.

Kohlberg, L. "Stage and Sequence: The Cognitive Developmental Approach to Socialization." In D. Goslin (ed.), *Handbook of Socialization Theory and Research.* Skokie, Ill.: Rand McNally, 1969.

Kohlberg, L. "The Future of Liberalism as the Dominant Ideology of the West." In R. Wilson and G. Schochet (eds.), *Moral Development and Politics.* New York: Praeger, 1980.

Kohlberg, L. *The Philosophy of Moral Judgment.* New York: Harper & Row, 1981.

Kraus, E., and Fendrich, J. "Political Socialization of U.S. and Japanese Adults: The Impact of Adult Roles on College Leftism." *Comparative Political Studies,* 1980, *13,* 3–33.

Kraut, R. E., and Lewis, S. H. "Alternate Models of Family Influence on Student Political Ideology." *Journal of Personality and Social Psychology,* 1975, *31,* 791–800.

Lamare, J. "Language Environment and Political Socialization of Mexican-American Children." In R. G. Niemi and Associates, *The Politics of Future Citizens: New Dimensions in the Political Socialization of Children.* San Francisco: Jossey-Bass, 1974.

Landes, R. G. "The Use of Role Theory in Political Socialization Research: A Review, Critique, and Modest Proposal." *International Journal of Comparative Sociology,* 1976, *17,* 59–72.

Landes, R. G. "Political Socialization Among Youth: A Comparative Study of English-Canadian and American School Children." *International Journal of Comparative Sociology,* 1977a, *18,* 63–80.

Landes, R. G. "Pre-Adult Orientations to Multiple Systems of Government: A Comparative Study of English-Canadian and American School Children in Two Cities." *Publius,* 1977b, *7,* 27–39.

Langeveld, W. "Political Education." In D. Heater and J. Gillespie (eds.), *Political Education in Flux.* Beverly Hills, Calif.: Sage, 1981.

Lazarsfeld, P., and Katz, E. *Personal Influence.* New York: Free Press, 1955.

Leach, E. *Culture and Communication.* Cambridge, England: Cambridge University Press, 1976.

LeoGrande, W. M. "Civil-Military Relations in Cuba: Party Control and Political Socialization." *Studies in Comparative Communism,* 1977–78, *10,* 278–291.

Lickona, T. (ed.). *Moral Development and Behavior.* New York: Holt, Rinehart & Winston, 1976.

Long, S. "Political Alienation Among Black and White Adolescents: A Test of the

Social Deprivation and Political Reality Models." *American Politics Quarterly,* 1976, *4,* 267-304.

Lyons, S. "The Political Socialization of Ghetto Children: Efficacy and Cynicism." *Journal of Politics,* 1970, *32,* 288-304.

Mann, J. M. *Consciousness and Action Among the Western Working Class.* London: Macmillan, 1973.

Maravall, J. M. "Political Socialization and Political Dissent: Spanish Radical Students, 1955-1970." *Sociology,* 1976, *10,* 63-82.

Marsh, A. "The 'Silent Revolution,' Value Priorities, and the Quality of Life in Britain." *American Political Science Review,* 1975, *69,* 21-31.

Marsh, D. "Political Socialization: The Implicit Assumptions Questioned." *British Journal of Political Science,* 1971, *1,* 453-465.

Martin, R. "The Socialization of Children in China and Taiwan: An Analysis of Elementary School Textbooks." *China Quarterly,* 1975, *16,* 242-262.

Massey, J. *Youth and Politics in Japan.* Lexington, Mass.: Lexington Books, 1976.

Merelman, R. M. "The Development of Political Ideology: A Framework for the Analysis of Political Socialization." *American Political Science Review,* 1969, *63,* 75-93.

Merelman, R. M. "The Development of Policy Thinking in Adolescence." *American Political Science Review,* 1971a, *65,* 1033-1047.

Merelman, R. M. *Political Socialization and Educational Climates.* New York: Holt, Rinehart & Winston, 1971b.

Merelman, R. M. "The Structure of Policy Thinking in Adolescence: A Research Note." *American Political Science Review,* 1973, *67,* 161-166.

Merelman, R. M. "Changing Class Awareness Among British Working Class Youth: The Effects of an Election Campaign." Unpublished manuscript, University of Wisconsin, 1974.

Merelman, R. M. *Political Reasoning in Adolescence: Some Bridging Themes.* Beverly Hills, Calif.: Sage, 1976.

Merelman, R. M. "Democratic Politics and the Culture of American Education." *American Political Science Review,* 1980a, *74,* 319-333.

Merelman, R. M. "The Family and Political Socialization: Toward a Theory of Exchange." *Journal of Politics,* 1980b, *42,* 461-486.

Merelman, R. M. "Culture and Political Education: A Comparative Perspective." *Micropolitics,* 1981, *1,* 215-238.

Merelman, R. M., and McCabe, A. "Evolving Orientations Toward Policy Choice in Adolescence." *American Journal of Political Science,* 1974, *18,* 665-680.

Milbrath, L., and Goel, M. L. *Political Participation.* (2nd ed.) Skokie, Ill.: Rand McNally, 1977.

Miliband, R. *The State and Capitalist Society.* London: Quartet Books, 1969.

Mill, J. S. *On Representative Government.* London: Dent, 1910. (Originally published 1861.)

Mladenka, K., and Hill, K. "The Development of Political Orientations: A Partial Test of a Cognitive Developmental Hypothesis." *Youth and Society,* 1975, *7,* 130-146.

Moore, S. W., and others. "The Civic Awareness of Five and Six Year Olds." *Western Political Quarterly,* 1976, *29,* 410-424.

Morgan, E. *Inequality in Classroom Learning.* New York: Praeger, 1977.

Mosca, G. *The Ruling Class.* (H. Kahn, trans.) New York: McGraw-Hill, 1939.

Newman, F. "Political Participation." In D. Heater and J. Gillespie (eds.), *Political Education in Flux.* Beverly Hills, Calif.: Sage, 1981.

Niemi, R. G. "Political Socialization." In J. N. Knutson (ed.), *Handbook of Political Psychology.* San Francisco: Jossey-Bass, 1973.

Niemi, R. G., Katz, R. S., and Newman, D. "Reconstructing Past Partisanship: The Failure of the Party Identification Recall Questions." *American Journal of Political Science,* 1980, *24,* 633–652.

Niemi, R. G., Ross, R. D., and Alexander, J. "The Similarity of Political Values of Parents and College-Age Youths." *Public Opinion Quarterly,* 1978, *42,* 503–520.

Niemi, R. G., and Sobieszek, B. "Political Socialization." *Annual Review of Sociology,* 1977, *3,* 209–233.

Nyomarky, J. *Charisma and Factionalism in the Nazi Party.* Minneapolis: University of Minnesota Press, 1967.

O'Connor, R. "Political Activism and Moral Reasoning: Political and Apolitical Students in Great Britain and France." *British Journal of Political Science,* 1975, *5,* 53–78.

O'Dell, F. *Socialization Through Children's Literature.* New York: Cambridge University Press, 1979.

Page, B., and Jones, C. C. "Reciprocal Effects of Policy Preferences, Party Loyalties, and the Vote." *American Political Science Review,* 1979, *73,* 1071–1089.

Parkin, F. *Marxism and Class Theory.* London: Tavistock, 1979.

Parry, G. "Trust, Distrust, and Consensus." *British Journal of Political Science,* 1976, *6,* 129–142.

Parsons, T. *The Social System.* New York: Free Press, 1951.

Patterson, J. "Moral Development and Political Thinking: The Case of Freedom of Speech." *Western Political Quarterly,* 1979, *32,* 7–20.

Percheron, A. *Les 10–16 ans et la politique* [10 to 16 year olds and politics]. Paris: Fondation Nationale des Sciences Politiques, 1978.

Phizakalea, A. M. "A Sense of Political Efficacy: A Comparison of Black and White Adolescents." In I. Crewe (ed.), *British Political Sociology Yearbook.* Vol. 2. London: Croom Helm, 1975.

Piaget, J. *The Moral Judgment of the Child.* (M. Gabain, trans.) New York: Free Press, 1965. (Originally published 1932.)

Pierce, J. C., and Sullivan, J. L. *The Electorate Reconsidered.* Beverly Hills, Calif.: Sage, 1980.

Pride, R., and Richards, B. "The Denigration of Political Authority in Television News: The Ecology Issue." *Western Political Quarterly,* 1975, *28,* 635–645.

Rawls, J. *A Theory of Justice.* Cambridge, Mass.: Harvard University Press, 1972.

Renshon, S. A. (ed.). *Handbook of Political Socialization Theory and Research.* New York: Free Press, 1977.

Riker, W., and Ordeshook, P. *An Introduction to Positive Political Theory.* Englewood Cliffs, N.J.: Prentice-Hall, 1973.

Roberts, D., Pingree, S., and Hawkins, R. P. "Do the Mass Media Play a Role in Political Socialization?" *Australian and New Zealand Journal of Sociology,* 1975, *11,* 37–42.

Robinson, R. V., and Bell, W. "Equality, Success, and Social Justice in England and the United States." *American Sociological Review,* 1978, *43,* 125–143.

Rousseau, J. J. *The Social Contract.* In F. Watkins (ed.), *The Political Writings.* Edinburgh: Nelson, 1953. (Originally published 1762.)

Runciman, W. G. *Relative Deprivation and Social Justice.* Berkeley: University of California Press, 1966.

Russell, J. "Replication of Instability: Political Socialization in Northern Ireland." *British Journal of Political Science,* 1977, *7,* 115–128.

Rutter, M., and others. *Fifteen Thousand Hours.* Cambridge, Mass.: Harvard University Press, 1979.

Sapiro, V. *The Political Integration of Women: Roles, Socialization, and Politics.* Urbana: University of Illinois Press, 1983.

Schank, R. G., and Abelson, R. *Scripts, Plans, Goals, and Understanding.* Hillsdale, N.J.: Erlbaum, 1977.

Schlesinger, P. *Putting "Reality" Together: BBC News.* London: Constable, 1978.

Schneider, D. *American Kinship: A Cultural Account.* Englewood Cliffs, N.J.: Prentice-Hall, 1968.

Schoenfeld, W. *Obedience and Revolt: French Behavior to Authority.* Beverly Hills, Calif.: Sage, 1976.

Schumpeter, J. *Capitalism, Socialism, and Democracy.* (3rd ed.) New York: Harper & Row, 1950.

Searing, D., and Stern, A. "The Stratification Beliefs of English and American Adolescents." *British Journal of Political Science,* 1976, *6,* 177–203.

Searing, D., Wright, G., and Rabinowitz, G. "The Primacy Principle: Attitude Change and Political Socialization." *British Journal of Political Science,* 1976, *6,* 83–113.

Sears, D. O. "Political Socialization." In F. I. Greenstein and N. W. Polsby (eds.), *Handbook of Political Science.* Vol. 4. Reading, Mass.: Addison-Wesley, 1975.

Sigel, R. S., and Hoskin, M. B. *The Political Involvement of Adolescents.* New Brunswick, N.J.: Rutgers University Press, 1981.

Simmons, R., and Rosenberg, M. "Functions of Children's Perceptions of the Stratification System." *American Sociological Review,* 1971, *36,* 235–249.

Singer, B. "Mass Media and Communication Processes in the Detroit Riot of 1967." *Public Opinion Quarterly,* 1970, *34,* 236–246.

Sluckin, A. *Growing Up in the Playground: The Social Development of Children.* London: Routledge & Kegan Paul, 1981.

Smelser, N. *Theory of Collective Behavior.* London: Routledge & Kegan Paul, 1962.

Sniderman, P. *A Question of Loyalty.* Berkeley: University of California Press, 1982.

Stacey, B. *Political Socialization in Western Society.* New York: St. Martin's Press, 1977.

Stevens, A. J. "The Acquisition of Participatory Norms: The Case of Japanese and Mexican American Children in a Suburban Environment." *Western Political Quarterly,* 1975, *28,* 281–296.

Styskal, R. A., and Sullivan, H. J. "Intergenerational Continuity and Congruence on Political Values." *Western Political Quarterly,* 1975, *28,* 516–527.

Sullivan, J. L., Piereson, J. E., and Marcus, G. E. *Political Tolerance and American Democracy.* Chicago: University of Chicago Press, 1982.

Sullivan, J. L., Piereson, J. E., Marcus, G. E., and Feldman, S. "The More Things Change, the More They Stay the Same: The Stability of Mass Belief Systems." *American Journal of Political Science,* 1979, *23,* 176–186.

Tapper, T., and Salter, B. *Education and the Political Order.* London: Macmillan, 1978.

Tedin, K. L. "The Influence of Parents on the Political Attitudes of Adolescents." *American Political Science Review,* 1974, *68,* 1579–1592.

Tedin, K. L. "Assessing Peer and Parent Influence on Adolescent Political Attitudes." *American Journal of Political Science,* 1980, *24,* 136–154.

Tolley, H., Jr. *Children and War.* New York: Teachers College Press, 1973.

Tomlinson, P. "Political Education: Cognitive Developmental Perspectives from Moral Education." *Oxford Review of Education,* 1975, *1,* 251–268.

Tuchman, G. (ed.). *The TV Establishment: Programming for Power and Profit.* Englewood Cliffs, N.J.: Prentice-Hall, 1974.

Turiel, E. "The Development of Social-Conventional and Moral Judgments Among Children." In M. Windmiller, N. Lambert, and E. Turiel (eds.), *Moral Development and Socialization.* Newton, Mass.: Allyn & Bacon, 1980.

Vaillancourt, P. M., and Niemi, R. G. "Children's Party Choices." In R. G. Niemi and Associates, *The Politics of Future Citizens: New Dimensions in the Political Socialization of Children.* San Francisco: Jossey-Bass, 1974.

Verba, S., Nie, N. H., and Kim, J. *Participation and Political Equality.* Cambridge, England: Cambridge University Press, 1978.

Weber, M. *The Theory of Social and Economic Organization.* (T. Parsons, trans.) New York: Free Press, 1947. (Originally published 1919.)

Weiner, R. R. *Cultural Marxism and Political Sociology.* Beverly Hills, Calif.: Sage, 1981.

Weiner, T., and Eckland, B. K. "Education and Political Party: The Effects of College or Social Class?" *American Journal of Sociology,* 1979, *65,* 911–928.

Weissberg, R. "The Politics of Political Competence Education." In D. Heater and J. Gillespie (eds.), *Political Education in Flux.* Beverly Hills, Calif.: Sage, 1981.

Wentworth, W. *Context and Understanding: An Inquiry into Socialization Theory.* New York: Elsevier Science, 1980.

White, S., "Political Socialization in the USSR: A Study in Failure?" *Studies in Comparative Communism,* 1977, *10,* 328–342.

Whyte, M. K. "Child Socialization in the Soviet Union and China." *Studies in Comparative Communism,* 1977, *10,* 235–259.

Wildavsky, A. "Three Cultures: Explaining Anomalies in the American Welfare State." *The Public Interest,* 1982, *69,* 45–58.

Williams, R. "Base and Superstructure in Marxist Cultural Theory." *New Left Review,* 1973, *82,* 3–17.

Williams, R. *Television: Technology and Cultural Form.* New York: Schocken Books, 1975.

Willis, P. *Learning to Labour: How Working Class Kids Get Working Class Jobs.* Farnborough, Hampshire, England: Teakfield, 1977.

Wilson, R. "Political Socialization and Moral Development." *World Politics,* 1981, *33,* 153–178.

Wright, J. D. "Political Socialization Research: The 'Primacy' Principle." *Social Forces,* 1975, *54,* 243–255.

Wright, J. D. *The Dissent of the Governed.* Orlando, Fla.: Academic Press, 1976.

Wright, J. D., and Holub, D. "Social Cleavage and Party Affiliation Revisited: A Comparison of West Germany and the United States." *Sociology and Social Research,* 1979, *33,* 671–698.

Zellman, G., and Sears, D. O. "Childhood Origins of Tolerance for Dissent." *Journal of Social Issues*, 1971, *27*, 109–136.

Zureik, E. "Major Issues in Political Socialization Research." In E. Zureik and R. M. Pike (eds.), *Socialization and Values in Canadian Society*. Vol. 1. Toronto: McClelland & Stewart, 1975.

Zureik, E., and Pike, R. M. (eds.). *Socialization and Values in Canadian Society*. Vol. 1. Toronto: McClelland & Stewart, 1975.

ELEVEN

ⵊⵊⵊⵊⵊⵊⵊⵊⵊⵊⵊⵊⵊⵊⵊⵊ

Identifying
a Society's Belief Systems

Ofira Seliktar

The interest in societal belief systems is fundamental to all social science. At the most general level, it stems from the fact that humans have normally been studied within the conceptual framework of a society. This focus is captured in the traditional definition of culture in anthropology and sociology. As described by Edward Tylor, in his work *Primitive Culture,* culture is "that complex whole which includes knowledge, beliefs, arts, morals, law, custom, and other capabilities acquired by man as a member of society" (quoted in Wiseman, 1966, p. 21). The study of societal belief systems is especially important in political science. Ever since Aristotle, political scientists have been interested in the structures and processes that consolidate and subsequently sustain a social group as a polity. Ascertaining the nature of the national belief system may contribute to a better understanding of four important areas in political science.

The first area pertains to the ongoing debate about how political systems are shaped. Following the work on political culture, it has been widely accepted that political systems are characterized by the orientation of the citizens toward the political domain. Almond and Verba's (1965) parochial, subject, and participant orientations have been universally applied in contemporary political research. Relatively little attention has been focused on the companion questions of why particular orientations are likely to emerge or how they are related to the broader belief system or "world view" of a society. These questions are particularly important because most contemporary theorists accept Easton's (1965a) view that a political system constitutes an "authoritative allocation of values" or Lasswell's (1936) view that it is a process through which a society decides who gets what, when, and how. These theories clearly call for an interpretation of the political system through the investigation of its collective values. It is only by understanding the belief system that one can explain why different societies choose to sanction different patterns of resource distribution.

More specifically, such an investigation can contribute to the perennial debate among political philosophers about the precise way in which belief systems reflect and sustain the underlying social conditions in which they are generated. Broadly speaking, political science accepts the thesis of the sociology of knowledge developed by Émile Durkheim and Karl Mannheim—namely, that groups formulate belief systems on the basis of the prevalent social conditions and economic modes of production. Beyond this consensus, there is little agreement as to whether belief systems represent the coercive or the voluntary adaptation of a collectivity to its social and economic environment.

One important theory, normally associated with Thomas Hobbes and the economic school in politics, maintains that universal scarcity has created a condition of permanent conflict among men. To avoid violence men are coerced into civil society. The subsequent belief system reflects and legitimizes both this coercion and the allocation of scarce resources. In the stark words of Moore (1967, p. 486), "to maintain and transmit a value system, human beings are punched, bullied, sent to jail."

Another variant of the coercionist theory is based on the classic Marxist notion that the capitalist modes of production, and especially private property, create artificial scarcity. In order for such societies to survive, a stringent division of labor and coercive assignment of roles must be imposed. The fundamental inequality of the system necessitates the shaping of a belief system that justifies the dominance of the elite and the regimentation it applies to maintain the stability of the system (Dahrendorf, 1954; Johnson, 1966).

The voluntaristic theory of integration is mostly associated with the work of Talcott Parsons, who draws on both Max Weber and Émile Durkheim. In his *Social Systems*, Parsons (1964, p. 42) argues that coercion alone cannot explain social acceptance of stratification and inequality. What facilitates integration is the fact that social groups form "moral communities": collectivities sharing certain "definitions of situations" or "values" that legitimize stratification. Moreover, the stability of any political system depends on the degree to which its constituent members internalize these values in order to produce an integrative collective belief system.

Quite obviously, an understanding of the dynamics involved in both coercionist and voluntaristic theories depends on political psychology. Johnson (1966, p. 21), in his analysis of the Parsonian perspective, comments that it raises numerous psychological questions. For example, are values internalized by individuals through socialization, or are they agreed on in a social contract? And can belief systems be manipulated so that citizens will perceive coercion as natural? Moreover, the pioneering research of Gurr (1970) and Tilly (1978) on civil unrest makes it clear that psychological states, such as relative deprivation, rather than objective inequalities explain human beliefs about social order.

Perhaps the most ambitious attempt to use social psychology to integrate the coercionist and voluntaristic perspectives has been undertaken by the contemporary German psychosociological schools—most notably by Habermas (1975) in his work on the crisis of legitimacy. Habermas argues that class societies based on "privileged appropriation of socially produced wealth" (p. 96) face the problem of the inequitable distribution of surplus social products. To legitimize the lack of equality, the extant belief system has built norms that presuppose an "asymmetrical distribution of legitimate chances to satisfy needs." The social acceptance of such norms of distributive justice is based not only on their legitimacy but also on an individual's perception of "his own powerlessness," which is related to "threatened sanctions and coercion." Billig (1976, pp. 261-268), in his imaginative psychological explanation of the phenomenon of "false consciousness," stresses the manipulative way in which a dominant group shapes the ideology of a subordinate group.

The second area in which political science can profit from a more systematic knowledge about belief systems pertains to systemic stability and change. The question of what constitutes stability and change in a political system has never been satisfactorily resolved, primarily because some of the methodologies employed focused on maintenance of stability, whereas others emphasized conflict and change (Hessler, Kong-Ming, and May, 1980). The related issue of the causes that promote stability, as opposed to the factors underlying change, has raised an even bigger controversy. The debate was partially mitigated when the notion of systems became widely accepted in political science. According to the systems theories, which were modeled on mechanical (Easton, 1965b) or cybernetic (Deutsch, 1953) systems in the natural sciences, a system is in "homeostatic equilibrium" as long as "society's values and the realities with which it must deal in order to exist" are synchronized (Johnson, 1966, p. 60). Conversely, a failure in the synchronization triggers a disequilibrium and a subsequent change in the system. The inventories compiled to explain the causes of disequilibrium, however, generally do not account for the process through which a society's belief system becomes aligned with the evolving realities.

An explicit focus on belief systems can provide a more ordered explanation of stability and change by introducing the notions of delegitimization and transvaluation. *Delegitimization* is a collective outcome of personal psychological states. Individuals may experience cognitive dissonance when their beliefs and values clash with new realities. When enough individuals in a society go through the same dissonant process, they eventually discard their old beliefs and values. *Transvaluation* is the companion process whereby new and more consonant values are generated and sanctioned as part of the evolving collective belief system.

Smith's (1970, pp. 85-123) model of modernization presents a good application of this approach. In his view, modernization is brought about by the gradual transvaluation of a society's belief system. Religious values are delegitimized as a source of political authority and replaced by a secular group identity associated with the nation. Concurrently, there is an emphasis on "nontranscendent, temporal goals and rational pragmatic means," which are the key to a secular value orientation in politics.

A model that focuses on the role that belief systems play in stability and change is particularly fruitful because its internal logic stipulates that the transvaluation process is reversible. Traditional studies of development, which were based on economic and social indices, often assumed that modernization is a linear and irreversible process. The notion of dissonant psychological states can explain why relatively rational and pragmatic belief systems occasionally revert to transcendent goals or even delegitimize the secular authority in favor of a religious one.

The investigation of belief systems also deserves a greater emphasis in democracies because it illuminates the reciprocal influence of party identification and the perceptual elements in voting decisions that derive from a citizen's system of values (Miller, 1976). The concept of realigning elections is an early but not fully developed reflection on this process. The realignment of the electorate during the New Deal, which led to an extended Democratic supremacy, is an example of such mass changes in the American belief system. The emergence of the British Labour party, which eclipsed the Liberal party after World War I, is explained by similar changes.

Research in political socialization and analyses of cohort voting have demonstrated that societal beliefs are instrumental in forming an individual's partisan preference. The Michigan studies of the American voter (Campbell, Converse, Miller, and Stokes, 1960; Nie, Verba, and Petrocik, 1976) and a major British voting study (Butler and Stokes, 1971) show this effect. Rose (1974) discusses the equivalent experience in European and Commonwealth countries.

The third area in which political science could benefit from systematic knowledge about belief systems is the complex problem of national cohesion. Traditional analysis postulated that ethnically and religiously homogeneous societies are more cohesive than pluralistic societies. These studies assumed that homogeneous societies have relatively unified belief systems whose core values are adhered to by all, whereas pluralistic societies harbor vestiges of ethnic or religious subcultures with their own belief systems, which detract from the cohesion of the national society. Since cohesion is a prerequisite for governability, it was further assumed that pluralistic societies have developed mechanisms for regulating intergroup conflict. Perhaps the most famous of such constructs is Lijphart's (1968) model of consociationalism, which envisaged a general agreement on a limited number of core values and bargaining and tradeoffs between conflicting subcultural beliefs.

This rather schematic representation of the two models obscures important complexities in the process through which national belief systems generate cohesion or fragmentation. The first point to be considered is that fragmentation of a national belief system is not necessarily contingent on the survival of historical subcultures. Recent writings on American and Western political culture indicate that the system has been progressively fragmented because of new cleavages. For instance, in *The Crisis of Democracy,* a major scholarly effort to assess the future of democracy, Crozier (1975) points out that liberal rationality was replaced by subjective rationality. The outcome of such a process is the loss of encompassing goals and the fragmentation of the national belief system. Rosenau and Holsti (1983) go so far as to assert that, in the domain related to American foreign policy, the "consensus broke down" and was replaced by a host of "competitive and conflictual belief systems." This fragmentation was apparently linked to the much-debated political malaise in Western democracies in the 1970s. Whether the new conservative consolidation has reversed this process is yet to be seen. Whatever its outcome, it does not invalidate the methodological argument that the process of unification and fragmentation of national belief systems is reversible.

Another point that merits attention is the function of ideological salience or the level of individual commitment to societal values in maintaining national cohesion. The "end-of-ideology" debate, which was allegedly started by the famous "Future of Freedom Conference" in 1955, illustrates the difficulty of relating ideological salience to social cohesion. In this theory—espoused by Daniel Bell,

Edward Shils, Raymond Aron, and Seymour Martin Lipset, among others—a slightly misleading term was used to describe what the scholars viewed as a process of diminishing commitment to ideological beliefs in postwar societies (Billig, 1982, p. 129). It is beyond the scope of this work to describe the enormous controversy generated by this debate. Nevertheless, at least one argument emphasized that decreased salience in traditional ideological beliefs would reduce social cleavages and promote national cohesion and governability.

Recent studies in social psychology indicate that lessened ideological commitment at the individual level can produce other types of fragmentation and anomie in a polity. As will be shown in this chapter, the new theme of "privatized attitudes" is a reflection of a process whereby individuals lose commitment to values beyond their most personal interests. Such a decrease in ideological salience can create a fragmented polity populated by numerous small interest groups. Indeed, this decrease in salience may well have contributed to the disintegration in the 1970s of some of the fairly cohesive Western belief systems and created what Crozier (1975, p. 49) has called a society that "possesses no sense of mission."

The fourth area in political science that depends heavily on an understanding of national belief systems is foreign policy. Historically, research in foreign policy has evolved from single- or multicountry studies to studies of general systems. One product of this conceptual development is an integrated systemic analysis of the foreign policy of single countries. These studies view the foreign policy of a country as a system composed of the operational environment of the country, the psychological environment of the decision makers, and the process through which decisions are formulated and implemented (for a good example, see Brecher, 1972).

Whereas the operational environment and the structure of the decision-making process of a foreign policy system are relatively easy to analyze, the psychological environment of the decision maker is conceptually more challenging. Following the pioneering work of Kenneth Boulding and his followers, it became almost commonplace to assume that decision makers act on their perceptions of reality rather than "objective" reality. "Cognitive behaviorism," as the principle is sometimes called, means that elites (as well as followers) have "cognitive maps" or sets of images that condition their foreign policy behavior (Boulding, 1959, 1963; Sprout and Sprout, 1961). These "cognitive maps" and their related images are used to order and make inferences about complex realities in the decision makers' operational environment.

Yet the terms "cognitive map" and "image" share the problem of other theoretical constructs—namely, that their links with observed reality do not lend themselves easily to empirical analysis. Boulding (1959, p. 128) himself admitted this difficulty when he stated that, in reality, the image cannot be represented as a "set of quantities or variables" and is the product of a weighted interaction between the images of a large number of people.

Perhaps the most difficult part of the construct pertains to Boulding's notion that individual images grow out of a complex process of interaction with the national images disseminated through the value system of a society. In other words, in order to understand the psychological environment of the foreign policy system, the analyst must account for the idiosyncrasies of decision makers, the national belief system of the society of which they are a part, and the patterned interactions between these two.

Definitions of "Belief System"

The term "belief system" is extremely popular in political psychology, but two problems have obscured its clarity. The first is that of diverse meanings—including, among others, ideology, political culture, and even culture. It is impossible to discuss the enormous literature on this subject, but it is safe to assume that there is a fair degree of implied overlap among these terms, even though they are not identical. In a sense, they all refer to sets of ideas that men use to position and explain physical and social realities, as well as to justify social actions aimed at ordering these realities (for representative treatments, see Minar, 1961; Seliger, 1970; Schmid, 1981; Szalay, Kelly, and Moon, 1972; Abercombie and Turner, 1978; Ashcroft, 1980; Asad, 1979; Wuthrow, 1981). The second, and more difficult, problem stems from the need to reconcile what may be broadly termed the macrosociological or "holistic" perspective with the microsociological orientation, which focuses on individual psychological processes.

The "holistic" position—that emergent group properties are not reducible to the sum properties of the individuals—is an intellectual outgrowth of the sociology-of-knowledge perspective. This view is most clearly associated with Karl Mannheim, but it has also been influenced by Karl Marx, Émile Durkheim, and Louis Althusser. In their respective approaches, they all share the view that belief systems are formed through a complex interaction between intellectual viewpoints and a sequence of human experience (Mannheim, [1929] 1955, in particular pp. 264–311). This approach has been featured either explicitly or implicitly in extremely diverse intellectual traditions, ranging from the concept of "ideal" in neo-Marxist sociology (Godelier, 1978) to "social myth" in psychoanalysis (Arlow, 1961; Rolle, 1980). More common uses include the concept of "collective consciousness," corresponding to Durkheim's collective representation (Larrain, 1980), "prophecy" (Merton, 1968, p. 475), "definition of situation" (Thomas, 1928, p. 572), and "ideational codes" in mainstream sociology and political science (Geertz, 1964). The term "working consensus as the emergent collective product" is current in interactionist sociology (Handel, 1979), and "mental collective consciousness" is implied in the notion of *ethos* and *eidos* in cultural anthropology (Berry and Dasen, 1974, p. 2).

The microsociological perspective derives from a number of disciplines that deal with individual psychological states. Cognitive psychology postulates that, in order to survive, human beings have developed the ability to extract essential clues out of the extensive flow of information to which they are constantly exposed. This selective perception is called "perceptual representation," "cognitive representation," "cognitive map," or "perceptual-representational system" (Szalay and Kelly, 1982). At the most fundamental level, such a private belief system informs the individual about the nature of reality by providing him with a series of explicit and implicit assumptions about causality, time and space orientation, and ethical codes of social morality and justice.

Motivational psychology, known also as the functional school, assumes that "manifest" attitudes and beliefs are instrumental in expressing and imposing order on the individual's repressed conflicts and drives. Perhaps the best-known work of the functional school is Adorno and his colleagues' (1950) study of the authoritarian personality, which found that anti-Semitism and strong ethnic prejudice correlate with repressed aggression and hostility (see also Smith, Bruner, and

White, 1956; Katz, Sarnoff, and McClintock, 1956). Seen in this way, beliefs are used by the individual to resolve problems arising from interactions between self and society.

Structurally, a person's belief system constitutes a configuration of ideas constrained by some form of interdependence between the constitutive elements. Popularized by Converse (1964, p. 207) in his seminal study on the belief systems of the mass public, the concept of constraint has a probabilistic meaning: "the success we would have in predicting, given initial knowledge that an individual holds a specific attitude, that he holds certain further ideas and attitudes." The constitutive relations between the elements of an ideational set may derive from the mathematically exacting logic of functional interdependence but more often are loosely generated and "packaged" by the social experience of the collective. Finally, an individual's belief system is also action oriented, because it specifies both the ends to be achieved and the normative contours of the means to be used (Frank, 1977).

The respective analyses of the collective and the individual belief system can be conceptually reconciled if one adopts an *interactionist view*. Because societal beliefs constitute complex symbolic sets, they are seen as both a product and a determinant of individual beliefs generated through continuous social interaction (Merkl, 1970, p. 144). This perspective was articulated in the phenomenological analysis of Berger and Luckmann (1966), which postulates a cyclical phenomenon whereby "the subjective mind creates a subjective reality (externalization), which, as time goes by, turns into institutions, tradition, and 'culture' (objectification), and then finally acts back on the subjective mind and shapes it (internalization)" (Schmid, 1981, p. 62).

Bronfenbrenner (1977) provides perhaps the most systematic exposition of this view in his model of the ecology of human development. Based on Kurt Lewin's concept of topological territories, Bronfenbrenner's model envisages human development as a "progressive, mutual accommodation, throughout the life span, between a growing human organism" and the changing ecological environment in which he lives. The ecological environment is conceptualized topologically, as a "nested arrangement of structures" ranging from microsystems to the macrosystem. Bronfenbrenner conceives of each system as both an interaction-creating structure and a carrier of ideational information. The complex network of interactions between the individual and the environment and the interactions within and between the environments reciprocally shape the development of the human and the environment. This perspective, though conceptually elegant, cannot solve the question of what unit of analysis should be used in an empirical investigation of a societal belief system.

The "holistic" approach is most rigid in its insistence that the "collective consciousness" should not be constructed as the sum total of the various types of "individual consciousness." The most emphatic advocate of this view is, of course, Mannheim himself. Converse (1964) once argued that Mannheim's objection to using the individual as the basis of inference about the belief of a group was methodological. It allegedly stemmed from the early antibehaviorist stand, which doubted the possibility of measuring subjective states. Nonetheless, Mannheim ([1929] 1955, p. 59) seems to go beyond mere methodology when he emphasizes that "the analysis derived from the content of individual thought can never achieve this basic reconstruction of the whole outlook of a social group."

The macrosociologists are more equivocal about the best empirical way to identify and reconstruct a societal belief system. While there is an implicit agreement that the belief system is the property of a certain collectivity—nation, class, ethnic group, religious community—it is not clear who are the ideational bearers of the system. One extreme view, which was quite prevalent in Enlightenment philosophy, conceived the carrier of "collective consciousness" as an almost metaphysical, abstract, supertemporal, and supersocietal entity. Ashcroft (1980) argues that indirectly this view of an extratemporal and extrasocial unit of consciousness pervades some of contemporary political theory, especially in its discourse on the great philosophers.

The alternative approach is nurtured by Mannheim's dictum that the identification of a belief system belonging to a group requires the "reconstruction of the systematic theoretical basis underlying the single judgment of the individual" ([1929] 1955, p. 59). It is within the broad confines of this prescription that sociology, anthropology, and political science look at group interaction in both institutional and informal settings, with a view toward decoding the belief system of the different collectivities. A potentially promising but empirically underdeveloped variant of this approach is to study policy "backward through behavior to the ideational antecedents" (Minar, 1961, p. 329). Theodore Lowi's discussion of the "public philosophy," Michel Crozier's work on the "bureaucratic phenomenon," and the "operational code" research are representative of this approach (see Elkins and Simeon, 1979).

The individual psychological approach is uncompromisingly clear in its choice of the single individual to be the basic unit for the empirical analysis of collective belief systems. Perhaps the most cogent statement of this perspective is provided by Almond and Verba (1965), who define political culture as the internalization of the political system in the cognition, feelings, and evaluation of the population: "The political culture is the particular distribution of orientations toward political objects among the members of the nation" (p. 13). The conceptual premise underlying this perspective is that a belief system can be described in terms of statistically derived modal characteristics and modal personalities in a given population. The use of the individual as the basic unit of analysis is widely employed in the social sciences. The various shortcomings of the two major approaches cannot be discussed here. We should note, however, that it is empirically impossible to determine the extent to which a societal belief system is the equivalent of the collective attitudes of its constituent individuals.

In the absence of conceptual clarity, research on group belief systems has used a bewildering number of approaches. Billig (1976, pp. 45, 220), who reviewed some of them, found that one of the common analytical devices is reductionism. Classical reductionism—which was based on the work of Geza Roheim, Karl Menninger, Anthony Storr, and Konrad Lorenz—assumed that social phenomena can be conceptualized in terms of individual psychological processes, which reflect unconscious psychological motives. Another common device is to treat the group and the individual as isomorphic constructs. Such an approach has produced the "group mind fallacy"—that is, the "attribution of mental predicates to social collectives."

A more systematic way to discern a societal value system is to study the beliefs of elites. The notion that elites represent the collective belief system more faithfully than ordinary citizens has a long intellectual tradition, dating from Plato's philosopher-kings. Writers as varied as Karl Mannheim, Vilfredo Pareto, Antonio Gramsci, C. Wright Mills, and Clifford Geertz have suggested that each society has a special group of individuals whose major task is to interpret social reality. These groups are variously known as "power elites," "castes," "networks of meaning," "strategic social groups" (Elliot and Schlesinger, 1979), and leaders of "communication communities" *(Kommunikationsgemeinschaft)* (Habermas, 1975, p. 105).

Extensive empirical research indicates that elite beliefs are indeed more representative of what is assumed to be the belief system of the collectivity. Because of the pioneering work of McClosky (1964) and others, this fact is among the best-documented findings in American political science. Analysis of elite utterances is routinely used to discern the belief systems of Communist and other nondemocratic regimes. Nonetheless, the study of collective belief systems through the attitudes of the elites is vulnerable to a "circular effect." Elites define the parameters of the belief system and invest psychologically in established patterns of thought. Measuring the beliefs of elites may not take account of what Elliot and Schlesinger (1979, p. 58) call the "disjunction between administrative and electoral politics."

A different way of ascertaining collective belief systems is based on studies of national identity in political psychology. These are also known as studies in ethnocentrism or by the popular and often misused term "national character" analysis. This research indicates that sociocultural systems can operate as selective and normative environments. They exert pressure, through the socialization process, toward the enhancement of individual traits that are functional in performing salient societal roles. The statistically measurable outcome is a skew in the distribution of personality characteristics toward the socially desirable modes. Frenkel-Brunswik (1948) was perhaps the first to uncover an empirically defensible connection between ethnocentrism and personality organization.

Follow-up studies postulate a relationship between ethnocultural situations and modal personality traits, such as dogmatism, prejudice, and submissiveness. Studying the attitudes of whites toward blacks in South Africa, Pettigrew (1970) made the important discovery that externalization processes, such as authoritarianism or personal aggression, cannot explain the inordinately high level of prejudice and hostility toward blacks. An alternative hypothesis is that the political culture positively sanctions prejudice and exerts strong pressure on individuals to conform. A study of child-rearing practices and economic development revealed that children in economies that give low priority to accumulation of food are taught to be more individualistic than are children in economies that give high priority to accumulation of food (Barry, Child, and Bacon, 1959).

A relatively new avenue of research is the contextual treatment of attitudinal characteristics. Examining political tolerance in various societies, Sullivan and associates (forthcoming) found that the chief differentiating agent is not personality type but the differing political contexts of the countries. In societies such as Israel, which face a large amount of threat, the level of personal tolerance is lower than in countries such as New Zealand, whose international environment is virtually nonthreatening.

McClosky's (1967, p. 56) concept of phenotypical as opposed to genotypical characteristics is one interesting application of ethnocentric insights to the study of foreign policy. Genotypical characteristics derive from personality dispositions and refer to such things as ego defense mechanisms, needs, and motives. They often underlie attitudes and "furnish the motive force that impels them." Phenotypical characteristics "depend upon social learning" and are influenced by an ethnic or national context. The border between genotypes and phenotypes is permeable enough to raise the intriguing possibility that characteristics such as pessimism, social responsibility, and contempt for weakness may be culturally conditioned.

A more promising approach to solving the dilemma of the unit of analysis would be to condition the choice on the specific aim of a given piece of research. In studies that focus on the role of belief systems as mediators of individual decisions and behavior, the only logical unit of analysis is the individual. Most of the research on voting behavior has used this approach, although the theoretical rationale was not always articulated. In any case, there is a sound political reason for analyzing individuals. Even without the typical democratic bias, which views numbers as a basis of power, it can be argued that "critical masses"—which can range from small oligarchies to unstructured mobs—sustain all belief systems. On the other hand, studies that deal with decision-oriented complex organizations—most notably, the foreign policy system—should at least touch on the macrosociological definition of the belief system. Defined in this way, a belief system may be seen as a set or range of discrete rather than deterministic alternatives on which decision makers can act. Given the constraints imposed by the external and internal environment of the foreign policy system, one cannot infer directly from a collective belief sytem to a particular decision. Nevertheless, the belief system can serve as a collective "cognitive map" of the foreign policy environment.

General Belief Systems and Political Beliefs

Another major difficulty in studying belief systems in political science is relating political beliefs to general beliefs. This difficult stems from what Goffmann (1959) calls "boundary collusion"—that is, the problem of interpreting a social phenomenon in the context of a larger unknown social paradigm. It is commonly assumed that the political belief system (or political culture) is the part of a general belief system (the *Weltanschauung*) that comprises a people's orientation toward the political realm. Yet the fact that political beliefs are embedded in the broader cognitive and affective organization of beliefs raises the perplexing question of the boundary of the political belief system. We can best discuss this problem by introducing the concept of autonomy—that is, the degree to which political beliefs are separated from general beliefs (Tucker, 1973).

The question of autonomy has not been systematically discussed in the literature. Rather, the boundaries of the political belief sytem have been defined ad hoc, to a large extent implicitly, by the methodological thrust of the various studies. Empirical studies of individual political beliefs have ranged widely in the degree of inferred autonomy. By definition, studies that probe political beliefs at the level of political opinion imply a fairly autonomous system. Political opinions are normally specific responses to particular issue stimuli and are more likely to reflect clearly identifiable individual and group interests.

Attitudes are more deeply rooted in the individual value system and are less likely to be dependent on the external stimuli of issues. Compared to opinion studies, research investigating attitudes conveys a diminished sense of autonomy, but even then the boundaries of political beliefs fluctuate greatly, depending on the methodology used. Early research on political attitudes normally used paper-and-pencil attitude scales, which provided a phenomenological report on the respondents' thinking about the issue. Although the cognitive-affective-evaluative trichotomy was used, the findings were normally skewed toward the cognitive meaning of ideational elements. This was the result of the widespread use of the Likert type of questionnaire, which is known to tap the more cognitive attitudes of the individual. The semantic differential, developed by Osgood and his associates (1957), is known to touch off more affective responses (Hofman, 1983). Although it has been widely used in psychology, it has only recently gained popularity in political science.

Moreover, recent and more sophisticated studies demonstrate that powerful ideational labels such as liberal-conservative serve as symbols that have both cognitive and evaluative meanings. Such studies show that many individuals respond in affective terms to the labels and the issues subsumed under them, although they may lack the appropriate cognitive information about the terms. One recent work found that symbolic affective meaning can introduce considerable cognitive distortion. Moreover, affective meaning is associated with symbols of social differentiation in the respondents' more general value system (Johnston-Conover and Feldman, 1981). Since symbols of group differentiation are intimately bound up with such characteristics as prejudice, scapegoating, and marking off, these findings imply an ever decreasing autonomy of the political realm.

An additional cause for fluctuation in the boundaries of the political belief system is based on what Bank and her associates (1977) called the "wondrous confusion" stemming from the interchangeable use of norms, preferences, and beliefs in attitude research. Depending on whether an attitude taps a norm, a preference, or a belief, the boundaries of the political system may shrink or expand. Preferences are most intimately related to the affective structure of the individual, thus implying minimum autonomy. Norms are the most externalized forms of cognitive learning and are usually expressed for the benefit of others. As a result, norm-oriented attitudes would convey a greater sense of autonomy.

The assumption of high interdependence between the political and the general belief systems is accorded a more systematic treatment in the functional theory of attitude structure and change. This theory differentiates between the utilitarian and the adaptive functions of beliefs. The latter category is based on a systematic elaboration of some of the insights derived from the use of psychoanalytic approaches in social science. It includes a variety of expressive functions, such as self-assertion, and ego defense functions, such as displacement and projection (Smith, Bruner, and White, 1956; Katz, Sarnoff, and McClintock, 1956). Known also as the "need source of arousal interaction" (Waldman, 1972), "restorative" or "defensive" functions of the belief system, or simply "salience," these adaptive functions conjure up a vision of the political domain as subordinate to nonpolitical and largely affective dimensions of an individual's psychology.

Perhaps the least autonomous vision of the political belief system is offered by the psychoanalytic perspective. As explained by Tajfel and Fraser (1978, p. 23), the choices and decisions made by humans "appear to us as self-determined and explained in terms of subjectively 'obvious' reasons which can be analyzed in terms of social causation. However, this level of causation is only like the 'tip of the iceberg'; a great deal of what is submerged can only be properly understood . . . against the background of social causation." Of course, the "tip of the iceberg" hides the "unconscious mind"—the least observable human characteristic and the least amenable to rigorous research (Rolle, 1980, p. 404). Lane (1969, p. 314), in his study of political consciousness, argues that many of the motivations stemming from the unconscious parts of the self are not obvious to the individual. They are also inaccessible to the researcher, thus hampering his ability to empirically delineate the borderline of the political belief system.

Difficult to fathom at the individual level, the question of autonomy becomes even less tractable at the level of the collective political system. Traditional historical and political science studies imply the existence of a fairly autonomous realm of the "political" and its corresponding political beliefs. These studies are permeated by what Frank (1977, p. 555) has described as "the humanistic-scientific belief system which dominates the American scientific community." They assume a single reality existing independently of the actors and a relatively simple cause-and-effect structure. Moreover, the scholars impute rationality, as they define it, to the actors.

An influential school of thought in political science derives from mathematical game theory and economic models of "political man." A central tenet in this approach is that humans are rational thinkers in the minimax sense of the term. The minimax principle predicts that people maximize their utilities and minimize their losses. Coalition theory (Riker, 1962) and the economic model of democracy (Downs, 1957), which apply the insights of game theory to an analysis of broad political processes, translate the minimax principle into functional rationality. Riker's (1962, p. 24) notion of a "fiduciary morality" is especially pertinent. When individuals come to perform political roles, they are forced to adhere to strict political rationality. It is not difficult to imagine that, if such rationality were to exist, the collective political belief system would be fairly autonomous from nonpolitical inferences (Goodin, 1976).

Yet the bulk of the studies seem to imply an almost intuitive agreement that collective political belief systems reflect both the rational cognitive and the conscious and subconscious inner needs of individuals. Even before the Freudian psychoanalytic tradition took intellectual root, not all theorists agreed that historical political belief systems rested on solid rational foundations. Friedrich Nietzsche, Henri Bergson, Søren Kierkegaard, Vilfredo Pareto, and Georges Sorel, among others, dwelt extensively on the "undercurrents" in man's "stream of consciousness" (Rolle, 1980, p. 426). Jung systematized these linkages by introducing the notion of "archetypal images"—archaic types of mental imagery embedded in man's collective unconscious. These images originated in a specific historical milieu but later became intrapsychic constructs, which surfaced subsequently as national and social myths (Rolle, 1980, p. 404). As a special form of shared fantasy, the myth brings the individual into a relationship with other group members and through this interaction becomes fused in complex belief systems (Arlow, 1961). The concept of myth as a hallowed belief pattern, which is almost blindly and unconsciously accepted by the society, is also quite central in cultural anthropology. Responding to these trends, Lasswell (1951, p. 184) went so far as to assert that politics is not a special demonstration of social action but rather a corrective or compensatory mechanism for social interactions arising from stratification and conflict that are only dimly recognized. Thus, politics is the process by which the irrational bases of society are brought into the open.

Whether "psychoanalytic sociology" is capable of becoming a paradigm, with a scientific community turning this assumption into research prescriptions, is quite doubtful. Even without accepting this perspective, one can still support the view that different belief systems imply varying degrees of political autonomy. Within the Western culture, the constant transvaluation of the belief system has produced a sharp dichotomy between the cognitively oriented philosophers of the age of rationalism and the highly emotive, *Volksgeist*-inspired thinkers of the Romantic era.

Cross-cultural studies reveal a wide range of belief systems reflecting the emotive, metaphysical, and transcendental needs of humans. The ideology of the utopian and millenarian movements is a particularly good case in point. An intriguing, but difficult-to-verify, assumption derived from neurological research is that collective beliefs of people whose mode of thinking is skewed toward the use of the right brain hemisphere—the more affective of the two hemispheres—will reflect a higher degree of nonpolitical emotive content (Frank, 1977; Stakes, 1982).

The work on social conflict in general and social change in particular provides more limited but complementary testimony to the lack of autonomy. As indicated, these studies rest on the theoretical assumption that the transvaluation of the belief system, which is seen as a prerequisite for social action ranging from civil unrest to revolution, is based on psychological states such as the perception of relative deprivation (Gurr, 1970; Tilly, 1978) and the "demonstration effect" (Spengler, 1980).

Other studies of social conflict point to displacement mechanisms, which lead to ethnic strife, "scapegoating," and the emergence of anti-out-group beliefs that have become fimly embedded in the collective belief system. The role that anti-Semitism, which at least partially derives from ego need-oriented displacement, plays in many belief systems is perhaps the best-researched case; but other examples abound in the literature (Allport, 1979; Pettigrew, Allport, and Barnett, 1958). Even the more structure- and process-oriented studies of mobilization often argue that certain types of political mobilization rely heavily on potent affective symbols as a means of manipulating the emotional responses of individuals. Occasionally this type of manipulation leads to mass outbursts of the difficult-to-research "mercurial variables," such as collective aggression, murderous frenzy, hysteria, and vindictive warfare (Rolle, 1980).

The porous nature of the collective political system is perhaps best illustrated by studies linking individual psychological responses to ideational consolidation at the collective level. For instance, Socialist Zionism is said to have included elements derived from a personal rebellion against the father (Diamond, 1957; Gonen, 1975). Tucker (1973) gives an impressive account of how Stalin's neurotic childhood caused him to strive toward omnipotence, which was subsequently institutionalized in the personality cult of official Soviet ideology. Similar illustrations can be found in studies of other totalitarian regimes.

Political Belief Systems and Cognitive Styles

Popularized by Rokeach's (1960) studies on dogmatism, the assumption that beliefs are linked with cognitive styles has surfaced under a bewildering array of terms, such as "superordinate values," "core beliefs," "cultural referents," "latent attitudes," and "rockbed sedimentation." The vision of the less-than-universal process of thought that the concept of cognitive style invokes is most systematically explored by comparative cognitive psychology (Berry and Dasen, 1974). The findings most relevant to our concern are that considerable perceptual differences exist among various cultures and among groups within one culture in relating to different epistemological constructs of reality. Among the politically related concepts that reveal a high intercultural perceptual variability are the concepts of reality (time, space, and causation), authoritarian knowledge (rational-scientific versus supranational), resources (scarcity versus abundance), and morality (absolutist versus relativist). Yet these higher-level abstract constructs have not been systematically incorporated into the study of political beliefs—in part because, rather paradoxically, they are so integrated into the belief system that they are taken for granted. In Lane's (1969, p. 315) eloquent phrase, "consciousness of these most fundamental beliefs, embedded in the cultural matrix of behavior and expectation, [can be] so persuasive and dense that one mistakes it for the natural environment." Schutz (1962, p. 74) calls such shared definitions acquired unconsciously "a world taken for granted."

A second reason that these constructs have not been systematically incorporated into the study of political beliefs involves the difficulties in estimating whether a particular core construct is related to issues or to belief systems. Rosenau (1967) suggests, for example, that Almond and Verba's concept of "subjective competence" can be subject to competing interpretations. "Subjective competence" may be issue oriented, in the sense that individuals may feel more competent in influencing domestic rather than foreign policies; or it may be systemic, in the sense that some belief systems, regardless of the issue area, involve more "subjective competence" than others. Controlling for issue areas, scaled from domestic to foreign, would undoubtedly improve the prediction, but very few studies employ the rather sophisticated design required for such research.

A third, and more serious, reason is the presence of ethnocentrism in the methodology of political science—that is, the "privileging" of the researcher's own cultural conceptual system and the tendency to use it in analyzing aspects of other cultures (Booth, 1979, p. 15). Whether such bias is caused by beliefs in the superiority of one's own culture, by a lack of cross-cultural sophistication, or by the scientific socialization that results in equating one's cultural "givens" with universal laws of human behavior, it inevitably distorts the theoretical perspective and hampers empirical research. Jervis (1976), who surveyed the topic of perceptions and misperceptions in international relations, reports that such distortions are quite common. Even when the investigator is aware of the pitfalls of ethnocentric methodology, finding cross-cultural conceptual equivalents is not easy. Among the difficulties involved, Wilson (1970, pp. viii-ix) lists the "philosophical problems of . . . translating the meaning of one culture into the language of another," using scientific terms in order to explain empirically oriented beliefs, and "interpretation of the behavior that is not self-purposive." The culture-bound nature of meaning is also noted by Przeworski and Teune (1970). They emphasize the nonequivalences in the meaning of reality and time across cultural boundaries. Cross-cultural problems in the operational code literature are another testimony to these difficulties (Hermann, 1977).

Nowhere is this problem more acute than in determining what constitutes a "rational" belief system at either the collective or the individual level. Lukes's (1970, p. 207) remark that "the use of the word 'rational' and its cognates has caused untold confusion and obscurity" is probably an accurate comment on the state of the art. Because of different meanings and diverse semantic usage, the concept of "rationality" ("rational decision making" or "rational behavior") is one of the most complex constructs in the social sciences. In this chapter, only a brief presentation of the problem of discerning rationality within a cross-cultural context can be attempted.

One major definition of rationality derives from formal logic. The science of logic is aimed at converting the concrete to the abstract by the "replacing of concrete individual elements by *formalized* elements of variable meaning" (Langer, 1967, p. 24). The process of formalization, which goes through a number of stages, results in the creation of a deductive system. Such a system is based on a number of postulates or "primitive propositions," which are taken for granted. Other propositions are derived from these axioms. In order to fulfill the deductive requirements of the system, the postulates have to be coherent, contributive, consistent, and independent.

The requirements of formal logic define the parameters of a rational decision. Such a decision must satisfy three criteria: consistency, instrumentality, and transitivity. Consistency is defined in terms of preferences about outcomes (O). If one prefers O_1 to O_2, he cannot prefer at the same time O_2 to O_1. Instrumentality is defined in terms of the relation between action (A) and outcome. If one prefers O_1 to O_2, one should also prefer A_1 to A_2, assuming that A_1 leads to O_1 and that A_2 leads to O_2. Transitivity is a preference in the pattern of options of a triad. If one prefers O_1 to O_2 and O_2 to O_3, then one should prefer O_1 to O_3.

Because of the restrictive nature of these parameters, violation of logical rationality is extremely pervasive in human actions. Some types of violations are related to cross-cultural differences. Rapoport (1969, p. 9) points out that consistency can be undermined "when a decision maker changes his mind for no apparent reason." Such a change can be whimsical or patterned, as in the example of the man who prefers meat to fish but chooses fish on Friday. Such behavior can be labeled "irrational" only at the peril of ignoring cultural factors. If the man is a Catholic, the pattern may be consistent in religious terms. Rapoport suggests that we can redefine the situation by adding to the list of outcomes. That is, instead of the original two outcomes, "eating meat" and "eating fish," we can adopt four outcomes: "meat on Friday," "fish on Friday," "meat on non-Friday," and "fish on non-Friday." This is a relatively easy adjustment, but other cross-cultural situations may necessitate redefinition of situational scripts beyond the permissible number of outcomes.

A more serious problem in logical rationality arises out of the ongoing debate between anthropologists and psycholinguists about the extent to which constructs that express logical relations are universally incorporated in human culture. Sparked by the controversy over "prerational mentality" and the subsequent Sapir-Whorf hypothesis, which postulates that language shapes thought habits, the discussion focuses on the question of whether every language possesses the concepts of conjunction, disjunction, and negation. These concepts, along with concepts such as implication and equivalence, form the backbone of the formal logic structure. Cole, Gay, and Glick (1974), in attempting to determine why African children experience difficulties in studying mathematics, found that the speed at which an individual can identify logical rules is related to linguistic structure. Nevertheless, there is no conclusive evidence to indicate whether some belief systems are more logically rational than others.

Finally, the use of formal logic in evaluating individual or collective belief systems may reveal that some of them are not empirically "rational." This seems paradoxical if one accepts the popular belief that logic somehow equates with "empirical truth." Unfortunately, deductive systems deal with logical certainty or *validity*, not with "factual certainty": "We may start with premises that have no foundation in fact at all and elaborate a perfectly . . . consistent deductive system,- . . .for in logic we require that our assertions shall be valid, not that they convey truth about the evidence" (Langer, 1967, p. 189). Only if the society is committed to the scientific paradigm as well is there some guarantee that its belief system will be empirically rational (Kuhn, 1962, p. 93). In the absence of such a commitment, culturally derived, formal logical rationality will deviate from empirical rationality. Traditional or religious belief systems can often be logically constrained but are never structured in such a way that their theorems lend themselves to empirical verification.

Another definition of rationality derives from Von Neumann and Morgenstern's (1947) theory of games, where the paradigm of the rational behavior of an individual is based on the minimax principle. As already indicated, this principle postulates that a rational decision maker will use a technique for maximizing his utilities at a minimum cost. The major pitfall of this formulation is that the rationality of a decision can be evaluated only if the individual's subjective scale of utility can be converted to some objective and comparable scale. Subsequent efforts to find empirical techniques to scale individual utilities have proved difficult. Because of individual and cross-cultural differences, the assumption of rationality had to be relaxed to the point where utilities were defined simply as social choices. Laboratory tests of gaming theories, such as the Prisoner's Dilemma or the Acme-Bolt trucking game, reveal that subjects deviate from the rational behavior prescribed by these games (Billig, 1976). Empirical studies of coalition formation indicate that national differences often override the principle of the minimal winning coalition as prescribed by Riker's (1962) classical coalition theory (De Swaan, 1973).

Rationality is most often regarded as the process through which individuals select means in order to achieve their ends. The means-ends rationality is subjective; it is based on the phenomenological assumption that individual perceptions define the context of the decision. An objective evaluation of the quality of the means-ends rationality involves an analysis of the processes through which an individual reaches a decision. Scholars offer three models for evaluating this process: the analytical, the cybernetic, and the cognitive. The analytical model assumes that decision makers go through the following steps: comprehensive search for options, optimal revision, complete evaluation, and value maximization. This model incorporates elements of both formal logic and minimax rationality. The cybernetic model assumes that decision makers use a programmed operation to select appropriate means for the given ends. The core of the cybernetic procedure is known as "satisficing"—that is, the reduction of uncertainty and complexity by small and marginal changes. The cognitive model assumes that decision makers act somewhat like "intuitive scientists"; they can construct causal explanations and show a capacity for formal logical rigor (for a good review of the models, see Gross-Stein and Tanter, 1980, pp. 23–62).

Extensive research devoted to evaluating these processes is quite unanimous in documenting that the quality of means-ends rationality is rather low regardless of which of the models is adopted. Deviations from rationality are caused by numerous factors. Some stem from an individual's cognitive errors, such as flaws in logical reasoning (Ross, 1977), low tolerance of cognitive dissonance (Abelson and Rosenberg, 1958), commitment to a central concept (Alker and Hermann, 1971), cognitive simplicity (Suedfeld, Tetlock, and Ramirez, 1977), and a low level of probabilistic thinking (Wright and Phillips, 1979). Other deviations are the result of an individual's affective states, such as a lack of "coolheadedness" (Verba, 1961), or crisis-induced stress (Brecher, 1977). Still others are caused by group biases, such as "groupthink" (Janis, 1972) or "risky shifts" (Vinokur and Burnstein, 1974). Individual difficulties in ordering values across dimensions (Simon, 1956) are compounded by the problem of trading off values in a group.

Not surprisingly, such a catalogue makes it doubtful whether means-ends rationality can be analyzed across cultures. This difficulty is epitomized by the classic anthropological query as to whether praying for rain is a rational act, given the fact that, objectively, prayer is less likely to produce rain than cloud seeding is (Jarvie, 1970). The means-ends rationality of this act can be evaluated only within the context of a particular societal belief sytem and depends on the extant knowledge of means (options) in this society and on their legitimacy. In prescientific societies extraordinary events that seemed opposed to the order of nature—events such as drought, flood, eclipse, or aurora borealis—were regarded as signs of heaven's wrath. Prayer was used in order to mollify God or the Heavens and, therefore, can be seen as quite rational given the context. In addition, not all known means are accepted by societies as legitimate in problem solving. Taboos and sanctions are used against certain means, especially "foreign cultural imports." Even in contemporary society, birth control techniques, though objectively effective in controlling population growth, are not perceived as legitimate in a number of belief systems.

Another cross-cultural problem involved in means-ends rationality pertains to the calculus of probability in estimates of outcomes. Individuals and collectivities, whether consciously or not, calculate the probability of successful outcomes whenever they make a decision. Yet the "probability that an event will occur" has more than one meaning. Theoretical probability can be inferred from events that have a known number of outcomes. Empirically defined probability is inferred from the observed frequency of an event, given that the situation is "identical." It can also mean the ratio of the number of "favorable" outcomes to the number of all possible cases.

In decisions involving social realities, the "probability that an event will occur" is often not an objective property of an event but is inferred from one's degree of belief about the outcome. A belief-based calculus implies that "the probability of an event changes in the light of what we know" (Rapoport, 1969,

p. 30). In order to make probability estimates in complex situations, decision makers utilize beliefs derived from analogous reasoning. Analogous thinking is basic to all cognitive activity; yet, paradoxically, it can introduce biases in probability estimates. A considerable number of studies have demonstrated that reliance on such analogous or "heuristic" devices can affect the ways in which individuals estimate probability (for a review, see Nisbett and Ross, 1980, pp. 17–41).

Such biases may become more prominent in traditional or religious belief systems, where analogous thinking is normatively reinforced. The great mathematician Pierre Simon de Laplace, in his work on the philosophy of probability, dating from 1795, listed a number of possible fallacies stemming from the use of historical analogies. One is the "degradation of the probability of events" because of transgenerational repetition. The accuracy of presentation of a historical event, which is originally estimated at a fraction less than unity, diminishes with each repetition. The probability of the accuracy of repetitions is equivalent to the original fraction raised to the power indicated by the number of repetitions. For instance, if the probability of each testimony is estimated at $9/10$ and it is transmitted by twenty "witnesses," the probability that the last testimony will be as accurate as the first is less than $1/8$ (see Laplace, [1814] 1950, p. 13).

An even more serious bias in the use of historical analogies is related to the fact that estimates of probabilities increase or diminish according to the mutual combination of events. For instance, if the events are considered to be independent of one another, the probability of their occurring together is the product of their individual probability of occurring. When two events are dependent on each other, the probability of the compound event is the product of the probability of the occurrence of the first event and the probability that, the first event having occurred, the second will occur. Analogous thinking is apparently skewed toward a compound perception of events at the cost of underestimating the frequency of independent events.

This necessarily brief review demonstrates that means-ends rationality can fluctuate widely according to the collective belief system. Societies whose belief systems are underlaid by the scientific paradigm are more likely to score higher on the means-ends rationality scale than those that skew their estimates of outcomes because of what Jervis (1976, p. 217) calls the "tyranny of the past upon imagination." In the most extreme cases, belief systems and the individuals who act on them turn from probabilistic to deterministic thinking because they "know" the outcome.

The growing realization that cognitive styles can influence political beliefs has already led to a reinterpretation of some traditional themes in political science. For instance, Prandy's (1979) cognitive analysis of perceptions of interest and alienation among the British working class proves that the traditional lower-class acceptance of social status quo is not necessarily related to normative deference. (The concept of deference dominated the hypothesis of the working-class Tory—that is, the phenomenon of blue-collar support for the Conservative party.) Rather, this acceptance of the status quo can be traced to the cognitive style of certain groups and particularly to perceptions of authority and self-direction. Workers accept the status quo, then, because of their perception that the social arrangement is inevitable, not because they believe that it is morally justified (as the notion of deference implies).

In an important contribution to the theory of relative deprivation, Yuchtman-Yaar (1983) argues that social expectations involve two perceptual elements.

One is the level of expectancy, a reality-bound way in which individuals evaluate their remuneration. The other is entitlement, a moral or normative judgment about what they deserve. When people believe that their entitlement is legitimate, they will accept a low level of remuneration. Perceptions of expectancy and entitlement are related to subjective feelings of welfare, which, in turn, create the attitude of relative deprivation. Such a sophisticated causal model of cognitive status explains, among other things, the changes in the belief system of blacks in America. Before the civil rights movement, blacks apparently accepted their low socioeconomic entitlement as legitimate. Recently, black employees were found to be more dissatisfied with their low remuneration than whites, although there was no racial difference with regard to expectancy.

The discussion of cognitive style has an immense but largely unrealized potential for explaining belief systems as they relate to domestic and foreign policy matters. In a generative reevaluation of the concept of political culture, Elkins and Simeon (1979) advocate the use of superordinate values—such as assumptions about order in the universe or the nature of causality or perceptions of competitiveness—in comparative studies of political beliefs. They point out that the absence of these overarching dimensions in research has frequently led to a bifurcated view of human behavior, such as Barry's (1970) distinction between the utility-maximizing "economic" approach and Parsons's (1964) value-analysis perspective underlying the "sociological" approach.

Elkins and Simeon's cogent argument that the utility calculus and assessment of costs and benefits are profoundly influenced by cultural cognitive styles has been echoed by others. Lane (1969) asserts that perceptions of resources, dichotomized into scarcity and abundance, may become embedded in a society's belief system. If the former predominates, it can create a zero-sum-game perception (that is, a competitive outlook); if the latter predominates, it can create a variable-sum-game perception (a cooperative outlook). Rapoport (1969, pp. 86–87), a leading authority on game theory applications in political science, argues that rationality is context bound. The cost and benefit calculations, which are based on the functional relations implied by the concept of rationality, are influenced by different settings. Rapoport illustrates this point by noting that even the calculation of the marginal benefit of saving human life varies with the specific context. Perceptions of the marginal utility of human life may depend on such factors as the relative anonymity of the victim. Thus, a lower value may be placed on reducing fatal traffic accidents than on saving the lives of a small group of coal miners. Calculations involving the marginal utility of human life can, of course, also vary dramatically in different cultural-religious settings.

Another construct that is not easily accommodated in traditional research, although it has relevance for the study of the belief system, is the perception of time. One instance of the variability in perceptions of time is the religiously inspired cyclical notion of time, as opposed to Western-secular concepts of time, which postulate a linear progression from one event to another. Cyclical concepts of time imply a fusion of past, present, and future. One such cycle is the Chinese conception of time or world age. According to this conception, time starts all over again every twenty-three million years (Sivin, 1966). Cyclicality is also implied in the Talmudic concept of redemption, which, though consigned to the remote future, would restore the glory of the past.

The perception of time can influence the belief system of a society in many ways. Sivin argues that the cyclical notion of time created an ambivalence in the way Chinese perceived progress and modernization. On the one hand, there was an awareness of progress and change; on the other, the recurrence of situational contexts made past relevant to present. The notion of fused time can hold a major moral significance because it organizes events in a moral sequence leading to a certain transcendental goal, such as the redemption (Seliktar, 1983). The normative purposiveness implied in such a time concept has quite different implications for a political belief system than the value-neutral notion of linear progression. Indeed, Mannheim ([1929] 1955, p. 235) generalized the notion of time sense by arguing that the "conservative mode of experiencing time found the best corroboration of its sense determinateness in the discovery of time as the creator of value."

Another instance where time can be differentially perceived is in what Lane (1969, p. 315) calls utopian as opposed to incremental thinking. The utopian mode has a certain "timeless" quality in experiencing time, which influences profoundly the perception of political possibilities in the belief system. In some ways the utopian sense of time, with its perceptual corollary of unlimited possibility, can produce a more initiating posture in national or group policies than the more cautious incremental appreciation of time (see also Fraisse, 1963).

Comparative cognitive psychology provides three additional insights of potential importance to understanding conflict and cooperation. The first is cultural variability in perceptions of the moral order. Each group moralizes its code of behavior in order to enhance collective commitments to laws and customs, to increase group cohesion, and to provide sanctions against "defectors, heretics, and deviants of all kinds" (Lane, 1969, p. 190). Yet societies differ greatly in the degree to which they perceive their code as the ultimate form of universal morality. In the extreme case of the absolutist perception of morality—or, as Mannheim ([1929] 1955, p. 57) calls it, "total conception of ideology"—we refer to "fundamental modes of experiencing and interpretation" and the neologically derived "conceptual framework of a mode of thought." The "total conception of ideology" questions the opponent's *Weltanschauung*, including his conceptual apparatus. With a more relativist perception—that is, Mannheim's "particularist ideology"—one can still "refute lies and eradicate sources of error [in the adversary's belief system] by referring to accepted criteria of objective validity common to both parties." Needless to say, the absolutist morality involves a much sharper zero-sum-game perception of intergroup relations and the external environment than the alternative outlook does.

The second insight derives from attribution theory, which comprises the set of theoretical principles proposed to explain how people draw causal inferences about other people's behavior. Based on Heider's (1958) work on phenomenal causality, attribution theory asumes that the means by which individuals predict social events are essentially similar to those used in predicting physical events. The attribution of events to causal sources is of immense importance to human perceptions of international or social environments. As Heider (1958, p. 16) notes, "It makes a real difference . . . if a person discovers that a stick that struck him fell from a rotten tree or was hurled by an enemy."

Perceptions of causality depend on perceptions of intention, and it is here that large cultural differences exist. For instance, in the Jewish Talmudic culture, an action is scrupulously evaluated according to the actor's intention. Moreover, in some instances the intention is judged to be more important than the action. In deliberating on the various restrictions of labor on the Sabbath, the Talmud judges the act on the basis of intention, which precedes the action (Steinsaltz, 1977, p. 110). Anthropological research has documented the elaborate procedures used for ascertaining intentions in tribal cultures.

The notion that different perceptions of intentionality may affect causality is of great importance for theories of international relations and even for some applied fields, such as intelligence. When acts are ambiguous and difficult to interpret, as most acts in international relations are, the reaction, including the "benefit-of-the-doubt" calculus, will depend on variable national perceptions of intentionality.

The third insight derives from Abelson's (1967) work on cognitive strategies of intrapersonal conflict resolution in instances where a person is faced with a situation that clashes with his beliefs. Abelson identifies four modal strategies: (1) *denial,* which is a direct attack on the elements underlying the conflict situation; (2) *bolstering,* which attempts to resolve the conflict by generating beliefs supportive of one of the unbalanced elements; (3) *differentiation,* which separates the conflict situation into discrete parts—that is, different dimensions of experience; (4) *transcendence,* which seeks a concept of a higher order to reconcile the disparate elements.

Miller (1978) has shown that these strategies for intrapersonal conflict resolution may be culturally formed. North Americans are more likely to use transcendence; South Americans opt for denial; Asians do not exhibit any modal preference. These findings acquire an added importance when viewed within the context of intergroup relations. The most cooperative posture is implied in the strategy of transcendence. It involves the development of superordinate goals that may supersede existing differences. In cases of strongly conflictual ethnic identities, the groups may utilize transcendence to create a superordinate civic identity. The history of the various international organizations and cooperation schemes may represent the application of transcendence to interstate conflicts.

Differentiation can diminish the conflict through the acquiescence of one group to another. In superordinate-subordinate group relations, the subordinate group often resolves the cognitive dissonance stemming from split identity by differentiating between levels of emotional discourse and action-oriented attitudes. For instance, in colonial situations many "natives" caught between the need to reassert their independence and the fact of foreign domination apply the strategy of differentiation. There is evidence to indicate that they perceive their commitment to independence and their lack of action to achieve it as two separate dimensions of intrapersonal discourse (Mannoni, 1964). The implications of denial and bolstering for intergroup conflict have not been fully elaborated in empirical research, but it seems safe to assume that bolstering increases the probability of intergroup conflict.

Correlation Between Domestic Belief Systems and Foreign Policy Beliefs

The correlation between domestic belief systems and foreign policy beliefs is difficult to ascertain, as the linkage literature in international relations demonstrates. For instance, Rosenau's (1969) representative volume on the subject reveals that— for a variety of reasons, ranging from the structure of domestic advocacy groups to geographical insularity—national foreign policies may be either interactionist or isolationist. For a number of reasons, the collective domestic belief system is a poor predictor of a country's foreign policy. First, countries are universally committed to preserving basic values such as physical survival of the population, territorial integrity, and political sovereignty. More national variation can be expected in what Brecher (1979, p. 447) has called "context-specific" beliefs; that is, foreign policy issues defined by countries as "high priority." Unlike the internal sovereignty of the domestic environment, rules of international interaction allow less leverage in pursuing such subjectively defined beliefs. As a result, foreign policy beliefs exhibit less national variation than domestic beliefs.

Second, extant typologies of political systems are normally based on the structure and legitimacy of domestic authority. The history of international relations, however, does not provide enough evidence to support the hypothesis that authoritarian or even totalitarian regimes are systematically more aggressive than other regimes. When such a correlation does exist, it is normally mediated by the power of the countries involved. Occasionally, as in Franco's Spain, a totalitarian regime may abstain from international conflict; or, like Pol Pot's Cambodia, it may become "psychologically insular." Such complexities indicate that a multivariate causal model is needed in order to improve prediction.

Third, domestic belief systems may affect the international outlook of a country in indirect and empirically difficult-to-investigate ways. Jervis (1976, p. 62) raised the intriguing possibility that some societies tend to develop a more Hobbesian foreign policy culture than others. A Hobbesian outlook tends to create a zero-sum-game perception of the external environment and can prompt a country to choose the spiral model of international competitions. Other countries have a more cooperative foreign policy cognition and abide by the rules of the deterrence model.

Fourth, there is the theoretical and methodological difficulty in delineating foreign policy issues and beliefs. Rosenau (1967) and others have dealt with the formidable theoretical and operational problems that have to be overcome in order to isolate foreign policy issues from domestic problems. Yet Rosenau's conclusion that foreign policy issues may or may not constitute an area with clear-cut boundaries and distinguishable characteristics bears testimony to the confusion surrounding the problem.

This confusion arises from two interrelated elements, which can be separated only in analytical terms. One is the degree of correlation between domestic and foreign policy beliefs, and the other is the respective degrees of autonomy among beliefs within the framework of the total societal belief system. We can best understand the first issue by looking at the structure of individual beliefs.

At the most general level of discourse, we accept McClosky's (1967, p. 67) opinion that "foreign policy attitudes are in principle no different from other political and social attitudes: they spring together with other attitude phenotypes from common personality genotypes." As a consequence, many of them can be more correctly understood "as part of a substantively diverse network of attitudes than as a unique stance arising wholly or largely out of elements intrinsic to the domain of international politics." A perusal of the empirical literature, however, raises doubts that domestic and foreign policy beliefs correlate at the personal level. For example, the research aimed at identifying clusters of domestic and foreign policy opinions that can be scaled along the traditional left-right or liberal-conservative continuum indicates that such a cluster is at best not universal and at worst nonexistent. Axelrod (1967) has demonstrated that the statistical correlation between holding liberal opinions on domestic and on international issues is quite weak in the general public. Moreover, a number of studies have shown that this correlation may disappear or become inverse when one controls for social class. Lower social strata, which normally form the backbone of liberal strength on domestic issues, can be quite conservative or rightist in foreign policy matters and in the treatment of minorities (Almond, 1965; Bell, 1964; Melikian, 1959).

A number of explanations for these findings can be offered. One pertains to the conceptual and methodological difficulties in using ideological scales in attitude research. The traditional undimensional scaling of issues, in terms of right-left or liberal-conservative, was inspired by the historical cleavages in Western industrial societies. The undimensional scale became increasingly strained in trying to accommodate a host of postindustrial issues that do not easily fit the traditional label. These undimensional scales are even less likely to fit foreign policy issues, since it is subjectively difficult for an individual to identify what constitutes a liberal or conservative issue in international relations. The use of multidimensional scaling, which has alreay been discussed in relation to domestic beliefs, may somewhat improve the fit. Nevertheless, spatial representation is susceptible to different interpretations according to the techniques used. One promising way in which special scaling techniques can be used is demonstrated by Ben-Sira's (1979) application of Guttman's smallest-space analysis. Ben-Sira found that domestic and foreign policy attitudes correlate to the extent that they pose a direct threat to the individual but not according to ideological proximity.

An alternative way to explain this lack of correlation is derived from what may be broadly called the "structure-of-meaning" literature. Extensive research in cognitive psychology and related fields has revealed that the meaning of ideological labels may vary culturally; that the meaning of issues and ideological labels is defined by a specific salient belief, known as a "referent"; and that salient issues vary widely among people. Consequently, different people use different "referents" in positioning themselves on the liberal-conservative continuum (Kerlinger, 1972; Szalay and Kelly, 1982). This perspective is especially promising in research on non-Western societies whose cleavage systems do not reflect the fissures of the industrial revolution. A multinational study that tested the validity of the meaning of left and right in thirteen countries provides conclusive evidence that this construct is "Western oriented." The authors found that the left-right division lacks clarity in Third World countries and "that such divisions should be interpreted only within the context of a particular nation or culture" (Finley, Simon, and Wilson, 1974, p. 213). The notion of "referents" is flexible enough to discern the particular issues that are most salient in different societies and provides an economic way of identifying the underlying meaning of the ideological labels. Research on Israeli political behavior routinely indicates that ideological labeling is influenced by foreign policy attitudes toward territorial concessions (Arian and Shamir, 1983). Lebanese political scientists Ghassan Salameh and Sofir Saadeh (quoted in the New York Times, March 12, 1984, p. A10) argue that traditional ideology is marginal; the terms of left and right are most conveniently used to describe attitudes toward foreign powers.

The third explanation derives from the sociologically oriented perspective, which argues that belief systems in postindustrial societies cannot be understood in terms of the traditional ideological apparatus. Instead, the notion of privatism is proposed as the new base for a mass belief system. Privatized orientation is defined as a purely "instrumental interest in those features of the social and political order which are central for the maintenance of private life." This outlook is opposed to the more publicly oriented commitment to collective goals (Turkel, 1980, p. 222). Privatism tends to produce issue-specific responses toward foreign policy, which are evaluated on the basis of private interests. The more theoretical implication is that foreign policy opinions are formed ad hoc, on the basis of privatist concerns, and may "swing" in all directions, reminiscent of the "issue voting" behavior identified in recent electoral literature. Hacker (1970) found that privatism in America is related to isolationism, but Turkel (1980) points out that privatism may easily lead to interventionism, depending on the future availability of resources. Of course, demands for protectionism, which are normally detrimental to the international collective, are another manifestation of privatism.

The fourth, and perhaps most important, explanation is based on the functional rationale behind belief formation. We have already indicated that individual belief systems are functional in relating the self to society. Societal beliefs are functional in solving group conflicts arising out of problems concerning the authoritative allocation of values. The domestic context provides what Abelson (1976) calls "episodic concrete information," with which the individual can formulate and shape his beliefs. Such nationally focused beliefs are difficult to apply to an international context, which may be equivalent to Abelson's "abstract information" environment. Rosenau and Holsti (1983, p. 384), in their description of the foreign policy thinking of the American elite, provide an especially insightful illustration of this difficulty: "In thinking about domestic affairs, one is inclined to develop integrated beliefs about justice, equality, representation . . . values that have little applicability to the conditions to which foreign policy is addressed."

In addition to examining the correlation between domestic and foreign policy beliefs, we need to explore whether foreign policy opinion enjoys a greater autonomy in the individual's total belief system than domestic political beliefs do. The rather limited number of studies on this issue are quite uniform in concluding that opinions about foreign policy are even less autonomous than opinions about domestic policy. Given the remote and abstract nature of foreign policy, these findings are somewhat surprising. They can be explained by motivational and cognitive psychology.

First, people have normally only a limited knowledge about a foreign environment. Under conditions of information scarcity, individuals tend to rely more on stereotyped thinking. Research on perceptions of out-groups and foreign nationals has documented that only a small number of ethnic and national stereotypes are positive. Negative stereotypes and prejudice are often used by members of a national group to channel aggression and build up internal cohesion (Greenstein, 1967; Rosenblatt, 1964).

Second, an unfamiliar environment over which the individual and his country have no control appears to be potentially threatening, regardless of the intrinsic character of the issue involved. Moreover, the content of foreign policy debates is often ambiguous; the messages are confused, contradictory, and unfamiliar to the person. Such a confusing set of stimuli can generate cognitive dissonance, anxiety, and fear. These reactions can trigger defense mechanisms or dissonance reduction, which gloss over cognitive ambiguity.

Third, foreign policy issues are often invested with symbolic meaning; that is, they are ideal "sources of arousal" and can give rise to highly affective responses. Attacks on officially designed national symbols abroad, such as diplomatic posts and personnel, are especially arousing; but even more pedestrian issues, such as international water rights, can provoke highly affective responses. Decolonization, even when only marginal possessions are involved, can create a massive psychological trauma, as Lijphart's (1966) study on the Netherlands' divestiture of its West New Guinea colony showed. Indeed, highly emotive responses to foreign policy issues have been occasionally manipulated for mobilization purposes. It is a truism that political leaders, especially in nondemocratic regimes, use highly symbolic foreign policy issues in order to overcome domestic difficulties and promote national cohesion. In some cases domestic failures are redefined in such a way as to be perceived as an outcome of the hostile international environment.

Of course, the least autonomous response is elicited in international conflicts that threaten the physical survival of a group or in clashes between total belief systems. Religious wars; the clash between the big "isms," such as nazism, fascism, communism, and capitalism; and the emergent bitter fissures between the international North and South pose an immense threat to the very identity of an individual. This type of conflict, which mobilizes one's entire psychological defense system, produces the most profound emotive responses (Stagner, 1967; Strachey, 1957).

Actually, a number of studies have demonstrated that foreign policy opinions reflect an individual's total belief system as mediated by personality. For instance, Smith and Rosen (1958) found that world-minded persons are likely to have fewer stereotypes, and Puttney and Middletown (1962) documented that college students' opinions on the arms race were influenced by concerns about their social status and by their intellectual outlook. McClosky's (1967) excellent study on the psychological bases of isolationism reveals a virtual panoply of both genotypical and phenotypical sources, including inflexibility, inclination toward polarization, black-white dichotomous distinctions, stimulus fixation, and selective attention. Moreover, in an instance of admirable intellectual honesty, McClosky (1967, p. 59) acknowledged that the exact boundaries of foreign policy beliefs are virtually indeterminable: "Isolationism is really a complex political orientation that can originate in different ways and from diverse motives. It may spring from psychological needs and impulses as well as from social, intellectual, or political elements and it need not serve the same function or possess the same meaning to all persons who embrace it."

A Decision-Making Approach to Analyzing Societal Belief Systems

The view expressed in McClosky's statement—that social reality is an incredibly complex and difficult-to-decipher network of motives, interactions, and structures arranged in an ever changing kaleidoscopic pattern—poses enormous problems for describing and analyzing such phenomena. At the risk of simplifying the problem, we can identify two broad approaches.

One approach may be loosely described as traditional. It includes a variety of historical, philosophical, legal, and institutional studies as well as a host of case studies concerned with "contemporary history." This approach does not attempt to apply the rigor of the scientific paradigm of inquiry, including operationalization of epistemological constructs, hypothesis testing, causal analysis, and theory formulation (Kuhn, 1962). From the sociology-of-knowledge perspective, this approach has a number of advantages. It is heuristic in the Renaissance sense of the term; that is, it identifies, albeit intuitively, latent, abstract, and empirically nonobvious dimensions of social reality, which subsequently inform more rigorous research. The major disadvantage of this approach is that, in the absence of scientific rigor, it gives the observer great latitude in interpreting reality. Even if we disregard normative or politically tendentious writing and assume a fair degree of objectivity and integrity, scholars still follow their personal predilections and professional socialization when they interpret complex social networks of reality. Thus, Theodor Mommsen's legalistically informed view of the Roman Empire, Charles Beard's economically inspired vision of American history, the Whig interpretation of British history, and Kenneth Clark's humanistic vision of civilization, to name just a few examples, have become embedded in the collective view of reality. In some cases, such as in the famous encounter over Arnold Toynbee's perception of Jews as a "fossilized civilization" or the controversy over Margaret Mead's view of coming of age in Samoa, this latitude is apparently of such magnitude as to obfuscate the thin boundary between the social objective and the normative.

The other approach, the "behavioral" approach, includes studies that try to implement, with varying degrees of accuracy, the principles of scientific investigation. These studies provide a more structured and systematic and less arbitrary view of social reality. They are also integrationist in the sense of striving to build up systematic inventories of knowledge, especially by generating new knowledge through the use of survey methods. Because of the self-imposed rigor of scientific inquiry, this approach provides less latitude for personal and value-oriented interpretations. A major drawback of this approach stems from the fact that it is geared toward explaining the stable rather than the changing, occasionally at the cost of overemphasizing the status quo. Moreover, interpretations often are results of the methodology employed. One of the better-known statistical artifacts stems from assumptions about bipolarity. The term "bipolar" implies a distribution along a single continuum, ranging from positive to negative (or right to left). There is a widely held assumption in the social sciences that certain psychological constructs are bipolar in nature, thus implying a competitive situation between the ends of the range. The notion of bipolarity, which was particularly popular in identity studies, was challenged by Kerlinger (1967), who demonstrated that attitudes can be orthogonal—that is, posited at a right angle. Such a structure would make some attitudes complementary rather than conflicting. Under the bipolar assumption, American national versus ethnic identity, for example, is viewed as conflictual, whereas the orthogonal assumption allows for a complementary interpretation.

Another drawback of the behavioral approach is that, because of the constraint of scientific design, it can handle only a limited number of variables and tends to produce a narrow vision of reality. Yet, because of statistical rigor, some of the findings become perceived as scientific rules, almost akin to the physical laws of the universe. Almond and Verba's (1965) civic culture is a case in point. The conceptually sound and statistically derived categories of subject, parochial, and participant cultures provide an invaluable contribution to the understanding of the working of the "invisible hand" of democracy. The immense appeal of civic culture is at least partially due to the psychological relief function that it performs for contemporary political science, overburdened by the generations-long deliberation on the "spirit of democracy." Included in almost every textbook, the concept of civic culture has become one of the "iron laws" of political science.

There are many grounds on which the concept of civic culture can be criticized and, indeed, has been criticized. Perhaps the point most pertinent to our concern is that the willingness to criticize or take action against the government, one of the hallmarks of participatory culture, is not necessarily an exclusive reflection of an individual's sense of personal efficacy. An alternative argument is that an individual's reluctance to criticize the authorities may stem from a "siege mentality." That is, in highly mobilized societies where physical existence or survival depends on maximal communal cohesion, consensus may be regarded as the highest moral value. Such a belief system, if generationally transmitted, can even inhibit criticism in the future. While such a pattern may generate parochialism, it also might produce a sophisticated voluntary restraint on an individual's urge to exercise political efficacy. Presumably, in such a context, subordinating one's personal efficacy to the collective goals will be perceived as a more civic stand. Whether democracy is possible under such conditions is not relevant to our discussion. The concept of civic culture is culture bound because it derives from the implicit assumption that homeostasis is the natural condition of human existence.

No research design can eliminate all or even most of the shortcomings implied in both the traditional and behavioral approaches or utilize all the advantages that they offer. Nevertheless, a researcher might produce a more balanced picture of the reality under investigation by systematically combining the traditional and the behavioral approaches in one framework. More specifically, we propose to study the societal belief system as an interaction of the macrosociological and microsociological levels of beliefs.

A useful way to accomplish this end may be to adopt a decision-oriented definition of a collective belief system. Derived from the anthropological concept of culture pattern, a belief system is defined as the range of acceptable possible alternatives from which groups or individuals may choose a course of action, other circumstances permitting (see Elkins and Simeon, 1979). Belief systems, in effect, set the agenda for decision making. In Handel's (1979, p. 858) words, a belief system is a "formulation of a preferred course of action for a specific class of actors in a specific class of situations." Such a conceptualization of belief system has a number of advantages:

1. It introduces a notion of probability into the explanation; the alternatives within the range (or set) are treated as permissive rather than as deterministic events. Each individual event does not have to happen, but it has a certain probability of occurring. Such a definition is most appropriate for complex political systems in which personalities, social and political structures, role definitions, and external circumstances mediate the relationship between the range of belief options and policy decisions and behavior.

2. The notion of a range or set of alternatives (A, B, C, or X, Y, Z) may instruct us about the range of choices the policy elite will consider in response to certain given contingencies. In spite of personal idiosyncrasies, elites are rarely known to exceed the permissible range of alternatives for any given contingency.

3. The notion of range can help us identify and compare the degree of var-

iance among belief systems, either between nations or within one country. This is especially crucial when one is analyzing incrementally changing collective beliefs in a political system. The comparison of the old and new set of alternatives would reveal whether there is a complete discontinuity (A, B, C ~ E, F) or whether there is a degree of overlap between the systems (A, B, C ~ B, C, D or A, B, C ~ C, D, E).

4. The identification of the sets can also help us analyze the degree of salience (an increase in probability of occurrence) that the belief system attaches to a given alternative. Two belief sets often contain the same options but accord them each a different salience. For example, the literature on ecological sociology indicates that attachment to a certain territorial expanse can range from the instrumental to the sentimental. Those who hold the instrumental view perceive the territorial tract as a property, resource, or military asset, whereas those who hold the sentimental view perceive the expanse as the center of the moral and religious order of their society (Toennis, 1955; Eliade, 1958). When there is a dispute over a territory, the international ramifications of the degree of salience can be quite different. Whereas one can offer material substitutes or territorial security arrangements to those who hold an instrumental view, one can use little reasoned argument with those who possess the sentimental perspective.

5. It is possible to identify assorted groups by the subset of alternatives they hold within the range. Such identification is especially important with regard to the power elite because their preferred alternatives have a higher probability of turning into policy choices. Moreover, the positions of ethnic, religious, and other pressure and challenge groups should be located. In coalition governments the preferences of such groups may receive disproportionate weight, increasing the probability that the alternatives in their subsets will turn into policies. In addition, policy makers will normally defer to the views of groups that invoke the specter of *Kulturkampf*.

6. One can use the range of options as a framework in constructing questionnaires to measure individual attitudes. The major advantage of such a framework is that the questionnaires can cover a wide variety of issues arranged in several dimensions that may not be obvious when one constructs such surveys in a more random and intuitive way. With regard to attitude surveys, two research strategies commend themselves. One would measure the empirical fit among the attitudes of the various elites with a view toward isolating areas of high overlap (consensus). The researcher would assign policy options in these areas a higher score in terms of their probability of occurrence and give a lower probability score to options featured in less consensual areas. The second strategy would focus on estimations of the empirical fit between elite and mass beliefs. Sharp disparities between the attitudes of elite and mass can serve as early indicators that the ruling belief system is being delegitimized. Delegitimization and its twin concept transvaluation are normally difficult to detect in incrementally changing situations; the measure of fit can improve our predictions.

7. The analysis of mass attitudes can provide an empirical indicator of the probability that the elite will turn its beliefs into political decisions. We can consider the relation between elite beliefs and decision making in power terms. Whenever there is massive popular support for elite beliefs, there is a high probability that the elite will act on these beliefs. It is also possible to look at the same relationship through the psychological concept of "anticipated reaction." Elites frequently screen alternatives in anticipation of a positive or negative popular reaction. The effect of

anticipated reaction on elite behavior is difficult to determine empirically, because the process of screening may be at least partially subconscious. Knowledge of the distribution of mass attitudes within the range of options can provide an empirical substitute for investigating the effects of anticipated reactions.

Conclusion

In this chapter we have tried to demonstrate that the study of societal belief systems can contribute to a better understanding of political science problems. The four issues that can profit most from such understanding are the process of formation and maintenance of political systems, systemic stability and change, political cohesion in homogeneous and plural societies, and decision making in foreign policy.

A discussion of societal belief systems involves a number of conceptual and methodological problems: the need to reconcile the macrosociological and microsociological perspectives in the study of belief systems; the need to delineate the degree of autonomy of the political belief system; the need to consider the implications of cognitive styles; and the need to determine the degree of fit between domestic and foreign policy beliefs.

We have argued that, in order to overcome some of the complexities involved, one should adopt a decision-making approach to the study of societal belief systems. This approach views a belief system as a range or set of alternatives that may instruct us about the spectrum of choices which the policy-making elite can pursue in response to certain given contingencies. There are three major advantages to this approach: It introduces the notion of probability in the relation between beliefs and decision making; it provides a framework for investigating the interaction of collective and individual beliefs; and it enables more systematic study of the variations in belief systems across time and space.

References

Abelson, R. P. "Modes of Resolution in Belief Dilemmas." In M. Fishbein (ed.), *Attitude Theory and Measurement.* New York: Wiley, 1967.

Abelson, R. P. "Script Processing in Attitude Formation and Decision Making." In J. S. Carroll and J. W. Payne (eds.), *Cognition and Social Behavior.* Hillsdale, N.J.: Erlbaum, 1976.

Abelson, R., and Rosenberg, M. "Symbolic Psycho-Logic: A Model of Attitudinal Cognition." *Behavioral Science,* 1958, *3,* 1-13.

Abercombie, N., and Turner, B. S. "The Dominant Ideology Thesis." *British Journal of Sociology,* 1978, *29,* 149-167.

Adorno, T. W., and others. *The Authoritarian Personality.* New York: Harper & Row, 1950.

Alker, H., and Hermann, M. G. "Are Bayesian Decisions Artificially Intelligent? The Effect of Task and Personality on Conservatism in Processing Information." *Journal of Personality and Social Psychology,* 1971, *19,* 31-41.

Allport, G. W. *The Nature of Prejudice.* Reading, Mass.: Addison-Wesley, 1979.

Almond, G. *The Appeal of Communism.* Princeton, N.J.: Princeton University Press, 1965.

Almond, G., and Verba, S. *The Civic Culture.* Boston: Little, Brown, 1965.

Arian, A., and Shamir, M. "The Primary Political Function of the Left-Right Continuum." *Comparative Politics,* 1983, *16,* 139–158.

Arlow, J. A. "Ego Psychology and the Study of Mythology." *Journal of the American Psychoanalytic Association,* 1961, *9,* 371–393.

Asad, T. "Anthropology and the Analysis of Ideology." *Man,* 1979, *14,* 607–627.

Ashcroft, R. "Political Theory and the Problem of Ideology." *Journal of Politics,* 1980, *42,* 687–721.

Axelrod, R. "Structure of Public Opinion on Policy Issues." *Public Opinion Quarterly,* 1967, *21,* 51–60.

Bank, B. J., and others. "Normative, Preferential, and Belief Modes of Adolescent Prejudice." *Sociological Quarterly,* 1977, *18,* 574–588.

Barry, B. *Sociologists, Economists and Democracy.* New York: Macmillan, 1970.

Barry, H., Child, I. L., and Bacon, M. "Relation of Child Training to Subsistence Economy." *American Anthropologist,* 1959, *61,* 51–63.

Bell, D. "The Depressed." In D. Bell (ed.), *The Radical Right.* New York: Doubleday, 1964.

Ben-Sira, Z. "Towards a Facet Theory of a Sequential Order of Societal Needs." *Quality and Quantity,* 1979, *13,* 223–253.

Berger, P., and Luckmann, T. *The Social Construction of Reality.* New York: Doubleday, 1966.

Berry, J. W., and Dasen, P. R. "Introduction: History and Method in the Cross-Cultural Study of Cognition." In J. W. Berry and P. R. Dasen (eds.), *Culture and Cognition: Readings in Cross-Cultural Psychology.* London: Methuen, 1974.

Billig, M. *Social Psychology and Intergroup Relations.* London: Academic Press, 1976.

Billig, M. *Ideology and Social Psychology: Extremism, Moderation, and Contradiction.* New York: St. Martin's Press, 1982.

Booth, K. *Strategy and Ethnocentrism.* New York: Holmes & Meier, 1979.

Boulding, K. N. "National Images and International Systems." *Journal of Conflict Resolution,* 1959, *3,* 120–137.

Boulding, K. N. *The Image: Knowledge in Life and Society.* Ann Arbor: University of Michigan Press, 1963.

Brecher, M. *The Foreign Policy System of Israel.* Oxford, England: Oxford University Press, 1972.

Brecher, M. "Toward a Theory of International Crisis Behavior." *International Studies Quarterly,* 1977, *21,* 39–74.

Brecher, M. "State Behavior in International Crisis." *Journal of Conflict Resolution,* 1979, *23,* 446–480.

Bronfenbrenner, U. "Toward an Experimental Ecology of Human Development." *American Psychologist,* 1977, *32,* 513–531.

Butler, D., and Stokes, D. E. *Political Change in Britain.* Harmondsworth, Middlesex, England: Penguin Books, 1971.

Campbell, A., Converse, P. E., Miller, W. E., and Stokes, D. E. *The American Voter.* New York: Wiley, 1960.

Cole, M., Gay, J., and Glick, J. "Some Experimental Studies of Kpelle Quantitative Behaviour." In J. W. Berry and P. R. Dasen (eds.), *Culture and Cognition: Readings in Cross-Cultural Psychology.* London: Methuen, 1974.

Converse, P. E. "The Nature of Belief Systems in Mass Publics." In D. E. Apter (ed.), *Ideology and Discontent*. New York: Free Press, 1964.

Crozier, M. J. "Western Europe." In M. J. Crozier, S. P. Huntington, and J. Watanuki (eds.), *The Crisis of Democracy: Report on the Governability of Democracies to the Trilateral Commission*. New York: New York University Press, 1975.

Dahrendorf, R. *Class and Class Conflict in Industrial Society*. Stanford, Calif.: Stanford University Press, 1954.

De Swaan, A. *Coalition Theories and Cabinet Formations*. Amsterdam: Elsevier Science, 1973.

Deutsch, K. W. *Nationalism and Social Communication*. Cambridge, Mass.: MIT Press, 1953.

Diamond, S. "Kibbutz and Shtetl: The History of an Idea. *Social Problems*, 1957, *5*, 71–99.

Downs, A. *An Economic Theory of Democracy*. New York: Harper & Row, 1957.

Easton, D. *A Framework for Political Analysis*. Englewood Cliffs, N.J.: Prentice-Hall, 1965a.

Easton, D. *A Sytems Analysis of Political Life*. New York: Wiley, 1965b.

Eliade, M. *Patterns of Comparative Religion*. London: Sheen & Ward, 1958.

Elkins, D. J., and Simeon, R. E. B. "A Cause in Search of Its Effects, or What Does Political Culture Explain?" *Comparative Politics*, 1979, *11*, 127–146.

Elliot, P., and Schlesinger, P. "On the Stratification of Political Knowledge: Studying Eurocommunism, An Unfolding Ideology." *Sociological Review*, 1979, *27*, 55–81.

Finley, D. J., Simon, D. W., and Wilson, L. A. "The Concept of Left and Right in Cross-National Research." *Comparative Political Studies*, 1974, *7*, 209–211.

Fraisse, P. *The Psychology of Time*. (J. Leith, trans.) New York: Harper & Row, 1963.

Frank, J. D. "Nature and Function of Belief Systems: Humanism and Transcendental Religion." *American Psychologist*, 1977, *32*, 555–559.

Frenkel-Brunswik, E. "A Study of Prejudice in Children." *Human Relations*, 1948, *1*, 295–306.

Geertz, C. "Ideology as a Cultural System." In D. E. Apter (ed.), *Ideology and Discontent*. New York: Free Press, 1964.

Godelier, M. "Infrastructure, Society and History." *Current Anthropology*, 1978, *19*, 763–771.

Goffman, E. *The Presentation of Self in Everyday Life*. New York: Doubleday, 1959.

Gonen, J. Y. *A Psychohistory of Zionism*. New York: New American Library, 1975.

Goodin, R. E. *The Politics of Rational Man*. London: Wiley, 1976.

Greenstein, F. "The Impact of Personality and Politics: An Attempt to Clear Away Underbrush." *American Political Science Review*, 1967, *61*, 629–641.

Gross-Stein, J., and Tanter, R. *Rational Decision-Making: Israel's Security Choices, 1967*. Columbus: Ohio State University Press, 1980.

Gurr, T. R. *Why Men Rebel*. Princeton, N.J.: Princeton University Press, 1970.

Habermas, J. *Legitimation Crisis*. Boston: Beacon Press, 1975.

Hacker, A. *The End of the American Era*. New York: Atheneum, 1970.

Handel, W. "Normative Expectations and the Emergence of Meaning as Solution to Problems: Convergence of Structural and Interactionist Views." *American Journal of Sociology*, 1979, *84*, 855–881.

Heider, F. *The Psychology of Interpersonal Relations.* New York: Wiley, 1958.

Hermann, M. G. (ed.). *A Psychological Examination of Political Leaders.* New York: Free Press, 1977.

Hessler, R., Kong-Ming, M., and May, J. T. "Conflict, Consensus and Exchange." *Social Problems,* 1980, *27,* 320-329.

Hofman, J. E. "Social Identity and Intergroup Conflict: A Conspectus." Paper presented at conference of European and Israeli social psychologists, Shefayim, Israel, Oct. 1983.

Janis, I. L. *Victims of Groupthink: A Psychological Study of Foreign Policy Decisions and Fiascoes.* Boston: Houghton Mifflin, 1972.

Jarvie, I. C. "Explaining Cargo Cults." In B. R. Wilson (ed.), *Rationality.* New York: Harper & Row, 1970.

Jervis, R. *Perception and Misperception in International Politics.* Princeton, N.J.: Princeton University Press, 1976.

Johnson, C. *Revolutionary Change.* Boston: Little, Brown, 1966.

Johnston-Conover, P., and Feldman, S. "The Origins and Meaning of Liberal-Conservative Self-Identifications." *American Journal of Political Science,* 1981, *25,* 617-645.

Katz, D., Sarnoff, I., and McClintock, C. "Ego Defense and Attitude Change." *Human Relations,* 1956, *9,* 27-46.

Kerlinger, F. "The First and Second Order Factor Structure of Attitudes Towards Education." *American Educational Research Journal,* 1967, *4,* 191-205.

Kerlinger, F. "The Structure and Content of Social Attitude Referents: A Preliminary Study." *Educational and Psychological Measurement,* 1972, *32,* 613-630.

Kuhn, T. S. *The Structure of Scientific Revolutions.* Chicago: University of Chicago Press, 1962.

Lane, R. E. *Political Thinking and Consciousness.* Chicago: Markham, 1969.

Langer, S. K. *An Introduction to Symbolic Logic.* (3rd ed.) Mineola, N.Y.: Dover, 1967.

Laplace, P. S. de. *A Philosophical Essay on Probabilities.* (F. W. Truscott and F. L. Emory, trans.) Mineola, N.Y.: Dover, 1950. (Originally published 1814.)

Larrain, J. "Durkheim's Concept of Ideology." *Sociological Review,* 1980, *28,* 129-139.

Lasswell, H. *Politics: Who Gets What, When and How.* New York: New American Library, 1936.

Lasswell, H. *The Political Writings of Harold Lasswell.* New York: Free Press, 1951.

Lijphart, A. *The Trauma of Decolonization: The Dutch and West New Guinea.* New Haven, Conn.: Yale University Press, 1966.

Lijphart, A. *The Politics of Accommodation.* Berkeley: University of California Press, 1968.

Lukes, S. "Some Problems About Rationality." In B. R. Wilson (ed.), *Rationality.* New York: Harper & Row, 1970.

McClosky, H. "Consensus and Ideology in American Politics."*American Political Science Review,* 1964, *58,* 366-382.

McClosky, H. "Personality and Attitude Correlates of Foreign Policy Orientation." In J. N. Rosenau (ed.), *Domestic Sources of Foreign Policy.* New York: Free Press, 1967.

Mannheim, K. *Ideology and Utopia.* San Diego: Harcourt Brace Jovanovich, 1955. (Originally published 1929.)

Mannoni, O. *Prospero and Caliban*. (2nd ed.) New York: Praeger, 1964.

Melikian, L. H. "Authoritarianism and Its Correlates in the Egyptian Culture and in the United States." *Journal of Social Issues*, 1959, *15*, 58–69.

Merkl, P. H. *Modern Comparative Politics*. New York: Holt, Rinehart & Winston, 1970.

Merton, R. K. *Social Theory and Social Structure*. New York: Free Press, 1968.

Miller, R. L. "Preferred Strategies for Resolving Belief Dilemmas." *Journal of Social Psychology*, 1978, *104*, 133–141.

Miller, W. E. "The Cross-National Use of Party Identification as a Stimulus to Political Inquiry." In I. Budge, I. Crewe, and D. Farlie (eds.), *Party Identification and Beyond*. London: Wiley, 1976.

Minar, D. "Ideology and Political Behavior." *Midwest Journal of Political Science*, 1961, *5*, 317–331.

Moore, B., Jr. *Social Origin of Dictatorship and Democracy: Lord and Peasant in the Making of the Modern World*. Harmondsworth, Middlesex, England: Penguin Books, 1967.

Nie, H. N., Verba, S., and Petrocik, J. R. *The Changing American Voter*. Cambridge, Mass.: Harvard University Press, 1976.

Nisbett, R., and Ross, L. *Human Inference: Strategies and Shortcomings of Social Judgment*. Englewood Cliffs, N.J.: Prentice-Hall, 1980.

Osgood, C. E., and others. *The Measurement of Meaning*. Urbana: University of Illinois Press, 1957.

Parsons, T. *Social Systems*. New York: Free Press, 1964.

Pettigrew, T. F. "Personality and Sociocultural Factors in Intergroup Attitudes: A Cross-National Comparison." In R. S. Sigel (ed.), *Learning About Politics: A Reader in Political Socialization*. New York: Random House, 1970.

Pettigrew, T. F., Allport, G. W., and Barnett, E. O. "Binocular Resolution and Perception of Race in South Africa." *British Journal of Psychology*, 1958, *49*, 265–279.

Prandy, K. "Alienation and Interest in the Analysis of Social Cognition." *British Journal of Sociology*, 1979, *30*, 442–471.

Przeworski, A., and Teune, H. *The Logic of Comparative Social Inquiry*. New York: Wiley, 1970.

Puttney, S., and Middletown, R. "Some Factors Associated with Student Acceptance and Rejection of War." *American Sociological Review*, 1962, *27*, 655–667.

Rapoport, A. *Strategy and Conscience*. New York: Schocken Books, 1969.

Riker, W. H. *The Theory of Political Coalitions*. New Haven, Conn.: Yale University Press, 1962.

Rokeach, M. *The Open and Closed Mind*. New York: Basic Books, 1960.

Rolle, A. "The Historic Past of the Unconscious." In H. D. Lasswell, D. Lerner, and M. Speier (eds.), *Propaganda and Communication in World History*. Vol. 3: *A Pluralizing World in Formation*. Honolulu: University of Hawaii Press, 1980.

Rose, R. (ed.). *Electoral Behavior: A Comparative Handbook*. New York: Free Press, 1974.

Rosenblatt, P. "Origins and Effects of Group Ethnocentrism and Nationalism." *Journal of Conflict Resolution*, 1964, *8*, 131–146.

Rosenau, J. N. "Foreign Policy as an Issue-Area." In J. N. Rosenau (ed.), *Domestic Sources of Foreign Policy*. New York: Free Press, 1967.

Rosenau, J. N. *Linkage Politics*. New York: Free Press, 1969.

Rosenau, J. N., and Holsti, O. R. "U.S. Leadership in a Shrinking World: The Breakdown of Consensus and the Emergence of Conflicting Belief Systems." *World Politics*, 1983, *35*, 368–392.

Ross, L. "The Intuitive Psychologist and His Shortcomings: Distortions in the Attribution Process." In L. Berkowitz (ed.), *Advances in Experimental Social Psychology*. Orlando, Fla.: Academic Press, 1977.

Schmid, H. "On the Origin of Ideology." *Acta Sociologica*, 1981, *24*, 57–73.

Schutz, A. *Collected Papers*. Vol. 1: *The Problem of Social Reality*. The Hague: Nijhoff, 1962.

Seliger, M. "Fundamental and Operative Ideology: The Two Principal Dimensions of Political Argumentation." *Policy Sciences*, 1970, *1*, 325–338.

Seliktar, O. "New Zionism." *Foreign Policy*, 1983, *51*, 118–138.

Simon, H. A. "Rational Choice and the Structure of the Environment." *Psychological Review*, 1956, *63*, 129–138.

Sivin, N. "Chinese Conception of Time." *Erlham Review*, 1966, *1*, 82–92.

Smith, D. K. *Religion and Political Development*. Boston: Little, Brown, 1970.

Smith, H. P., and Rosen, E. W. "Some Psychological Correlates of World Mindedness and Authoritarianism." *Journal of Personality*, 1958, *26*, 170–183.

Smith, M. B., Bruner, J. S., and White, R. W. *Opinions and Personality*. New York: Wiley, 1956.

Spengler, J. J. "Rising Expectations: Frustration." In H. D. Lasswell, D. Lerner, and H. Speier (eds.), *Propaganda and Communication in World History*. Vol. 3: *A Pluralizing World in Formation*. Honolulu: University of Hawaii Press, 1980.

Sprout, H., and Sprout, M. "Environmental Factors in the Study of International Politics." In J. N. Rosenau (ed.), *International Politics and Foreign Policy*. New York: Free Press, 1961.

Stagner, R. *Psychological Aspects of International Conflict*. Monterey, Calif.: Brooks/Cole, 1967.

Stakes, G. "Cognitive Style and Nationalism." *Canadian Review of Studies in Nationalism*, 1982, *9*, 1–14.

Steinsaltz, A. *The Essential Talmud*. New York: Bantam Books, 1977.

Strachey, A. *The Unconscious Motives of War*. New York: International Universities Press, 1957.

Suedfeld, P., Tetlock, P., and Ramirez, C. "War, Peace and Integrative Complexity." *Journal of Conflict Resolution*, 1977, *21*, 427–442.

Sullivan, J. L., and others. "Pluralistic Intolerance, Focused Intolerance and Tolerance: Mass Attitudes in the U.S., Israel and New Zealand." *Comparative Political Studies*, forthcoming.

Szalay, L. B., and Kelly, R. M. "Political Ideology and Subjective Culture: Conceptualization and Empirical Assessment." *American Political Science Review*, 1982, *76*, 585–602.

Szalay, L. B., Kelly, R. M., and Moon, T. W. "Ideology: Its Meaning and Measurement." *Comparative Political Studies*, 1972, *35*, 151–173.

Tajfel, H., and Fraser, C. "Social Psychology as Social Science." In H. Tajfel and C. Fraser (eds.), *Introducing Social Psychology*. Harmondsworth, Middlesex, England: Penguin Books, 1978.

Thomas, W. I. *The Child in America*. New York: Knopf, 1928.

Tilly, C. *From Mobilization to Revolution*. Reading, Mass.: Addison-Wesley, 1978.

Toennis, F. *Community and Association*. London: Routledge & Kegan Paul, 1955.

Tucker, R. *Stalin as Revolutionary*. New York: Norton, 1973.

Turkel, G. "Privatism and Orientation Toward Political Action." *Urban Life*, 1980, *9*, 217–235.

Verba, S. "Assumptions of Rationality and Non-Rationality in Models of the International System." In K. Knorr and S. Verba (eds.), *The International System: Theoretical Essays*. Princeton, N.J.: Princeton University Press, 1961.

Vinokur, A., and Burnstein, E. "Effects of Partially Shared Persuasive Arguments on Group Induced Shifts: A Group Problem-Solving Approach." *Journal of Personality and Social Psychology*, 1974, *29*, 305–315.

Von Neumann, J., and Morgenstern, O. *The Theory of Games and Economic Behavior*. (2nd ed.) Princeton, N.J.: Princeton University Press, 1947.

Waldman, S. R. "Exchange Theory and Political Analysis." In A. Effrat (ed.), *Perspectives in Political Sociology*. New York: Bobbs-Merrill, 1972.

Wilson, B. R. "A Sociologist's Introduction." In B. R. Wilson (ed.), *Rationality*. New York: Harper & Row, 1970.

Wiseman, H. V. *Political Systems: Some Sociological Approaches*. New York: Praeger, 1966.

Wright, G. N., and Phillips, L. D. "Personality and Probabilistic Thinking: An Exploratory Study." *British Journal of Psychology*, 1979, *70*, 295–303.

Wuthrow, R. "Comparative Ideology." *International Journal of Comparative Sociology*, 1981, *22*, 121–140.

Yuchtman-Yaar, E. "Expectancies, Entitlements, and Subjective Welfare." In E. Yuchtman-Yaar (ed.), *Evaluating the Welfare State: Social and Political Perspectives*. Orlando, Fla.: Academic Press, 1983.

TWELVE

Protest Movements
as a Form of Political Action

Gerda Lederer

The prominence of political protest in the advanced industrial democracies beginning in the late 1960s reflects the politicization of mass publics and the emergence
of new styles of political action. The causes of this increase and proliferation in
protest behavior and its effects on the decision-making processes in the Western
democracies have been of major concern to social scientists in the 1970s and 1980s
and have given rise to the development of theories and analyses dealing with
protest movements.

The manifestations of protest behavior are functions of the historical context
in which they occur. Both the repertory of political action and the significance
attributed to it change with time. Whereas early analysts saw political protest
movements as a threat to political stability and as a bid for system change, later
analysts have regarded protest behavior as an extension of the conventional democratic political behavior repertory, frequently manifested in limited, issue-based
group actions addressing themselves to unresponsive government bodies.

After a brief examination of protest behavior from the seventeenth to the
nineteenth century, this chapter will focus on the study of social conflict in the
twentieth century. Theories relevant to protest in the 1980s will be reviewed, and
empirical studies that operationalize the hypotheses of these theories will be examined.
We will trace the subject from its theoretical origins to the complex studies presently
being carried out; thus, we will illustrate the contribution that political psychology
can make to an understanding of these complex political issues of our time.

Political Protest in Historical Perspective

Through the records of the authorities in power and through historical
reports, we can trace the history of collective protest in Western Europe and North

America from the middle of the seventeenth century to the present. By 1660 many of the European states had acquired approximately the same boundaries that they have today. Dynastic and commercial rivalry had superseded religious and feudal disputes as primary incentives to war, and the unity of medieval Christendom had given way to a system of centralized territorial states, most of them ruled by absolute monarchies. Notable exceptions were Switzerland; some of the Italian states, which were republics; and the Dutch Netherlands, where an elected officer exercised the power of a king. In England a Parliament controlled by the ruling classes limited the royal prerogative. The great majority of the people lived in rural surroundings, their horizons bounded by the limits of the local hamlet or feudal estate. Their lives were hard, filled with unending toil; they had no leisure or luxury and were subject to cruel laws. Yet few people protested against the system. It was in the spirit of the time to accept the established customs in government and society without much question. When citizens did get together to act on shared interests, they made use of a limited repertory of protest behavior. When innovations in this behavior occurred, they took place at the margin of existing forms.

In an analysis of popular collective action in Western Europe and North America, Tilly (1983, p. 465) distinguishes between the "old" repertory, in use roughly from 1650 to 1850, and the "new" repertory, in use roughly from 1850 to 1980. Whereas the "old" repertory was parochial in scope and appealed to imme-diately available power holders to convey grievances or settle disputes, the "new" repertory is generally wider in scope and challenges established, often national, authorities in the name of an unrepresented constituency. A short overview of the "old" repertory will be given here. The "new" repertory will be discussed later in the chapter.

One form of protest in the "old" repertory was the "turnout," a forerunner of the modern "strike." Workers in a given craft in a specific locality would stop work, march through town, and hold a meeting at the edge of town. There a vote was generally taken concerning a specific set of demands; if the workers voted in favor of the demands, a delegation was sent to the employers, and a work stoppage was organized to force the employers' compliance.

Citizens also took advantage of ceremonial occasions to express their plea-sure or disapproval. Since they had a right and even a duty to assemble on state occasions, such as official visits by church dignitaries and royalty, they were not in danger of being dispersed as "unlawful assemblies" and thus had the oppor-tunity to present pleas for mercy, to complain about municipal administrations and high taxes, and on occasion to attack the dignitaries' entourage. Great cele-brations, such as those for the birth of a royal heir, not only offered occasion to express satisfaction and dissatisfaction but also provided the public with models for protest behavior. The lighting up of the windows at a royal birth, for example, was adopted by protesters for popular causes in Paris and London when they ran through the streets, forcing householders to light up their windows as a sign of solidarity. Public punishments, such as hangings and placing people in the pillory, were other occasions for mass gatherings and the expression of approval or indignation.

Another early form of protest behavior was the "food riot," undertaken by citizens in response to food shortages and profiteering. Protesters would seize shipments of grain to keep them from leaving town. Sometimes protesters would "sack" the houses, shops, or mills of the profiteers and throw the precious goods into the street. During the era of the American Revolution, collective protest of this type flourished. Innovations in protest behavior were introduced, for example, when a conventionally small petitioning delegation in behalf of the imprisoned popular leader John Wilkes became a march of thousands and a forerunner of mass demonstrations.

Political protest frequently addressed itself to symbols. In Wilkes's time the burning of stamp paper and the christening of Liberty Trees became the manner of opposition to royal policy on both sides of the Atlantic. Participation early in the French Revolution involved gathering outside the headquarters of an assembly or an administration, marching on other centers of power, and attacking both symbols and supporters of the opposition. In Paris in 1789, French protesters burned the newly built tollhouses and broke into arsenals to arm the militia. They then used those militias to capture the great symbol of arbitrary rule, the Bastille. In 1792 Parisians tore down their king's statue in the Place des Victoires, just as citizens of New York had done with their king's statue across the Atlantic in 1770.

The tools of protest used in revolution were essentially imitations and adaptations of the repressive measures used by the authorities in power. The killing of royal officials accused of profiteering in grain by French revolutionaries, and displaying their heads on pikes, mimicked the official old-regime ceremonial for the execution of traitors (Tilly, 1983, p. 471).

In the French revolutions of 1830 and 1848, the routines and symbols of the eighteenth-century revolution were revived. At the same time, a movement for parliamentary reform emerging in England used the holding of public meetings, the mounting of petition drives, the organization of street marches and associations, and the constant dialogue with power holders to accomplish its ends. These activities are part of the "new" repertory of protest behavior that gained prominence in the twentieth century.

Early Theories of Social Conflict

The first meeting of the American Sociological Society in 1907 had "Social Conflict" as its main topic. American sociologists at the turn of the century saw themselves as reformers and addressed themselves to an audience of reformers, who, in turn, gave them positive response and recognition. This first generation of sociologists saw social conflict as performing positive functions, as responsible for social change and progress. The sociologists, however, did not agree on the nature of the needed reform. "Structural reformers"—such as Lester Ward, Albion W. Small, Edward A. Ross, Robert E. Park, Thorstein Veblen, and Charles Horton Cooley—advocated social changes so profound that, if adopted, they would have changed the very structure of society. Others, such as Franklin H. Giddings and William Graham Sumner, were concerned with more limited, specific reforms that would not have fundamentally altered the status quo.

A major departure from the cosmological style of thought typical of early contributors such as Auguste Comte and Herbert Spencer occurred with German sociologist Georg Simmel (1858–1918). A contemporary of Max Weber and founder of "formal" sociology, Simmel devoted himself to the study of association on a higher level of abstraction than had previously been used. He regarded conflict as a form of socialization, since, in his view, a group entirely harmonious would be devoid of process and structure. He believed that groups require disharmony as well as harmony, dissociation as well as association.

During the three decades that followed, a shift in the self-image and the role of American sociologists contributed to changing the focus of their attention, from concern with conflict to concern with consensus and adjustment, from social dynamics to social statics. Talcott Parsons (1949, 1951) is representative of this school of thought. He regarded conflict as dysfunctional and disruptive, a form of sickness in the body social. Although he made significant contributions to the theory of social control and to an understanding of the stresses and strains on social systems, he failed to advance the theory of social conflict.

Coser and Simmel: The Sociology of Conflict. In the 1950s Lewis Coser (1956) contributed to the theory of social conflict with a conceptual analysis of the term. Building on the work of Simmel and others, Coser hoped to bridge the gap between theory and research, a failing he held responsible for many of the short-comings of American sociology. In Coser's view, conflict helps to establish group identity and to maintain group boundaries against the surrounding social world. Integrating insights gained from advances that had been made in psychology in Vienna with assertions of Simmel, Coser differentiated between conflict behavior and hostile feelings. He found that conflict allows the release of pent-up feelings and the expression of dissent and, thus, is frequently not dysfunctional for the relationship within which it occurs. While conflict changes the terms of the relationships of the participants, mere hostility does not have that effect.

Coser (1956, p. 48 ff.) expanded on a distinction made by Simmel between "realistic" and "nonrealistic" types of conflict. Realistic conflicts are prompted by conflicting claims to scarce status, power, and resources and the adherence to conflicting values. Nonrealistic conflicts arise from the deprivations and frustrations of the socialization process or from a conversion of originally realistic antagonisms that were not allowed expression. The first type of conflict is viewed by the participants as a means toward the achievement of realistic ends—a means that might be abandoned if other, more effective, means are identified; the second leaves no such alternative, since satisfaction is derived from the aggressive act itself.

Yet realistic conflicts are often invested with affective energies, since, as Simmel ([1908] 1955, p. 33) suggested, "it is expedient to hate the adversary with whom one fights." As a matter of fact, hostile feelings are generally an important element of close social relations; and if conflicts occur in these relationships, they are likely to be intense. Thus, the absence of conflict cannot be taken as an index of strength and stability. The absence of conflict may be due to the fear that conflict might endanger the social structure and might signify the accumulation of ambivalent and hostile feelings.

Simmel believed that outside conflict will strengthen the internal cohesion of the group and increase centralization. Coser agreed that external conflict has an integrative rather than a disruptive effect but asserted that whether an increase in centralization accompanies this increase in cohesion depends on both the character of the conflict and the type of the group—its relative size and the degree of members' involvement. He found that small groups whose members are highly involved tend to be intolerant of internal dissent. Social cohesion in such groups depends on total sharing of all aspects of group life and is reinforced by the assertion of group unity against the dissenter. In contrast, large groups that do not expect total personal involvement of the membership permit expression of dissent, and hence conflict, within their ranks and draw their strength and cohesion from their flexibility.

Since outside conflict increases group cohesion, it follows that groups may seek continued conflict as a condition of survival. From that perspective it is unimportant whether the group has been victorious in obtaining its goals or whether there are other reasons why the original goals no longer exist. As a matter of fact, outside conflict need not be objectively present to accomplish the group's purpose; it suffices for the members to perceive the outside threat. Similarly, search for, or invention of, a dissenter within may serve a group structure that is threatened from the outside.

Examining the relationship between the intensity of conflict and the content of conflict, Coser (1956, p. 118) concluded, with Simmel ([1908] 1955, pp. 39-40), that conflicts in which the participants feel that they are fighting for the ideals of the group they represent are likely to be more radical and merciless than those where the participants are motivated by personal goals.

Conflict itself is seen as establishing relations between groups where none may have existed before. Simmel ([1908] 1955, pp. 26, 35) claimed that conflict tends to give rise to regulations and norms governing conduct and restraining conflict behavior. Once relations have thus been established, he believed, other types of relations are likely to follow. Seen in this light, conflict acts as a stimulus for the establishment of new rules, norms, and institutions, thus serving as an agent of socialization for both contending parties.

In view of the advantages of unity within a group for purposes of winning a conflict, it might be supposed that each party would strongly desire the absence of unity in the opposing party. In effect, however, Coser contended that conflict calls for a common organizational structure to facilitate the acceptance of common rules and to ensure that hostilities will cease once the specific results have been attained. Centralization of the internal structure of each contending party ensures that peace can be concluded and maintained effectively as long as the same conditions prevail.

Smelser's Theory of Collective Behavior. Writing in the 1960s and building on foundations laid down by Parsons, Neil Smelser (1963) developed an elaborate analytical framework for dealing with a wide variety of collective behavior, including protest movements. Like Parsons, he identified four basic "action components" guiding social behavior: (1) values, the general ends of social action; (2) norms, the rules that regulate the pursuit of these goals; (3) social organization, the mobilization of people for coordinated action; and (4) situational facilities, the means and resources used in achieving these goals. The four components were ordered hierarchically, with values at the top and situational facilities at the bottom. Smelser defined collective behavior in relation to these abstract dimensions as "an uninstitutionalized mobilization for action in order to modify one or more kinds of strain on the basis of a generalized reconstitution of a component of action" (p. 71). Here "strain" was defined as "an impairment of the relations among and consequently inadequate functioning of the components of action" (p. 47). If "strain" appears on one action level, and institutionalized means for overcoming the "strain" are limited, it is likely that a higher level will be drawn on to solve the problem. Thus, Smelser argued that "strain," the degree of generalization in the action hierarchy, and a number of other factors jointly determine the timing and the type of collective behavior likely to be manifested.

Smelser's examples of social problems that qualify as a "strain" include discrimination against minority groups, unemployment, and national competition with the "Communist world." Moreover, he contended that what may be a "strain" in one society at one time might not be a "strain" in another. Unseem (1975, p. 9) has criticized the circular nature of Smelser's argument: "Strain, then, can be readily identified only when the reaction has already occurred. With no means of discovering the strain apart from the appearance of collective behavior, the argument becomes a tautology."

Smelser reached his first goal: "to reduce this residue of indeterminacy which lingers in explanations of collective outbursts" (p. 25). He was less successful in answering the question he posed at the outset: "Why do collective episodes occur *where* they do, *when* they do, and *in the ways* they do" (p. 1)? Smelser certainly did not anticipate the widespread conflicts of the late 1960s when he wrote about collective behavior only a few years earlier.

Approaches such as Smelser's can be classified as involving "structural-functional" concepts. Among their weaknesses is their failure to consider the role of the individual in the relationship between social conditions and protest movements.

Theories of Relative Deprivation

Among the psychological approaches to protest movements are the theories that view individual and collective psychological factors as intervening variables that link and shape the connection between social conditions and protest movements. One of the most important of these theories is based on the concept of "relative deprivation"—the disparity between what people perceive they have and what they believe they deserve to have.

Theories based on this concept of relative deprivation go back to Aristotle (384-322 B.C.), who saw the principal cause of revolution as the aspiration for economic or political equality on the part of the common people, who lack it, and the aspiration of oligarchs for greater inequality than they have. In both instances the underlying cause is the discrepancy between the political and economic goods people have and what they think is justly theirs.

Alexis de Tocqueville, writing about the French Revolution, pointed to "rising expectations" as the cause for revolutionary fervor. "The evil, which was suffered patiently as inevitable, seems unendurable as soon as the idea of escaping from it is conceived" (de Tocqueville, [1856] 1951, p. 186). Davies (1962), in his "J-curve" hypothesis, discerned a similar pattern. He studied economic and social developments preceding a variety of movements, ranging from Dorr's rebellion to the Russian Revolution, and found that, when a group's economic and social situation is suddenly reversed after a period of substantial gain, expectations continue to rise despite the objective setback. The resulting frustrations tend to create political upheaval.

Drawing on prior studies to develop a comprehensive theory of relative deprivation, Gurr (1970, p. 11) attempted to "analyze and develop testable general hypotheses about three aspects of political violence: its courses, magnitude, and forms." He defined the term "political violence" as "all collective attacks within a political community against the political regime, its actors—including competing political groups as well as incumbents—or its policies. The concepts represent a set of events, a common property of which is the actual or threatened use of violence, but the explanation is not limited to that property" (p. 4).

To describe patterns of relative deprivation, Gurr related aspects of Festinger's (1957) cognitive dissonance theory, Galtung's (1967) work on conflict, and Durkheim's ([1897] 1951) understanding of anomia. However, while cognitive dissonance is mostly concerned with the individual and conflict theory deals with the interaction of groups, Gurr's theory of relative deprivation mediates between the individual and the group. Gurr (1970, p. 50 ff.) identified three distinct patterns of disequilibrium of societal conditions in which there is discrepancy between sought and attainable value positions: "In *decremental deprivation* a group's value expectations remain relatively constant but value capabilities are perceived to decline; in *aspirational deprivation,* capabilities remain relatively static while expectations increase or intensify; in *progressive deprivation,* there is a substantial and simultaneous increase in expectations and decrease in capabilities." All three patterns have been cited as causal or predisposing factors for political violence. Gurr examined three forms of political violence in his analysis—turmoil, conspiracy, and internal war—and related them to relative deprivation in a long list of hypotheses and corollaries. In his effort to employ theory to guide research, Gurr elected to test the proposition that the psychological variable, relative deprivation, is the basic precondition for civil strife of any kind and that the more widespread and intense deprivation is among members of a population, the greater the magnitude of strife in one form or another (Gurr, 1971).

Gurr (1971) based his work on an underlying causal mechanism derived from psychological evidence—namely, that one response to perceived deprivation is discontent or anger and that anger is a motivating state for which aggression is an inherently satisfying response. According to Gurr, the relationship between discontent and participation in strife is, however, mediated by a number of intervening social conditions. In an empirical test of his hypothesis, he chose as his universe of analysis 114 distinct national and colonial political entities, each with a population in excess of one million in 1962. The dependent variable, the magnitude of civil strife, was carefully defined and operationalized with a number of measures, and extensive data collection and estimation were undertaken.

The underlying variables examined in his study are unmeasured and must be inferred from indicators. Gurr found that these variables are, in fact, unmeasurable by aggregate data, since one of them, deprivation-induced discontent, relates to a state of mind, and the intervening social conditions have their effect only insofar as the discontented perceive them as relevant to their response to deprivation. Gurr dealt with this problem by using summary measures derived by combining a number of indicators of the underlying variables.

Analyzing the results of his study, Gurr found that eight summary indicators accounted jointly for two thirds of the variance among nations in the relative magnitude of civil strife during 1961–1965. He concluded that the fundamental proposition—that strife varies directly in magnitude with the intensity of relative deprivation—was strongly supported. While Gurr admitted that his research did not constitute a "direct" test of the relevance of the variables, he maintained that no scientific proposition is ever *directly* confirmed or disproved. Therefore, he claimed, unless and until a reasonably parsimonious alternative explanation can be found, his results must be accepted as strong indirect evidence for the psychological propositions relating deprivation to civil violence.

There are a number of difficulties with Gurr's operationalization of the theory linking relative deprivation and protest movements. Gurr (1970, p. 56) writes, for example, that one can infer decremental relative deprivation "from such patterns as short-term declines in productivity following a period of stable production" and "progressive relative deprivation" from "short-term changes in inflation rates, commodity prices, or total productivity relative to rates in the more distant past." Similarly, he links "status relative deprivation" and "interpersonal relative deprivation" to structural variables, as if a direct link between feelings of frustration and economic indicators could be inferred without first being empirically established. Gurr's concept of relative deprivation rests on the perception of deprivation, but his empirical studies are not investigations of perceptions.

Gurney and Tierney (1982, pp. 38–39) point out that relative deprivation theorists "typically pose a unidirectional rather than a cyclical or feedback model in describing RD/SM [relative deprivation/social movement] linkage," while social movements themselves may be instrumental in producing perceptions of relative deprivation. Though structural inequalities may exist before protest movements form, the perception of deprivation may arise only after the movements have begun to do their work. Gurney and Tierney also note that relative deprivation theorists pay little attention to the possibility of alternative responses to relative deprivation. In other words, had Gurr established that feelings of frustration coexist with the inequities indicated by his structural indicators, he would have had to demonstrate that political protest is the prevalent response. Protest movement participants as well as nonparticipants may be experiencing feelings of relative deprivation; in fact, there may even be greater variation in relative deprivation levels among movement participants than between participants and nonparticipants (Marx and Holzner, 1977).

Relative deprivation theorists who turn to microlevel analysis in order to avoid the fallacies growing out of the macrolevel approach find themselves confronted with the classic problem of lack of attitude-behavior congruence. Also, when societal-level analysis is replaced by self-report data on individuals, there is a tacit assumption that protest movements can be treated as aggregates of persons sharing common tendencies and predispositions.

Studies of Political Participation

As a result of the widespread eruption of political protest in the Western democracies of Europe and the United States in the second half of the 1960s, an international group of researchers decided to collaborate in a multinational study of the new range of political participation and protest behavior. They observed that in the Western democracies broad sociopolitical movements for system change had waned and that limited, issue-based, and frequently regional ad hoc group actions had increased. Moreover, they noted that very little empirical cross-sectional and longitudinal survey evidence was available, nationally or cross-nationally, on styles of political participation beyond the institutionalized, electorally oriented activities. The group agreed that the classical theories of collective violence, which regard unconventional political behavior as a threat to political stability, were too limited for an analysis of the newly emerging participatory political culture of advanced industrial societies. Therefore, using national multistage probability samples in five countries, they collected data on a wide variety of issues related to political action. The report of their study (Barnes and Kaase, 1979) represents an important contribution to the understanding of political protest in cross-cultural perspective.

The five participating nations were the United States, Great Britain, West Germany, Austria, and the Netherlands. The main dependent variables under examination were the use of conventional and unconventional political participation. "Political participation" was taken to mean "all voluntary activities by individual citizens intended to influence either directly or indirectly political choices at various levels of the political system" (Kaase and Marsh, 1979c, p. 42). Unconventional political participation, also referred to as "protest behavior," was defined as behavior that does not correspond to the norms of law and custom that regulate political participation under a particular regime.

The measures used in the analyses were based on survey responses concerning actual activities of the respondents as well as on the respondents' attitudes towards protest activities and evaluation of their effectiveness. In addition, the respondents' attitudes toward repression of protest were examined. Conventional political activities included in the study were reading about politics in the newspapers, discussing politics with others, seeking to influence voting, working on community problems, attending political meetings, contacting politicians or public officials, and spending time working for a political party or candidate. Unconventional political actions included the use of petitions, demonstrations, boycotts, rent or tax strikes, unofficial industrial strikes, occupation of buildings, boycotts, rent or tax damage to property, and personal violence. Participation in such activities or approval of their use became the basis of a measure of "protest potential."

The measure called "repression potential" was based on the willingness of individuals who themselves oppose protest action to support the authorities in their use of power to control protest. To what extent are subjects willing to sanction police violence against demonstrators, judicial punishment, the use of troops to break strikes, and the banning of all public protest demonstrations? In the opinion of Barnes and Kaase and their associates, the extent to which political protest is likely to occur in a given situation depends, among other things, on the complementary interaction between the will and the means to resist by the authorities and the support such resistance receives from those members of the society not in agreement with the protesters on some particular issue.

On the basis of survey results, individual propensity to protest was shown to be much more widespread than actual behavior would suggest. The belief that protest can be effective was even more widespread. Marsh and Kaase (1979, pp. 92-93) conclude that "involvement in protest behavior is governed far more by local political opportunity than consensual feelings of deferrence and loyalty to normative values of public order or to the institutions that enforce them. . . . The custodians of civil authority in Europe and the United States do not have carte blanche when confronted with unorthodox forms of political action. Nor are the legitimate pathways of political action laid down by tradition and practice any antidote to noisy and disrespectful forms of protest."

In each country examined, analysis showed a pronounced negative correlation between "protest potential" and "repression potential." Not surprisingly, the more likely a citizen is to engage in unconventional political action, the less likely he is to be in favor of repression of such activity. However, results also showed a negative correlation between conventional participation and the repression potential, though of a lower order. Thus, even citizens engaged in conventional political activities tend to oppose repression of protest, and, conversely, citizens likely to sanction police violence against demonstrators themselves tend to be inactive politically.

An important feature of the analysis is the finding of consistent, though modest, *positive* correlations between protest potential and conventional participation (Pearson correlation coefficients from .17 in the United States to .28 in West Germany). On the basis of these results, Marsh and Kaase (1979, p. 94) conclude that both protest and conventional political behavior clearly lie within a similar general sphere of "politics for social change" and in contrast to "politics for social control" as measured by the "repression potential" scale.

One of the difficulties facing the cross-cultural project of Barnes and Kaase and their associates was the paucity of available earlier data to provide a longitudinal basis for comparison concerning unconventional political participation. That this circumstance can be attributed to the rarity of such behavior in the 1950s and early 1960s can be concluded on the basis of empirical evidence reported in a study by Almond and Verba (1965). This work, *The Civic Culture*, was one of the first cross-national studies using sample survey techniques to analyze the complex macropolitical problem of democratic stability and citizen participation. Like the study of Barnes and Kaase and their associates, the focus of Almond and Verba's research was "the participation explosion" in five Western democracies. Data dealing with citizens' attitudes and values were collected in 1959–60 in five nations—the United States, Great Britain, West Germany, Italy, and Mexico.

Since three of the countries in *The Civic Culture* were also included in *Political Action* (Barnes and Kaase, 1979), a limited longitudinal analysis was possible. Responses dealing with subjective political competence—the extent to which individuals believe they can exert political influence—on the local as well as on the national level were compared (Kaase and Marsh, 1979b, pp. 138–149). The data indicated that a substantial rise in overall competence on both the local and the national level had occurred over the fifteen-year period in all three countries. The results also corroborated that in the late 1950s direct-action techniques were practically nonexistent among mass publics as perceived means of political influence, whereas fifteen years later about 7 percent of the respondents in the three nations in question indicated willingness to engage in unconventional political actions to influence specific political outcomes.

Other studies support similar conclusions. Almond and Verba (1980) revisited the civic cultures of their first volume and found results similar to those of Barnes and Kaase and their associates. In a chapter about the United States, Abramowitz (1980, p. 199) writes that "the total number of protest incidents recorded [in the United States] during the decade of the 1950s was less than the number recorded in every single year between 1960 and 1967" and "by 1973 a Harris survey found that 11 percent of the adult population had taken part in a street demonstration of some kind and 2 percent had taken part in a demonstration involving violence." Merelman and Foster (1978, p. 454) report on protest behavior in the Federal Republic of Germany: "It also appears that many [Germans] have begun to move beyond conventional political activity into more activist and assertive roles. Since the 1960s about 15,000 different grass-roots groups have emerged to try to influence policy decisions, particularly concerning the environment, atomic energy, consumer, and neighborhood issues. These groups, while clearly expressing the frustration and dissatisfaction of citizens against powerful government and business interests, nevertheless reflect the internalization of democratic values and rising participation."

Antecedents of Political Action. One of the purposes of the multinational study of Barnes and Kaase and their associates was to examine demographic variables and social values relevant to protest behavior. The independent variables regarded by the international team of social scientists as the most important antecedents of political action were *social structure* and *sociopolitical values.* Social structure variables (1) locate the individual in his society, with regard to social status relative to others; (2) focus on the degree of integration into secondary associations, such as interest groups; and (3) consider age, in terms of generation and position in the life cycle. The variables dealing with sociopolitical values were based on Maslow's (1954) psychological theory of need hierarchy and its extension by the value theory of Inglehart (1977). Maslow postulated that individual needs are hierarchically organized and that satisfaction of each respective lower stage leads to the activation of needs of the next higher level. Inglehart found that, contrary to earlier expectations, satisfaction of the physical and safety needs does not eliminate political conflict. Instead, conflict in the societies where satisfaction of these needs is in sight shifts to "postmaterialist" values.

Another group of variables identified by the sociologists of the political action project dealt with the motivational and cognitive conditions that make it possible for citizens, once they have identified needs, to make relevant choices from the repertory of available political means. Klingemann (1979, p. 281 ff.) contributed to this aspect of the cross-cultural research project by adapting Converse's (1964) measurement approach for estimating the cognitive abilities of mass publics to the development of cross-national indicators of levels of political conceptualization.

The political action study included a fourth block of variables in its model, for the purpose of assessing relative deprivation. This concept, which has played a major role in macropolitical empirical research, is analyzed in terms of its significance in a cross-national microstudy of protest. The authors acknowledge that relative deprivation can become politically relevant only as a collective property of groups. In order to cross the threshold of awareness, deprivations have to be put into a common frame of reference through the activities of political elites, thus overcoming the isolation of the individual. According to Dahl (1971, p. 95), five conditions are necessary for collective deprivation to have an impact on the political process: perception of deprivation; high relevance for the individual and the group; evaluation of deprivation as illegitimate; feelings of anger, frustration, and resentment over it; and the actual demand for removal of deprivation. Barnes and Kaase and their associates added two conditions as also crucial for the process of politicization: that political authorities be held responsible for the felt deprivation and that the performance of the authorities in the areas of deprivation be negatively evaluated.

On the basis of their analyses of the measured dimensions within and between countries, the authors of the political action study (Barnes and Kaase, 1979, p. 106) found that there is, within Western political communities, a substantial and widely distributed constituency for radical political action, with the most important groups, in terms of the actual mobilization of activists, to be found in the populations under forty. Marsh and Kaase (1979, p. 106) report that, in this age group, "nearly half the Dutch, a third of the Americans, and at least a quarter of the Germans and British (if rather few Austrians) are all seriously committed to the idea of using unconventional and even some illegal forms of political protest." The evidence suggested that the protest-prone political activists in the countries under study were young, but not necessarily youths, and that a good education "accelerated the will to protest." Protest potential, it was found, was not even predominantly a middle-class characteristic. Marsh and Kaase (1979, pp. 134–135) observe:

> Overall, men are more ready than women to be mobilized, but *young* women have an impressive political potency that, unlike the even-handed versatility shown by men, is pointed sharply in the direction of protest methods. . . . The feminist movement is one of a number of new political forces to emerge since the peace movement of the 1960s demonstrated, quite literally, that protest was a potent and even legitimate pathway toward political redress. . . . What really appears to have happened—what is really significant—is that what was extremism in the 1960s is becoming the legitimacy of the 1970s. In passing from the vanguard to the masses, political protest has obviously been modified, toned down. On the way, it has picked up increased connections with conventional politics. . . . The governments of our five nations, and probably the governments of most similar nations, now have to contend with a polity full of young, well-educated men and women who do not accept that their political efficacy is bounded by officially sanctioned channels of representative democracy.

A Follow-Up Study. Many of the results of the political action study proved to be of such general interest that major efforts were made to continue the work into the 1980s, and an internationally comparative longitudinal project was undertaken. Data were collected in 1980–81 in three of the original five countries of the political action study: the Netherlands, West Germany, and the United States. In addition to the relatively large number of respondents who could be located and reinterviewed (65 percent in the Netherlands, 55 percent in the United States, and 40 percent in West Germany), these panels were supplemented by new respondents in order to achieve cross-sectional representation for 1981. Thus, the researchers could evaluate changes in the distribution of participation measures and their sociodemographic correlates from 1974 to 1981, and they also could analyze the individual stability of these measures over time.

Reporting on preliminary findings of this research, Kaase (1983) found that the initial distribution of the four measures employed in the earlier study (conventional political participation, protest potential, repression potential, and political action repertory typology) was largely maintained. The picture of aggregate stability was further supported by the finding that the positive correlations between conventional political participation and protest potential had remained virtually unchanged in all three countries examined over the seven-year interval.

Examination of such change as did occur showed that, of the four measures involving political action, conventional political participation displayed the highest degree of aggregate stability over time. In the Netherlands and West Germany, changes in the measures of protest potential indicated a minor tendency toward less involvement, whereas in the United States a slight increase could be noticed.

Another result of the new political action study was the realization that the thrust of unconventional, direct-action politics "is as much or more aimed at preventing some undesirable outcome, rather than at achieving a desirable one, while conventional participation is aimed at getting and not preventing something" (Kaase, 1983, p. 33).

Some of the panel data cast doubt on a key hypothesis of the original political action study. Barnes and Kaase and their associates believed that the figures indicating increasing participation in protest activities in the Western democracies represented an increase in the political action repertory of the individual, and that the positive correlation between conventional and unconventional activities was indicative of the individual's adding items from the unconventional realm to his political participation repertory. The fact that the measures employed—the conventional political participation scale and the protest potential scale—were "conceptualized and empirically found to hold up as one-dimensional Guttman scales" (Kaase, 1983, p. 3) gave rise and support to this interpretation.

This view of protest behavior would explain an individual's moving from support of lesser, conventional participation to support of more forceful, unconventional participation; but it would not explain a move in the opposite direction. Citizens should not lose an action dimension once it had been acquired. Examination of individual stability with respect to the political action repertory of individuals in the panel study revealed, however, that 28 percent of the American subjects, 33 percent of the Dutch, and 45 percent of the West Germans had made such "incorrect" transitions, an outcome Kaase (1983, p. 19) describes as "dealing a devastating blow to the repertory concept . . . requiring some rethinking on the conceptual level as well as with regard to the operationalization of the scales."

Muller: The Expectancy-Value-Norms Model. Muller (1979, 1982) also has focused on the different types of political participation in the Western democracies. He differentiated between legal, democratic participation, which he subclassified into "conventional" and "unconventional" behavior, and illegal, aggressive participation, such as civil disobedience and political violence. He cited a number of studies to show that positive nontrivial correlations have been consistently observed between indicators of democratic and aggressive participation (Citrin and others, 1973; Muller, 1977, 1979; Barnes and Kaase, 1979; Seligson, 1980). In contrast to Barnes and Kaase and their associates, however, Muller (1982, p. 8) saw "no compelling a priori theoretical reason for expecting that individuals will necessarily begin participating in one type of activity but not the other."

Muller attempted to construct an integrated explanatory model that would investigate the causal antecedents of both democratic and aggressive political participation simultaneously. In this way he hoped to differentiate between unique and common causes and to identify direct and intervening variables. Building on a general behavior theory proposed by Fishbein (1967) and on the "economic model" used by Opp, Burow-Affarth, and Heinrichs (1981), Muller developed the expectancy-value-norms model of democratic and aggressive political participation.

Opp and his associates had estimated the parameters of two separate prediction equations, one for aggressive participation and the other for democratic participation. The structure of this model assumed, in effect, that zero correlation exists between aggressive and democratic political participation. Using a set of personal interviews conducted by Infratest in West Germany in 1974 ($N = 2,662$) to test their model, Opp and his associates calculated standardized partial regression coefficients for seven variables. They were able to account for 42 percent of the variance in aggressive participation and 46 percent of the variance in democratic participation.

Muller made use of Opp's "economic model," with a number of modifications. To allow for the possibility of reciprocal causation of democratic and aggressive political participation, Muller included aggressive political participation in the prediction equation for democratic political participation and vice versa. Also, Muller included two variables in his model not used by Opp: a respondent's belief in the efficacy of collective aggression and the subject's position on a left-right ideological continuum.

Using the same data that Opp and his associates had used to test their model, and incidentally a population very similar in time and place to that used by Barnes and Kaase and their associates for the German data of their comparative study, Muller was able to account for 53 percent of the variance with regard to aggressive participation and 46 percent of the variance with regard to democratic participation. The expectancy-value-norms model thus showed superior predictive accuracy in regard to aggressive participation, compared with Opp's economic model.

Muller found the presence of a sizable direct effect of aggressive participation on democratic participation ($r = .32$) but only a very slight effect ($r = .09$) of democratic participation on aggressive participation. Muller (1982, p. 14) concluded that "in this sample there appears to be a fairly strong tendency for respondents who have participated aggressively to subsequently expand their behavioral repertoire to include democratic activities." According to Muller (1982, p. 14), the "results indicated that people who are alienated, or hold left-wing ideology, or feel relatively deprived are likely to become politically active by taking part in aggressive behavior, then go on to include democratic activity in their behavioral repertoire." He found the same thing to be true about people with a low sense of personal political efficacy but a high psychological involvement in politics. Muller found, on the other hand, that people who feel that it is important to be involved politically and who feel a strong sense of personal political efficacy tend to take part in democratic political activities; these people, however, tend to limit their behavioral repertory to the democratic type.

Muller's findings confirm the presence of a positive correlation between conventional and unconventional political participation as reported by Barnes and Kaase (1979). However, they contradict the political action study's hypothesis concerning the relationship between different types of participation. Muller's results explain the "incorrect" transitions that Kaase (1983) reports as a result of his panel studies and support the contention that aggressive political participation does not represent escalation in political participation and that the repertory of political action is frequently not perceived as a Guttman scale by protesting citizens.

Dimensions of Political Participation

Schmidtchen and Ühlinger (1983; see also Ühlinger, 1983) used a different approach in their study of political participation. They did not use Kaase and Marsh's (1979b) scales of conventional participation and protest potential or Muller's (1982) equations for aggressive and democratic participation. Instead, they attempted to obtain an integrated view of political participation, identifying possible clusters of different types of activities and the dimensions underlying all kinds of political participation. In 1980 they asked 5,000 West Germans between sixteen and thirty-five years of age the following three questions concerning twenty-two forms of political activity: What would you do if you wanted to gain influence? If these actions did not have any effect, what would you do then? What have you already done?

Analyses of the data by nonmetric multidimensional scaling of similarities and by hierarchical cluster analysis yielded a two-dimensional solution. The first dimension was interpreted as reflecting the extent of pressure on the political system; the second dimension, as a measure of personal investment. The cluster analysis revealed that the twenty-two forms of political activity were divided into two large and clearly separated clusters, one containing all items considered illegal, the other the legal items. The structure of these two clusters suggested further subdivision. The illegal participation items were grouped into those with violence and those without. Within the other cluster, three subgroups could be identified. One expressed the traditional role of the citizen as a voter; a second included those items with which the actor influences the political system via representatives; and the third consisted of the direct-action or "unconventional" participation items.

Schmidtchen and Ühlinger found a large amount of overlap among the different types of political participation. People who engaged in one kind of political activity generally also used other kinds of participation. Also, the respondents preferred to influence the political system through direct action than to influence it through representatives. Forty-three percent of the respondents had already engaged in some direct action; only 20 percent had tried to influence the system through representatives. The most important criterion of distinction was the legality of the form of participation, not its conventionality. A secondary analysis by Schmidtchen and Ühlinger of the data used by Barnes and Kaase and their associates in the political action study yielded a similar clustering of types of political activity as they had found in their own study.

These results confirm the findings of Muller (1982), Barnes and Kaase (1979), and others that there is a positive correlation between different forms of political participation. They cast further doubt on the hypothesis that unconventional political participation represents an escalation in a citizen's political participation repertory.

It becomes increasingly clear that empirical studies, though they answer many questions, leave many others unanswered. Powerful computer programs enable us to make comparative intercultural and longitudinal analyses; yet these analyses fail to communicate a sense of the individual behind the statistics. There is a need for a dual approach—the joining of quantitative and qualitative methodology. Unfortunately, social scientists are generally expert in only one of these two branches of research and give less than full credence to the work of the other. In a rare attempt to blend the two approaches, the German research institute Infratest, in collaboration with the Bundeszentrale für Politische Bildung (National Office for Political Education), combined qualitative and quantitative methods in its study of political protest in the Federal Republic of Germany (Infratest, 1980).

Political Protest in West Germany: The Extremism Potential

The Infratest study tried to overcome some of the problems of earlier studies and illustrates how classical theories and imaginative research design can be used to advantage.

Using the scales of Barnes and Kaase (1979), the investigators sought to answer the following questions: What is the size and nature of the extremism potential in West Germany? What social and political conditions lead to extremist political behavior? Are there personal-psychological factors that can be regarded as causal for the development of extremist views and behavior? What circumstances contribute to the manifestation of violent political action? Under what circumstances do individuals relinquish their readiness to participate in acts of political violence?

The theory guiding the research was developed by Kaase (1976) and is derived from the theories of relative deprivation. Kaase specified the circumstances that mediate between collective relative deprivation and the readiness to participate in political protest. He found that a systematic relationship between discontent (Kaase uses the word "Unzufriedenheit," which is not really synonymous with "deprivation") and political protest can be expected only when (1) the discontent is collective in nature, in the sense that a significant portion of the population is affected; (2) the discontent involves matters that are the responsibility of government and where people feel that the government has not lived up to its responsibility; and (3) the discontent involves issues of great importance to the individuals. Kaase calls this specific discontent "political deprivation" (Infratest, 1980, p. 36). In Kaase's theory the changing values explored by Inglehart, rather than the economic deprivation postulated by Gurr, are the catalysts of political discontent. When political discontent is coupled with little confidence in the political leadership and high assessment of personal political efficacy, the result is unconventional political protest behavior.

The design of the Infratest study included six distinct stages: (1) A search of the literature led to the formulation of hypotheses. (2) The hypotheses were examined in a pretest, from which questionnaires were developed. (3) A representative sample of 4,008 West Germans between the ages of sixteen and fifty were interviewed and their responses to the scales of the questionnaire reported. (4) In-depth interviews were conducted with subjects identified as belonging to the "left-wing protest potential." (5) Target groups of teachers, journalists, students, and unemployed youths were surveyed, since these groups were considered relevant to provision of insight into the research questions. (6) Sixty case histories of members of the extreme left were included in the study, in order to provide information about the biographical constellation of events that might have contributed to the development of these political attitudes.

The Infratest researchers found that only 8 percent of the representative sample belonged to the "protest potential" group (that is, those who approve of participation in the more extreme forms of unconventional protest). Of these, 1.7 percent identified with the political right; 1.9 percent, with the center of the political spectrum; and 4.4 percent, with the political left. The protest potential on the right tended to consist of members of the lower socioeconomic levels and showed a high degree of acceptance of violence. The left-wing group tended to be young and well educated. Since the first two groups (right and center) were numerically very small, the researchers decided that these data did not lend themselves to further statistical analysis, and the remainder of the study focused only on the left-wing protest potential.

In the phase of the study calling for in-depth interviews, ninety-one subjects (52 percent) of those identified as belonging to the "left-wing protest potential" were examined. Subjects were encouraged to talk about a number of specific topics, such as their perceptions of everyday reality, their ideological views of the world, their acceptance of (political) violence, their personal emancipation, their experiences with alternative lifestyles, and their psychopathic tendencies.

The collected data were quantified and categorized. Twenty-one indices (for example, the "resignation index" and the "tolerance-of-violence index") were calculated and assigned to ten overriding dimensions (such as "determinism/indeterminism" and "idealism/materialism"). This information was used, in turn, to classify the ninety-one subjects into seven political categories (such as "orthodox Communists," "unorthodox Marxists," "civilization critics," and "left-wing socialists").

On the basis of this part of the study, the authors concluded that the members of the left-wing protest potential have a high degree of sensitivity to social inequality and injustice, coupled with an unwillingness to compromise by accepting flawed reality. Violence as a political tool, rejected by more than 98 percent of the subjects of the large-scale study, was rejected by more than half of the interviewees belonging to the left-wing protest potential. Of those agreeing to the use of moderate violence, almost all regarded such use as a last desperate resort, preferring passive resistance. However, they accepted violence more readily if it could be legitimized as resistance to violence. The political extremists were the group most willing to accept the use of political violence and judged its use on the basis of effectiveness rather than on moral grounds.

The purpose of the last segment of the project was to seek biographical correlates for the genesis of left-wing extremism. The case histories of sixty subjects were taken by psychologists in an effort to discover the relationship between political socialization, personality structure, and the political attitudes of the subjects. Five political subgroups were identified and typical radicalization patterns discovered.

Summing up their findings from the different parts of the investigation, the Infratest group made the following observations:

1. The protesters are less satisfied with their achievements than the average for the population, and the difference between their goals and their achievements is greater.

2. The members of this group hold postmaterialist values, and their dissatisfaction can be accounted for by the discrepancy between their expectations, on the basis of these values, on the one hand, and the realization of these values, on the other. The perception of economic insecurity reinforces their criticism of the political system.

3. The protesters hold the government responsible for what they perceive to be inadequate coping with issues of social justice (and thus suffer "political deprivation").

4. Though the majority of these members of the left-wing protest potential have little confidence in the government, most are close to the Social Democratic party, and most believe that their demands can be met by democratic, parliamentary means. Exceptions are found largely among the unemployed members of the left-wing protest potential, among whom there are disproportionately many members of the Communist party.

Two distinct reactions to the perceptions of discrepancies between political value expectations and the realization of these expectations in society were found. If the perception of discrepancy was coupled with great confidence in the readiness of the system to respond, as was the case with most members of the left-wing protest potential, then the government was thought to carry the blame. However, if the perception of discrepancy was coupled with little faith in the responsiveness of the system, then the system itself was held responsible for the perceived failure.

Although the Infratest (1980) study did not rely solely on survey data, as the investigation of political action had done (Barnes and Kaase, 1979), it still failed to capture and convey some important aspects of the subject of its study—political protest in the Federal Republic of Germany. It continued to focus on self-reported data of individuals, though questionnaire information was augmented by in-depth interviews. Limiting the research to this microplane of the individual as the unit of analysis implies that collective action is no more than the sum total of individual behavior. This assumption cannot be made without evidence, and it is especially questionable with respect to unconventional and violent political action.

One of the most serious problems of studies dealing with political protest concerns the noncooperation of the target group. It is a point of principle with young West German protesters, for example, to oppose sociological surveys. They distrust assurances that their anonymity will be respected and believe that information they give may be used against them. They believe that studies of protest will be used to help curb this protest, and, for many, it is an article of faith that social science can only serve the interests of the establishment.

Another research group (Prognos, 1982) studying West German youth protest reports that, on one occasion, only 2 of 30 protesters approached were willing to participate in the research and that even these ultimately did not take part. Only 7 of 120 Catholic Youths for Peace approached by the Prognos team consented to be interviewed. The Infratest team (1980, pp. 110, 149) acknowledged similar problems and suggested that the more extreme the positions of the subjects, the less likely they were to submit to an interview. However, no attempt was made to evaluate the effect of these considerations on the results of the study. Thus, it seems likely that the percentage of the protest potential in the probability sample of the Infratest survey is considerably larger than indicated and that the findings reported on the basis of the 91 of 175 protesters identified in the survey and willing to be interviewed may be subject to systematic error. In the latter parts of this study, focusing on the individual representatives of the left-wing protest potential, a quota system for the recruitment of subjects was used—a method that gives no information about refusal rates and also does little to preclude systematic error.

Other sources of error in the studies of protest based on self-report data are the acquiescence response set (the tendency of subjects to respond positively to questions asked) (Couch and Keniston, 1960) and the social desirability response set (Edwards, 1957). The authors of the Infratest study were aware of the problem of the acquiescence response set and tried to take it into consideration by formulating a number of items so that, to express a liberal attitude, some items would have to be rejected and others would have to be approved. They report that the items requiring rejection were significantly less often rejected than the positive items were agreed to and, furthermore, that this tendency applied far less frequently to subjects with more education (Infratest, 1980, p. 84). These factors were not considered in the report of the results. Social desirability—the tendency of a subject to give the answer perceived as socially desirable—may, for example, have prompted 91.6 percent of the West German subjects to respond that they read the political section of the newspaper sometimes or often (Infratest, 1980, p. 48). A report of July 1981 by the Institut für Demoskopie Allensbach, to the effect that more than 80 percent of the general public were unable to answer general questions concerning long-standing political issues, casts doubt on this claim.

In Search of New Methods: A Qualitative Approach

In 1981 I was commissioned by the Institut für Konfliktforschung, Vienna, to investigate the nature and the causes of political protest and violence in the Federal Republic of Germany. In an attempt to augment the numerous studies available with a contribution that would not be subject to the difficulties discussed above, I used a qualitative method (Glaser and Strauss, 1967; Kleining, 1982) that relies on text analyses. The data used consisted of published autobiographical accounts by protesters; of essays, articles, and statements by members of the protest movement; of eye-witness accounts; and of protocols of protest meetings. The focus of the analysis was the systematic organization of the themes discussed in the literature and the recurrent relationships between these themes.

It was possible, in this way, to include the feelings and attitudes of subjects who would have been unwilling to cooperate with social surveys and to avoid problems of the acquiescence response set. A three-dimensional picture of the West German protest movement emerged that went beyond anything the statistical studies had been able to give. Other analyses (Oltmanns, 1980; Haller, 1981; Prognos, 1982) independently prepared at about the same time using other qualitative methods corroborated many of my findings.

My investigation of the West German protest movement revealed a deep cleavage in the West German public, with traditional society on one side and a varied and fluctuating counterculture on the other. The heterogeneous members of this alternative culture live in surprising isolation from the establishment. Many live in communal arrangements, some in houses occupied by squatters. Self-help projects, shops, and organizations provide employment. It has been estimated that in 1979 there were in West Germany and Berlin about 10,000 such projects of various kinds involving roughly 70,000 active members and about 250,000 sympathizers (Huber, 1980, p. 28). The members of this protest movement regard their way of life as an important part of their protest. They want to abolish the rigid separation of the three components of their lives—housing, working, and leisure—and seek autonomy and self-determination in all three areas. They demand "Freiräume" (literally, "free spaces")—politically, socially, and physically—and refuse to conform to what they experience as the extreme regimentation and constraints imposed by society.

These protesters feel that work should be an integral part of their lives—meaningful and socially useful, not consumption or profit oriented. Brainwork and menial tasks should be shared equally by all, and decisions should be made jointly. Hours should be flexible. The protesters reject hierarchical structures and the delegation of authority. They practice "basic democracy," calling meetings where everyone who comes may participate. Only if everyone agrees on an action is it carried out. Finally, they are very critical of the political establishment, although they do not have an alternative plan for society and do not occupy a conventional niche in the left-right spectrum. They mobilize large numbers of participants around the citizens' initiatives against atomic power, for peace, for women's liberation, and for ecology. They enjoy spontaneity and advocate acting out in preference to thinking and reasoning things out. They see protest not only as a means to an end but also as an end in itself. The confrontation with the police is, for some, a lustful physical experience in an alienating world (Lederer, 1982).

Unanswered Questions

In this chapter I have outlined the evolution of some theories of social conflict and the operationalization of these theories by means of empirical research design. Although there have been valuable contributions in the field, relatively little systematic research has been carried out. Much of what is most relevant remains unknown, and the research that has been carried out seems to miss essential aspects of the phenomenon on which it focuses.

The phenomenon of political protest in the modern industrial democracies is hard to capture with theories and research projects. Vast and diverse assemblages of activists form coalitions around a complex of disparate issues. The protest movements are in general highly decentralized and have strong religious components, strong secular components, and little ideological purity. It has been difficult to identify leaders and to predict strength and influence. The line between political participation and political protest is difficult to draw. Much protest originates with citizen initiatives that blend conventional political participation with protest activities.

It is, after all, a fundamental principle of democratic societies to guarantee citizens the chance to influence the decision-making process. Lack of system responsiveness leads to various direct-action techniques. At a time when the media make the transmission of events immediate and personal, the frustration of the individual who perceives himself unable to influence the decision-making process leads to new types of participation. Protest activities that were relatively rare in the first half of the twentieth century and that were perceived as promoting political unrest and system change have gained widespread acceptance in the second half of the twentieth century as legitimate tools of political participation—an indication of value change in the mass publics.

Technological developments have facilitated the process of establishing ad hoc groups and single-issue movements. This type of political protest has tended to manifest itself in waves. Its periodic, issue-linked recurrence leads to the conclusion that this is not a passing phenomenon but instead an integral part of Western politics and a pathway to political redress in the future.

Important questions remain to be answered by the interdisciplinary efforts of political scientists, sociologists, and psychologists:

1. What has been the effect of direct-action politics on the major issues that such actions have addressed? For example, what was the effect of the protest movement on the outcome of the war in Vietnam? What effect has the West German peace movement had on party platforms and national policy? What is the relationship between public protest and the abandonment of major nuclear projects in the United States?

2. Is the spreading political protest movement a threat to the rational democratic decision-making process; or is it a positive, legitimate pathway toward political redress, with the power to focus political thinking on urgent issues? It remains for social scientists to assess the influence that the more generalized political activism will have on the traditional processes of representative democracies, to answer the questions of legitimacy and representation raised by this increased activism.

3. The widespread public acceptance of new forms of political participation signals a change in values in the political culture of the Western democracies. Is it possible for social science to extrapolate from the evolution of needs and values to anticipate change? The changing values and consequent changes in structure of political cleavages in Western Europe have been the subject of investigation by Inglehart (1977, 1981, 1982) and others. There is evidence that political protest has become divorced from party alignment, giving the terms "political left" and "political right," so important in the European context, new meaning. What is the nature of this new meaning, and what are its political implications?

4. Can social science keep pace with change? One of the major weaknesses of research on political participation has been that it has lagged behind the rapidly changing political realities. By the time the deliberate process of analysis has run its course, the data base of the research has lost congruence with time. Whereas it is true that changing manifestations of societal behavior do not necessarily indicate profound changes in the underlying variables, little work has been done to pinpoint the extent and significance of such change.

Modern society is involved in an evolutionary process that is proceeding at an accelerating rate of change. It is important for research in the social sciences to address this problem. The role this research will play will depend on its ability to develop a sensitivity to societal change. Imaginative use of the new tools of technology could confer on researchers the capability to record and analyze the dialectic process instead of recording, or at best comparing, specific points in time.

5. Will social research meet the special problems of its subjects with flexibility and imagination? In the Federal Republic of Germany, for example, it is a shared belief among the protesters that social research represents a threat to them and their protest activities, leading to a widespread refusal of cooperation. A probability sample will thus automatically exclude these members of the protest movement. This example suggests that attention needs to be paid to the subjects who fail to participate in a survey.

Another problem is the inability of the social survey to reveal unanticipated motivations, feelings, and interrelations between feelings and motives. The realization of this shortcoming has given rise to a plethora of qualitative research that throws light on a few subjects in depth. Unfortunately, these studies do not furnish measures of the problems they examine. In an attempt to assess thinking and motivation of the participants of the West German protest movement, Lederer (1982) combined the results of available empirical research with a qualitative analysis of the speeches and writings of protesters. The picture that emerges of deeply alienated young people living isolated in a society within a society underscores the need for innovative research methods. No survey would capture their values, their reconciliation of apparently irreconcilable ideas, their understanding of violence, democracy, or political participation.

The questions raised here point to some of the challenges that political psychology research faces in its efforts to grasp and interpret political protest movements. Since there can be no doubt that protest movements will play a major, perhaps a decisive, role in shaping modern society, it will be increasingly important for political psychologists to live up to these challenges.

References

Abramowitz, A. I. "The United States: Political Culture Under Stress." In G. A. Almond and S. Verba (eds.), *The Civic Culture Revisited*. Boston: Little, Brown, 1980.

Almond, G. A., and Verba, S. *The Civic Culture: Political Attitudes and Democracy in Five Nations*. Boston: Little, Brown, 1965.

Almond, G. A., and Verba, S. (eds.). *The Civic Culture Revisited*. Boston: Little, Brown, 1980.

Barnes, S. H., and Kaase, M. (eds.). *Political Action: Mass Participation in Five Western Democracies*. Beverly Hills, Calif.: Sage, 1979.

Citrin, J., and others. "Sources and Consequences of Political Alienation: A Progress Report on Indicator Development." Paper presented at the Conference on Public Support for the Political System, Madison, Wisc., Aug. 1973

Converse, P. E. "The Nature of Belief Systems in Mass Publics." In D. Apter (ed.), *Ideology and Discontent*. New York: Free Press, 1964.

Coser, L. A. *The Functions of Social Conflict*. New York: Free Press, 1956.

Couch, A., and Keniston, K. "Yeasayers and Naysayers: Agreeing Response Set as a Personality Variable." *Journal of Abnormal and Social Psychology*, 1960, *60*, 151-174.

Dahl, R. A. *Polyarchy*. New Haven, Conn.: Yale University Press, 1971.

Davies, J. C. "Toward a Theory of Revolution." *American Sociological Review*, 1962, *27*, 5-19.

Durkheim, E. *Suicide: A Study in Sociology*. (A. Spaulding and G. Simpson, trans.) New York: Free Press, 1951. (Originally published 1897.)

Edwards, A. L. *The Social Desirability Variable in Personality Assessment and Research*. New York: Dryden Press, 1957.

Festinger, L. *A Theory of Cognitive Dissonance*. Stanford, Calif.: Stanford University Press, 1957.

Fishbein, M. "Attitude and the Prediction of Behavior." In M. Fishbein (ed.), *Readings in Attitude Theory and Measurement*. New York: Wiley, 1967.

Galtung, J. *Theory and Methods of Social Research*. New York: Columbia University Press, 1967.

Glaser, B. G., and Strauss, A. L. *The Discovery of Grounded Theory: Strategies for Qualitative Research*. Hawthorne, N.Y.: Aldine, 1967.

Gurney, J. N., and Tierney, K. J. "Relative Deprivation and Social Movements: A Critical Look at Twenty Years of Theory and Research." *Sociological Quarterly*, 1982, *23*, 33-47.

Gurr, T. R. *Why Men Rebel*. Princeton, N.J.: Princeton University Press, 1970.

Gurr, T. R. "Model Building and the Test of Theory." In J. C. Davies (ed.), *When Men Revolt and Why*. New York: Free Press, 1971.

Haller, M. (ed.), *Aussteigen oder Rebellieren: Jugendliche gegen Staat und Gesellschaft* [Acting out or rebelling: Youth against state and society]. Hamburg: Rowohlt, 1981.

Hibbs, D. A., Jr. *Mass Political Violence: A Cross-National Causal Analysis*. New York: Wiley, 1973.

Huber, J. *Wer soll das alles ändern? Die Alternativen und die Alternative Bewegung* [Who shall change things? The alternatives and the Alternative Movement]. Berlin: Rotbuch, 1980.

Infratest. *Politischer Protest in der Bundesrepublik Deutschland* [Political protest in the Federal Republic of Germany]. Stuttgart: Kohlhammer, 1980.

Inglehart, R. *The Silent Revolution: Changing Values and Political Styles Among Western Publics*. Princeton, N.J.: Princeton University Press, 1977.

Inglehart, R. "Post-Materialism in an Environment of Insecurity." *American Political Science Review*, 1981, 75 (4), 880-900.

Inglehart, R. "The Changing Structure of Political Cleavages Among West European Elites and Publics." Paper presented at the Workshop on Empirical Elite Research, European University Institute, Florence, Italy, Oct. 1982.

Kaase, M. "Bedingungen unkonventionellen politischen Verhaltens in der Bundesrepublik Deutschland" [Training of unconventional behavior in the Federal Republic of Germany]. *Politische Vierteljahresschrift*, 1976, Special Issue no. 7, 179-216.

Kaase, M. "Political Action in the 80s: Structures and Idiosyncrasies." Paper presented at 6th annual meeting of the International Society of Political Psychology, Oxford University, July 1983.

Kaase, M., and Marsh, A. "Distribution of Political Action." In S. H. Barnes and M. Kaase (eds.), *Political Action*. Beverly Hills, Calif.: Sage, 1979a.

Kaase, M., and Marsh, A. "Political Action Repertory: Changes over Time and a New Typology." In S. H. Barnes and M. Kaase (eds.), *Political Action*. Beverly Hills, Calif.: Sage, 1979b.

Kaase, M., and Marsh, A. "Political Action: A Theoretical Perspective." In S. H. Barnes and M. Kaase (eds.), *Political Action*. Beverly Hills, Calif.: Sage, 1979c.

Kleining, G. "Umriss zu einer Methodologie qualitiver Sozialforschung" [Outline of a qualitative methodology for social research]. *Kölner Zeitschrift für Soziologie und Sozialpsychologie*, 1982, 34, 224-253.

Klingemann, H. D. "Ideological Conceptualization and Political Action." In S. H. Barnes and M. Kaase (eds.), *Political Action*. Beverly Hills, Calif.: Sage, 1979.

Lederer, G. "Neue Jugendbewegungen und Protestformen: Bedingungen des Umschlagens politischen Protests in Gewalt" [New youth movements and forms of protest: Conditions relevant to violent political protests]. Paper prepared for the Institut für Konfliktforschung, Vienna, 1982.

Lederer, G. *Jugend und Autorität* [Youth and authority]. Opladen: Westdeutscher Verlag, 1983.

Marsh, A., and Kaase, M. "Measuring Political Action." In S. H. Barnes and M. Kaase (eds.), *Political Action*. Beverly Hills, Calif.: Sage, 1979.

Marx, J., and Holzner, B. "The Social Construction of Strain and Ideological Models of Grievance in Contemporary Movements." *Sociological Perspectives*, 1977, 18, 411-433.

Maslow, A. *Motivation and Personality*. New York: Harper & Row, 1954.

Merelman, R. M., and Foster, C. R. "Political Culture and Education in Advanced Industrial Societies: West Germany and the United States." *International Review of Education*, 1978, *26*, 443–465.

Muller, E. N. "Behavioral Correlates of Political Support." *American Political Science Review*, 1977, *71*, 454–467.

Muller, E. N. *Aggressive Political Participation*. Princeton, N.J.: Princeton University Press, 1979.

Muller, E. N. "An Explanatory Model for Differing Types of Participation." *European Journal of Political Research*, 1982, *10*, 1–16.

Oltmanns, R. *Du hast keine Chance, aber nutze sie* [You have no opportunity, but they benefit]. Hamburg: Rowohlt, 1980.

Opp, K. D., Burow-Affarth, K., and Heinrichs, U. "Conditions for Conventional and Unconventional Political Participation: An Empirical Test of Economic and Sociological Hypotheses." *European Journal of Poltical Research*, 1981, *9*, 147–168.

Parsons, T. "Social Classes and Class Conflict." *American Economic Review*, 1949, *34*, 16–26.

Parsons, T. *The Social System*. New York: Free Press, 1951.

Prognos. "Jugendprotest: Einstellungen und Motive von Jugendlichen in achten ausgewählten Gruppen" [Youth protest: Attitudes and motives in eight selected groups]. Unpublished research report by the European Center for Applied Economic Research, Basel, Switzerland, Sept. 1982.

Schmidtchen, G., and Ühlinger, H. "Jugend und Staat" [Youth and the state]. In U. Matz and G. Schmidtchen (eds.), *Gewalt und Legitimität* [Power and legitimacy]. Opladen: Westdeutscher Verlag, 1983.

Seligson, M. A. "Trust, Efficacy and Modes of Political Participation: A Study of Costa Rican Peasants." *British Journal of Political Science*, 1980, *10*, 75–98.

Simmel, G. *Conflict*. (K. H. Wolff, trans.) New York: Free Press, 1955. (Originally published 1908.)

Smelser, N. J. *Theory of Collective Behavior*. New York: Free Press, 1963.

Tilly, C. "Speaking Your Mind Without Elections, Surveys, or Social Movements." *Public Opinion Quarterly*, 1983, *47*, 461–478.

Tocqueville, A. de. *L'Ancien Régime et la Révolution* [The old regime and the revolution]. (M. W. Patterson, trans.) Oxford, England: Oxford University Press, 1951. (Originally published 1856.)

Ühlinger, H. M. "The Dimensionality of Political Participation." Paper presented at 6th annual meeting of the International Society of Political Psychology, Oxford University, July 1983.

Unseem, M. *Protest Movements in America*. New York: Bobbs-Merrill, 1975.

Verba, S., and Nie, N. H. *Participation in America*. New York: Harper & Row, 1972.

THIRTEEN

❧❧❧❧❧❧❧❧❧❧❧❧❧❧❧❧❧❧❧❧❧❧

The Psychology
of Political Terrorism

Martha Crenshaw

Violence is a perennial problem of politics. Scholars and policy makers are rarely satisfied with their understanding of its sources or consequences—other than the manifest results of death and destruction, which only deepen frustration over being unable to prevent its occurrence. Terrorism used by underground organizations against state institutions and policies is a specific type of political violence, one that has attracted much attention in the past fifteen years. As terrorism has affected Western liberal democracies, it has shaken their faith in the possibility of the eradication of civil strife through political and social reform or through the material benefits of the welfare state. Terrorism has shown that the end of colonialism does not bring an end to struggles for national liberation. Indeed, Third World violence has inspired imitation in the West, as ethnic minorities revive hopes of separatism and as radical political organizations, often growing out of the student movements of the 1960s, move to join what they perceive as a global struggle against imperialism. After 1968 in Western Europe terrorism seemed to replace riots and protest demonstrations as a dramatic and violent disruption of stability, often disturbing to the public because of its unexpectedness in societies hitherto thought immune to serious domestic violence. Ideology has also motivated terrorist resistance to regimes in Latin America and the Middle East. In the latter region, religious fundamentalism is now combined with secular opposition as a source of violence. Although terrorism is not a historical novelty, changes in its form and scope have appeared in the past fifteen years.

As Greenstein (1973, p. 464) has noted: "It would seem necessary to identify functionally discrete types of violence and aggression in order to identify reasonably stable and distinctive antecedents." This observation is equally appropriate to the analysis of the consequences of violence. Terrorism is one of these discrete types of violence. The purpose of this chapter is to use terrorism as the basis for a case study of the relationship between political violence and psychology. Terrorism, a rare and extreme form of political behavior, is dependent on the motivations of the small numbers who practice it. Because its effectiveness in influencing political events depends on arousing emotions, the psychological reactions of its target audiences are significant.

Before attempting to analyze the problem of terrorism from a psychological perspective, we must complete several preliminary tasks. First, the concept of terrorism must be defined. Second, a review of existing approaches to the subject of terrorism is needed to sketch the general state of theoretical advance in the area. Third, an explanation of the complexity of the phenomenon of terrorism suggests caution in generalization. Proceeding to the application of psychological theory to terrorism, a logical beginning is the question of individual motivation. Why do people resort to terrorism? A concept that serves to unify diverse interpretations of motivation is Erikson's (1963, 1968) theory of identity. An exclusive focus on the individual is, however, incomplete, since terrorism usually involves group activity. Patterns of small-group interaction are a significant part of the explanation of terrorism activity. The psychology of terrorism also concerns the effects of terrorism on audiences and victims. The fate of hostages, as the most intense experience of victimization, will be examined in some depth.

Definitions and Approaches

Defining the concept of terrorism has proved difficult, in part because judgments about what terrorism is frequently depend on the circumstances in which violence occurs. Most writers on this subject rely on one of the earliest definitions, that of Thornton (1964, p. 73), who proposed: "In an internal war situation, terror is a symbolic act designed to influence political behavior by extranormal means, entailing the use or threat of violence." The violence of terrorism is distinguished from other types of political violence by its extranormality (terrorism exceeds the bounds of socially acceptable violence) and by its symbolic nature (the targets of terrorism are symbols of the state or of social norms and structure) (see Thornton, 1964, pp. 73–78). Terrorism is based on systematic and purposive violence, designed to influence the political choices of other actors more than to inflict casualties or material destruction. To achieve political influence, terrorism depends on its power to arouse emotions in audiences, including the neutral, the supportive, and the antagonistic. The emotional reactions to terrorism (which, of course, may be unanticipated by the terrorists although they strive to control them) may thus range from terror or acute anxiety to enthusiasm (see Hutchinson, 1972).

Thornton's conception, as expanded here, is restricted to terrorism against the state; that is, terrorism from below rather than from above. Terrorism is also practiced by governments, and some characteristics of its processes, effects, and perpetrators are similar to the characteristics of insurgent or agitational terrorism. For example, insurgent terrorist organizations may use terrorism to control their supporters and to enforce obedience. There are, however, such critical differences in the power, authority, and status of governments as opposed to nongovernments that an undifferentiated analysis would be misleading. The potential magnitude of most government violence is incomparably greater than that of nongovernments.

The literature in the field of terrorism is unsystematic, despite great popular and governmental interest in terrorism and the promise that the social sciences and psychology hold for its theoretical development. There are numerous ahistorical or alarmist treatments, but few scholars have turned their attention to terrorism, and among them fewer are familiar with the literature and attempt to build on the work of others. Nevertheless, there are signs that terrorism is becoming an established subject for research in the mainstream of American political science, including both quantitative as well as conceptual studies (for the former approach, see Hamilton and Hamilton, 1983; Sandler, Tschirhart, and Cauley, 1983). Even so, few psychiatrists, psychologists, or social psychologists have worked in this area. The present analysis of the state of the field is as much a sketch of what needs to be accomplished as an overview of achievements. It attempts to synthesize existing findings, to point out the areas of psychology from which future theoretical contributions might come, and to define the directions that psychological approaches to the study of political terrorism might take.

There are a number of reasons for the weak state of theoretical development in this area. First, terrorism is a controversial subject; it possesses normative connotations that make the mere use of the term a statement of approval or disapproval of the activity. As a consequence, Jenkins (1981, pp. 4-5), noting that the normative implications and controversiality of terrorism impede clear definition, proposes that terrorism be considered simply as criminal violence directed against civilian targets for political motives.

Second, despite its historical antiquity, terrorism is relatively new as a concept that has interested scholars, whose interest followed that of governments and the public when hijackings, hostage seizures, and attacks on diplomats became sensational news in the late 1960s and early 1970s. Within the past ten years, the number of citations on the subject of terrorism has grown from fewer than ten to thousands (see Mickolus, 1980). The dramatic nature of the topic and the extremely rapid growth of the field have understandably produced uneven results.

Third, because terrorism is perceived as a threat to a government's reputation and international image, if not always to its stability, official bureaucracies are much more interested in the study of terrorism than in that of many other topics in scholarly research. Government attention has resulted in an emphasis on the particular aspects of terrorism that concern public safety—notably, the response to terrorism and the anticipation of future threats. Policy analysis and criminal justice approaches are more common than attempts to explain the motivations of terrorists and terrorist groups. These approaches frequently deny that the intentions of the terrorist are relevant at all, concentrating instead on terrorist capabilities and on government countermeasures.

Last, the difficulty of acquiring the sort of detailed information that would support psychobiographical studies of individuals or make histories of group dynamics possible inhibits psychological theory building. Difficulties stemming from the mutual suspicion of terrorists and governments are inevitable, given the illegality and consequent secretiveness of terrorist organizations. Security and intelligence considerations can impede access to data. West German social scientists, for example, found it very difficult to interview members of the Red Army Faction and its successors; most were unwilling to meet with researchers (Jäger, Schmidtchen, and Süllwold, 1981). They also found, somewhat paradoxically, that local government authorities were reluctant to cooperate even though their study was commissioned by the federal Ministry of the Interior. The West German effort, however, was hampered most because researchers attempted to interview suspected terrorists who were under arrest or undergoing trial but who had not been convicted. Since interviews with social science researchers did not have the status of privileged communications, the researchers could have been subpoenaed to give evidence in the cases. Such conditions, as well as the often hostile and uncooperative attitudes of accused terrorists toward researchers whom they perceived as representatives of the establishment, made trust between interviewer and subject impossible to achieve.

On the other hand, Knutson (1980, 1981) did succeed in interviewing convicted terrorists in United States prisons. She found the authorities helpful and the prisoners eager for a chance to express themselves to a sympathetic listener; most felt that during their trials they had not been given an opportunity to explain the reasons for their actions. Differences both in method and in situation may explain Knutson's relative ease of access compared to the West German problems. Nevertheless, requirements of confidentiality mean that findings based on this research must be carefully formulated and that access to interview transcripts and other data is restricted.

In sum, although the total number of materials on terrorism is large, including primary documents such as trial records, research specifically relevant to this analysis is limited. This survey as a result is based on a small amount of available psychological data and analysis. It also considers some autobiographical materials, although these generally lack self-perception. Analysis of terrorism must be interdisciplinary, relying on secondary sources from history, political science, and sociology that provide case studies of individual terrorists and terrorist groups. Theoretical insights are often borrowed from other sources in psychology and adapted to an interpretation of terrorist activity and its consequences.

Complexity of the Problem

In order to generalize about psychological influences on terrorism, one must take into account the diversity and variation of the phenomenon. One reason for the imprecision or bias of many definitions of terrorism is that the activity assumes different forms. For instance, terrorists claim to be inspired by ideological goals ranging from social revolution or national self-determination to reactionary or conservative defense of the status quo. Terrorist organizations range in structure from extremely hierarchical and centralized, with rigid role distinctions, to a decentralized or anarchical model. Terrorist strategies vary in degree of selectivity in targeting and in preferences for specific methods; some involve bargaining with governments by seizing hostages, while others are designed only for immediate effect. Some terrorists choose to operate on an international scale, while others restrict themselves to their domestic surroundings. Terrorist modes of operation change constantly, often as a result of technological opportunities or government pressures.

Furthermore, the situations in which terrorism occurs vary along a number of dimensions. Political contexts include democracies as well as authoritarian regimes and states ranging from strong to weak in coercive capability and political stability. Legal systems may be flexible or rigid in dealing with violent opposition. Target societies may be homogeneous or heterogeneous, and history and political culture may be tolerant or intolerant of violence against the state. The international environment can be permissive or discouraging. Several types of terrorism occur in this range of contexts. The organizational forms and capabilities of terrorist organizations and the environments they operate in are related to both motivations and psychological consequences. Any model of terrorism must take into account the varieties and the interactive dynamics of the process.

To illustrate briefly differences in motivation, context, and status among contemporary terrorist organizations, one can compare the Provisional Irish Republican Army (IRA) in the United Kingdom and Ireland to the Red Army Faction (RAF) and its successors in the Federal Republic of Germany. The Provisional IRA is the heir to a tradition of violent resistance to British rule, the "physical force" tradition that has its roots not only in Oliver Cromwell's depredations but in the mythology of the French Revolution. Although the majority of the citizens of Ireland and Northern Ireland do not actively support the IRA, belonging to the IRA in the divided society of Northern Ireland is more socially acceptable than belonging to the RAF in West Germany, where memories of violence against the regime derive primarily from the paramilitary extremists of both right and left under the Weimar Republic. In West Germany neither religious nor national divisions legitimize violence against the state. Most West German terrorists, whose organizations emerged from student protest movements, are from the middle or upper-middle classes; in contrast, members of the IRA are from working-class backgrounds. Whereas the aims of Irish Republicans focus sharply on creating a united and non-British Ireland, the vague and unrealistic goals of German terrorism center on the creation of an ill-defined socialist order. Many Irish, northern, southern, and American, sympathize with the IRA's goals of national unity and British withdrawal if not its methods. Few Germans (despite the publicity over "sympathizers") want a revolution. The IRA generally restricts its activities to the traditional methods of terrorism and guerrilla warfare—selective assassinations, bombings, troop ambushes, sniper fire—that accord with its self-image as an army against the British. The RAF, on the contrary, progressed to kidnappings and hijackings in order to compel the government to release imprisoned fellow terrorists. This form of bargaining with governments has since 1968 represented a significant innovation in terrorist strategies.

Even this brief description indicates that psychological motivations, processes, and effects differ from case to case and that one should exercise caution in proposing generalizations. Answers to the questions of why individuals are attracted to terrorism, why terrorism finds supporters among the population, why a terrorist organization chooses particular strategies, and why terrorism has extreme effects in some cases but not in others depend on political and social context and type of terrorist organization as well as on psychological theory.

Another element in the complexity of modern terrorism is its transnational character. The fact that terrorism is a transnational phenomenon—one that in crossing national boundaries escapes the control of governments—blurs distinctions among different national groups and their contexts. As terrorists collaborate among themselves, imitate each other, and seek foreign support, it becomes difficult to isolate causes and effects. Furthermore, transnationalism (a product of modernization) means that terrorists can be both mobile and anonymous. Consequently, terrorists can be either close to or distant from the populations they target. Palestinian terrorism against Israelis in West Germany, for example, and Armenian terrorism against Turks in the United States will not have the same effects on its respective national audiences as indigenous terrorism would have.

Further complexities in analyzing terrorism arise from the widely held assumption that terrorism is intentional behavior, in which motivations of whatever sort, rational or irrational, lead to action that can be objectively identified as terrorism. However, the translation of intention into action is modified by chance and opportunity, neither of which can be satisfactorily predicted. Furthermore, in asking why terrorism happens, one must distinguish between the initiation of a campaign of terrorism and its continuation in the face of government reaction. One must also distinguish between why an individual becomes a terrorist and why an organization (already formed as a group) collectively turns to terrorism. Why terrorists persist despite the risks involved and the uncertainty of reward is an important question. Why terrorist organizations choose the particular strategies they do—bombings, kidnappings, or armed attacks, for example—is also significant.

Scholarly analysis should also be attentive to what is meant by becoming a "terrorist" or a member of a terrorist organization. Most people probably oversimplify the role of the "terrorist" into a mental picture of a wild-eyed nineteenth-century anarchist. Actually, complex role differentiation exists within terrorist organizations. First, there are significant differences between leaders and followers. The latter group is further divided into those who are active within the organization and those who are passive supporters, remaining outside the underground structure but providing needed services as well as channels for recruitment into the organization. Among active followers, one can distinguish a number of separate functions: public relations, propaganda, fund raising, forgery, weapons purchases, and logistics, as well as those related to planning and engaging in violence. A terrorist may be a sharpshooter, a builder of bombs, a specialist in armed attacks or kidnappings, or a guard for hostages. Terrorist violence need not involve physical interaction with victims.

Finally, constructing theories to explain the effects of terrorism on victims and on audiences is also hampered by the elusiveness of the phenomenon. It is difficult to separate the effects of terrorism from the effects of other social phenomena to which the public responds. It is somewhat easier to analyze the reactions of victims, especially former hostages. Yet even here, analysts are hard pressed to specify what it is about terrorism that accounts for its effects, or how much the strength of reaction lies in the predispositions of the victim or target audience.

Explanations of Individual Motivation

It would be simplistic to base an argument about motivation on the premise that terrorism is solely a result of specific personality patterns or traits. As with all forms of political behavior, terrorism cannot be studied in isolation from its political and social context. The analysis of terrorism clearly deals with the intersection of psychological predispositions (which may be derived as much from prior experience and socialization as from psychological traits emerging from early childhood and infancy) and the external environment. This interrelationship is the more compelling because the ostensible purpose of terrorist groups is to change that environment; terrorists invariably claim, in fact, that their behavior is the only logical response to external circumstances. Many indignantly reject psychological explanations. Terrorism, furthermore, is a result of group interactions as much as individual choice. Although isolated, individually motivated acts of terrorism can occur, the most important terrorist events are part of campaigns led by organizations.

Another problem with the study of individual motivation or predisposition toward terrorism is that it is difficult to go beyond a series of unrelated psychobiographies and focus on common themes. Most analysts agree that there is no common "terrorist personality." Terrorism is not purely expressive violence; it is also instrumental. We are thus dealing with individuals who are extremely goal oriented but whose goals and means of pursuing their goals are influenced (not determined) by psychological considerations in interaction with the situation.

Nor does terrorism in general appear to be a result of mental pathologies. Rasch (1979, p. 80), a psychiatrist who has analyzed several members of the West German terrorist organizations, warns that "no conclusive evidence has been found for the assumption that a significant number of them are disturbed or abnormal." In Rasch's (1979, p. 79) view, the argument that terrorism is pathological behavior is an attempt to avoid discussion of the political and social issues raised by terrorism. Rasch's position is reinforced by the studies performed under the aegis of the West German Ministry of the Interior, which include information on 227 leftist terrorists in West Germany (Jäger, Schmidtchen, and Süllwold, 1981, particularly Süllwold, pp. 101-102 and conclusions by Jäger and Böllinger, p. 235). Similarly, Ferracuti and Bruno (1981, p. 206), who studied Italian terrorists, note that "a general psychiatric explanation of terrorism is impossible. To define all terrorists as mentally ill would be an easy way to solve the problem, simply by invoking evil spirits in order to exclude from normality those from whom we want to be as different as possible." Heskin (1980, pp. 84-85), in a study of the psychology of Northern Ireland, similarly concludes that IRA members are not psychopaths, predisposed to violence, or mentally abnormal. Corrado (1981) has critically reviewed theories that regard terrorism in Western societies as rooted in sociopathy, narcissism, the death wish, or physiological impairment (such as neurological disorders leading to antisocial behavior). He found that the mental disorder approach lacks the systematic clinical observation and reliable diagnostic criteria necessary for its substantiation; furthermore, he suggests, terrorism is more likely to be a product of frustrated but rational idealism.

A possible reason for the apparently small numbers of pathologically ill individuals among the ranks of terrorists is that most terrorist organizations, as conspiratorial undergrounds, are careful about whom they recruit. Centralized, efficient organizations screen out potential members who could be dangerous to the survival of the group. This practical rule of organizational security and maintenance excludes the person of unpredictable or uncontrolled behavior. In less hierarchical organizations, those with a loose structure and relaxed central direction in the anarchist model, there is less control over membership. Hence, group exclusivity would be less of an obstacle to mentally ill persons who might be attracted to terrorism. Thus, according to Ferracuti and Bruno (1981, pp. 208-209), clinical analyses based on the few available case histories of individual left-wing Italian terrorists reveal that they rarely suffered from serious personality defects; in contrast, right-wing terrorists (who are more frequently examined by psychiatrists than are left-wing revolutionary terrorists because the insanity defense is more frequently employed at their trials) showed a much higher incidence of borderline or even psychotic personalities and of drug addiction. The glorification of violence in right-wing ideologies of terrorism may also explain their attraction for mentally disturbed individuals. The West German study, however, did not conclude that right-wing terrorists (of whom twenty-three cases were included) are more likely to be unbalanced, although it noted several distinctive personality traits (see Süllwold, 1981, pp. 110–113).

To argue that terrorism does not result from a single personality constellation or from psychopathology is not to say that the political decision to join a terrorist organization is not influenced or, in some cases, even determined by subconscious or latent psychological motives. The problem is to find some commonality in a heterogeneous group of individuals, especially in considering cross-national terrorism. One facet of personality or one predisposition to which analysts have been drawn is the individual's attitudes toward and feelings about violence and aggression. The question is complex, since for most of its adherents terrorism does not necessarily involve direct participation in violent activities. An attraction to violence does not appear to be the dominant aspect of their personalities—unlike, for example, the most violent of the Nazi stormtroopers studied by Merkl (1980), who notes that these individuals showed an early, single-minded, and "awesome bent for violence" (p. 235). Terrorism involves reflective, not impulsive, violence and requires the ability to delay gratification through long and tedious planning stages.

Knutson (1981, p. 109) found that the terrorists she interviewed in American prisons were ambivalent in their attitudes toward the use of violence. Highly uncomfortable at being called "terrorists," they nevertheless admitted that a purpose of their action had been to cause fear. Yet they insisted that creating fear was less important than demonstrating their commitment to a cause through personal sacrifice. They also regarded terrorism as a last desperate alternative; it was almost an act of personal futility, used after all other options were exhausted, when there was nowhere else to go (Knutson, 1981, pp. 143–144). Certainly, the theme of "we had no choice" dominates terrorists' self-explanations, but it is difficult to distinguish motivation from rationalization.

Knutson (1981) also analyzed a single case in depth, that of Zvonko Busic, the Croatian hijacker of an American airliner to Paris in 1975, who in addition had placed a bomb in Grand Central Station that killed one policeman and injured three others. Busic had chosen hijacking precisely because he considered it "humane" violence, involving as it did the use of fake bombs. His attitude toward violence was conflicted; he looked forward not to frightening his hostages but to their relief, acceptance, and forgiveness when he exposed the reality that there were no explosive devices. He was unable to accept his own anger, felt remorse when he did have to face it, and thus denied it in order to preserve personality integration. Being unable to recognize or accept his own violent impulses, he separated the violent act from his own control and responsibility. Therefore, the bomb that Busic left at Grand Central was accompanied by instructions on how to dismantle it; Busic did not consciously mean to cause deaths. Someone else had to be blamed: in this case the police. A trace of sadism is also revealed in Busic's direction of violence toward "safe" targets—airline passengers—who were unable to respond in kind. Knutson's analysis leads us to suspect that psychological motives may influence the particular form that terrorism takes (for example, seizure of hostages as opposed to assassination) as much as the decision to become a terrorist.

Indeed, Knutson (1980, p. 197) maintains generally that "many terrorist events are carefully, painstakingly engineered to avoid ultimate responsibility for violent death." Many terrorists are "psychologically nonviolent" and spend much time trying to resolve the dilemma, devising ways to instill fear without assuming responsibility for deaths. Similar ambiguities in attitudes toward violence may lead other terrorists to adopt hostage taking as a mode of terrorism, a means by which the final responsibility for causing harm can be laid to the government that refuses to accommodate terrorist demands.

On the other hand, some evidence suggests that not all terrorists are ambivalent. Morf (1970), in an analysis of the early members of the Front de Libération de Québec (FLQ), found more explicit signs of an early interest in violence. Several FLQ members had already engaged in violent resistance to authority. As an adolescent, one had fought with the Belgian partisans in World War II. Another had lived through wartime air raids and subsequently fought with the French Foreign Legion in Vietnam and Algeria. Morf interprets the fascination with violence that he discovered in some individuals as compensation for feelings of inferiority.

Böllinger (1981), a member of the West German study team, also found that some of the terrorists he interviewed were attracted to violence—which he attributes to unconscious aggressive motives. Such motives, in his view, differentiate the terrorist from people with similar psychological features (resulting from early childhood traumas) who do not show the same behavioral outcome—some conforming to social norms and others choosing nonviolent yet nonconformist roles, such as membership in religious cults. The terrorist group represents an outlet for archaic aggressive tendencies, frequently rooted in youthful conflicts with stepfathers. Such aggressive tendencies reflect fantasies of omnipotence corresponding to the individual's own inner feelings of impotence and inferiority. The attraction to violence may also be a result of identification with the violent acts of father figures (a violence several individuals had actually experienced); that is, an identification with the aggressor (see especially Böllinger, 1981, pp. 222-224).

Jäger (1981, pp. 167-169), however, found no common pattern in attitudes toward violence, neither ambivalence nor attraction, among the West German terrorists. Some individuals reported a strong prior aversion to aggression. They were conscious of a need to justify their behavior and felt a sense of limitation. Others reported that violence was simply not a problem for them. Jäger concludes that these attitudes depend on individual socialization and are not particularly significant.

Possibly, rather than being attracted to the inherent violence of terrorism, some individuals are seduced by the lures of omnipotence and grandeur to compensate for feelings of inferiority or impotence. Kaplan (1981, pp. 41-42) contends that the self-righteousness of terrorism conceals the terrorists' insecurities and that "terrorism is a response to a lack of self-esteem." Süllwold (1981) believes that West German terrorists are people who have high aspiration levels but are internally conflicted and prone to failure because of unrealistic demands on themselves. They react to failure not by adapting to their realistic level of capability but by raising the level of their aspirations. Such neurotic behavior involves clinging to irrational goals regardless of outcomes, while refusing to engage in any activity that might test one's abilities. Failure leads to aimlessness and dissatisfaction, which make the individual susceptible to the appeal of terrorist organizations, whose goals are equally unrealistic. Such individuals are also prone to external attribution: to blame others for their failures and consequently to feel hostility toward the outside world (see Süllwold, 1981, pp. 89–96). Knutson (1981) noted a similar tendency to blame others. Böllinger (1981) observed in a limited number of West German terrorists the need to overcome feelings of inferiority.

Another possible psychological trait, which appears to have been neglected thus far by researchers, is stress seeking. Terrorism differs from other counterculture activity not only in its violence but also in its stress-producing character. The glamor and excitement of terrorism, perhaps the attraction for some individuals, lie partially in the physical danger it comports. Terrorists may be "stress seekers," who are attracted to "behavior designed to increase the intensity of emotion or level of activation of the organism" (Klausner, 1968, p. 139). Stress seekers carefully plan their behavior; they respond more to internal than to external imperatives; and they return repeatedly to stressful situations. Moreover, repetition of the stressful activity becomes not only obsessive but escalatory; the stress seeker is compelled to perform more and more difficult acts (see Klausner, 1968, pp. 143, 145). Not all stress seeking is socially destructive behavior; in fact, in many Western societies, the sort of adventurism it may produce is admired. Stress seeking would have to occur in conjunction with other predispositions to encourage violent defiance of government and society.

Stress seekers seem to fall into two types. The individualistic stress seeker is uncomfortable as a follower; he seeks attention to the point of being narcissistic. Such a person seeks self-affirmation in the face of danger. The group stress seeker, in contrast, wishes to abandon the self in the group. This type of stress seeker identifies with the group and merges himself completely in the collective personality (Klausner, 1968, pp. 143–145). This observation leads to an important distinction among terrorist roles between leaders and followers. Whereas leaders may be more likely to possess latent dispositions and traits (acquired through socialization) that make violent, stressful oppositional behavior attractive, followers may be attracted more to the group than to its activities. Followers exhibit strong affiliative needs. Süllwold (1981, pp. 103–106), for example, argues that a notable difference exists between leaders and followers. While there is no such thing as a typical terrorist, leaders are more likely to be people who combine a lack of scruples with extreme self-assurance. She found that leaders often lead by frightening or pressuring their followers.

Süllwold noted two types of personality traits among terrorist leaders. The first type is the extremely extroverted personality, whose behavior is unstable, uninhibited, inconsiderate, self-interested, and unemotional. (Although Süllwold does not suggest the concept of narcissism, these attributes resemble those of the narcissistic personality; see Rubins, 1983). Emotional deficiencies blind such individuals to the negative consequences of their actions. Such people also possess a high tolerance for stress. It is possible that this person is a stress seeker, for whom the excitement of danger compensates for the absence of feeling. Such persons, furthermore, do not accept responsibility for their actions and dislike boredom and inactivity. The second type of terrorist leader is neurotically hostile. Suspicious, aggressive, defensive, and intolerant, he rejects criticism and is extremely sensitive to external hostility. For this type of individual, the terrorist movement serves as a projection of inner hostility. Süllwold (1981) asserts, as does Pomper (1979) in his biography of the nineteenth-century Russian terrorist Sergei Nechaev, that terrorism is a field of action in which personality defects that would be punished in a normal social setting are rewarded. The psychology of terrorist leadership has otherwise been little studied, although several leaders—Boris Savinkov (1931) of the Combat Organization of the Socialist-Revolutionary Party in prerevolutionary Russia, Saadi Yacef (1962) of the Algerian FLN, and Menachem Begin (1977) of the Irgun zvai Leumi—have written autobiographies.

The available evidence strongly suggests that, for the majority of terrorists who are followers, to become a member of the group is a dominant motive. Terrorists, in contrast to assassins, are not usually comfortable acting alone; terrorism is a small-group activity. The path to joining a terrorist organization is often through other groups, such as in West German residential cooperatives, communes, and prisoners' help groups. The recruitment process of the Basque Euzkadi ta Askatasuna (ETA) is slow and gradual, moving like the West German organizations from legal to illegal assistance, and is based on groups in Basque youth culture (Clark, 1983). Kaplan (1981, p. 45) also emphasizes the importance of the "merged collective identity."

In West Germany the communal life from which terrorist groups emerged was extraordinarily homogeneous; it formed a counterculture dominated by leaders with extreme political views. Almost three quarters of the terrorists in Schmidtchen's (1981) sample lived in a commune or residential cooperative before their involvement in terrorism. Many were also individuals whose break with family and society and whose rejection of bourgeois culture and values preceded the politicization of their discontent and was intensified by association with like-minded individuals in closed communities (see Jäger, 1981, pp. 147–150). To many individuals the group substituted for family and filled needs for recognition, acceptance, warmth, and solidarity. Jäger (1981, pp. 151–153) argues that it was above all in this phase of entering a group that latent motives rather than the group's political goals influenced individual actions. The group itself becomes the aim of many people. Jäger also found that many terrorists expressed a need for the structure, discipline, and commitment they found in group life.

For West Germans entrance into the terrorist group was a gradual process—as it was for recruits into the Basque ETA—rather than an instantaneous conversion. As individuals joined groups that became more and more radical, they were drawn closer to the inner circles that espoused violence. Thus, the decision to use violence came only after association with the group; the choice was then between participating in violence or leaving the group. The individual who was already in need of the things a group could supply and who had over time become dependent on the group found it costly, in psychological terms, to go back.

Observers of terrorism in West Germany have also noted the importance of personal connections and relatives in the process of joining a group (Jäger, Schmidtchen, and Süllwold, 1981; Wasmund, 1982). Wasmund discovered a large number of couples and brothers and sisters participating in terrorism. This finding reinforces his argument that the terrorist group is a family substitute. Jäger (1981, pp. 156-157) noted that in some cases relationships with other influential persons were so significant that without them the terrorist's personal development would have taken a different course. Leaders of terrorist groups often fill the role of mentor, becoming substitute parents. Similarly, in the Basque resistance, young recruits frequently joined under the influence of older militants (Clark, 1983). Couples also are commonly found in Italian terrorist groups, and Japanese terrorist Kozo Okamoto followed the lead of his older brother.

A last issue that should be discussed in relation to individual psychological traits and the turn to terrorism concerns the role of women. Some authors believe that female participation in terrorism is unique in character or motivation. For example, Cooper (1979, pp. 151-155) describes the presence of women in terrorist organizations as shocking and their behavior as "vicious," "ferocious," and "intractable." Cooper refers to "fatal proclivities" and unusually intense and personal emotional involvement—the results of women's sexual nature—and to the low self-image, alienation, and bitterness of women terrorists. Knight (1979), in analyzing the significant female participation in the terrorist branch of the Russian Socialist Revolutionary party, contends that terrorism would not have developed as strongly as it did without the critical role of women. Although, Knight argues, the women terrorists whom she studied were more emotionally than rationally inspired, their emotional needs were derived less from inherently feminine traits than from their isolated and frustrated position in a society that offers few outlets for women. She found women terrorists distinctively ethical and moral in their approach to violence, determined and absolutely committed, and bent on self-sacrifice and martyrdom. Their view of terrorism was highly subjective and personal; women valued the sense of importance they gained from participation. The fact that several later showed signs of instability Knight attributes to the trauma of the experience rather than predisposition.

Süllwold (1981, pp. 106-110) does not regard the causes of female participation in terrorism as unusual. She views such assumptions as the result of social stereotyping rather than objective analysis. Süllwold suggests that the significant contribution of women to left-wing West German terrorism, especially to its leadership, was not the result of social frustration and attempts at emancipation. Instead, this participation stemmed from the same factors that drove men to terrorism, although the influence of personal contacts might have been somewhat greater. (An account that illustrates the role of emotional dependence in terrorism is found in Alpert's 1981 autobiography.)

Identity as an Organizing Concept

A theory is needed to integrate existing findings and link the psychological characteristics analysts have noted in individual terrorists to empirical observations. For example, take the fact that most terrorists are young. Many are students or recent students. Often they have already rejected society, choosing to live in a deviant subculture, or are members of ethnic minorities who reject the dominant culture and society. One attempt to link these factors is Feuer's (1969) theory of the "conflict of generations," which is based on a Freudian interpretation of terrorism as a psychological reaction of sons against fathers, a generational phenomenon rooted in the Oedipus complex and, thus, in maleness. Terrorism is seen as a universal and inevitable outgrowth of student movements, independent of political and social context. Authority figures are identified as fathers against whom adolescent sons inevitably rebel. With maturity, terrorism ceases. Liebert (1971, pp. 187–188) criticizes Feuer's monocausal explanation and his confusion of psychodynamics and psychopathology. He contends that Feuer fails to explain why some students do not become activists, although they share the same unconscious impulses as others, or why females are present in contemporary student and terrorist groups.

A more sophisticated theory connecting individual psychology to society is found in the developmental psychology of Erik Erikson (especially 1963 and 1968). Erikson's sensitivity to the interaction between psychoanalytic and social explanations of human behavior is highlighted in his concept of identity, which is a reflection of the individual in a setting, familial or social. To Erikson (1963, p. 242) identity is as central to today's world as sexuality was to Freud's. The successful development of personal identity is essential to the integrity and continuity of the personality. Identity enables the individual to experience the self as something that has continuity and sameness, to act accordingly, and to be confident that one's sense of self is matched by one's meaning for others. Erikson's theory has influenced at least two specific analyses of the personalities of terrorists.

To introduce and clarify these contributions, it is useful to review briefly the part of Erikson's work that pertains to the study of terrorism. Erikson based his concept of personality on the child's development through a series of cumulative developmental stages, each of which is a "crisis" (in the sense of a turning point rather than a catastrophe) that results either in matured integration of the personality or in the persistence of unresolved conflicts, which may torment the individual through later life (see Erikson, 1968, p. 96). Erikson considers the development of basic trust in the infant as the cornerstone of a vital personality. Early mistrust, accompanied by rage and fantasies of domination or destruction of the sources that give pleasure or provide sustenance, is revived when society fails to provide needed assurances. These conflicts of infanthood and early childhood resurface in later extreme circumstances, especially in adolescence, when the crisis facing the individual involves finding a stable identity. Earlier failures to establish trust, autonomy, initiative, or industry handicap the adolescent's search for positive identity, leading in some cases to extreme identity confusion and in others to the formation of a negative identity. Identity is something found not alone but in a collectivity and is rooted in one's ethnic, national, or family past. It cannot, therefore, be separated from historical circumstances.

At the stage of identity formation, individuals seek both meaning and a sense of wholeness or completeness as well as what Erikson (1968, especially p. 232) terms "fidelity," a need to have faith in something or someone outside oneself as well as to be trustworthy in its service. Ideologies, then, are guardians of identity. Erikson further suggests that political undergrounds utilize youth's need for fidelity as well as the "store of wrath" held by those deprived of something in which to have faith. A crisis of identity (when the individual who finds self-definition difficult is suffering from ambiguity, fragmentation, and contradiction) makes some adolescents susceptible to "totalism" or to totalistic collective identities that promise certainty. In such collectivities the troubled young find not only an identity but an explanation for their difficulties and a promise for the future.

Erikson's theories form the basis for Böllinger's (1981) psychoanalytic study of eight indicted or convicted members of West German terrorist groups. Böllinger found that his subjects had suffered serious traumas during critical stages of development, especially in failures to establish trust, autonomy, and initiative. Individuals who lacked the quality of basic trust failed to integrate excessive aggressive tendencies or maintain successful social relations. Böllinger believes that these disruptions at the stage where autonomy is developed were the fault of a nonsupportive environment. Failure to develop autonomy resulted in destructive tendencies, insecurity, and fear of personality disintegration. In Böllinger's subjects overcontrolling and unaffectionate parents had turned all relations with the child into a struggle for power, leading the child to clash repeatedly with outside authority. Upon reaching the formative identity period, these individuals found an ideology based on conflict between oppressed and oppressor highly attractive. Acquisition of weapons in an underground group made the "child" feel less small, weak, and helpless before the powerful authority. Böllinger found in these revivals of earlier power struggles an individual's need to control, to dominate, or even to inflict pain bound to feelings of childhood impotence, which were compensated for by illusions of grandeur and omnipotence.

According to Erikson, the rage that an individual feels at being helpless is projected onto the controlling figures; it may also engender guilt feelings, which lead to self-punitive actions. Thus, Erikson's theory can help explain the theme of self-sacrifice in terrorist behavior. Similarly, some individuals fail to surmount the crisis of initiative, so that on top of feelings of suspiciousness, self-doubt, powerlessness, and shame come inferiority and incompetence, feelings often resulting from social deficiencies and obstacles beyond the individual's control (such as weak educational background). Thus, for the individuals Böllinger studied, layer on layer of development and experience did not smooth over scars but reopened old wounds. Such individuals reached puberty and the crisis of identity formation already seriously impaired. They found themselves in social and political circumstances that for different reasons were not favorable to the acquisition of a positive identity.

Böllinger argues that joining a terrorist organization was the last of a series of attempts at identity formation. These potential terrorists were searching for meaning, structure, and a stable social role. They hoped to gain purpose and assurance from the terrorist organization. The group became the family that had never provided the warmth, protection, security, and support the individual had needed. The opportunity to join a terrorist organization allowed the individual to submerge himself in a collective identity and, thus, to lay down the burden of personal responsibility. The group met a need to idealize authority figures, to express aggressive tendencies, to feel omnipotent, and to belong. Its ideology of violent resistance to the state and to imperial domination allowed collective identification simultaneously with the victims of oppression and the aggressive authority figure, while neutralizing guilt through intellectual and emotional justifications. The group provided the structure and integration lacked by the isolated individual.

Knutson (1981) also used Erikson's conceptualization, especially his concept of negative identity. Erikson (1968, p. 174) defines negative identity as "an identity perversely based on all those identifications and roles which, at critical stages of development, had been presented to them [patients] as most undesirable or dangerous and yet also as most real." It involves what Erikson frequently terms a "vindictive" rejection of the roles considered desirable and proper by the individual's family and community; it may result from excessive normative ideals demanded by ambitious parents or actualized by superior ones. This interpretation accords with the findings of Schmidtchen (1981) that many terrorists come from families who exert strong pressure for achievement. If a positive identity is not possible, the individual prefers being a "bad" person to being nobody or partially somebody. If early steps toward the acquisition of a negative identity are interpreted and treated by society as final, individuals may be pushed into conformity with the worst that people expect of them (Erikson, 1968, p. 88). Not only may such confused individuals find refuge in radical groups where certainty is assured, but they may be forced into a choice by others' interpretations of their behavior.

Knutson (1981, p. 112) also emphasizes the theme of government actions narrowing choices and pushing an individual into the assumption of a negative identity. Croatian terrorist Zvonko Busic was a member of an oppressed minority in a dominant culture, a situation Erikson (1968, p. 303) considers likely to engender negative identities because minorities may fuse the negative image held of them by the majority with the negative self-image of the group. Knutson found that economic constraints prevented Busic from pursuing his early goal of a university education. This disappointment, which Knutson compares to life disappointments experienced by several other terrorists, blocked the path to a positive identity and led to his assuming negative roles. As a child in Yugoslavia, Busic was socialized into strong beliefs in the cause of Croatian separatism and had a nationalistic cousin who was a role model. Similarly, many German terrorists came from families where the parents were social activists. Knutson's contention is that the negative identity is not totally negative; although deviant in some ways, it is based on values acquired through early socialization. This fact seems to contradict Erikson's original theory of negative identity as the antithesis of what parents and society value.

In cases of nationalist or separatist terrorism, the concept of negative identity acquires a more subtle meaning. To become a violent revolutionary in the cause of Croatian, Basque, or Irish independence is not a totally negative identification. There is much more social approval within the minority community for such actions than there is for violent undergrounds in homogeneous Western societies or liberal states, where nonviolent means for expressing opposition exist. The choice of becoming a terrorist is extreme; but, for example, in the Basque region of Spain, the young man who becomes a member of the ETA receives strong social support from the Basque small-town milieu, although his family does not approve of the decision (mainly because of the dangers involved). After a period of under three years as an *etarra*, a young man usually returns to society (Clark, 1983). The opprobrium attached to violent dissent in Germany, Italy, or the United States is absent; the choice of joining the ETA would not represent an absolutely negative identity. Knutson argues that the negative identity actually reflects values instilled early in life and may reaffirm, albeit in a radical manner, ethnic roots and traditions. One should therefore be cautious about attributing all terrorist activity to the individual's rejection of, or inability to pursue, a positive identity. Furthermore, not all acquisitions of negative identities are politicized; many young people rebel socially—in clothes and manners—without political purpose. Such individuals may have neither the inner needs (which are impossible to ascertain from the outside observer's viewpoint) nor the opportunity to join violent undergrounds.

Both Böllinger and Knutson agree that the government often plays a critical role in pushing certain individuals into violent opposition. Government surveillance or persecution were factors in closing off the path to a positive identity for Busic, who encountered suspicious police in Yugoslavia, Austria, and the United States. In West Germany people who were only on the fringes of radical movements found their way back blocked by government records that marked them as sympathizers. Böllinger found, for example, that many of his interviewees had been harassed or, in one case, jailed for quite minor offenses. In the Basque region of Spain, in the Franco era, even cultural activities had to be clandestine because of government persecution. In the nineteenth century, the Russian government's repression of nonviolent reformist activities was a factor in convincing a minority of activists that terrorism was their only mode of self-expression.

To individuals already suffering from identity confusion, the attention paid them by the government not only confirms a negative identity but makes them feel like "somebody." They are gratified to be sufficiently important to be the object of excessive attention, even if that attention is negative. Harassment or surveillance is preferable to being ignored by society.

Another contribution of Erikson's, apparently unnoticed by students of terrorism, helps to confirm the relevance of his theory to an understanding of terrorism. Discussing the developmental stage of initiation, Erikson observes that, in addition to aggressive "ideals," the child develops a sense of guilt and, thus, a conscience. Individuals whose conscience (or superego) becomes too controlling and overinhibiting may become moralistic. If the parent who early served as a model for the conscience—that is, as the external authority imposing moral rules which are subsequently internalized in an inflexible way—subsequently proves unworthy of such a position, that parent can become the target of violent opposition and resentment. According to Erikson (1968, p. 119), the child becomes suspicious, vindictive, and prone to the suppression of others. Moreover, the assumption of a negative identity is rooted in a latent death wish against the parents and may result from overdemanding parents. Early feelings of moral betrayal by parents may be the basis for later acute sensitivity to perceived injustices by authorities, a trait noted in many terrorists. In West Germany, for example, children discovered that strict and puritannical fathers had been, if not Nazis, accomplices in the evil of the Hitler period. Such disillusionment, rooted in history and politics, can interact with excessive guilt or conscience to produce an individual disposed to violent action against a perfidious substitute for parental authority.

Erikson (1963, p. 189) also emphasizes a Freudian contribution that may explain an individual's choice of terrorism as a form of conflict with authority: "The individual unconsciously arranges for variations of an original theme which he has not learned either to overcome or to live with: he tries to master a situation which in its original form has been too much for him by meeting it repeatedly and of his own accord." The child who feared to mount a violent challenge to parents may later try to overcome that fear by attacking external authorities, such as political or social elites.

An interesting question is the relevance of the theories of Frantz Fanon (see McCulloch, 1983) to this framework. Fanon's conception of violence as a part of the self-liberation of the colonized person can be compared to Erikson's view of violence as reflecting unresolved childhood conflicts, the expression of which is not necessarily therapeutic. Certainly, Fanon's theory of the relationship between colonialism and personality links individual to social setting in a way compatible with Erikson's model. What Fanon saw as the psychopathology of the colonized could be the assumption of a negative identity.

The Social Psychology of the Group

The foregoing discussion indicates that the group is central to terrorist behavior. The individual's path to becoming an active terrorist is often through groups and through personal contacts who introduce him to the organization. Student political groups in the United States, West Germany, and Italy, as well as Basque cultural and political youth groups, often perform this initiatory function. Belonging to the group, as has been suggested, can be critical to the integration of some personalities; the collective identity becomes the individual's identity. Therefore, the maintenance of this primary group or family substitute may become as important as political aims or events. Terrorist organizations are likely to be composed of people whose need is the group and others whose goals are to change their social and political environment. But both types are dependent on the organization.

The social psychological dynamics of terrorist organizations help determine not only why individuals join them but why they stay in and why they choose terrorism as a strategy. Some features are characteristic of all small groups; others are specific to underground conspiracies.

Terrorist organizations become countercultures, with their own values and norms, into which new recruits are indoctrinated (see Wolfgang and Ferracuti, 1982). They are in this respect similar to youth gangs or nonpolitical cults and sects (see Bainbridge and Stark, 1979; Balch, 1980; Levine, 1978; Stark and Bainbridge, 1980). They tend, as Erikson (1968) suspected, to be "totalistic," demanding the complete allegiance of members. Relations with "outsiders" are discouraged if not prohibited. (Security considerations also make this a rational precaution.) Clandestine organizations are isolated from the outside world, an isolation often reinforced by living "underground" with false identities. Even in more open situations, such as in Spain or Ireland, members of the terrorist organization tend to be exclusive and to trust only one another.

A similarity between terrorist organizations and religious cults underscores the group's dominance over individual members and the collective drive toward totalistic control. Both types of groups strictly regulate the sexual relations of their members. In some groups sexual contact with outsiders is banned. In others, such as the Weather Underground, monogamy is discouraged. Some exceedingly puritanical groups, such as the People's Will, encourage celibacy and asexual comradeship. It is impossible to know the meaning of these restrictions, beyond their implication of total control by the group. In puritanical groups the image of rigid morality (it is not clear that obedience to such precepts is absolute) may be a reflection of the overcontrolling superego and a rejection of society as immoral and inadequate. The appearance of morality may also be an attempt to prove that the group's political stand is equally superior, despite its deviation from the social norm. The deliberate promiscuity of the Weathermen seems to have stemmed in part from a male drive to dominate the females in the organization (Stern, 1975). Terrorist groups are similar to other groups whose goal is to transform not only society but the individual (see Wilson, 1973).

All primary groups strive toward cohesion and uniformity (Cartwright, 1968; Verba, 1961), and terrorist organizations exhibit stronger than usual tendencies toward solidarity and conformity. Terrorist organizations are formed of like-minded individuals who build their association on prior homogeneity, at least in political attitude, and on explicit commitment to political goals. The terrorist group is an association whose members share a "common fate," in that their futures and the achievement of group goals—indeed, their lives—are bound together. Members must trust each other not to betray the group or endanger it in any way. Under these conditions of mutual interdependence, members of groups have been shown to develop the high interpersonal attraction that creates cohesiveness (Collins and Guetzkow, 1964, pp. 140-145). The group necessarily stands or falls together. In such circumstances members have more influence over each other; they feel more responsibility toward each other and more agreement with each other's views. Hence, the group's power over its members increases with cohesiveness.

A distinctive characteristic of terrorist groups is that they exist under conditions of extreme danger and corresponding stress. As Janis (1968, p. 80) observes, "When people are exposed to external danger, they show a remarkable increase in group solidarity. That is, they manifest increased motivation to retain affiliation with a face-to-face group and to avoid actions that deviate from its norms." Janis's (1968) studies of soldiers under combat conditions are relevant to this analysis of terrorist behavior. He notes, for example, that social isolation—something that terrorists choose—also increases dependence on the group. External danger stimulates needs for reassurance, which are satisfied through interaction with other members of the group, leading to a strong individual motivation to stay in the group and to avoid the risk of expulsion. The threat of group disapproval suppresses inclinations to deviate from group norms.

A further source of increased cohesion and ideological solidarity is the individual's reaction to the death of comrades. Survivors often try to adjust to death and to counteract group demoralization by unconsciously identifying with dead (or, as is often the case in terrorism, captured) comrades. Via a process of introjection, or internalization of the lost object, this reaction leads to a form of "postponed obedience," or strengthened adherence to the standards represented by the fallen comrade. This "blood price" contributes powerfully to group conformity (Janis, 1968, pp. 84-85).

Members of terrorist organizations are also well aware of the unattractiveness of alternatives to membership in the group. Their former life was sufficiently unsatisfactory that they abandoned it; in any event, for revolutionary terrorists in Western countries, the path back to the outside world is closed. In groups less isolated from society and for whom the option of return is open, one would expect less cohesiveness.

The consequences of strong cohesiveness and pressure to conform in terrorist groups are numerous. Naturally strong affective ties are formed among members, so that the dependence with which most members entered deepens. The rewards that members seek probably become more "interpersonal" than "task-environmental" (Collins and Guetzkow, 1964, pp. 74–80). That is, the approval of other group members becomes more important than the achievement of group goals. Approval is awarded not only for actions that move the group toward its political goals but also for conformity and correct ideological thinking. Under these conditions the goal of the terrorist organization may become self-maintenance more than the transformation of the political system (as happens with other political organizations; see Wilson, 1973). Members are now motivated by the desire to keep the group together. For example, terrorist organizations emerged from student movements in part because some activists were unwilling to see the group dissolved.

Another consequence of group cohesiveness is the tendency to encourage the pursuit of violence. As isolation deepens, most communication comes from within the group, and information about the outside world is filtered through the group. Growing misperceptions reinforce group beliefs and values. It becomes easier to depersonalize victims and to see the enemy as unmitigatingly hostile. The need to deflect internal conflict that might disturb a vital harmony may lead to extreme aggressiveness toward outside enemies. Desperate attempts by terrorists to free imprisoned comrades are clearly related to the mutual interdependence of the group. They may also be related to survivor guilt, as well as to what Janis (1968, pp. 85–86) terms the "old sergeant" syndrome, in that the individual is unable to see new group members as acceptable emotional substitutes for former comrades and leaders.

Because terrorism takes place in a group setting, a phenomenon known as the "risky shift" may occur. Individuals in groups are more likely to take risks than they would when acting alone. The increase in risk-taking propensity may encourage escalation, as terrorists become less inhibited by the prospect of negative consequences. Studies in experimental social psychology (Wallach and Kogan, 1965; Wallach, Kogan, and Bem, 1962, 1964; Wehman, Goldstein, and Williams, 1977) have shown that individuals associated in small, face-to-face groups will accept greater risks—largely as a consequence of group discussion—than they would if unassociated with a group. Although it would be incautious to equate the behavior of experimental subjects faced with loss of small amounts of money with that of committed political radicals confronting death or disgrace, participation in the terrorist group itself may increase the individual's propensity to accept the significant risks that participation in terrorist activity entails.

Membership in a primary group may also help individuals cope with guilt. Research has not established that individual terrorists actually feel guilt over their behavior. The group both creates and imposes its own standards and norms and forms a counterculture in which violence against the enemy is morally acceptable and, indeed, may even be a duty. Degree of guilt probably varies with individual personality and the strength of group influence over members. Nevertheless, peer pressure can induce people to perform acts that they would ordinarily be prevented from doing by moral restraints. If guilt creates more stress for the individual, dependence on the group surely increases—with the result that group influence over the individual is strengthened, leading to the commission of more guilt-inducing acts. It then becomes difficult to leave the terrorist group, because the reformed terrorist would confront not only social opprobrium and legal sanctions but also remorse. Most individuals probably find it easier to continue to believe in the values and standards of the terrorist group. Some, however, do "repent," although their motivations remain obscure to researchers.

Other components of terrorist belief systems, common to most groups, may also provide means of coping with guilt. The often-encountered theme of self-sacrifice, for example, may be a form of atonement. Terrorists engage in what Bandura (1973, pp. 238–239) calls "slighting aggression by advantageous comparison"—that is, emphasizing the gross misdeeds of the government as justification for terrorism against it. Schmidtchen (1981, pp. 54–55) noted in West German terrorist groups a process of socialization resulting in a demarcation between friend and enemy that reserved all positive identifications for friends, all negative identifications for the enemy. The enemy was perceived as an abstraction, a structure rather than a group of individuals. Victims have no personal value to terrorists; they are merely representatives of institutions. In this regard it is useful to compare the process of dehumanization of the enemy in military combat units to that in terrorist organizations.

The image that terrorists often present of themselves—as soldiers acting only in the name of duty and a higher call—may also be a way of avoiding personal responsibility for acts of violence. This identification is a form of self-presentation as well as of self-perception. It is a method of coping with the prospect of physical danger as well as with the emotional consequences of harming others. Being a soldier means being part of a collective enterprise that is externally sanctioned. Ferracuti and Bruno (1983, pp. 308–310) have argued that Italian terrorists, by imagining themselves to be in a state of war with the government, are engaging in an important fantasy mechanism that makes their participation in violence possible.

A further consequence of group interaction, which may explain the escalation of terrorist violence, is the possibility of brutalization, or "graduated desensitization" (Bandura, 1973, p. 241), as the performance of acts of terrorism progressively extinguishes discomfort and self-censure. Dicks (1972, pp. 253–256) saw Nazi violence emerging over time from a triggering process shared by fellow Nazis in a facilitating group setting. This conditioning process, through which the individual comes to seek destructive power, is termed brutalization, a result of succumbing to group pressures and conforming to a new ethos. Even individuals who had at first shown anxiety and reluctance gave in to the group in the end.

In comparison, Liebert (1971) explains the shift in the Columbia University student movement from nonviolent protest to terrorism as a generational phenomenon; the second generation is recruited into a value system and socialized into a group that may be entirely different from the group that influenced the first generation. Value changes profoundly affect socialization: "When 'temporary' deviations from the humanistic tradition (such as terrorism) begin to characterize the tactics used to obtain the ends, these compromised values become internalized in the psychological organization of the members of the movement, particularly the younger ones who enter and are indoctrinated at that phase of the revolution.

The corrupted values then are passed on through the generations" (Liebert, 1971, pp. 244-245). For example, whereas the initial decision to use terrorism is probably a topic of heated discussion in the early stage of the development of the organization, the more violence is used, the less controversial its value and acceptability become. The ends and means of actions are no longer separable; not only are values corrupted but the use of terrorism is tied irrevocably to the values it serves.

Another group characteristic that helps explain the conduct of a terrorist strategy concerns relationships between leaders and followers. Janis (1968, pp. 81-83) refers to the Freudian concept of transference to explain the motivation for group solidarity in military units. The individual's feelings of dependency, an unconscious need from childhood, are redirected to new objects. Janis describes in combat situations a "fear-ridden" dependency, based on the reactivation of early separation anxiety, which is likely to develop toward authority figures perceived as able to ward off danger. Social isolation is further likely to enhance such dependency. Transference also causes the follower to overestimate the power of the surrogate parent and to seek that parent's approval.

Verba (1961, p. 149) notes that while followers depend on their leaders, the reverse also holds: "The conflict between directing the group and maintaining one's acceptance by the group would seem to be the unique problem of the group leader." Leaders must spend as much time maintaining the group as in achieving instrumental goals. This balance is easier to attain when the leader is perceived as acting as an agent of impersonal forces and in the service of group norms (Verba, 1961, pp. 172-175). In terrorist as in revolutionary organizations, the ideological purity of the leader must be above question; the leader must be the chief interpreter and communicator of the group's beliefs and aims. Leaders are, thus, under great pressure to conform to group norms, making innovation or compromise difficult. Since the external power sources of terrorist leaders are surely few, their position depends on their interpretation of group goals and efficient direction of terrorist operations. In effect, the behavior of both leaders and followers is restricted by the terrorist group.

Another way the group facilitates terrorism is by creating an appropriate context for social learning. Bandura (1973) has argued that aggressive patterns of behavior are learned from observation or experience, rather than emerging from instinctual drives or frustration. His theory underscores the argument that participation in violent acts desensitizes the individual to guilt. Not only do individuals learn from their experiences in the organization, but they also are exposed to powerful external role models, whom they are encouraged to imitate. The narrow band of communication from the outside world, filtered through the perceptions of leaders, emphasizes the dramatic exploits of other terrorist groups. Terrorism, a symbolic action, is highly memorable; for this reason, as well as the ease with which it can be implemented, terrorism is almost ideally imitable (Bandura, 1973, p. 213; Midlarsky, Crenshaw, and Fumihiko, 1980). The terrorist subculture forms an environment in which violence is valued, and models such as the Tupamaros of Uruguay may be endowed with great prestige. The power of such models is not diluted by their objective failures. The 1960s revolutionary campaign of the Tupamaros, for example, culminated in a military dictatorship. The mass media, especially television, are often thought to be critical to the communication of information about models, but their actual influence remains undocumented.

If members of terrorist groups receive most of their information from other sources in the group or from an underground press, the popular news media would not be a primary determinant of the social contagion of terrorism.

Bandura (1973, pp. 215-216) has suggested that symbolic modeling may help to explain the surge and decline of terrorist incidents: "Social contagion of new styles and tactics of aggression conforms to a pattern that characterizes the transitory changes of most other types of collective activities: New behavior is initiated by a salient example; it spreads rapidly in a contagious fashion; after it has been widely adopted, it is discarded, often in favor of a new form that follows a similar course." Decline is explained by the development of effective counter-measures, the discrepancy between anticipated and experienced consequences, and routinization of the activity. The decline of an activity, then, may depend on its not being rewarded.

The dynamics of reward and punishment in the case of terrorism are as yet poorly understood. Since the individual motivation for terrorism may be psychological, involving the acquisition of an identity or affiliation with a substitute family, the failure to achieve the organization's instrumental goals may not be a sufficient "aversive stimulation." Individuals who resort to terrorist behavior as part of the assumption of a negative identity expect and even seek social disapproval, which confirms their self-expectations. Some terrorists become disillusioned when anticipated social and political changes do not occur, but others continue despite the absence of positive external reinforcements. Given the small numbers of people required for the implementation of a terrorist strategy and a ready availability of recruits, terrorism can show remarkable persistence. A punitive government response may confirm terrorist expectations of coercive "enemy" behavior, provide a needed reward of attention and publicity, and generate resentment not only among terrorists but among the larger political or ethnic minorities from which they sprang. The government may wish, instead, to avoid creating obstacles to the reintegration of dissidents into society.

Psychological Effects of Terrorism

The political effectiveness of terrorism is importantly determined by the psychological effects of violence on audiences. The physical destructiveness of terrorism is in general minimal, despite the tragedy it may cause for individual victims. There is some feeling that the significance of terrorism has been exaggerated, perhaps as a result of the media's adoption of international terrorism as a news issue. Whether because of the intrinsic drama of terrorist violence or because of press and television hyperbole, hijackings, kidnappings, and other terrorist assaults have created large public concern (see de Boer, 1979).

In part because of public reaction, terrorism has become a salient policy issue for many governments. The general thrust of both public reaction and government response has been to resist giving in to terrorist demands or admitting the justice of their claims. The forceful reactions of the Israeli, West German, Egyptian, and American governments, respectively, in the crises of Entebbe, Mogadishu, Larnaca, and Iran were, in part, determined by the blow that terrorism dealt to domestic authority and international prestige. Terrorism is more a threat to image and reputation than to physical security.

Even Israel, surely the most directly endangered of all states affected by terrorism, is said to overreact (Alon, 1980). Although terrorism is perceived as a major threat by Israeli society, this assessment is based on subjective probabilities rather than a realistic estimate of the number of casualties caused by terrorism. Individuals feel both fearful and angry at the damage done to national prestige. Such perceptions are affected not only by the nature of terrorism but also by media portrayals and government countermeasures, which serve as a constant reminder of the threat. Alon (1980) concludes that the effect of terrorism should be downgraded; terrorism should be treated simply as one among many sources of casualties. Government resources should be allocated accordingly.

Despite the obvious importance of society's reactions to terrorism, there has been little research on general psychological and social effects. Gutmann (1979) argues that psychological studies neglect the audience for terrorism, although terrorists are shrewdly aware of the composition and attitudes of viewing groups. Even though the social arena—especially critical elites—is decisive to the success of terrorism, "liberals" have permitted the development of a terrorist mystique. Gutmann (1979) contends that academic elites are victims of a fatal fascination for terrorism, derived from their bourgeois midlife crises, the comfortable life they despise, and their idealization of the terrorist as a hero. In his opinion, those who study terrorism have made it respectable.

The practice of blaming intellectuals for the social ills they seek to explain, although common, is hardly conducive to the advancement of knowledge. Gutmann also reveals an ignorance of terrorism—placing the Tupamaros in Ecuador instead of Uruguay, for example—but his point that the study of audiences is neglected is obvious. However, neglect of the subject is due as much to the difficulties of studying audience reactions as to lack of recognition of their importance. Responses to terrorism are difficult to conceptualize and to measure.

Freedman (1983, pp. 399-400) has proposed a theoretical framework, a "model of terroristic resonance," to solve what he considers a significant puzzle. The reaction to terrorism depends on the audience's perception of the terrorist as single-minded, willful, fearless, and unremorseful. Terrorism must be seen as violence of human agency. Terrorist acts appear to the audience as anonymous, sudden, and random. The awareness of vulnerability undermines the victim's sense of autonomy and security. In this way terrorism arouses awe, anxiety, and a mystical dread. The id seems to be assaulting the superego, evoking infantile apprehensions.

The metaphor of resonance appropriately describes terrorism's effects, since acts of terrorism constitute a reasonably small stimulus that causes and intensifies an echo or vibration in the social system. This concept implies that the act of terrorism has to be properly attuned to its audience, to strike a chord, if it is to be effective. When the audience is responsive, the act of terrorism resonates or continues to sound beyond its immediate impact. However, a conceptual distinction must be drawn between direct and indirect audiences. The direct audience is composed of persons who identify with the victims of terrorism; they are potential victims because they belong to the same social category as the victims (such as judges, police, diplomats, airline passengers, foreign business executives). The indirect audience, in contrast, is not directly affiliated with the victims. Its members may be neutral or may even identify with the terrorists. The act of terrorism, if it seems a threat at all, is experienced only vicariously. The indirect audience is not a party to the struggle the terrorists have initiated. Most terrorists, of course, try to choose their audiences strategically. They may widen the scope of the conflict by incorporating new direct audiences. For example, Palestinian attacks on non-Israeli targets, such as foreign tourists or pilgrims, converted people who were uninvolved into direct audiences.

For the indirect audience, terrorism is a spectacle more than a personal experience. Terrorism shocks because its milieu and its specific victims are unpredictable. Terrorism attracts attention because it unexpectedly breaks social taboos. For most indirect audiences, terrorism is a geographically distant phenomenon. Information about it is communicated primarily by the news media, especially television. In these cases the manner of presentation of information about terrorism can significantly influence audience reactions. Furthermore, in order to maintain its psychological effectiveness, terrorism must become more dramatic as the distance, both geographical and psychological, between the act and the audience increases. Otherwise, competing with other newsworthy events and with more immediate personal concerns, terrorism may lose the salience upon which its influence over audiences depends. Most terrorists, aware of the risk of audience distraction, direct their actions accordingly and strive for innovativeness and timeliness.

The same factors that make terrorism a source of concern and interest for indirect audiences make it a source of personal anxiety for direct audiences, whose feelings of invulnerability are diminished. The reactions of direct audiences to terrorism can usefully be compared to those of the victims of aerial bombing (see Hutchinson, 1972; Janis, 1951). Extreme anxiety, disorientation, feelings of helplessness and defenselessness, and demoralization can characterize reactions to terrorism, which is the type of indefinite and unidentifiable threat that classical studies indicate as difficult to understand or to act against (see Lowenthal, 1946, pp. 2–5; May, 1940, pp. 191–195; Riezler, 1950, pp. 129, 131; Sullivan, 1941, p. 282).

Since fear of terrorism is the fear of death or mutilation, extremely powerful emotional drives direct the political behavior of potential victims. The fear of terrorism often leads to popular demands for protection and prevention. Democratic procedures can also be undermined. Judicial processes, for example, can be subverted. In April 1977 the assassination of the president of the Turin Bar Association was followed by a request to be excused for medical reasons by thirty-six of the forty-two jurors preliminarily selected for the trial of Renato Curcio and twelve other terrorist leaders of the Red Brigades. This postponement followed an earlier delay resulting from the June 1976 assassination of the attorney general of Genoa (Pisano, 1979, pp. 186–187).

Terrorism and reactions to it can also effect broad and diffuse social changes in the direction of decreased openness and trust. Officials in both czarist Russia and contemporary Italy hesitated to appear in public. Businessmen travel with bodyguards in bullet-proof limousines, altering their route for each journey. Diplomats live unostentatiously. The White House is ringed with concrete barriers. The long-term psychological effects of suspiciousness, isolation, and mistrust are largely unknown; they are surely destructive of political community.

Northern Ireland, an extreme case of the effects of terrorism, has been the subject of several studies (for example, Fields, 1980; Heskin, 1980). Researchers are divided on the question of how serious the psychological effects of terrorism have been in Northern Ireland. (This case is a reminder that it is difficult to isolate the effects of terrorism from those of other conflicts, social prejudice, and government countermeasures.) On the one hand, Fields (1980) and Fraser (1973) argue that terrorism has produced dramatic consequences, especially in the children of Northern Ireland. To Fraser children are being socialized into "a perpetual chaotic state of imminent violence" (p. 8). He notes the very high rate of youth involvement in the violence of Northern Ireland as a sign of how deeply children are affected. Although Fields is primarily concerned with the consequences of British repression more than of IRA or Protestant terrorism, she also foresees grave physical and mental harm and predicts a new generation of "militaristic automatons" who will require significant rehabilitation efforts if Northern Ireland is to survive as a society (p. 55).

Heskin (1980) is less pessimistic. He concludes, as have other observers of people living under conditions of pervasive insecurity, that life goes on as usual. Minor inconveniences no longer seem unusual; dramatic stress is seen in only a few places. He is cautious in interpreting the results of studies of the effects of violence on children; violence does seem to become more acceptable and normal, but this seems to come as much from watching it on television as from actually experiencing it. Violence also seems to have reinforced antisocial behavior, although to what extent is difficult to gauge. The data on the incidence of mental illness, most of which come from Belfast, are mixed and inconclusive. He agrees that increased psychiatric disturbance in the intermediate rather than the serious trouble spots may occur. These problems are more common in women than in men. There is less depression than usual, although attempted suicides (while still infrequent) increase (see Heskin, 1980, pp. 52-73). Heskin also warns, however, that the social and psychological resilience he observed may obscure hidden costs of adaptation to acute stress.

These studies point to a need to distinguish between different levels of terrorism as they affect audiences. In situations where the threat of terrorism is so constant as to be normal, it may be accepted as a fact of life. However, where the threat remains sufficiently random and unusual, its targets cannot adjust to uncertainty. For example, the "Document on Terror" (1952), purportedly a Communist instruction manual for the takeover of Eastern Europe after World War II, recommends that terrorism be applied scientifically in waves, in order to avoid producing the insensitivity that would diminish its effectiveness. The use of an analytical framework that distinguishes among levels of threat as well as among types of audience is essential to understanding the general psychological effects of terrorism.

Hostage Taking

Interest in the psychological and physical effects that terrorism has on its victims has taken its most direct form in the literature on hostage taking and victimization (see Ochberg and Soskis, 1982). The seizure of hostages is a modern form of terrorism; it results from attempts by terrorists to bargain with governments rather than to make a declaration through an act of violence. It has usually involved holding passengers on airlines or trains, diplomats, or school children and demanding some government concession for their release. Government concern over this problem has dominated research, leading to a focus on hostage reactions and terrorist behavior in order to improve negotiating tactics and policies. The issue, which first acquired relevance because of the rash of diplomatic kidnappings and seizures of embassies in the 1970s, became acute with the Iran crisis of 1979–80. The efforts of government and private psychologists and psychiatrists were concentrated on how hostages, held for long periods in captivity, coped with their plight.

The issue has been analyzed most frequently from a criminal justice perspective, not only because it is intrinsically important to policy makers but also because hostage taking as a tactic is not the exclusive domain of political terrorists. Most hostage takers with whom police have to deal are criminals or psychotics. Consequently, psychological advice to practitioners is often based on a uniform model of the hostage taker. For example, one such work (Miron and Goldstein, 1979, p. 11) assumes that "Many acts of terrorism are really acts of expressive suicide. They have as their sole purpose the establishment of the significance and importance of the perpetrator. They are acts designed to establish the perpetrator's importance through media coverage. Often the perpetrators mask these true intentions through the facade of some worthy, or at least respectable, cause."

Although Knutson (1980, pp. 195, 219) agrees that terrorism is more often expressive than instrumental, she criticizes the government approach as "myopic." Governments need a flexible and varied response, not one tailored to a single view of the hostage taker based on criminal and psychotic behavior. Negotiators, Knutson (1980, p. 202) claims, are reluctant to appear sympathetic to terrorists who are politically motivated: "This refusal is based upon the ill-advised wholesale transfer to the terrorist event of a rule which *can* alleviate similar events perpetrated for gain or out of major mental disorder: do nothing to enhance the psychological status of the adversary." Endowing a terrorist with formal adversary status is perceived as a loss of power and esteem. Because terrorism is a threat to the government's legitimacy, policy makers are under intense psychological pressure to act forcefully to end the crisis. Resisting this pressure to act in order to wait for a peaceful resolution of the incident is probably the most difficult problem the policy maker confronts.

In addition to recommendations on how to bargain with terrorists, governments have sought psychological explanations of the behavior of hostages in cases of kidnapping and temporary captivity. Recent research has applied many of the theories of stress, coping, and adaptation that were developed from the experiences of World War II (see Hamburg, 1974). The literature on concentration camp victims and prisoners of war has been found relevant (see, for example, Bettelheim, 1960; Stein and others, 1960). Some research is notable for establishing links between mental and physical effects of exposure to life-threatening circumstances.

In general, the experience of being a hostage is highly stressful, given individual variations in personality, situation, and duration of the incident. Eitinger (1982) has emphasized the deprivation of freedom and of physical movement or activity that might make extreme emotional stress more bearable. The victim suffers a loss of power and autonomy, becoming a symbolic object without personal identity or meaning. The outcome is unpredictable, but death is a realistic possibility. The hostage is forced to relate to the adversary, often in conditions of physical intimacy and extreme dependence, isolated from the support systems of family and society.

Accounts offered by former hostages (Jackson, 1974; Jacobson, 1973; Ochberg, 1982) confirm the threatening and uncomfortable aspects of the hostage situation. Although Roth (1982) finds that the hostage situation is theoretically interesting because it is stressful mainly for psychological reasons, physical deprivations—such as the lack of sanitary facilities, extreme temperatures, or inadequate food—weigh heavily with the hostages themselves. These discomforts may seem minor in comparison to those suffered by concentration camp prisoners or some prisoners of war, but they are, nevertheless, painfully real to those who experience them. Dwelling on physical details may also be a method of coping with the fear of death as much as an objective appraisal of conditions.

The stress of being a hostage has complex and, as yet, incompletely specified emotional and physiological consequences. Physical effects may include changes in the autonomic nervous system and in hormonal balance, which, depending on their severity and duration, may cause illness or even death (Roth, 1982; see also Bourne, 1971). Psychologically, the individual's ability to think and act is modified. Ochberg and Soskis (1982, pp. 113-114) found that, in addition to stress, victims also suffer guilt over not having fought back, over having lived when other hostages were killed, or over having been released early.

Most analysts agree that the effects of having been a hostage can be long-lasting. According to Fields (1981, p. 69), for example, traumatic effects that are both mentally and physically destructive can last as long as fifteen years. (Her study extends to the effects of government treatment on terrorist prisoners.) Most authors advise subsequent therapeutic intervention to minimize the effects of the experience.

Research on coping and adaptation has also been extended to terrorism. Researchers (Roth, 1982; Tinklenberg, 1982) draw a distinction between the largely unconscious psychological defenses that hostages first erect in order to handle the situation and the later coping strategies that they consciously adopt in order to survive. Various well-known defenses—such as denial of reality, task orientation, counterphobias, reaction formation, intellectualization, creative elaboration, and humor—have been observed in the victims of terrorism. Coping with terrorism often requires deliberation and reflection. The victim must relinquish control over his fate; all psychological studies agree that it is best to submit and avoid provocation, within the bounds of retaining one's self-esteem. Maintaining self-control and emotional stability can be aided by various strategies, such as gathering information about the situation, establishing positive contacts with terrorists (in hopes of creating emotional bonds that will inhibit subsequent terrorist violence), establishing relationships with other victims, focusing on survival, and maintaining a will to live (see Tinklenberg, 1982, pp. 68-70). The memoirs of Geoffrey Jackson (1974), kidnapped British ambassador to Uruguay, are cited as a handbook of successful coping (Eitinger, 1982, p. 84).

If hostages are multiple, the individual's ability to cope with being a hostage may depend on the nature of the group. According to Caplan (1981), neurophysiological and other medical evidence indicates that social support reduces the likelihood of illness as a result of stress. As this chapter suggested earlier, with reference to the effects of stress on the cohesiveness and mutual interdependence of terrorist groups: "Individuals under stress usually show a spontaneous increase in their affiliative needs, accompanied by a rise in suggestibility and compliance"

(Caplan, 1981, p. 416). Whereas terrorists possess a preexisting social support system and concrete opportunities for collective action to relieve anxiety, their victims have not usually enjoyed prior association. Targets of opportunity, they are surprised and unprepared, in contrast to their calculating adversaries. Under such circumstances division seems as likely as unity, further hampering the individual's ability to cope successfully (see Jacobson, 1973, for an account of these problems in a hijacked airliner). The emergence of strong and adaptive leaders seems to be critical; for example, see Ochberg's (1982) biographical analysis of the experience of Gerard Vaders, a hostage on a train held in the Netherlands by South Moluccan terrorists in 1975.

Prior experience and training affect the individual's capacity for responding constructively to frightening situations; hence, government and business organizations devote extensive resources to preparing their representatives for hostage situations (Ochberg, 1979; Silverstein, 1979). A common prescription is to pursue adaptive coping mechanisms, such as planning physical activity and establishing positive personal relationships with one's captors.

The potential hostage reaction that seems to have most preoccupied policy makers is the "Stockholm syndrome," a phenomenon initially noted during a bank siege in Stockholm in 1973 (Lang, 1974). Officials, reporters, and the public were astounded and puzzled by the apparent friendliness that developed between bank robbers and hostages and by the corresponding hostility the hostages exhibited toward the police and the government. Swedish psychologists suggested that what had transpired was a neurotic mechanism termed "identification with the aggressor" (Lang, 1974, p. 78). This form of identification is an essentially passive and regressive defense that had been noted among concentration camp inmates and prisoners of war. The concept of identification with the aggressor has been employed in both popular and academic circles. Miller (1980, pp. 37–60), for example, sees the Stockholm syndrome as a version of the process of transference. As a result of physical intimacy and stress, hostage and captor develop emotional bonds that make it difficult for the terrorist to kill the hostage. Miller urges government negotiators to stall for time, in hopes that the terrorists will become reluctant to kill their hostages. At the same time, he reminds negotiators that the development of affective bonds is not automatic. Intimacy may be precluded by terrorists who are particularly abusive or in situations where ethnic, religious, or political differences between terrorists and hostages make identification impossible. Miller also contends that it is more likely for hostages to feel an emotional tie to their captors than vice versa and that terrorists manipulate such dependencies.

The diagnosis of the Stockholm syndrome as a form of identification with the aggressor has been criticized. Eitinger (1982, pp. 78–80) sees it as a misinterpretation; emotional closeness between victim and terrorist is a result not of latent needs but of relief, as the hostage's initial fear of death dissipates. Intimacy grows as terrorist and hostage are forced to solve practical problems together. Nor should observers assume that hostility between hostage and terrorist is natural; "neutral" victims who do not have a side in the political conflict the terrorists represent may become sympathetic if the terrorists are sufficiently persuasive. Brockman (1976), a passenger on the airliner hijacked by Zvonko Busic and his Croatian compatriots, observed with some indignation that the pilot of the aircraft and many passengers applauded the terrorists as heroes. Eitinger (1982) points out, as does Miller (1980), that emotional ties are unlikely to emerge in situations where strong differences between terrorists and hostages are manifest from the start, as in the 1976 Entebbe crisis, when Palestinian terrorists held exclusively Jewish passengers.

Other analysts (Knutson, 1980, p. 204; Strentz, 1982, pp. 149–163) argue that affinity between hostage and terrorist has a realistic basis. Hostages are aware that governments are under pressure to act and that any moment may bring the use of force. They may also know that hostages are most endangered during police or military assaults. Hostages are in a situation of extreme dependency, one in which they are encouraged not only by their situation but by professionals to be friendly to their captors. In order to avoid the cognitive dissonance that must arise from pretending to be sympathetic, hostages must surely come to believe in the positive feelings they express. It is also natural that hostages should blame the government for their misfortunes. Displacement of aggression is a familiar phenomenon. The government is blamed not only because it is responsible for the hostages' plight (having failed to protect them) but also because, being absent, it cannot punish the hostages for their anger. The physical discomfort of the situation is blamed on the government, on whose account is laid the responsibility to provide food, clothing, blankets, and sanitary materials. Grievances of a practical nature, bitterly felt, are attributed to government neglect or incompetence. Since what the hostages can do to influence the government is minimal, they must orient their attempts at persuasion and conciliation toward the authority in place.

Another problem with interpretations of the "Stockholm syndrome" is that they often assume sexual implications. For example, Miller (1980, p. 46) reports that a woman hostage in the original bank robbery initiated sexual relations with her captor. According to the original account of the episode (Lang, 1974, especially pp. 90 and 92), such was not the case. There does not appear to be any factual evidence that women hostages experience stronger emotional dependencies than men.

Conclusion

Although uneven and sparsely developed, psychological studies of political terrorism against the state are important to understanding this extreme form of political behavior. Psychology helps answer questions of why the individual becomes a terrorist, how terrorist groups are formed and act, and why publics and governments react with alarm despite the minor physical menace of terrorism. Psychological findings dispute the assumption that personality abnormalities explain terrorism. Instead, they point to the significance of the small cohesive group in determining behavior. In many cases the purpose of the terrorist organization becomes the maintenance of the group as much as the achievement of its external political goals. Moreover, the psychological effects of terrorism are critical to its political effectiveness. Because terrorism is both frightening and dramatically symbolic, it influences distant as well as immediate audiences.

Existing psychological research on terrorism suffers from a lack of coherence. Some inconsistency is explained by the ambiguity of the central concept of terrorism. Terrorist activity is extraordinarily complex and varied; the very definition is disputed. For example, recommendations on how to handle negotiations with political terrorists who have seized hostages are not likely to be appropriate, and may even be harmful, if based on an analysis of what is actually criminal behavior. The field lacks systematic inquiry that builds on the work of other scholars and integrates psychology with what is known about the historical phenomenon of terrorism. More systematic and comprehensive theories are needed to develop cumulative knowledge and to fit the analysis of terrorism into larger theories of political behavior and social change. Definitive statements about the relationship between terrorism, psychological determinants, and sociopolitical change must be preceded by tentative and middle-range hypotheses closely linked to empirical data. Many puzzles remain to be solved.

These puzzles include questions related to both the causes and the consequences of terrorism. On the one hand, terrorist decision making is imperfectly understood. Studying this problem is difficult: Researchers usually have access to terrorists only after the fact, not while they are engaged in the activity, and there are impediments to conducting interviews, such as government reluctance and terrorist hostility. Research on the perceptions and beliefs of terrorists ultimately depends on government cooperation. Despite these complexities, comparative inquiry should work toward answering questions such as why terrorists exercise restraint. Apparently, some terrorist organizations have not taken advantage of the technological resources available to them, such as the possibility of exploiting nuclear capabilities. On the other hand, psychological factors may be at the root of the escalation of terrorism. Perhaps under pressure from the government, members of terrorist organizations grow desperate and lose control. What kinds of pressures and perceptions increase tendencies toward counterproductive violence? Innovation in terrorist strategies is another area of research to which psychology could contribute. Why, for example, did terrorist organizations shift to bargaining tactics after 1968? The answer to the question of why terrorism ends may also lie in the psychology of the terrorists rather than in the countervailing power of the government. Why some terrorists "repent" while others persist to their deaths is an important question. The role of terrorist leaders in restraint, escalation, and innovation may be critical. What are the bases of authority in violent undergrounds?

Understanding the psychology of the terrorist is also relevant to analysis of the government policy response. Appropriate countermeasures must be tailored to accurate assessment of terrorist behavior. How terrorists perceive the threat of government coercion may determine whether or not policies of deterrence will work. How terrorists interpret success and failure may be critical to policy effectiveness, since what the government regards as a threat of punishment may be considered by the terrorist as a reward. Policies intended to inhibit terrorism may instead lead to its escalation.

Surveys of the attitudinal reactions of different audiences could also help explain the consequences and effectiveness of strategies of violence. Is the seriousness with which governments take terrorism justified by the public insecurity it causes? Additionally, government decision making in terrorist crises is an important but neglected subject. Stress affects policy makers as well as terrorists. Are there similarities in government and terrorist reactions to each other, leading to conflict spiral syndromes? Do policy makers perceive foreign and domestic terrorist crises differently? Are terrorists considered to be unusual adversaries? The literature on crisis management could be useful in examining policies toward terrorism. It seems especially important in dealing with terrorism that political and military leaders learn to expect the unexpected and to cope with adversaries they perceive as irrational. Part of the explanation of why terrorist surprise succeeds lies in the mind-sets of government officials. Reliance on operational routine, inflexible doctrines, and narrow conceptions of the normal in politics may prevent policy makers from successfully anticipating terrorist innovations.

References

Alon, H. *Countering Palestinian Terrorism in Israel: Toward a Policy Analysis of Countermeasures.* Santa Monica, Calif.: Rand, 1980.

Alpert, J. *Growing Up Underground.* New York: Morrow, 1981.

Bainbridge, W. S., and Stark, R. "Cult Formation: Three Compatible Models." *Sociological Analysis,* 1979, *40,* 283-295.

Balch, R. W. "Looking Behind the Scenes in a Religious Cult: Implications for the Study of Conversion." *Sociological Analysis,* 1980, *41,* 137-143.

Bandura, A. "Social Learning Theory of Aggression." In J. F. Knutson (ed.), *The Control of Aggression: Implications from Basic Research.* Hawthorne, N.Y.: Aldine, 1973.

Begin, M. *The Revolt.* (S. Katz, trans.) Los Angeles: Nash, 1977.

Bettelheim, B. *The Informed Heart.* New York: Free Press, 1960.

Böllinger, L. "Die Entwicklung zu terroristischem Handeln als psychosozialer Prozess: Begegnungen mit Beteiligten" [The development of terrorist actions as a psychosocial process: Encounters with participants]. In H. Jäger, G. Schmidtchen, and L. Süllwold, *Analysen zum Terrorismus* [Analysis of terrorism]. Vol. 2: *Lebenslauf-Analysen* [Biographical analysis]. Opladen: Westdeutscher Verlag, 1981.

Bourne, P. G. "Altered Adrenal Function in Two Combat Situations in Viet Nam." In B. E. Eleftheriou and J. P. Scott (eds.), *The Physiology of Aggression and Defeat.* New York: Plenum, 1971.

Brockman, R. "Notes While Being Hijacked." *Atlantic,* Dec. 1976, pp. 68-75.

Caplan, G. "Mastery of Stress: Psychosocial Aspects." *American Journal of Psychiatry,* 1981, *138,* 413-420.

Cartwright, D. "The Nature of Group Cohesiveness." In D. Cartwright and A. Zander (eds.), *Group Dynamics: Research and Theory.* (3rd ed.) New York: Harper & Row, 1968.

Clark, R. P. "Patterns in the Lives of ETA Members." *Terrorism: An International Journal,* 1983, *6,* 423-454.

Collins, B. E., and Guetzkow, H. *A Social Psychology of Group Processes for Decision-Making.* New York: Wiley, 1964.

Cooper, H. H. A. "Women as Terrorists." In F. Adler and R. J. Simon (eds.), *The Criminology of Deviant Women.* Boston: Houghton Mifflin, 1979.

Corrado, R. R. "A Critique of the Mental Disorder Perspective of Political Terrorism." *International Journal of Law and Psychiatry,* 1981, *4,* 293-310.

de Boer, C. "The Polls: Terrorism and Hijacking." *Public Opinion Quarterly,* 1979, *43,* 410-419.

Dicks, H. V. *Licensed Mass Murder: A Socio-Psychological Study of Some S.S. Killers.* New York: Basic Books, 1972.

"Document on Terror." *News from Behind the Iron Curtain,* 1952, *1,* 44-57.

Eitinger, L. "The Effects of Captivity." In F. M. Ochberg and D. A. Soskis (eds.), *Victims of Terrorism.* Boulder, Colo.: Westview Press, 1982.

Erikson, E. H. *Childhood and Society.* (2nd ed.) New York: Norton, 1963.

Erikson, E. H. *Identity: Youth and Crisis.* New York: Norton, 1968.

Ferracuti, F., and Bruno, F. "Psychiatric Aspects of Terrorism in Italy." In I. L. Barak-Glantz and C. R. Huff (eds.), *The Mad, the Bad and the Different: Essays in Honor of Simon Dinitz.* Lexington, Mass.: Heath, 1981.

Ferracuti, F., and Bruno, F. "Italy: A Systems Perspective." In A. P. Goldstein and M. H. Segall (eds.), *Aggression in Global Perspective.* Elmsford, N.Y.: Pergamon Press, 1983.

Feuer, L. *The Conflict of Generations: The Character and Significance of Student Movements.* New York: Basic Books, 1969.

Fields, R. M. *Northern Ireland: Society Under Siege.* New Brunswick, N.J.: Transaction Books, 1980.

Fields, R. M. "Psychological Sequelae of Terrorization." In Y. Alexander and J. M. Gleason (eds.), *Behavioral and Quantitative Perspectives on Terrorism.* Elmsford, N.Y.: Pergamon Press, 1981.

Fraser, M. *Children in Conflict: Growing Up in Northern Ireland.* New York: Basic Books, 1973.

Freedman, L. Z. "Why Does Terrorism Terrorize?" *Terrorism: An International Journal,* 1983, *6,* 389-402.

Greenstein, F. I. "Political Psychology: A Pluralistic Universe." In J. N. Knutson (ed.), *Handbook of Political Psychology.* San Francisco: Jossey-Bass, 1973.

Gutmann, D. "Killers and Consumers: The Terrorist and His Audience." *Social Research,* 1979, *46,* 517-526.

Hamburg, D. A. "Coping Behavior in Life-Threatening Circumstances." *Psychotherapy and Psychosomatics,* 1974, *23,* 13-25.

Hamilton, L. C., and Hamilton, J. D. "Dynamics of Terrorism." *International Studies Quarterly,* 1983, *27,* 39-54.

Heskin, K. *Northern Ireland: A Psychological Analysis.* New York: Columbia University Press, 1980.

Hutchinson, M. C. "The Concept of Revolutionary Terrorism." *Journal of Conflict Resolution,* 1972, *16,* 383-396.

Jackson, G. *Surviving the Long Night: An Autobiographical Account of a Political Kidnapping.* New York: Vanguard Press, 1974.

Jacobson, S. R. "Individual and Group Responses to Confinement in a Skyjacked Plane."*American Journal of Orthopsychiatry,* 1973, *43,* 459-469.

Jäger, H. "Die individuelle Dimension terroristischen Handelns: Annäherungen an Einzelfälle" [The individual dimension of terrorist actions: Approaches to individual cases]. In H. Jäger, G. Schmidtchen, and L. Süllwold, *Analysen zum Terrorismus* [Analysis of terrorism]. Vol. 2: *Lebenslauf-Analysen* [Biographical analysis]. Opladen: Westdeutscher Verlag, 1981.

Jäger, H., Schmidtchen, G., and Süllwold, L. *Analysen zum Terrorismus* [Analysis of terrorism]. Vol. 2: *Lebenslauf-Analysen* [Biographical analysis]. Opladen: Westdeutscher Verlag, 1981.

Janis, I. L. *Air War and Emotional Stress: Psychological Studies of Bombing and Civilian Defense.* New York: McGraw-Hill, 1951.

Janis, I. L. "Group Identification Under Conditions of External Danger." In D.

Cartwright and A. Zander (eds.), *Group Dynamics: Research and Theory*. (3rd ed.) New York: Harper & Row, 1968.

Jenkins, B. G. "The Study of Terrorism: Definitional Problems." In Y. Alexander and J. M. Gleason (eds.), *Behavioral and Quantitative Perspectives on Terrorism*. Elmsford, N.Y.: Pergamon Press, 1981.

Kaplan, A. "The Psychodynamics of Terrorism." In Y. Alexander and J. M. Gleason (eds.), *Behavioral and Quantitative Perspectives on Terrorism*. Elmsford, N.Y.: Pergamon Press, 1981.

Klausner, S. Z. "The Intermingling of Pain and Pleasure: The Stress-Seeking Personality in Its Social Context." In S. Z. Klausner (ed.), *Why Man Takes Chances: Studies in Stress-Seeking*. New York: Doubleday, 1968.

Knight, A. "Female Terrorists in the Russian Socialist Revolutionary Party." *Russian Review*, 1979, *38*, 139–159.

Knutson, J. N. "The Terrorists' Dilemmas: Some Implicit Rules of the Game." *Terrorism: An International Journal*, 1980, *4*, 195–222.

Knutson, J. N. "Social and Psychodynamic Pressures Toward a Negative Identity: The Case of an American Revolutionary Terrorist." In Y. Alexander and J. M. Gleason (eds.), *Behavioral and Quantitative Perspectives on Terrorism*. Elmsford, N.Y.: Pergamon Press, 1981.

Lang, D. "A Reporter at Large: The Bank Drama." *New Yorker*, Nov. 25, 1974, pp. 56–126.

Levine, S. V. "Youth and Religious Cults: A Societal and Clinical Dilemma." *Adolescent Psychiatry*, 1978, *6*, 75–89.

Liebert, R. *Radical and Militant Youth: A Psychoanalytic Inquiry*. New York: Praeger, 1971.

Lowenthal, L. "Crisis of the Individual: Terror's Atomization of Man." *Commentary*, 1946, *1*, 1–8.

McCulloch, J. *Black Soul, White Artifact: Fanon's Clinical Psychology and Social Theory*. Cambridge, England: Cambridge University Press, 1983.

May, R. *The Meaning of Anxiety*. New York: Macmillan, 1940.

Merkl, P. *The Making of a Stormtrooper*. Princeton, N.J.: Princeton University Press, 1980.

Mickolus, E. F. *The Literature of Terrorism: A Selectively Annotated Bibliography*. Westport, Conn.: Greenwood Press, 1980.

Midlarsky, M. I., Crenshaw, M., and Fumihiko, Y. "Why Violence Spreads: The Contagion of International Terrorism." *International Studies Quarterly*, 1980, *24*, 262–298.

Miller, A. H. *Terrorism and Hostage Negotiations*. Boulder, Colo.: Westview Press, 1980.

Miron, M. S., and Goldstein, A. P. *Hostage*. Elmsford, N.Y.: Pergamon Press, 1979.

Morf, G. *Terror in Quebec: Case Studies of the FLQ*. Toronto: Clarke, Irwin, 1970.

Ochberg, F. M. "Preparing for Terrorist Victimization." In Y. Alexander and R. A. Kilmarx (eds.), *Political Terrorism and Business: The Threat and the Response*. New York: Praeger, 1979.

Ochberg, F. M. "A Case Study: Gerard Vaders." In F. M. Ochberg and D. A. Soskis (eds.), *Victims of Terrorism*. Boulder, Colo.: Westview Press, 1982.

Ochberg, F. M., and Soskis, D. A. (eds.). *Victims of Terrorism*. Boulder, Colo.: Westview Press, 1982.

Pisano, V. "A Survey of Terrorism of the Left in Italy: 1970-1978." *Terrorism: An International Journal,* 1979, *2,* 171-212.

Pomper, P. *Sergei Nechaev.* New Brunswick, N.J.: Rutgers University Press, 1979.

Rasch, W. "Psychological Dimensions of Political Terrorism in the Federal Republic of Germany." *International Journal of Law and Psychiatry,* 1979, *2,* 79-85.

Riezler, K. *Man: Mutable and Immutable.* Chicago: Contemporary Books, 1950.

Roth, W. T. "The Meaning of Stress." In F. M. Ochberg and D. A. Soskis (eds.), *Victims of Terrorism.* Boulder, Colo.: Westview Press, 1982.

Rubins, J. L. "Narcissism and the Narcissistic Personality: A Holistic Reappraisal." *American Journal of Psychoanalysis,* 1983, *43,* 3-20.

Sandler, T., Tschirhart, J. T., and Cauley, J. "A Theoretical Analysis of Transnational Terrorism." *American Political Science Review,* 1983, *77,* 36-54.

Savinkov, B. *Memoirs of a Terrorist.* (J. Shaplen, trans.) New York: A. and C. Boni, 1931.

Schmidtchen, G. "Terroristische Karrieren: Soziologische Analyse anhand von Fahndungsunterlagen und Prozessakten" [Terrorist careers: Sociological analysis based on investigation and trial documents]. In H. Jäger, G. Schmidtchen, and L. Süllwold, *Analysen zum Terrorismus* [Analysis of terrorism]. Vol. 2.: *Lebenslauf-Analysen* [Biographical analysis]. Opladen: Westdeutscher Verlag, 1981.

Silverstein, M. E. "Counterterrorist Medical Preparedness: A Necessity for the Corporate Executive." In Y. Alexander and R. A. Kilmarx (eds.), *Political Terrorism and Business: The Threat and the Response.* New York: Praeger, 1979.

Stark, R., and Bainbridge, W. S. "Networks of Faith: Interpersonal Bonds and Recruitment to Cults and Sects." *American Journal of Sociology,* 1980, *85,* 1376-1395.

Stein, M. R., and others (eds.). *Identity and Anxiety.* New York: Free Press, 1960.

Stern, S. *With the Weathermen: The Personal Journal of a Revolutionary Woman.* New York: Doubleday, 1975.

Strentz, T. "The Stockholm Syndrome: Law Enforcement Policy and Hostage Behavior." In F. M. Ochberg and D. A. Soskis (eds.), *Victims of Terrorism.* Boulder, Colo.: Westview Press, 1982.

Sullivan, H. S. "Psychiatric Aspects of Morale." *American Journal of Sociology,* 1941, *47,* 277-301.

Süllwold, L. "Stationen in der Entwicklung von Terroristen: Psychologische Aspekte biographischer Daten" [Stages in the development of terrorists: Psychological aspects of biographical data]. In H. Jäger, G. Schmidtchen, and L. Süllwold, *Analysen zum Terrorismus* [Analysis of terrorism]. Vol. 2.: *Lebenslauf-Analysen* [Biographical analysis]. Opladen: Westdeutscher Verlag, 1981.

Thornton, T. P. "Terror as a Weapon of Political Agitation." In H. Eckstein (ed.), *Internal War: Problems and Approaches.* New York: Free Press, 1964.

Tinklenberg, J. "Coping with Terrorist Victimization." In F. M. Ochberg and D. A. Soskis (eds.), *Victims of Terrorism.* Boulder, Colo.: Westview Press, 1982.

Verba, S. *Small Groups and Political Behavior: A Study of Leadership.* Princeton, N.J.: Princeton University Press, 1961.

Wallach, M. A., and Kogan, N. "The Roles of Information, Discussion, and Consensus in Group Risk Taking." *Journal of Experimental Social Psychology,* 1965, *1,* 1-19.

Wallach, M. A., Kogan, N., and Bem, D. J. "Group Influence on Individual Risk Taking." *Journal of Abnormal and Social Psychology,* 1962, *65,* 75-86.

Wallach, M. A., Kogan, N., and Bem, D. J. "Diffusion of Responsibility and Level of Risk Taking in Groups." *Journal of Abnormal and Social Psychology*, 1964, *68*, 263-274.

Wasmund, K. "Political Socialization in Terrorist Groups—West Germany." Paper presented at Conference of Europeanists, Washington, D.C., May 1982.

Wehman, P., Goldstein, M. A., and Williams, J. R. "Effects of Different Leadership Styles on Individual Risk-Taking in Groups." *Human Relations*, 1977, *30*, 249-259.

Wilson, J. Q. *Political Organizations*. New York: Basic Books, 1973.

Wolfgang, M. E., and Ferracuti, F. *The Subculture of Violence: Towards an Integrated Theory in Criminology*. Beverly Hills, Calif.: Sage, 1982.

Yacef, S. *Souvenirs de la bataille d'Alger* [Memories of the battle of Algiers]. Paris: Julliard, 1962.

FOURTEEN

༄༅༄༅༄༅༄༅༄༅༄༅༄༅༄༅༄༅༄༅

Political Psychology
in Latin America

Maritza Montero

Political psychology is at present not a significant member of the academic and applied social science scene in Latin America. Social psychology has developed fairly well in many countries in the area. But when it comes to political topics, what we find is a rather blank page or in some cases timid approaches that are sprinkled sporadically through journals and reports on social psychological research. There are few samples of sustained work, and such studies as do exist are designed so that they will not clash with the views of the political system that is dominant in the country where the study is being conducted. This dearth of research is not the result of backwardness, ignorance, or lack of interest. Instead, authoritarianism, expressed through dictatorships, can be considered the main obstruction to the development of psychopolitical explanations of behavior. In other words, in Latin America democracy and the political analysis of society are linked.

Looking at Latin American history, one finds a sequence of military coups and de facto governments implemented by force and through force, erupting now and then, from the Caribbean basin to the Patagonia. Some of them (for instance, the Trujillo government in the Dominican Republic and the Gómez government in Venezuela) have ended only with the dictator's death; others (such as the Rosas government in Argentina) have lasted as long as twenty years. Currently, several Latin American countries have totalitarian governments with different political tendencies and different levels of repression but sharing the fact that such political objects of study as voting, electoral attitudes, and perceptions of political parties and candidates are nonexistent in them. Other areas of study, such as political socialization (that is, the acquisition of political ideologies, values, beliefs, attitudes, and stereotypes) cannot be examined unless the researcher is prepared to take great personal risks and to be subjected to persecution and violence.

414

In addition to the problems involved in undertaking political psychology research in a totalitarian political system, there are the general problems of social science research in Latin America. Not all Latin American countries have the ways and means to publish research reports—or even an academic or policy community with a scientific point of view. And if these exist, the publications and information reach only the local scientific community, having little or no international diffusion. Journals do not always go beyond a country's boundaries. Nor are all libraries equally equipped, since periodical publications sections were just recently created in many places and give precedence to scientific journals from Europe and the United States, something that also happens to books. Moreover, many Latin American psychological journals were started at the beginning of the 1960s and initially were devoted mainly to clinical issues. For these reasons it is difficult to know where studies are being done or who are the appropriate persons to contact to learn what is going on in political psychology in a particular country. Tables 1 and 2 show the sources of information on political psychology that I was able to find.

Given that Latin America is a dependent region struggling to develop economically, certain fields of psychology (such as child development, industrial psychology, assessment, and clinical problems) have priority and receive preference when it comes to research and teaching. Therefore, researchers generally will choose to study, for example, learning abilities or teaching styles rather than political issues. Of course, one can reason that political issues influence educational or mental health policies and cannot be separated from the general understanding of a given society, but the needs stemming from a specific urgent reality cannot be overlooked.

Consequently, political psychology can be considered only a budding new field of study. What is found at the moment reflects the current state of the political climate in any country. Usually, during a period of democratic rule, there are attempts to explain political behavior and political phenomena from a psychological point of view. That is, there is the need to understand and to explain the people and their government as well as the relationship between them; the need to learn about certain attitudes and ideologies; the need to study the style of political life found in a particular country. Under authoritarian rule these efforts disappear. They are suppressed by government action or by enforced individual censorship. For these reasons most of the research reviewed for this chapter comes from Mexico, Colombia, Venezuela, Brazil, and Argentina. The first three countries currently have democratic governments elected by the people. Argentina had a democratic government until 1972; as soon as the "dirty war" began, however, I was unable to find any more articles about political psychology in the journals from Argentina that are known across Latin America. Nor were any books on the subject published. The studies on political psychology coming from Brazil are primarily dated between 1980 and 1982, coinciding with the beginning of a change in the military regime, oriented toward more democratization.

I could find studies on political psychology being conducted in only nine other countries: Chile, Cuba, the Dominican Republic, Guatemala, Nicaragua, Panama, Peru, Puerto Rico, and El Salvador. In some cases there is only one reference, usually a cross-cultural study directed or coordinated by an external researcher.

An examination of the materials that I was able to find on political psy-

Table 1. Journals Consulted and Number of Articles in Them.

Journals	Country of Origin	Number of Articles Found
Acta psiquiátrica y psicológica de América Latina	Argentina	2
Applied Cross-Cultural Psychology	Netherlands	1
Arquivos brasileiros de psicologia	Brazil	2
Arquivos brasileiros de psicologia aplicada	Brazil	
Boletim técnico—SENAC	Brazil	1
Boletín bibliográfico de FACES	Venezuela	1
Boletín de la Asociación Nicaraguense de Psicólogos	Nicaragua	1
Boletín de AVEPSO	Venezuela	3
Boletín de Psicología	Cuba	1
Cadernos de pesquisa	Brazil	3
Ciencia e cultura	Brazil	1
Cuadernos de psicología	Colombia	1
Cuadernos de psicología	Venezuela	1
Cuadernos de sociología	Colombia	1
Dialéctica	Mexico	1
Enseñanza y investigación en psicología	Mexico	1
Estudios centroamericanos	El Salvador	2
Interamerican Journal of Psychology	USA	1
International Social Science Journal	UNESCO	1
Journal of Social Psychology	England	1
PSICO	Brazil	
Psicodeia	Spain	1
Psicología	Venezuela	8
Revista argentina de psicología	Argentina	3
Revista chilena de psicología	Chile	1
Revista de ciencias sociales	Puerto Rico	1
Revista latinoamericana de psicología	Colombia	4
Revista latinoamericana de psicología social	Mexico	
Revista de psicoanálisis, psiquiatría y psicología	Mexico	
Revista de psicología	Colombia	1
Revista de psicología	Peru	
Revista de psicología fundapsive	Venezuela	1
Revista de psicología de la Universidad de La Plata	Argentina	
Revista de psicología general y aplicada	Spain	1
Revista de psicologia geral e aplicada	Brazil	1
Revista de psicologia normal e patológica	Brazil	
Revista dos pós-graduados em psicologia social	Brazil	
Revista peruana de análisis de la conducta	Peru	1
SIC	Venezuela	1
Spanish Language Psychology	Netherlands	
Sumarios de periódicos em psicologia	Brazil	
Total Number of Political Psychology Articles Found		50

chology indicates four trends in the political psychological research being done in Latin America. Studies are being conducted on nationalism, political socialization, and political participation. Discussion concerning the political role of psychology represents the fourth trend. Table 3 indicates the studies that were examined by topic and country. The rest of this chapter will illustrate the kinds of research and debate that are occurring in each of these areas.

Table 2. Other Sources of Political Psychology Works in Latin America.

	Countries					
Sources	Brazil	Colombia	Mexico	Peru	Venezuela	Total
Books	1				2	3
B.A. Theses		1		2	4	7
Papers in Congresses (national and international)		1	2		15	18
Anthologies		1	2		5	8
Other[a]					3	3
Total	1	3	4	2	29	39

[a]Unpublished papers for internal circulation.

Table 3. Research in Political Psychology by Country and Topic (1956–1983).

Country	Reference	Topic
Argentina	Aguad, 1983	Political role of psychology
	Baron de Neiburg and others, 1983	Political role of psychology
	Brignardello, 1978	Political participation
	Isaacson, 1977	Political role of psychology
	Kogan, 1976	Political role of psychology
	Margulis, 1971	Political role of psychology
	Tobar, 1972	Political role of psychology
Brazil	Araujo, 1982	Nationalism
	Campos, 1968	Political role of psychology
	Ginsberg, 1982	Nationalism
	Pereira, 1982	Nationalism
	Szmrecsanyi, 1982	Political role of psychology
Chile	Barudy, 1979, 1980	Political role of psychology
	Barudy and others, 1977, 1980a, 1980b, 1980c	Political role of psychology
	Corral, 1980	Political role of psychology
	Gissi, 1982	Nationalism
	Hernandez, W., n.d.	Political socialization
	Lira and Kovalskis, 1983	Political role of psychology
	Paez, 1980a, 1980b	Political role of psychology
	Paez and others, 1980	Political role of psychology
	Peralta, 1979	Political role of psychology
	Vasquez, A., 1976	Political role of psychology
	Verro, 1981	Nationalism
Colombia	Acevedo and others, 1975	Political participation
	Alvarez Cuadros, 1973–1975	Political participation
	Castillo and others, 1980	Nationalism
	López del Rey, 1983	Political socialization

Table 3. (continued)

	Reyes and others, 1974	Nationalism
	Rojas and others, 1980	Political participation
	Romero, 1978	Political role of psychology
	Urdaneta, 1979	Political role of psychology
Cuba	Asis Córdova, 1979	Political role of psychology
	Sorin, 1981	Political role of psychology
El Salvador	Hernandez, R., 1983	Political role of psychology
	Martín-Baro, 1980	Political role of psychology
	Martín-Baro, 1981	Political participation
Guatemala	Flores Osorio, 1983	Political role of psychology
Mexico	Bleichmar, 1979	Political role of psychology
	Dávila and others, 1956	Nationalism
	Fortes, 1975, 1978	Political socialization
	Ribes Iñesta, 1976	Political role of psychology
	Talento and Ribes Iñesta, 1979	Political role of psychology
Nicaragua	Pineda and Whitford, 1983	Political role of psychology
Panama	Escovar, 1977, 1980	Political role of psychology
Peru	Franco, 1980	Political participation
	Pinzas, 1980	Political socialization
Peru *(cont'd.)*	Roncagliolo, 1969	Political socialization
	Tueros, 1977	Political socialization
Puerto Rico	Vasquez, O., 1973	Political socialization
Venezuela	Amarista and others, 1976	Political participation
	Betancourt, 1980	Political participation
	Brice, 1973	Political role of psychology
	De Castro Aguirre, 1968	Nationalism
	Montero, 1975	Political socialization
	Montero, 1976	Political participation
	Montero, 1980, 1983, 1984	Nationalism
	Montero and others, 1972	Political participation
	Olivo de Celli, 1980	Political participation
	Pulido de Briceño and Piñango, 1979	Political role of psychology
	Queiros de Ramos, 1979	Nationalism
	Quintero, 1979	Political role of psychology
	Rincon, 1979	Political participation
	Rodríquez, 1979	Political participation
	Salazar, 1960, 1970a, 1970b, 1974, 1975, 1976, 1977, 1978, 1979, 1980, 1981, 1982, 1983a, 1983b, in press	Nationalism
	Salazar, 1961, 1964	Political socialization
	Salazar and Marin, 1975a, 1975b, 1977	Nationalism
	Salazar and others, 1982, 1983	Nationalism
	Santoro, 1975	Nationalism
	Serbin, 1980	Nationalism
	Valladares, 1980	Political socialization
	Welsch and others, 1984	Political participation

Nationalism

Nationalism is an area of long-standing interest in Latin America. Ever since Latin American countries achieved their independence from Spain, scientists, intellectuals, and politicians have been posing a recurrent question: Who are the Latin American people? And their writings contain descriptions of traits to identify Latin Americans as a group, each country's major beliefs, and the supraidentity that is shared by all countries in the region as a result of their colonial experience.

Sociopolitical literature, from the Rio Grande downward, is abundant with interest in nationalism. The desire for independent identity is most dramatically expressed in the crisis generated at the beginning of the nineteenth century all through Spanish Latin America that culminated in the independence of almost all the territory. (Cuba remained a colony until 1899.) Thus, the concept of Americanism (Latin Americanism today)—meaning a kind of individualism and differentiation from Europe—is expressed in the works of the liberators (Simón Bolívar, for example) and of the intellectuals of the postindependence period. Bolívar's writings present a vision of Latin America united by common characteristics from Mexico to Argentina. He believed that these shared traits surpassed the differences among countries, making possible a sort of pan-American confederation "consolidating the New World into a single nation" (Bolívar, [1815] 1951, p. 172) and yet permitting local governments or the recognition of diversity inside the unity.

The same feeling and idea is found in Uruguay's José Artigas and José Enrique Rodó, in Cuba's José Martí, in Argentina's José Ingenieros, in Venezuela's Cesar Zumeta and Rufino Blanco Fombona, in Mexico's José Vasconcelos, in Guatemala's Juan José Arévalo, in Brazil's Manuel de Oliveira Lima, in Nicaragua's Rubén Darío, and in Colombia's José Vargas Vila. All proposed the presence of a continental identity. These proposals were made between the second half of the past century and the first quarter of the present one. More recently José Miguel Salazar (1983b), a Venezuelan social psychologist, has raised the point again and has presented empirical data sustaining it.

Salazar (1983b, p. 306) concludes that Latin Americanism "encompasses strongly felt 'myths of descent' and cultural and linguistic homogeneity." His conclusions are supported by his finding that, in five of a group of six Latin American countries (Brazil, Colombia, the Dominican Republic, Mexico, Peru, and Venezuela) participating in a cross-cultural study, there was "a more positive attitude toward Latin America as a whole than toward restricted [national] groups" (Salazar, 1983b, p. 303). (The exception was Brazil, where no difference was found.) A factor analysis of the data produced three main factors: a social-affective factor (being "happy" or "hospitable"), an instrumental factor (being "lazy" or "hard-working"), and a cultural factor (being "cultured"). Some 89 percent of the traits in the cultural factor, 78 percent in the instrumental, and 97 percent in the social-affective were more favorable to Latin Americans in general than to more restricted national groups.

The concept of "myths of descent," taken from Smith (1982; quoted by Salazar, 1983a), refers to origins (when and from where did nationals come), descent (who bore them and how did they develop and descend from common ancestors), the heroic age (the saga about liberation with all its great deeds and glories), and decline and rebirth (how descendants declined and suffered many afflictions, leading to today's subjugation, corruption, and decay, from which, nevertheless, they can be reborn). We find in Latin America a common origin from two main ethnic groups—the Spaniards and the Indians. A third group, the black Africans, whose presence was felt in the Caribbean basin and in Brazil, were brought to Latin America as slaves in the eighteenth century.

We also find a common history, with unions between conquerors and aborigines and later with the blacks. This history has made Latin Americans conscious of their mixed blood. The positivist philosophers and scientists of the late nineteenth and early twentieth centuries blamed all Latin American faults on this mixed blood—that is, they adopted the racist explanation then dominant in Europe. Black and Indian blood, they claimed, produced a disaggregation and degeneration of white blood and was responsible for a collection of traits (for example, laziness, violence, anarchism, passivity, fatalism) that have led Latin Americans to lag behind in development. Other writers have proposed that mixed racial origin is, on the contrary, responsible for a more robust condition, for more creativity, and for the absence of racist attitudes.

Latin Americans also share similar independence traditions. Between 1808 and 1899, wars of liberation took place from Mexico to Argentina. The past glories are a recurrent theme in all these countries. The greatness that was achieved during the nineteenth century is difficult to equal, this theme suggests. Men like the founding fathers have not been born since. People of today need to look back and gain inspiration from the great deeds accomplished during the past century. People must look backward in order to overcome the wrongs done by the corrupt governments that succeeded the founding regimes. This theme recurs in the works of intellectuals and in the addresses of politicians. In fact, throughout Latin America there is evident a continuous and strong urge to study all sorts of expressions of nationalism—not only to define and describe the continental nationalism but also to define, explain, and examine local nationalisms.

The first study on nationalism, by Dávila and associates, appeared in 1956. This research dealt with the image of North Americans held by the Mexican child. Although the study's main purpose was to determine the perceptions of neighboring nationals, it also provides information on Mexican traits, especially about a phenomenon found in other Latin American countries—an overevaluation of the North American.

In 1968 we find a work by De Castro Aguirre from Venezuela, exploring the nationality stereotypes in Latin Americans. The group whose stereotypes were measured considered that Germans, Russians, North Americans, and Jews were alike and could be characterized as scientific, ambitious, materialistic, tenacious, and hard-working. Chinese, Africans, and Russians were viewed as sly, distrustful, and superstitious. Spaniards, Italians, Latin Americans, and Portuguese were considered to be talkative, religious, and artistic. The English and North Americans were perceived as methodical, practical, and ambitious, while the French and Italians were seen as frivolous, courteous, artistic, and sensuous.

The fact that Latin Americans were clustered with their colonizers (the Spaniards and Portuguese) seems to lend support to the "myths of descent" ideas—specifically, those related to origins. The data also support the decline aspect of the "myths of descent." That is, the Latin Americans exhibited an inferiority complex in the sense that they did not attribute any positive traits to themselves. De Castro Aguirre explains this finding by noting that the stereotypes his subjects held about themselves were not clearly defined.

The study of nationalism was given impetus by the work of Salazar, who began examining the political attitudes of university students during the late 1950s and early 1960s (see Salazar, 1960, 1961, 1964). According to Salazar, nationalism is composed of both positive and negative affect—positive affect toward one's own nation (a positive attitude toward nationals, toward the state, toward the national geographical milieu, and toward the symbols of nationhood); negative affect toward other nations (ethnocentrism, group self-perception, identification and assumption of the national group as reference group). In one study Salazar (1970a) had subjects choose from a list of thirty-seven adjectives those identifying three groups—Venezuelans, Italians, and North Americans. Salazar's findings show that the Venezuelan students considered themselves lazy, passionate, generous, temperamental, and impulsive. Italians were seen as hard-working, musical, passionate, thrifty, and temperamental. North Americans were considered practical, scientific, intelligent, materialistic, and ambitious.

Salazar's Venezuelan subjects, then, regarded North Americans in much the same way that De Castro Aguirre's Latin American group did. But Salazar's main conclusion is that his subjects shared a negative perception of themselves as Venezuelans. This conclusion comes as somewhat of a surprise, since the general psychological literature shows that self-stereotypes are more positive than heterostereotypes. Salazar argues, however, that what his subjects manifested was an underevaluation of themselves in relation to other national groups.

Queiros de Ramos (1979) and Salazar (1983a) have explored the relationship between dependency and underevaluation. In the Queiros de Ramos research, a group of Venezuelan students evaluated their own country and compared it with England, Colombia, the United States, and Argentina, using a semantic differential. The Venezuelan students underevaluated their nation in relation to the developed countries.

Salazar (1983a) has observed a linkage between dependence, ideology, and underevaluation. Latin American countries can be classified as dependent nations. Dependent countries are controlled by nations that are power centers. Salazar has noted that many Latin American countries, like many other Third World countries, have their socioeconomic and cultural development conditioned by these power centers. But dependency is not only an externally imposed phenomenon. In dependent countries internal processes exist that reinforce and reproduce the policies of the centers of power. The people in the dependent nation learn to compare themselves with those in the centers of power and, in turn, to devalue themselves.

People in countries such as Venezuela, who engage in self-deprecation, tend to exhibit a United States–dependent ideology—the United States being the country with the highest evaluation (see Salazar, 1983a). These people perceive progress, culture, and observation of law as desirable characteristics for countries, while freedom, natural beauty, democracy, and richness are given less importance. Subjects exhibiting this ideology emphasize the importance of being hard-working, responsible, and thrifty; they deemphasize being hospitable, intelligent, dishonest, or exploitive. The Venezuelans with this ideology tend to view themselves as lazy, spendthrift, and irresponsible.

Montero (1980, 1984), working from a psychohistorical point of view, has corroborated Salazar's and Queiros de Ramos's findings. A content analysis of Venezuelan sociopolitical works published from 1890 to 1982 shows how undere-valuation has developed in Venezuela. The negative national image appears to become more or less marked and negative as the type of government in power becomes more or less authoritarian. When authoritarianism prevails, the people begin to manifest characteristics such as externality, learned helplessness, and blocking of self-efficacy, as well as a sense of dependency on countries such as the United States. To a certain extent, the phenomenon is self-fulfilling; individuals and groups contribute to it, reproducing and echoing it, blaming themselves, denying their possibilities, and devaluing their identity.

Castillo, Correa, and Salas (1980) and Reyes, Barroso, and Pérez (1974) have demonstrated experimentally how easily this self-deprecation can be manipulated. Their research was done in Colombia. Children from three socioeconomic levels were given Likert-type attitude scales to measure their attitudes toward political, economic, and cultural autonomy and toward patriotic objects. The researchers then used two animated stories. The story presented to the experimental group emphasized the superiority of the United States and its nationals; the story for the control group described the life of a composer. The children in the experimental group showed an increase in their underevaluation of their country; the children in the control condition did not.

Montero (1984) has proposed that the underevaluation in which many Latin Americans engage results in a negative national identity. The reference point for the social self is located outside one's own country in those nations and peoples evaluated positively. Instead of ethnocentrism, there is an "altercentrism" among the Latin American people.

Political Socialization

A second line of research in political psychology in Latin America focuses on how political attitudes are formed—that is, on political socialization. Six studies were found that examined political socialization directly (Fortes, 1975, 1978; López del Rey, 1983; Montero, 1975; Roncagliolo, 1969; Tueros, 1977; Vasquez, 1973). This research is exploratory and descriptive, probing the major variables that influence the process of political socialization. The studies focus on adolescents and young adults in Colombia, Mexico, Peru, Puerto Rico, and Venezuela.

This research shows that for most young people the family is the principal influence in the socialization process; in late adolescence, however, young people also are influenced by peer groups—sometimes more so than by the family. López del Rey (1983) found an interaction among school, peer groups, and family in the socialization process. Students from the working class who were placed in heter-ogeneous school groups were resocialized in the direction of the upper-class polit-ical norms as a result of their school experience. These students were more politically active, more tolerant of minority groups, less protectionistic, and less supportive of the present political system than students in schools composed of homogeneous groups. Students from the working class in schools with homogeneous groupings had the political norms of their families reinforced, as well as the differences they perceived between social classes. This same set of findings applied to students from the middle class. Homogeneous and heterogeneous grouping had little effect on upper-class students.

Exploring the effect of information on the political socialization process in a sample of young people in Caracas, Venezuela, Montero (1975) found that socioeconomic class was associated with interest in political information. Interest was higher in the upper and middle classes than in the lower class. Seeking political information was not related to political participation for any of the classes. Montero found a difference between men and women in the amount of information they sought and where they learned political information. Women tended to get their information from their families and to accept the family political traditions. Women were generally more passive politically than men, participated in fewer political discussions at work, and showed less interest in politics. Montero's research, however, suggests that—as radio, television, press, films, and posters become more widely available—the mass media are beginning to challenge the family as a vehicle for political socialization. A similar tendency was found in the Colombian and Peruvian samples (López del Rey, 1983; Roncagliolo, 1969; Tueros, 1977).

Fortes (1978) and Vasquez (1973) found a relationship between activity and involvement in university functions and social/political activity. The more active the individual was generally in university functions, the more active he became in the social and/or political arenas. Students who were assertive and explored their environments were likely to become involved in social and political causes. The more passive students were found to value external environmental stimuli as prods to action and showed a strong belief in external control of their behavior.

In Cuba Sorin (1981) has attempted to determine how notions of socialism, capitalism, humanism, patriotism, and internationalism can be developed in school children of seven and eight years of age. How can schools be used more effectively as agents for political socialization? The goal of the research was to design a set of training materials around these concepts. Sorin developed a series of workshops illustrated with slides, poems, and songs for the children to experience. In addition to the workshops, the children engaged in activities of the following kinds: wrote letters and sent keepsakes to the children of a Latin American "combatant" woman, met and interviewed a Latin American combatant, wrote letters to children in a Soviet school, attended plays, and met an "international worker." Pre- and postintervention measures and an experimental design were used.

The results showed some change in the breadth of the children's ideas about these concepts. For example, the children at first perceived nationalism through the symbols for the country—the flag and the national anthem. After going through the program, they began to link the concept of Cuban nationalism to humanitarianism: Cuba "is a place where men and women get prepared to help other countries such as Angola; one should not only love his or her country but all countries in the world" (Sorin, 1981, p. 95). The activities that provided the children with opportunities to interact with different kinds of people had the greatest effect on their assimilation of attitudes.

Sorin proposes that development of social attitudes has to begin with consideration of a child's needs. Needs must be satisfied in such a way as to link them to social values. Experience in social situations and with different kinds of people helps to forge this link. Openness and self-confidence on the part of the children also facilitate this process.

Political Participation

A third line of research in political psychology in Latin America focuses on what motivates people to participate in the political arena. Why do people vote? Venezuela, with its almost three decades of democracy, has provided a laboratory for examining this question. Montero, Roncayolo, and Rengel (1972) surveyed the electoral attitudes among the population of Caracas during the 1968 Venezuelan presidential campaign. Although some of the left-wing parties were urging people to abstain from voting in the election, there was a strong interest in voting among the general public. According to Montero and her associates, this decision was motivated less by ideology than by the desire to react against the government in office at the moment (a "punishment vote"). In this election there was a strong tendency to vote for candidates on the basis of their personalities, independently of their political qualifications. Those voting appeared to be influenced by the slogans of the candidates diffused through the mass media—slogans stressing personal virtues and traits.

Another study of Caracas voters during the 1973 election—a sample of first-time voters—showed that, in spite of a profusion of presidential candidates (some thirteen), the voters had clear images about only three of the candidates (Montero, 1976). The other candidates in the campaign lacked any kind of image. The best-defined image was that of the social democratic candidate, who won the election, but the most positive image was that of the leftist candidate. This finding suggests that the positive image did not provide the motivation to vote. In general, men had more negative images of the candidates than women did.

Rincon's (1979) study of the 1978 election campaign suggests the influence on the Venezuelan candidates of campaign techniques and expertise from the United States. During the course of the campaign, the candidates imported procedures and technicians from the United States, with an increase in the shaping of materials for different audiences and an increase in the political use of the mass media.

Several researchers have examined the relationship between attitudes and participation. Rodríguez (1979) was interested in the factors influencing the political participation of working women. Those who were more active politically (voting, attending political party and trade union meetings) believed that they had some control over events, were from smaller families, were more "curious" about things in their environment, had taken assertiveness courses, considered culture an important value, had better-educated parents, and had been raised to have a nontraditional view of feminine roles. These politically active women considered among their major goals (in order of importance, with most important first) (1) economic welfare, (2) family stability, (3) an internationally respected country, and (4) equal rights.

Franco (1980) has studied the relationship between image of society, personality, and style of participation in political organizations. Peruvian university students were given the *F* scale, Rokeach's Dogmatism scale, the Mach IV scale, Rosenberg's Interpersonal Confidence scale, and the Fatalism scale and also were asked questions about their image of society. Those individuals who expressed a preference for a society with extensive opportunities for participation were less authoritarian, less dogmatic, less Machiavellian, less distrustful, and less fatalistic than those favoring societies where political power is either delegated or highly controlled.

Political Role of Psychology

The kind of role that psychology can play in the political development of Latin America is a fourth area of discussion and debate among Latin American political psychologists. Can psychology be used as a tool to change the Latin Americans' undervalued image of themselves? Can psychology be used to accelerate the growing consciousness about Latin America's place in the world, about its history, about its struggle to develop, and about its achievements?

Ribes Iñesta (1976) believes that psychology should have a role to play in social change in Latin America. Psychologists need to develop a technology based on the learning paradigm that can be directed toward deprived groups in society. By enabling these people to learn to help themselves, psychology becomes deprofessionalized but diffuse throughout the developing countries. Ribes Iñesta argues that only in this way can psychology have some influence on social transformations and break the existing social divisions of labor.

Escovar (1977, 1980) has described a psychosocial model for development in Latin American countries. According to Escovar, the role of psychologists is to set goals according to a scientific model of man and to define development, taking into account psychological variables. Psychology should be understood as the process through which man acquires greater control over his environment. Beginning with this definition and taking elements from theories and paradigms dealing with the behavioral correlates of alienation, Escovar has developed a model of socioeconomic development that includes the following factors: structural factors (for example, subordinated place in social structure, lack of control over one's physical and sociocultural milieu), dimensions of alienation (for example, external locus of control, learned helplessness, normative alienation, and lack of predictive control), and attitudinal/behavioral consequences (for example, lack of initiative, lack of political interest, negative attitudes). The causal sequence runs from structure to alienation to consequences, with a feedback effect from consequences to structure giving the whole phenomenon a cyclical nature. Social change can occur in both the structural factors and the dimensions of alienation. Escovar urges psychologists to intervene in the alienation part of the process by building a program for social change that takes into account the attitudinal and behavioral consequences of alienation.

Taking an orthodox Marxist view as a point of departure, Pineda and Whitford (1983) discuss the role of psychology in a revolutionary country such as Nicaragua. Means of production and class position produce a kind of ideology that is reflected in psychology as practiced. They argue that any form of psychology is political, since it responds to a certain ideology and certain interests: those of capitalism or those of the revolution.

Some researchers in Latin America (for example, Asis Córdova, 1979; Margulis, 1971; Pulido de Briceño and Piñango, 1979; Quintero, 1979; Romero, 1978; Vasquez, 1976) have begun to question the relevance of classic psychological and political theories for explaining what is happening in Latin America. A growing realization about Latin America's place in the world, about its history, and about the struggle to develop the region has led to a growing sense of uniqueness and the need to find theories and concepts that permit application and intervention leading to social change. What is resulting is an eclectic point of view that assumes some Marxian and post-Marxian ideas, uses some psychological notions and methods, and considers society as its laboratory.

An example of such thinking is found in Isaacson's (1977) proposal for the quantification of alienation. He differentiates between estrangement (what the society takes from the individual) and alienation (what the individual perceives he loses to society). Estrangement is seen as objective, alienation as subjective. Alienation is viewed as being a function of estrangement. As Isaacson envisions it, people are somewhat estranged in every Latin American society, since estrangement depends not only on one's means of production but on the whole complex situation in which one lives and develops. The degree of estrangement that results from the relation between the individual and society, in turn, affects degree of alienation. By focusing on estrangement, we can begin to work on alienation.

Finally, some Latin American psychologists, working in exile (for example, Barudy, 1979, 1980; Barudy and others, 1977, 1980a, 1980b, 1980c), have strongly denounced the role of certain psychologists who serve dictatorships. At the same time, these writers urge psychologists in Latin America to study and treat the effects of torture, exile, and political persecution. Argentina, Brazil, Chile, and Uruguay are the focus of these discussions.

Conclusion

Looking back at this review and summarizing its main points, we note that there are two general foci to the research and debate. The first centers around traditional themes in political psychology—that is, nationalism, political socialization, and political participation. The second involves the search for a genuine Latin American approach to political psychology.

Research on the traditional themes has produced a need for frames of reference that is only partially filled by theoretical explanations from established European and North American theorists. One can detect a strong interest among Latin American political psychologists in developing theoretical constructs and models that explain the Latin American social reality that they are seeing. The theoretical constructs and models must take into account the phenomenon of dependency, the effects of different types of political systems, the presence of political instability, and clear class distinctions.

This chapter has also presented evidence on what Latin American political psychologists perceive their role to be. They attribute a significant role in society to political psychology. Political psychologists, instead of being observers or witnesses of sociopolitical processes, are seen as participants in the processes. Political psychologists are urged to participate in social interventions, to advocate them, and to analyze them. This view of political psychology may be responsible for the absence of this field in some of the Latin American countries that we surveyed. The active role prescribed for political psychology, directly linking it to social intervention, makes the relationship between the presence of political psychology and the type of political system in a Latin American country more understandable.

In conclusion, despite the obstacles that I encountered in gathering information and despite the obstacles to political psychology as a field discussed in this review, there continues to be work in this area. Thin and halting as the research may be, it shows a strong tendency to develop along with the societies in which it is present, to become a part of the social processes of these societies, and to generate a body of theoretical explanations that are typically Latin American.

References

Acevedo, M. I., Alzate, G. M., and Duran, A. S. "Influencia del partido político y el sexo en la percepción social" [Influence of sex and political party on social perception]. In G. Marin (ed.), *La psicología social en Latinoamérica* [Social psychology in Latin America]. Mexico: Trillas, 1975.

Aguad, B. "Prisión política y suicidio: Muertes en las cárceles argentinas" [Political prisoners and suicide: Death in Argentinian jails]. In S. Marcos (ed.), *Manicomios y prisiones* [Madhouses and prisons]. Mexico: Red-Ediciones, 1983.

Alvarez Cuadros, R. "Análisis psicosocial del poder: Un marco conceptual" [Psychological analysis of power: A conceptual framework]. *Revista de psicología*, 1973-1975, *18-20* (1-2).

Amarista, R., and others. "Análisis del contenido sobre la problemática agrícola en una muestra de discursos del ex-presidente Rafael Caldera y del presidente Carlos Andres Pérez" [Content analysis concerning agricultural problems in a sample of addresses by Ex-President Rafael Caldera and President Carlos Andres Pérez]. *Psicología*, 1976, *3* (2), 159-170.

Araujo, D. M. "O carácter nacional, as organizações e a personalidade: Uma reflexão para educadores" [National character, organizations, and personality: A guide for teachers]. *Boletim técnico—SENAC*, 1982, *8* (1), 33-40.

Asis Córdova, M. "Psicología de la tortura: Premisas para una nueva especialidad científica" [Psychology of torture: Premises for a new scientific specialty]. *Boletín de psicología*, 1979, *2* (1), 19-27.

Baron de Neiburg, and others. "Identidad y exilio" [Identity and exile]. In S. Marcos (ed.), *Manicomios y prisiones* [Madhouses and prisons]. Mexico: Red-Ediciones, 1983.

Barudy, J. "La integración crítica: Método de una terapia liberadora en el exilio latinoamericano" [Critical integration: A liberating therapy technique for the Latin American Exile]. In Colectivo Latinoamericano, *Escritos No. 2* [Writings No. 2]. [Name of publisher not given], 1979.

Barudy, J. "Modelo e instrumentos de una intervención psicosocial destinada a prevenir y tratar los problemas de los hijos de exilados políticos latinoamericanos en Europe" [Model and instruments for a psychosocial intervention to treat and prevent problems in the children of exiled Latin American politicians in Europe]. In Colectivo Latinoamericano (ed.), *Psicopatología de la tortura y el exilio* [Psychopathology of torture and exile]. Madrid: Fundamentos, 1980.

Barudy, J., and others. "Los problemas provocados por la tortura en los refugiados chilenos y latinoamericanos" [Psychic problems provoked by torture in Chilean and Latin American refugees]. [Paper published by Colectivo Latinoamericano; place of publication not given], 1977.

Barudy, J., and others. "La carrera moral del prisionero político latinoamericano" [The moral career of the Latin American political prisoner]. In Colectivo Latinoamericano (ed.), *Psicopatología de la tortura y el exilio* [Psychopathology of torture and exile]. Madrid: Fundamentos, 1980a.

Barudy, J., and others. "El mundo del exilado político" [The world of the political exile]. In Colectivo Latinoamericano (ed.), *Psicopatología de la tortura y el exilio* [Psychopathology of torture and exile]. Madrid: Fundamentos, 1980b.

Barudy, J., and others. "La reconstrucción del sí mismo traumatizado por la tortura: El proceso terapéutico" [Reconstruction of the traumatized self: The therapeutic process]. In Colectivo Latinoamericano (ed.), *Psicopatología de la tortura y el exilio* [Psychopathology of torture and exile]. Madrid: Fundamentos, 1980c.

Betancourt, O. "Influencia que ejerce la campaña electoral sobre los votantes en la elección de candidato" [Influences exerted on voters in an election campaign]. *Psicología*, 1980, 7 (4), 465-474.

Bleichmar, S. "Los hijos de la violencia: Psicoanalizar, contemplar o transformar?" [The children of violence: To psychoanalyze, to contemplate, or to transform?] *Dialéctica*, 1979, *4*, 6.

Bolívar, S. "Carta de Jamaica" [Jamaica letter]. In V. Lecuna (ed.), *Selected Writings of Bolívar*. (L. Bertrand, trans.) New York: Colonial Press, 1951. (Originally published 1815.)

Brice, O. *Fascismo en Venezuela?* [Fascism in Venezuela?] Caracas: Venezuela Central University, School of Psychology, 1973.

Brignardello, L. "Motivación de los dirigentes estudiantiles universitarios" [Motivation of university student leaders]. *Revista latinoamericana de psicologia*, 1978, *10*, 165-171.

Campos, F. "La psicologia como arma contra el subdesarrollo" [Psychology as a weapon against underdevelopment]. *Revista de psicología general y aplicada*, 1968, *23*, 537-552.

Castillo, O. H., Correa, E., and Salas, M. "Modelamiento de actitudes nacionales por medio de historietas cómicos" [Modeling of national attitudes through comic books]. *Revista latinoamericana de psicología*, 1980, *12*, 51-61.

Corral, N. "Reflexiones sobre la problemática de la mujer en el exilio" [Reflections on women's problems in exile]. In Colectivo Latinoamericano (ed.), *Psicopatología de la tortura y el exilio* [Psychopathology of torture and exile]. Madrid: Fundamentos, 1980.

Dávila, G., and others. "Image of Americans in the Mexican Child." In *Psychological Approaches to Intergroup and International Understanding*. Austin, Texas: Hogg Foundation for Mental Hygiene, 1956.

De Castro Aguirre, C. "Estereotipos de nacionalidad en un grupo latinoamericano" [Nationality stereotypes in a Latin American group]. *Revista de psicología general y aplicada*, 1968, *23*, 235-268.

Escovar, L. "El psicólogo social y el desarrollo" [The social psychologist and development]. *Psicología*, 1977, *4* (3-4), 367-378.

Escovar, L. "Hacia un modelo psicológico-social del desarrollo" [Toward a psychosocial model of development]. *Boletín de la Asociación Venezolana de Psicología Social*, 1980, *3* (1), 1-6.

Flores Osorio, J. M. "Represión y lucha política: Connotaciones psicológicas" [Repression and political struggle: A psychological interpretation]. In S. Marcos (ed.), *Manicomios y prisiones* [Madhouses and prisons]. Mexico: Red-Ediciones, 1983.

Fortes, J. "Actividad y passividad estudiantil: Sus aspectos académicos y políticos" [Active and passive students: Their academic and political lives]. Paper presented at 1st Congress of Clinical Psychology, Mexico, Sept. 1975.

Fortes, J. "Passividad y falta de involucración en estudiantes" [Passivity and lack of involvement in college students]. *Interamerican Journal of Psychology*, 1978, *12* (2), 143–151.

Franco, C. "Imagen de la sociedad: Valoración de la participación política y personalidad" [Image of society: Personality and value given political participation]. *Revista latinoamericana de psicología*, 1980, *12* (2), 277–292.

Ginsberg, A. "Projeto de pesquisa sobre as atitudes nacionalistas de jovens brasileiros de diferentes origens nacionais, pertencentes a diferentes grupos sociais e etnicos" [Nationalistic attitudes of Brazilian young people from different social and ethnic groups]. *Arquivos brasileiros de psicologia*, 1982, *34* (3), 96–101.

Gissi, J. "Identidad, 'caracter social' y cultura latinoamericana" [Identity, "social character," and Latin American culture]. Unpublished paper, Pontificia Universidad Católica, Santiago, 1982.

Hernandez, R. "La tortura: Causas y efectos psicológicos" [Torture: Causes and psychological effects]. In S. Marcos (ed.), *Manicomios y prisiones* [Madhouses and prisons]. Mexico: Red-Ediciones, 1983.

Hernandez, W. A. *Educación de transición en los hijos de los refugiados políticos* [Transition education of children of political refugees]. Copenhagen: Institut fur Klinik Psykologi Nyalsgade, n.d.

Isaacson, J. "Cultura y persona: Una propuesta para cuantificar la alienación" [Culture and person: A proposal for quantifying alienation]. *Acta psiquiátrica y psicológica de América Latina*, 1977, *23*, 6–11.

Kogan, A. A. "Un enfoque psicológico de la prevención de la guerra" [A psychological approach to the prevention of war]. *Acta psiquiátrica y psicológica de América Latina*, 1976, *22*, 225–231.

Lira, E., and Kovalskis, J. "Exilio y retorno: Una approximación psicosocial" [Exile and return: A psychosocial approach]. *Revista chilena de psicología*, 1983, *6* (1), 41–46.

López del Rey, A. "Los grupos coetáneos y la socialización política" [Peer groups and political socialization]. *Cuadernos de sociología*, 1983, 7 (17), 2–7.

Margulis, M. "Condiciones de producción e ideologización de la ciencia social en países dependientes" [Ideological conditions and production in dependent countries]. *Revista argentina de psicología*, 1971, *8*.

Martín-Baro, I. "Ocupación juvenil: Reflexiones psicosociales de un rehen por 24 horas" [Takeover by youth: Psychosocial reflections of a hostage for 24 hours]. *Estudios centroamericanos*, 1980, *379*, 463–474.

Martín-Baro, I. "El liderato de monseñor Romero (Un análisis psicosocial)" [Monsignor Romero's leadership: A psychosocial analysis]. *Estudios centroamericanos*, 1981, *389*, 151–172.

Montero, M. "Socialización política en jóvenes Caraqueños" [Political socialization of the young people of Caracas]. In G. Marin (ed.), *La psicología social en Latinoamérica* [Social psychology in Latin America]. Mexico: Trillas, 1975.

Montero, M. "Imagen de partido políticos e imagen de candidatos presidenciales" [Images of political parties and presidential candidates]. Paper presented at 16th Interamerican Congress of Psychology, Miami, Summer 1976.

Montero, M. "Bosquejo para una teoría explicativa de la conducta de alienación" [Sketch of a theory of alienation behavior]. *Boletín de la Asociación Venezolana de Psicología Social*, 1980, *3* (3), 6–10.

Montero, M. "An Explanation for the Psychosocial Level of Dependency Ideology." Paper presented at annual meeting of the International Society of Political Psychology, Oxford University, July 1983.

Montero, M. *Ideología, alienación e identidad nacional* [Ideology, alienation, and national identity]. Caracas: Ediciones de la Biblioteca de la Universidad Central (EBUC), 1984.

Montero, M., Roncayolo, M., and Rengel, J. "Actitudes electorales en la población de Caracas" [Electoral attitudes in the population of Caracas]. Paper presented at 23rd International Congress of Sociology, Caracas, 1972.

Olivo de Celli, V. "Maquiavelismo de los líderes empresariales y de los partidos políticos" [Machiavellianism in leaders of business and political parties]. In E. Granell de Aldaz (ed.), *Simposia*. Caracas: Equinoccio, 1980.

Paez, D. "La psicología social de los movimientos de masas en un período dictatorial" [The social psychology of mass movements during a dictatorial government]. In *Asi buscamos rehacernos* [Thus we search to rebuild ourselves]. Lima: CELADEC, 1980a.

Paez, D. "Psicología social del reflujo de los movimientos sociales y metodología del trabajo psicosocial: Los efectos ideológicos de la represión" [The social psychology of social movements and methodology of psychosocial work: Ideological effects of repression]. In Colectivo Latinoamericano (ed.), *Psicopatología de la tortura y el exilio* [Psychopathology of torture and exile]. Madrid: Fundamentos, 1980b.

Paez, D., and others. "Crisis política e intervención psicosocial: Terapia familiar y animación comunitaria en el exilio" [Political crisis and psychosocial intervention: Family therapy and community in exile]. In Colectivo Latinoamericano (ed.), *Psicopatología de la tortura y el exilio* [Psychopathology of torture and exile]. Madrid: Fundamentos, 1980.

Peralta, T. "Psychological Damage of Political Repression and Torture on Chilean Political Prisoners." Unpublished paper, 1979.

Pereira, J. C. "Ideologia e alienação" [Ideology and alienation]. *Ciencia e cultura*, 1982, *34* (1), 48–49.

Pineda, G., and Whitford, J. "La psicología como ciencia ideológica-política" [Psychology as a political-ideological science]. *Boletín de la Asociación Nicaraguense de Psicólogos*, 1983, *2* (3), 11–13.

Pinzas, J. R. "El desarrollo de conceptos sociales en niños peruanos" [Development of social concepts in Peruvian children). *Revista latinoamericana de psicología*, 1980, *12* (1), 29–35.

Pulido de Briceño, M., and Piñango, R. "La política social de la democracia venezolana" [The social policy of the Venezuelan democracy]. *SIC*, 1979, *42*, 394–397.

Queiros de Ramos, A. *Relación entre minusvalía social y externalidad* [Relationship between externality and national underevaluation]. Caracas: Venezuela Central University, School of Psychology, 1979.

Quintero, M. "Contribuciones a la teoría para el estudio de la consciencia social en América Latina" [Contributions to a theory for the study of social consciousness in Latin America]. Paper presented at 2nd National Conference of Social Psychology of the Venezuelan Association of Social Psychology, 1979.

Reyes, M. L., Barroso, C. J., and Pérez, C. E. "Estereotipos de niños colombianos hacia diferentes grupos nacionales en función de la educación que reciben" [Stereotypes of Colombian children toward different national groups as a function of type of education]. Paper presented at 15th Interamerican Congress of Psychology, Bogotá, Summer 1974.

Ribes Iñesta, E. "Papel de la psicología en el cambio social" [The role of psychology in social change]. *Psicología*, 1976, *3* (3-4), 267-278.

Rincon, O. *La propaganda electoral venezolana de 1978: Una expresión de dependencia en el orden científico-técnico* [Venezuelan electoral propaganda in 1978: An expression of dependency on the scientific-technological order]. Caracas: Venezuela Central University, School of Psychology, 1979.

Rodríguez, B. B. *Factores que influyen en la participación de la mujer obrera en la política a través del estudio de una organización sindical* [Factors influencing the participation of working women in politics: A study of a union]. Caracas: Venezuela Central University, School of Psychology, 1979.

Rojas, X., and others. *Representación cognoscitiva de conceptos políticos en votantes y abstencionistas y su influencia en la votación presidencial* [Cognitive representation of political concepts in voters and nonparticipants and its influence on presidential voting]. Bogotá: University Javeriana, Faculty of Psychology, 1980.

Romero, L. "Las toma del poder" [Power takeover]. *Cuadernos de Psicología*, 1978, *2* (2), 85-96.

Roncagliolo, R. *Estudiantes y política* [Students and politics]. Lima: Universidad Católica, 1969.

Salazar, J. M. "La Psicología social y la posibilidad de investigación sobre el carácter nacional venezolano" [Social psychology and the possibility of doing research on Venezuelan national character]. *Cuadernos de psicología*, 1960, *2* (5-6), 175-181.

Salazar, J. M. *Determinantes y dinámica de las actitudes políticas de estudiantes universitarios* [Dynamics and determinants of political attitudes in university students]. Caracas: Venezuela Central University, School of Psychology, 1961.

Salazar, J. M. "Influencia de la experiencia universitaria en la modificación de las actitudes políticas" [Influence of university experience on the change in political attitudes]. *Boletín bibliográfico de FACES*, 1964, *2*, 273-284.

Salazar, J. M. "Aspectos psicológicos del nacionalismo: Autoestereotipo del Venezolano" [Psychological aspects of nationalism: Venezuelan self-stereotypes]. *Revista de psicología fundapsive*, 1970a, *1*, 15-18.

Salazar, J. M. "Relaciones entre actitudes y diferentes aspectos del nacionalismo entre estudiantes Venezolanos" [Relationship between attitudes and several aspects of nationalism among Venezuelan students]. Paper presented at 20th convention of the Venezuelan Association for the Advancement of Science, Caracas, 1970b.

Salazar, J. M. "Orientaciones políticas y actitudes hacia lo nacional" [Political orientations and attitudes toward nationality]. *Psicología*, 1974, *1*, 7-15.

Salazar, J. M. "Actitudes de estudiantes Venezolanos de secundaria y de sus padres hacia la patria, los simbolos nacionales y el estado" [Attitudes of Venezuelan high school students and their parents toward motherland, national symbols, and the state]. In G. Marin (ed.), *La Psicología social in Latinoamérica* [Social psychology in Latin America]. Mexico: Trillas, 1975.

Salazar, J. M. "Contribuciones de la psicología social al estudio del nacionalismo" [Contributions of social psychology to the study of nationalism]. Paper presented at 3rd Conference of Psychology, Brasilia, 1976.

Salazar, J. M. "Modelos actitudinales, actitudes nacionalistas e intención electoral" [Attitude models, nationalist attitudes, and electoral intentions]. Paper presented at 1st National Conference of Social Psychology, AVEPSO, Caracas, 1977.

Salazar, J. M. "Psicología social y nacionalismo" [Social psychology and nationalism]. Paper presented at 2nd Latin American Seminar of Social Psychology, Oaxtepec, Mexico, 1978.

Salazar, J. M. "Creencias y actitudes nacionales en la población metropolitana de Caracas" [National beliefs and attitudes in the population of Caracas]. Paper presented at 29th Convention of the Venezuelan Association for the Advancement of Science, Barquisimeto, Venezuela, 1979.

Salazar, J. M. "Etnocentrismo, patriotismo y nacionalismo" [Ethnocentrism, patriotism, and nationalism]. *Boletín de la Asociación Venezolana de Psicología Social*, 1980, *3* (3), 11–16.

Salazar, J. M. "Creencias y actitudes hacia lo nacional y extranjero en la población de Caracas" [Beliefs and attitudes toward what is national and what is foreign in the population of Caracas]. Unpublished paper, Institute of Psychology, Venezuela Central University, 1981.

Salazar, J. M. "Creencias, actitudes nacionales e ideología dependiente" [Beliefs, nationalistic attitudes, and dependent ideology]. In *Contribuciones recientes a la psicología en Venezuela* [Recent contributions to psychology in Venezuela]. Caracas: Institute of Psychology, Venezuela Central University, 1982.

Salazar, J. M. *Bases Psicológicas del nacionalismo* [Psychological bases of nationalism]. Mexico: Trillas, 1983a.

Salazar, J. M. "On the Psychological Viability of 'Latin Americanism.' " *International Social Science Journal*, 1983b, *35* (2), 295–308.

Salazar, J. M. "Beliefs About Nations and Their Relationship to 'Nationalistic Behavior.' " In E. Roth (ed.), *Perspectives in Attitude Research*. Toronto: Hografe, in press.

Salazar, J. M., Banchs, M. A., and Marin, G. "Valoración de la categoría 'Latinoamericano' entre estudiantes de seis países" [Evaluation of the category "Latin American" among students from six countries]. Paper presented at 2nd Conference on Research of the Humanities and Education Faculty, Venezuela Central University, Caracas, 1983.

Salazar, J. M., and Marin, G. "El fenómeno de la imagen de espejo en las percepciones mutuas de Colombianos y Venezolanos" [Mirror-image phenomena in mutual perceptions of Colombians and Venezuelans]. *Psicología*, 1975a, *2* (4), 3–12.

Salazar, J. M., and Marin, G. "Stereotypes and Mirror Image." In J. W. Berry and W. J. Loner (eds.), *Applied Cross-Cultural Psychology*. Lisse, Netherlands: Swets & Zeitlinger, 1975b.

Salazar, J. M., and Marin, G. "National Stereotypes as a Function of Conflict and Territorial Proximity: A Test of the Mirror-Image Hypothesis." *Journal of Social Psychology*, 1977, *101*, 13–19.

Salazar, J. M., and others. "Degree of Development and Distance as Related to Mutual Perceptions and Attitudes Among Students in Seven Latin American Countries." Paper presented at 6th International Congress of Cross-Cultural Psychology, Aberdeen, Scotland, 1982.

Santoro, E. "Estereotipos nacionales en habitantes de una zona marginal de Caracas" [National stereotypes in slum dwellers in Caracas]. In G. Marin (ed.), *La Psicología social in Latinoamérica* [Social psychology in Latin America]. Mexico: Trillas, 1975.

Serbin, A. "Un estudio exploratorio sobre el desarrollo de una ideología nacional en la conformación del estada Guyanes: La visión de los intelectuales" [An exploratory study of a national ideology in the Guyanese state: The intellectual's point of view]. In E. Granell de Aldaz (ed.), *Simposia*. Caracas: Equinoccio, 1980.

Smith, A. D. "Ethnic Identity and World Order." Paper presented at 5th annual Millennium Conference, London School of Economics, 1982.

Sorin, M. "Desarrollo de actitudes vinculadas al humanismo, patriotismo e internacionalismo en escolares cubanos" [Development of attitudes linked to humanism, patriotism, and internationalism in Cuban school children]. *Boletín de Psicología*, 1981, *4* (3), 80-102.

Szmrecsanyi, M. I. "Determinações sociais do planejamento: Estado, educação e legitimação do poder na obra de Karl Mannheim" [Social determinants of planning, education, and legitimation of power in the works of Karl Mannheim]. *Cadernos de pesquisa*, 1982, *40*, 15-22.

Talento, M., and Ribes Iñesta, E. "Algunas consideraciones sobre el papel social de la profesión psicológica" [Some considerations of the social role of the psychological profession]. *Psicología*, 1979, *6* (4), 225-242.

Tobar, N. "La psicología y el ser nacional" [Psychology and the national being]. *Revista argentina de psicología*, 1972, *11*, 151-156.

Tueros, M. *Apuntes para el estudio de la socialización político de los adolescentes de Lima urbana* [Notes for the study of the political socialization of adolescents in urban Lima]. Lima: Universidad Nacional Mayor de San Marcos, 1977.

Urdaneta, O. "Psicología, ética y política" [Psychology, ethics, and politics]. *Psicodeia*, 1979, *4* (38), 7-136.

Valladares, L. *El sesgo de la respuesta por efecto del orden de los items en la medición de opiniones asociadas a un gobierno socialista en Venezuela* [Response bias as an effect of item order in measuring opinions associated with a socialist government in Venezuela]. Caracas: Venezuela Central University, School of Psychology, 1980.

Vasquez, A. "Ethical Questions Submitted to Psychologists About Some Torture Techniques Used in Chile." *Psicología*, 1976, *3* (3-4), 525-532.

Vasquez, O. "Elementos de socialización formal e informal en el ambiente universitario: Congruencias e incongruencias" [Elements of formal and informal socialization in the university milieu: Congruity and incongruity]. *Revista de ciencias sociales*, 1973, *17*, 363-439.

Verro, L. "Cultura y liberación" [Culture and liberation]. Unpublished doctoral dissertation, Arzobispado, [Catholic University Archbishopric], Santiago, 1981.

Welsch, F., and others. "Cultura política: Miembros de la elite dirigente venezolana" [Political culture: Members of the Venezuelan leading elite]. Unpublished paper, Caracas, 1984.

FIFTEEN

❧❧❧❧❧❧❧❧❧❧❧❧❧❧❧❧❧❧❧❧❧❧

Political Psychology
in Western Europe

Tom Bryder

In the twentieth century, Europe has experienced two world wars, the turmoil and
distress of a great depression, several successful and unsuccessful political revolutions and coups d'état, and a gradual transition from aristocratic autocracy to
liberal democracy in many countries. Yet a coherent or comprehensive political
theory, in the strict scientific sense, indicating—on the basis of contemporary or
past historical evidence or logical argument—that all these things were possible
or even likely has not appeared. Among the academic political scientists who were
witnesses to all these events, few saw—before it was clear for all who had eyes to
see—the deadly menace to the civil political order posed by totalitarian movements
with world-hegemonic and destructive mass appeals. With a few exceptions
(Stenelo, 1980; Hörberg, 1983), the idea of political predictions on the basis of
theory and research is largely underdeveloped in political science as an academic
discipline.

In the psychological discipline, things have generally been worse, not better.
In the first half of the century, psychologists paid little attention to the question
of social relevance in those areas where they actually were able to predict human
behavior with some degree of statistical probability. Able researchers and clinicians
were so concerned with the experimental, clinical, and technological developments
in their normal science paradigms that, in most cases, they forgot the wider applicability of their findings—even when the researchers were, for example, Jews in
countries controlled by National Socialists (Bettelheim, 1970; Sanford, 1973).

How could this happen? Was it merely because the disciplines of political
science and psychology were in some respects theoretically and empirically underdeveloped, or did other social and scientific factors contribute to this lacuna? Can
we be certain that political psychology, as it is taught at universities and practiced

in research today, adequately captures the main currents of the politically significant trends in ways that will enable us to describe, explain, and predict, with some degree of scientific accuracy, what type of political life we may face tomorrow? The answers to these questions suggest that political psychologists must abandon any type of scientific parochialism or national, historical, and intradisciplinary prejudices. In political psychology we can afford no limits to trade or travel.

To survey political psychology in Western Europe is a complex task involving difficulties. In the first place, few social scientists in Western Europe would call themselves political psychologists. Rather, they would tend to call themselves sociologists, political scientists, psychologists, or social psychologists, and the traces of their works would typically appear in the specialized journals of these more narrow and traditional disciplines. In the second place, Western Europe— with its many countries, cultures, and academic traditions—is almost impossible to cover in a way that would do justice to all approaches, national patterns, and specific research results. Add to this, thirdly, that the scientific pluralism of political psychology makes it more a field than an actual academic discipline. So, in the end, the idiosyncrasies of the surveyor somehow make themselves felt; there can be no presupposed objectivity or full coverage, since these complexities simply defy any attempt to do justice to all the research out there (Greenstein, 1973).

Although biases cannot be avoided, nevertheless an attempt is made here to keep them within limits and to make them as explicit as possible. For linguistic reasons there may be a bias toward Scandinavian, English, German, and French research, and an underemphasis on Italian, Belgian, and Dutch work. Spanish, Portuguese, and Greek studies are not covered at all. Moreover, since my own professional background includes political science, psychoanalysis, and social psychology, the idiosyncratic limits of these disciplines will inevitably make themselves apparent. In dealing with the past, we already have two good records: that of Stone (1981), describing the development of political psychology from the perspective of psychology, and that of Sanford (1973), dealing with the origins, development, and consequences of studies in authoritarianism, originally conceptualized by members of the Frankfurt School and elaborated on within a wider intellectual community. Far less is known about many of the outstanding scholars whose impact is still felt, but seldom acknowledged, in what we have come to take for granted as basic knowledge in political psychology. Although I will attempt to paint the broader lines of European developments in political psychology, I will give special attention to scholars who are virtually unheard of today (for example, Gabriel Tarde) but who, nevertheless, in their times exercised important influences in the intellectual community, both in Europe and the United States.

As we look back, survey the present, and gaze into the future of political psychology theory and research, we shall be able to discover how research increasingly moves toward integration and how theory becomes more and more dispersed, influencing developments both in the traditional parental disciplines of political science and psychology and in what has emerged as a nascent discipline in its own right, political psychology.

Freud ([1932] 1973, p. 34) has noted the difficulty of conducting scientific research in psychology: "No reader of an account of astronomy will feel disappointed and contemptuous of the science if he is shown the frontiers at which our knowledge of the universe melts into haziness. Only in psychology is it otherwise.

There mankind's constitutional unfitness for scientific research comes fully into the open. What people seem to demand of psychology is not progress in knowledge, but satisfaction of some other sort; every unsolved problem, every admitted uncertainty is made into a reproach against it." Resistance to psychologizing politics has been even more pronounced than that experienced by clinical analysts in the past. In some countries such resistance silenced not only political psychology as an empirical social science discipline but also empirical political science, social psychology, and political sociology. As the following account will try to demonstrate, this was the case in France for half a century; in Germany such resistance influenced in important ways the patterning of political psychology into a tripartite discipline. In general, political psychology in Western Europe since World War II increasingly has modeled itelf on research done across the Atlantic. At present, however, there are signs that political psychology may be breaking new paths in Europe, which Americans may come to understand only as time passes. The rebirth of social science in the backwaters of the National Socialist dictatorship has brought about a quantity and quality of theory and research that in the long run may play as important a role as did the intellectual emigration of the Frankfurt Institute of Social Research to the United States in the 1940s.

A note on the style of presentation and themes in this chapter seems in order at this point. In what follows little attempt is made at focusing on individual countries. National and disciplinary labels are of little use for those comparisons and judgments that will be made. It is not the goal of the present chapter to make assessments of which national contribution was most important or to estimate whether political science, psychology, psychoanalysis, social psychology, or political sociology did most to further political psychology in Western Europe. These issues are, strictly speaking, immaterial. What matters is which contributions— in theory, results, and methods, in that order—have been made by individuals and groups of individuals concerned with political psychology as a field of research. The themes selected for exposition derive their rationale from the idea that politics is always about people. To most political psychologists, the idea of studying politics without focusing on people seems a contradiction in terms. To better understand protest movements, parties, parliaments, and transnational organizations, we need to learn about the people who are involved.

The style of presentation will be partly "presentist" and partly "historicist." According to Stone (1981, p. 2), "Presentism refers to history written from the standpoint of the present, with little attempt to understand the situation as experienced by the actors of the past." "Historicism" is used here as the logical opposite of "presentism." "Historicism" helps us understand the effects that the historical context had on the development of ideas. These ways of presenting the material are meant to complement and supplement each other.

Irrationality and Consciousness in Mass Behavior

In Western Europe, as contrasted with later developments in the United States, the relationship between political psychology and its variegated social environments has always been close and transparent. Both as a speculative philosophy in medieval times, and as an increasingly self-conscious science in the late nineteenth and early twentieth centuries, political psychology was by and large a response to major and conspicuous historical events in those countries where it found practitioners and audiences. The growth of the field was a *response to,* rather than merely a *reflection of,* these events and conditions; for the values, aspirations, hopes, and fears of those who wrote the classics are omnipresent in their works.

In the last decades of the nineteenth century, the impact of industrialization, urbanization, colonialism, and socialism became apparent in most Western European countries. The hardships of factory work and poor urban housing; a widespread compulsory school system, which was required for the foundation, maintenance, and expansion of the factory system; and the consciously propagated nationalisms after Germany and Italy had been unified—all combined to increase political consciousness and unrest among the people of Europe. Unsuccessful wars, compulsory military conscription, and trade union organization added to this picture a widespread demand for an enlarged popular influence on national and local politics. It was an age of political mass expectations and demands.

Many of these trends culminated in the unsuccessful Paris Commune of 1871 and the defeat of the first Russian revolution of 1905. These events demonstrated a growing political identity among the underdogs in society, but since theoretical studies were then the privilege of an elite, successful attempts to formulate the contents of this new identity had to be expressed by literate intellectuals. That the intellectuals had partisan biases was often openly admitted in their writings, but then one should not take their respective partisan attitudes to indicate that they were unable to use both their intellectual abilities and analytical skills. What we today regard as serious prejudices in the works of these authors by no means prevented them from making valuable contributions to our knowledge of political behavior, thought, and emotions.

The most convenient way of illustrating the early work done in the psychology of mass political behavior, from a historicist point of view, is to compare the apparently opposite views of Gustave Le Bon and Vladimir Lenin. Whereas Le Bon was preoccupied with irrationality, traits, instincts, and individuality, Lenin concerned himself with the problems of political consciousness. Lenin was interested in the question of how political behavior can be stimulated through experience and learning in contexts designed for collective action. One could say, in a somewhat simplified fashion, that each of them stood on *his* side of the barricades, both in theoretical and practical matters of politics. The pessimistic and conservative views held by Le Bon, in politics as well as in psychology, were largely the result of the role he ascribed to inheritance and emotions; the optimistic views of Lenin were closely tied to his cognitive theory and, above all, the potentialities for human betterment he saw in organization. Both were interested in the problem of political leadership, and the relationships each described, in different terms, between "masses" and "leaders" make their inclusion important to a discussion of contemporary views and research.

Gustave Le Bon (1841–1931). Le Bon was trained as a physician, but he had a mixture of wide-ranging interests, including theoretical physics, archeology, public hygiene, and physical anthropology. Yet it would be wrong to see him as a neo-Machiavellian, as Thierc and Tréanton (1983, p. 120) do; for, despite his connections with Mussolini, he lacked the synthetic abilities of the Renaissance intellectuals. Today Le Bon is remembered for his books on group behavior, one of which, *La Psychologie des foules* (1895; trans. as *The Crowd,* 1896), in many ways inspired Freud to reformulate his theory of personality in structural terms and to advance a psychoanalytic theory of leadership and group behavior.

Since Le Bon accepted Joseph de Gobineau's theories concerning the roles of superior and inferior races in the evolution of civilization, he was an outspoken racist. He also had a romantic conception of national character, which he blended with a homespun myth of a "racial soul." As pointed out earlier, for Le Bon emotion, rather than cognition and intelligence, constituted the determining factor in the evolution of history and culture.

Although his works were widely translated, Le Bon was not a popularizer of his own writings. That would, of course, have been a major self-contradiction. Nevertheless, his works reflect aristocratic and antidemocratic prejudices, which we today might see as forerunners to the nascent ideology of fascism. He held, for example, that most people are devoid of reason and beyond intellectual persuasion; in popular government he saw nothing but mob rule. He regarded women as inferior to men and was convinced that all major achievements of Europe's civilization were the outcome of (male) elite genius. He had a peculiar idea of the impact of nationality and race on political ideology and behavior. In his early works, he attributed to the Germans and the Anglo-Saxon peoples a capacity for individual political accomplishment, while he saw the Latins as predisposed to mob behavior and collectivism. With his noteworthy strange disregard for empirical data, logical coherence, and proof, he was not hesitant to maintain that after World War I the Germans, in particular, were innately prone to state socialism, whereas true individualism became the outstanding trait of the Latins.

The more lasting influence of Le Bon's writings comes, however, from his condemnation of revolutions. In *La Psychologie des foules,* he maintained that revolutionary behavior is, in the main, the outcome of mass hysteria. His ideas closely resembled those of Scipio Sighele (1895), probably because they were both influenced by contemporary French abnormal psychologists, particularly Hippolyte Bernheim and Pierre Janet, whose studies of suggestion, hysteria, and hypnosis they both reformulated to fit crowd and mob phenomena (Thierc, 1981).

While it would probably be most appropriate to see *The Crowd* as a contemporary partisan political pamphlet because of its prejudices and illustrations from the Paris Commune of 1871, the book contains much more than that. In fact, it contains a social theory which states that—as a result of the industrial revolution, the rise of modern cities, and the growth of communications—social life has become more and more crowdlike. Le Bon regarded the masses as organized aggregations of people who substitute subconscious, primitive urges for their conscious individualities. This deindividuation of group members tends to provide a common ground for collective action, tying participants together. What we call *group syntality* today was, thus, conceived by Le Bon as transcending individual participant control, but he did not develop any detailed theory of how group properties, environments, and internal group dynamics interact. His preoccupation with inheritance and a strict social and racial determination blinded him to further development of thoughts for which there undoubtedly was some observational foundation.

Le Bon tried to relate the "mob mentality" described in *The Crowd* to a variety of observables, all of which he appeared to take more or less for granted.

He alleged, for example, that group size is an influential factor in making human aggregates volatile, although his major thesis was that the charismatic properties and skills of the group leader inevitably determine the outcome of the collective process. His tendency to equate socialism with theft and criminal behavior was widespread among the property-owning classes of the time. What made him different from the rest of his contemporary conservatives was his insistence on generalizing his political observations of society to lower-level aggregates, and on maintaining the instinctual nature of what happens at this level.

In addition to *The Crowd*, Le Bon also wrote *La Psychologie du socialisme* (The psychology of socialism) (1896); *La Psychologie politique et la défense sociale* (Political psychology and social defense) (1910); and *La Révolution Française et la psychologie des révolutions* (The French Revolution and the psychology of revolutions) (1912). From the standpoint of theoretical political psychology today, these later works are of lesser importance, since all are marked by an almost incredible reiteration of previous generalizations, and, as was previously pointed out, Le Bon's primitive political "anthropology" remains incoherent throughout. Le Bon's impact on early French sociology is analyzed in Moscovici's (1981) scholarly treatise *L'Age de foule: Une traité historique de psychologie des masses* (The age of the crowd: A historical treatise on the psychology of the masses). As a classic thinker in the area of political psychology, Le Bon still deserves to be studied today, more for the sake of hypothesis formation than for confirmation and proof.

Vladimir Ilich Lenin (Ulyanov) (1870-1924). It may, perhaps, appear strange to include Lenin—a Russian—in an overview of Western European political psychology, and to compare him with Le Bon, of whom he had probably never heard. Yet, for a long period in his life (1900-1905, 1907-1917), Lenin was an exile in France, England, and Switzerland, and he was a "Westerner" as a Marxist and social philosopher. Besides, his theory of revolutionary class consciousness has *paradigmatic significance* for a group of political psychologists who, despite their ignorance of Lenin's ideas, have perceived the positive goals that can ensue from collective behavior and have played down the role of inheritance and instincts.

By profession Lenin was a lawyer; he got his law degree in 1891, four years before Le Bon published *The Crowd*. As a political type, he combined the skills and interests of an agitator, an administrator, and a theorist (Lasswell, 1951, p. 54; Bryder, 1975, pp. 16-17). It is his theoretical skills that justify his inclusion in the present discussion. For even though he was a man by, of, and for the socialist revolution, he devoted considerable time to theoretical studies. Although Lenin occasionally would engage in studies of the philosophy of science—most notably in *Materialism and Empirio-Criticism* ([1909] 1967)—he lacked Le Bon's dilettante predilection for polyhistoricism.

In a recent study of Lenin's political theory, Lundquist (1982)—in the rigorous tradition of *The Organizational Weapon* (Selznick, 1950), *A Study of Bolshevism* (Leites, 1953), and *Soviet Attitudes Toward Authority* (Mead, 1951)—convincingly shows that an authentic interpretation of Lenin's normative political theory requires a deep knowledge of his dialectical materialism, as it appears in his psychological assumptions about relationships between the masses and the Communist party. In fact, Lundquist manages to show that the basic elements in Lenin's model for the socialist revolution formed a consistent pattern and were already established before Lenin went abroad. What, then, to the occasional reader would appear as fragmented comments on various contemporary events were all variants of the basic model, the outline of which is most explicit in the 1902 pamphlet *What Is to Be Done?*

Whereas in Le Bon's works the *social* side of mass psychology remains very much at the level of political prejudice, the *psychological* details in Lenin's earlier conceptions of political consciousness were influenced by a certain physicalistic and mechanical view, derived from Georgii Plekhanov's monistic philosophy. In *Materialism and Empirio-Criticism,* for example, Lenin ([1909] 1967) maintains that our mental lives are little more than neurophysiology, with fixed structures mirroring the external world. In those works where he is less explicit, such as *What Is to Be Done?* ([1902] 1967) and *Left-Wing Communism: An Infantile Disorder* ([1920] 1967), a more subtle theory emerges, in which two levels—an axiomatic, basic level and an operational level—stand out in a complex argument about experience and basic political principles (Lundquist, 1982, pp. 37-38).

Not unlike Le Bon, Lenin argued that, without external guidance from an elite, the masses are doomed to "false consciousness." But unlike Le Bon, who maintained that this false consciousness was likely to overthrow culture and the achievements of civilization, Lenin saw it as a conservative force, which he called "trade union consciousness" and which he believed was defective precisely because it did *not* alter the status quo. Although Lenin proposed the vanguard role of the Communist party in the process of preparing the masses for a new political order, he was eager to emphasize that it could not be accomplished simply by agitation, propaganda, and indoctrination.

Mann (1973), in his empirical study *Consciousness and Action Among the Western Working Class,* outlines the conditions and process that occur in the shaping of class consciousness according to the Leninist model:

> Firstly, we can separate class *identity*—the definition of oneself as working class, as playing a distinctive role in common with other workers in the productive process. Secondly comes class *opposition*—the perception that the capitalist and his agents constitute an enduring opponent to oneself. These two elements interact dialectically; that is to say, opposition itself serves to reinforce identity, and vice versa. Thirdly is class *totality*—the acceptance of the two previous elements as the defining characteristics of (a) one's total social situation and (b) the whole society in which one lives. Finally comes the conception of an *alternative* society, a goal toward which one moves through the struggle with the opponent. True revolutionary consciousness is a combination of all four, and an obviously rare occurrence [p. 13].

According to Lenin, consciousness grows as the worker generalizes from his own concrete experience to the wider conditions of society and to a vision of an alternative political order. It is through coming to terms with this alternative reality—not as it is immediately given through experience but, rather, as it can be reshaped on the basis of a generalized knowledge of society—that the masses overcome their false consciousness.

For Le Bon the role and the character of leadership were primary in group behavior. But since he held that crowd situations can only produce leaders with criminal intentions and mediocre skills, epitomizing the group "soul," he disregarded the potentiality of the purposes to which group psychology can be put. With Lenin the reverse was true. According to Lenin's theory the process of group leadership is dynamic, not between an individual and an amorphous crowd but between a collectivity—a revolutionary and politically conscious party organization—and a loosely organized set of organizations, mainly designed to protect unionists' rights against the owners of the means of production. The emphasis in Lenin's theory on the role of education reveals an optimistic view with regard to human nature, and the stress on experience deemphasizes the role of emotions at the expense of cognition. For these reasons Lenin's theory of mass political behavior and consciousness is still worth studying today, for where Le Bon fails, Lenin seems to have an answer. Both offer an explanation for the agonies of the masses in industrial society and suggestions for remedying these agonies. That modern political psychology has chosen diagnoses and interpretations that resemble Lenin's ideas more than Le Bon's is, perhaps, a sign of a growing preference for intellectualism in industrialized society. The strength of Le Bon's work is that he nowhere takes perception and cognition to be simple processes devoid of emotion. Whereas his idea of a "group soul" is nonsense, and needs to be replaced by Lenin's emphasis on *relations* between individuals and groups of individuals at an observational level, Le Bon's subtle analysis of unconscious psychological processes and his recognition of the importance of group fantasies are still pertinent areas for empirical field and laboratory research.

Interregnum, Continuities, and Developments

"The state phenomena," wrote Jellinek (1914) in his widely read *Allgemeine Staatslehre* (General theory of the state), "are both human acts and the effects of human acts. All action is, however, psychological activity. Therefore, *psychology*, the theory of psychological conditions and actions, is the precondition for the theory of the state, as it is for the theory of all the humanities" (p. 81; my trans.). At the beginning of the century, however, there were few political scientists who knew much about psychology. In 1879 Wilhelm Wundt had established scientific psychology when he set up a laboratory and started experimental research, and in the United States, William James worked on a major textbook. But for most Europeans, psychology was little more than introspective philosophy, and a crude one at that. Lenin, for example, who was against introspection for philosophical reasons, had attacked Ernst Mach and his Russian followers in *Materialism and Empirio-Criticism* ([1909] 1967), and in France Émile Durkheim was engaged in polemics with Gabriel Tarde on the role of mental phenomena in social life. Jellinek's statement above was probably more a statement of faith or an idealistic philosophy than a well-grounded opinion on the role of psychology vis-à-vis politics.

One of the demonstrable exceptions to this pattern of ignorance in political science appears in a treatise written by Fredrik Lagerroth at the University of Lund, Sweden, which earned him a professorship in 1925. *Psykologisk verklighet och juridisk fiktion vid tillämpningen av sveriges grundlager* (Psychological reality and legal fiction in the application of Swedish constitutional law) is a remarkable work in light of the prevailing views of what was academically respectable at the time. Not only was Lagerroth familiar with Le Bon's work on group psychology; he also knew, and on logical and scientific criteria preferred, the interpretations of Sigmund Freud and William McDougall. Lagerroth contested the ideas behind Le Bon's conception of the innately immoral and criminal tendencies in the spiritual constitution of collectivities and, on the basis of Freud's ([1921] 1968) *Group Psychology and the Analysis of the Ego,* constructed his own version of "methodological individualism" in an argument against certain codifications of constitutional practices.

Neither in Sweden nor elsewhere did psychology have any deeper impact on political science in the years before and between the two world wars. In the period immediately following World War II, political science almost everywhere was firmly tied to the legal profession and the law faculties, although in the Netherlands philosophers took over the study of politics from the outset. Influential skeptics did not want to entrust the science of statecraft to the students of jurisprudence.

The general attitude that prevailed in most Western European countries is epitomized best in a quotation from an overview of political science in Belgium (van Kalken and Lepses, 1950, p. 327): "The jurists of our country have a predilection for practical and realistic projects, and they are not interested in trying out procedures which are somewhat spectacularly introduced into the social sciences from time to time. For this reason survey methods like those widely used in certain countries—the United States, for example—have hardly been put into practice at all in Belgium. Their illusory character is distrusted. . . . Informed opinion also distrusts methods derived from applied psychology, or what is called collective psychology. In any case, there exist no serious works or important publications based on these types of investigation."

In psychology and sociology, however, abortive attempts were made to use psychology in political analyses. In Italy Vilfredo Pareto developed a theory of "residues"; in France Gabriel Tarde wrote an important book on imitations, which—through the philosophy of James Mark Baldwin and the sociology of Charles H. Cooley—influenced George Herbert Mead and helped to clarify important issues in what later became known as "symbolic interactionism." Freud ([1911] 1948) pioneered the study of political leaders "at a distance" when, on the basis of an autobiographical account and his psychopathological theory, he diagnosed a judge in Saxony, Daniel Paul Schreber, as suffering from psychotic paranoia. After World War I, Freud also undertook the task of reformulating his theory of personality in terms of id, ego, and superego. In England Graham Wallas (1908) had reacted against the prevailing tendency in political science and law to see political deliberations as enlightened statecraft; and toward the end of the 1920s, George Catlin, on Hobbesian assumptions, tried to formulate his own version of political man. In Germany Willy Hellpach (1952), a social psychologist trained in what Wundt had called *Völkerpsychologie,* advocated the use of psychology for political analysis. But the real "takeoff" for political psychology was the assimilation of psychoanalysis in the research done by the Institute of Social Research in Frankfurt.

Vilfredo Pareto (1848-1923). Pareto's interest in social science arose in the 1890s; that is, at the time when Émile Durkheim, Henri Bergson, and Max Weber began to formulate their theories. "At the outset," says his British interpreter (Finer, 1976, p. 7), "he was a devout, albeit critical, believer in the dominant philosophies of reason, democracy, and progress. Within ten years, however, in complete independence of these contemporaries, he had run up against their common problem and came up with a similar answer. Like them he sensed the intrusion of the human personality into the framing of what had hitherto been regarded as objective laws established by naked intellect."

The works of Pareto are voluminous. As was customary at the time, he tried to formulate a general theory of the subjects to which he directed his attention. It was a quest for holism in science that began to disappear as expertise rose and encyclopedism declined. In place of a search for general theories, the social sciences became compartmentalized into such subjects as "criminal psychology," "work sociology," "school psychology," and "leisure sociology." To Pareto and his contemporaries, such narrowness indicated a lack in education and was, consequently, deplorable.

Pareto had a background in civil engineering and was an able mathematician as well as a pioneer in economics. As a matter of fact, like Weber, he regarded sociology as a supplement to economics in areas where its theory of value, as determined by market factors, could not be applied. Although an aristocrat, he despised aristocracy and was for a time an ardent supporter of republicanism, free trade, democracy, and disarmament. In the late 1890s, however, he became an antidemocrat, having concluded that the rise of working-class power through trade unionism and universal suffrage would merely mean the replacement of one set of privileges for another and the rise of a new form of oppression. He was, so to speak, caught between the mainstreams of the two major political tendencies of his time—namely, capitalism and socialism. He despised both as perversions of reason. He also opposed conservative autocracy and believed mainly in the eternal rule of elites.

From a scientific standpoint, Pareto held that nonlogical actions are often treated as if they are matters of fact even if they have no other basis than prejudice. He attributed this process to an inherent tendency in human nature to "logicalize"—a Freudian would say "rationalize"—nonrational actions so as to make them seem logical. Introducing a conception of political utility borrowed from economics, Pareto then argued that whether beliefs, concepts, and theories are logical or not is a matter separate from their political utility. Therefore, in sociology propaganda and irrational beliefs, what his contemporary Gaetano Mosca called "myths," should not be judged by rational criteria but by their utility. In this respect Pareto closely resembles Machiavelli.

According to Pareto, beliefs, concepts, and theories—at both the scientific and the everyday levels—contain two elements: a constant element, the *residue,* expressing psychological states of mind; and a logical or pseudological element, the *derivation,* tricking and masking the residue. Whereas, in Pareto's view, it is necessary to purify science by disclosing the derivations, in political life such purification is not absolutely essential. Since his economics predisposed him toward value relativism, his essential goal for sociology was to investigate the patterns of preference in culture and politics by means other than economic ones.

In one of his first systematic attempts to analyze nonlogical action, *Les Systèmes socialistes* (The socialist systems), Pareto (1902) tried to come to terms with his own previous political activism and to reconcile it with his new sociology. At the end of the 1890s, he lectured in Lausanne, Switzerland, and finally was appointed to an academic chair there. He developed a synthesis between value relativism and social relativism, which is the outstanding property of the above-mentioned book.

According to Pareto, genuine liberals tend to regard opinions and beliefs as something that people choose; in contrast, conservatives and socialists regard them as predetermined. For the conservatives opinions and beliefs are genetically determined; for the socialists they are socially determined. Pareto, however, saw these different orientations as associated with social stratification. And he interpreted social stratification in power terms—that is, in the language of political relations. He held that the great majority of people in industrial countries—those lacking power—are moved, in the main, not by logical reason but by the impact of derivations: "Reason is of little or no importance in shaping social phenomena. The operative forces are different ones; this is what I want to prove in my sociology. Men think they are choosing their opinions, but instead these are imposed on them by their mode of life just as it is imposed on fish that they must breathe through gills and on mammals that they must breathe through lungs" (quoted by Finer, 1976, p. 20).

Pareto's diagnosis here resembles Lenin's more than Le Bon's. Both Pareto and Lenin were, of course, familiar with Max Scheler's "sociology of knowledge" and with the Marxist theory of ideology. They were both influenced by this mode of analysis. In their "predictions"—or should one say preferred expectations—they differed because Lenin had a dynamic view of social structure, whereas Pareto's was static. Although Pareto formulated a theory of circulating elites, his view was nevertheless static, since he held that the rule of the few over the many is an inevitable fact of history, nature, and human society.

Pareto died ten months after the Fascist march on Rome. His insistence on denouncing both capitalism and socialism, along with his disbelief in democracy and conservative autocracy, justifies the allegations sometimes made that he was the great theorist of fascism. For the day-to-day political events in Italy, however, Pareto could not even in an indirect way be held responsible. Mussolini's men were not in any sense *literati* but people who had suffered psychological injuries in World War I, often together with considerable losses in economic and personal security. They were the victims of conditions that Pareto had described and tried to explain, first as a radically optimistic young liberal and later as a detached and pessimistic scholar.

Raymond Aron (1937), in an article on Pareto's sociology published by the *Zeitschrift für Sozialforschung*, criticized both the psychological assumptions and the historical analyses at the core of Pareto's social theory. Particularly in the second part of his article, Aron compared Pareto's method with the results of psychoanalysis and the Marxist theory of ideology, in order to show that Pareto was unable to demonstrate—both empirically and logically—the psychological roots of the derivations or to assess their significance within a wider historical context. Aron convincingly alleged that the weakness in Pareto's theory is its inability to account for change. To Pareto the nature of man and society are eternally the same; there are no short circuits to individual or cultural betterment.

Nonetheless, Pareto occupies an important position in political psychology today, through the work of Talcott Parsons and Elton Mayo. Although Pareto's cynical views on social engineering lurk behind the "human relations school" that Mayo (1949, 1951) helped to shape, it is not far-fetched to say that indirectly Pareto helped to humanize factory work in both the United States and Western Europe. His early dreams of social and material progress, his search for human perfectibility, and his insistence on using the scientific method, however inadequate his own may appear today, have, thus, come to play an important role in the social reaction against views he held as an old and politically cynical man on the eve of Fascist violence and antihumanism.

Gabriel Tarde (1843-1904). "We have lost the habit of reading Tarde," says Boudon (1980, p. 62) in *The Crisis in Sociology,* "and certainly not just recently. Even very old sociology textbooks include scarcely more on Tarde than a more or less paraphrased version of Durkheim's critique." Although there was a single attempt to rescue the contributions of Tarde in an American reader toward the end of the 1960s (Tarde, 1969), nobody seems to know very much about Gabriel Tarde these days—especially not in France, where the Durkheimians in general and Marcel Mauss in particular have made major attempts to conceal the ideas of a man who, as a contemporary of Durkheim, was once regarded as equally if not more important.

As an example of the successful impact of the Durkheimians' concealment, we may quote from *The Discovery of Society* (Collins and Makowsky, 1972, p. 82), where an attempt to explain Durkheim's antipsychological theories is made: "In 1885 [Durkheim] had paid a visit to the laboratory of Wilhelm Wundt in Germany, who had just created the science of experimental psychology out of an old philosophical field of speculation. But psychology in France was overshadowed by conservative crowd-psychologists like Gabriel Tarde and Gustave Le Bon. Durkheim, instead, adopted the sociology of Comte and Spencer, which emphasized a realm of phenomena above the psychological level." One does no justice to Tarde by lumping him together with Le Bon, whose idea of a "racial soul" Tarde explicitly attacked. Whereas it is correct that Tarde was critical of Herbert Spencer's conception of evolution, since he took it to be too ambitious and preferred the term "transformations," he was hardly a conservative of the sort that Le Bon was.

It is symptomatic that in Parsons's ([1937] 1968) *The Structure of Social Action,* Tarde is mentioned only once: in a second source reference in a footnote outlining Sorokin's (1928, p. 212) description of the differences between Tarde and Durkheim (see p. 385 of 1968 edition), a reference that does no justice to Sorokin's extensive treatment of Tarde as a pioneer in the social sciences who tried to ward off such speculative organismatic theories as Le Bon's.

Among the social scientists at the end of the nineteenth century, Tarde occupied one of the very few prominent academic positions available. He came to social psychology and political sociology through law and criminal statistics; and, according to Boudon (1980, p. 75), he "directly envisages the notions behind Guttman scales, linear scales, scales to show saturation effects, etc." Tarde held the chair of modern philosophy at the Collège de France between 1899 and 1904. His philosophical inclinations made his otherwise friendly reviewer Sorokin (1928, p. 637) say of him that he "was rather a social philosopher than an accurate scientific scholar. Many of his theories lack the necessary accuracy and clearness; and some others are rather speculative."

Unlike Durkheim and Pareto, Tarde did not provide a systematic statement of his methodology. In his early works on criminal statistics, Tarde criticized the classical and Italian criminologists, especially Cesare Lombroso, and claimed that crime is caused primarily by social conditions—although individuals still must be held responsible for the commission of crimes. He harbored a chronic suspicion of dogmatism, and in many of his polemical works, he maintained that the complex aspects of social reality cannot be subsumed or reduced to the properties of rigid systems. He thought that Durkheim was too doctrinaire in his positivism, whereas Durkheim constantly alleged that Tarde was too inclined to subjectivism to be included in the new science of sociology.

Tarde's theories may be summarized as follows: Human society is basically psychical in nature. The beliefs and desires of interacting individuals are the cornerstones on which to construct a theory of society; for where there is psychical interaction, there is also society. Where no psychical interaction can be observed, there is no society. As Sorokin (1928, p. 637) says, "Tarde, although a psychological sociologist, at the same time refuses to join either psychosocial or biological organicism. He emphatically rejects all theories of a 'social mind' or 'collective soul,' and so on."

The mental interaction that Tarde had in mind consists of an exchange and circulation of beliefs and desires, this being the essence of the social process. He distinguished three basic forms of this process: repetition or imitation, opposition, and adaptation or invention. According to Tarde, any new fashion, idea, or belief originating in the mind of an individual will sooner or later be repeated or imitated by other people. There ensues a wave of imitations, which spread through society. At some point in this process of diffusion, these new ideas collide with the old or with other new ideas. Such collisions may have three types of outcomes: (1) If the diffusion processes are equally strong and incompatible, they may destroy each other. (2) There may be a mutual adaptation; that is, a new combination of original ideas, which for Tarde is equal to a new invention. (3) The stronger diffusion process may destroy the weaker.

Tarde paid special attention to convergent patterns in the process of ideational diffusion and applied his basic propositions to political and other social phenomena. Sorokin (1928, p. 320 n.) rightly points out that Tarde was one of the earliest theorists who classified the phenomenon of opposition into three basic forms—that is, war, competition, and polemics—although this classification is usually attributed to Georg Simmel. Tarde did not regard social opposition as eternally determining progress, as Lenin and the Marxists had done in their consideration of class antagonisms or as Le Bon and the heirs of Hegel had done with respect to the relations between states. Instead, Tarde and some of his contemporaries believed that the disappearance of war and physical violence in the struggle for existence in human societies was more or less inevitable.

An example of this optimism in Tarde's theory is found in *Penal Philosophy:* "The effect of militarism is to exhaust the criminal passions scattered through every nation, to purify them in concentrating them, and to justify them by making them serve to destroy one another, under the superior form which they thus assume. After all is said and done, war enlarges the sphere of peace, as crime formerly used to enlarge the sphere of honesty. This is the irony of history" ([1912] 1968, p. 422). Unfortunately, Tarde's philosophy here did not stand up to empirical proof. In his own statistical investigations of criminality after the 1870–71 war between Germany and France, he himself discovered that crime rates were actually rising. In *Les Transformations du pouvoir* (The transformations of power) Tarde (1899) tried to give political science its sociological baptism; but in this area, as well as in most other areas where he tried new ways to make the study of society more scientific, he was premature and did not manage to solve many of the substantial problems which he, through intuition, actually saw (Boudon, 1980, p. 76).

As late as 1950, Aron (p. 52) could still say of politics as an academic field in France: "So far, political science has been either the pet hobby of scholars of other disciplines or the work of amateurs." Aron attributed this state of affairs to the psychology of the French university system. In two recent studies, however, Apfelbaum (1981) and Lubek (1981) show that the emancipatory tendencies in French sociology, and Durkheimian sociology in particular, were much more influential than these factors.

The political scientist Pierre Favre presents more details. In particular, Favre (1982) points out that in the bibliographical section of *L'Année sociologique*, Durkheim set up and used a systematic classification of the social sciences that failed to cover the entire field of social science—specifically, politics and psychology. Other Durkheimians, after 1918, were willing to modify the classification, but they systematically ruled out any separate place for political sociology and political psychology. These areas were denied the status of social science—unlike, for example, legal, moral, and economic sociology and the sociology of religion. Thus, the concern of sociology to emancipate itself from economics, medicine, and the humanities caused a delay in the development of political psychology and political science for nearly half a century. The delay was bolstered by a debate in which exaggerated emphasis was placed on the difference between macro and micro social artifacts. The coterie of the Durkheimians, in the end, managed to submerge the ideas and research of their opponents almost in the manner described by Kuhn (1963). But in the aftermath of World War II, the French colonial defeat in Indochina and Algeria, and the rise of Charles de Gaulle, students of politics as a science tried new paths to academic acceptance.

Sigmund Freud (1856–1939). The role of Freudian psychoanalysis in the developing science of political psychology was rather indirect and very general. As a young and ambitious man, Freud had been inclined to liberal ideas. He particularly took an interest in the British utilitarian doctrines. During his life he also at times reflected on Marxism but admitted that he found many of its ideas strange and awkward.

"It is proper to speak of Freud's 'political psychology' only in a very limited sense," says Roazen (1970, p. 242), who has successfully reconstructed the fragments of Freud's scattered notes on politics, society, and psychoanalysis. Freud regarded social analysis as nothing but an instance of applied psychology; and, as Billig (1976, p. 9) has pointed out, Freud "claims that all psychoanalysis is in fact social psychology and that there is no sharp distinction between individual and social psychology." In this respect Freud resembles Tarde, with whose work he was familiar (Freud, [1921] 1968, p. 27).

The case of Daniel Paul Schreber (Freud, [1911] 1948) was not primarily intended as a study in political psychology. Since he was a judge in Saxony, Schreber was widely discussed among psychological experts and an informed public after his *Memoirs* were published in 1903. However, Freud did not concern himself with the case until 1910, although earlier in his career as a psychopathologist he had worked on the etiology of paranoid psychotic delusions. The Schreber analysis, and the diagnosis of paranoia that Freud was able to distill out of it, has played a vital role in psychiatric work in this area of psychopathology, which is strange considering that Freud's major interest was *not* psychosis but neurosis. What made Freud pay special attention to Schreber's case were the open confessions of homosexual fantasies that appeared in Schreber's autobiographical account and the precision with which the details of the illness could be made to fit into Freud's basic theory.

A modern approach to what Freud saw would, perhaps, have taken into account more of the political environment than Freud did. According to Zamansky (1968), for example, it is now a well-established fact that paranoia operates selectively—that is, in fields such as politics, religion, and science, and more often in males around fifty than, say, among other groups of people in other walks of life. The "social psychology" in these Freudian interpretations, as in Freud's other case studies, was by and large limited to the interaction patterns in childhood and the repression of instinctual wishes, on the one hand, and, on the other hand, to the regressions that appear later in adult life when subjects encounter vicissitudes similar to those that were submerged at earlier stages of psychobiological development. In *Massenpsychologie und Ich-Analyse* (Group psychology and the analysis of the ego), Freud ([1921] 1968) still operated within the confines of this conception. *Massenpsychologie*, which is an abstract theoretical work, had three major sources: Le Bon's *La Psychologie des foules* (1895), Freud's own *Totem and Taboo* ([1913] 1952), and various papers on narcissism written during the war. Like Tarde, Freud in his social psychology used the individual as the basic unit for an explanation of changes and more static characteristics of groups. However, he got most of his ideas for a social psychology from Le Bon. He then adapted those ideas to fit his own previously developed conceptions.

As Billig (1976, p. 11) has pointed out, "It [was] not so much the political contents of Le Bon's theses that most attracted Freud—rather, it was the similarities between Le Bon's descriptions of the mental states of crowd members with some of the formulations of psychoanalytic theory." Le Bon's discussion of the role that the crowd or masses can play in the appearance of irrationality supplied a link for Freud in his search for a relation between individuals and aggregates. Like Le Bon, Freud recognized a hypnotic relationship among the crowd members, on the one hand, and between these crowd members and the leader, on the other. But unlike Le Bon, Freud did not simply debunk leadership; instead, he treated it as analogous to family relationships. Freud particularly emphasized the ambivalent emotions in the leader-follower relationship and explained them by means of a theory in which the *narcissism of minor differences* is central.

"Narcissism of minor differences" means that as social animals we tend to dislike those in our environment who differ only slightly from us with respect to such values as skill, strength, power, prestige, and possession. Those who are totally different can be "boxed in" and regarded as outside legitimate boundaries of social comparison. If Tarde was right about imitation in groups, then narcissism of small differences would introduce an ambivalent element in interpersonal and interorganizational relations. Lenin as a political leader is a suitable case in point.

He constantly engaged in conflicts with people he was trying to lead whose views were close to his own. His attempts to distance himself from such people through polemics and ideological persecution, on the one hand, and through emphasizing his own virtues, on the other, is suggestive of the phenomenon of narcissism of minor differences. An alternative psychoanalytic theory, used by Leites (1953, p. 403 ff.), poses a far more speculative set of propositions to account for the same type of phenomenon—namely, the theory of latent homosexuality. This theory, however, requires data that are usually not available to political analysts. It would, consequently, be less useful for empirical study as long as it is not specified in greater detail and validated on the basis of nonclinical data.

For the sake of completeness, a theory of such conflicts would also have to take into account the typology of in-group "deviants" suggested by Coser (1956, p. 101), where "heretics," "renegades," and "dissenters" are distinguished and discussed in a manner compatible with Freud's theory. Tendencies toward such an integration are presently visible in the phenomenological approach of Peter L. Berger and Thomas Luckmann (1967) and in the political psychology of Thomas Leithäuser, Walter Heinz, Birgit Volmerg, Gunther Salje, Ute Volmerg, and Bernhard Wutka (Leithäuser, 1976; Leithäuser and Heinz, 1980; Leithäuser and others, 1981).

Other Contributions Before the 1930s. Among the many noteworthy contributions of political psychology in Western Europe before the 1930s were those of Graham Wallas and George Catlin in England, Willy Hellpach and Karl Jaspers in Germany, and the Bühlers in Vienna, Austria. In France Georges Politzer attempted to formulate a concrete psychology, and Paul Federn wrote an optimistic essay on what he believed would be the blessings of the new society that Lenin and the Bolsheviks had tried to create. Already in 1909 Alfred Adler had presented a paper on Marxism before the psychoanalytic association of Vienna (Dahmer, 1967, p. 273 ff.; Hydén, 1980), but he had obviously misunderstood the philosophy of Marx, regarding it as a sort of hedonism. Under the growing menace of fascism and national socialism, the Frankfurt Institute of Social Research invited psychoanalysts such as Erich Fromm to participate in a research project on authoritarianism and family life, a project greatly stimulated by the writings of Wilhelm Reich (Jay, 1973, p. 86 ff.; Sanford, 1973). Where a juxtaposition between Marxism and psychoanalysis was attempted, what mattered was that the scientific method became more and more accepted, and introspective philosophy tended to decline. Charlotte and Karl Bühler, with the aid of Paul Lazarsfeld, Marie Jahoda, and Hans Zeisel, pioneered empirical sociological research in Vienna with a study of unemployment. At the same time, Karl Jaspers ([1919] 1960) in Heidelberg completed his *Psychologie der Weltanschauungen* (The Psychology of world views), and Martin Heidegger ([1927] 1962) wrote *Being and Time*, which influenced Theodor Adorno's intellectual development.

According to Murphy (1949, p. 434), "In Germany the cleavage had widened during the nineteenth century between 'natural science psychology,' concerned with laboratory activities, and 'cultural science psychology', concerned with the critical and philosophical study of man in society." The sociologist Theodor Geiger was, however, a living example to the contrary. Influenced by the Danish epistemologist Herbert Iversen and by the Swedish philosopher of justice Axel Hagerström, he made both intensive and extensive studies of totalitarianism. In

1910 Wilhelm Wundt published a ten-volume set of research reports on *Völkerpsychologie*, despite the fact that he was the founder of experimental studies; and Willy Hellpach similarly wrote books in both the cultural and the experimental tradition.

Before we continue our overview, let us, however, take a somewhat closer look at two British contributors who in many respects are still valuable and inspiring, although widely neglected—namely, Graham Wallas and George Catlin. As Stone (1981, p. 2) correctly has remarked, "The emergence of political psychology in the twentieth century bears witness to Harold Lasswell's preeminence in the field but suggests that Graham Wallas has a prior claim to foundership." Rowse, in his introduction to the 1947 edition of Wallas's *Human Nature in Politics* ([1908] 1947), likewise said that Wallas was a pioneer in the application of psychology to political thinking.

Besides being a teacher at the London School of Economics and Political Science, where Harold Lasswell had been his student in 1923–24, Wallas was also a Fabian Socialist and a political activist. One may suspect that the critical attitude of the Fabians in their view of day-to-day politics motivated Wallas to see political life as permeated by irrationalism. In the Fabian analysis of politics, ideology was regarded as essential for a correct social diagnosis, just as it was to the Leninists— although the Fabians espoused philosophical idealism, in contrast to the materialism of the Leninists. Ultimately, after extensive study, Wallas came to the same conclusions that Freud had come to through clinical work. However, when Wallas wrote *Human Nature in Politics,* he was ignorant of Freud's work. Freud never played a major role in Wallas's political psychological ideas—a fact that makes him all the more interesting since virtually all political psychology since the 1920s has had a Freudian twist to it. It was rather through William McDougall's instinctivism that Wallas saw the political world.

Wallas was, however, a man divided against himself. As Allport (1954, p. 18) has pointed out: "A few years [after the publication of *Human Nature in Politics*] . . . Wallas became alarmed at the onesidedness of the resulting picture, and wrote a second treatise to counteract the irrationalism of his first production." In the preface to his second book, *The Great Society,* Wallas (1914, p. v) published a letter to Walter Lippmann, to whom he admitted: "The earlier book was an analysis of representative government, which turned into an argument against nineteenth-century intellectualism. . . . This book is an analysis of the general social organization of a large modern state, which has turned, at times, into an argument against certain forms of twentieth-century anti-intellectualism."

It is, perhaps, an irony of the epoch in which Wallas lived that in 1908 he could write (p. 21), "Whoever sets himself to base his political thinking on a reexamination of human nature must begin by trying to overcome his own tendency to exaggerate the intellectuality of mankind," only to claim, on the eve of World War I, when evidence told heavily against it, "The biological and psychological arguments against the possibility of organized peace among the Great Powers seem insufficient" (1914, p. xi).

Not surprisingly, George Catlin's (1930) book *A Study of the Principles of Politics* was dedicated to Edward Titchener and Graham Wallas. Catlin and Harold Laski at the London School of Economics had belonged to the same circle as Wallas and had influenced Lasswell when he attempted to make political psychology a field of study in the United States in the early 1930s. For Catlin a main line of intellectual stimulation had come from an intensive study of Thomas Hobbes (Catlin, 1922, 1932, 1950; Eulau, 1970, p. 133). Catlin (1950, p. 232) noted that "Hobbes was a psychologist, perhaps the first observational psychologist. Very properly and significantly he bases his politics on his psychology." But Catlin (1927, p. 134, p. 143) was critical of both the single-value postulate of Hobbes (power sought for its own sake as a basic human trait) and contemporary political science, which, Catlin thought, failed "to deliver the goods." He was somewhat more optimistic about the potentialities of psychology, although he issued a warning note (Catlin, 1927, p. 184): "Politics certainly cannot afford to be independent of psychology, but it will not be wisely advised to make use dogmatically of psychological concepts of which psychologists of authority dispute the validity. Its use of these concepts should be hypothetical, selective, and derivative, not primary and dogmatic."

It was central to Catlin's concern to distinguish political science from political philosophy: "Modern psychology forbids us to copy Hobbes or Helvetius, Bentham or Tarde" (1930, p. 29). Eulau (1970, p. 133) is, nevertheless, right in saying that "A work such as George E. G. Catlin's *The Science and Method of Politics*, perhaps the only systematic attempt to investigate the assumptions of political science as science, had no influence whatsoever on the course of the discipline, possibly because its strong individualistic and Hobbesian premises did not square with immediate realities as experienced by most political scientists."

Like Tarde, Catlin was prematurely discussing new and systematic ways to explore the multiverses of political psychology. Symptomatically, Catlin (1930, p. 125, p. 243 ff.) also derived inspiration from Tarde's (1899) *Les Transformations du pouvoir* (The transformation of power). This inspiration permitted him to make an outline of the premises, processes, and consequences of *dynamic equilibrium* before there was any discussion of this concept outside Marxist sociology— that is, outside the version of Bukharin's ([1921] 1969) *Historical Materialism.*

On approximately the same grounds as those discussed in the present overview, Catlin (1930, p. 253 n.) alleged that Pareto was "the godfather of fascism." Nevertheless, he (p. 31 n.) approvingly quoted Pareto's (1909, p. 40) *Manuel d'économie politique* (A Manual of political economy), to the effect that "La psychologie est évidemment à la base de l'économie politique et, en général, de toutes les sciences sociales" ("Psychology is, obviously, at the bottom of political economy and, generally, of all the social sciences").

Catlin's psychological analysis of fascism was later to be confirmed by empirical political psychology. According to Catlin (1930, p. 253 n.): "The technical merit of fascismo is that it appeals, as usually only war does, both to the conservative and adventurous elements in man, to his desire for discipline, for being ordered and led—every man, as every woman, occasionally likes an emotional surrender of responsibility to his self-abasing (masochistic) and his self-asserting (or even sadistic) impulses."

With Catlin there emerged in political psychology a distinction between form and content, between utility and truth, in what was judged to be science. According to Catlin (1927, p. 145): "Science, as such, is concerned neither with what ought to be nor with what happens to be, but with what must be when the conditions are fulfilled, with 'what must be, if.' " Like Pareto before him, Catlin

(1950, p. 3) maintained and stressed the amoral element in science by insisting that the study of politics is a study of how to gain control over men and things. "It is a study of power. But, like the humanities, it involves discussion and assessment of values. The first of these fields is that of political science. The second is that of political philosophy."

Thus, with Catlin the scientific study of politics is back where Machiavelli left off. We reach a point in the development of political psychology where logical empiricism and positivism once more become emphasized. As adequate new techniques for the measurement and observation of human motives and behaviors developed in response to the requirements of the war exigencies, this stance tended to dominate the patterns and developments of social science in general and political psychology in particular. It was, simultaneously, a stance whose roots could no longer be described as genuinely European.

New Edifices and Patterns

The qualifications for advancing a Western European science of political psychology turned out to be exacting. The impact of fascism and national socialism made social scientists in general, and political scientists in particular, aware of the need to look for patterns of interaction among social structures and mental processes in the industrial societies (Billig, 1976; Horn, 1982; Mitscherlich, 1970). Horn (1972, p. 189) points out: "An adequate problem consciousness demands the transcendence of existing disciplinary boundaries. Political psychology must be as open to economic as to science-theoretical issues."

In the early 1950s, the division between the cultural and the experimental approaches to political psychology had, nevertheless, not been completely overcome. In West Germany the two major personalities associated with the pathbreaking studies of fascism and authoritarianism, Max Horkheimer and Theodor Adorno, returned to Frankfurt to set up, anew, the Institute for Social Research, which in the 1930s had been driven into American exile by political developments in Germany and France. They continued their work on what they themselves had called a "critical theory" of society; that is, a type of theory that puts emphasis on the social and political relevance of research premises, problem selection, and the projected consequences of presented results. While there was caution in other quarters not to engage in normative arguments and to stress the social utility of political psychology research, Horkheimer and Adorno, as former refugees, were in a position to claim social relevance and, indeed, social foundation for any type of research—social as well as natural science—that became the object of their investigations. They continued to launch criticisms against objectifying social science where no explicit mention was made of the total human condition. They also reacted against the scientific integration advocated by, for example, proponents of general systems theory. "Das Feldgeschrei nach der Integration der Wissenschaften ist Ausdruck der Hilflosigkeit, nicht des Fortschritts" ("The battle cry for an integration of the sciences is an expression of helplessness, not of advance") wrote Adorno (1955, p. 18) in an article against Parsons's attempt to integrate sociology and psychoanalysis.

An explicit appeal for political psychology studies was made in West Germany by Walter Jacobsen at the Second Congress of the German Psychological

Association in 1949. His appeal did not, however, have much result. "Only in 1958 did the German Psychological Association succeed in establishing a 'Political Psychology Section.' Most of the colleagues greeted the publication of its aims and tasks with reserve. . . . One must remember that in addition to a general tendency to suppress the past during that time, the slogan 'Politics?—Without me!' was popular" (Jacobsen, 1978, p. 2). Other psychologists who participated in setting up the section were Max Simoneit, Eduard Weisner, Heinz Wolf, and Karl-Dieter Hartmann (Wolf, 1972, p. 777 n.).

In addition to the approaches of the Frankfurt school and those of traditional German psychology, a third center of gravity for the growth and dispersion of political psychology came through the "behavioral revolution" in sociology, mainly an American influence which in the late 1950s also asserted itself in political science in Europe. Behavioralism—which should not be confused with behaviorism—was, however, not mainly a plea for the psychological study of politics, although many of its American founders were inspired by psychoanalysis. Most often in the early "behavioral studies" of politics, the psychological aspect was "blackboxed," and anthropomorphism—the imputation of motives to collectivities—tended to substitute for a genuine psychological analysis of political decision making at both intra- and international levels of analysis.

Reestablishment of Political Studies in Germany. In the late 1940s, the Allied military forces in Germany carried out a massive denazification program in all the occupied zones (Fürstenau, 1969). After the more spectacular events of the Nuremberg trials, the whole German population was surveyed, interrogated, and labeled for degrees of Nazi involvement. This process was carried out by popular tribunals, and people were classified by means of a five-point scale. No one was to be considered totally innocent. There were several scandals where active Nazi party members bought themselves "Persilscheine"—that is, papers saying that their pasts were "white as snow." According to Horkheimer (1950, p. 236), the denazification program was generally felt to be a failure.

In political science and psychology, practitioners in social science professions who were of non-Jewish descent had managed in many cases to continue their studies under the pretext of value neutrality, legal positivism, or collaboration with the dictatorship. In sociology in general, and political sociology in particular, there was, however, a virtual extinction of the profession and, thus, a revival after 1945. In sociology, for example, two thirds of all academic personnel had emigrated, in most cases to the United States. Others, such as Alfred Weber, had resigned with pensions, and still others had chosen new professions that were less vulnerable to national socialist criticism. Leopold von Wiese came back to Germany, and on his initiative the German Association for Sociology was reestablished in 1946. He was elected president and remained in this position until 1955 (Lepsius, 1979, p. 26).

In the reemergence of empirical political science in West Germany, Berlin soon became a major center. Otto Stammer, one of the major driving forces behind the new political science, had been a student of Hermann Hellers, who in turn was one of the most important contributors on political science to the *Encyclopedia of the Social Sciences* (1932). In 1954 Stammer became the director of Berlin's Institute of Political Science. The influence of his students slowly began to make itself felt in the academic world. It was, at this time, important to have a center for the empirical study of political processes, since sociologists were often reluctant to approach political issues for approximately the same reasons as the psychologists were (Lepsius, 1979, p. 39 ff.).

The growth of empirical political studies in West Germany during the 1950s was, however, quite modest. New centers began to appear as the democratic processes started to produce material for study, and political science itself became in some places—for example, at the University of Freiburg—a contributor to the growth of political education. Arnold Bergstrasser's contribution to enlightened political citizenship was a major element in political science in West Germany in the 1950s.

At the business school of Mannheim, which later became a university, Rainer Lepsius, Rudolf Wildenmann, and Wolfgang Hirsch-Weber were wholly in the mainstream of what we today call modern empirical political analysis; that is, the analysis of politics by means of scientific sociological and sociopsychological methods. Hirsch-Weber and Klaus Schütz (who later became mayor of Berlin), for example, together published an impressive study of the German electorate in 1957. Other names of importance were Iring Fetscher and Wolfgang Abendroth at the universities of Frankfurt and Marburg, respectively, whose interest in Marxism as a set of theoretical and empirical propositions was only paralleled by the sociologist Ralf Dahrendorf's, then at the University of Tübingen.

Much of what had developed in the German-speaking tradition before and during the years when many able scholars worked abroad never seemed to come back once the Nazi period was over. In Austria neither the Vienna tradition of science theory (Karl Popper and the logical empiricists) nor the methodologically pioneering empirical sociology (Lazarsfeld, Jahoda, and Zeisel, 1933) had any deep impact in the 1950s.

Cologne, however, had a research institute for social and behavioral sciences, where the important *Kölner Zeitschrift für Soziologie und Sozialpsychologie* began to reappear in 1948. Although inspired by American scholarship, the analyses flowing from this source were not merely a product of a Germanized version of Chicago or Ann Arbor. Lepsius (1979, p. 51) summarizes the American impact in the following way (my trans.): "The reception of American sociology remained selective and from an early date eclectic. It does not seem justified to talk of an 'Americanization' of sociology, if one does not thereby simply mean the adoption of the newer methods of empirical social research."

In political science it was not, perhaps, surprising that a split gradually developed between those who, during the Nazi regime, had remained in Germany and those who came back from abroad or who were raised in the modern tradition of political studies. The differences sometimes masqueraded as an enmity between *Allgemeine Staatslehre* ("general theory of the state") and political sociology, sometimes with a third party, the Marxists, attacking both of these positions. In 1960 Stammer tried to reconcile the differences between these groups, but without much success.

At the Frankfurt Institute, the attitude toward the new American emphasis on technique and methodology remained skeptical, to put it mildly. Adorno, Horkheimer, and Jurgen Habermas used Marxist and Freudian concepts in their social analyses, attacking advanced capitalism and the role of science in this social formation. Often they used a polemic where the vernacular balanced on the edge of pompous trash and pejorative accusations. Adorno, in particular, talked of the "pseudoproblems of behaviorism," of "odd values in the conception of value," and of "coarse and rough-mannered use of language" when describing Parsons's sociology. Words such as "positivism," "scientism," and "behaviorism" were afterward imputed, with pejorative connotations masking more precise meanings.

In summary, until about 1960 the growth of political psychology in West Germany, like that in the United States, resulted from a restless and deep concern with the traditional boundaries between politics, sociology, and psychology. Academic social scientists were driven to revise the old and to formulate new hypotheses with respect to political decision making, political order, and political personality. But political psychology remained, by and large, an amorphous field rather than a well-defined area of empirical and theoretical research.

Italy, France, and Scandinavia. Italy has had a long tradition of scholarly study in political psychology. The scientific credo of Machiavelli had been taken up anew by Vilfredo Pareto, Gaetano Mosca, and Roberto Michels in the period of classical social science—that is, from approximately 1880 to 1920. Although to some extent nourished by this development, fascism discontinued the social scientific tradition. Antonio Gramsci, one of the few important Marxists after the death of Lenin, was imprisoned but, nevertheless, managed to contribute substantially to contemporary political analysis through his *Prison Notebooks* ([1948] 1971), in which the concepts of skill, ideology, and power were put into a new conceptual framework, emphasizing *hegemony* over society as a whole, not just economic power, as a socialist goal. Gramsci, like many non-Marxist Italian intellectuals, was brought up in the tradition of Antonio Labriola and Pareto. His theoretical roots were also derived from Benedetto Croce's historiography. Unlike Croce, Gramsci did not allow his Hegelianism to develop into a full-blown antipositivism, although he—in contradistinction to many contemporary Marxists, notably Nikolai Bukharin—was prone to accept mental phenomena in political processes as equally important as the legal ownership of the means of production. In the 1950s social studies in Italy experienced a renewed empirical interest founded on theoretical influences from existentialism, phenomenology, and the Marxism of Gramsci. Croce's antitheoretical views, as far as social phenomena were concerned, gradually began to lose ground; that is, the idiographic emphasis gradually gave way to a more nomothetically inspired interest in politics and political psychology.

In political science a strict legal tradition—which had been strengthened during the years of Fascist rule—delayed the behavioral movement. The close boundaries in the rigid university system also contributed to the delay. Doctoral degrees were awarded from eight political science faculties (Bologna, Florence, Milan, Cattolica, Padua, Pavia, Perugia, and Rome). At the same time, eleven law faculties were entitled to award Ph.D. degrees in political science, and they often set the substantive standards and structured the content of courses. In political science the burden of the legal tradition was equal only to that in France, Belgium, and the Scandinavian countries.

Around 1960 the picture began to change. In both *Quaderni di sociologica* and *Il politico,* the two leading journals of sociology and political science, respectively, articles on political behavior, voting, alienation, and participation were increasingly published. Scholars with affiliations on both sides of the Atlantic— such as Joseph La Palombara, Mattei Dogan, Giovanni Sartori, and Gordon di

Renzo—were only the most conspicuous tips of an iceberg of growing interest in political psychology.

Italian political psychology, as it became known throughout political science and sociology publications, was often more Anglo-Saxon in its viewpoints than its other Western European counterparts. A crude content analysis of Passigli's (1971) overview of modern political analysis in Italy reveals, for example, that, despite its ambition to be an overview of *Italian* political studies, American and British sources made up 65 percent of all quoted sources, followed by Italian sources (17.5 percent), Italian-translated French sources (5.7 percent), French sources (5.1 percent), other—mostly German—sources (3.9 percent), and Italian-translated English sources (2.7 percent) (N = 331). One might question whether there was really an autonomous Italian approach at all.

In the French-speaking areas, there was no political science in the singular, and it is doubtful whether one could really speak of empirical political studies before the 1950s. In his overview article from 1950, Aron could still say of France: "Political science is not recognized either as a scientific discipline or as a university school" (p. 50). There was, for sure, an "École Libre de Science Politique," the original purpose of which had been to fill the lacunae of political leadership training after the military defeat against Germany in 1870. But—very much as in Denmark, where *statsvidenskab* (literally "state science") was being taught—the content of academic courses and research was jurisprudence, economics, and statistics rather than politics in the strictest sense. The impact of psychoanalytic and anthropological studies on the study of political phenomena was, even outside academia, marginal.

In Belgium Hendrik de Man (1928) had written *The Psychology of Socialism,* in which he advocated the application of psychoanalytic concepts, particularly those of Alfred Adler, to the study of political ideology. Like Harold Lasswell, de Man emphasized the importance of psychological compensation, and—also like Lasswell—he alleged that totalitarianism had its roots in the insecurity of the upwardly mobile middle-class power seekers. He could, for example, say: "Up to now a strong man has never come because he was called upon; real leaders are not elected by the masses; they impose themselves on them. Movements calling for a strong leader are movements of cowards and cowards are envious. They cannot stand strong leaders. At the bottom of their hearts they want leaders that are weak as compared to themselves" (de Man, 1928, p. 200; my trans.). The trouble with de Man's idea, like that of Lasswell, was that it was only a hypothesis with some face validity, not a statistically supported observation.

In France the scientific study of public opinion was not introduced until Jean Stoetzel in two books—*Théorie des opinions* (A theory of opinions) (1943) and *L'Étude experimentale des opinions* (The experimental study of opinions) (1945)—demonstrated what could be accomplished. These studies contributed to the status of the French Institute of Public Opinion and its bulletin, *Sondages,* as Gognel (1950, p. 508) has pointed out.

There is one name particularly associated with the behavioral breakthrough in French political science—namely, Maurice Duverger. In his textbook *Introduction à la politique* (1964), both psychological and psychoanalytic factors were adequately treated in a way that had up to then been unknown. Perhaps even more important, Duverger introduced scientific method in political science through an earlier textbook, *An Introduction to the Social Sciences with Special Reference to Their Methods* (1959). However, it was still the idea of a political sociology and a political geography, rather than a social psychology of politics, that attracted the attention of French political science scholars.

Interest in psychoanalysis, as far as political studies were concerned, was limited to a small group of existentialist philosophers with Marxist inclinations, such as the group around Jean-Paul Sartre. Georges Politzer's premature attempts to bridge the gap between experimental psychological studies, humanism, and Marxism in the late 1920s and early 1930s were nowhere revived, although Lucien Sève, a philosopher, tried to reconcile the various Soviet attempts to formulate a psychology with his own brand of Marxist social analysis. Jacques Lacan, though not a Marxist himself, probably played a more important role in the development of leftist political psychology in France, particularly through his influence on Louis Althusser and Nicos Poulantzas (Turkle, 1979). Unfortunately, however, the leftist interest in political psychology remained very much at the parlor and philosophical level. It produced no experimental or quasi-experimental results; and in its isolation from the mainstream, academic behavioral research failed to integrate results that could have given it a firmer foundation.

In the Scandinavian countries during the 1950s, the advances of political analysis as a separate academic discipline were uneven. In Sweden, for example, political science had a long tradition, going back to the seventeenth century (Bryder, 1980); but here, as in the other Scandinavian countries, or in Western Europe generally for that matter, the behavioral breakthrough did not occur before the 1950s and 1960s.

In Denmark there was no academic political science discipline outside history, law, and philosophy before 1959. Then Erik Rasmussen (1983), who had intellectual roots in historiography and philosophy, was appointed to a new chair in political science at the University of Aarhus. Together with Poul Meyer, one of Europe's leading experts in the field of public administration, he laid the institutional foundation for empirical—mostly sociological—studies of politics in Denmark. They soon coopted Erling Bjöl, an international relations expert, and H. P. Clausen, who was trained in history. With the expansion of the Danish welfare state, the department rapidly grew to become one of the biggest in Europe.

At the University of Copenhagen, political studies, like their French counterparts, were really not studies of politics but involved training for service in the central government's administration. In the 1950s and 1960s, however, an emphasis on electoral studies at the Institute of Political Studies paved the way for behavioral analysis. Outstanding contributions by experts on voting behavior and electoral statistics, such as Torben Worre and Hans Jorgen Nielsen, contributed both to the more orthodox study of political behavior and to the emerging, social psychologically inclined research of democratic electorates. In their efforts to make the study of the Danish electorate viable, they also collaborated with Ole Borre at the Department of Political Science at Aarhus, whose studies of nonvoting correlates and political volatility had a firm empirical basis.

In Norway, as in Italy, the exchange of social researchers with the United States left a deep imprint. In Bergen, Stein Rokkan and Knut Dahl Jacobsen were introducing behavioral analysis into political science and sociology, emphasizing the distinction between center and periphery and ideological cleavages. At Oslo

University Henry Valen became *the* expert on Norwegian voting behavior. In numerous research projects, often with the benign collaboration of American scholars such as Daniel Katz and Seymour Martin Lipset, Valen, like Rokkan and Dahl Jacobsen, helped to elevate the quality of Norwegian social research above that in many other European countries. The open attitude and stimulating research environment they encouraged became a valuable asset in the later part of the 1960s, when the total volume of social and political studies increased.

In the psychology department of the University of Oslo, Bjorn Christiansen in the late 1950s wrote an impressive political psychology study of citizen attitudes toward foreign policy, partly inspired and encouraged by Herbert Hyman (Christiansen, 1959). Several theoretical hypotheses concerning the individual roots of political involvement and participation were tested in a methodologically rigorous way. In a sense, this focus set a standard for later studies, of which those of Daniel Heradstveit—director of the Norwegian Institute of Foreign Affairs—are, perhaps, most outstanding. Using cognitive mapping and operational code techniques as frameworks for analysis, Heradstveit (1974, 1979) made detailed and complex in-depth probings of elite perceptions and cognitions in the Middle East, and helped to clarify several methodological issues in political psychology.

In Sweden the interest in behavioralism came mainly with Gunnar Sjöblom's (1968) *Party Strategies in a Multiparty System,* which influenced a whole generation of political scientists in Scandinavia. There had, in a sense, been previous behavioral studies of politics—for example, Ulf Himmelstrand's (1960) *Social Pressures, Attitudes, and Democratic Processes.* But Swedish political scientists seldom read sociological works in those days and, as a result, alienated themselves from the major research trends of empirical social studies in the outside world. Sjöblom's work, however, reversed this trend toward navel gazing. Many of his conceptions derived from Anthony Downs's (1957) theory of democracy and the framework for analyzing foreign policy devised by Richard Snyder (Snyder, Bruck, and Sapin, 1962). This behavioral compound was discussed within the confines of David Easton's (1965) theory of political systems.

Behavioralism as a mode of analyzing party behavior seldom resulted in explicit social psychological explanations. The assumptions of a social psychological framework underneath the analysis of goals and means of strategic behavior were, by and large, left open to empirical investigation. There was seldom any explicit reference to experimental or quasi-experimental research that could have provided a causally safer basis than the postulates usually singled out as governing principles of rationality. For political analysis, however, behavioralism meant that functional analysis had finally been able to assert itself against the institutional and legal approaches of previous generations. The plea for attention to the subjective element implied a break with the cruder forms of positivistic political sociology.

Toward New Foci and Autonomy

Summarizing the importance of behavioralism for Western European political psychology, one might say that the focus on standards of scientific as opposed to speculative thought, the emphasis on method and technique, and the concern with field data were the most important contributions. Often there were differences of opinion about what characterized *the* scientific element in social research. Such clashes of opinion were more frequent in Germany than in other Western European countries.

Niklas Luhmann (1983, p. 991) has alleged that "Germans use the concept of science *(Wissenschaft)* in a very broad sense. It includes the humanities, education, history, law, theology, and so on. Within this general field, which comprises everything that is taught at the universities, we find a kind of interdisciplinary commerce. Ideas are imported and exported and reimported. Concepts in one science become metaphors in another."

Around the end of the 1960s, psychological concepts were no longer used in a metaphorical sense among scholars studying politics as a science. The American behavioral movement had put a strong emphasis on psychological structures and processes as determinants of political thought and decisions, thereby neglecting the other side of the micro-macro relationship of power, influence, and authority in society. But, as Morton Deutsch (1983, p. 222) has pointed out: "European political psychology, although much influenced by American political psychology, has been less one-sided. The greater impact of the Marxist perspective in Europe has evoked more awareness of the role of political processes in shaping psychological processes and personalities."

It is, nevertheless, true that when this other side of the psycho-social interaction process began to receive attention, the traditional focus of behavioralism was not lost. As Franz Lehner (1974), a Swiss scholar trained at the University of Mannheim in both social psychology and political science, remarked a decade ago, there actually never was such a thing as a postbehavioral revolution in empirical political analysis, except in the sense that the psychological foundations of such things as voting behavior and elite studies became objects for more intense scrutiny, analysis, and critique. A new generation of scholars, educated in both politics and psychology, had grown up and were consciously opting for interdisciplinary scholarship.

The old problem of individualism *versus* society was gradually being replaced by a new political psychology and sociology, which emphasized relationships, mutual interaction, and change. More sophisticated methods—including time-series analysis, simulation, and factor analysis—were important in this process but not decisive. Primarily, theory shifted focus, and out of the criticism emerged an autonomous new field of political psychology. Michael Billig's (1976) *Social Psychology and Intergroup Relations,* a solid criticism of the old literature, positively contributed to the new trend in the English-speaking world. In a later application of the ideas put forward in this path-breaking study, Billig (1978) analyzed the fascism of the British National Front in ways that transcended many previously held views on authoritarianism, nazism, conservatism, and dogmatism.

Billig's work is, however, simply an example of a much more widespread tendency in political psychology, especially strong in the Federal Republic of Germany. After the abortive attempts to create a "Political Psychology Section" in the German Psychological Association in 1949, Walter Jacobsen began to edit a series of books in political psychology, starting in 1963. He was assisted by Kurt Aurin, Wanda von Bayer-Katte, Walter Jaide, Hans Wiesbroch, and Klaus Hartmann. Together the group managed to publish eight volumes of exceptional quality. In the early 1970s, a second major breakthrough came with the two-volume edition *Marxismus, Psychoanalyse, Sexpol (Socialism, psychoanalysis, sex)*, collected by Hans-Peter Gente (1970–71). In the first volume, the old controversy within the psychoanalytic movement concerning Marxism and political psychology was extensively redocumented. In the second volume, the new generation presented its views. There were contributions by Helmut Dahmer, Klaus Horn, and Peter Brückner, among others. Herbert Marcuse also had a chapter on instinct theory and freedom.

One of the outstanding features of German academic life in both the nineteenth and the twentieth centuries has been its tendency to divide into "schools of thought" on any major question or academic controversy. In the second volume of Gente's aforementioned edition, a group of political psychologists around Horn presented their contributions under the heading "Critical Theory of the Subject." Moser (1979) has pointed out that, in addition to this group, there also exist a more "traditional" group ("Critical Rationalists") and a Marxist group ("Critical Psychologists"). Many of the issues that distinguish these three groups from one another began to surface during the student revolts in the late 1960s, but they were already being given a more precise formulation during the so-called positivism dispute in sociology starting around 1961. Whereas the Marxists were not really party to this controversy in any other than an indirect way, the arguments of Adorno versus Popper, of Habermas versus Albert, and all the echoes of this fundamental—indeed, fundamentalistic in many respects—debate could lead to nothing but a reevaluation of the purpose and functions of social research (Adorno and others, 1976; Lenk, 1979). But, as with all genuine philosophical debates, the positivism debate did not lead to any solutions. This is not to say that it was valueless, for it had considerable value. But the positivism debate showed, above all, that conflicting views about the normative implications of social research and science generally can coexist in a pluralist scientific community, something unthinkable only a decade earlier.

Throughout the 1970s and during the early 1980s, this period of "peaceful coexistence"—which should not be mistaken for its lack of mutual criticism—began to produce many substantial results. Two major volumes, each called *Politische Psychologie* (Political psychology), were published. One was edited by Moser (1979); the other, by Klingemann, Kaase, and Horn (1981). Bernhard Claussen and Klaus Wasmund (1982) together undertook to edit a German handbook of political socialization, and Wasmund (1982) alone edited another first-class volume on the political attitudes and behaviors of adolescents. At the moment, political psychology is actually teeming with new publications. More as an introduction to political psychology than as a comprehensive overview, Ekkehard Lippert and Roland Wakenhut (1983) have recently edited a *Handwörterbuch der politischen Psychologie* (Dictionary of political psychology). The Political Psychology Section of the German Psychology Association is presently issuing eight new volumes on political psychology, of which three have already appeared at Beltz Verlag, a publishing company that specializes in political psychology (Moser, 1981; Preiser, 1982, 1983). In these volumes the theme is that neither cognitive nor emotive aspects can stand alone in a theory of political behavior but, rather, that these aspects should be studied together, not isolated. Nor should they be studied in terms of a simple functional tradeoff but in terms of patterns of actual political and historical evidence.

This brings us to the close of this examination of political psychology in Western Europe. But before we end, let us return to the initial theme of this chapter. Has political psychology begun, at last, to grasp in a more scientific manner the problems of peace and war, of revolutions and acquiescence as they manifest themselves in the human mind and in the political system? Are we any better off today in terms of theory than we were some hundred years ago, when the first prospects for a political psychology began to appear? We cannot, of course, know for sure, but books such as Volmerg, Volmerg, and Leithäuser's (1983) *Kriegsängste und Sicherheitsbedürfnis* (War anxiety and security needs) and Horn and Senghaas-Knobloch's (1983) *Friedensbewegung: Personlisches und politisches* (Peace movement: Personal and political factors) seem to indicate that we are heading in the right direction, with "warm hearts and cool brains."

References

Adorno, T. W. "Zum Verhältnis von Soziologie und Psychologie" [On the relationship between sociology and psychology]. In T. W. Adorno and W. Dirks (eds.), *Beiträge zur Soziologie*. Vol. 1. Frankfurt on Main: Europäische Verlagsanstalt, 1955.

Adorno, T. W., and others. *The Positivist Dispute in German Sociology*. London: Heinemann, 1976.

Allport, G. W. "The Historical Background of Modern Social Psychology." In G. Lindzey (ed.), *Handbook of Social Psychology*. Vol. 1. Reading, Mass.: Addison-Wesley, 1954.

Apfelbaum, E. "Origine de la psychologie sociale en France" [The origins of social psychology in France]. *Revue française de sociologie*, 1981, *22*, 397–407.

Aron, R. "La Sociologie de Pareto" [Pareto's sociology]. *Zeitschrift für Sozialforschung*, 1937, *6*, 489–521.

Aron, R. "Political Science in France." In *Contemporary Political Science*. Paris: UNESCO, 1950.

Berger, P. L., and Luckmann, T. *The Social Construction of Reality*. New York: Doubleday, 1967.

Bettelheim, B. *The Informed Heart*. London: Paladin Books, 1970.

Billig, M. *Social Psychology and Intergroup Relations*. London: Academic Press, 1976.

Billig, M. *Fascists: A Social Psychological View of the National Front*. San Diego: Harcourt Brace Jovanovich, 1978.

Boudon, R. *The Crisis of Sociology: Problems of Sociological Epistemology*. London: Macmillan, 1980.

Bryder, T. *Power and Responsibility: Contending Approaches to Industrial Relations and Decisionmaking in Britain 1963–1971*. Lund, Sweden: Gleerup, 1975.

Bryder, T. "A Brief Guide to the History, Locus and Focus of Swedish Political Science." *P.S. Newsletter of the American Political Science Association*, 1980, *12*, 89–91.

Bukharin, N. *Historical Materialism*. Ann Arbor, Mich.: University of Michigan Press, 1969. (Originally published 1921.)

Catlin, G. *Thomas Hobbes as Philosopher*. Oxford, England: Blackwell, 1922.

Catlin, G. *The Science and Methods of Politics*. New York: Knopf, 1927.

Catlin, G. *A Study of the Principles of Politics.* London: Allen & Unwin, 1930.

Catlin, G. "Thomas Hobbes." In *Encyclopedia of the Social Sciences.* Vol. 7. London: Macmillan, 1932.

Catlin, G. *A History of Political Philosophers.* London: Allen & Unwin, 1950.

Christiansen, B. *Attitudes Towards Foreign Affairs as a Function of Personality.* Oslo: Oslo University Press, 1959.

Claussen, B., and Wasmund, K. (eds.), *Handbuch der politischen Sozialisation* [Handbook of political socialization]. Braunschweig, West Germany: Agentur Pedersen, 1982.

Collins, R., and Makowsky, M. *The Discovery of Society.* New York: Random House, 1972.

Coser, L. *The Functions of Social Conflict.* New York: Free Press, 1956.

Dahmer, H. *Libido und Gesellschaft* [Libido and society]. Frankfurt on Main: Fischer Taschenbuch Verlag, 1967.

de Man, H. *Socialismens psykologi* [The psychology of socialism]. Vols. 1 and 2. Stockholm: Tiden, 1928.

Deutsch, M. "What is Political Psychology?" *International Social Science Journal,* 1983, *35*, 211–236.

Downs, A. *An Economic Theory of Democracy.* New York: Harper & Row, 1957.

Duverger, M. *An Introduction to the Social Sciences with Special Reference to Their Methods.* New York: Harper & Row, 1959.

Duverger, M. *Introduction à la politique* [Introduction to politics]. Paris: Presses Universitaires de France, 1964.

Easton, D. *A Systems Analysis of Political Life.* New York: Wiley, 1965.

Eulau, H. "Political Science." In B. F. Hoselitz (ed.), *A Reader's Guide to the Social Sciences.* New York: Free Press, 1970.

Favre, P. "L'Absence de la sociologie politique dans les classifications Durkheimiennes des sciences sociales" [The exclusion of political sociology in the Durkheimians' classifications of social science]. *Revue française de science politique,* 1982, *32*, 5–31.

Finer, S. "Introduction to Vilfredo Pareto's Sociological Writings." In V. Pareto, *Sociological Writings.* Oxford, England: Blackwell, 1976.

Freud, S. "Psychoanalytische Bemerkungen über einen autobiographisch beschriebeben Fall von Paranoia" [Psychoanalytic remarks on an autobiographically described case of paranoia]. In S. Freud, *Gesammelte Werke* [Collected works]. Vol. 8. London: Imago, 1948. (Originally published 1911.)

Freud, S. "Totem and Taboo." In *The Standard Edition of the Works of Sigmund Freud.* Vol. 13. London: Hogarth Press, 1952. (Originally published 1913.)

Freud, S. "On Narcissism: An Introduction." In *The Standard Edition of the Works of Sigmund Freud.* Vol. 14. London: Hogarth Press, 1952. (Originally published 1914.)

Freud, S. *Massenpsychologie und Ich-Analyse* [Group psychology and the analysis of the ego]. Frankfurt on Main: Fischer Taschenbuch Verlag, 1968. (Originally published 1921.)

Freud, S. *New Introductory Lectures on Psychoanalysis.* London: Pelican Books, 1973. (Originally published 1932.)

Fürstenau, J. *Entnazifizierung: Ein Kapitel deutscher Nachkriegspolitik* [Denazification: A chapter in German postwar politics]. Neuwied/Berlin: Luchterhand, 1969.

Gente, H.P. (ed.). *Marxismus, Psychoanalyse, Sexpol* [Socialism, psychoanalysis, sex]. Vols. 1 and 2. Frankfurt on Main: Fischer Taschenbuch Verlag, 1970–71.

Gognel, F. "The Study of Political Parties, Public Opinion and Elections in France." In *Contemporary Political Science.* Paris: UNESCO, 1950.

Gramsci, A. *Selections from the Prison Notebooks.* (Q. Hoare and G. N. Smith, eds. and trans.) New York: International Publishers, 1971. (Originally published 1948.)

Greenstein, F. I. "Political Psychology: A Pluralistic Universe." In J. N. Knutson (ed.), *Handbook of Political Psychology.* San Francisco: Jossey-Bass, 1973.

Heidegger, M. *Being and Time.* New York: Harper & Row, 1962. (Originally published 1927.)

Hellpach, W. "Beiträge zur Individual- und Sozialpsychologie" [Contributions to individual and social psychology]. In *Abhandlungen der Heidelberger Akademie der Wissenschaften.* Heidelberg: Akademie der Wissenschaften, 1952.

Heradstveit, D. *Arab and Israeli Elite Perceptions.* Oslo: Oslo University Press and Humanity Press, 1974.

Heradstveit, D. *The Arab-Israeli Conflict: Psychological Obstacles to Peace.* Oslo: Universitetsforlaget, 1979.

Himmelstrand, U. *Social Pressures, Attitudes, and Democratic Processes.* Stockholm: Almqvist & Wiksell, 1960.

Hirsch-Weber, W., and Schütz, K. *Wähler und Gewählte: Eine Untersuchung der Bundestagswahlen 1953* [Electors and elected: An investigation of the Bundestag election 1953]. Munich: Vahlen, 1957.

Hörberg, T. *Prediktion, osäkerhet och risk i internationella förhandlingar* [Prediction, uncertainty, and risk in international negotiations]. Lund, Sweden: Studentlitteratur, 1983.

Horkheimer, M. "The Lessons of Fascism." In H. Cantril (ed.), *Tensions That Cause Wars.* Urbana: University of Illinois Press, 1950.

Horn, K. "Politische Psychologie" [Political Psychology]. In G. Kress and D. Senghaas (eds.), *Politikwissenschaft: Ein Einführung in ihre Probleme* [Political science: An introduction to its problems]. Frankfurt on Main: Fischer Taschenbuch Verlag, 1972.

Horn, K. "Occasion and Historical Cause for the Development of Political Psychology in the Federal Republic of Germany." Paper presented at 5th scientific meeting of International Society of Political Psychology, Washington, D.C., June 1982.

Horn, K., and Senghaas-Knobloch, E. (eds.). *Friedensbewegung: Personliches und politisches* [Peace movement: Personal and political factors]. Frankfurt on Main: Fischer Information zur Zeit, 1983.

Hydén, L. C. *Psykologi och Marxism* [Psychology and Marxism]. Stockholm: Norstedt, 1980.

Jacobsen, W. "Development of Political Psychology in Germany." Paper presented at annual meeting of the German Psychological Association, Hamburg, May 1978.

Jaspers, K. *Psychologie der Weltenschauungen* [The psychology of world views]. Berlin: Springer, 1960. (Originally published 1919.)

Jay, M. *The Dialectical Imagination: A History of the Frankfurt School and the Institute of Social Research, 1923–50.* London: Heinemann, 1973.

Jellinek, G. *Allgemeine Staatslehre* [General theory of the state]. Berlin: Häning, 1914.

Klingemann, H. D., Kaase, M., and Horn, K. (eds.). *Politische Psychologie* [Political psychology]. Opladen: Westdeutscher Verlag, 1981.

Kuhn, T. *The Structure of Scientific Revolutions.* Chicago: University of Chicago Press, 1963.

Lagerroth, F. *Psykologisk verklighet och juridisk fiktion vid tillämpningen av sveriges grundlager* [Psychological reality and legal fiction in the application of Swedish constitutional law]. Lund, Sweden: Gleerup, 1925.

Lasswell, H. D. "Psychopathology and Politics." In *The Political Writings of Harold D. Lasswell.* New York: Free Press, 1951.

Lazarsfeld, P., Jahoda, M., and Zeisel, H. *Die arbeitslosen von Marienthal* [The unemployed from Marienthal]. Leipzig: Sternhem, 1933.

Le Bon, G. *La Psychologie des foules* [trans. as *The Crowd*]. Paris: Alcan, 1895.

Le Bon, G. *La Psychologie du socialisme* [The psychology of socialism]. Paris: Alcan, 1896.

Le Bon, G. *La Psychologie politique et la défense sociale* [Political psychology and social defense]. Paris: Flammarion, 1910.

Le Bon, G. *La Révolution Française et la psychologie des révolutions* [The French Revolution and the psychology of revolutions]. Paris: Flammarion, 1912.

Lehner, F. "Nostalgie einer Disziplin oder die Revolution, die nie stattgefunden hat" [The nostalgia of a discipline or the revolution that never occurred]. *Politische Vierteljahresschrift,* 1974, *15,* 245-256.

Leites, N. *A Study of Bolshevism.* New York: Free Press, 1953.

Leithäuser, T. *Formen des Alltagsbewusstseins* [Forms of everyday consciousness]. Frankfurt on Main: Campus Verlag, 1976.

Leithäuser, T., and Heinz, W. R. (eds.). *Produktion, Arbeit, Sozialisation* [Production, work, socialization]. Frankfurt on Main: Suhrkamp, 1980.

Leithäuser, T., and others. *Entwurf zu eine Empirie des Alltagsbewusstseins* (An outline of the empirical foundations of everyday consciousness]. Frankfurt on Main: Suhrkamp, 1981.

Lenin, V. I. "What Is to Be Done?" In V. I. Lenin, *Selected Works in Three Volumes.* Vol. 1. Moscow: Progress Publishers, 1967. (Originally published 1902.)

Lenin, V. I. *Materialism and Empirio-Criticism.* Moscow: Progress Publishers, 1967. (Originally published 1909.)

Lenin, V. I. "Left-Wing Communism: An Infantile Disorder." In V. I. Lenin, *Selected Works in Three Volumes.* Vol. 3. Moscow: Progress Publishers, 1967. (Originally published 1920.)

Lenk, H. "Zur wissenschaftstheoretische Situation der deutschen Soziologie" [On the state of theoretical knowledge in German sociology]. *Kölner Zeitschrift für Soziologie und Sozialpsychologie,* 1979, Special Issue no. 21.

Lepsius, M. R. "Die Entwicklung der Soziologie nach dem Zweiten Weltkrieg" [The development of sociology since World War II]. *Kölner Zeitschrift für Soziologie und Sozialpsychologie,* 1979, Special Issue no. 21.

Lippert, E., and Wakenhut, R. (eds.). *Handwörterbuch der politischen Psychologie* [A dictionary of political psychology]. Opladen: Westdeutscher Verlag, 1983.

Lubek, I. "Histoire de psychologie sociales perdues: Le cas de Gabriel Tarde" [History of lost social psychology: The case of Gabriel Tarde]. *Revue française de sociologie,* 1981, *22,* 361-395.

Luhmann, N. "Sociology in Germany: Insistence on Systems Theory." *Social Forces*, 1983, *61*, 987–998.

Lundquist, L. *The Party and the Masses: An Interorganizational Analysis of Lenin's Model for the Bolshevik Revolutionary Movement.* Dobbs Ferry, N.Y.: Transnational Publishers, 1982.

Mann, M. *Consciousness and Action Among the Western Working Class.* London: Macmillan, 1973.

Mayo, E. *The Social Problems of an Industrial Civilization.* London: Routledge & Kegan Paul, 1949.

Mayo, E. *The Psychology of Pierre Janet.* London: Routledge & Kegan Paul, 1951.

Mead, M. *Soviet Attitudes Toward Authority.* New York: McGraw-Hill, 1951.

Mitscherlich, A. *Society Without the Father.* New York: Schocken Books, 1970.

Moscovici, S. *L'Age de foule* [The age of the crowd]. Paris: Fayard, 1981.

Moser, H. (ed.). *Politische Psychologie* [Political psychology]. Basel, Switzerland: Beltz, 1979.

Moser, H. (ed.). *Fortschritte der politischen Psychologie* [Advances in political psychology]. Vol. 1. Basel, Switzerland: Beltz, 1981.

Murphy, G. *Historical Introduction to Modern Psychology.* San Diego: Harcourt Brace Jovanovich, 1949.

Pareto, V. *Les Systèmes socialistes* [The socialist systems]. Paris: Giard & Brière, 1902.

Pareto, V. *Manuel d'économie politique* [A manual of political economy]. Paris: Giard & Brière, 1909.

Parsons, T. *The Structure of Social Action.* Vols. 1 and 2. New York: Free Press, 1968. (Originally published 1937.)

Passigli, S. "Politische Wissenschaft in italienisches Sicht" [Political science from an Italian perspective]. *Politische Vierteljahresschrift*, 1971, *12*, 162–200.

Preiser, S. (ed.). *Kognitive und emotionale Aspekte politischen Engagements* [Cognitive and emotional aspects of political involvement]. Vol. 2 of H. Moser (ed.), *Fortschritte der politischen Psychologie* [Advances in political psychology]. Basel, Switzerland: Beltz, 1982.

Preiser, S. (ed.). *Soziales und Politisches Engagement: Kognitive und sozioökologische Bedingungen* [Social and political involvement: Cognitive and social-ecological conditions]. Vol. 3 of H. Moser (ed.), *Fortschritte der politischen Psychologie* [Advances in political psychology]. Basel, Switzerland: Beltz, 1983.

Rasmussen, E. "En filosof og to historikere" [One philosopher and two historians]. *Statsvetenskaplig tidskrift*, 1983, *86*, 109–116.

Roazen, P. *Freud: Political and Social Thought.* New York: Random House, 1970.

Rowse, A. L. "Foreword." In G. Wallas, *Human Nature in Politics.* London: Constable, 1947. (Originally published 1908.)

Sanford, N. "Authoritarian Personality in Contemporary Perspective." In J. N. Knutson (ed.), *Handbook of Political Psychology.* San Francisco: Jossey-Bass, 1973.

Selznick, P. *The Organizational Weapon.* New York: Free Press, 1950.

Sighele, S. *La Foule criminelle* [The criminal crowd]. Paris: Ballière, 1895. (Original Italian edition 1891.)

Sighele, S. *Psychologie des sects* (The psychology of sects]. Paris: Giard & Brière, 1898.

Sjöblom, G. *Party Strategies in a Multiparty System*. Lund, Sweden: Studentlitteratur, 1968.

Snyder, R. C., Bruck, H. W., and Sapin, B. (eds.). *Foreign Policy Decision Making: An Approach to the Study of International Politics*. New York: Free Press, 1962.

Sorokin, P. *Contemporary Sociological Theories*. New York: Harper & Row, 1928.

Stenelo, L. G. *Foreign Policy Predictions*. Lund, Sweden: Studentlitteratur, 1980.

Stoetzel, J. *Théorie des opinions* [A theory of opinions]. Paris: Fayard, 1943.

Stoetzel, J. *L'Étude experimentale des opinions* [The experimental study of opinions]. Paris: Fayard, 1945.

Stone, W. F. "Political Psychology: A Whig History." In S. L. Long (ed.), *The Handbook of Political Behavior*. Vol. 1. New York: Plenum, 1981.

Tarde, G. *Les Transformations du pouvoir* [The transformations of power]. Paris: Alcan, 1899.

Tarde, G. *Penal Philosophy*. (R. Howell, trans.) Montclair, N.J.: Patterson Smith, 1968. (Originally published 1912.)

Tarde, G. *On Communications and Social Influence*. (T. Clark, ed.) Chicago: University of Chicago Press, 1969.

Thierc, Y. J. "Gustave Le Bon: Prophète de l'irrationalisme de masse" [Gustave Le Bon: Prophet of mass irrationalism]. *Revue française de sociologie*, 1981, 22, 409–428.

Thierc, Y. J., and Tréanton, J. R. "La Foule comme objet de 'science' " [The crowd as object of "science"]. *Revue française de sociologie*, 1983, 24, 119–125.

Turkle, S. *Psychoanalytic Politics: Jacques Lacan and Freud's French Revolution*. New York: Basic Books, 1979.

van Kalken, F., and Lepses, J. "Political Science in Belgium." In *Contemporary Political Science*. Paris: UNESCO, 1950.

Volmerg, B., Volmerg, U., and Leithäuser, T. *Kriegsängste und Sicherheitsbedürfnis: Zur Sozialpsychologie des Ost-West Konflikts im Alltag* [War anxiety and security needs: On the social psychology of East-West conflict in everyday life]. Frankfurt on Main: Fischer Taschenbuch Verlag, 1983.

Wallas, G. *Human Nature in Politics*. London: Constable, 1947. (Originally published 1908.)

Wallas, G. *The Great Society: A Psychological Analysis*. New York: Macmillan, 1914.

Wasmund, K. (ed.). *Jugendliche: Neue Bewusstseinsformen und politische Verhaltensweisen* [Adolescents: New forms of consciousness and political behaviors]. Stuttgart: Ernst Klett, 1982.

Wolf, H. E. "Zu einigen Problemen ideologischer Einflüsse auf die Vorurteilsforschung" [On some problems of ideological influences on the study of prejudice]. *Kölner Zeitschrift für Soziologie und Sozialpsychologie*, 1972, 24, 747–789.

Zamansky, H. S. "Paranoid Reactions." In *International Encyclopedia of the Social Sciences*. Vol. 11. New York: Free Press, 1968.

SIXTEEN

Political Psychology in Asia

Lucian W. Pye

Asia's rich cultural diversity offers exciting possibilities for research in comparative political psychology. In East Asia there are the bewildering similarities and differences in the Confucian culture area, which encompasses China, Japan, Korea, and Vietnam. In the subcontinent of South Asia, Hindu and Moslem contrasts accentuate national differences. And in Southeast Asia there are several hundred subcultures with their separate language variations that give form to innumerable subnational political identities. The historical experiences of the countries have been such that it is readily possible to make comparisons, controlling for such important variables as different durations and forms of Western colonial rule, different religions, different patterns of economic development, and modernization.

Unfortunately, the extraordinary research potential of Asia, especially for comparative analysis, has not yet been exploited, although the stage has been set for significant advances. Earlier work in anthropology, particularly on Southeast Asian cultures, can provide the basis for the beginning of systematic political psychology research. Solid studies have been done in the fields of historical and institutional analyses and on ideologies and political movements.

The growth of political psychology in Asia is likely to follow somewhat different paths in the various countries because of the different starts that have been made and the different degrees of interest in the subject among indigenous scholars. These are the people who in the end are likely to be decisive in determining the level of advancement the field will achieve in the study of each of the countries. At present the greatest interest among Asian scholars in political psychology has been in Japan and India, while work on China and the Southeast Asian countries is still at a stage in which Western scholars are largely setting the pace.

Note: I appreciate the helpful assistance of Akuto Hiroshi, Richard J. Samuels, and Myron Weiner.

In carrying out this survey of the state of the art, our only objective was to identify the most promising research trends; we had no intention of looking for any single characteristics for the whole continent. Yet, when the first draft was completed, it was apparent that, surprisingly, there was such a theme—that of various manifestations of psychological dependency. Aspects of the dynamics of dependency are to be found in the leadership styles in some countries, in the ties that produce political groupings in others, and in the motivations behind much of individual political behavior in nearly all the cultures. In the end, however, we hesitate to make much of this finding, and we certainly would not suggest that it is an attribute of the dominant religions or even the secular political philosophies of Asia. Rather, it seems more a reflection of the continued positive role in Asia of traditional values and such basic institutions as family and community. Since manifestations of dependency are as strong in highly industrialized Japan, Taiwan, and Singapore as in the less developed parts of Asia, it seems possible that Asia may modernize without abandoning appreciation for paternalistic modes of authority, the personal security that comes from submerging the self into a larger group, or the simple comforts of conformity. In any case, it is clear that Asians now show little of the Westerner's obsession with self-identity and individualization. Consequently, the suggestion that dependency is a major theme in Asian political culture has far less pejorative overtones for Asians than it would have for Westerners. On the contrary, most Asians probably see in a most positive light those features of social life and personal development that Westerners associate with psychological dependency.

Japan: Fascination with the Self and with Methodology

The appropriate starting point for understanding current trends in Japanese political psychology is still Ruth Benedict's *The Chrysanthemum and the Sword: Patterns of Japanese Culture,* published in 1946 and based on research "done from afar" during the war. Benedict's thesis—that Japanese society revolves centrally around the feelings of *giri* and *on,* of binding obligations and debts—stimulated among the Japanese both fascination at a foreigner's understanding of their national psyche and defensive criticism that such "old-fashioned" ideas no longer applied to modern Japanese. The book provoked extensive reactions among Japanese and set in motion two quite different traditions, which still dominate political psychology in Japan. The first, which had its seeds in prewar days, involves highly speculative and introspective attempts to describe the uniqueness of the Japanese spirit. Even Americans are no match for the Japanese when it comes to fascination with the national self. The second tradition has been almost the exact opposite of the first, in that it involves extremely rigorous quantitative measurements of attitudes and opinions, with almost no room for speculation and, in fact, little attempt at interpretation. The second tradition in a sense denied the significance of Benedict's work by simply saying that it was not "scientific."

The first tradition, which is well established in Japan, possessing even a name, *Nihonjinron* or "Theory of Japaneseness," dates back to the Japanese reaction to earlier attempts by foreigners to describe the Japanese personality. Percival Lowell's *The Soul of the Far East* ([1888] 1973) and *Occult Japan, or the Way of the Gods: An Esoteric Study of Japanese Personality and Possession* (1895), as well as Lafcadio Hearn's *Japan: An Attempt at Interpretation* (1904), invited Japanese intellectuals to ruminate about what makes the Japanese distinctive and in most cases an interesting people. But with surprising frequency they also described themselves as having inferior or flawed characteristics.

Ruth Benedict in a sense legitimized for her Japanese admirers and critics the methodological practice of taking key Japanese social concepts and analyzing their psychological implications. For Benedict the door to understanding was the tremendous feeling of obligation and indebtedness that the Japanese accumulates from the moment he passes beyond the bliss of early childhood irresponsibility. The task of working off deep feelings of indebtedness provides the disciplining guidelines and compulsive drive so characteristic of Japanese behavior in a well-structured and familiar social context.

Other students of *Nihonjinron* have identified further concepts as the keys to Japanese character. Maruyama (1963), the foremost analyst of Japanese ultra-nationalism, has emphasized the group orientedness of Japanese. This character-istic—combined with their strong sense of hierarchy, in which there is no individualization of either superior or inferior—tends to produce an authoritarian political culture. Maruyama's key word is *takotsubo shakai*, or "octopus-pot society," by which he means to suggest that in Japanese society, as in a pile of octopus pots, similar groups are arranged in a single hierarchy with no commu-nications among them. Austin (1975), following the same lead, has noted that in the Japanese religious tradition little distinction was made between this world and another world; consequently, the sentiments of awe, respect, and obedience, which in the West have been diffusely and differentiatedly focused on sacred and secular institutions, must in Japan be concentrated on here-and-now relations. There is, thus, a tremendous psychic attachment to concrete role relationships. The extraor-dinary emotional intensity of Japanese commitments to specific role performances is stressed by De Vos (1973).

The social anthropologist Nakane (1970) has further refined the picture of the individual's place in society by stressing the balance that must be maintained in favor of one's vertical ties to a superior (parent, teacher, supervisor, boss) over one's horizontal ties to colleagues, both of which define the boundaries of whatever group, organization, or company becomes the basis of the individual's identity. It is her contention that Japanese expect to find in their vertical group identifi-cations—their circles *(kai)*, cliques *(batsu)*, factions *(ha)*, professional worlds *(dan)*, and companies or departments—the warmth and security of their original family membership.

Sato, Murakami, and Kumon (1975) have modified the picture of Japanese culture as stressing only harmony and consensus by developing the theory that Japanese society is composed of the spirit of both *ie* ("family"), warm group orientations, and *mura* ("village"), in which there is contending and factional competition. The dual qualities of *ie* and *mura* thus help to explain the capability of Japanese to work closely together in an organization while also being highly competitive in a larger context—but not so competitive as to destroy the ultimate unity of the "village" or, in general terms, the nation. The main political effect of *ie-mura* is an exaggerated concern for consensus, an overdramatized fear of potential national disunity, and a leadership style that must at all costs avoid the appearances, and not just the reality, of using power against the minority and thereby committing the political sin of the "tyranny of the majority."

This strong sense of group identification is coupled in Japanese political culture with a highly paternalistic leadership style. As Austin (1975) has quantitatively demonstrated, Japanese executives expect leaders to be essentially supportive, protecting, and nurturing authority figures, concerned above all with building consensus, and not at all like the American ideal of the hard-driving, demanding, and fully in command leader. The absence in Japanese culture of the ideal of the executive type of leader has meant that "Even the word 'leader' has had to be imported into Japan and naturalized imperfectly as *rida*—or even more implausibly as *wan man rida*" (Austin, 1975, p. 128; Samuels, 1982).

The complex relationship between superiors and subordinates in Japanese culture has contributed to the development of a distinctive style in decision making, which tends to operate in a manner that provides considerable scope for initiative among subordinates and at the same time protects the self-esteem of the superior. Decision making takes the form of *nemawashi*, or root "brinding," which means that before there can be a change in policy every loose end, or "root," must be tidied up and everyone informed and involved, much as the roots of a tree must be trimmed and balled before the tree is transplanted. Traditional Japanese administration employs the system of *ringi* (best described by Tsuji, 1968), in which every decision begins at the lowest level of the particular administrative command with a subordinate's draft and then is passed up the hierarchy, so that by the time it reaches the top it represents the consensus of the entire organization. The ultimate authority is, thus, at the mercy of his subordinates; yet, if the decision is criticized by another department, the leader can pass off the proposal as merely the work of one of his minions.

The psychological ties between paternalistic leader and loyal group-oriented subordinate have been illuminated by the psychoanalyst Doi (1962) in his analysis of the Japanese concept of *amae*, or "dependency." Subordinates constantly seek to evoke from their superiors the qualities of kindness and sympathetic understanding, which are associated in the Japanese mind with the best qualities of paternal authority. Superiors in their turn also seek to be shielded by their subordinates so that they can likewise gain the security of dependency.

Foreign scholars working on Japanese character have sought in recent years to reduce stress on the exotic while still identifying what is distinctive in Japanese political and social behavior. The efforts of sociologists such as Dore (1973) and Vogel (1975) have brought greater precision to our understanding of Japanese social and psychological concepts. On the other hand, Western awe of Japanese economic successes has produced a stream of books on Japanese management style (Clark, 1979; Ouchi, 1981; Pascale, 1980), which are directed toward influencing American management practices through explaining Japanese behavior.

It is significant, however, that Western interest in learning from the Japanese how to be more efficient industrially has coincided with a noticeable change in the Japanese perceptions of their own national character. When in 1970 Herman Kahn predicted that the Japanese would shortly have the world's second largest economy, the Japanese immediately discounted the possibility that they could be so successful and much preferred Zbigniew Brzezinski's (1972) more qualified forecast, which was reflected in the title of his book *The Fragile Blossom: Crisis and Change in Japan*. Even as Japan continued to have astonishing economic progress, the Japanese, according to Reischauer (1950), persisted in manifesting their traditional inferiority complex, reveling in the idea that much of the world was against them. This sense of persecution was graphically illustrated with the popularity in the early 1970s of a strange book in the *Nihonjinron* tradition, written under the pseudonym Isaiah Ben-Dasan (1972) and entitled *The Japanese and the Jews,* which advanced the astonishing thesis that the two races shared virtually a common tradition and a common fate.

By the next decade, however, the Japanese mood dramatically changed, as could be witnessed in the spectacular best-seller success of Vogel's (1979) *Japan as Number One.* Japanese writers of *Nihonjinron* were suddenly beginning to discover that the personality traits and national character qualities they had been criticizing as feudal faults were now admirable qualities deserving of praise. Intellectuals, who had earlier believed that Japan's salvation required a Marxist, socialist transformation, discovered a need to cherish features of old, pre–American Occupation Japan.

The other tradition of Japanese study of political psychology, which was also initially stimulated by Ruth Benedict's *The Chrysanthemum and the Sword,* has had a more straightforward history. This is the rigorous and scientific tradition of measuring attitudes and opinions through sample surveys. The Japanese were in a sense introduced to national sample surveys and polling during the American Occupation by the work of the Strategic Bombing Survey. Since the Occupation the Japanese have, with great interest and increasing sophistication, taken to national surveys, and by now they have probably gone ahead of the United States in having the most continuous and intensive polling of their population for all manner of attitudes.

The three huge national newpapers of Japan invest heavily in regular national polls. The *Ashahi Shinbun,* the largest, conducts at least ten surveys a year, based on national samples of 3,000 to 4,000 people, while the somewhat smaller *Yomiuri* and *Mainichi* carry out six or so polls each a year. Work on public opinion has been further supported, particularly at universities and research centers, by grants from a foundation set up by NHK, the Japanese national broadcasting and television service, from a capital endowment established from the profits the network made by selling its main headquarters in downtown Tokyo when moving to the suburbs.

Japanese work in the universities on political psychology has been of outstandingly high quality in methodology, particularly in the use of statistical and mathematical methods, but it has been quite atheoretical. Professors Hayashi Chikio and Akuto Hikoshi have produced a four-volume study, *Japanese National Character* (Hayashi and Akuto, 1956, 1961, 1965, 1972), based on surveys five years apart, and are working on a fifth volume. This work shows significant changes in various items, but there is no attempt at a summation picture comparable to the theories of Japanese character produced by writers in the *Nihonjinron* tradition. Tazaki Tokuro, a professor at Gumma University, did attempt, through survey interviewing, to test Benedict, Doi, and Nakane's theories of Japanese character, but he found it exceedingly difficult to arrive at definitive conclusions (Tazaki, 1980).

Part of the problem of moving from survey studies to a deeper analysis of

Japanese character is that polling, which is dominated by newspapers, has produced a tradition of tracing opinion according to responses to only the issues of the day. In a sense it can be said that in Japan the newspapers both shape opinion and then measure what they have produced. The problem, however, is even more complicated because of a peculiar feature of Japanese political culture: the Japanese rule that the strong should always remain silent, while it is the weak who are allowed to determine the course of public discussions. Hence, the media in Japan are filled consistently with the pleas of the opposition; they provide disproportionately little attention to explaining the government's actions. The Japanese rule goes beyond just the principle that those with power should not be vulgarly verbose; it includes the idea that, whereas ritualized apologizing is becoming, explaining is an unacceptable form of excuse making among the powerful. Instead of the American politicians' dictum "Never apologize, never explain," Japanese leaders follow the practice "Merely apologize, so as not to explain."

If we pull back from examining current trends, the broader perspective reveals some surprising omissions in the work on Japanese political psychology. For example, the very essence of power relations in day-to-day Japanese politics is the interplay of factions within the Liberal-Democratic party; yet there has been no systematic work on the psychological bases of such factional groupings. What is the nature of the loyalty commitments? How do the leaders maintain and expand their followings? What are the pressures in the initial recruitment? How does advancement take place? And are there significant stresses on the individual Diet member to choose among different objects of loyalty? Although we have masterful studies of the electoral processes and the nature of campaigning in Japan (Curtis, 1971; Richardson, 1974; Thayer, 1969), as well as of the formal processes of law making in the Diet (Campbell, 1977; Pempel, 1977), we know little about the actual political life of party members.

Another neglected area is the study of the relationship between the media and the politicians. The analysis of the media has been almost entirely focused on its role in shaping public opinion and attitudes. Little has been done to unearth the ground rules that govern the relations between politicians and journalists and the ways in which they use each other.

With respect to mass psychology, it would seem that the time has come for fresh studies of the character of Japanese nationalism. What are the underlying forces in the apparent new wave of national pride that seems to be strongest among urbanites, whereas the traditional Japanese nationalism had its strongest roots among rural people? What is likely to change in Japanese political behavior if the traditional Japanese sense of inferiority and anxiety about catching up with the West is replaced with a sense of superiority toward the outside world?

Clearly, there is more to be done in the study of Japanese political psychology, but what is important is that a great deal has been accomplished, many interesting ideas are contending for acceptance, and a host of technically qualified researchers are available to get on with the job. The great danger is that this situation may lead to undue caution as more and more energy is expended to test rigorously less and less startling propositions and too few people will feel that they can take the risk of being unconventional by exploring novel topics. In short, the dangers of pedantry are great in Japanese studies.

India: Western Concepts Merged into Traditional Theories

Moving from one side of Asia to the other, we find that political psychology in India also has a bifurcated character, as in Japan, but the two approaches in India are along different lines. The first Indian tradition involves the direct application of Western theories and concepts to an Asian population. The assumption behind this approach is that the people of industrial and Third World societies are all a part of mankind and that there are universal qualities to human psychology. Hence, Indian behavior can and should be measured according to the standards and norms appropriate for understanding political behavior in the West. The second, and newer, tradition begins with the belief that Hindu culture is distinct enough from Western to justify the use of quite different theories about the range of mental and emotional states in the subcontinent. More specifically, this second approach is sensitive to traditional Indian concepts about human nature and mental illness and is prepared to accept the idea that, just possibly, schools of thought based on ancient observations and experiences in Hindu society may command unexpected and valid insights for this non-Western culture.

Unquestionably, Hindu character has been more intensely analyzed by both foreigners and indigenous people than any other Asian culture. First the British and then Westerners in general have been fascinated, and at times repelled, by their perceptions of the Indian personality. Indians themselves have been only slightly less caught up than the Japanese in self-analysis, but they have been probably more bluntly self-critical; there is, for example, no Japanese writer who has been as savage and insightful in criticizing his own national psychology as Chaudhuri (1951, 1966).

It would be incorrect to suggest that the two traditions of studying Indian psychology represent a split between Westerners and Indians, because there has been a mix of scholars working on both approaches. The tradition of using Western psychology concepts came first as both Europeans and Westernized Indian intellectuals sought to become more "scientific" and to go beyond the long tradition of interpreting Hindu character in the context of Indian literature and the analysis of the Hindu religion. Thus, the more systematic analysis of Indian personality began against the background of an illustrious tradition of insightful novelists and writers extending from Rudyard Kipling to Rabindranath Tagore and R. K. Narayan. There was, however, from the beginning some feeling, which was made much stronger by Mahatma Gandhi's success with the tactics of nonviolence, that Indian political behavior includes dimensions that cannot be understood in Western terms alone, so that traditional Indian theories would also have to be employed.

It would be neither appropriate nor possible in the space available to review here the huge body of literature that constitutes the foundations upon which all current work on Indian political psychology must be constructed. We can, however, identify a few trends and present a brief summary view of the psychological bases of political man in India.

In contrast to Japan, where sample surveys have provided the basis for the modern study of political psychology, in India research about political behavior has been built largely on interview studies that follow anthropological and even clinical psychology approaches. There has also been a strong tradition, almost totally absent in Japan, of in-depth biographical and autobiographical studies of political leaders.

In contrast to the remarkable cultural homogeneity of Japan, India—with its confusing diversity of religions, languages, regions, castes, classes, and urban-rural differences—represents the extreme of cultural heterogeneity. Yet, in spite of this diversity, which on first sight would suggest the impossibility of generalizations, all the various approaches to the analysis of Indian culture and personality tend in the end to accentuate certain common themes, although the explanations differ considerably. This tendency is especially surprising since among scholars working on India there are sharp cleavages that are not bridged by even the conventions of mutual respect. (We shall consciously ignore these academic, sectarian differences and concentrate only on the common themes.)

There are two explanations for why, in spite of the manifest diversity of India, it is still possible to find a striking degree of commonality in descriptions of Hindu character and behavior. First, there seems to be a very clear pattern of childhood socialization with little variation across caste *(jati)* and class lines. Second, the insights of Hindu religion and traditional concepts about the nature of man and his life cycle inform the thinking of nearly all Indians (Narain, 1957).

With respect to socialization processes, there seems to be nearly universal agreement that the early years of Indians, boys slightly more than girls, are almost a cocoon stage because of the strong, all-enveloping, nurturing support of the mother—a stage that may contribute to the marked idealization of the mother in Indian culture. The father is seen as more distant and as a somewhat fearful figure. At the same time, the child is early made aware of his place in an extended family and also learns of its collective caste *(jati)* role. At an extremely early age, the child is taught the obligations of loyalty to family and caste, and he also discovers that he can expect positive rewards and further nurturing support if he manifests the expected signs of such loyalty (Dinnage, 1981).

This warm sense of belonging to a secure and protecting family, in which one is constantly adored by an admiring mother, is suddenly brought to an end for boys by the shock of the "second birth," which occurs at between five and six years of age, precisely when the Oedipal crisis might be expected to be greatest. This second birth involves the boy's introduction to the expected discipline of his ultimate traditional role. The supporting mother is, however, still at hand, but the father becomes more difficult to identify with than ever. Kakar (1978, p. 128) is speaking for most students of Indian personality development when he writes: "The consequences of the 'second birth' in the identity development of Indian men are several: a heightened narcissistic vulnerability, an unconscious tendency to 'submit' to an idealized omnipotent figure, both in the inner world of fantasy and the outside world of making a living; the lifelong search for someone, a charismatic leader or a *guru*, who will provide mentorship and a guiding world view, thereby restoring intimacy and authority to individual life."

The theme of narcissism in Indian personality has been stressed by numerous writers (Akhilananda, 1948; Bose, 1966; Spratt, 1966). It seems to lie at the root of the Indian penchant for self-absorption and of their apparent unawareness that moralizing can be an annoyingly aggressive act and not, as Indians would have it, merely a manifestation of one's virtues, which should provoke universal praise. "The relative lack of tension between the superego and the ego in Indian personality" (Kakar, 1978, p. 136) means that there are fewer problems of guilt and less awareness of the ways in which moral constraints can be tied to feelings of aggression. In other cultures such moral constraints produce the generally understood sentiments of "Don't preach at me unless you want a fight" (because you are not my father, my priest, my conscience) and "If I have to obey all these rules, then, dammit, everyone else should."

In political behavior the effect is a widespread acceptance that people will express lofty sentiments, in order to manifest their strivings for virtue, while displaying little sense of social consciousness. The turning of libidinal energies inward upon the ego reduces the capacity for empathy for the feelings of others. Everyone is engaged in finding his own inner self and becoming exhilarated by the fascination of self-realization. The appeal of problems in this world is secondary to the appeal of religion when the basic craving is to recapture the ecstasy of being once again, as in infancy, completely one with a nurturing, adoring "other" who provides a sense of omnipotence by instantly responding to every need, thus turning the wish into reality.

The "second birth" shock also seems to reinforce the tolerant acceptance of hierarchy and authority and to set in motion the search for a mentor or *guru* to whom one can completely give oneself and who will, in return, acknowledge one's virtues as one seeks perfection in an inner world. The search for a *guru* is another manifestation of narcissism (Carstairs, 1957).

After the "second birth" comes the learning of religious doctrines and especially the concept that every individual must seek to follow the laws of his *dharma* (Kakar, 1979). The idea that each person has his own *karma*, which must govern his particular life cycle, suggests to the Indian that there are no universal rules applicable to everyone but rather that he should be tolerant and accepting of different lifestyles and, in effect, different economic circumstances. The political consequences of such views are an acceptance of hierarchy, which can be modified by strong support for essentially "affirmative action" and protective quotas for the "scheduled castes" (untouchables) but not because of egalitarian values. Thus, ironically, the Indian belief in inherent differences has made it politically easier to employ quotas and "affirmative action" plans than in the United States, where belief in equality produces unease and tension over such measures (Weiner and Katzenstein, 1981).

Although violence is commonplace in Indian social and political life, the ideal of nonviolence has considerable appeal. To expound doctrines of nonviolence is in a sense to perform the *guru* or holy man role, to demonstrate to all that one does not have rude sentiments but only a craving for virtue.

The Indian socialization process and Hindu religious doctrines appear to combine and to contribute equally to the idealization of planning in Indian political culture and to the discounting of the importance of implementing policies. Plans, as expressions of wishful aspirations, are seen as having inherent merit, while the Hindu cosmic order stresses proper classification over explanations of cause and effect. In much of Hindu philosophical thinking, the intellectual task is seen as completed with the act of classification, whereas in the West classification is usually seen as only the first step before analysis is possible. Weiner (1967) has documented the fact that in Indian politics patronage considerations take precedence over policy concerns. Neither Jawaharlal Nehru nor Indira Gandhi consistently treated public policy as practical attempts to solve concrete problems. The father adhered to his idealized plans and had little sense of pragmatic experimentation; the daughter increasingly showed less and less interest in policy innovations and concentrated her energies on building and maintaining favor through patronage decisions.

The central place of patronage in Indian politics is a reflection of the importance of dependency in Hindu political psychology. The search for a *guru* becomes in politics the need for a protecting powerful figure who can provide security in return for loyalty. The politics of patronage, and not of policy, is also consistent with a psychology that emphasizes overachieving, which was one of Erikson's (1969) themes about Indian personality. The Indian will pour his psychic energies into winning the favor and respect of his particular superior figure.

We should note here the profound difference in the ways in which dependency feelings are played out in Indian and Japanese culture. For the Indian the drive is a competitive one, or at least it ignores the place of others and focuses only on gaining the approving attention of a superior. Hence, it often leads to conspicuous, self-dramatizing actions, and it can be very corrosive for feelings of group solidarity. Once security is achieved in an organizational situation, the tendency is for ritualization and routinization of behavior in which everyone merely does his or her own thing. In contrast, dependency in Japan encourages the anonymity of group identification and a powerful need for loyalty and dedication. To support the group and hold the esteem of the leader, one needs to be productive and effective, because the group has competitors. Thus, whereas dependency in Japanese culture produces group-oriented behavior that can be effectively directed toward purposeful action, in Indian culture the sense of security found in dependent relationships means that one has passed beyond the need to meet any tests of effectiveness. Indeed, the bonds of the relationship become ends in themselves and save all concerned from the Indian dread of having to prove one's ability for the consummation of actions. This problem of consummation seems to be related to the widely observed Indian anxiety about potency, distrust of sexuality, and respect for, and possible relief over, pledges of celibacy and commitments to asceticism (Carstairs, 1957, pp. 72–87; Erikson, 1969, pp. 229–254). Ashir Nandy has gone even further and has made the observation that—in spite of, or perhaps more accurately because of, the idealization of mothers—Indians have a hostility toward women, as in the practice of *suti*, or widow suicide, although they admire womanliness, as in Gandhi's reverence for nonviolence (Nandy, 1980, pp. 1–47).

All these considerations contribute to making Indian politics, according to Nandy, a politics of self-redefinition, self-affirmation, and autonomy, in that the focus of action is not on grand policy objectives or even the implementation of, or experimentation with, probing policies; instead, people usually turn to politics in search of contacts and connections that will help with their "banal" problems. All this suggests that the psychology of dependency—rather than abstract ideals or the imperatives of conscience and the dictates of law—is the cohesive force that holds together the Indian political system. The subcommunities of caste, region, and language—which form the basis of India's rich diversity—are held together by their separate systems of dependency; and, in turn, the subgroups are, at another and generally more elite level, brought together again by a system of patronage, the rules of which are deeply understood because of the shared psychology of dependency.

In looking ahead for promising research trends, we can find grounds for both optimism and pessimism. On the positive side, researchers in sociology and anthropology are on the verge of producing rich new findings about a variety of aspects of Indian life. The Joint Committee on South Asia of the Social Science Research Council and the American Council of Learned Societies, under the chairmanship of Myron Weiner, has been carrying out an impressive array of projects, including a projected four-volume study of the concept of *karma* over time; a study of *adab*, the Islamic concept of appropriate behavior; and a multidisciplinary analysis of the Indian concept of the self. In addition, the joint committee is collaborating with the Indian Council on Social Science Research in a series of studies of political economy that will include household and marriage arrangements. All these studies will provide an ever more solid basis for political psychology work. On the debit side is the increasing reluctance of Indian officials to sanction social science research by foreigners and a growing defensiveness of Indian intellectuals about the analysis of Hindu culture.

Southeast Asia: Variations of Patron-Client Relations

Dependency is also the key phenomenon that provides a central theme for the even more culturally diversified societies of Southeast Asia. In spite of the extraordinary variations among and within the nine main countries of Southeast Asia, with their nearly one hundred different languages and dialects, all of them manifest dependency at the core of their cultures, albeit in different forms.

This psychological characteristic is to be seen in the pervasive patron-client relationships that are basic to the social structures of all the countries in the region. In Indonesia the relationship takes the form of the *bapak–anak buah* ties— ties between a *bapak* or "father" and his *anak buah* or "children." The relationship is filled with paternalistic and filial sentiments. A *bapak* is expected to assume diverse responsibilities for all his *anak buah*, and they, in return, will owe him an incalculable debt of moral obligation, known as *hutan budy* (Jackson, 1980). In the Indonesian version of the patron-client relationship, stress is placed on the importance of the *bapak's* providing advice and practical guidance as well as protection and material help. There is also a gratifying sense of pride on the part of the *anak buah* about the sacrifices they have made for their *bapak*, regardless of the costs or risks. These psychologically reinforced adviser-advisee bonds readily become the basic relationship of Indonesian politics, more important in building parties or groupings than ideology or religion. Indeed, the framework of both ostensibly ideological and religious parties consists at a latent level of networks of such patron-client relations (Jackson, 1980).

In Thailand the comparable patron-client relationship puts somewhat more emphasis on the nurturing powers of the superior, who by displaying *metta*, a form of kindness and compassion, is able to give to his subordinates the gift of *kamlangcaj*, a vital sense of will, of energy or force, which helps inferiors overcome their feelings of inadequacy. Without a superior to provide *kamlangcaj*, the individual would feel helpless and vulnerable from all quarters (Rubin, 1972.) At the same time, Thai culture insists that superiors must be psychologically protected from the excessive demands of inferiors; therefore, in gaining *kamlangcaj* an inferior is expected to experience *krengcaj*—that is, humbleness, or self-effacement. The feeling of awe of the leader establishes sharp bounds on how far inferiors feel they can go in imposing on the compassion of their benevolent superiors. Thus, at the heart of the Thai patron-client relationship is a blending of will and awe on the part of subordinates and a balancing of compassion and unapproachability for the superior.

The patron-client pattern in Burmese politics produces not single hierarchies of power but scattered groupings consisting of circles and entourages (Hanks, 1968). It is precisely because of the more limited reach of these networks, as compared with those in Indonesia, that Embree (1950) speaks of Burma and Thailand as being "loosely structured" societies. Among the elites in these societies, and particularly in Burma, there is not a single pyramid of power but, rather, numerous semiautonomous clusters of influential people who focus their attention on those in their own grouping and try to ignore others as much as possible. Because the people in each cluster distrust all outsiders, it is difficult to establish effective nationwide institutions. At the same time, the capacity to disregard others also means that a crisis for some of the elite is not translated into an automatic problem for all. It can be hard to accomplish much, but it is also hard for the society to be jarred by events.

Analysis of the patron-client relations in Vietnam, as well as elsewhere in Southeast Asia, has stimulated two competing theories with significant psychological implications. The first is the theory of "moral economy" advanced by Scott (1980); the second is Popkin's (1980) "rational peasant" theory. Arguing along lines similar to those first developed by Furnivall (1948), Scott maintains that before the Western influence—or, in his words, "the world economic system"—disrupted village life in Southeast Asia, peasants lived in integrated communities, in which everyone helped each other out and the needy were taken care of by the more fortunate. Because the peasants wanted to avoid the "bourgeois" calculus of risk and profit, they developed a "subsistence ethic," which became a "moral economy" whereby the weakest were protected from disaster. Western "capitalism" destroyed this harmonious "moral economy" by introducing a competitive, materialistic economy, thereby corrupting the essence of what had been an ethical patron-client relationship in each village community.

Popkin argues that Scott's view of the past is grossly sentimental, that he has no evidence to prove his contention that village life was ever so blissfully harmonious, and that he exaggerates the difference between past and present peasant behavior. Popkin marshals considerable evidence to support his contention that peasants in Vietnam historically and at present have consistently acted according to rational calculations for maximizing their self-interest. Patron-client ties are not, in his view, based on moral imperatives but, rather, represent mutually beneficial tradeoffs that are finely calculated and rationally understood, even when dressed up in the language of ethics and moral obligation .

The debate between the "moral economy" and the "rational peasant" schools is significant for political psychology because it focuses attention on the problem of determining what blend of reasoned calculation, sentimental attachment, and moral judgment supports the dependency syndrome in the various forms of patron-client relations in the region. The one school stresses calculations of utility and rational choice, while the other concentrates on traditional ethical norms. For those outside of the debate, it seems easy to combine elements of both approaches and to add the further dimension of the particular culture and personality common to each society in explaining patterns of association in each country. Popkin's rational peasants are obviously influenced in their perceptions and judgments by cultural and ethical considerations. Indeed, it is easy to move from his models of rational behavior to incorporate other considerations. The "moral economy" perspective causes more problems of adjustment, for it carries an essentially ideological overtone of extolling the past and attacking the "capitalistic modes of production" of the "world economy." Yet, if one discounts the presumed significance of such code words, it becomes clear that rational calculations and cultural predispositions must both influence peasant decisions.

What is important in all these approaches is that elite and mass political life are each built around the sentiments and calculations of reciprocity basic to the psychology of dependency. The importance of dependency is historically well established in the various traditions of Southeast Asian cultures, but it appears that, with modernization and increased urbanization, the search for individual security has produced even greater cravings for dependency. Social change in Southeast Asia has not led to greater striving for autonomy or more impersonal role relationships. On the contrary, the very uncertainty of change has seemingly caused people to seek out new dependency relationships. In particular, dependency relationships are important for those who deal with power and authority. Hence, in the political life of all of the countries, we find a growing reliance on forms of patron-client relations. Behind the rhetoric of ideologies, there are usually concrete networks of personal ties, which can be fully understood only if their essentially psychological dimensions are appreciated.

Over the last two decades, studies of political motivation in Southeast Asia have focused primarily on the various manifestations of nationalism that were largely the culmination of earlier anticolonial sentiments. The recent relative successes at economic development of especially the five countries of the Association of Southeast Asian Nations (ASEAN) have brought other issues to the fore in their politics. Because these countries' leaders are no longer being obliged to react according to Western norms, there has been a decline in commitment to constitutional rule, with its legal constraints, and a marked trend toward more authoritarian practices. For students of political psychology, it would seem desirable to learn more about how public opinion in such countries as the Philippines and Indonesia will respond to such increased authoritarian rule, particularly if there should be a decline in the rates of economic growth.

Other areas that call for research include the politics of religion in several of the countries, and especially the dynamics of Islamic revivalism; the redefinitions of ethnic identities as economic change takes place; and the question of what incipient ideologies are likely to fill the void caused by the declining appeal of communism—which is particularly noticeable in the region because of the general awareness of how China was set back by its immersion in Maoism.

China: The Bonds of *Guanxi*

Political psychology studies of China have not been immune to the vacillations of Chinese politics or to China's relations with the West. In the early years of the People's Republic, there was, for example, considerable emphasis on Chinese practices of "thought reform" or "brainwashing." The attempts of the Chinese to use "coercive persuasion" on American prisoners of war in Korea and Western civilians in China produced several psychologically insightful studies of Chinese techniques of ideological combat (Lifton, 1961; Schein, 1961).

During the early years of Communist rule, it was presumed that the Communist party was extraordinarily successful in changing Chinese cultural patterns and altering Chinese psychology (Schurmann, 1966). The madness of the Cultural Revolution and the fanaticism and violence of the Red Guards seemed to be further proof that Chinese psychology had broken from its traditional Confucian roots and had taken on a completely new form. Psychologically oriented theories were advanced to try to explain the apparently "irrational" developments in China. Lifton (1968) related the Cultural Revolution to Mao's concern about death and his need to find "immortality" in revolutionary rhetoric and practice. Hiniker (1977) advanced the interesting theory that the Maoists were responding to "cognitive dissonance" by ignoring reality in favor of reaffirmation of their faith.

Other scholars, while taking into account the impact of Mao's rule, have tended to see the problems of Chinese political psychology in the context of continuities and discontinuities from the traditional Confucian social and political order. One theory (Pye, 1968), which bridges past and contemporary Chinese political behavior, contends that in Chinese culture the obligation of filial piety has tended to create (1) exaggerated expectations about what authority should be able to accomplish (hence, in modern China the concept of revolution is related not to a demand for individual autonomy but, rather, to a craving for stronger, more effective "authority") and (2) a general repression of aggression, manifested in an emphasis on correct behavior, disciplined control of emotions, fear of disorder, and extreme outbreaks of hate and hostility whenever the social order is disrupted. Solomon (1971), in an outstanding work on Chinese political culture, argues that Mao was seeking to rid the Chinese of their deep psychological fears of *luan,* or disorder. Solomon's study was based on interviews with, and psychological testing of, refugees in Hong Kong. The extent to which there is a distinctive Chinese psychology encompassing those socialized in China, Hong Kong, Taiwan, and Singapore has been documented in numerous studies (Scofield and Sun, 1960; Wilson, 1970). Now that it is possible to have direct contacts with people in China, it appears that thirty years of Communist indoctrination have done less to change Chinese character than might have been expected.

Indeed, the continuities in Chinese culture and personality may be more impressive than the changes; and in many respects the hold of tradition, particularly in rural areas, is greater in China than among overseas Chinese (Parish and Whyte, 1978). Because of the policy of preventing internal migration, rural people have had little exposure to urban trends; furthermore, the elimination of many of the specialists in traditional practices—such as marriage brokers, priests, supervisors of funerals, astrologers, and geomancers—has meant that laymen in surprisingly large numbers have had to acquaint themselves with all manner of esoteric traditional lore. Above all, child-rearing practices have remained much the same even in the cities, where both parents may be employed. The children are attended by grandparents and, thereby, socialized in traditional ways.

Even in the political realm, where the impact of ideology has been the most intense and hence the likelihood of change the greatest, there are numerous examples of pre-Communist behavior traits. Behind the ideological rhetoric of Marxist-Leninist-Mao thought, the Chinese conduct many features of party and government affairs in typical Chinese fashion. Deference to age, stress on correctness of behavior, fear of disorder, a need for consensus, the use of Aesopian language, belief in the power of shaming, and a host of other characteristics long associated with Chinese political behavior continue to prevail.

Possibly the most significant continuity in Chinese political behavior is the continuing practice of Chinese to seek out personal relationships as the most natural responses to any feelings of insecurity. The basis of factional politics in the post-Mao era, for example, has been largely the need for officials, behind the protective screen of consensus, to seek such personal bonds, which can result in groups of friends and foes (Pye, 1981). The deeply felt need to establish personal and reliable friendships and to protect oneself against potential enemies tends to intensify and provide a strong emotional dimension to policy disagreements.

The word that the Chinese use in describing such mutually supportive relationships is *guanxi*. *Guanxi* does have some resemblance to the patron-client relations common in Southeast Asia. Yet, although the Chinese place almost all human relations in a hierarchy and there is always a superior and a subordinate, the claims of *guanxi* allow for such uninhibited requests that the parties can hardly be classified as clients or patrons. Also, the basis for the existence of such a relationship can be almost any form of shared identity—family or clan membership, classmates, common origins (whether village or even province), or maybe nothing more than a shared third friend. The Chinese will speak of *guanxi* as though it were an objective quantity: "Do *A* and *B* have *guanxi*?" If so, "How much?" The measurement of the degree of *guanxi* that exists is often put in quantitative terms, even to the point of specifying how much money each feels he could borrow from the other. Any form of friendship can be readily turned into a *guanxi* relationship.

Because *guanxi* stresses particularistic rather than universalistic norms, modernizing Chinese have usually regarded it as an old-fashioned concept that should be eliminated. The communists decry it as a feudal remnant. Yet the travails of modernization and its associated uncertainties have apparently contributed to ensuring an enduring place for *guanxi* in Chinese culture. It certainly exists in the highest reaches of the Communist party and is widely practiced by the very people who denounce its pernicious effects on China's modernization.

Psychologically, *guanxi* must be understood as a positive response to sentiments of dependency. Both parties in a *guanxi* relationship find psychic value in their dependency on the other. To violate the expectations of a *guanxi* relationship is to cut oneself off from human society by demonstrating that one lacks the capacity for loyalty and self-respect. The positive support for *guanxi*, however, arises from the sense of security that the acceptance of dependency can provide. The source for welcoming the security of dependency lies no doubt in Chinese socialization practices, which stress early warm nurturance, a strong sense of group identity, and the notions that conformity will be rewarded and that authority in return for deference will generally be supportive. The fear of shame, which is early instilled, also suggests that shaming can be a tool of the weak in checking the strong. In Chinese politics the use of moralistic criticisms is even more commonplace than in India, and it is usually more effective.

There are many dimensions of Chinese political culture that call for further research. The process of change in the post-Mao era also raises uncertainties about evolving Chinese attitudes and sentiments. The Chinese have historically preferred to live with a clearly defined political orthodoxy—Confucianism, communism, Sun Yat-senism. Therefore, it will be interesting to evaluate their acceptance of greater political pragmatism. Related is the question of the Chinese reactions to de-Maoification. In other developing countries, the ideological "patricide" of their "founding fathers" has resulted in widespread cynicism and opportunism. Can the Chinese escape such a development if they officially admit that Mao had previously unacknowledged flaws?

Above all, there is the question of whether the Chinese will be successful in finding a form of political authority compatible with the requirements of modernization and industrial development. In the past the Chinese predisposition to dependency produced a craving for an omnipotent political authority that would be appropriately in command in all major spheres of life. Modernization, however, requires respect for specialization and hence differentiated authorities, each with its limited sphere of competence. As of now the Chinese political authorities have been willing to grant little scope to subordinate authorities in such fields as economics, education, and the arts. Whenever these specialists have begun to assert themselves, the ultimate authorities have felt threatened and reasserted their domination.

On the other hand, products of the Confucian culture elsewhere in Asia have been remarkably adept in modern professions and in the building of economic organizations. Therefore, should China experience a period of political stability, major changes may well take place in the country. The Chinese people would then be joining their neighbors in effectively transforming their economic and social conditions.

Of all the specialists in the various social science disciplines watching to determine the direction in which China is most likely to move, those who are best able to fathom Chinese psychology probably will be the first to know. Many critical factors in China's modernization hinge on psychological developments. Understanding these developments presents a major challenge to political psychology as a discipline.

Dependency and Power

As indicated at the beginning of this chapter, we unexpectedly discovered in this review of political psychology in Asia that a major common theme was psychological dependency. The finding that in Asian cultures there may be less craving for individual autonomy and more comfortable identification with groups should have profound implications for understanding differences in Asian and Western political behavior. For example, this difference might be translated into quite a different understanding of the nature of power. In Western political thought, power has conventionally involved commanding and controlling the behavior of others for one's own purposes; power is, thus, participation in the making of significant decisions; and legitimate authority is expected to be directed toward the realization of public policy goals. People seek power in order to gain ends and to maximize their values. Furthermore, in the West there is a general assumption that authority and popular participation are opposites and must clash. It is a natural condition in society for people to seek to check authority. The spirit of revolution and freedom involves the toppling or constraining of authority.

The view of power and authority is somewhat different in Asian cultures, where the security of dependency is accepted and the ideal of power is a paternalistic form of authority. In these cultures power becomes a dynamic process of positive interaction between superiors and inferiors, which may only incidentally yield public policies. Those who seek the security of dependency feel that they cannot realize their true selves without a leader, a teacher, a *guru* (Neki, 1973, 1976). Since the end of the imperial system, the Chinese have talked of "revolution," by which they mean not the elimination of authority so that all can be free but, rather, the replacement of ineffectual (and corrupt) authorities with strong (and more heroic) authorities. The Cultural Revolution was only an extreme caricature of this instinct for improving and making more omnipotent authorities that are seen as inadequate.

Power as a process suggests also a need for community. People feel more comfortable when consensus prevails. Consequently, in Asian societies leaders can achieve considerable freedom for their policies as long as they are able to provide the people with a sense of belonging. Conversely, leaders are not held strictly accountable for the consequences of their policies as long as they are able to maintain the sense of community. Once people are excluded, however, and feel isolated, they will shrilly complain about the "corruption" of their "selfish" leaders and will call for another leadership.

We see this pattern of power—as community building and not the calculated implementation of policy choices—in the upholding of conformity and the paternalistic leadership of Japanese politics, in the patronage practices of Indian politics, in the patron-client politics of Southeast Asia, and in the building of power out of *guanxi* in Chinese politics.

This discussion should suggest to political psychologists that the tensions and strains caused by modernization and industrialization may not be the same in Asian societies as they have been in the West. As a guide in forecasting the conditions that might lead to political crises in Asian societies, attention should probably not be unduly focused on the effectiveness of the government in achieving its announced policies; instead, the more sensitive indicators are likely to be the level of cohesion and the degree to which people feel reassured about belonging to a secure community. The search is, thus, for basic security, not policy promises.

This does not mean, however, as the Japanese case dramatically demonstrates, that such people, once given security, cannot be extremely effective in furthering public policies. Indeed, as more Asian societies succeed in achieving impressive economic growth while preserving some traditional values, there should be even greater Western interest in learning about the political psychology of such successful societies. The result could be some very fundamental rethinking of basic Western political theory.

References

Akhilananda, S. *Hindu Psychology*. London: Routledge & Kegan Paul, 1948.

Austin, L. *Saints and Samurai*. New Haven, Conn.: Yale University Press, 1975.

Ben-Dasan, I. (pseudonym for Yamamoto Shichihei). *The Japanese and the Jews*. New York: Weatherhill, 1972.

Benedict, R. *The Chrysanthemum and the Sword*. Boston: Houghton Mifflin, 1946.

Bose, M. *A Psychiatrist Discovers India*. Calcutta: Rupa, 1966.

Brzezinski, Z. *The Fragile Blossom: Crisis and Change in Japan*. New York: Harper & Row, 1972.

Campbell, J. C. *Contemporary Japanese Budget Politics*. Berkeley: University of California Press, 1977.

Carstairs, K. M. *The Twice-Born*. London: Hogarth Press, 1957.

Chaudhuri, N. C. *The Autobiography of an Unknown Indian*. New York: Macmillan, 1951.

Chaudhuri, N. C. *A Continent of Circe*. New York: Oxford University Press, 1966.

Clark, R. *The Japanese Company*. New Haven, Conn.: Yale University Press, 1979.

Curtis, G. L. *Election Campaigning Japanese Style*. New York: Columbia University Press, 1971.

De Vos, G. "Role Narcissism and the Etiology of Japanese Suicide." In *Socialization for Achievement: Essays on the Cultural Psychology of the Japanese*. Berkeley: University of California Press, 1973.

Dinnage, R. "Going Crazy in India." *New York Review of Books*, 1981, *28* (18), 52–56.

Doi, L. T. "Amae: A Key Concept for Understanding Japanese Personality Structure." In R. K. Beardsley and R. J. Smith (eds.), *Japanese Culture: Its Development and Characteristics*. Chicago: University of Chicago Press, 1962.

Dore, R. *British Factory—Japanese Factory*. Berkeley: University of California Press, 1973.

Embree, J. F. "Thailand—A Loosely Structured Social System." *American Anthropologist*, 1950, *52*, 181–193.

Erikson, E. H. *Gandhi's Truth*. New York: Norton, 1969.

Furnivall, J. S. *Colonial Policy and Practice*. New York: New York University Press, 1948.

Hanks, L. "Entourage and Circle in Burma." *Bennington Review*, Summer 1968.

Hayashi, C., and Akuto, H. *Nihonjin no kokuminsei* [Japanese national character]. 4 vols. Tokyo: Shiseidu, 1956, 1961, 1965, 1972.

Hearn, L. *Japan: An Attempt at Interpretation*. New York: Macmillan, 1904.

Hiniker, P. J. *Revolutionary Ideology and Chinese Reality*. Beverly Hills, Calif.: Sage, 1977.

Hoch, E. "A Pattern of Neurosis in India." *American Journal of Psychoanalysis*, 1966, *25*.

Jackson, K. D. *Traditional Authority, Islam, and Rebellion*. Berkeley: University of California Press, 1980.

Kahn, H. *The Emerging Japanese Superstate*. Englewood Cliffs, N.J.: Prentice-Hall, 1970.

Kakar, S. *The Inner World: A Psycho-Analytical Study of Childhood and Society in India*. Delhi: Oxford University Press, 1978.

Kakar, S. *Identity and Adulthood.* Delhi: Oxford University Press, 1979.

Lifton, R. J. *Thought Reform and the Psychology of Totalism.* New York: Norton, 1961.

Lifton, R. J. *Revolutionary Immortality: Mao Tse-Tung and the Chinese Cultural Revolution.* New York: Knopf, 1968.

Lowell, P. *The Soul of the Far East.* Philadelphia: R. West, 1973. (Originally published 1888.)

Lowell, P. *Occult Japan.* Bowling Green Station, N.Y.: Gordon Press, n.d. (Originally published 1895.)

Mandelbaum, D. G. *Society in India.* 2 vols. Berkeley: University of California Press, 1970.

Maruyama, M. *Thought and Behavior in Modern Japanese Politics.* Oxford, England: Oxford University Press, 1963.

Nakane, C. *Japanese Society.* Berkeley: University of California Press, 1970.

Nandy, A. *At the Edge of Psychology.* Bombay: Oxford University Press, 1980.

Narain, D. *Hindu Character.* Bombay: University of Bombay Press, 1957.

Neki, J. S. "Guru-Chela Relationship: The Possibility of a Therapeutic Paradigm." *American Journal of Orthopsychiatry,* 1973, *43,* 755-766.

Neki, J. S. "An Examination of the Cultural Relativism of Dependence as a Dynamic of Social and Therapeutic Relationships." *British Journal of Medical Psychology,* 1976, *56,* 11-22.

Ouchi, W. *Theory Z.* Reading, Mass.: Addison-Wesley, 1981.

Parish, W., and Whyte, M. K. *Village and Family in Contemporary China.* Chicago: University of Chicago Press, 1978.

Pascale, R. T. *The Art of Japanese Management: Applications for American Executives.* New York: Simon & Schuster, 1980.

Pempel, T. J. (ed.). *Policymaking in Contemporary Japan.* Ithaca, N.Y.: Cornell University Press, 1977.

Popkin, S. L. *The Rational Peasant: The Political Economy of Rural Society in Vietnam.* Berkeley: University of California Press, 1980.

Pye, L. W. *The Spirit of Chinese Politics.* Cambridge, Mass.: MIT Press, 1968.

Pye, L. W. *The Dynamics of Chinese Politics.* Cambridge, Mass.: Oelgeschlager, Gunn, & Hain, 1981.

Reischauer, E. O. *The United States and Japan.* Cambridge, Mass.: Harvard University Press, 1950.

Richardson, B. *The Political Culture of Japan.* Berkeley: University of California Press, 1974.

Rubin, H. "Will and Awe: Illustrations of Thai Villagers' Dependency upon Officials." *Journal of Asian Studies,* 1972, *32,* 425-495.

Samuels, R. J. "Power Behind the Throne." In T. MacDougall (ed.), *Political Leadership in Contemporary Japan.* Ann Arbor: East Asia Monographs, University of Michigan, 1982.

Sato, S., Murakami, Y., and Kumon, S. "Intellectual Perspectives on Japanese Modernity." *Japan Echo,* 1975, *2* (3).

Schein, E. *Coercive Persuasion.* New York: Norton, 1961.

Schurmann, F. *Ideology and Organization in Communist China.* Berkeley: University of California Press, 1966.

Scofield, R. W., and Sun, C. "A Comparative Study of Differential Effect upon

Personality of Chinese and American Child Training Practices." *Journal of Social Psychology*, 1960, *52*, 221–224.

Scott, J. C. *The Moral Economy of the Peasant*. New Haven, Conn.: Yale University Press, 1980.

Solomon, R. H. *Mao's Revolution and the Chinese Political Culture*. Berkeley: University of California Press, 1971.

Spratt, P. *Hindu Culture and Personality*. Bombay: Manaktalas, 1966.

Tazaki, T. *Nihonjinron no kensho* [An examination of the theory of Japaneseness]. Tokyo: 1980.

Thayer, N. B. *How the Conservatives Rule Japan*. Princeton, N.J.: Princeton University Press, 1969.

Tsuji, K. "Decision-Making in the Japanese Government: A Study of Ringisei." In R. Ward (ed.), *Political Development in Modern Japan*. Princeton, N.J.: Princeton University Press, 1968.

Vogel, E. (ed.). *Modern Japanese Organization and Decision-Making*. Berkeley: University of California Press, 1975.

Vogel, E. *Japan as Number One: Lessons for America*. Cambridge, Mass.: Harvard University Press, 1979.

Weiner, M. *Party Building in a New Nation*. Chicago: University of Chicago Press, 1967.

Weiner, M., and Katzenstein, M. F. *India's Preferential Politics*. Chicago: University of Chicago Press, 1981.

Wilson, R. W. *The Political Socialization of Children in Taiwan*. Cambridge, Mass.: MIT Press, 1970.

EPILOGUE

Toward an Agenda
for Political Psychology

Margaret G. Hermann

In the previous chapters contributors to this volume have covered a wide range of topics that are part of the field of political psychology. Each has examined how psychological and political phenomena interact in determining political behavior. The authors have explored the effects of psychological factors on political factors as well as the effects of political factors on psychological factors. They have also provided insights into three of the issues described in the Prologue that political psychologists are currently debating; namely, is there an underlying paradigm in political psychology, what is the appropriate unit of analysis in political psychology, and how important is a comparative approach to political psychology.

This Epilogue will consider how the contributors have dealt with these three issues. It will examine several general themes the chapters suggest undergird the study of political psychology. And it will explore how the unit of analysis and context problems affect what is studied in each theme area. The aim of the Epilogue is to show how the chapters help to structure an agenda for political psychology by indicating alternative ways of coping with the problems presently confronting political psychologists.

But before turning to these issues, some definition of terms is in order. Throughout this book we have referred to political psychology as involving the study of what happens when psychological and political phenomena interact. What kinds of psychological and political phenomena are we talking about and what do we mean by interact? The chapters in this book suggest that the psychological phenomena we are interested in have to do with how an individual perceives, interprets, feels about, and reacts to the environment. These processes, the authors argue, are influenced, in turn, by human nature (biological and physiological factors), motives, beliefs, cognitive styles, values, emotions, and early psychological experiences. The chapters emphasize an array of political phenomena: voting, protest behavior, terrorism, expression of public opinion, policy making, international relations, political socialization, conflict resolution, political leadership. These activities have to do with governing or the making of public policy— that is, with how the material and human resources of a collectivity are to be allocated. And these activities are shaped by and affect those who are involved in making allocations for a collectivity. They indicate who can make authoritative decisions. The activities also suggest a result; that is, the individual or collectivity does something that has implications for public policy.

Political psychology marries these two types of phenomena. It specifies that the environment individuals are perceiving, interpreting, developing feelings about, and reacting to is one in which public policy is being made. Sometimes, as in the chapters in the first part of this book, we emphasize the bride in this marriage and examine what it is about the individual that makes for a particular way of perceiving, interpreting, feeling about, or reacting to a public policy issue. The focus is on the psychological phenomena with the political phenomena forming the context for study. At other times, as in the chapters in part three of this book, we turn to the groom in this marriage and examine who makes public policy, how, and with what effect on members of the collectivity. The focus becomes the political phenomena but at the individual or psychological level of analysis. And at still other times, as in the Hermann, Crenshaw, and Pye chapters (Chapters Six, Thirteen, and Sixteen, respectively), the emphasis is on both parties to the marriage and their interaction. A particular psychological factor leads to different kinds of effects in different kinds of governing bodies—for example, the various effects psychological dependence has in Asian countries. Or a particular reaction to the way public policy is being made takes different forms depending on the psychological makeup of those exercising it—for example, terrorism. Or the political behavior to be observed depends on how specific psychological and political factors combine—for example, the motives of a political leader combine with the expectations of those he leads to determine the nature of the political leadership the individual will have to exert to be effective.

This way of conceptualizing political psychology suggests that there are several underlying themes that have piqued the curiosity of political psychologists. One of the themes focuses on how people's perceptions, interpretations, and feelings about politics are developed and maintained. A second is concerned with the effect that people's perceptions, interpretations, and feelings have on their political behavior. A third centers on how decisions about public policy are made. And a fourth focuses on where the authority for making political decisions is located— who has the right to make public policy and with what effect. The chapters in this book have explored these four themes. The contributors have proposed ways of thinking about these issues that begin to shape crude maps of what is involved in each of these domains. Let us examine what they have said.

Development and Maintenance of Political Views

The chapters in the first part of the book focus on the theme of development and maintenance of political views, as do the chapters by Kinder and Fiske, Merelman, and Seliktar later in the book. What factors do these authors suggest influence the way people view politics? Somit and Peterson (Chapter One) propose that an individual's physiological state can influence how the person perceives, interprets, and feels about political issues. Davies (Chapter Two) examines how human needs structure what people seek in their environment and what they are willing to tolerate politically. Sniderman and Tetlock (Chapter Three) suggest that most people develop their views of politics based on their likes and dislikes of politically strategic groups. Milbrath (Chapter Four) elaborates two particular ways of viewing the world and the kinds of people who are attracted to each view. Cocks (Chapter Five) explores how an individual's life experiences shape how he views issues of public policy. Kinder and Fiske (Chapter Seven) describe the ways in which people in the United States both understand and make judgments about presidents and presidential behavior. Merelman (Chapter Ten) shows how the political environment works on molding people's views of politics. And Seliktar (Chapter Eleven) considers how we know when individual views of the world become shared and a part of a societal political view.

The chapters indicate that the way people perceive, interpret, and feel about political issues is determined both by what they themselves are like and the political environment in which they live. An individual's physiological makeup, needs, likes and dislikes, and way of processing information help to shape the kinds of cues that will be highlighted in the political environment. But the range of cues that is available as well as expectations about how the cues are interrelated and evaluated is a function of the political environment in which the individual finds himself. The political environment can frustrate some political views and reinforce others just as individuals' predispositions can lead them to seek out political environments where their views are shared or obstinately hold on to views at variance with the environment.

The chapters suggest that there is a difference between how mass and elite views are formed and maintained. There is evidence that the general public neither knows much nor cares much about politics. When forced to pay attention to political issues, the general public tends to grasp at simple rules to suggest they have a view. One such rule is the likeability heuristic that Sniderman and Tetlock (Chapter Three) describe. Kinder and Fiske (Chapter Seven) have suggested how the general public uses schemas or prototypes to understand politics. And, indeed, Merelman (Chapter Ten) describes the way elites configure the political environment to ensure that the general public adopts a particular way of viewing politics. Each configuration of elites engages the general public in an attempt to perpetuate its system and itself. Sniderman and Tetlock (Chapter Three) propose that elites are more likely to succeed if they have a consensus themselves on the issue and the issue does not engage conflicting values. Even the general public can become more thoughtful about problems that call their values into conflict or over which they see their opinion leaders disagreeing. Seliktar (Chapter Eleven) indicates some of the ways that we can assess when elites are in agreement—that is, when they share a set of beliefs—as well as how successful elites are in communicating their beliefs to the general public. Milbrath (Chapter Four) describes an issue on which elites' beliefs and values differ—whether the environment is a "home for mankind" or a "sustenance base"—and shows how the general public distributes itself between the two positions.

The chapters suggest that much of the research on how peoples' political

views are developed and maintained has been conducted in the Western industrialized, democratic societies. We know less about the development of political views
in third- and fourth-world countries and in communist countries. Montero's chapter on political psychology in Latin America (Chapter Fourteen) proposes that
political views in these other parts of the world may have different roots. She
describes how ethnocentrism and, in turn, nationalism for Latin Americans is
based on individuals' perceptions of how well their group or country compares
with highly valued other groups and countries rather than on characteristics of
their own group or country. Ethnocentrism is altercentrism. The highly valued
others tend to be in the more developed countries and countries on which the
Latin Americans feel they are dependent. Davies (Chapter Two) suggests that
political views are associated with the level of development of the vast majority
of people in a country. If meeting survival needs occupies most people in a country
then concerns for food, housing, and security temper political views; if status
needs drive the majority of the people, then concerns for recognition and independence affect political views. The reader may wonder if Merelman's (Chapter
Ten) search for a general theory of political socialization leads us to overlook the
importance of context. The political theories Merelman examines suggest different
types of political regimes. If we were able to isolate instances of each type of
polity, would the political socialization practices suggested by the theory be in
evidence? At issue is how far we can generalize the data and propositions in these
chapters on political views without examining whether they change or remain
the same as the political context—for example, level of development, type of political regime, degree of dependence on other countries or cultures, and degree of-
stability—changes.

Much of the analysis of how peoples' political views are developed and
maintained focuses on the individual: What are individuals—members of the
general public or an elite—concerned about in public policy and why? The single
person is not so much the center of attention in these studies, however, as is
ascertaining what political views are representative of a particular political constituency and how they are formed and can be changed. Knowledge about what
views characterize a specific group provides us with clues about what the political
leadership of the group will need to pay attention to, about how successful the
leadership is in inculcating its own political views into followers, and about the
conditions under which group members' views can be molded or shaped. As V. O.
Key (1961, p. 535) has said, there is an interest in understanding how the "preferences, aspirations, and prejudices of the public can be connected with the workings of governmental systems." The problem becomes defining whose views must
be considered before we can determine what political views are representative of
a particular constituency. Is it the elite, the opinion leaders, the media, the politically active, those who are politically aware, the general public, or all or some
of the just named? The chapters differ in their answer to this question. Davies
(Chapter Two) argues that it is only by learning where most members of a political
group are located that we can understand the consensual political expectations
that guide the group. Seliktar (Chapter Eleven), on the other hand, proposes that
we need to compare and contrast the political views of all these various parts of
a constituency to understand what political views are likely to emerge for the
whole. And Merelman (Chapter Ten) focuses on the political views of the agents

of political socialization to suggest the political views of the group while Milbrath (Chapter Four) examines the views of particular types of elites. Since whose views are assessed has implications for what views are considered representative, careful thought needs to be given to who constitutes the political group under study and their internal dynamics in deciding where to focus. Whose political views are sought or paid attention to, whose political views would need to be included to capture all aspects of political life in the group; who shape and mold the views of the group; who help define the norms of the group are questions that can help to suggest whose views should be assessed.

In the Prologue to this book, Smith's (1973) map placing political attitudes in context is presented and posed as one way of organizing information in political psychology. The chapters dealing with how political views are developed and maintained elaborate the proposed relationships in that part of Smith's map suggesting how attitudes are formed. Each of the chapters we have been discussing focuses on one of the arrows in the map spelling out in detail how the two types of variables at either end of the arrow are related. For example, Kinder and Fiske (Chapter Seven) in describing how people appraise the president (arrow P in the map) outline several perspectives on the ways in which people understand and judge political objects in their environment and the effect on political views. A close reading of the chapters suggests that while Smith's map identifies important sets of variables that affect political views, each of his relationships may demand a map itself to understand the specifics of the relationship. The relevance of Smith's map to political psychologists, however, is it indicates that to ultimately understand how political views are developed and maintained we are going to have to stipulate how the sets of relationships themselves interrelate. Focusing exclusively on one of the arrows or relationships that Smith (1973) suggests gives us only a partial picture of the ways in which political views are developed.

Effects of Political Views on Political Behavior

In one way or another, most of the chapters in this book deal with how people's perceptions, views, beliefs, motives, feelings, and experiences influence what they do politically. Judging from the chapters, examining this relationship has formed an important part of what political psychologists study. The authors propose a number of processes that individuals use in translating their views into actions. A discussion of these processes suggests how psychological and political phenomena interact in determining the kind of political activities people choose to engage in.

Several of the chapters show how political views act as filters for environmental stimuli, helping individuals organize and understand the political arena in which they are operating. Political views as filters sort out stimuli, focus attention, and restrict the range of likely responses to a situation. Seliktar (Chapter Eleven) has captured this process in her description of a decision-oriented definition of collective belief systems. Kinder and Fiske (Chapter Seven) suggest the effects of political views as filters in their discussion of attribution error and understanding through the use of schema in the appraisal of presidents. Mandel (Chapter Nine) has organized his discussion of psychological approaches to international relations around the distortions or biases these filters encourage.

Most of us have a cultural filter that suggests how our political views in general are going to relate to our political behavior. Pye's (Chapter Sixteen) description of how psychological dependency acts as an organizing theme for political behavior in Asia illustrates the effect of such a cultural filter. He contrasts this Asian theme with the Western focus on individual autonomy. Deutsch and Shichman (Chapter Eight) suggest that individuals in countries that are adversaries, such as the United States and the Soviet Union, often have filters that promote malignant social conflict. Somit and Peterson (Chapter One), in their survey of biopolitics, propose that there may be hereditary filters that are common to all people such as the "norm of reciprocity." And Mandel (Chapter Nine) indicates that many of us have filters that derive from the political roles we play, the political groups we belong to, and the types of situations we regularly encounter. Mandel provides examples of these filters as they affect foreign policy activity.

A second process that seems to affect the relationship between political views and political behavior centers around the discrepancy between expectation and reality. Political views act as a standard of comparison against which political stimuli are gauged and judged. Political behavior becomes more likely the greater the discrepancy between what the individual expects and what he is experiencing. Lederer (Chapter Twelve) and Crenshaw (Chapter Thirteen) describe how protest behavior and terrorism result from what is perceived as a deprivation. Kinder and Fiske (Chapter Seven) indicate that most Americans' reactions to their president are formed by comparing him with some standard or set of expectations. Milbrath (Chapter Four) notes how environmental calamities provide consciousness raising experiences for individuals, predisposing them to become more environmentally active.

The discrepancy between expectation and experience poses a problem for the individual. When a similar discrepancy is perceived by a number of people, political groups can coalesce in response to the problem and seek to change the environment. Lederer (Chapter Twelve) suggests that whether such action will be relatively peaceful and within society's rules or become violent depends on how politically efficacious the people in the group perceive they are and how much resistance they engender in the process of seeking change, violence being associated with a low sense of efficacy and a high degree of resistance. Crenshaw (Chapter Thirteen) suggests that if such groups resort to violence, they may generate an overreaction on the part of those whose position is challenged. If this overreaction gives the group notoriety—highlights their cause—they are likely to perceive violence as the means to redressing the problem and continue this course of action.

A third process the chapters identify as a means for linking political views to political behavior focuses on what Merelman (Chapter Ten) calls "sentimental attachments." People's political views are often enmeshed with their feelings about certain groups through whom they act politically. By identifying with the group, the individual shares accountability as well as gains support for his political behavior. Crenshaw (Chapter Thirteen) and Bryder (Chapter Fifteen) talk about the process as one of deindividuation.

Merelman (Chapter Ten) suggests that in modern, industrialized societies these attachments are transient and informal in the general public. While Crenshaw (Chapter Thirteen) observes that for some people who lack a sense of identity or are confused about that identity—notably terrorists—the attachments are lasting and all-consuming. In many cases the terrorist group becomes a second family, its cohesiveness enhanced by the stress conditions under which it exists as well as its relative social isolation and rigid norms and values. Mandel (Chapter Nine) observes how group attachments can change the emphasis in policy making from decisions that attack the problem at hand to decisions that promote the group or maintain its cohesiveness. The political behavior reinforces the attachment to the group.

Most people probably use all three of these processes in linking their political views to behavior, often simultaneously. The chapters suggest the following crude model for how these three processes function. The filters generally arise as a result of an attachment to a group; the information the filters provide alert the individual to a discrepancy in the environment and, in turn, the likelihood of joining with others who perceive a similar problem in trying to do something about it. Thus, one's political views configure the cues in the environment that will receive attention; the political environment interacts with one's views in setting occasions for action; and the action occurs in conjunction with others with somewhat similar political views and interests in acting. The type of political behavior that results will depend on the interaction among those involved in acting and, therefore, may not be directly predictable from any one person's political beliefs. In effect, the chapters propose that political beliefs help to define the occasion for action and probably set limits on what the nature of the action will be, but interaction with the environment determines the specific action that occurs.

How Public Policy Decisions Are Made

The chapters in Part Two of the book examine political decision making as do the chapters by Seliktar (Chapter Eleven) and Pye (Chapter Sixteen). The authors appear to proceed from the idea that decisions exhibit bounded rationality. That is, they evince "a reasonable process for choosing" based on "the choosing organism's goals, the information and conceptualization it has of the situation, and its abilities to draw inferences from the information it possesses" (Simon, 1985, p. 294). The chapters emphasize the forces that influence goals, perceptions and definition of the situation, and reasoning processes. The focus is on decision making as part of leadership, negotiation, conflict resolution, voting, domestic and foreign policy making, and international relations.

Thus, Hermann (Chapter Six) discusses the characteristics of leaders that are likely to affect how they make decisions for and with their constituents as well as why particular constituents choose to work with particular leaders. Kinder and Fiske (Chapter Seven) describe the bases on which the general public in the United States chooses a president. Deutsch and Shichman (Chapter Eight) focus on the conditions that lead to different ways of resolving interpersonal, intergroup, and international conflicts. Mandel (Chapter Nine) explores the psychological constraints on how individuals, groups, and governments make foreign policy. And Seliktar (Chapter Eleven) and Pye (Chapter Sixteen) explore how cultural beliefs and values influence the political decision making of members of the culture.

The chapters differ in their approach to whether the influences on decision making are similar or different as one moves from the level of the individual to groups to organizations and governments to international entities. Deutsch and Shichman (Chapter Eight) make what they call the brash assumption that there is no difference. Similar processes and conditions hold across these various types of decision making. And, indeed, Deutsch and Shichman are examining a situation at all these levels in which there are two parties, each with a position and a set of political views that have helped generate the position, who are trying to reach a decision together. But what if there is dissension among members of one of the parties on what the position should be or disagreement among the members on what their representative is doing? This is unlikely to happen at the individual or interpersonal level; it becomes more likely as we move from individuals to groups to organizations and governments. Mandel (Chapter Nine) explores some of the literature that has examined group, organizational, and bureaucratic decision making, suggesting how the structural relationships among the people involved in the decision making and the decision-making process give some indication of whose political views are having an impact on the decision. Thus, for example, if a group has a strong leader, an organization is hierarchically structured so that authoritative decisions are centralized in one person at the top, or a government has a predominant leader, the knowledge about one person's political views may enable us to understand the nature of the decisions that are made. But if we move to a situation where power is more evenly distributed among members of a group or among groups in an organization or bureaucracies in a government, understanding how the political views of the different members of the group interact and are affected by the group context becomes relevant. It is difficult to account for the group, organization, or government's decision on the basis of one individual's political views. Yet the tendency of political psychologists is to treat a group, organization, and nation as if each were an individual with its own political views instead of a set of interacting individuals often with differing political views.

It is exactly in these types of situations that ascertaining how political and psychological phenomena interact becomes important. As Seliktar (Chapter Eleven) suggests, we may want to use political variables to isolate which individuals' political views in a group, organization, or government need to be considered in a particular situation and, in turn, use political variables to determine how the positions these people take will affect one another or combine in influencing decision making. The following are the kinds of questions we need to ask: Does the structure of authority in the political unit suggest that one person, a group, or several groups is likely to be involved in making decisions? If a group, are there coalitions; is there a dominant leader; are there formal rules specifying functions in the group; do the members represent outside groups or is the membership primarily loyal to this group? All these questions help us identify whose political views are important to understand or take into account in considering the nature of the decision. Once we know who is likely to be involved in making the decision, we need to ask some questions about the political relationships among these people before ascertaining their views on the particular decision under consideration. Are there some agreed upon rules of the game? Has this usually been an adversarial relationship where some members lose while others win? Is dissension permitted? When we have information about or some hunches on who is likely to make the decision and how they are likely to interact, we can begin looking at the people involved and what they are like. We know enough at this point to begin to give some weighting to the political views of each of the individuals as it is likely to affect the decision that is made.

Although we have been focusing here on the point when a decision is made, it is important to recognize that the decision-making process in groups, organizations, and governments generally involves a series of steps with different people at each step. There are people who perceive that there is a need for a decision—who define the occasion for decision, people who stipulate what the alternatives are among which decision makers are to decide, and people who implement the decision. What these people are like can influence the kind of decision that is made and the effect the decision will have on the political system. In analyzing how people's political views impact on public policy decisions, the easiest thing to do is to focus on how one individual makes a political decision, such as a decision to vote for a particular candidate in an election. Much more difficult is ascertaining the effect of people's political views on decisions made in groups, organizations, or governments. The point of the present discussion is to suggest that inroads on this more difficult task are possible by dissecting the situation and determining where in the group or organization the decision is likely to be made as well as who will have input before the decision reaches these ultimate decision makers and after it leaves them. (For an application of this procedure see Hermann, Hermann, and Hagan, forthcoming.) Without a process like this we will continue to get caught in the three fallacies of cross-level analysis, namely, reducing the group, organization, or government to a single entity; personifying the group, organization, or government and treating it as an individual; or extrapolating directly from what we know about decision making at the individual level to studies of decision making in groups, organizations, or governments (see Eulau, 1968).

Who Makes Authoritative Decisions

The chapters in Part Three of this book examine where the authority for making public policy decisions is located. (Chapters Two, Six, Seven, Nine, and Sixteen also address this issue.) The authors are interested in who assumes the right to make authoritative decisions for others on public policy and with what effect on the policy. In exploring this question a series of other questions are raised. Does it make a difference in the public policy that gets generated who is in charge? How do those in authority assure themselves of continuing to exercise influence? When is a change in authority likely? How do those who perceive themselves without authority attempt to influence what happens in the public policy arena? And on what bases do those affected by public policy decisions judge the behavior of the policymakers? The chapters pose some answers to these queries.

Hermann (Chapter Six) and Mandel (Chapter Nine) suggest that what the people are like who are involved in making the authoritative decisions for a political body has implications for resulting policy. In examining political leadership and foreign policy making, these two chapters show that characteristics of the leaders influence what happens. But both chapters suggest that the influence of leader characteristics on policy is often mediated by the nature of the context—for example, how accountable the leader is to others for his decisions, how much opposition there is to the leader and how strong it is, what the "fit" is between what the leader wants and what the followers (constituents) want, how many layers there are in the organization between the leader and those implementing his policy. In effect, the situation can act as a constraint on what the leader wants to do and force a decision not necessarily reflective of the leader. We are just beginning to understand and be able to identify situations in which leaders' characteristics impinge on the policy of the political unit as opposed to situations in which the leaders' characteristics have little effect.

Hermann (Chapter Six), Kinder and Fiske (Chapter Seven), and Merelman (Chapter Ten) examine how those with authority try to ensure that they continue to exercise influence. These chapters describe several processes that those in authority use: socialization, image building, and building coalitions or networks of supporters. Through socialization those in authority try to inculcate their political views into the next generation and reinforce the present generation's views by using them as the socializing agents. Through image building, those in authority are interested in projecting the idea that they are effective in getting done what constituents want done and are in charge. By engaging in coalition building and networking, those in authority increase the number of people who define problems and solutions as they do and who owe them some allegiance. How those in authority go about doing these things will depend on what they are like, their political views, and the nature of the political situation in which they find themselves.

Davies (Chapter Two) and Seliktar (Chapter Eleven) explore how we can ascertain when a change in authority is likely. Davies proposes that we can judge the type of political system a nation is likely to have by learning something about the needs of the people. A nation's political system reflects its stage of political development which, in turn, parallels the individual development of the majority of the people in that country. We can detect when a change in political system is likely to be advocated by noting when there is no longer a majority of the population at any one level or there is a dramatic increase in the number of people at a higher level of development. Seliktar adds to the Davies' proposal by suggesting that the match between the beliefs among the power elite and the masses or between the power elite and important interest groups can signal when change may be coming. Identifying and observing the fit between the beliefs of these various groups provides us with information on which to gauge the legitimacy of those in authority and to note where the erosion of support is occurring.

Lederer (Chapter Twelve) and Crenshaw (Chapter Thirteen) discuss how those not in authority try to influence those in power to give them what they want. These authors examine legal and illegal means of exerting such influence and suggest some of the psychological bases for choosing among alternative ways of protesting to those in authority. They suggest that the very act of protesting and being part of a protest group—violent or nonviolent—can take on a life of its own, often becoming divorced from the reality of the situation and can lead those involved to form a counterculture. Crenshaw observes that those in authority, perceiving the protesters (or terrorists) as a threat to their way of doing things, generally assume that such groups are challenging their right to power rather than a particular issue, expanding rather than limiting the problem. Lederer and Crenshaw both indicate a certain catch-22 in the relationship between those in authority and those protesting: If those in authority respond as if the protesters were challenges to their very existence, the protesters receive a signal that they can have an impact and try harder, becoming, in turn, more of a threat to the base of power of those in authority. Understanding better the nature of the individuals at either end of this relationship and the circumstances in which they find themselves will help improve our understanding of how each is likely to respond to the other.

Kinder and Fiske (Chapter Seven) present some rules of thumb that the general public often uses to judge those in authority. By assessing how the public is appraising their leaders, we learn how successful those in authority are with their image building and maintenance programs as well as how legitimate and effective the public believes they are. Seliktar (Chapter Eleven) observes that the power elite also often use their knowledge or perceptions of the public's yardsticks in policy making. That is, those in authority try to anticipate how they might evoke a positive public response and then frame their actions accordingly. At issue is how much of the behavior of public policy makers is guided by their perceptions of "what will sell" as opposed to other considerations. Are there certain types of people for whom such information is critical?

Pye (Chapter Sixteen) throws a monkey wrench into this discussion, however, because his analysis of political psychology in Asia suggests that there may be a cultural overlay to any discussion of who has and who gives authority to make public policy decisions. How one answers the questions we have just been examining may depend on where in the world one is looking. Since most of the authors of the other chapters were drawing from materials about the United States, Canada, and Western Europe, they have been looking at these issues through a specific lens. Pye suggests there may be at least one other lens through which to view the answers to our queries. His discussion implies that the idea of what constitutes power and authority and the relationship between those who have it and those who do not may be different in various parts of the world.

Cross-Cutting Themes

The four themes just described and discussed appear to underly both the chapters and the field of political psychology. In the chapters in this book, they act as cross-cutting themes indicating that there are several common interests among political psychologists. In the Prologue we observed that those involved in political psychology tend to focus on particular problems (topics) or areas of the world and that there is little contact among persons working in these various arenas. The four themes examined in this Epilogue provide a basis for establishing communication among these different networks of people. Those working on the same theme have information of relevance to exchange, even though they may not be studying the same substantive area. Thus, for example, in learning about how political views are developed and maintained, Crenshaw (Chapter Thirteen) may find help with her study of the psychological roots of terrorism by reading what the authors in Part One of the book who examine political views have to say, and vice versa.

The cross-cutting themes also suggest that instead of one over-arching paradigm in political psychology, there are several interests that drive the field. In this Epilogue, we have only begun to construct maps of the terrain that each of these themes covers. The chapters have pointed to what topics share a focus on which themes and have highlighted some of the important political and psychological variables to consider in examining the themes. Much work remains, but the themes, nonetheless, pose useful ways to organize information in the field and to structure future work in political psychology.

Conclusion

We began this book with the statement that political psychology is coming of age. The ensuing chapters have tried to suggest the appropriateness of this claim by providing an outline of the field of political psychology. Thus, in the

Prologue we indicated a series of tenets that appear to undergird political psychology and some issues about which there is debate and dialogue. In the chapters between the Prologue and this Epilogue we have presented perspectives on a set of topics that seem to capture the most prominent areas of research and action for those calling themselves political psychologists. The chapters posed alternative ways of dealing with the issues raised in the Prologue. And in this Epilogue we have discussed four themes that stand out after reading the chapters and have suggested how the chapters elaborate these themes. In this process, the field of political psychology has begun to take on a more definite shape. Like the young person moving from childhood into adolescence, the field is gaining a sense of identity as well as some sense of direction. The challenge for the future is to retain the momentum of the last decade and a half and to continue the exponential growth in our understanding of the psychological roots and effects of political behavior.

References

Eulau, H. "Political Behavior." In D. L. Sills (Ed.), *International Encyclopedia of the Social Sciences.* Vol. 12. New York: Macmillan, 1968.

Hermann, M. G., Hermann, C. F., and Hagan, J. D. "How Decision Units Shape Foreign Policy Behavior." In C. Kegley, C. F. Hermann, and J. N. Rosenau (Eds.), *New Directions in the Comparative Study of Foreign Policy.* New York: Allen Unwin, forthcoming.

Key, V. O., Jr. *Public Opinion and American Democracy.* New York: Knopf, 1961.

Simon, H. A. "Human Nature in Politics: The Dialogue of Psychology with Political Science." *American Political Science Review,* 1985, 79, 293–304.

Smith, M. B. "Political Attitudes." In J. N. Knutson (Ed.), *Handbook of Political Psychology.* San Francisco: Jossey-Bass, 1973.

Name Index

Name Index

Subject Index

A

B